A CENTRAL ASIAN PERSPECTIVE ON INTERNATIONAL LAW

This book offers the first full-length, systematic account of international law as seen and applied from the perspective of Central Asia.

Since gaining independence from the Soviet Union in 1991, Kazakhstan, Kyrgyzstan, Tajikistan, Turkmenistan and Uzbekistan have gradually emerged as active participants in the international legal order. Drawing on their evolving statehood and regional cooperation, this book explores how the Central Asian States engage with the rules, principles and institutions of international law.

Across 15 chapters, the book covers key areas of international law – from the nature and sources of international law to the law of treaties, international responsibility, and peaceful settlement of disputes – as well as specialist regimes including international human rights, humanitarian and criminal law, international peace and security, and international trade law. Dedicated chapters address the status of the Caspian Sea, the role of international organisations and non-state actors, and the domestic implementation of international norms.

Through rigorous legal analysis and rich empirical references, the book also examines Central Asian constitutional and policy approaches to international law, regional mechanisms of dispute settlement, and case studies such as the legal status of the Caspian Sea, the Central Asian Nuclear-Weapon-Free Zone, and the development of institutional arbitration in the region, including the Astana International Financial Centre and the Tashkent International Arbitration Centre. The analysis highlights how the region's engagement with international law reflects both adaptation to global norms and the emergence of context-specific legal practices.

This is an essential resource for scholars, practitioners, and students of international law, comparative law, and Central Asian studies, as well as diplomats and policymakers.

Volume 103 in the series Studies in International Law

Studies in International Law

Recent titles in this series

Territorial Status in International Law
Jure Vidmar

Marine Bioprospecting, Biodiversity and Novel Uses of Ocean Resources: New Approaches in International Law
Edited by Niels Krabbe and David Langlet

The Standard of Review Before the International Court of Justice: Between Principle and Pragmatism
Felix Fouchard

Global Lawmaking and Social Change: The Varieties of Customary International Law
Gregor Novak

The Effectiveness of the Inter-American Court of Human Rights: The Case of Indigenous Territorial Rights
Gabriela CB Navarro

Individuals in International Humanitarian Law: A Historical Analysis
Sarina Landefeld

The Pathology of Plenty: Natural Resources in International Law
Lys Kulamadayil

The United Nations Security Council and the Authorisation of Force: Form, Character and Nature
Marko Svicevic

Protecting the Right to Leave in an Era of Externalised Migration Control
Emilie McDonnell

Pluralising Actors and Norms in Human Rights Treaties: Beyond Monolithic States
Hinako Takata

Systemic Economic Offences as International Crimes: Theorising a New Paradigm of Mass Criminality
Nicole Citeroni

A Central Asian Perspective on International Law
Sergey Sayapin

For a complete list of titles in this series see www.bloomsbury.com/uk/series/studies-in-international-law/

A Central Asian Perspective on International Law

Sergey Sayapin

•HART•
OXFORD • LONDON • NEW YORK • NEW DELHI • SYDNEY

HART PUBLISHING

Bloomsbury Publishing Plc

Kemp House, Chawley Park, Cumnor Hill, Oxford, OX2 9PH, UK

1385 Broadway, New York, NY 10018, USA

Bloomsbury Publishing Ireland Limited, 29 Earlsfort Terrace, Dublin 2, D02 AY28, Ireland

HART PUBLISHING, the Hart/Stag logo, BLOOMSBURY and the Diana logo are trademarks of Bloomsbury Publishing Plc

First published in Great Britain 2026

A catalogue record for this book is available from the British Library.

A catalogue record for this book is available from the Library of Congress.

Library of Congress Control Number: 2026933083

ISBN: HB: 978-1-50993-549-9
ePDF: 978-1-50993-551-2
ePub: 978-1-50993-550-5

Typeset by Compuscript Ltd, Shannon

For product safety related questions contact productsafety@bloomsbury.com

To find out more about our authors and books visit www.hartpublishing.co.uk. Here you will find extracts, author information, details of forthcoming events and the option to sign up for our newsletters.

To my mother, Olga Sayapina – you chose Central Asia as your home, and made it mine as well.

In memory of my professor and LLM thesis supervisor at the University of Essex, Françoise J. Hampson (1951–2025). You visited Central Asia twice, and many here still remember your brilliant lectures and your remarkable sense of humour.

For my friends – who understand that in Central Asia, international law is best discussed over tea.

To M. – for reminding me that international law, like all human endeavours, draws strength not only from rules, but from those who endure with dignity.

For my students – past, present, and future.

Foreword

SERGEY SAYAPIN'S TREATISE offers us an introduction to international law and does so from Central Asian perspectives. Central Asia in the book is primarily defined by five countries which once were part of the Russian Empire and then the Soviet Union – Kazakhstan, Kyrgyzstan, Tajikistan, Turkmenistan, and Uzbekistan. Students from the region are a specific target group of the book.

Being an Uzbek national and living and working in Almaty, Kazakhstan, Professor Sayapin is in a very good position to judge what unites and what separates the five Central Asian republics. What matters is the main conceptual perspective itself: to take the Central Asian experiences in the context of international law seriously. We already have textbooks which highlight Australian, European and, for example, South African perspectives on international law. To examine international law from the perspective of Central Asian countries is a welcome and also bold addition and should be of interest also to scholars and students from outside the region. Whoever wants to understand international law must also learn about the world and its different perspectives, regions and even 'corners'. By now, a lot has been said and written about the Euro- or Western-centric history of international law; what we need now to balance this history is to take seriously other regional-national circumstances and perspectives.

Central Asian republics emerged relatively recently, in December 1991, from the Soviet Union when the latter disintegrated. The Soviets were a decisive factor in Central Asian history because they reformed the political map of Central Asia and, by and large, drew the contemporary borders of the five States of the region which are examined in Professor Sayapin's book. Before that, Tsarist Russia used the institute of protectorates in polities such as Khiva and Bukhara. The Tsarist Russian conquest of Central Asia was essentially not so different from the British and other European conquests, approaching Central Asia from India and Afghanistan. The two Empires, the British and Russian, 'met' in places like Afghanistan and Persia (nowadays Iran), clashing and drawing spheres of influence with each other. The famous Tsarist Russian international lawyer Fyodor (Friedrich) Martens (1845–1909) was not just the author of the Martens Clause in international humanitarian law but also made proposals on how the Russian and British Empires should work together and not start fighting with each other in their *mission civilisatrice* in Central Asia.

One fascinating keyword for Central Asian history in international law is the right of self-determination of peoples. Soviet Russia and, since

30 December 1922, the Soviet Union claimed that they were global pioneers in terms of practising the right of peoples to self-determination. The reorganisation of Central Asia served as a key example in this discourse and non-Soviet visitors to republics such as Uzbekistan were proudly given the message: being part of the Soviet federation could be the future after decolonisation. At the same time, the Soviet Union can also be understood as a continuation of the Russian Empire, on a completely different and reformed constitutional basis, but still. The Soviet legal theory emphasises that all 15 Soviet republics were 'sovereign', along with the Soviet Union as a whole, but historians have observed that it nevertheless remained a very centralised country, a peculiar Empire of sorts, which liked to highlight the realisation of the right of peoples to self-determination. In any case, I am convinced that the history of Central Asia will continue to offer food for thought in discussions about the history of international law more generally. It is just that Eurocentrism had a specific feature in Central Asia as experts all too often got used to looking at the region and its history primarily from Russian and Soviet perspectives.

One important aspect for the future is the question of regional integration. Professor Sayapin offers his own interesting thoughts and proposals on what political and economic integration in the region should look like. However, the two great powers bordering with the region, China and Russia, have not disappeared anywhere. They will want to have a say in the regional integration, and have their own interests in such processes: Russia, for example, in the Eurasian Economic Union and in the Collective Security Treaty Organisation. Some Western international lawyers, such as Professor Tom Ginsburg of the University of Chicago, have observed authoritarian values and tendencies in some regional organisations such as in the Shanghai Cooperation Organization. I hope that international law students in Central Asia can also engage with such arguments and outside criticisms during their studies. Central Asian States are often responding to their complex geopolitical situation with their multi-vector politics in diplomacy. For example, as a member of the Venice Commission of the Council of Europe, I have noted with interest the political engagement of Kazakhstan and Kyrgyzstan in that expert body, and thus also their ideas and practices related to democracy.

The most important aspect of the right of people to self-determination is that people themselves can be in charge of their destiny. Students of international law can discuss to what extent this promise was fulfilled in Central Asia in and after 1917, to what extent in and after 1991, or to what extent realising this can only be a process which is still ongoing. In any case, Professor Sayapin's treatise offers much information and ideas for students and scholars who want to learn about what international law and Central Asia have got to do with each other.

Lauri Mälksoo
Professor of International Law at the University of Tartu (Estonia)
Member of the Institut de Droit International

Preface

THIS BOOK WAS conceived in response to a glaring absence: the lack of a comprehensive, critically grounded, and regionally contextualised introduction to international law for and about Central Asia. While countless volumes have been written on the foundations and evolution of international law, few – if any – seriously examine how international law is received, practised, contested, and developed in one of the world's most legally and geopolitically dynamic regions. This book seeks to fill that gap, not by merely 'applying' global legal principles to Central Asia, but by reimagining international law through the lens of Central Asian legal experience.

A defining feature of the book is its integrative methodological approach. Rather than viewing international law as static or closed, the book presents it as shaped by history, society, and political processes. Another core strength of this book is its regional grounding. Each doctrinal chapter is anchored in the legal systems, constitutional traditions, treaty practice, and policy frameworks of Kazakhstan, Kyrgyzstan, Tajikistan, Turkmenistan, and Uzbekistan. Far from treating Central Asia as a monolith, the book highlights both shared legacies (such as Soviet legal traditions and Islamic legal influences) and national divergences (such as differing approaches to treaty ratification, human rights implementation, and economic integration). For each area of law, the chapters carefully trace how international norms have been internalised, resisted, or reshaped within domestic legal systems.

The book also explores regional institutions in depth. In addition to analysing the legal structures of global organisations such as the United Nations, World Trade Organization, and International Criminal Court, it examines in detail the Eurasian Economic Union, the Collective Security Treaty Organization, the Shanghai Cooperation Organization, the Organization of Turkic States, and the OSCE. These institutions are explored not only as legal frameworks, but as arenas of contested authority and shifting regional influence – particularly in light of Russia's evolving role, China's economic presence, and post-2022 geopolitical realignments.

While rooted in law, this book is also designed with an interdisciplinary perspective. Scholars of political science, international relations, economics, development studies, history, and Central Asian studies will find in its pages a wealth of data, interpretation, and reflection on how international norms intersect with national identity, regional strategy, and institutional change. The analysis of human rights law integrates gender studies and sociology; the trade law chapter draws on development economics; the environmental and humanitarian law discussions engage with postcolonial and ecological critiques. In this sense, the book invites conversation across disciplines, helping to close the gap between law and the broader study of global order.

Above all, the book aspires to be more than an academic reference work – it aims to inspire, connect, and empower the next generation of international lawyers in Central Asia. It affirms that Central Asia plays an active role in shaping the development, complexity, and future of international law. By showcasing the region's legal evolution and interpretive agency, the book encourages students and scholars to see themselves as participants in the shaping of international norms. I hope that readers – whether lawyers, scholars, diplomats, or students – will find in these pages not only knowledge, but also intellectual tools with which to question, analyse, and ultimately engage with international law as a living, pluralistic, and globally shared project.

The book has benefitted from the insights of students in my Public International Law (Advanced) course taught at KIMEP University in the Autumn 2024 semester. I thank Arystan Akbiyev, Aruzhan Amangeldy, Alua Amirzhanova, Malika Aslambekova, Farrukh Baratov, Renata Kristina Benavides Maldonado, Andong Ding, Diana Dolgashova, Akhmadsiar Dorani, Inzhel Gadylzhan, Madina Kenzhebay, Kirsan Kulmagambetov, Karima Lukpanova, Marzhan Muslimova, Alina Salakhunova, Nurly Saparali, Adele Sarsembayeva, Natan Tsoy, Nuray Zhaksybay, and Roman Zhelak for their helpful comments on the text and excellent in-class discussions. Malika Aslambekova also provided valuable assistance with formatting the manuscript for publication.

I extend my sincere thanks to Professor Lauri Mälksoo (University of Tartu, Institut de Droit International) for his thoughtful and supportive Foreword. Likewise, I am deeply grateful to Fred Mitchell Isaacs JD, my former Dean at KIMEP University's School of Law and currently an Associate Justice of the Supreme Court of the Republic of Palau, for his valuable linguistic and substantive suggestions on the manuscript.

My sincere thanks go to Sinead Moloney, Sasha Jawed, and Verity Stuart at Hart Publishing for their unwavering support and professionalism throughout this project. From the very outset, their guidance, responsiveness, and commitment to excellence have been invaluable. I am also grateful to the wider team at Hart Publishing for their behind-the-scenes work and dedication, all of which have contributed significantly to bringing this book to fruition. I would also like to thank Joanne Choulerton for her meticulous and thoughtful copyediting, which greatly enhanced the clarity and precision of the manuscript. I am further indebted to the Centre for International Law at the National University of Singapore, where the final work on this manuscript was completed, and to Dr Nilüfer Oral, Director of the Centre, for providing excellent working conditions during my tenure as Distinguished Visiting Global Scholar.

All errors and omissions are my own. I would be grateful to receive any comments or suggestions at sergey.sayapin@yahoo.com, and will do my best to incorporate them in future editions of the book.

Sergey Sayapin
Almaty – Batumi, August 2025

Contents

PART II
INTERNATIONAL LAW-MAKING PROCESSES

PART III
INTERNATIONAL DISPUTES AND RESPONSIBILITY

PART IV
CURRENT CHALLENGES

Part I

Central Asia in the International System

1

A Critical Introduction to International Law

THIS CHAPTER OFFERS a critical introduction to international law, and places it in its interdisciplinary context. The chapter will be of particular interest to students who are taking their first steps in studying international law. More advanced readers are familiar with the fundamentals. For them, the chapter will serve as a helpful introduction to the structure and logic of the book.

I. WHAT IS THE INTERNATIONAL SYSTEM?

This world is existentially interdependent. Currently, communication between most nations is so intensive that ongoing developments in one place may quickly have vital repercussions in many others. For example, the COVID-19 pandemic, having originated in Wuhan (China) in December 2019, by 5 May 2023 affected 676 million individuals worldwide (8.4 per cent of the world's population).[1] The amount of data created is growing at an unprecedented pace: it is estimated that it will 'hit a staggering 163 zettabytes by 2025. This is about ten times the amount in 2017'.[2] This exceptional development enables us to process increasing volumes of constructive information but also creates opportunities for misinformation and disinformation.[3] Online tools enable us to communicate in real time with people around the world but also make our personal data and assets ever more vulnerable: by 2025, global losses from cybercrime are projected to reach USD 10.5 trillion per year.[4] Armed

[1] 24.KG, 'Number of infected with coronavirus exceeds 676 million people globally', 7 March 2023. available at 24.kg/english/260194_Number_of_infected_with_coronavirus_exceeds_676_million_people_globally/.

[2] T Taulli, *Artificial Intelligence Basics: A Non-Technical Introduction* (New York, Apress, 2019), 23.

[3] Die Bundesregierung, 'What is disinformation?', available at www.bundesregierung.de/breg-de/schwerpunkte/disinformation-definition-1911048; N Molina-Clemente and S Zarmsky, 'Digital Clarity: Why International Law Needs Clearer Application in the Digital Space', OpinioJuris, 23 June 2025, available at opiniojuris.org/2025/06/23/digital-clarity-why-international-law-needs-clearer-application-in-the-digital-space/.

[4] Cobalt, 'Top Cybersecurity Statistics for 2025', 23 December 2024, available at www.cobalt.io/blog/top-cybersecurity-statistics-2025.

conflicts and other situations of violence annually affect hundreds of millions of people as victims, missing persons, refugees and internally displaced persons.[5] Climate change is a truly global issue with ecological, political, economic, and humanitarian implications.[6] International terrorism and other transnational organised crime are threatening the well-being of societies on all continents.[7] We are living at the most interesting but also the most dangerous time in history.

No State is able to cope with global challenges like those mentioned above on its own. Even the wealthiest and most powerful nations are vulnerable in the face of dangers affecting everyone. To facilitate communication, exchange experiences and share resources in response to shared threats and challenges, an international system consisting of sovereign States, international institutions and non-State actors has emerged. It is sometimes referred to as the 'international society', to emphasise its diversity and relative decentralisation.[8] At other times, it is called the 'international community'[9] or 'world community', to accentuate its shared interests and values.[10] In this book, the focus is on the 'international system',[11] which, in addition to international actors and their relations, also includes the rules of international law helping make those relations more constructive and friendly.

II. WHY HAVE A LAW FOR THE INTERNATIONAL SYSTEM?

All human interactions are subject to some regulation. Some regulators (such as morals[12] or custom[13]) vary from one society to another, whereas others (such as religion[14]) are more global. In all cases, the purpose of regulation is to make human interactions more consistent. Law is the most stringent of all regulators

[5] Council on Foreign Relations, 'Conflicts to Watch in 2025', available at www.cfr.org/report/conflicts-watch-2025.

[6] Climate Home News, 'Scientists predict global warming of more than 1.5C for 2025–2029 period', 28 May 2025, available at www.climatechangenews.com/2025/05/28/scientists-predict-global-warming-of-more-than-1-5c-for-2025-2029-period/.

[7] Institute for Economics and Peace, 'Global Terrorism Index', available at www.economicsandpeace.org/global-terrorism-index/.

[8] P Allott, *The Health of Nations: Society and Law beyond the State* (Cambridge, Cambridge University Press, 2002), 297.

[9] This term is consistently used in P Gaeta, JE Viñuales and S Zappalà, *Cassese's International Law*, 3rd edn (Oxford, Oxford University Press, 2020).

[10] MN Shaw, *International Law*, 9th edn (Cambridge, Cambridge University Press, 2021), 2–3.

[11] ibid, 5–9.

[12] VM Korelskiy and VD Perevalov (eds), *Teoriya gosudarstva i prava* [*Theory of State and Law*] (Moscow, Norma–Infra M, 1998), 249–52. See also MN Marchenko (ed), *Obshchaya teoriya gosudarstva i prava* [*General Theory of State and Law*], 4th edn, vol 2 (Moscow, Norma–Infra M, 2013), 120–25.

[13] Korelskiy and Perevalov (n 12), 253–55, Marchenko (n 12), 117–18.

[14] Marchenko (n 12), 118–20. See also II Lukashuk, *Mezhdunarodnoye pravo: Obshchaya chast* [*International Law: General Part*] (Moscow, Wolters Kluwer, 2008), 61–64.

in that, in addition to substantive and procedural rules,[15] it also contains provisions prescribing sanctions for violations of the primary rules.[16] For the most part, societies consist of persons sharing those societies' tenets and values – but even then, some individuals act against those common values, and societies take coercive measures against transgressors.[17] A fortiori, the international system where collective (and sometimes, individual) actors are very heterogeneous – and whose original values are very diverse – requires clear and enforceable rules. This is why the international system needs international law.[18]

III. IS INTERNATIONAL LAW REALLY LAW?

At times, international law is denied its legal nature. Its critics often regard it as 'institutionalised politics'[19] or even 'gentlemen's agreements'.[20] The main ground for such condescending criticisms is the absence of a higher or centralised law-making authority in the international system. It is true that the UN General Assembly is not a 'World Parliament' and the UN Security Council is not a 'World Government'; that the jurisdiction of the International Court of Justice (ICJ) – and, for that matter, of other international judicial organs – is not universal; and there are no international police at all.[21] But it does not mean that all rules governing relations within the international system lack legal force. Indeed, some types of international rules – such as international usage or international comity (*comitas gentium*) – lack enforcement mechanisms akin to legal sanctions.[22] However, general international law and its thematic areas *do* provide for bilateral and multilateral mechanisms of legal responsibility,[23] and this circumstance in itself distinguishes international law

[15] On the significance of procedural rules, see AH Saidov, *Sravnitelnoye pravovedeniye* [*Comparative Law*] (Moscow, Yurist, 2003), 249.

[16] MN Marchenko (ed), *Obshchaya teoriya gosudarstva i prava* [*General Theory of State and Law*], 4th edn, vol 3 (Moscow, Norma–Infra M, 2013), 655–98.

[17] F Schmalleger, *Criminology Today: An Integrative Introduction*, 7th edn (Boston MA, Pearson Education Inc, 2015), 166.

[18] HT Adilkariyev, *Mezhdunarodnoye pravo* [*International law*] (Tashkent, Tashkent State Law Institute, 2003), 5–25; II Lukashuk and AH Saidov, *Hozirgi zamon xalqaro huquqi nazariyasi asoslari* [*The theoretical fundamentals of modern international law*] (Tashkent, Adolat, 2006), 8–27; VN Repetsky and VV Gutnyk, 'Sotsialnaya tsennost mezhdunarodnogo prava' ['The Social Value of International Law'] in A Melnyk, S Melnyk and T Korotkyi (eds), *Mezhdunarodnoye pravo kak osnova sovremennogo miroporyadka* [*International Law as the Foundation of Modern World Order*] (Odessa, Phoenix Press, 2012).

[19] For an excellent analysis of the evolving relationship between politics and international law, see M Koskenniemi, *The Politics of International Law* (Oxford, Hart Publishing, 2011).

[20] Britannica, 'Gentlemen's Agreement', available at www.britannica.com/event/Gentlemens-Agreement.

[21] P Malanczuk, *Akehurst's Modern Introduction to International Law*, 7th revised edn (London, Routledge, 1997), 3.

[22] See Chapter 7, section I.A below.

[23] On responsibility under international law, see Chapter 9 below.

from other international regulators. Furthermore, the very fact that the rules of international law are created and enforced by subjects who are equal in their sovereignty (and not by a superior authority, as is the case in domestic legal systems) may be interpreted as evidence of international law's more democratic character.[24]

IV. A NOTE ON APPLICABLE TERMINOLOGY

There are several interchangeable terms to denote the principles and rules of law applying within the international system. The most common term suggested by Jeremy Bentham (1748–1832) is 'international law'.[25] Literally, it implies that there is a 'law among nations' (*ius inter gentes*). This term is most frequently used throughout this book, for reasons of convenience. Similar terms are used, for example, in Italian ('*diritto internazionale*'), Portuguese ('*direito internacional*'), and Spanish ('*derecho internacional*'). Alternative terms are not fully identical to 'international law' but are frequently encountered in academic discourse. Thus, in Roman law, *ius gentium* was 'a system of equity applying to cases between foreigners and Roman citizens'.[26] Similarly, in Islamic law, *al-siyar* are rules applicable to relations involving a Muslim State, or relations between Muslims and non-Muslims.[27] Upon the publication of a seminal treatise by Emer de Vattel (1714–67) in 1758,[28] the term 'law of nations' became popular. It has influenced, in particular, the academic terminology used by German-speaking ('*Völkerrecht*') and French-speaking lawyers ('*droit de gens*'), although these terms literally mean 'the law of peoples'. In Eastern Europe,[29] South Caucasus,[30] and Central Asia,[31] the relevant terms literally mean 'the law among peoples' or 'the law among nations'. For comparison, the Chinese phrase 國際法 ('*Guójìfǎ*') literally stands for 'law between nations', as does the Hindi term अंतरराष्ट्रीय कानून ('*antararaashtreey kanoon*'). The Japanese expression 国際法 ('*Kokusai-hō*') and the Korean term 국제법 ('*gugjebeob*') literally mean 'law between nations'. These traditional designations suggest that the main

[24] J Klabbers et al, 'International Law and Democracy Revisited: Introduction to the Symposium' (2021) 32 *European Journal of International Law* 9.

[25] MN Shaw, *International Law*, 8th edn (Cambridge, Cambridge University Press, 2017), 1, fn 1.

[26] 'Jus gentium', Britannica: www.britannica.com/topic/jus-gentium-Roman-law.

[27] See generally M Khadduri, *The Islamic Law of Nations: Shaybani's Siyar* (Baltimore MD, The Johns Hopkins Press, 1966).

[28] E de Vattel, *The Law of Nations* (Indianapolis IN, Liberty Fund, 2008).

[29] cf, for example, '*mizhnarodnaye prava*' in Belarusian, '*rahvusvaheline õigus*' in Estonian, '*starptautiskās tiesības*' in Latvian, '*tarptautinė teis*' in Lithuanian, '*prawo międzynarodowe*' in Polish, '*mezhdunarodnoye pravo*' in Russian, and '*mizhnarodne pravo*' in Ukrainian.

[30] The relevant terms are միջազգային իրավունք ('*mijazgayin iravunk*') in Armenian, '*beynəlxalq hüquq*' in Azerbaijani, and საერთაშორისო სამართალი ('*saertashoriso samartali*') in Georgian.

[31] The relevant terms are '*halyqaralyq quqyq*' in Kazakh, '*el aralyk ukuk*' in Kyrgyz, '*huquqi baynalmilali*' in Tajik, '*halkara hukugy*' in Turkmen, and '*xalqaro huquq*' in Uzbek.

actors under international law are 'nations', 'peoples', or 'States' but as will be seen, the range of international actors is now much broader.

V. ORIGINS AND NATURE OF INTERNATIONAL LAW

A. European Origins of Modern International Law

Although numerous cultures had rules pertaining to the conduct of international relations, until the twentieth century, international law was largely regarded as a phenomenon with European origins.[32] It was often traced back to the Roman concept of *ius gentium*,[33] and later to the Christian religion.[34] Friedrich Fromhold (Fyodor Fyodorovich) Martens (1845–1909) went as far as to divide peoples into 'civilised' and 'uncivilised' for the purpose of his theory of international law.[35] Such views completely overlooked contributions to the formation of international law by cultures such as Ancient Egypt,[36] Mesopotamia,[37] India,[38] China,[39] the Islamic world,[40] and nomadic cultures,[41] as well as by traditional and informal legal systems.[42]

The idea of modern international law is often associated with names such as Francisco de Vitoria (circa 1483–1546), Francisco Suárez (1548–1617),[43] Alberico Gentili (1552–1608), and most remarkably, Hugo de Groot (Hugo Grotius, 1583–1645). More particularly, de Groot authored two books, which are commonly regarded as the foundations of modern international law scholarship. In 1609, he published *Mare liberum* ('*The Free Sea*') where he expounded the idea that all nations should be free to use the high seas for the purpose of travel and trade.[44] In 1625, *De iure belli ac pacis* ('*On the Law of War and Peace*') followed,[45] which institutionalised the doctrinal division of the law of nations into the 'law of war' and the 'law of peace'. The influence of these books was

[32] J Klabbers, *International Law*, 3rd edn (Cambridge, Cambridge University Press, 2021), 4.
[33] DV Dozhdev, *Rimskoye chastnoye pravo* [*Roman Private Law*], 3rd edn (Moscow, Norma–Infra M, 2018), 41.
[34] H Grotius, *The Truth of the Christian Religion* (Indianapolis IN, Liberty Fund, 2012).
[35] FF Martens, *Sovremennoye mezhdunarodnoye pravo tsivilizovannyh narodov* [*The Contemporary International Law of Civilised Peoples*], vols 1 and 2 (Moscow, Zertsalo, 2008).
[36] OA Zhidkov and NA Krasheninnikova (eds), *Istoriya gosudarstva i prava zarubezhnyh stran* [*History of the State and Law of Foreign Countries*], vol 1 (Moscow, Norma–Infra M, 2001), 25–38.
[37] ibid, 39–52, 77–93.
[38] ibid, 53–65, 94–114.
[39] ibid, 66–76, 115–28.
[40] ibid, 498–504.
[41] MA Sarsembayev and KM Sarembayev, *Mezhdunarodnoye pravo* (Almaty, Zhety Zhargy, 2009), 20–33.
[42] Saidov (n 15), 295–344.
[43] F Suárez, *Selections from Three Works* (Indianapolis IN, Liberty Fund, 2015).
[44] H Grotius, *The Free Sea* (Indianapolis IN, Liberty Fund, 2004).
[45] H Grotius, *The Rights of War and Peace*, vols I–III (Indianapolis IN, Liberty Fund, 2005).

great and enduring. They were essential in making international law a tool for consolidating Europe's colonial domination over peoples of the Global South.[46]

B. Natural Law

According to de Groot, laws obliging peoples were of a natural (*ius naturale*) and positive (*ius voluntarium*) character.[47] Natural law was binding on all human beings, irrespective of religion (and, for that matter, also on animals and inanimate objects).[48] The natural law theory has declined over time but its elements are still present in the concept of customary international law (see Chapter seven, section I below). Quite a few key areas of international law – such as the law of the sea,[49] the laws and customs of war,[50] and diplomatic and consular law[51] – have developed as international custom, and were not codified until relatively recently.

C. Positive Law

The positive law approach has prevailed in that international law is now predominantly positive – that is, treaty-based. On the law of treaties, see Chapter six in this book.

D. Universal International Law

With the proliferation of sovereign States after the Second World War,[52] and given the current interdependence within the international system,[53] international law has become a universal phenomenon. Almost all areas of international law affect almost all States and are managed by universal

[46] E Masters, 'The Berlin Conference and the New Imperialism in Africa', 7 March 2023, available at: www.amdigital.co.uk/insights/blog/the-berlin-conference-and-the-new-imperialism-in-africa.

[47] S Sayapin, *The Crime of Aggression in International Criminal Law: Historical Development, Comparative Analysis and Present* State (The Hague, TMC Asser Press, 2014), 22.

[48] See generally S Pufendorf, *The Whole Duty of Man, According to the Law of Nature* (Indianapolis IN, Liberty Fund, 2003); S Pufendorf, *Two Books of the Elements of Universal Jurisprudence* (Indianapolis IN, Liberty Fund, 2009).

[49] See Chapter 12 below. See also A Proelß (ed), *United Nations Convention on the Law of the Sea* (Baden-Baden, Nomos, 2017).

[50] See Chapter 14 below.

[51] G Yuldasheva, *Diplomaticheskoye i konsulskoye pravo* [*Diplomatic and Consular Law*] (Tashkent, Tashkent State University of Law, 2014).

[52] With only 51 founding Members in 1945, the United Nations now consists of 193 sovereign States: www.un.org/en/about-us/member-states.

[53] See section I.A above.

international institutions.[54] International courts such as the ICJ[55] and many others, arbitral institutions and other mechanisms are there to help settle disputes among States and other international actors. Customary rules on the international responsibility of States and international organisations for internationally wrongful acts have been codified. Importantly, international law is not static, and new areas – such as climate change law,[56] cyberspace law,[57] and animal law[58] – are emerging.

E. Regional International Law

At the same time, regional international law and institutions are developing,[59] especially in such strategic areas as the promotion and protection of human rights,[60] security,[61] and trade.[62] Regional institutions are 'more flexible than the UN, may claim to have a better understanding of regional contexts and issues, and, probably most importantly, share common legal and political ideologies and values'.[63] Especially in the area of international security, '[i]t may reasonably be predicted that [in the future, there will be] multiple regional security organisations ensuring their members' security against potential threats emanating from [non-member States] and armed non-State actors'.[64] Along with obvious benefits, a distinct challenge brought about by regional institutions is the so-called fragmentation of international law.[65] It requires a balanced approach, so that the integrity of the international legal system is not endangered.

[54] See Chapter 3, sections II and III below.
[55] See Chapter 3, section II.F below.
[56] II Lukashuk and AH Saidov, *Hozirgi zamon xalqaro huquqi nazariyasi asoslari* [*The theoretical fundamentals of modern international law*] (Tashkent, Adolat, 2006), 277–86.
[57] IJ Lloyd, *Information Technology Law*, 9th edn (Oxford, Oxford University Press, 2020); N Tsagourias and R Buchan (eds), *Research Handbook on International Law and Cyberspace*, 2nd edn (Cheltenham, Edward Elgar Publishing, 2021); S Chesterman, *We, the Robots?* (Cambridge, Cambridge University Press, 2021).
[58] RN Fasel and SC Butler, *Animal Rights Law* (Oxford, Hart Publishing, 2023); F Dalpane and M Baideldinova (eds), *Animal Law Worldwide: Key Issues and Main Trends Across 27 Jurisdictions* (The Hague, TMC Asser Press, 2024).
[59] A Simonyan, *Regional International Law in Eurasia* (Tartu, University of Tartu Press, 2024).
[60] S Sayapin, 'International Law in Central Asia: Practices and Doctrines' (2022) 47 *Review of Central and East European Law* 322, 341–43.
[61] On the Collective Security Treaty Organisation (CSTO), see Chapter 3, section IV.D below.
[62] On the Eurasian Economic Union (EAEU), see Chapter 12, sections II and III below.
[63] S Sayapin, 'Institutional Attitudes Towards Acts of Aggression' in S Bock and E Conze (eds), *Rethinking the Crime of Aggression: International and Interdisciplinary Perspectives* (The Hague, TMC Asser Press, 2022), 146 (footnotes omitted).
[64] ibid, 147.
[65] M Koskenniemi (ed), *Fragmentation of International Law: Difficulties Arising from the Diversification and Expansion of International Law: Report of the Study Group of the International Law Commission* (Helsinki, Erik Castren Institute, 2007).

F. Comparative International Law

In recent years, a novel (but already influential) trend has emerged in international legal scholarship, suggesting that traditional views of the universality of international law and its 'monolithic' character are somewhat exaggerated, and that States' attitudes towards international law are in fact determined by their prevailing national interests, political, religious, cultural, and societal attitudes and priorities, and therefore, a 'comparative' understanding of international law might be a better methodology. Since the publication of Anthea Roberts' seminal book in 2017,[66] this approach is becoming ever more popular. The book you are reading right now follows this trend and discusses the theory and practice of international law from a Central Asian perspective. While the author has taken care to interpret the relevant law and practice with maximum accuracy, the book is not intended to represent any official views. It is an academic doctrine in the sense of Article 38(1)(d) of the ICJ Statute, intended to serve as the first English-language textbook of international law for students and scholars of the subject in Central Asia, and to be used as a reference work on Central Asia and international law by colleagues outside the region.

VI. CRITICAL THEORIES OF MODERN INTERNATIONAL LAW

Most international law theories focus on the rules of international law and their application by international actors. However, since the twentieth century, a few critical theories have emerged, which consider connections between international law and international relations, economics, politics and political science, sociology, psychology, and other areas. This trend makes full sense, for none of these fields exist in isolation, and strong mutual influences are present. The following subsections offer brief insights into some critical theories of international law and explain this book's integrative methodology.

A. Psychological Theory of International Law

The psychological theory of international law has its origins in the more general psychological theory of law proposed by Leon Petrażycki (1867–1961). The key concept in the theory is 'legal emotion': according to Petrażycki, 'law in its essence is, first and foremost, not something outside the consciousness of a person, but the content of [his or her] consciousness, a phenomenon

[66] See A Roberts, *Is International Law International?* (Oxford, Oxford University Press, 2017). See also A Roberts, PB Stephan, PH Verdier, M Versteeg (eds), *Comparative International Law* (Oxford, Oxford University Press, 2018).

of [his or her] psyche'.[67] This idea is fundamental for our understanding of international law and the values underlying it[68] inasmuch as international law always is a product of a specific time and historical context. For example, slavery had been a normality since antiquity until attitudes towards it started changing worldwide in the late eighteenth century. During the nineteenth century, slavery was made illegal throughout the British Empire, the Americas, in Eastern Europe and some parts of Asia. The Convention to Suppress Slave Trade and Slavery was adopted on 25 September 1926,[69] and after the Second World War, the prohibition of slavery was reaffirmed in the Universal Declaration of Human Rights (UDHR),[70] the International Covenant on Civil and Political Rights (ICCPR),[71] and in regional human rights instruments.[72] In the 1960s–1970s, slavery was abolished in the Arab world, and the last State to abolish slavery in 1981 was Mauritania.[73] Similarly, war was an acceptable state of affairs until after the First World War, and the new attitudes were embodied in the Peace Treaty of Versailles (which included the Covenant of the League of Nations),[74] the Kellogg-Briand Pact,[75] and the Charter of the United Nations.[76] Now both slavery and wars of aggression are crimes under international law, along with some other acts, and the mental health of individuals perpetrating such acts or supporting such conduct is a matter of professional attention for psychiatrists and criminologists.[77]

B. Feminism and International Law

Until the twentieth century, international law was a male profession, and women were excluded from the scholarship and practice of international law. A close reading of Article 97 of the UN Charter suggests that the Secretary-General

[67] A Merezhko, *Psihologicheskaya teoriya mezhdunarodnogo prava (publichnogo i chastnogo)* [*The Psychological Theory of International Law (Public and Private)*] (Odessa, Phoenix Press, 2012), 16. See also A Merezhko, *Psihologicheskaya shkola prava L.I. Petrazhitskogo: istoki, soderzhaniye, vliyaniye* [*L.I. Petrażycki's Psychological School of Law: Origins, Content, Influence*] (Odessa, Phoenix Press, 2016).

[68] See section I.H below.

[69] On the 1926 Slavery Convention, see: www.loc.gov/item/2021667888/.

[70] UDHR, Art 4.

[71] ICCPR, Art 8(1).

[72] European Convention on Human Rights, Art 4(1); American Convention on Human Rights, Art 6(1); African Charter on Human and Peoples' Rights, Art 5.

[73] JD Sutter, 'Slavery's last stronghold', March 2023, available at https://edition.cnn.com/interactive/2012/03/world/mauritania.slaverys.last.stronghold/index.html.

[74] For the text of the Covenant of the League of Nations, see: www.ungeneva.org/en/about/league-of-nations/covenant.

[75] On the 1928 Kellogg-Briant Pact, see Britannica, 'Kellogg-Briand Pact': www.britannica.com/event/Kellogg-Briand-Pact. See also Sayapin (n 47), 34–36.

[76] For the text of the Charter of the United Nations, see: www.un.org/en/about-us/un-charter.

[77] L Goldensohn, The Nuremberg Interviews: *An American Psychiatrist's Conversations with the Defendants and Witnesses* (New York, Vintage Books, 2005).

of the Organisation can only be a man.[78] In its entire history to date, the ICJ has had only five female Judges, compared to 106 male Judges.[79] The first woman who became an ICJ Judge in 1995 – and in 2006, was elected the first female President of the Court – was Dame Rosalyn Higgins.[80] The situation is gradually changing for the better. At present, four out of 15 ICJ Judges are women.[81] Among the current members of the International Law Commission, there are five women (out of 34 members).[82] Many exceptional international law academics are women, and international law classes attract increasing numbers of female students worldwide, including in Central Asia. It is hoped that these dynamics will result in a more balanced international legal profession in the future.

C. Third World Approaches to International Law (TWAIL)

As the number of sovereign States grew substantially as a result of the post-World War II decolonisation, the making of international law rules was no longer a prerogative of their former colonial masters. The Asian-African Conference, which took place at Bandung (Indonesia) on 18–24 April 1955, made clear the beginning of a new era for international law.[83] The new States, conscious and proud of their newly acquired sovereignty, contributed to the development of key areas of international law – such as international human rights law, the law of the sea, international trade law, law of international security, and many others. This intellectual movement focusing on the role of developing nations in the progress of international law is known as the Third World Approaches to International Law (TWAIL).[84] More recently, the Second World Approaches to International Law (SWAIL) narrative began taking shape.[85] Since 1991, the States of Central Asia have made significant contributions to various areas of international law,[86] and this book offers perspectives on some of those.

[78] cf the last sentence of Art 97: '*He* shall be the chief administrative officer of the Organization' (emphasis added).

[79] UN News, 'Women in justice: Three trailblazing World Court judges send a powerful message', 10 March 2023: news.un.org/en/story/2023/03/1134487.

[80] ibid.

[81] ICJ, 'Current Members', available at https://www.icj-cij.org/current-members.

[82] International Law Commission, 'Membership': legal.un.org/ilc/ilcmembe.shtml.

[83] L Eslava, M Fakhri and V Nesiah (eds), *Bandung, Global History, and International Law: Critical Pasts and Pending Futures* (Cambridge, Cambridge University Press, 2017).

[84] See A Anghie, 'Rethinking International Law: A TWAIL Retrospective' (2023) 34 *European Journal of International Law* 7. See also A Anghie, *Imperialism, Sovereignty and the Making of International Law* (Cambridge, Cambridge University Press, 2004).

[85] Central European University, 'In Search of Second World Approaches to International Law', 21 February 2025, available at https://events.ceu.edu/2025-02-21/search-second-world-approaches-international-law.

[86] Sayapin (n 60).

D. Economic Analysis of International Law

In order for rules of international law – and, for that matter, any law – to be effective, it is not enough simply to have good rules. The relevant actors need sufficient resources – first of all, economic resources – to enforce the rules. States need funds to enable the functioning of their organs.[87] International organisations need budgets, and deficits result in inadequate performance. Indeed, the operation of each treaty requires funds,[88] as does the domestic implementation of all treaties.[89] Therefore, where appropriate, this book refers to relevant macroeconomic indicators, and discusses applicable macroeconomic trends.

E. Integrative Methodology

Overall, the book employs an integrative methodology – that is, it places the rules of international law in their historical, political, economic, social, and sometimes religious context, and discusses the influences of those non-legal factors on the shaping and application of the rules of law as well as international law's own impact on those adjacent areas. Obviously, international law does not operate in isolation from those essential factors, and understanding them should help to increase the effectiveness of international law as such.

VII. FUNCTIONS OF INTERNATIONAL LAW

International law has a few important and mutually complementary functions in the international system. It applies alongside other international regulators, and is an eminent factor in international relations (and often, in domestic affairs as well), owing to the binding character of its rules.

A. Common Language

With due regard to differences inherent in States as the main international actors – such as the sizes of their territories and populations, economic and military strengths, political influences, attitudes towards religion, prevailing ideologies, and other factors[90] – they need a common language to communicate with one

[87] BL Coggins and I Kala, 'The economics of state emergence and collapse' in E Kontorovich and F Parisi (eds), *Economic Analysis of International Law* (Cheltenham, Edward Elgar Publishing, 2016).
[88] PB Stephan, 'Treaty enforcement' in Kontorovich and Parisi (n 87).
[89] T Ginsburg, 'The interaction between domestic and international law' in Kontorovich and Parisi (n 87).
[90] On statehood and international law, see Chapter 2 below.

another, and with other international actors. International law enables States and other international actors to set the 'rules of the game' applicable to all irrespective of their differences, to express their legitimate concerns and goals, and to formulate shared solutions to challenges they are facing by reference to universal ideals and ideas which are understandable and acceptable to all. In a way, international law is a *lingua franca* for international actors to identify their common ways and approaches, despite their objective differences. The following chapters show the Central Asian States' many substantive contributions to the international legal discourse.

B. Pacification

By setting common rules of behaviour, international law helps reduce the conflict potential in the international system. In the past, wars were nothing exceptional.[91] However, after the First World War (1914–18), the founders of the League of Nations attempted to limit States' capacity to lawfully resort to military force, and after the Second World War (1939–45), the threat or use of force was outlawed, save in very limited circumstances.[92] International law now offers States and other international actors a wide range of means for the pacific settlement of disputes (see Chapter eight below). In the twenty-first century, trading is more beneficial than making wars,[93] and the substantial development of the 'law of peace' since the mid-twentieth century certainly attests to that.

C. Stability

Any law – domestic or international – contributes to stability in the society where it applies, by allowing or encouraging some behaviours and disallowing and penalising others. In doing so, law seeks to multiply behaviours that are acceptable to most members of a given society, and to reduce ways of conduct that are less or not acceptable due to their relative danger.[94] In the same way, international law reinforces the stability of the international system by promoting peace, respect for human rights and fundamental freedoms[95] and advancing free trade, international communication and mutual understanding; discourages the threat or use of force, crimes under international law and transnational crimes;[96] and sets up mechanisms of responsibility for violations.

[91] Sayapin (n 47), 4.
[92] See Chapter 10 below.
[93] On international trade law, see Chapter 11 below.
[94] Schmalleger (n 17).
[95] On human rights, see Chapter 13 below.
[96] On transnational and international criminal law, see Chapter 15 below.

D. Predictability

Ultimately, international law contributes to making the behaviour of all international actors more predictable (and therefore reliable). Whether we assume that international actors tend to comply with international law because they think such compliance is the right ethical choice, or is in their best interest, or because they fear responsibility and its related negative consequences, we expect compliance to be the norm, and deviations an exception. As a matter of fact, 'almost all nations observe almost all principles of international law and almost all of their obligations almost all of the time'.[97] If such efficiency is taken as a criterion to measure international law's success, then probably international law is among humanity's most successful inventions.

VIII. VALUE-BASED INTERNATIONAL LAW

International law safeguards a few key values which are essential to the modern international society. Indeed, these values are so fundamental that they transcend specific areas of international law and underlie its entire system. They reveal its philosophy and are embodied in numerous (universal and regional) sources of 'hard' and 'soft' international law.[98]

A. Humanity

According to Atadjanov, '[i]t is hard to imagine a more compelling and global idea … in the modern public discourse worldwide than the idea of humanity'.[99] The notion has several mutually complementary meanings:

> The first, and apparently the most widespread understanding of it is humanity as 'humankind' or 'mankind', i.e., the aggregation of all human beings, as a collectivity. The second definition encompasses the quality of being human, or humanness, or the very human condition itself. These first two figure prominently in various legal scholarly works dealing with international criminal law … The third definition foresees the set of strengths focused on tending others, or humanity as a virtue (benevolence). Yet another meaning represents a combination of natural human characteristics (such as ways of thinking, feeling and acting), or humanity as 'human nature'; this one may serve as a distinguishing characteristic of human beings as opposed to animals.[100]

[97] L Henkin, *How Nations Behave* (New York, Columbia University Press, 1979), 47.

[98] On the sources of international law, see Chapters 6 and 7 below.

[99] R Atadjanov, 'Humanity' in S Sayapin et al (eds), *International Conflict and Security Law: A Research Handbook* (The Hague, TMC Asser Press, 2022), 4.

[100] ibid, 5 (footnotes omitted).

Crucially, modern international law is increasingly human-centric.[101] In the past, it was a body of law exclusively for States and international organisations but now, numerous non-State actors – such as individuals, non-governmental organisations (NGOs), and others – have rights and duties under international law, and contribute to its development. For details, see Chapter four in this book.

B. Self-determination and Sustainable Development

Kashnikov notes that '[s]elf-determination is a many-faceted principle, belonging simultaneously to three overlapping realms: the realm of politics, of international law and of morals'.[102] He suggests that self-determination of a people is similar to individual self-determination, and therefore is a 'mix of two … systems of values – liberalism and collectivism'.[103] Freedom is a precondition for development, for there is no development without personal freedom. In turn, the concept of sustainable development originates in the collective dimension of self-determination: 'Sustainable development … meets the needs of the present without compromising the ability of future generations to meet their own needs'.[104] Self-determination is democratic in that it is 'the right of a people to political freedoms'.[105] It is therefore correct that the right to self-determination features in Article 1 of the International Covenant on Civil and Political Rights.[106] It is also an inalienable collective human right 'of a group to exist and … to resist'.[107] Importantly, '[a]s soon as the group is deprived of its culture and modes of expression, of its unique cultural codes as well as the ways of transmission of these codes, the existence of people as collective entities is threatened'.[108] The right of peoples to self-determination is so fundamental that it has acquired the status of a peremptory norm of general international law (*jus cogens*).[109]

C. International Peace and Security

The maintenance of international peace and security is a fundamental objective of the modern international legal order,[110] and a Purpose of the United Nations

[101] A Cassese, *The Human Dimension of International Law: Selected Papers* (Oxford, Oxford University Press, 2008).

[102] B Kashnikov, 'Self-determination of Peoples' in Sayapin et al (n 99), 32.

[103] ibid, 29.

[104] 'Report of the World Commission on Environment and Development: Our Common Future' (Brundtland Report, 1987), available at www.un-documents.net/our-common-future.pdf, 41.

[105] ibid.

[106] See Chapter 13, section II.A below.

[107] Kashnikov (n 102), 31.

[108] ibid.

[109] See Chapter 7, section II.B below.

[110] S Sayapin, 'International Law and the Use of Force: from the Charter of the United Nations to the Rome Statute of the International Criminal Court' (2009) 15 *Asian Yearbook of International Law* 3.

(Article 1(1) of the Charter of the United Nations). The UN Charter contains at least 35 direct references to 'peace',[111] and related words – such as 'peaceful', 'pacific', 'peace-loving' – are mentioned in nine further articles of the Charter.[112] The concept of peace is comprehensive and means more than the absence of armed conflict. It also means respect for human rights and fundamental freedoms, preservation of the environment, sustainable development, and other aspects. For details, see Chapter ten in this book.

D. Natural Resources

As Schrijver noted, after 1945, 'permanent sovereignty over natural resources emerged as a new principle of international law'.[113] The origins of the principle are in the UN Charter.[114] On 14 December 1962, the UN General Assembly adopted Resolution 1803 (XVII) 'Permanent sovereignty over natural resources'.[115] Its first operative paragraph provides that the right of peoples and nations to permanent sovereignty over their natural wealth and resources must be exercised in the interests of their national development and of the well-being of the people of the State concerned. The significance of the principle extends well beyond economic aspects: the resolution's seventh operative paragraph states that violation of the rights of peoples and nations to sovereignty over their natural wealth and resources is contrary to the spirit and principles of the Charter of the United Nations and hinders the development of international cooperation and the maintenance of peace.

E. Cooperation

Cooperation is a fundamental idea underlying international law. As a 'horizontal' legal system, the latter comprises rules made by actors, which are equal in their sovereignty (States), and relies on their voluntary cooperation in order for those rules to be complied with and enforced. Cooperation is the only method of creating the rules of international law and making them work.[116] Cooperation is also essential for holding the delinquent actors responsible for violations of international law in bilateral or multilateral formats.[117]

[111] See Preamble, paras 5, 6, Articles 1(1), (2), 2(3), (6), 11(1), (2), (3), 12(2), 15(1), 18(1), 23(1), 24(1), 26, 33(1), 34, 37(2), 39, 42, 43(1), 47(1), 48(1), 51, 52(1), 54, 73, 76, 84, 99, 106.

[112] See Articles 1(1), 2(3), 4(1), 14, 33(1), 35(2), 38, 52(2), (3), 55.

[113] N Schrijver, 'Self-determination of peoples and sovereignty over natural wealth and resources', available at www.ohchr.org/sites/default/files/Documents/Issues/Development/RTDBook/PartIIChapter5.pdf.

[114] ibid.

[115] For the text of the Resolution, see: www.ohchr.org/en/instruments-mechanisms/instruments/general-assembly-resolution-1803-xvii-14-december-1962-permanent.

[116] See Chapters 6 and 7 below.

[117] See Chapter 9 below.

F. International Rule of Law

Cullen and Gorobets observe that '[t]he concept of the international rule of law belongs to the most complicated and debatable topics in international legal scholarship'.[118] They single out three main approaches towards the phenomenon. First, 'the international rule of law is supplementary to the domestic rule of law in the sense that international institutions become actively involved in promoting and strengthening the rule of law within states'.[119] This approach appears to underlie the theory of primacy of domestic law over international law.[120] The second approach treats the international rule of law 'as an independent set of principles relevant to the international legal system'.[121] In other words,

> [s]uch an understanding of the international rule of law traces back to the Grotian tradition of international law and implies that the international rule of law is not a weaker or defective version of the rule of law but its independent manifestation.[122]

It manifests itself in the dualist theory of relationship between international law and domestic law.[123] The third approach argues

> that the international rule of law concerns three levels of relations: horizontal state-to-state relations; relations in respect of the execution of governmental authority in regard to individuals and non-state actors; and relations in respect of the execution of authority by international institutions.[124]

This approach reflects the monist theory and the theory of primacy of international law over domestic law,[125] and most comprehensively matches this book's integrative concept and methodology.[126]

[118] A Cullen and K Gorobets, 'The International Rule of Law' in Sayapin et al (n 99), 48.
[119] ibid.
[120] See Chapter 5, section I.C below.
[121] Cullen and Gorobets (n 118).
[122] ibid.
[123] See Chapter 5, section I.A below.
[124] Cullen and Gorobets (n 118), 49–50.
[125] See Chapter 5, sections I.B and I.D below.
[126] See section VI.E above.

2

The Central Asian States as Sovereign Actors

Although Central Asia is sometimes said to include Eastern Iran, Afghanistan, Mongolia, Western China, and parts of Russia,[1] this book focuses on post-Soviet Central Asia – namely Kazakhstan, Kyrgyzstan, Tajikistan, Turkmenistan, and Uzbekistan – as sovereign actors and primary subjects of international law. This chapter offers an overview of statehood in the region since antiquity and examines the key elements of modern statehood from the perspective of international law.

I. STATEHOOD IN CENTRAL ASIA

There is a misconception that statehood in Central Asia is a recent development. In 2014, Vladimir Putin claimed that Kazakhstan's first President, Nursultan A Nazarbayev, had done 'a unique thing. He created a State on a territory where there had never been a State. Kazakhs have never had statehood [of their own]'.[2] In 2020, State Duma member Vyacheslav Nikonov asserted that 'Kazakhstan simply did not exist' and that its territory was 'a big present from Russia and the Soviet Union'.[3] The following sections refute such claims. In fact, Central Asia's political culture and traditions of statehood pre-date those of Russia by centuries. Moreover, the emergence of modern sovereign statehood in Central Asia compellingly reflects the peremptory principle of the self-determination of peoples.[4]

[1] Geohistory, 'Central Asia: Core and Periphery', 18 May 2025, available at geohistory.today/central-asia/.

[2] BBC News, 'V Kazahstane ozadacheny slovami Putina o russkom mire' ['In Kazakhstan, [People are] Puzzled by Putin's Words about the Russian World'], 2 September 2014: www.bbc.com/russian/international/2014/09/140901_kazakhstan_putin.

[3] A Mamashuly, 'Bolshoy podarok'. Vyskazyvaniya rossiyskih deputatov o territorii Kazahstana vyzvali vozmushcheniye' ['A Big Present'. Statements by the Russian Deputies about the Territory of Kazakhstan Caused Outrage], 15 December 2020, available at rus.azattyq.org/a/kazakhstanis-reaction-to-the-statements-of-russian-deputies-about-the-kazakh-territory/31002411.html.

[4] UA Mansurov, *Mezhdunarodnaya pravosubyektnost Respubliki Tadjikistan, Chast 1: Pravo na chlenstvo v mezhdunarodnyh organizatsiyah* [*The international legal personality of the Republic of Tajikistan, Part 1: The right to membership in international organizations*] (Dushanbe, Russian-Tajik

A. Kazakhstan[5]

Humans have inhabited the territory of modern-day Kazakhstan since the Lower Paleolithic period. Archaeologists have found tools used by *Homo erectus* around 1,000,000–800,000 BCE near Qaratau, Mangyshlaq, and Lake Balqash. Climate warming between 12,000 and 5,000 BCE enabled widespread settlement across present-day Kazakhstan, with over 500 dwellings identified. The Neolithic Revolution saw advances in hunting, fishing, agriculture, and the production of sophisticated tools. The Koskuduk I site near Aktau on the Caspian Sea (circa 5000–4000 BCE) contains the oldest known grave in Kazakhstan. Another grave, of a cremated woman, was found near Zhelezinka (Pavlodar region). The Qaraunkur cave in southern Kazakhstan yielded stone and bone tools, ceramics, and animal remains (bears, deer, pigs, horses, and others).[6] Copper tool production began between 4000 and 3000 BCE.[7] By 2700 BCE, millet was cultivated in the Dzunghar Alatau to feed sheep and goats during winter. From 2000 BCE to 800 CE, nomadic cattle breeding developed alongside the consolidation of sun, sky, and fire cults. The first written records of tribes inhabiting the region date to the mid-first millennium BCE. Herodotus (circa 484–425 BCE) described the Scythians (Saka, Sakae) and their interactions with Achaemenid Iran.[8] Between 300 and 200 BCE, proto-Mongol and proto-Turkic nomadic tribes from the steppes south and southeast of the Altai Mountains formed the Xiangnu confederation. It lasted until the first century CE, when some Xiangnu settled in the Dzunghar Alatau, while others moved westward into Kazakhstan and, in 375, into Europe, initiating the Migration Period.[9]

In the mid-first millennium CE, the first Turkic Khaganate (552–603) emerged between the Altai Mountains and the Caspian Sea, and cities such as Otrar, Sygnaq, Taraz, and Balasagyn developed along the Great Silk Road. By the sixth century, the region was known as 'Turkestan' (land of the Turks), and in the seventh century, it split into Eastern and Western Khaganates.[10] During the seventh and eighth centuries, the area witnessed a power struggle between China and the Umayyad Caliphate, which ended with the latter's victory at the Battle of Talas (751). This led to the replacement of ancient Turkic script

(Slavonic) University, 2019); RT Hakimov, *Mezhdunarodnaya pravosubyektnost: voprosy istorii, teorii i praktiki* [*International legal personality: Issues of history, theory, and practice*] (Tashkent, Yangi asr avlodi, 2012).

[5] This section uses the author's material published in S Sayapin, 'Kazakhstan' in M Porsche-Ludwig and Ying-Yu Chen (eds), *Handbook of Asian States: Geography – History – Culture – Politics – Economy, Part 1* (LIT Verlag, 2021), pp 267–76. Permission to use published material is gratefully acknowledged.

[6] GV Kan, *Istoriya Kazahstana* [*History of Kazakhstan*] (Almaty, Almatykitap baspasy, 2013), 17–25.

[7] ibid, 25–38.

[8] ibid, 38–47.

[9] ibid, 47–52.

[10] ibid, 53–65.

with the Arabic alphabet and the gradual decline of the indigenous religion, Tengrianism (Tengrism).[11]

In the ninth and tenth centuries, two new Turkic states arose in what is present-day Kazakhstan: the Qarakhanids in the south and east, and the Oghuz Yabgu State in the west.[12] The Kara-Khitans later established control in 1140,[13] ruling Central Asia until defeated by the Naimans in 1211[14] and by Genghis Khan in 1218.[15] In 1391, Amir Temur ('Tamerlane') triumphed over the Golden Horde Khanate, leading to its division into the western (White Horde) and eastern (Blue Horde) wings.[16]

In 1459, several tribes led by Kerei Khan (1425–74) and Janibek Khan (1428–73) settled in Moghulistan. The Kazakh Khanate, founded by Kerei and Janibek, was established in 1465 and formally existed until 1847.[17] By the mid-eighth century, the Khanate began to decline due to conflicts with the Dzunghars and Oirats.[18] Russian colonisation of present-day Kazakhstan began around the same period and was completed in the second half of the nineteenth century.[19] Colonial policies sparked uprisings, including those led by Isatay Taymanuly (1836–37), Makhambet Utemisuly (1836–38), and Eset Kotibaruly (1847–58).[20] Between 1906 and 1913, over 430,000 farms from European Russia were relocated to the Akmola, Torgay, Ural, and Semipalatinsk regions under Pyotr Stolypin's (1862–1911) agrarian reform, while Kazakhs were forcibly displaced to the central and southern steppes. Under the electoral law of 3(16) June 1907, indigenous peoples of Siberia, Central Asia, and Kazakhstan were disenfranchised. These reforms prompted some Kazakhs to migrate, particularly to China.[21]

Soon after the Russian Revolution, on 13 December 1917, a group of Kazakh politicians established Alash Orda, a provisional government of 25 members (including 10 non-Kazakhs) and 15 member candidates. During the Russian Civil War, Alash Orda manoeuvred between rival factions before surrendering to the Soviets in December 1919. It was dissolved in early 1920, and nearly all

[11] S Akimbekov, *Kratkaya istoriya kazahov: Ot pervyh kochevnikov do nashih dney* [*A Brief History of Kazakhs: From the First Nomads to Our Days*] (Almaty, Institute of Asian Studies, 2023), 41–42.

[12] Kan (n 6), 71–72; Akimbekov (n 11), 43–44.

[13] Kan (n 6), 65–71.

[14] Kan (n 6), 72–73.

[15] Akimbekov (n 11), 53–73. See also R Rahmanaliyev, *Imperiya tyurkov: Istoriya velikoy tsivilizatsii* [*Turkic Empire: History of a Great Civilisation*] (Moscow, Ripol Classic, 2021), 242–450.

[16] Kan (n 6), 88–100; Rahmanaliyev (n 15), 451–628.

[17] Akimbekov (n 11), 92–171. See also M Sarsembayev, *Mezhdunarodnoye pravo v istorii Kazakhstana i Sredney Azii* [*International law in the history of Central Asia*] (Astana, Foliant, 2011), 5–22.

[18] Kan (n 6), 101–24. See also R Temirgaliyev, *Epoha poslednih batyrov* [*The Epoch of the Last Batyrs*] (Almaty, Meloman Publishing, 2024).

[19] Kan (n 6), 125–33; Sarsembayev (n 17), 23–27. See also R Temirgaliyev, *Kazahi i Rossiya* [*Kazakhs and Russia*] (Almaty, Meloman Publishing, 2024).

[20] Kan (n 6), 134–50.

[21] Kan (n 6), 151–86; Akimbekov (n 11), 172–92.

its leaders were later executed.[22] On 26 August 1920, the Autonomous Kyrgyz Socialist Soviet Republic (within the RSFSR) was established on its territory, with Orenburg as its capital. In 1925, it was reorganised as the Kazak Autonomous Socialist Soviet Republic (Kazak ASSR), with the capital moved to Qyzylorda, and in 1927 to Alma-Ata. In 1936, the Kazak ASSR was renamed the Kazakh ASSR and, on 5 December 1936, was separated from the RSFSR and reorganised as the Kazakh Soviet Socialist Republic (Kazakh SSR).[23] Under Soviet rule,[24] Kazakhstan experienced industrialisation and significant educational reforms – some serving to impose Russian language and culture[25] – as well as mass deportations (including Poles, Ukrainians, Koreans, Greeks, Chechens, Ingush, and Crimean Tatars), two man-made famines (1919–22 and 1932–33),[26] and 456 nuclear tests at the Semipalatinsk site (1949–89).[27] The latter would later position independent Kazakhstan as a leader in the international anti-nuclear movement.[28]

Kazakhstan declared independence from the Soviet Union on 16 December 1991, becoming the last Soviet republic to do so.[29] Independence Day is celebrated annually on that date. On 21 December 1991, Alma-Ata (now Almaty) hosted a summit where the leaders of Azerbaijan, Armenia, Belarus, Kazakhstan, Kyrgyzstan, Moldova, Russia, Tajikistan, Turkmenistan, Uzbekistan, and Ukraine signed a Protocol to the Agreement on the Establishment of the Commonwealth of Independent States.[30] Kazakhstan's current Constitution was approved by referendum on 30 August 1995.[31] It grants broad powers to the President (Articles 40–48), establishes a bicameral Parliament (Articles 49–63), and a Government accountable to both President and Parliament (Articles 64–70). It also provides for a Constitutional Court (Articles 71–74), and a judiciary comprising the Supreme Court and other courts (Articles 75–82). The Prosecutor's Office oversees legality, represents the State in court, and conducts criminal prosecutions (Article 83). The Commissioner for Human Rights promotes and restores human and civil rights and freedoms (Article 83-1). The first President, Nursultan A Nazarbayev (born 1940), assumed power on 24 April 1990 as First Secretary of the Communist Party of the Kazakh SSR, was elected President on 1 December 1991, and remained in office until resigning on 19 March 2019. He was succeeded by Dr Kassym-Jomart K Tokayev (born 1953), a career diplomat and former Chairman of the Senate, who was elected President on 9 June 2019.

[22] Kan (n 6), 207–12; Akimbekov (n 11), 192–214.
[23] Akimbekov (n 11), 256–68.
[24] Sarsembayev (n 17), 115–75.
[25] Kan (n 6), 213–31; Akimbekov (n 11), 256–322.
[26] Akimbekov (n 11), 215–55.
[27] Kan (n 6), 232–41. See also T Kassenova, *Atomnaya step: Kak Kazahstan otkazalsya ot yadernogo oruzhiya* [*Atomic Steppe: How Kazakhstan Gave Up the Bomb*] (Almaty, Steppe & World Publishing, 2024).
[28] See Chapter 10, section IX.H below.
[29] Sarsembayev (n 17), 176–91.
[30] See Chapter 3, section IV.B below.
[31] For the text of the Constitution of the Republic of Kazakhstan (in Russian), see: www.akorda.kz/ru/official_documents/constitution.

Since 1991, Kazakhstan has undertaken significant economic, political, and social reforms. In October 1997, the country's first President introduced a Strategy for Development until 2030, outlining seven long-term priorities: national security; domestic political stability and social cohesion; economic growth based on an open market economy with strong foreign investment and domestic savings; citizens' health, education, and welfare; energy resources; infrastructure, particularly transport and communication; and a more professional State. According to the World Bank in 2025:

> In 2025, Kazakhstan's economic growth is projected to moderate to 4.5%, supported by a one-off increase in oil production and further fiscal stimulus, before slowing towards its 3.5% growth potential. Household spending is expected to remain resilient, bolstered by social transfers and steady consumer borrowing. Exports are anticipated to expand, driven by strong crude oil shipments …
>
> The poverty rate is projected to decline gradually to 4.9% by 2027 (at the [US]$6.85/day threshold). However, higher-than-projected inflation could disproportionately impact low-income households and delay poverty reduction.[32]

Measures were adopted to reform the civil service based on merit, combat corruption, and strengthen judicial independence. Several world-class higher education institutions were established, including Maqsut Narikbayev University (MNU)[33] and Nazarbayev University (NU)[34] in Astana, and KIMEP University[35] in Almaty. These institutions employ national and international academics with competitive doctoral degrees and educate undergraduate and postgraduate students from Kazakhstan, Central Asia, and beyond. Ongoing reforms include economic digitalisation, renewable energy development, improved law enforcement, and armed forces modernisation. Kazakhstan's foreign policy follows a multi-vectoral approach, fostering relations with Central Asian States, Russia, China, the EU, the United States, and international organisations.[36] In 2017–2018, Kazakhstan became the first Central Asian State to serve on the UN Security Council as a non-permanent member, using the opportunity to advance its international agenda on nuclear non-proliferation, counter-terrorism, and conflict resolution.

B. Kyrgyzstan

The territory of present-day Kyrgyzstan has been inhabited since the Paleolithic era, with archaeological evidence of early human presence in the Tien Shan

[32] The World Bank, 'Kazakhstan – Overview': www.worldbank.org/en/country/kazakhstan/overview.

[33] Maqsut Narikbayev University, available at mnu.kz/.

[34] Nazarbayev University, available at nu.edu.kz/.

[35] KIMEP University, available at https://www.kimep.kz/en/.

[36] Kan (n 6), 244–93; Akimbekov (n 11), 357–435.

mountains and Fergana Valley predating recorded history. The history of the Kyrgyz people dates back to at least the second century BCE.[37] Their early settlements were probably in the upper Yenisey River valley in central Siberia, possibly linked to the Tashtyk culture (first century BCE – fifth century CE).[38] By the mid-ninth century, the Kyrgyz, now Turkic-speaking, overthrew the Uighur Empire in Mongolia, though they did not establish lasting control and remained in forested regions. In 1207, they capitulated to Jochi (circa 1182–1227), eldest son of Genghis Khan, maintaining a degree of separation from the spread of Islam.[39]

In the sixteenth and seventeenth centuries, most remaining Kyrgyz tribes lived as nomadic herders in the Tien Shan mountains, organised into two factions (left and right). In 1703, under pressure from the Dzunghars – a western Mongolian tribe – the Yenisey Kyrgyz migrated to the Semirechye region. Nevertheless, conflicts continued until the Qing dynasty defeated the Dzunghars in 1757. By the mid-eighteenth century, the Kyrgyz had nominally become part of the Qing (Manchu) Empire. Between 1825 and 1830, they were subjugated by Muhammad Ali Khan of Qo'qon (also known as Madali Khan, circa 1808 – circa 1842). In the following decades, southern Kyrgyz mounted sporadic uprisings against the Qo'qon Khanate.[40] Another major threat to Kyrgyz life arose from the simultaneous influx of Russian settlers. In 1916, widespread dissatisfaction culminated in a major uprising, which was met with harsh and prolonged repression – even after the fall of the tsarist regime.[41]

Under Soviet rule, the Kyrgyz faced considerable challenges in asserting their identity as a distinct ethnic group.[42] In 1924, an autonomous Kirgiz oblast (province) was created within the Russian Soviet Federated Socialist Republic (RSFSR), elevated to an autonomous republic in 1926, and upgraded to the Kirgiz Soviet Socialist Republic in 1936. In the late twentieth century, Kyrgyzstan showed one of the strongest desires for independence among the Central Asian Soviet republics.[43] After more than a millennium of external domination, it became a sovereign nation on 31 August 1991.[44]

Since 1991, 'the Kyrgyz Republic has experienced political instability, with several political upheavals leading to the overthrow of presidents in 2005, 2010, and 2020'.[45] During Askar A Akayev's presidency (born 1944),

[37] OJ Osmonov, *Istoriya Kyrgyzstana (S drevneyhih vremen do nashih dney)* [*The History of Kyrgyzstan (From the Ancient Times to Our Days)*] (Bishkek, Mezgil, 2024), 40–49.
[38] Rahmanaliyev (n 15), 121–36.
[39] Osmonov (n 37), 50–151.
[40] ibid, 151–252.
[41] ibid, 305–403.
[42] ibid, 404–24.
[43] ibid, 424–520.
[44] ibid, 557–80.
[45] The World Bank, 'Kyrgyz Republic – Overview': www.worldbank.org/en/country/kyrgyzrepublic/overview. See also Osmonov (n 37), 581–622.

Kyrgyzstan was often called an 'island of democracy in Central Asia'.[46] However, his administration faced widespread corruption allegations, triggering mass protests in March 2005. The resulting 'Tulip Revolution' led to Akayev's swift ouster; he left the country on 24 March 2005 and resigned shortly thereafter.[47]

In the July 2005 elections, Kurmanbek Bakiyev (born 1949) was elected President. His presidency was marked by significant political turbulence as he sought to consolidate power. Mounting protests over authoritarianism and corruption culminated in violent unrest in April 2010. Riot police, unable to disperse crowds with tear gas and stun grenades, used live ammunition, killing around 80 people and injuring many more. A state of emergency was declared on 7 April amid protests in Naryn, Tokmak, and Talas, where demonstrators seized government buildings. By the morning of 8 April, Bakiyev had fled the capital by air, and the opposition formed an interim government. Roza I Otunbayeva (born 1950) served as Interim President from 7 April 2010 to 1 December 2011 – the first, and to date only, female Head of State in Central Asia.[48]

In October 2010, Kyrgyzstan held its first parliamentary elections under the new Constitution enacted on 27 June 2010. A coalition government was formed, and Almazbek S Atambayev (born 1956) of the Social Democratic Party of Kyrgyzstan (SDPK) became Prime Minister. He resigned in September 2011 to run for president and was elected in October 2011 with over 60 per cent of the vote. Barred by term limits from seeking re-election, Atambayev was succeeded by Sooronbai S Jeenbekov (born 1958), who was elected President in October 2017. Jeenbekov resigned on 15 October 2020, and Prime Minister Sadyr N Japarov (born 1968) became Acting President. Japarov was elected to a full term in January 2021. A referendum in April 2021 approved a new Constitution expanding presidential powers, which came into force in May.[49]

According to the World Bank,

> [t]o unlock strong, sustainable growth, reforms are needed to attract private investment, boost international trade, and promote sustainable energy. By focusing on these areas, the Kyrgyz Republic can build resilience, drive domestic growth, and reduce dependence on external factors, ultimately securing a brighter future for its citizens.[50]

[46] B Pannier, 'Kyrgyzstan: Central Asia's Island of Democracy Sinks Into Authoritarianism', Foreign Policy Research Institute, 12 April 2024, available at www.fpri.org/Art/2024/04/kyrgyzstan-central-asias-island-of-democracy-sinks-into-authoritarianism/.

[47] T Wood, 'Reflections on the Revolution in Kyrgyzstan' (2006) 30 *The Fletcher Forum of World Affairs* 43.

[48] S Akiner, 'Kyrgyzstan 2010: Conflict and Context', Silk Road Studies Program, July 2016, available at silkroadstudies.org/resources/2016-Akiner-Kyrgyzstan_2010-Conflict-Context.pdf.

[49] On developments in Kyrgyzstan since 2021, see Pannier (n 46).

[50] The World Bank (n 45).

C. Tajikistan

The Tajiks are closely related to the Iranian peoples whose presence in Central Asia dates back to the first millennium BCE. Their ancestors were part of the Persian and Alexandrian empires and later assimilated with invaders such as the Kushans and Hephtalites between the first and sixth centuries CE. Arab conquests began in the mid-seventh century but were weakened by internal conflicts. With the rise of the Samanid dynasty (819–999), the Tajiks came under Iranian rule. In 999, Turkic forces captured Transoxiana. As both groups were Muslim, many Tajiks – especially in the Syrdaryo and Amudaryo river valleys – eventually became Turkicised. Until the mid-eighteenth century, they were part of the Emirate of Bukhara. Afghan forces later seized territories south and southwest of the Amudaryo, and in 1849–50, took the historic city of Balkh, a key Tajik cultural centre.[51]

Russian imperial expansion in the 1860s and 1870s led to the incorporation of Tajiks from the Zaravshon and Fergana valleys into the Russian administrative system. By 1873, the Emirate of Bukhara had become a Russian protectorate. After the 1917 Russian Revolution, much of the Tajik population was included in the Turkestan Autonomous Soviet Socialist Republic, established in April 1918. The Bukhara People's Soviet Republic was proclaimed in October 1920, and in early 1921, Soviet forces captured Dushanbe and Kulob (Kulyab). The Basmachi uprising followed in 1922–23, with insurgents led by Ibrahim Bek (1889–1931) active in eastern Bukhara until 1931. In 1925, the Tajik Autonomous Soviet Socialist Republic was formed within the Uzbek SSR, and the Gorno-Badakhshan autonomous region was created in December that year. The Tajik ASSR was upgraded to a Soviet Socialist Republic in 1929. In the following decades, major infrastructure projects, including dams for power and irrigation, were undertaken. Dushanbe (renamed Stalinabad from 1929 to 1961) developed into a modern capital, home to the Tajik State University (established 1951) and the Tajik Academy of Sciences (founded 1948).[52]

Tajikistan declared independence from the Soviet Union on 9 September 1991. Rahman N Nabiyev (1930–93), a former Communist leader, won the presidential election in November 1991. In March 1992, large-scale peaceful protests broke out in Dushanbe following his dismissal of opposition groups. The situation escalated in May when government forces opened fire on demonstrators. In September, opposition forces ousted Nabiyev and briefly seized control, but by November, a government led by Emomali S Rahmonov (born 1952), with Russian military backing, had retaken power – ending the war's first phase.[53] By the mid-1990s, tens of

[51] BBC News, 'Tajikistan country profile', 30 October 2024, available at www.bbc.com/news/world-asia-16201032. See also K Nourzhanov, *Tajikistan: A Political and Social History* (Canberra, Australian National University Press, 2013), 11–26.

[52] Nourzhanov (n 51), 27–192.

[53] ibid, 193–338.

thousands had died, and over half a million were displaced. A 1994 cease-fire led to Rahmonov's election as President. Sporadic clashes continued until June 1997, when a UN-, Russia-, and Iran-brokered peace agreement ended the conflict.

In 1999, Rahmonov was re-elected with support from some former opponents. In 2003, constitutional amendments he considered vital for modernisation were adopted, including a provision allowing him to remain in office until 2020. He won a new seven-year term in November 2006 with nearly 80 per cent of the vote. In March 2007, he shortened his surname to Rahmon, and was re-elected again on 6 November 2013. In 2015, he was conferred the title 'Leader of the Nation'.

In May 2016, Tajikistan's electorate approved removing term limits for President Rahmon and lowering the minimum age for presidential candidates from 35 to 30 – widely seen as a move to enable the rise of his eldest son, Rustam Emomali (born 1987). By 2020, Rustam had become Chairman of the Majlisi Milli (the upper house of Parliament), placing him first in the presidential line of succession. The 2016 referendum also banned political parties based on religious principles. On 11 October 2020, Rahmon won another presidential election with little opposition.

For decades, poverty has remained Tajikistan's primary economic challenge.[54] As reported by the World Bank:

> Over the last decade, Tajikistan experienced strong economic performance, with growth rate averaging above 7.1%. The economy grew by 8.4 % in 2024, driven by remittance inflows. Strong growth, higher wages, and international remittances helped reduce the number of people living in poverty from 32% of the population in 2009 to an estimated 9.1% in 2024 (at the international poverty line of [US]$3.65/ day) …
>
> The Government of Tajikistan has set an ambitious target – to more than double or triple domestic incomes between 2016 and 2030 – which will require a new growth model centered around a dynamic private sector. Boosting growth and jobs requires structural reforms, improved competition, investment climate, and access to finance, energy sector efficiency, trade, transport and digital connectivity, and human capital development.[55]

D. Turkmenistan

Human settlements in southern Turkmenistan date back to the Paleolithic Age. Some of the earliest evidence of agriculture in Central Asia was discovered about 32 km north of Ashgabat, linked to the Neolithic Jeitun civilisation (fifth millennium BCE). This was followed by other Neolithic cultures between

[54] Asian Development Bank, 'Poverty Data: Tajikistan', available at www.adb.org/where-we-work/tajikistan/poverty.

[55] The World Bank, 'Tajikistan – Overview': www.worldbank.org/en/country/tajikistan/overview.

roughly 2500 and 2000 BCE. In the following centuries, several urban centres emerged, including Namazga-Tepe, which spanned about 60 hectares. From the mid-third century BCE to the Sasanian conquest in the fourth century CE, the area of present-day Turkmenistan formed part of the Parthian Empire.[56]

Historians associate the Turkmens with the Oghuz, a loose alliance of Turkic tribes established in the region since the ninth century. Some Turkmens came under Seljuq rule (1038–1194), after which southern tribes joined the Il-Khanid empire (1256–1335), while northern groups became part of the Golden Horde. In the sixteenth and seventeenth centuries, the Chaudor tribe formed a major confederation in the north, while the Salor tribe dominated the south. During the seventeenth and eighteenth centuries, power shifted to the Yomuts, Tekkes, Ersaris, and Saryks, who migrated from the desert to the fertile oases of Khorezm and along the Atrek, Tejen, and Morghab rivers, gradually adopting a more settled lifestyle. The Tekkes led resistance against Russian expansion in the 1860s and 1870s. In 1869, Russian forces landed on the eastern Caspian shore and founded the port of Krasnovodsk (now Türkmenbashy). The Transcaspian military district was established in 1874 and elevated to provincial status in 1881. In 1899, it was incorporated into the Turkistan Governorate-General. In 1916, Turkmens played a major role in an uprising against Russian rule.[57]

Following the Russian Revolution, the Red Army seized Ashgabat in July 1919 and Krasnovodsk in February 1920. In 1921, the Transcaspian province was renamed Turkmen province and integrated into the Turkistan Autonomous Soviet Socialist Republic. The Turkmen Socialist Soviet Republic was established in October 1924, incorporating the Turkmen province and Turkmen rayons (districts) from the former Khorezm and Bukhara Republics. It formally joined the USSR on 13 May 1925.[58]

Turkmenistan declared independence on 27 October 1991, and its Constitution of 18 May 1992 formalised the name. The first President, Saparmurad A Niyazov (1944–2006), remained in power until his death in December 2006, when he was succeeded by Gurbanguly M Berdimuhamedow (born 1957). In February 2012, Berdimuhamedow was re-elected for a second five-year term. In 2016, the presidential term was extended to seven years, and the age cap of 70 for candidates was removed. He secured a seven-year term in February 2017, winning 98 per cent of the vote. In 2021, his son Serdar was appointed Deputy Prime Minister. In February 2022, Berdimuhamedow announced an early election for March and his decision not to run. Serdar Berdimuhamedov was elected President with over 70 per cent of the vote.[59]

[56] *BBC News*, 'Turkmenistan country profile', 24 March 2023, available at www.bbc.com/news/world-asia-16094646.

[57] Refworld, 'Turkmenistan. Political Conditions in the Post-Soviet Era', 1 December 1993, available at www.refworld.org/reference/countryrep/uscis/1993/en/94014.

[58] ibid.

[59] ibid.

Turkmenistan's post-1991 isolationist policy has led to persistent systemic economic challenges. As observed by the World Bank:

> Tight administrative controls and the public sector's dominant role in economic activity have hindered private sector development. Despite the growth of the private sector's share in segments of the economy, public sector and state-owned monopolies continue to govern the economy and the formal labor market. Apart from the hydrocarbon sector, foreign direct investment (FDI) remains limited.
>
> Opening the economy, improving the business regulatory environment, accelerating the corporatization and privatization of state-owned enterprises (SOEs), and investing more heavily in human capital would be vital to boosting private sector development and achieving medium- and long-term national development goals.[60]

E. Uzbekistan[61]

Lower Paleolithic dwellings and tools were discovered near present-day Samarqand, and in 1938–39, the remains of an 8–9-year-old Neanderthal girl were found in the Teshik-Tash cave in the Surkhondaryo region. Numerous Mesolithic and especially Neolithic sites have been uncovered along the Amudaryo river, in Surkhondaryo, as well as in the Tashkent, Fergana, and Samarqand regions. During the Bronze Age (3000–1000 BCE), settlements such as Sappali-Tepe, Jarkutan, and Kuchuk-Tepe developed along the Amudaryo. In the ninth–eighth centuries BCE, the Khorezm civilisation established advanced irrigation systems and became a major regional centre of trade and culture. In the eighth–sixth centuries BCE, the Ancient Bactrian State, encompassing the Zarafshon and Kashkadaryo valleys (Sogd), gained renown in China, Persia, and Europe for its gold, stone, and bronze artefacts.

In the sixth century BCE, Central Asia was invaded by the Achaemenid Empire. While sedentary Bactria, Khorezm, and Sogd accepted its rule, the Massagetae and other nomadic tribes resisted. In 329 BCE, Alexander the Great conquered Bactria and the Sogdian capital, Maraqanda (now Samarqand). After his death, Sogd became part of the Seleucid Empire (312–63 BCE), and later of the Kushan State (30–350 CE), which was eventually overthrown by the Kidarites (circa 320–500 CE) and the Hephtalites, or White Huns (circa 440–710 CE). Following the Battle of Bukhara (circa 563–567 CE), where the Turkic Khaganate and Sasanian Empire triumphed, the Hephtalite Empire fragmented into smaller kingdoms. The territory of present-day Uzbekistan came under the

[60] The World Bank, 'Turkmenistan – Overview': www.worldbank.org/en/country/turkmenistan/overview.

[61] This section uses the author's material published in S Sayapin, 'Uzbekistan' in M. Porsche-Ludwig and Ying-Yu Chen (eds), *Handbook of Asian States: Geography – History – Culture – Politics – Economy, Part 2* (LIT Verlag, 2021), pp 737–44. Permission to use published material is gratefully acknowledged.

Western Turkic Khaganate, which was conquered by the Chinese Tang Empire in 658 CE.

In the seventh century CE, the Sasanian Empire was defeated by the Umayyad Caliphate (661–750 CE), and Arab forces began invading the lands between the Syrdaryo and Amudaryo rivers. Between 709 and 712, they captured Bukhara,[62] Khorezm, and Samarqand. In July 751, the Arabs defeated the Chinese at the Battle of Talas. The spread of Islam that followed had a mixed impact: it somewhat diminished the preservation of the region's pre-Islamic cultural heritage but also enabled many Central Asian scholars to make major contributions to the Islamic Golden Age (eighth–fourteenth centuries CE).

From 819 to 999, the Samanids ruled Khorasan and Transoxiana under Abbasid suzerainty. They were succeeded by the Qarakhanids in Samarqand until 1212, while the Ghaznavids (1017–40) and Seljuks (1040–1141) ruled Khorezm until their defeat by the Kara-Khitans at the Battle of Qatwan (1141). In 1194, the Khorezm Shah dynasty emerged, challenging both the Seljuks and Kara-Khitans, and ruled until 1219–21, when Genghis Khan overran their territories. His descendants governed the region until the mid-fourteenth century. In 1370, Amir Temur ('Tamerlane') took Samarqand and founded a dynasty that ruled Central Asia until 1500 (Timurids) and India until 1862 (Mughals).[63] In 1500, Muhammad Shaybani (1451–1510) captured Samarqand; his successors moved the capital to Bukhara in 1533. The Bukhara Khanate lasted until 1920, alongside the Khiva (Khorezm) Khanate (1512–1920) and the Qo'qon Khanate (1709–1876). The Tashkent State (1784–1808) was annexed by Qo'qon. After the Russian Revolution, the Turkestan Autonomy was declared on 27 November 1917 but was dissolved by the Bolsheviks in February 1918 and replaced by the Turkestan Autonomous Soviet Socialist Republic. The Khiva and Bukhara Khanates fell to the Red Army in February 1920 and became the Khorezm and Bukhara People's Soviet Republics. In September 1924, both became Socialist Republics, and on 27 October 1924, were reorganised into the Uzbek and Turkmen SSRs. Samarqand was initially the capital of Soviet Uzbekistan, until the capital moved to Tashkent in 1930.

Uzbekistan declared independence from the Soviet Union on 31 August 1991, with Independence Day celebrated annually on 1 September.[64] The Constitution was adopted on 8 December 1992. A new edition of the Constitution was adopted on 30 April 2023. It establishes a bicameral Parliament (Articles 91–104), broad presidential powers (Articles 105–113), a Cabinet of

[62] RN Fry, *Buhara v Sredniye veka* [*Bukhara in the Middle Age*] (Moscow, Tsentrpoligraph, 2016), 25–42.

[63] Rahmanaliyev (n 15), 596–628.

[64] HT Adilkariyev, *Mezhdunarodnoye pravo* [*International law*] (Tashkent, Tashkent State Law Institute, 2003), 90–93.

Ministers (Articles 114–119), and a judiciary comprising the Constitutional Court (Articles 132–133), the Supreme Court, and lower courts (Articles 130–131, 134–140). The first President, Islam A Karimov (1938–2016), assumed power in 1989 as First Secretary of the Communist Party of the Uzbek SSR, became President of the Uzbek SSR on 24 March 1990, and remained in office until his death in 2016.

Mr Karimov was succeeded as President by Shavkat Mirziyoyev (born 1957), who had served as Uzbekistan's Prime Minister from 2003 to 2016. Since 2016, notable economic and political reforms have been implemented. Steps were taken to ease convertibility of the national currency. The National Security Service (NSS) was restructured as the State Security Service (SSS), and a law on police was enacted in 2016. Efforts to combat corruption, particularly in law enforcement, were strengthened. From 2017, some progress in judicial independence became apparent. Customs laws were liberalised, and initiatives targeted the elimination of forced labour in the cotton industry. In 2018, a major reform of criminal law and procedure began to align with international standards.[65] That year, Uzbekistan introduced e-visas and streamlined its visa policy, including for Kyrgyz and Tajik nationals. The 'exit visa' system was abolished on 1 January 2019. In September 2019, individuals previously imprisoned for minor offences were allowed to vote.

At the regional level, Uzbekistan significantly improved relations with its Central Asian neighbours, particularly in transport, energy, and security, while further strengthening ties with Russia and China. In 2017 alone, President Mirziyoyev held around 20 meetings with the leaders of Kazakhstan, Afghanistan, Turkmenistan, and other States. In April 2018, Turkmenistan's President made his first State visit to Uzbekistan. By 2019, GDP growth reached 5.4 per cent, exceeding the World Bank's forecast by 0.1 per cent. Macroeconomic developments since 2020 have also been noteworthy:

> In Uzbekistan, real GDP growth increased to 6.5% in 2024 (from 6.3% in 2023). Real private consumption growth accelerated to 7.5% (compared to 7% in 2023). The 27.6% growth in real investment was driven by centralized investment and foreign direct investment (FDI), with the latter accounting for 30.5% of total investment …
>
> Uzbekistan is projected to grow by 5.9% in 2025, driven by domestic demand from high real wages, remittance inflows, and investment. The improved trade balance, supported by growth in gold, services, and manufactured exports, along with fiscal consolidation, is expected to keep the current account deficit around 5% of GDP over the medium term.[66]

[65] S Sayapin, 'Crimes against the Peace and Security of Mankind in the Revised Edition of the Criminal Code of the Republic of Uzbekistan' (2020) 45 *Review of Central and East European Law* 36.

[66] The World Bank, 'Uzbekistan – Economy', available at www.worldbank.org/en/country/uzbekistan/overview#economy.

II. STATEHOOD UNDER INTERNATIONAL LAW

The Montevideo Convention on the Rights and Duties of States of 26 December 1933 is commonly regarded as a foundational text for discussions on statehood in international law.[67] Article 1 of the Convention sets out the core criteria for statehood: (1) a permanent population; (2) a defined territory; (3) government; and (4) the capacity to enter into relations with other States. The following sections examine the relevance of these, and other, elements in the Central Asian context.

III. PERMANENT POPULATION AND NATIONALITY

Pursuant to Article 1(a) of the Montevideo Convention, the first essential element of statehood is a permanent population.[68] A territory lacking such a population – such as Antarctica – cannot qualify as a State. The Organisation for Economic Co-operation and Development (OECD) defines permanent population as 'the resident population, defined as all nationals present in, or temporarily absent from the country, and aliens permanently settled in the country'.[69] More specifically:

> The population includes the following categories: national armed forces stationed abroad; merchant seamen at sea; diplomatic personnel located abroad; civilian aliens resident in the country; and displaced persons resident in the country. Excluded are the following categories: foreign armed forces stationed in the country; foreign diplomatic personnel located in the country; and civilian aliens temporarily in the country.[70]

The nationals of a State fall under its personal jurisdiction.[71] The size of the permanent population is irrelevant for statehood: some States have vast populations (eg India, China, the United States, Indonesia, Pakistan), while others are home to only a few hundred or thousand nationals (eg Vatican City, Tuvalu, Nauru, Cook Islands, Palau). As of July 2025, Kazakhstan had 20,864,533 inhabitants;[72] Kyrgyzstan, 7,295,034;[73] Tajikistan,

[67] For the text of the Montevideo Convention, see: www.ilsa.org/Jessup/Jessup15/Montevideo%20 Convention.pdf.

[68] II Lukashuk and AH Saidov, *Hozirgi zamon xalqaro huquqi nazariyasi asoslari* [*The theoretical fundamentals of modern international law*] (Tashkent, Adolat, 2006), 136–45.

[69] OECD, 'Population', available at www.oecd.org/en/data/indicators/population.html.

[70] ibid.

[71] See section V below.

[72] Worldometer, 'Kazakhstan Population', available at www.worldometers.info/world-population/kazakhstan-population/.

[73] Worldometer, 'Kyrgyzstan Population', available at www.worldometers.info/world-population/kyrgyzstan-population/.

10,786,734;[74] Turkmenistan, 7,618,847;[75] and Uzbekistan, 37,053,428.[76] It is equally immaterial whether a population is settled or nomadic, or whether it is monoethnic or polyethnic. In fact, most States are polyethnic, including all in Central Asia. As nationals typically constitute the bulk of a State's permanent population, the key rules governing nationality are examined below. While a few multilateral treaties address specific aspects of nationality, most rules remain within domestic law.

A. International Law and Nationality

In addition to Article 15 of the Universal Declaration of Human Rights (UDHR)[77] and relevant treaty provisions concerning the rights of children,[78] women,[79] refugees,[80] persons with disabilities,[81] and migrant workers and their families,[82] nationality is addressed in several specialised instruments: the Convention Relating to the Status of Stateless Persons (28 September 1954),[83] the Convention on the Nationality of Married Women (20 February 1957),[84] and the Convention on the Reduction of Statelessness (30 August 1961).[85] Regional instruments, such as the European Convention on Nationality (6 November 1997), are also applicable.[86]

[74] Worldometer, 'Tajikistan Population', available at www.worldometers.info/world-population/tajikistan-population/.

[75] Worldometer, 'Turkmenistan Population', available at www.worldometers.info/world-population/turkmenistan-population/.

[76] Worldometer, 'Uzbekistan Population', available at www.worldometers.info/world-population/uzbekistan-population/. See also Fergana News, 'Rozhdayemost v Uzbekistane snizhayetsya vtoroy god podryad' ['Birth Rate in Uzbekistan Declines for Second Year in a Row'], 22 July 2025, available at fergana.agency/news/139064/.

[77] See UDHR, Art 15: 'Everyone has the right to a nationality. No one shall be arbitrarily deprived of his nationality nor denied the right to change his nationality'.

[78] See Art 7(1) of the Convention on the Rights of the Child.

[79] See Art 9 of the Convention on the Elimination of All Forms of Discrimination against Women.

[80] See Art 1 of the Convention Relating to the Status of Refugees.

[81] See Art 18 of the Convention on the Rights of Persons with Disabilities.

[82] See Arts 1(1), 7 and 29 of the International Convention on the Protection of the Rights of All Migrant Workers and Members of Their Families.

[83] For the text, see: www.ohchr.org/en/instruments-mechanisms/instruments/convention-relating-status-stateless-persons. At the time of writing, the Convention has 98 States parties, including Turkmenistan: treaties.un.org/Pages/ViewDetailsII.aspx?src=TREATY&mtdsg_no=V-3&chapter=5&Temp=mtdsg2&clang=_en.

[84] For the text, see: treaties.un.org/doc/Treaties/1958/08/19580811%2001-34%20AM/Ch_XVI_2p.pdf. At the time of writing, the Convention has 75 States parties, including Kazakhstan and Kyrgyzstan: treaties.un.org/Pages/ViewDetailsIII.aspx?src=TREATY&mtdsg_no=XVI-2&chapter=16&Temp=mtdsg3&clang=_en.

[85] For the text, see: www.ohchr.org/en/instruments-mechanisms/instruments/convention-reduction-statelessness. At the time of writing, the Convention has 80 States parties, including Turkmenistan: treaties.un.org/pages/ViewDetails.aspx?src=TREATY&mtdsg_no=V-4&chapter=5.

[86] For the text, see: rm.coe.int/168007f2c8.

B. Domestic Nationality Laws

All Central Asian States have enacted domestic laws on nationality (citizenship). In chronological order: the Law 'On Citizenship of the Republic of Kazakhstan' was adopted on 20 December 1991;[87] the Law 'On Citizenship of the Kyrgyz Republic', on 21 May 2007;[88] the Law 'On Citizenship of Turkmenistan', on 22 June 2013;[89] the Constitutional Law 'On Citizenship of the Republic of Tajikistan', on 8 August 2015;[90] and the Law 'On Citizenship of the Republic of Uzbekistan', on 13 March 2020.[91] All these laws define citizenship as a stable (or, in Uzbekistan, permanent) political and legal relationship between a person and the State, reflecting mutual rights and obligations.[92] Uzbekistan's law adds that this relationship entails mutual responsibility and is based on dignity and fundamental rights and freedoms.[93] In all Central Asian States, citizenship is equal regardless of how it is acquired.[94] Under Uzbekistan's law, citizens of the Republic of Karakalpakstan are also citizens of Uzbekistan.[95] Tajikistan may confer honorary citizenship on non-citizens with outstanding merit to the Republic or the world community, with their consent.[96] Citizens of Kyrgyzstan may not be expelled or extradited.[97] Kazakhstan, Tajikistan, and Uzbekistan prohibit extradition unless a treaty provides otherwise.[98] Marriage to or divorce from a foreigner does not affect citizenship.[99]

[87] For the text of the Law (in Russian, as amended), see: online.zakon.kz/Document/?doc_id=1000816&pos=429;-20#pos=429;-20.

[88] The current Law replaced the Law 'On Citizenship of the Kyrgyz Republic' of 18 December 1993. For the text of the Law (in Russian), see: cbd.minjust.gov.kg/202103/edition/1272039/ru.

[89] The current Law replaced the Law 'On Citizenship of Turkmenistan' of 30 September 1992. For the text of the Law (in Russian), see: www.refworld.org/ru/legal/legislation/natlegbod/2013/ru/135237.

[90] The current Constitutional Law replaced the Constitutional Law 'On Citizenship of the Republic of Tajikistan' of 4 November 1995. For the text of the Constitutional Law (in Russian), see: www.refworld.org/ru/legal/legislation/natlegbod/2015/ru/135476.

[91] The current Law replaced the Law 'On Citizenship of the Republic of Uzbekistan' of 2 July 1992. For the text of the Law (in Russian), see: lex.uz/docs/4761986.

[92] Art 1 (first part) of Kazakhstan's law on citizenship; Art 3 (first part) of Kyrgyzstan's law on citizenship; Art 1 (second part) of Tajikistan's law on citizenship; Art 1 of Turkmenistan's law on citizenship; Art 4 (first part) of Uzbekistan's law on citizenship.

[93] Art 4 (first part) of Uzbekistan's law on citizenship.

[94] Art 5 (first part) of Kazakhstan's law on citizenship; Art 4(4) of Kyrgyzstan's law on citizenship; Art 4 (second subparagraph) of Tajikistan's law on citizenship; Art 4(2) of Turkmenistan's law on citizenship; Art 4 (third part) of Uzbekistan's law on citizenship.

[95] Art 4 (second part) of Uzbekistan's law on citizenship.

[96] Art 9 of Tajikistan's law on citizenship.

[97] Art 10 of Kyrgyzstan's law on citizenship.

[98] Art 8 of Kazakhstan's law on citizenship, Art 5 of Tajikistan's law on citizenship, Art 11 of Uzbekistan's law on citizenship.

[99] Art 7 (second part) of Kazakhstan's law on citizenship; Art 8 of Kyrgyzstan's law on citizenship; Art 7 of Tajikistan's law on citizenship; Art 7 of Turkmenistan's law on citizenship; Art 8 of Uzbekistan's law on citizenship.

C. *Jus Soli*

Jus soli ('right of the soil') is a customary principle under which 'citizenship is acquired by birth within the territory of the state, regardless of parental citizenship'.[100] The principle is reflected in the citizenship laws of all Central Asian States.[101]

D. *Jus Sanguinis*

Jus sanguinis ('right of blood') is another customary principle providing that 'a person, wherever born, is a citizen of the state if, at the time of his or her birth, his or her parent is one'.[102] This principle is incorporated in the citizenship laws of all Central Asian States.[103]

E. Naturalisation

Naturalisation is defined as 'the act of investing an alien with the status of a national in a given state'.[104] It may result from 'voluntary application, special legislative direction, marriage to a citizen, or parental action'.[105] As it is not automatic but requires a legal process, customary requirements for naturalisation include:

> [A] certain period of residence, which varies from 2 to 15 years, intention to reside permanently, a minimum age, capacity to act according to the law of the state of the former nationality or of the state applied to or of both, good character, physical and mental health, a sufficient command of the language of the prospective adopting country, ability to earn a livelihood or to support oneself, and evidence that, upon naturalization, the applicant will lose his or her former nationality or has taken steps to renounce it.[106]

In the Central Asian States, naturalisation may occur on general, simplified, or privileged terms. A common requirement under all five citizenship laws for

[100] Britannica, '*Jus soli*', available at www.britannica.com/topic/jus-soli.
[101] Arts 10(1), 12 (first part), 13, 14 of Kazakhstan's law on citizenship; Arts 11(1), 12(4)–(6) of Kyrgyzstan's law on citizenship; Arts 12 (first subparagraph), 13(2), (7)–(9) of Tajikistan's law on citizenship; Arts 10(1)(1), 11(1)(3), 11(1)(6)–(8), 11(3) of Turkmenistan's law on citizenship; Arts 13 (first subparagraph), 14 (third and fourth parts) of Uzbekistan's law on citizenship.
[102] Britannica (n 100).
[103] Arts 11, 11-1, 12 (second, third, and fourth parts) of Kazakhstan's law on citizenship; Arts 12(1)–(3) of Kyrgyzstan's law on citizenship; Arts 13(1), 13(3)–(6) of Tajikistan's law on citizenship; Arts 11(1)(1)–(5), 11(2) of Turkmenistan's law on citizenship; Arts 14 (first and second parts) of Uzbekistan's law on citizenship.
[104] Britannica, 'Naturalization', available at www.britannica.com/topic/naturalization.
[105] ibid.
[106] ibid.

naturalisation on general terms is at least five years of permanent residence in the prospective State.[107] Other conditions may include compliance with the Constitution and laws,[108] proficiency in the State's language(s),[109] lawful source of income,[110] and a clean criminal record.[111] Uzbekistan's citizenship law also explicitly requires applicants to have renounced any foreign citizenship.[112]

Grounds for simplified naturalisation differ across Central Asian States. In Kazakhstan, it applies to *qandas* (foreigners of Kazakh ethnicity) with permanent residence, rehabilitated victims of mass political repressions and their ancestors, ethnic Kazakhs studying at Kazakh higher education institutions, and widows of Kazakh citizens residing permanently in the country.[113] Kyrgyzstan grants simplified naturalisation to persons who: (1) have at least one parent with Kyrgyz citizenship residing in the country; (2) were born in the Kyrgyz SSR and/or held USSR citizenship; or (3) are being reinstated as Kyrgyz citizens.[114]

Tajikistan waives the requirements of permanent residence and language proficiency for: (1) persons with outstanding achievements in science, healthcare, or sports, or contributions to Tajikistan's economic, social, and cultural development or the promotion of universal human values; (2) veterans of the Great Patriotic War [World War II] who held USSR citizenship and reside in Tajikistan; (3) children or incapacitated persons under the guardianship of a Tajik citizen; (4) children or incapacitated persons under full State care in an educational, medical, or social welfare institution in Tajikistan; and (5) persons born in the Tajik SSR who held USSR citizenship, resided in post-Soviet States, but became stateless.[115] In addition, Tajikistan halves the residence requirement for: (1) other stateless persons; (2) foreigners whose parent was a Tajik citizen at their birth and who acquired foreign citizenship at birth (these persons may apply for naturalisation within five years after turning 18); (3) foreigners with a Tajik parent; and (4) persons born in the Tajik SSR who held USSR citizenship.[116]

[107] Art 16 (first part, subparagraph 1) of Kazakhstan's law on citizenship; Art 13(1)(1) of Kyrgyzstan's law on citizenship; Art 15 (first subparagraph) of Tajikistan's law on citizenship; Art 12(1)(3) of Turkmenistan's law on citizenship; Art 19 (first part, subparagraph (b)) of Uzbekistan's law on citizenship.

[108] Art 13(1)(3) of Kyrgyzstan's law on citizenship; Art 12(1)(1) of Turkmenistan's law on citizenship; Art 19 (first part, subparagraph (d)) of Uzbekistan's law on citizenship.

[109] Art 13(1)(2) of Kyrgyzstan's law on citizenship; Art 15 (second subparagraph) of Tajikistan's law on citizenship; Art 12(1)(2) of Turkmenistan's law on citizenship; Art 19 (first part, subparagraph (e)) of Uzbekistan's law on citizenship. See also Fergana News, 'V Kazahstane snizyat trebovaniya k znaniyu gosyazyka pri priyome v grazhdanstvo' ['Kazakhstan to Reduce State Language Requirements for Citizenship'], 14 July 2025, available at fergana.agency/news/138901/.

[110] Art 13(1)(4) of Kyrgyzstan's law on citizenship; Art 19 (first part, subparagraph (c)) of Uzbekistan's law on citizenship.

[111] Art 13(1)(5) of Kyrgyzstan's law on citizenship; Art 15 (third subparagraph) of Tajikistan's law on citizenship.

[112] Art 19 (first part, subparagraph (a)) of Uzbekistan's law on citizenship.

[113] Art 16-1 of Kazakhstan's law on citizenship.

[114] Art 14 of Kyrgyzstan's law on citizenship.

[115] Art 16(1) of Tajikistan's law on citizenship.

[116] Art 16(2) of Tajikistan's law on citizenship.

Turkmenistan waives or may reduce the permanent residence requirement for: (1) Turkmens and their descendants (children, grandchildren, great-grandchildren, etc.); (2) former USSR citizens with close relatives in Turkmenistan who arrive with intent to take up permanent residence; (3) individuals with outstanding service to Turkmenistan, notable achievements in science, technology, culture, or sports, or professions of national interest; (4) those who previously held the right to Turkmen citizenship; (5) persons granted asylum; (6) individuals recognised as refugees under Turkmen law or treaties; and (7) those who previously resided permanently in Turkmenistan but were forcibly evicted or fled due to political or religious persecution, along with their descendants.[117]

Uzbekistan applies a simplified naturalisation procedure to compatriots who are foreign nationals or stateless persons if they: (1) have at least one direct ascendant residing in Uzbekistan and holding Uzbek citizenship; (2) have a lawful source of income; (3) pledge to comply with the Constitution; and (4) possess sufficient proficiency in the State language, as determined by law.[118] The first condition may be waived for compatriots and/ or their family members with notable achievements in science, technology, culture, or sports, or with a profession or qualification of interest to Uzbekistan.[119]

Privileged (or exceptional) naturalisation is granted at the discretion of the Head of State. Article 16(3) of Tajikistan's constitutional law on citizenship allows the President to confer citizenship on foreign nationals and stateless persons who do not meet the conditions of Article 15. Under Article 12(3) of Turkmenistan's law on citizenship, the President may, in exceptional cases, grant citizenship solely on the condition that the applicant agrees to comply with the Constitution and laws. Article 21 of Uzbekistan's citizenship law provides that, in the national interest, the President may confer citizenship without applying the requirements of Articles 19 and 20.

F. Procedures for Changing the Nationality of Children

In the best interests of the child, nationality procedures aim to (1) preserve the child's citizenship of a Central Asian State where possible, and (2) avoid statelessness. If both parents acquire citizenship of a Central Asian State, their child under 14 also acquires it.[120] If only one parent acquires citizenship, the child may do so upon that parent's (written) request.[121] Generally, if one parent

[117] Art 13(2) of Turkmenistan's law on citizenship.

[118] Art 20 (first part) of Uzbekistan's law on citizenship.

[119] Art 20 (second part) of Uzbekistan's law on citizenship.

[120] Art 22 (first part) of Kazakhstan's law on citizenship; Art 26(1) of Tajikistan's law on citizenship; Art 18(1) of Turkmenistan's law on citizenship; Art 32 (first and second parts) of Uzbekistan's law on citizenship.

[121] Art 23 of Kazakhstan's law on citizenship; Art 20 of Kyrgyzstan's law on citizenship; Art 27(1), 27(2), 27(3), 27(4) of Tajikistan's law on citizenship; Art 19 of Turkmenistan's law on citizenship; Art 34 of Uzbekistan's law on citizenship.

renounces citizenship, the child under 14 retains it unless the parent requests otherwise and provided that this does not render the child stateless.[122] If both parents renounce citizenship, the child's citizenship changes accordingly, again provided statelessness does not result.[123] For children aged 14 to 18, a change in parental citizenship affects the child only with his or her (written or notarised) consent.[124] A foreign or stateless child adopted by parents one or both of whom are citizens of a Central Asian State acquires the same citizenship.[125] Conversely, a child who is a citizen of a Central Asian State adopted by foreigners generally retains their citizenship.[126] A child under guardianship or trusteeship retains citizenship even if their parents renounce it.[127]

G. Grounds for Rejecting Applications for Naturalisation

An application for naturalisation will be rejected on imperative grounds, including the applicant's military, law enforcement, or security service in a foreign State; threats to national security; submission of false documents or knowingly false information; commission of terrorist crimes, crimes against peace and security of mankind, or other serious crimes; or, where applicable, possession of another State's citizenship.[128]

H. Dual (or Multiple) Nationality

Domestic nationality laws may sometimes overlap, resulting in dual or even multiple citizenship.[129] Advantages of holding more than one nationality include easier international travel and fewer bureaucratic hurdles when doing business across jurisdictions. However, drawbacks include potential obligations for

[122] Art 24 of Kazakhstan's law on citizenship; Art 27(5) of Tajikistan's law on citizenship; Art 20 of Turkmenistan's law on citizenship; Art 34 of Uzbekistan's law on citizenship.

[123] Art 22 (first part) of Kazakhstan's law on citizenship; Art 26(2) of Tajikistan's law on citizenship; Art 18(2) of Turkmenistan's law on citizenship; Art 32 (second part) of Uzbekistan's law on citizenship.

[124] Art 28 of Kazakhstan's law on citizenship; Art 21 of Kyrgyzstan's law on citizenship; Art 26(3) of Tajikistan's law on citizenship; Art 23 of Turkmenistan's law on citizenship; Art 36 of Uzbekistan's law on citizenship.

[125] Art 25 of Kazakhstan's law on citizenship; Art 17 of Kyrgyzstan's law on citizenship; Art 28 of Tajikistan's law on citizenship; Art 21(4), 21(5), 21(6), 21(7) of Turkmenistan's law on citizenship.

[126] Art 27 of Kazakhstan's law on citizenship; Art 18 of Kyrgyzstan's law on citizenship; Art 21(8) of Turkmenistan's law on citizenship.

[127] Art 26 of Kazakhstan's law on citizenship; Art 19 of Kyrgyzstan's law on citizenship; Art 29 of Tajikistan's law on citizenship; Art 22 of Turkmenistan's law on citizenship; Art 33 of Uzbekistan's law on citizenship.

[128] Art 17 of Kazakhstan's law on citizenship; Art 16 of Kyrgyzstan's law on citizenship; Art 18 of Tajikistan's law on citizenship; Art 14 of Turkmenistan's law on citizenship; Art 28 of Uzbekistan's law on citizenship.

[129] Britannica, 'Citizenship', available at www.britannica.com/topic/citizenship.

national service and taxation in all relevant States. More than 130 States reportedly permit dual citizenship.[130]

Kazakhstan, Turkmenistan, and Uzbekistan do not permit dual or multiple citizenship.[131] Under Turkmen law, individuals holding another nationality are recognised solely as Turkmen citizens.[132] In contrast, Kyrgyz citizens may acquire another nationality,[133] subject to restrictions – particularly, dual citizenship with neighbouring States is prohibited.[134] Dual nationals are barred from serving as President, a member of parliament or judiciary, in law enforcement or the armed forces, and from holding senior executive posts.[135] In Tajikistan, dual citizenship is governed by treaties; otherwise, those with an additional nationality are regarded only as Tajik citizens.[136]

I. Termination of Nationality

All Central Asian States recognise two common grounds for the termination of nationality: renunciation[137] and loss.[138] Additionally, Kazakhstan's law allows for deprivation of nationality;[139] Kyrgyzstan's and Turkmenistan's laws refer to other grounds specified in citizenship laws and applicable treaties;[140] and Tajikistan's law includes cancellation of a decision on admission to citizenship and the choice of another nationality due to changes in the State border of the Republic of Tajikistan.[141]

J. Renunciation of Nationality

Citizenship may be voluntarily renounced through a formal written request to the President of the respective Central Asian State, following procedures

[130] ENDEVIO, 'Understanding Dual Citizenship, the Benefits, and the Process', available at www.endevio.org/en/insights/countries-that-allow-dual-citizenship.

[131] Art 3 (second part) of Kazakhstan's law on citizenship, Art 5(2) of Turkmenistan's law on citizenship, Art 12 of Uzbekistan's law on citizenship.

[132] Art 5(2) of Turkmenistan's law on citizenship.

[133] Art 22(1) of Kyrgyzstan's law on citizenship.

[134] Art 22(2)(1) of Kyrgyzstan's law on citizenship.

[135] Art 22(4) of Kyrgyzstan's law on citizenship.

[136] Art 8(1) of Tajikistan's law on citizenship.

[137] Art 19(1) of Kazakhstan's law on citizenship; Art 23(1) of Kyrgyzstan's law on citizenship; Art 20 (first subparagraph) of Tajikistan's law on citizenship; Art 15(1) of Turkmenistan's law on citizenship; Art 23(a) of Uzbekistan's law on citizenship.

[138] Art 19(2) of Kazakhstan's law on citizenship; Art 23(2) of Kyrgyzstan's law on citizenship; Art 20 (second subparagraph) of Tajikistan's law on citizenship; Art 15(2) of Turkmenistan's law on citizenship; Art 23(b) of Uzbekistan's law on citizenship.

[139] Art 19(3) of Kazakhstan's law on citizenship.

[140] Art 23(3) of Kyrgyzstan's law on citizenship, Art 15(3) of Turkmenistan's law on citizenship.

[141] Art 20 (third and fourth subparagraphs) of Tajikistan's law on citizenship.

established by law.[142] Such a request will be rejected if a criminal prosecution is pending, the applicant has been convicted,[143] or the renunciation poses a threat to national security.[144] It will also be denied if the applicant has outstanding obligations to the State, individuals, or legal entities.[145] Additionally, under the laws of Tajikistan and Turkmenistan, renunciation is refused if it would render the applicant stateless.[146]

K. Loss of Nationality

Common grounds for the loss of nationality include enlistment in the armed forces, security services, police, judiciary, or other organs of a foreign State (except as permitted by treaties),[147] submission of false documents or information during the citizenship application,[148] and acquiring another State's citizenship.[149] Kazakhstan's and Uzbekistan's laws further list participation in foreign armed conflicts, extremist or terrorist activities abroad,[150] significant harm to State or societal interests, collaboration with foreign States, and crimes against peace and security[151] as additional grounds. Both also provide for loss of citizenship by children who, upon reaching majority, acquire a foreign nationality.[152]

[142] Art 20 (first part) of Kazakhstan's law on citizenship; Art 24 of Kyrgyzstan's law on citizenship; Art 21 of Tajikistan's law on citizenship; Art 16 of Turkmenistan's law on citizenship; Arts 24, 37, 39 of Uzbekistan's law on citizenship.

[143] Art 20 (third part) of Kazakhstan's law on citizenship; Art 25(2) of Kyrgyzstan's law on citizenship; Art 22 (second subparagraph) of Tajikistan's law on citizenship; Art 16(3)(1) of Turkmenistan's law on citizenship.

[144] Art 20 (third part) of Kazakhstan's law on citizenship; Art 22 (sixth subparagraph) of Tajikistan's law on citizenship; Art 16(3)(3) of Turkmenistan's law on citizenship.

[145] Art 20 (second part) of Kazakhstan's law on citizenship; Art 25(1) of Kyrgyzstan's law on citizenship; Art 22 (third subparagraph) of Tajikistan's law on citizenship; Art 16(3)(2) of Turkmenistan's law on citizenship.

[146] Art 22 (fifth subparagraph) of Tajikistan's law on citizenship, Art 16(3)(4) of Turkmenistan's law on citizenship.

[147] Art 21 (first part, subparagraph 1) of Kazakhstan's law on citizenship; Art 23(1) of Tajikistan's law on citizenship; Art 17(1) of Turkmenistan's law on citizenship, Art 25 (first part, subparagraph (a)) of Uzbekistan's law on citizenship.

[148] Art 21 (first part, subparagraph 2) of Kazakhstan's law on citizenship; Art 24 of Tajikistan's law on citizenship (on the cancellation of admission to citizenship); Art 17(2) of Turkmenistan's law on citizenship, Art 25 (first part, subparagraph (c)) of Uzbekistan's law on citizenship.

[149] Art 21 (first part, subparagraph 5) of Kazakhstan's law on citizenship; Art 26(2)(1) of Kyrgyzstan's law on citizenship; Art 23(2) of Tajikistan's law on citizenship (if a citizen acquires the nationality of a foreign State, which does not have a treaty on dual citizenship with Tajikistan); Art 17(2) of Turkmenistan's law on citizenship, Art 25 (first part, subparagraph (e)) of Uzbekistan's law on citizenship.

[150] Art 21 (first part, subparagraph 8) of Kazakhstan's law on citizenship.

[151] Art 25 (first part, subparagraph (d)) of Uzbekistan's law on citizenship.

[152] Art 21 (first part, subparagraph 7) of Kazakhstan's law on citizenship, Art 25 (first part, subparagraph (f)) of Uzbekistan's law on citizenship.

L. Deprivation of Nationality

Article 20-1 of Kazakhstan's law on citizenship allows for the deprivation of citizenship as a penal sanction for terrorist crimes and other offences listed in the Special Part of the Criminal Code that cause grave harm to the Republic's vital interests. Article 50-1(1) of the Criminal Code defines deprivation of citizenship as an additional sanction involving the State's forced termination of the stable political and legal bond between it and the convicted person.[153] Under Article 50-1(2), this penalty does not apply to crimes committed before the age of 18. At the time of writing, offences punishable by deprivation of citizenship include: planning, preparation, launching or waging a war of aggression (Article 160); use of prohibited means and methods of warfare (Article 163); violations of the laws and customs of war (Article 164); genocide (Article 168); ecocide (Article 169);[154] mercenarism (Article 170); attacks on persons or organisations under international protection (Article 173); treason (Article 175); attacks on the First President (Article 177) or President (Article 178); separatist activity (Article 180); armed mutiny (Article 181); establishing, leading an extremist group or participation in its activity (Article 182); diversion (Article 184); act of terrorism (Article 255); establishing or leading a terrorist group, or participation in its activity (Article 257); hostage-taking (Article 261); attacking or seizing buildings, structures, and means of communication (Article 269); hijacking as well as seizure of an aircraft or water vessel or railway rolling stock (Article 270); deliberate illegal crossing of the State Border of the Republic of Kazakhstan (Article 392); organisation of and participation in the activities of a public or religious association or other organisation after a judicial decision to ban their activities or liquidate them in connection with their engagement in extremism or terrorism (Article 405); and surrender or abandonment of means of warfare to the enemy (Article 455).

M. Other Grounds for the Termination of Nationality

In Kazakhstan, additional grounds for loss of nationality include using documents confirming foreign citizenship after acquiring Kazakh citizenship,[155] and a court's invalidation of a marriage to a Kazakh citizen that served as the basis for naturalisation.[156] Under Article 25 of Tajikistan's citizenship law, when the State border changes, residents of the affected territory may opt for foreign

[153] For the text of the Criminal Code (in Russian), see: online.zakon.kz/Document/?doc_id=31575252:.
[154] cf R Sharma, 'Ecocide as the Fifth International Crime: Is the Rome Statute Compatible with Ecocide?', *Völkerrechtsblog*, 16 January 2025, available at voelkerrechtsblog.org/ecocide-as-the-fifth-international-crime/.
[155] Art 21 (first part, subparagraph 5-1) of Kazakhstan's law on citizenship.
[156] Art 21 (first part, subparagraph 6) of Kazakhstan's law on citizenship.

citizenship pursuant to a relevant treaty. Uzbekistan's law provides for loss of citizenship if a citizen permanently residing abroad fails, without valid reason, to register with a consulate for seven years.[157] Treaties may also establish further grounds for the loss of nationality.[158]

N. Foreigners and Stateless Persons

Foreigners (or aliens) are individuals who hold the nationality of one or more foreign States but not that of the State where they reside temporarily or permanently.[159] Stateless persons (or *apatrides*) are individuals without the nationality of any State. The Convention Relating to the Status of Stateless Persons defines a stateless person as someone 'not considered as a national by any state under the operation of its law'.[160] Statelessness typically arises from 'the lack of uniform rules on citizenship acquisition and loss'.[161] Following the collapse of the Soviet Union in 1991, over 97,000 people became stateless in Uzbekistan alone.[162] The 2020 Law 'On Citizenship' enabled 49,228 of them to acquire Uzbek citizenship.[163]

Article 6 of Kazakhstan's law on citizenship states that aliens and stateless persons enjoy the rights and freedoms, and bear the duties, established for citizens, unless otherwise specified by the Constitution, national laws, or treaties. This mirrors Article 12(4) of Kazakhstan's Constitution. Similar provisions appear in Article 52(1) of Kyrgyzstan's Constitution, Article 16 (second part) of Tajikistan's, and Article 11 (first part) of Turkmenistan's. Article 24 of Uzbekistan's Constitution guarantees foreign citizens and stateless persons rights and freedoms in accordance with international law, while also holding them to responsibilities under the Constitution, national laws, and treaties of Uzbekistan. More detailed rules on their legal status (including permanent residents) are set out in specific legislation.[164]

[157] Art 25 (first part, subparagraph (b)) of Uzbekistan's law on citizenship.

[158] Art 21 (first part, subparagraph 3) of Kazakhstan's law on citizenship, Art 26(1)(3) of Kyrgyzstan's law on citizenship, Art 17(3) of Turkmenistan's law on citizenship.

[159] Britannica, 'Alien', available at www.britannica.com/topic/alien-law.

[160] For the text of the Convention, see: www.unhcr.org/ibelong/wp-content/uploads/1954-Convention-relating-to-the-Status-of-Stateless-Persons_ENG.pdf.

[161] Britannica, 'Citizenship', available at www.britannica.com/topic/citizenship.

[162] UNHCR, 'Uzbekistan reshit problemu bezgrazhdanstva dlya 50000 chelovek' ['Uzbekistan Will Solve the Problem of Statelessness for 50000 People'], 17 March 2020, available at www.unhcr.org/centralasia/11671-uzbekistan-to-end-statelessness-for-50000-people.html.

[163] ibid.

[164] For the text of Kazakhstan's Law 'On the Legal Status of Foreigners' of 19 June 1995 (as amended, in Russian), see: online.zakon.kz/Document/?doc_id=1003764&pos=5;-108#pos=5;-108. For the text of the Law 'On the Legal Status of Foreign Nationals in the Kyrgyz Republic' of 14 December 1993 (as amended, in Russian), see: cbd.minjust.gov.kg/772/edition/1264919/ru. For the text of the Law 'On the Legal Status of Foreign Nationals and Stateless Persons in the Republic of Tajikistan' of 2 January 2018 (in Russian, replacing the Law 'On the Legal Status of

IV. TERRITORY

In accordance with Article 1(b) of the Montevideo Convention, the second essential element of statehood is a defined territory. Each State exercises exclusive territorial jurisdiction over its entire territory.[165] The unlawful assertion of jurisdiction over another State's territory – such as Russia's occupation of Crimea and parts of Eastern Ukraine since 2014 – violates the rights of individuals, legal entities, and the affected States.

The territory of a State comprises its land, internal and territorial waters, airspace, and subsoil. The following subsections outline the key principles and rules governing territorial sovereignty and present illustrative cases concerning territorial developments, challenges, and disputes in Central Asia.

A. *Uti Possidetis Iuris*

Uti possidetis iuris (often shortened to *uti possidetis*) is a Roman law doctrine revived in international law 'to maintain the territorial stability of newly created states at the time of decolonization'.[166] More recently, 'the principle of *uti possidetis* has been stretched and applied to postcolonial borders to maintain the finality of borders in situations such as territorial breakups, an example being Yugoslavia',[167] – or, similarly, the former Soviet Union. Article 5 of the Agreement on the Establishment of the Commonwealth of Independent States (CIS) of 8 December 1991 explicitly affirms the High Contracting Parties' recognition and respect for each other's territorial integrity and the inviolability of existing frontiers.[168] Likewise, the third preambular paragraph of the Alma-Ata Declaration of 21 December 1991 affirms these same principles.[169] Notably, both texts refer to 'existing frontiers', clearly indicating that the former administrative borders between Soviet republics were meant to become the international borders of the newly independent States. Although 'the legal character of [the

Foreign Nationals in the Republic of Tajikistan' of 1 February 1996), see: www.consular.tj/zakon-respubliki-tadjikistan-o-pravavom-statuse-inostrannih-grajdan.html. For the text of the Law 'On the Legal Status of Foreign Nationals in Turkmenistan' of 13 November 2021 (in Russian, replacing the Law 'On the Legal Status of Foreign Nationals in Turkmenistan' of 26 March 2011), see: turkmenistan.gov.tm/ru/post/58786/zakon-turkmenistana-o-pravovom-polozhenii-inostrannyh-grazhdan-v-turkmenistane. For the text of the Law 'On the Legal Status of Foreign Nationals and Stateless Persons in the Republic of Uzbekistan' of 4 June 2021 (in Russian), see: lex.uz/ru/docs/5443901?ONDATE2=14.03.2022&action=compare.

[165] Lukashuk and Saidov (n 68), 123–35.

[166] F Lone, 'Uti Possidetis Iuris', available at www.oxfordbibliographies.com/display/document/obo-9780199796953/obo-9780199796953-0065.xml.

[167] ibid.

[168] For the text of the Agreement (in Russian), see: cis.minsk.by/page/176/soglasenie-o-sozdanii-sodruzestva-nezavisimyh-gosudarstv-gminsk-8-dekabra-1991-goda.

[169] For the text of the Declaration (in Russian), see: cis.minsk.by/page/178/alma-atinskaa-deklaracia-g-alma-ata-21-dekabra-1991-goda.

uti possidetis] principle is unclear', and 'depending on various situations, it has been referred to as a rule, principle, customary international law, technique, policy decision, and political tenet',[170] its critical importance in the region is beyond doubt – evident in Central Asian Constitutions, domestic laws, and scholarly international legal doctrine.

B. Inviolability of Frontiers

As participating States of the Organization for Security and Co-operation in Europe (OSCE), all Central Asian States are bound by its rules on the inviolability of frontiers. Section III of the 1975 Helsinki Final Act's Declaration of Principles affirms that participating States regard all frontiers – each other's and those of all States in Europe – as inviolable and pledge to refrain, now and in the future, from assaulting them.[171] The second part of this section obliges them to abstain from any demand for, or act of, seizure or usurpation of all or part of any participating State's territory. Their respective Constitutions[172] and domestic laws[173] set out more specific rules governing the legal regime of State borders.

C. Territorial Integrity

The principle of territorial integrity is enshrined in section IV of the 1975 Helsinki Final Act's Declaration of Principles. Its first part states that all participating States must respect each other's territorial integrity. With reference to Article 2(4) of the UN Charter,[174] the second part requires States to refrain from actions contrary to the Charter's purposes and principles, particularly those threatening or using force against a State's territorial integrity, political

[170] Lone (n 166).

[171] For the text of the Helsinki Final Act, see: www.osce.org/files/f/documents/5/c/39501.pdf.

[172] Arts 3, 80(1)(5), 85(5) of the Constitution of the Kyrgyz Republic, Art 81(12) of the Constitution of Turkmenistan, Arts 3 (second part), 17 (second part), 84, 88, 93(12)–(13) of the Constitution of the Republic of Uzbekistan.

[173] For the text of the Law 'On the State Border of the Republic of Kazakhstan' of 16 January 2013 (as amended, in Russian, replacing the Law 'On the State Border of the Republic of Kazakhstan' of 13 January 1993), see: online.zakon.kz/Document/?doc_id=31320511&pos=1314;-11#pos=1314;-11. For the text of the Law 'On the State Border of the Kyrgyz Republic' of 16 May 2015 (as amended, in Russian, replacing the Law 'On the State Border of the Kyrgyz Republic' of 19 March 1999), see: cbd.minjust.gov.kg/111141/edition/1278744/ru. For the text of the Law 'On the State Border of the Republic of Tajikistan' of 1 August 1997 (in Russian), see: www.adlia.tj/show_doc.fwx?rgn=984. For the text of the Law 'On the State Border of Turkmenistan' of 4 May 2013 (in Russian, replacing the Law 'On the State Border of Turkmenistan' of 1 October 1993), see: alpagama.org/pravovaya-baza-turista/zakon-turkmenistana-o-gosudarstvennoj-granitse-turkmenistana. For the text of the Law 'On the State Border of the Republic of Uzbekistan' of 13 September 2023 (in Russian, replacing the Law 'On the State Border of the Republic of Uzbekistan' of 20 August 1999), see: lex.uz/ru/docs/6605259.

[174] cf Chapter 10, section II below.

independence, or unity. Echoing Article 11 of the Montevideo Convention, the third part of section IV urges States not to subject each other's territory to military occupation or other coercive measures in violation of international law, nor to acquire territory by such means or the threat of them. No such occupation or acquisition may be recognised as lawful.[175]

The principle of territorial integrity is reflected, with some variation, in the Constitutions of all Central Asian States. Article 2(2) of Kazakhstan's Constitution affirms that the State ensures the integrity, inviolability, and inalienability of its territory. Article 3(1) of Kyrgyzstan's Constitution similarly provides that its territory is integral and inviolable. Article 7 of Tajikistan's Constitution declares the territory indivisible and inviolable; the State guarantees sovereignty, independence, and territorial integrity, while propaganda or actions aimed at undermining State unity are prohibited. Article 1 of Turkmenistan's Constitution states that the State sovereignty and territory are single and indivisible; it also obliges the State to protect independence, sovereignty, territorial integrity, and the constitutional order, and to ensure law and order. Article 2 calls on UN Member States to support Turkmenistan's permanent neutrality and to respect its independence, sovereignty, and territorial integrity. Article 17 of Uzbekistan's Constitution bases foreign policy on the principle of territorial integrity (and other principles of international law). Article 71 prohibits the establishment and activities of political parties and NGOs seeking to violently alter the constitutional order or undermine sovereignty, territorial integrity, or security. Article 109(1) designates the President as guarantor of citizens' rights and freedoms, the Constitution and laws, and the sovereignty, security, and territorial integrity of the Republic. Under Article 152, the Armed Forces protect Uzbekistan's sovereignty, territorial integrity, and public security. Acts undermining the territorial integrity of Central Asian States are criminal offences.

D. Land and Internal Waters

According to *Black's Law Dictionary Online*, land

> in the most general sense, comprehends any ground, soil, or earth whatsoever; as meadows, pastures, woods, moors, waters, marshes, furzes, and heath … Land is the solid material of the earth, whatever may be the ingredients of which it is composed, whether soil, rock, or other substance.[176]

[175] cf Art 11 of the Montevideo Convention: 'The contracting states definitely establish as the rule of their conduct the precise obligation not to recognize territorial acquisitions or special advantages which have been obtained by force whether this consists in the employment of arms, in threatening diplomatic representations, or in any other effective coercive measure. The territory of a state is inviolable and may not be the object of military occupation nor of other measures of force imposed by another state directly or indirectly or for any motive whatever even temporarily'.

[176] Black's Law Dictionary Online, 'Land', available at thelawdictionary.org/land/.

In international law, 'land' refers to all ground surface within a State's international boundaries. 'Internal (or inland) waters' are defined as

> permanent water bodies inland from the coastal zone and areas whose properties and use are dominated by the permanent, seasonal, or intermittent occurrence of flooded conditions … Inland waters include rivers, lakes, floodplains, reservoirs, wetlands, and inland saline systems.[177]

Kazakhstan is the ninth largest State in the world with an overall territory of 2,724,900 km^2 (including its territorial waters in the Caspian Sea).[178] Its topographic relief is diverse, with lowlands making up 'one-third of Kazakhstan's huge expanse, hilly plateaus and plains account[ing] for nearly half, and low mountainous regions about one-fifth'.[179] Astana is the second-coldest capital in the world (after Ulaanbaatar in Mongolia),[180] and the international border between Kazakhstan and Russia is the longest land border in the world (7,591 km).[181] Kazakhstan has about 8,500 rivers, and 48,000 lakes.[182] Lake Balqash (Balkhash) is about 600 km long with a maximum depth of about 25 metres.[183] Depending on seasonal precipitation, the lake's area varies between 15,500 km^2 and 19,000 km^2.[184] According to geological and paleontological data, Lake Zaysan is the most ancient lake in the world.[185] Its length is 105 km, with a maximum depth of 15 metres. Lake Alakol is 104 km long and 52 km wide with a maximum depth of 45 metres.[186]

With a land territory of 199,945 km^2, Kyrgyzstan is a largely mountainous country.[187] Valleys and plains occupy about one-seventh of the total area.[188] Kyrgyzstan has more than 40,000 rivers and streams,[189] and almost 2,000 lakes,[190] including Lake Ysyk (Issyk-Kul) – one of the largest and deepest mountain lakes in the world, having a surface area of some 6,280 km^2 and reaching 702 metres in depth.[191]

[177] GreenFacts, 'Inland waters', available at www.greenfacts.org/glossary/ghi/inland-waters.htm.

[178] Gov.Kz, 'About Kazakhstan', available at www.gov.kz/Art/19305?lang=en.

[179] Britannica, 'Kazakhstan', available at www.britannica.com/place/Kazakhstan.

[180] Al Jazeera, 'Kazakhstan: Capital Astana paralysed by cold weather', 19 November 2016, available at www.aljazeera.com/news/2016/11/19/kazakhstan-capital-astana-paralysed-by-cold-weather.

[181] Official Website of the President of the Republic of Kazakhstan, 'Republic of Kazakhstan', available at www.akorda.kz/en/republic_of_kazakhstan/kazakhstan.

[182] ibid.

[183] Britannica, 'Lake Balkhash Summary', available at www.britannica.com/summary/Lake-Balkhash.

[184] ibid.

[185] BF Dorfman, 'Zaysan – the Only Surviving Cretaceous Lake – May be Lost' (2011) 10 *Procedia Environmental Sciences* 1376, 1376.

[186] Britannica, 'Lake Alakol', available at www.britannica.com/place/Lake-Alakol.

[187] Britannica, 'Kyrgyzstan Summary', available at www.britannica.com/summary/Kyrgyzstan.

[188] ibid.

[189] Advantour, 'Rivers of Kyrgyzstan', available at www.advantour.com/kyrgyzstan/nature/rivers.htm.

[190] Advantour, 'Kyrgyzstan Lakes', available at www.advantour.com/kyrgyzstan/nature/lakes.htm.

[191] Britannica, 'Kyrgyzstan Summary', available at www.britannica.com/summary/Kyrgyzstan.

Tajikistan has a land area of 141,400 km^2,[192] with mountains covering 93 per cent of its territory, and about half of the territory lying at elevations above 3,000 metres.[193] The country has 947 rivers, their total length exceeding 28,500 km.[194] Notably, over 80 per cent of the Amudaryo river flow originates in Tajikistan.[195] The country has about 1,300 lakes covering 1005 km^2 (just below one per cent of the entire territory).[196]

The overall territory of Turkmenistan (including its territorial waters in the Caspian Sea) is 491,210 km^2.[197] The country has some hills and low mountains but about nine-tenths of its area are desert, predominantly the Karakum.[198] The main rivers are the Amudaryo and Morghāb. The country has many canals and reservoirs, including the Karakum Canal, which runs 1,400 km between the Amudaryo and the Caspian Sea.[199]

One of the world's two double-landlocked States,[200] Uzbekistan has a land area of 448,971 km^2.[201] It includes the Republic of Karakalpakstan, and lies largely between the Syrdaryo and Amudaryo rivers.[202] This region of ancient and medieval Central Asia was known as the 'land beyond the river' (*Mawara' al-Nahr*/ Mawarannahr).[203] Although Uzbekistan's territory 'contains fertile oases and high mountain ranges in the south and east, almost four-fifths of the country consists of flat, sunbaked lowlands. Two-thirds of the Aral Sea extends into Uzbekistan'.[204] On the Aral Sea, see subsection G below.

E. Enclaves and Exclaves

Enclaves and exclaves are the same territorial units, viewed from different perspectives. An enclave is defined for the purpose of international law as

> an isolated part of the territory of a State, which is entirely surrounded by the territory of only one foreign State – the surrounding, enclaving, or host State – so that it

[192] Britannica, 'Tajikistan Summary', available at www.britannica.com/summary/Tajikistan.
[193] ibid.
[194] Dushanbe Water Process, 'Facts and figures about water in Tajikistan', available at dushanbewaterprocess.org/facts-and-figures-about-water-in-tajikistan/.
[195] ibid. On transboundary rivers, see Chapter 2, section IV.F below.
[196] Dushanbe Water Process (n 194).
[197] Britannica, 'Turkmenistan Summary', available at www.britannica.com/summary/Turkmenistan.
[198] Britannica, 'Karakum Desert Summary', available at www.britannica.com/summary/Karakum-Desert.
[199] Britannica, 'Turkmenistan Summary', available at www.britannica.com/summary/Turkmenistan.
[200] The other double-landlocked State is Liechtenstein. On the latter, see Britannica, 'Liechtensten Summary', available at www.britannica.com/summary/Liechtenstein. See also United Nations, 'Third UN Conference on Landlocked Developing Countries, 5–8 August 2025', available at www.un.org/en/landlocked.
[201] Britannica, 'Uzbekistan Summary', available at www.britannica.com/summary/Uzbekistan.
[202] ibid. See also Fergana News, 'Prezident Uzbekistana utverdil Vodnyy kodeks' ['The President of Uzbekistan Promulgated the Water Code'], 31 July 2025, available at fergana.agency/news/139206/.
[203] The Free Dictionary, 'Sogdiana', available at www.thefreedictionary.com/Mawarannahr.
[204] Britannica, 'Uzbekistan Summary', available at www.britannica.com/summary/Uzbekistan.

> has no communication with the territory of the State to which it belongs – the mother or home State – other than through the territory of the host State. Seen from the latter's perspective, such territory is an exclave.[205]

In other words, an exclave is 'a portion of a country separated from the main part and constituting an enclave in respect to the surrounding territory'.[206]

The Soviet authorities set up eight enclaves in Central Asia, all of them in the Ferghana Valley. This approach laid the groundwork for potential territorial disputes, and

> enabled Moscow to rule over an expansive region without fear that a unified Central Asian state in the Ferghana Valley could mobilize against its authority. Following the collapse of the USSR, the Central Asian republics adhered to the border demarcations from the Soviet Union.[207]

As a result, four Uzbek enclaves – Chonkara (approximately 3 km^2), Jangali / Dzhangali (approximately 3 km^2), Shakhimardan (approximately 90 km^2), and Sokh (approximately 325 km^2) – are enclosed within the territory of Kyrgyzstan; and three Tajik enclaves are surrounded, respectively, by the territories of Uzbekistan (Sarvak, approximately 8 km^2), and Kyrgyzstan (Vorukh, approximately 96.7 km^2, and Lolazor, formerly Kairagach / Kayragach, less than 1 km^2).[208] As a result of a land swap announced in November 2022, the former Kyrgyz enclave Barak (approximately 4 km^2) was given to Uzbekistan in exchange for 208 hectares of land, and the resettlement of its residents to Kyrgyzstan was completed in 2024.[209]

F. Transboundary Rivers

According to UN Water, '[t]ransboundary waters are the aquifers and lake and river basins shared by two or more countries'.[210] Globally, '[t]ransboundary waters account for 60 per cent of the world's freshwater flows. 153 countries have territory within at least one of the 286 transboundary river and lake basins

[205] TH Irmscher, 'Enclaves', *Max Planck Encyclopaedia of Public International Law*, available at opil.ouplaw.com/display/10.1093/law:epil/9780199231690/law-9780199231690-e1037.

[206] Merriam-Webster Dictionary, 'Exclave', available at www.merriam-webster.com/dictionary/exclave.

[207] D Schulz, 'Mapping Central Asian Enclaves', available at www.caspianpolicy.org/research/security-and-politics-program-spp/mapping-central-asian-enclaves.

[208] ibid.

[209] Kun.Uz, 'Zaversheno pereseleniye kyrgyzskogo anklava Barak, nahodivshegosya na territorii Uzbekistana' ['The Resettlement of Residents of the Kyrgyz Enclave Barak, Located in the Territory of Uzbekistan, Has Been Completed'], 20 April 2024, available at kun.uz/ru/news/2024/04/20/zaversheno-pereseleniye-jiteley-kyrgyzskogo-anklava-barak-naxodivshegosya-na-territorii-uzbekistana.

[210] UN Water, 'Transboundary Waters', available at www.unwater.org/water-facts/transboundary-waters.

and 592 transboundary aquifer systems'.[211] In Central Asia, the two largest rivers – the Syrdaryo and the Amudaryo – are transboundary, and '[t]heir river basins provide 90% of the region's river water' for '[a]lmost 90% of the people living in Central Asia'.[212] The key issues in the transboundary water management in the region were correctly summarised by Zhiltsov et al:

> Nowadays many scientists and specialists say that in the twenty-first century, not hydrocarbons but water will be the key issue for economic development, well-being, and quality of life. This fully applies to the Central Asian countries where historically the problems of water resources have been in the focus of attention as the main factors determining stability in all sectors of the economy … The situation is aggravated by the fact that the river basins in this region are transboundary and their watersheds do not coincide with the existing state borders … The problem is aggravated by differing hydropower priorities of the countries located in the upper reaches of rivers, such as Tajikistan and Kyrgyzstan that control more than 80% of all freshwater supplies, and agricultural needs of the downstream countries – Uzbekistan, Kazakhstan, and Turkmenistan. In other words, some of the countries need electricity, while others [need] water for irrigated farming.[213]

The water scarcity problem is likely to deteriorate in Central Asia in the next few decades. It was reported in early 2024 that:

> The Central Asian water crisis, the product of climate change, inefficient water management, and growing water consumption, is not just a hypothetical problem anymore – it is affecting all parts of the region, and it is happening now. The past year underscored a pressing need for comprehensive and sustainable climate action, prompting an exploration of adaptive strategies and the fostering of collaborative efforts to mitigate far-reaching consequences on both ecosystems and local communities.[214]

According to the World Bank, the shortage of freshwater is likely to lead to massive migration within the region: by 2050, Central Asia could see as many as 5 million 'climate migrants'.[215]

In order to mitigate the adverse effects of water scarcity, the Central Asian States are now

[211] ibid.

[212] OSCE, 'Women in Water Management in Central Asia', available at www.osce.org/files/f/documents/8/a/521086_0.pdf.

[213] SS Zhiltsov, IS Zonn, OE Grishin, VG Egorov and MS Ruban, 'Transboundary Rivers in Central Asia: Cooperation and Conflicts Among Countries' in SS Zhiltsov, IS Zonn, AG Kostianoy, AV Semenov (eds.), *Water Resources in Central Asia: International Context* (Springer Nature, 2018), 61–62.

[214] J Taganova, A Shabanova-Serdechna and N Saida, 'Central Asia's Water Crisis Is Already Here', The Diplomat, 4 January 2024, available at thediplomat.com/2023/12/central-asias-water-crisis-is-already-here/.

[215] ibid. More generally on climate migration, see B Hernandez, C Bianco and Z Garcia, 'Refugees without Recognition: Climate Change and Ecological and Gender Inequality', EJIL:Talk!, 15 August 2024, available at www.ejiltalk.org/refugees-without-recognition-climate-change-and-ecological-and-gender-inequality/.

> strengthening efforts in coordinating [their national] water policies ... towards mutual goals ... The common desire of all five countries to promote economic welfare and growth [at] the national level, will more than likely also benefit future water security and planning on a regional level.[216]

Thus, at the sixth Consultative Meeting of the Heads of Central Asian States (Astana, 9 August 2024), Kazakhstan's President Tokayev suggested developing 'a new consolidated water policy based on equitable and fair water use and strict implementation of mutual obligations'.[217] At the same Consultative Meeting, Uzbekistan's President Mirziyoyev proposed adopting a Regional strategy for the rational use of water resources of transboundary rivers.[218] In practical terms, in 2024, Uzbekistan agreed to

> send another 500 million cubic metres of water to Kazakhstan by the end of the irrigation season ... Tashkent promised to send 3.7 billion cubic metres of [water] resources within six months. But [Uzbekistan has] even exceeded the plan: since 1 April [2024], Kazakh farmers have received over 4 billion cubic meters of water.[219]

G. The Aral Sea[220]

The Aral Sea was an endorheic lake (namely, one with no outlet to the ocean) within the State borders of Kazakhstan and Uzbekistan. Until the 1960s, the Aral Sea had a surface area of 68,000 km^2 and a volume of about 1000 km^3. At the time, it was the second largest intra-continental drainless lake (after the Caspian Sea), and the fourth largest lake in the world (after the Caspian Sea, Lake Superior and Lake Victoria). The name of the Aral Sea originates from the Turkic word for 'island': until 1961, the Aral Sea's waters were dotted with over 1100 islands each having a surface area of at least 0.01 km^2. In the 1960s, the influx of the Syrdaryo and Amudaryo rivers into the Aral Sea began to decrease sharply, due to the Soviet government's hardline irrigation policy. According to the International Fund for Saving the Aral Sea (IFAS), between 1910 and 1960, the Sea was fed with an annual average of about 62 km^3 of water, whereas in 1961–70, this volume declined to 43.3 km^3 per year, in 1971–80 – to 16.7 km^3, and in 1981–90 – to only 3.5 km^3. In 1974–86, Syrdaryo's runoff was

[216] Nazarbayev University, 'Water security in Central Asia: an overview', 25 July 2020, available at nu.edu.kz/news/water-security-in-central-asia-an-overview.

[217] Fergana News, 'Kurs na regionalnuyu identichnost' ['A Course Towards Regional Identity'], available at https://fergana.agency/articles/134581/.

[218] ibid.

[219] Fergana News, 'Uzbekistan dolopnitelno napravit v Kazahstan 500 mln kubometrov vody dlya nuzhd fermerov' ['Uzbekistan Will Additionally Send 500 Million Cubic Metres of Water to Kazakhstan for the Needs of Farmers'], 9 August 2024, available at: fergana.agency/news/134578/.

[220] This section uses the author's material published in S Sayapin, 'The Aral Sea' in S Lee et al (eds), *Encyclopedia of Public International Law in Asia*, Volume III: Central & South Asia (Leiden, Brill, 2021). Permission to use published material is gratefully acknowledged.

not reaching the Aral Sea at all, and Amudaryo's runoff was deficient in 1982–83, 1985–86, and 1989. As a result, the Aral Sea's level was declining in the 1960s by an average of 0.2 m per year, in the 1970s by 0.6 m, and in the 1980s by 0.85 m. In 1987, its level reached 36.4 m; that is, 16.6 m lower than the average long-term level before 1961. The consequential ecosystem collapse led to devastating effects for the environment, public health, and economy.[221]

H. The Caspian Sea

The Caspian Sea is the world's largest natural inland saltwater reservoir. Its legal status is governed by treaties among the coastal States – Azerbaijan, Iran, Kazakhstan, Russia, and Turkmenistan – and by their domestic laws. Territorial waters, extending up to 15 nautical miles, fall under the sovereignty of the respective States. For further details, see Chapter twelve below.

I. Subsoil

As Schrijver observed, after 1945, 'permanent sovereignty over natural resources emerged as a new principle of international law'.[222] Its roots lie in the UN Charter.[223] On 14 December 1962, the UN General Assembly adopted resolution 1803 (XVII) on 'Permanent sovereignty over natural resources'.[224] The first operative paragraph affirms that peoples and nations must exercise this right in the interest of national development and the well-being of their people. The principle's importance goes beyond economics: the seventh operative paragraph states that violating this right contradicts the UN Charter's spirit and principles and impedes international cooperation and peace. Reflecting this significance, Kazakhstan has adopted a Code on Subsoil and Subsoil Use,[225] while the other Central Asian States have also enacted laws on the subject.[226]

[221] See S Klötzli, 'The "Aral Sea Syndrome" and Regional Cooperation in Central Asia: Opportunity or Obstacle?' in NP Gleditsch (ed), *Conflict and the Environment* (Springer, 1997), pp 417–34. See also Chapter 10, section IX.I below.

[222] N Schrijver, 'Self-determination of peoples and sovereignty over natural wealth and resources' in *Realizing the Right to Development: Essays in Commemoration of 25 years of the United Nations Declaration on the Right to Development* (Office of the UN High Commissioner for Human Rights, 2013), 95, available at: www.ohchr.org/sites/default/files/Documents/Issues/Development/RTDBook/PartIIChapter5.pdf.

[223] ibid.

[224] For the text of the resolution, see: www.ohchr.org/en/instruments-mechanisms/instruments/general-assembly-resolution-1803-xvii-14-december-1962-permanent.

[225] For the text of the Code (in Russian), see: online.zakon.kz/Document/?doc_id=31764592&pos=4;-108#pos=4;-108.

[226] For Kyrgyzstan's Law 'On Subsoil' of 19 May 2018 (as amended, in Russian, replacing the Law 'On Subsoil' of 9 August 2012), see: cbd.minjust.gov.kg/111782/edition/12594/ru. For Tajikistan's

Article 10(1) of Kazakhstan's Code on Subsoil and Subsoil Use usefully defines subsoil as 'the part of the earth's crust located below the soil layer, and in its absence, below the earth's surface, the bottom of water reservoirs, and watercourses'. The Code regulates the use of subsoil with respect to (1) extractable resources, (2) technogenic mineral formations, and (3) subsoil space (Article 10(2)). Pursuant to Article 12(2), based on their economic significance, extractable resources are divided into the following groups: (1) groundwater; (2) hydrocarbon minerals (oil, crude gas and natural bitumen); and (3) solid minerals.[227] In turn, solid minerals can be metallic and non-metallic (Article 12(4), second part). Metallic solid minerals include native metals, ores of ferrous, non-ferrous, rare, radioactive metals, and rare earth elements. The other solid minerals are non-metallic (metamorphic rocks such as marble, igneous rocks such as granite, and sedimentary rocks such as gravel, clay, sand, and others). In turn, technogenic mineral formations are accumulations of waste from mining (dust or substandard / low-grade ore), mine processing (slags), and energy production (cinder), containing useful components and (or) minerals (Article 13). Finally, subsoil space is a three-dimensional spatial characteristic of the subsoil, which, with due regard to geotechnical, geological, economic and environmental factors, can be used as an environment for the placement of industrial, scientific or other activities (Article 16).

Central Asia's natural resources are immense. Kazakhstan's reserves include 34 billion tonnes of coal, 4,402 million tonnes of oil, 1,017,000 tonnes of uranium (second largest reserves in the world), 20 billion tonnes of iron, 37 million tonnes of copper, and 14 million tonnes of lead (fourth largest reserves in the world).[228] Kazakhstan ranks first in the world in chromium reserves, and third in zinc.[229] Reportedly, '[t]he extractive sector of the economy provides about 30% of the republic's GDP, and the entire mineral and raw materials complex provides up to 70% of GDP, and brings in the majority of the country's foreign exchange earnings'.[230] Kyrgyzstan has significant reserves of gold, mercury, antimony, rare earths, tin, tungsten, coal, non-metallic raw materials, and groundwater.[231] The country also has large reserves of 'iron, titanium, vanadium, aluminum, copper, molybdenum, and beryllium. The industrial

Law 'On Subsoil' of 20 July 1994 (as amended, in Russian), see: online.zakon.kz/Document/?doc_id=30514242. For Turkmenistan's Law 'On Subsoil' of 20 December 2014 (as amended, in Russian), see: online.zakon.kz/Document/?doc_id=31648769&pos=6;-108#pos=6;-108. For Uzbekistan's Law 'On Subsoil' of 23 September 1994 (in Russian, new edition adopted on 13 December 2002), see: lex.uz/docs/75839.

[227] A similar classification is contained in Art 4(13) of Kyrgyzstan's Law 'On Subsoil'.

[228] 24.Kz, 'Skolko poleznyh iskopaemyh v Kazahstane' [How Many Mineral Resources Are There in Kazakhstan], available at: 24.kz/ru/news/economyc/item/645821-skolko-poleznykh-iskopaemykh-v-kazakhstane.

[229] Kursiv Media, 'Pochemu v Kazahstane slozhno dobyvat poleznye iskopayemye' [Why is it Difficult to Extract Minerals in Kazakhstan?], available at: kz.kursiv.media/2023-07-14/skvr-altyn-2/.

[230] ibid.

[231] Kyrgyzstan Review, 'Poleznye iskopaemye Kyrgyzstana' [Kyrgyzstan's Extractable Resources], available at: rus.gateway.kg/geografiya-kyrgyzstana/poleznye-iskopaemye-kyrgyzstana/.

significance of tantalum-niobates, cobalt, zirconium, lithium, and coloured stones cannot be ruled out'.[232] In addition to the largest reserves of silver in Central Asia, Tajikistan has gold, tungsten, zinc, copper, bismuth, cadmium, tin and other minerals.[233] In Turkmenistan,

> proven reserves of natural gas amount to 44 trillion cubic metres. Oil, ozokerite, limestone, gypsum, bentonite clay, rock salt, granite, sulfur, Glauber's salt, inert materials, ornamental stones, brick and cement raw materials, mineral and fresh groundwater are also extracted. Turkmenistan has all known types of mineral salt deposits, [and there are] large reserves of native sulfur, iodine, bromine, table and potassium salts, sodium sulfate, and magnesium salts.[234]

In turn,

> about 100 types of mineral raw materials … have been identified in Uzbekistan's subsoil. More than 900 deposits have been explored, with proven reserves estimated at 970 billion US dollars. The total mineral resource potential is estimated at more than 3.3 trillion US dollars.[235]

Uzbekistan 'ranks fourth in the world in terms of gold reserves, and seventh in terms of its production level. In terms of gold production, Uzbekistan ranks second among the CIS countries (after Russia), and first in terms of quantity per capita. In terms of uranium and copper reserves, Uzbekistan is among the top ten countries in the world'.[236] Nonetheless, to remain continuously competitive in the world economy, the Central Asian States ought to cease relying primarily on their natural resources, and to diversify their national economies.[237]

J. Airspace

All Central Asian States are Members of the International Civil Aviation Organization (ICAO; see Chapter three, section III.D below) and have enacted domestic laws governing airspace use. Kazakhstan's Law 'On the Use of the Airspace of the Republic of Kazakhstan and Aviation Activities' was adopted on 15 July 2010,[238] while the other Central Asian States have introduced more

[232] ibid.

[233] Asia Plus, 'Kakiye est poleznye iskopayemye v Tadjikistane, i kto ih "vykachivayet"?' ['What Mineral Resources Are There in Tajikistan, and Who Is "Pumping Them Out"?'], available at: www.asiaplustj.info/ru/news/tajikistan/economic/20230616/kakie-poleznie-iskopaemie-est-v-tadzhikistane-i-kto-ih-vikachivaet-karta.

[234] TurkmenInform, 'Informatsiya o Turkmenistane' ['Information about Turkmenistan'], available at: turkmeninform.com/ru/turkmenistan.html.

[235] CatalogMineralov.Ru, 'Mestorozhdeniya poleznyh iskopayemyh Uzbekistana' ['Mineral Deposits of Uzbekistan'], available at: catalogmineralov.ru/deposit/uzbekistan/.

[236] ibid.

[237] For further details, see Chapter 11 on international trade law below.

[238] For the text of the Law (as amended, in Russian, replacing the Law 'On the Use of the Airspace of the Republic of Kazakhstan and Aviation Activities' of 20 December 1995), see: online.zakon.kz/Document/?doc_id=30789893&pos=3545;-52#pos=3545;-52.

comprehensive Air Codes.[239] Notably, not all these laws define airspace, and those that do omit its upper limits. Article 1(59) of Kazakhstan's law defines national airspace as 'airspace over the land and water territory of the Republic of Kazakhstan, including over its territorial waters'. Similarly, Article 1(2) of Turkmenistan's Air Code defines it as the airspace over its territory, including internal waters and territorial sea. Article 1(2) of Uzbekistan's Air Code states that its airspace forms part of the State's territory – a provision echoed in Article 2(2) of Kazakhstan's Law 'On the Use of the Airspace of the Republic of Kazakhstan and Aviation Activities' and Article 1(1) of Turkmenistan's Air Code. Article 1 of Tajikistan's Air Code, citing the Constitution, declares its airspace the exclusive property of the State. All Central Asian States affirm full and exclusive sovereignty over their respective airspaces.[240]

K. Outer Space

Outer space is space beyond Earth's atmosphere,

> most often thought to begin about 62 miles (100 kilometers) above sea level at what is known as the Kármán line. This is an imaginary boundary at an altitude where there is no appreciable air to breathe or scatter light.[241]

Other altitudes – for example, 73 miles (118 kilometres) or 76 miles (122 kilometres) – have also been suggested to designate the boundary between Earth's atmosphere and outer space for various practical purposes.[242] The major treaties of international space law, commonly referred to as the 'five United Nations treaties on outer space', are the Treaty on Principles Governing the Activities of States in the Exploration and Use of Outer Space, including the Moon and Other Celestial Bodies (Outer Space Treaty) of 27 January 1967,[243] Agreement on the Rescue of Astronauts, the Return of Astronauts and the Return of Objects Launched into Outer Space (Rescue Agreement) of 22 April 1968,[244] Convention

[239] For the text of the Air Code of the Kyrgyz Republic of 6 August 2015 (as amended, in Russian), see: cbd.minjust.gov.kg/111262/edition/929268/ru. For the text of the Air Code of the Republic of Tajikistan of 13 November 1998 (as amended, in Russian), see: base.spinform.ru/show_doc.fwx?rgn=2194. For the text of the Air Code of Turkmenistan of 10 January 2012 (in Russian), see: minjust.gov.tm/ru/hukuk/merkezi/hukuk/430. For the text of the Air Code of the Republic of Uzbekistan of 7 May 1993 (as amended, in Russian), see: lex.uz/acts/55599.

[240] See Art 2(1) of Kazakhstan's law, Art 1 of Kyrgyzstan's Code, Art 1 of Tajikistan's Code, Art 1(1) of Turkmenistan's Code, Art 1 (first part) of Uzbekistan's Air Code.

[241] E Howell, 'What is Space?', SPACE.com, 17 February 2022, available at www.space.com/24870-what-is-space.html.

[242] A Thompson, 'Edge of Space Found', SPACE.com, 9 April 2009, available at https://www.space.com/6564-edge-space.html.

[243] For the text of the Outer Space Treaty, see: www.unoosa.org/oosa/en/ourwork/spacelaw/treaties/outerspacetreaty.html.

[244] For the text of the Rescue Agreement, see: www.unoosa.org/oosa/en/ourwork/spacelaw/treaties/introrescueagreement.html.

on International Liability for Damage Caused by Space Objects (Liability Convention) of 29 March 1972,[245] Convention on Registration of Objects Launched into Outer Space (Registration Convention) of 14 January 1975,[246] and Agreement Governing the Activities of States on the Moon and Other Celestial Bodies (Moon Agreement) of 18 December 1979.[247] In Central Asia, only Kazakhstan has ratified all five space treaties; the other States are not yet parties.[248] The United Nations Office for Outer Space Affairs' collection of international and national instruments on space activities also includes several additional texts.[249]

The Outer Space Treaty sets out the key principles for the exploration and use of outer space. In accordance with the first part of Article I, the exploration and use of outer space is carried out for the benefit and in the interests of all countries and is the province of all mankind. Outer space is free for exploration and use by all States (Article I, second part). Outer space is not subject to national appropriation by claim of sovereignty, by means of use or occupation, or by any other means (Article II). The exploration and use of outer space should be carried out in accordance with international law, including the Charter of the United Nations, in the interest of maintaining international peace and security, and promoting international cooperation and understanding (Article III). States should not place nuclear weapons or other weapons of mass destruction in orbit or on celestial bodies, or station them in outer space in any other manner (Article IV, first part). The Moon and other celestial bodies should be used exclusively for peaceful purposes (Article IV, second part). Astronauts are regarded as the envoys of mankind in outer space and are entitled to all possible assistance in the event of accident, distress, or emergency landing on the territory of any State Party or on the high seas (Article V, first part). States are responsible for national space activities, whether carried out by governmental or non-governmental entities (Article VI). States are liable for damage caused by their space objects (Article VII). The State on whose registry an object launched into outer space is held retains jurisdiction and control over such object, and over any personnel thereof, while in outer space or on a celestial body (Article VIII). Importantly, States should avoid harmful contamination of space and celestial bodies (Article IX).[250]

[245] For the text of the Liability Convention, see: www.unoosa.org/oosa/en/ourwork/spacelaw/treaties/introliability-convention.html.

[246] For the text of the Registration Convention, see: www.unoosa.org/oosa/en/ourwork/spacelaw/treaties/introregistration-convention.html.

[247] For the text of the Moon Agreement, see: www.unoosa.org/oosa/en/ourwork/spacelaw/treaties/intromoon-agreement.html.

[248] Committee on the Peaceful Uses of Outer Space, 'Status of International Agreements relating to activities in outer space as at 1 January 2024', available at: www.unoosa.org/res/oosadoc/data/documents/2024/aac_105c_22024crp/aac_105c_22024crp_3_0_html/AC105_C2_2024_CRP03E.pdf.

[249] Accessing Space Treaty Resources Online (ASTRO), available at: astro.unoosa.org/astro/en/index.html.

[250] United Nations Office for Outer Space Affairs, 'Treaty on Principles Governing the Activities of States in the Exploration and Use of Outer Space, including the Moon and Other Celestial Bodies', available at: www.unoosa.org/oosa/en/ourwork/spacelaw/treaties/introouterspacetreaty.html.

The Central Asian States are developing national space programmes, taking into account their geography, economic conditions, and other capabilities. Kazakhstan hosts the world's largest spaceport.[251] In Kyrgyzstan, a non-governmental initiative is working to launch the first Kyrgyz satellite.[252] On 19 June 2023, the governments of Tajikistan and Russia signed an Agreement on Cooperation in the Exploration and Use of Outer Space for Peaceful Purposes. The Agreement 'regulates the procedure for the protection of intellectual property rights, issues of protection and exchange of information, export control, customs operations, protection of exported property, issues of handling various types of information and technology protection', and other aspects.[253] Turkmenistan established its National Space Agency in 2011.[254] Uzbekistan followed with the creation of the Space Research and Technology Agency under the Ministry of Digital Technologies ('Uzbekspace' Agency) on 30 August 2019.[255]

L. Baiqonyr

The world's largest operational space launch facility by area (6,717 km^2), Baiqonyr (or Baikonur) was established on 12 February 1955 in the Kazakh SSR's Qyzylorda region as a test site for the R-7, the world's first intercontinental ballistic missile (ICBM), and became operational with the first R-7 launch on 15 May 1957. Baiqonyr has been central to all major milestones of the Soviet and later the Russian space programme, including the launch of the first artificial satellite, Sputnik-1, on 4 October 1957, Yuri Gagarin's flight on 12 April 1961, Valentina Tereshkova's mission on 16–19 June 1963, Alexei Leonov's flight on 18–19 March 1965, the launch of the Mir space station on 20 February 1986, the Buran spaceplane on 15 November 1988, and the Zarya Functional Cargo Block of the International Space Station on 1 February 1999.

The legal status of the Baiqonyr Cosmodrome is currently governed by several treaties between Kazakhstan and Russia, along with relevant domestic laws. On 28 March 1994, the Agreement between the Republic of Kazakhstan and the Russian Federation on the Main Principles and Conditions of Use of

[251] See section IV.L below.

[252] 'Kyrgyz Space Program: defying barriers and reaching for the stars', available at kyrgyzspace-program.com/.

[253] Asia Plus, 'Tajikistan and Russia sign agreement on joint exploration of space', 3 October 2023, availableatasiaplustj.info/en/news/tajikistan/society/20231003/tajikistan-and-russia-sign-agreement-on-joint-exploration-of-space.

[254] Radio Free Europe / Radio Liberty, 'Turkmenistan Creates National Space Agency', 31 May 2011, available at www.rferl.org/a/turkmenistan_creates_national_space_agency/24211149.html.

[255] Space Research and Technology Agency under the Ministry of Digital Technologies of the Republic of Uzbekistan, 'Official name', available at uzspace.uz/en/page/overview.

the Baiqonyr Cosmodrome was concluded.[256] Article 2 (first part) states that, to enable continued use of the cosmodrome for Russian space activities, Kazakhstan leases the Baiqonyr complex's facilities to Russia. Under Article 7 (first part), the Agreement was concluded for 20 years and, per its second part, was subject to automatic prolongation for 10 years. Article 6 (first part) of the Agreement on the Development of Cooperation on the Effective Use of the Baiqonyr Complex of 9 January 2004 further extended the lease until 2050.[257] Article 4(5) (first part) of the 1994 Agreement provides that Russian military units supporting space operations at Baiqonyr are regarded as temporarily stationed in Kazakhstan. The second part of this paragraph stipulates that these units operate under Russian legislation and armed forces regulations, with due regard to Kazakh law. Within the Baiqonyr complex, Russian legislation applies to Russian military and civilian personnel and their families, and Russian authorities exercise jurisdiction over them.

On 10 December 1994, the governments of Kazakhstan and Russia concluded the Lease Treaty for the Baiqonyr Complex.[258] Article 5.1 sets the annual rent at 115 million USD. Under Article 6.1, all Baiqonyr complex property located in Kazakhstan as of 31 August 1991 belongs to Kazakhstan. Property created, acquired, or supplied after that date belongs to the party that financed it, while ownership of jointly funded assets is determined by separate agreements. Article 6.10 provides that Russia funds the essential functioning and infrastructure maintenance of the city of Leninsk. Kazakhstan contributes to funding in order to uphold the social rights of its citizens, as guaranteed by its legislation. According to Article 6.11, the commander of the Baiqonyr Cosmodrome is appointed and dismissed by the President of the Russian Federation, with the agreement of the President of the Republic of Kazakhstan.

On 23 December 1995, the Agreement between the Republic of Kazakhstan and the Russian Federation on the Status of the City of Baiqonyr, the Order of Formation and the Status of its Executive Organs was concluded.[259] Article 1(1) states that Baiqonyr is an administrative territorial unit of Kazakhstan, functioning under lease. Article 1(2) provides that the city administration building displays both States' flags. Under Article 6 (second part), the head of the city administration is jointly appointed by the Presidents of Kazakhstan and Russia, upon a Russian proposal. For the duration of the Lease Agreement, the city administration is formed by the Russian government on

[256] For the text of the Agreement (in Russian), see: www.baikonuradm.ru/index.php?mod1=npb1&npbid=46.

[257] For the text of the Agreement (in Russian), see: base.garant.ru/1156473/#block_6.

[258] For the text of the Agreement (in Russian), see: adilet.zan.kz/rus/docs/U950002195_.

[259] For the text of the Agreement (in Russian), see: www.baikonuradm.ru/userfiles/file/2020/jan/Baikonur_s.pdf.

the head's proposal (Article 6, third part). The head oversees all civilian executive functions (Article 7), manages the administration (Article 8), and exercises control (Article 9). The administration exercises property (Article 10) and land rights (Article 11). Financial and banking systems are jointly managed by Kazakhstan and Russia (Articles 12 and 13). Cooperation between Kazakh and Russian organisations, enterprises, and military units in Baiqonyr is coordinated by the Baiqonyr Complex Coordination Council (Article 15), which includes the city head and cosmodrome commander (Article 19). Disputes over the Agreement's interpretation or application are resolved through negotiations (Article 25, first part).

In 2024, it was reported that Kazakhstan planned to launch new commercial projects at the Baiqonyr Cosmodrome, following Russia's proposed transfer of over 200 facilities it sought to remove from the lease.[260] Members of the Senate of the Parliament of Kazakhstan 'were concerned about the current situation in the aerospace industry. According to them, there is a high risk that it will stop developing'.[261] For 2023–25, '4.9 billion tenge was approved for the space industry, but in practice, expenses in 2023–2024 [amounted] to 1.8 billion tenge; no funds are provided for 2025'.[262] In response, Prime Minister Olzhas Bektenov stated that work was 'underway to attract specialists from Serbia, China and India, [and] issues of technology transfer and organising internships for Kazakhstani specialists [were] being discussed'.[263] He added with respect to Kazakhstan's own 'Baiterek' space project that 'Kazakhstan [was] analysing modern technological solutions with Turkey, Italy, the USA and other countries'.[264]

V. GOVERNMENT

The third essential element of statehood, as codified in Article 1(c) of the Montevideo Convention, is government. The term is used generically to denote the existence of an apparatus capable of exercising legislative, executive, and judicial powers over the State's nationals (personal jurisdiction) and throughout its territory (territorial jurisdiction).[265]

[260] O Tonkonog, 'Rossiya peredast Kazahstanu bolee 200 obyektov na 'Baikonure'. Respublika planiruet zapustit tam proizvodstvo' ['Russia will transfer more than 200 facilities at Baikonur to Kazakhstan. The Republic plans to launch production there'], 16 May 2024, available at kz.kursiv.media/2024-05-16/lgtn-kazakstan-space/.

[261] ibid.

[262] ibid.

[263] ibid.

[264] ibid.

[265] See also Art 9 of the Montevideo Convention: 'The jurisdiction of states within the limits of national territory applies to all the inhabitants. Nationals and foreigners are under the same protection of the law and the national authorities and the foreigners may not claim rights other or more extensive than those of the nationals'.

A. Legislative Jurisdiction

Legislative jurisdiction refers to a State's authority to create rules of domestic and international law. In Central Asia, this authority is exercised by national Parliaments – unicameral in Kyrgyzstan[266] and Turkmenistan,[267] and bicameral in Kazakhstan (since 1995),[268] Tajikistan (since 1999),[269] and Uzbekistan (since 2005).[270] In relation to international law, Parliaments perform three key functions: (1) ratifying treaties, where required by treaty provisions or domestic laws;[271] (2) implementing treaties through domestic legislation;[272] and (3) participating in interparliamentary bodies such as the CIS Interparliamentary Assembly.[273]

B. Executive Jurisdiction

Executive jurisdiction denotes a State's authority to enforce domestic and international law. In all Central Asian States, the executive is subordinated to the President, who defines the main directions of foreign policy,[274] implemented through the Ministry of Foreign Affairs (MFA)[275] and its overseas missions (embassies and consulates). Executive organs are also responsible for implementing treaties within their respective competences.[276]

C. Adjudicative Jurisdiction

Adjudicative jurisdiction refers to a State's authority to resolve competing public or private claims involving the State, legal entities, or individuals under

[266] For the *Jogorku Kenesh* of the Kyrgyz Republic, see: kenesh.kg/ru.

[267] For the *Mejlis* of Turkmenistan, see: mejlis.gov.tm/?lang=tm. In 2021–23, the Parliament of Turkmenistan was bicameral but in January 2023, the *Halk Maslahaty* (People's Council) of Turkmenistan became a separate representative organ headed by the ex-President of Turkmenistan. For the *Halk Maslahaty*, see: maslahat.gov.tm/ru.

[268] For the *Mazhilis* of the Parliament of the Republic of Kazakhstan, see: www.parlam.kz/ru/mazhilis. For the website of the Senate, see: senate.parlam.kz/ru-RU.

[269] For the *Majlisi Namoyandagon* of the *Majlisi Oli* of the Republic of Tajikistan, see: www.parlament.tj/ru. For the website of the *Majlisi Milli*, see: majmilli.tj/.

[270] For the *Qonunchilik Palatasi* of the *Oliy Majlis* of the Republic of Uzbekistan, see: parliament.gov.uz/ru/. For the website of the Senate, see senat.uz/.

[271] See Chapter 6, section II.E below.

[272] See Chapter 6, section III.F below.

[273] For the CIS Interparliamentary Assembly, see: iacis.ru/.

[274] Art 40(1) of the Constitution of the Republic of Kazakhstan, Art 66(1) and (4) of the Constitution of the Kyrgyz Republic, Arts 64 (first para) and 69(1) of the Constitution of the Republic of Tajikistan, Arts 68 and 71(2) of the Constitution of Turkmenistan, Art 109 of the Constitution of the Republic of Uzbekistan.

[275] For the MFA of Kazakhstan, see: www.gov.kz/memleket/entities/mfa?lang=kk. For the MFA of Kyrgyzstan, see: mfa.gov.kg/ru. For the MFA of Tajikistan, see: mfa.tj/ru. For the MFA of Turkmenistan, see: www.mfa.gov.tm/ru. For the MFA of Uzbekistan, see: mfa.uz/ru/.

[276] See Chapter 6, section III.F below.

domestic and, where applicable, international law. Depending on a legal system's approach to the relationship between international and domestic law, treaty provisions may require implementation.[277] In some instances, domestic courts are obliged to apply treaty rules directly.[278] Constitutional Courts, in particular, play a key role in protecting human rights and fundamental freedoms.[279] For instance, in a landmark decision of 23 July 2024, Kazakhstan's Constitutional Court permitted unmarried men to adopt children.[280] The Constitutional Court ruled that 'restrictions established by the legislator for persons wishing to adopt a child must be adequate to legally justified purposes, and meet the requirements of fairness, proportionality and balance, based on the rights and interests of children'.[281] The Court directed that 'the Government, no later than within 6 months, submit to the Mazhilis a draft law aimed at improving the legal regulation of ... adoption, taking into account the specified legal positions of the Constitutional Court'.[282]

VI. CAPACITY TO ENTER INTO INTERNATIONAL RELATIONS

According to Article 1(d) of the Montevideo Convention, the fourth essential element of statehood under international law is the capacity to enter into relations with other States. In practice, this capacity depends on the degree and quality of recognition granted by existing States to entities claiming statehood or to governments that have assumed power unconstitutionally.

A. Recognition of States

Two main approaches exist regarding the recognition of new States. According to the declaratory theory, 'the act of recognition signifies no more than the acceptance of an already-existing factual situation – i.e., conformity with the criteria of statehood'.[283] In other words, '[i]nternational recognition is ...

[277] See Chapter 6, section III.F below.
[278] See Chapter 6, section III.E below.
[279] For the Constitutional Court of the Republic of Kazakhstan, see: www.gov.kz/memleket/entities/ksrk?lang=ru. For the Constitutional Court of the Kyrgyz Republic, see: constsot.kg/ru/. For the Constitutional Court of the Republic of Tajikistan, see: constcourt.tj/ru/. For the Constitutional Court of the Republic of Uzbekistan, see: www.konstsud.uz/ru.
[280] See Inbusiness.Kz, 'Nezhenatye muzhchiny smogut usynovlyat detey – Konstitutsionnyy sud RK' ['Unmarried Men Will Be Able to Adopt Children – the Constitutional Court of the [Republic of Kazakhstan'], 24 July 2024, available at inbusiness.kz/ru/last/nezhenatye-muzhchiny-smogut-usynovlyat-detej-konstitucionnyj-sud-rk.
[281] ibid.
[282] ibid.
[283] Britannica, 'States in international law', available at www.britannica.com/topic/international-law/States-in-international-law.

evidence that the factual criteria of statehood actually have been fulfilled'.[284] The declaratory theory was effectively codified in Article 6 (first sentence) of the Montevideo Convention: 'The recognition of a state merely signifies that the state which recognizes it accepts the personality of the other with all the rights and duties determined by international law'. In this sense, recognition of new States is rightly based

> on already existing facts, and does not generate them. This approach is shared by a number of scholars … It [was] also confirmed by the Institut de droit international, and [was] codified in a few international documents, in particular, [in] the Charter of the Organization of American States (Art[icle] 13).[285]

Moreover, Article 3 (first part) of the Montevideo Convention suggests that recognition is largely symbolic and not essential to statehood:

> The political existence of the state is independent of recognition by the other states. Even before recognition the state has the right to defend its integrity and independence, to provide for its conservation and prosperity, and consequently to organize itself as it sees fit, to legislate upon its interests, administer its services, and to define the jurisdiction and competence of its courts.

However, State practice appears more complex. If recognition merely 'confirmed' that an entity had a permanent population, defined territory, and government, then Kosovo, Taiwan, and some other entities would probably enjoy broader recognition. For instance, on 17 June 2022, the President of Kazakhstan stated at the St Petersburg Economic Forum:

> It has been calculated that if the right of a nation to self-determination is realized throughout the globe, then instead of 193 states there will be more than 500–600 States on Earth. It will be chaos. For this reason, we do not recognise Taiwan, Kosovo, South Ossetia, or Abkhazia. This principle will also be applied to quasi-state territories, which, in our view, are Luhansk and Donetsk.[286]

The other Central Asian States have likewise not recognised the aforementioned entities.[287] This practice may indicate the continued relevance of the

[284] ibid. cf M Milanovic, 'No, Recognizing Palestine Would Not Be Contrary to International Law', EJIL:Talk!, 31 July 2025, available at www.ejiltalk.org/no-recognizing-palestine-would-not-be-contrary-to-international-law/.

[285] SA Melnik, *Odnostoronniye akty gosudarstv v sovremennom mezhdunarodnom prave* [*Unilateral Acts of States in Contemporary International Law*] (Odessa, Phoenix, 2011), 140 (footnotes omitted).

[286] Radio Azattyq, 'Tokayev: Kazahstan ne priznaet "kvazigosudarstvennye" "DNR" i "LNR" ['Tokayev: Kazakhstan Does Not Recognise the "Quasi-State" ["Donetsk People's Republic"] and ["Luhansk People's Republic"]'], 18 June 2022, available at rus.azattyq.org/a/tokaev-o-priznanii-lnr-i-dnr/31903400.html.

[287] 'Ne stoit na nashey povestke. MID Kyrgyzstana ne hochet govorit, chey Krym, i priznayut li oni "DNR" i "LNR" ['Not on our agenda. The Ministry of Foreign Affairs of Kyrgyzstan Does Not Want to Say Whose Crimea Is, and Whether They Recognise the "DPR" and "LPR"'], 8 April 2022, available at kloop.kg/blog/2022/04/08/ne-stoit-na-nashej-povestke-mid-kyrgyzstana-ne-hochet-govorit-chej-krym-i-priznayut-li-oni-dnr-i-lnr/. 'Rossiysko-ukrainskiy konflikt: vzglyad

constitutive theory of recognition,[288] which 'contends that the act of recognition itself actually creates the [S]tate'.[289] Recognition is thus a *conditio sine qua non* for establishing diplomatic relations, invoking sovereign immunity, recognising and enforcing foreign judgments, and other forms of international cooperation. According to Article 6 (second sentence) of the Montevideo Convention, recognition is unconditional and irrevocable. While the latter is generally accepted, States sometimes make recognition conditional upon additional criteria. For example, in the early 1990s, the European Union proposed standards for recognising new States 'in order [for them] to be recognised as full members of the international community',[290] including 'inter alia, respect for minority rights, the inviolability of frontiers, and commitments to disarmament and nuclear nonproliferation'.[291] Such criteria appear reasonable, as they assess a new entity's ability to pursue the primary objective of States codified in Article 10 (first sentence) of the Montevideo Convention: the conservation of peace.

As a rule, State recognition occurs expressly (de jure), typically through a unilateral statement, but it may also occur tacitly (de facto), and may result 'from any act which implies the intention of recognizing the new state' (Article 7 of the Montevideo Convention). As Melnik explains, 'certain types of behaviour of States … constitute inferred, implicit or conclusive recognition. Such actions can give rise to international legal consequences similar to those of a unilateral act of recognition'.[292] To give some examples: on 16 March 1921, the United Kingdom concluded a trade agreement with the Russian Socialist Federal Soviet Republic; today, Taiwan maintains bilateral trade agreements with numerous States, including Mainland China;[293] and, similarly, Kosovo engages in trade with several nations, without prejudice to its legal status:

> Kosovo is a signatory of the Central European Free Trade Agreement (CEFTA) through the United Nations Mission in Kosovo (UNMIK) and has a Stabilization and Association Agreement (SAA) with the European Union that serves, among other things, as a free trade agreement. Kosovo also signed a trade and cooperation

iz Dushanbe. VIDEO' ['The Russian-Ukrainian Conflict: A View from Dushanbe. VIDEO'], 22 February 2022, available at rus.ozodi.org/a/31717227.html. 'Kto neytralen, a kto za Russiyu? Kak za god voyny menyalas pozitsiya stran Tsentralnoy Azii po konfliktu v Ukraine' ['Who is Neutral and Who is for Russia? How the Position of Central Asian Countries on the Conflict in Ukraine Has Changed Over the Course of a Year of the War'], 24 February 2023, available at www.currenttime.tv/a/32283122.html.

[288] Melnik (n 285).

[289] Britannica (n 283).

[290] Melnik (n 285).

[291] Britannica (n 283).

[292] Melnik (n 285), 136.

[293] International Trade Administration, available at www.trade.gov.tw/english/BilateralTrade/BilateralTrade.aspx?code=7030&nodeID=4639.

> agreement with the United Kingdom, a free trade agreement with Turkey, and has started the accession process for the European Free Trade Association …
>
> Kosovo has signed double-taxation treaties with Albania, Austria, Croatia, Hungary, Latvia, Lithuania, Luxemburg, Malta, Netherlands, North Macedonia, Saudi Arabia, Slovenia, Switzerland, Turkey, the United Arab Emirates, and the United Kingdom. Older treaties with Belgium, Finland, and Germany from the time of the former Yugoslavia are still in effect. Kosovo is member of the European Common Aviation Area and member of the Athens Process on Energy for the Southeastern Europe Energy Community Treaty.[294]

B. Recognition of Governments

The recognition of governments becomes relevant when a new administration assumes power within a State through non-constitutional means. Two main doctrines address this issue. The first, the Tobar Doctrine – named after Ecuadorian Foreign Minister Carlos Tobar (1853–1920) – holds that 'recognition of a government should only be granted if that administration came to power by legitimate democratic means'.[295] The second, the Estrada Doctrine – named after Mexican Secretary of Foreign Affairs Genaro Estrada (1887–1937) – maintains that 'recognition of a government should be based on its *de facto* existence, rather than on its legitimacy'.[296] In 1930, Secretary Estrada 'ordered that Mexican diplomats should issue no declarations that amounted to a grant of recognition: he felt that this was an insulting practice and offended against the sovereignty of other nations'.[297] Accordingly,

> [t]he contemporary trend is in fact no longer to recognize governments formally but to focus instead upon the continuation (or discontinuation) of diplomatic relations. By this change, states seek to avoid the political difficulties involved in deciding whether or not to 'recognize' new regimes taking power by nonconstitutional means.[298]

In Central Asia, the issue is particularly relevant to the recognition of, and relations with, the Taliban government in Afghanistan. None of the Central Asian States has recognised the Taliban de jure, but all cooperate with them de facto in strategic areas.[299] In 2024, Kazakhstan removed the Taliban from its list of

[294] International Trade Administration, 'Kosovo – Country Commercial Guide', available at www.trade.gov/country-commercial-guides/kosovo-trade-agreements.
[295] Oxford Reference, 'Tobar doctrine', available at www.oxfordreference.com/display/10.1093/acref/9780198802525.001.0001/acref-9780198802525-e-3986.
[296] Oxford Reference, 'Estrada doctrine', available at www.oxfordreference.com/display/10.1093/oi/authority.20110803095758788.
[297] ibid.
[298] Britannica (n 283).
[299] On 4 July 2025, Russia became the first State to formally recognise the Islamic Emirate of Afghanistan, see: https://fergana.agency/news/138757/.

terrorist organisations.[300] According to President Tokayev, '[t]he development of trade and economic cooperation with … Afghanistan is important, and we think that the current regime will be a long-term factor'.[301] In June 2024, Chingiz Aidarbekov, former Foreign Minister and currently a member of Kyrgyzstan's Parliament, stated:

> The decision to recognise the Taliban will be made jointly with the Ministry of Foreign Affairs … Based on this, the President will make a decision, and then the issue will be discussed with the executive branch at a meeting of the parliamentary committee on international relations and security.[302]

Tajikistan exports electricity to Afghanistan,[303] and has reportedly been in contact with the Taliban regarding bilateral security concerns.[304] In February 2024, the Taliban asked Turkmenistan to increase electricity supplies to Herat province, simplify visa procedures for Afghan entrepreneurs and transport personnel, and expand scholarship opportunities for (male) Afghan students in Turkmenistan.[305] On 12 March 2024, Uzbekistan's Foreign Minister, Bakhtiyor O Saidov, visited Kabul, and 'confirmed that Uzbekistan [was] committed to strengthening political and economic relations with Afghanistan, and offered the country technical support for the construction of modern irrigation systems and the Kosh-Tepa canal'.[306] Mr Saidov's own appraisal of his visit was pragmatic: 'Particular attention was paid to creating the most favourable conditions for strengthening economic ties and improving relations between business circles. We have a rich and common history, common traditions and future. There are many areas we can explore together'.[307] In addition to bilateral cooperation with

[300] Radio Liberty, 'Kazakstan isklyuchil "Taliban" is spiska terroristicheskih organizatsiy' ['Kazakhstan Removed the Taliban from the List of Terrorist Organizations'], 3 June 2024, available at www.svoboda.org/a/kazahstan-isklyuchil-taliban-iz-spiska-terroristicheskih-organizatsiy/32977458.html.

[301] ibid.

[302] 24.KG, 'Nuzhno li Kyrgyzstanu vyvodit dvizheniye 'Taliban' is spiska terroristicheskih organizatsiy?' ['Should Kyrgyzstan Remove the Taliban from the List of Terrorist Organisations?'], 7 June 2024, available at 24.kg/vlast/296008_nujnoli_kyirgyizstanu_vyivodit_dvijenie_taliban_izspiska_terroristicheskih/.

[303] Fergana News, 'SMI: Predstoyashchey zimoy Tadzhikistan sokratit postavki elektroenergii v Afganistan na 25%' ['Media: Tajikistan to Cut Electricity Supplies to Afghanistan by 25% This Coming Winter'], 30 July 2025, available at fergana.agency/news/139197/.

[304] *Radio Azattyk*, 'Issledovatelskiy institut: Tadjikistan prosil "Taliban" likdividirovat "Ansorullo" ['Research Institute: Tajikistan asked the "Taliban" to eliminate "Ansorullo"'], 23 February 2024, available at rus.azattyq.org/a/32831930.html.

[305] Fergana News, 'Taliby poprosili Turkmenistan uvelichit postavki elektroenergii i stipendii afganskim studentam' ['The Taliban Asked Turkmenistan to Increase Electricity Supplies and Scholarships for Afghan Students'], 27 February 2024, available at fergana.agency/news/133084/.

[306] Asia Plus, 'Glava MID Uzbekistana provel peregovory s dolzhnostnymi litsami "Taliban"' ['The Head of Uzbekistan's MFA Held Talks with Taliban Officials'], 13 March 2024, available at asiaplustj.info/ru/news/centralasia/20240313/glava-mid-uzbekistana-provel-peregovori-s-dolzhnostnimi-litsami-taliban.

[307] See Minister Saidov's Telegram channel: https://t.me/bakhtiyor_saidov/1307.

Afghanistan, Uzbekistan has in recent years hosted high-level international conferences on economic, security, and other strategic developments in the country.[308]

C. Membership of International Organisations

Admission to international organisations is sometimes regarded as evidence of 'collective recognition' – a persuasive interpretation. All Central Asian States joined the United Nations on 2 March 1992 and subsequently became members of numerous UN specialised agencies.[309] They are also founding members of several regional organisations.[310]

VII. OTHER ATTRIBUTES OF STATEHOOD

In addition to the essential elements of statehood listed in Article 1 of the Montevideo Convention, other implicit elements include armed forces, currency, and State symbols.

A. Armed Forces

Most States maintain standing armed forces.[311] Some use alternative designations – for example, Japan renounced war 'as a sovereign right of the nation' in its post-WWII Constitution and pledged not to maintain 'land, sea, and air forces, as well as other war potential'.[312] Today, its military is known as the Ground, Maritime, and Air Self-Defense Forces (SDF). At least 15 sovereign States – Andorra, Dominica, Grenada, Kiribati, Liechtenstein, Marshall Islands, Micronesia, Nauru, Palau, Saint Lucia, Saint Vincent and the Grenadines, Samoa, Solomon Islands, Tuvalu, and Vatican City – lack standing armed forces and rely on others for defence. At least six – Costa Rica, Iceland, Mauritius, Monaco, Panama, and Vanuatu – have no standing armies but maintain limited military forces.

[308] cf Chapter 10, section IX.G below. See also Fergana News, 'Glava SGB Uzbekistana obsudil s talibami transgranichnye ugrozy i borbu s narkobiznesom' ['Head of Uzbek State Security Service Discusses Cross-border Threats and Fight against Drug Trafficking with Taliban'], 23 July 2025, available at fergana.agency/news/139081/.

[309] See Chapter 3, sections II–III below.

[310] See Chapter 3, section IV below.

[311] For the 2025 Military Strength Ranking, see: www.globalfirepower.com/countries-listing.php.

[312] See Art 9 of the Constitution of Japan: japan.kantei.go.jp/constitution_and_government_of_japan/constitution_e.html.

All Central Asian States maintain standing armed forces, operating under domestic laws[313] and comprising both military professionals and conscripts. According to the 2025 Military Strength Ranking, Kazakhstan ranked 57th among 145 countries, with Uzbekistan ranked 58th, Turkmenistan 77rd, Kyrgyzstan 105th, and Tajikistan 108th.[314]

B. Currency

All States have financial systems, and most possess their own currencies. Some States and territories use the currencies of others,[315] while a few adopt collective currencies such as the euro.[316] All Central Asian States have national currencies. The Kyrgyz som (KGS) was launched on 10 May 1993 as the second post-Soviet currency after the Russian ruble.[317] The Turkmen manat (TMT) followed on 1 November 1993.[318] Two weeks later, on 15 November 1993, Kazakhstan introduced the tenge (KZT),[319] while Uzbekistan launched the soum coupon, later replaced by the Uzbek soum (UZS) on 1 July 1994.[320] Tajikistan introduced the somoni (TJS) on 30 October 2000, replacing the Tajik ruble, which had circulated from 10 May 1995 to 29 October 2000.[321]

[313] For the text of the Law 'On Defence and the Armed Forces of the Republic of Kazakhstan' of 7 January 2005 (as amended, in Russian, replacing the Law 'On Defence and the Armed Forces of the Republic of Kazakhstan' of 9 April 1993), see: online.zakon.kz/Document/?doc_id=1052592&pos=807;-57#pos=807;-57. For the text of the Law 'On Defence and the Armed Forces of the Kyrgyz Republic' of 24 July 2009 (as amended, in Russian, replacing the Law 'On Defence' of 13 April 1994), see: cbd.minjust.gov.kg/202668/edition/4265/ru. For the text of the Law of the Republic of Tajikistan 'On Defence' of 4 November 1995 (as amended, in Russian), see: online.zakon.kz/Document/?doc_id=30585225&show_di=1&pos=6;-108#pos=6;-108. For the text of the Law of Turkmenistan 'On Defence' of 25 September 2010 (as amended, in Russian), see: online.zakon.kz/Document/?doc_id=31344747&pos=6;-108#pos=6;-108. For the text of the Law of the Republic of Uzbekistan 'On Defence' of 3 July 1992 (in Russian, new edition adopted on 11 May 2001), see: lex.uz/acts/22317.

[314] 2025 Military Strength Ranking (n 311).

[315] For instance, more than 10 States and territories use the US dollar as their primary currency, and more than 20 States and territories use it alongside their own currencies. See Stripe, 'Which countries use the US dollar? Here's a complete list', 19 February 2024, available at stripe.com/resources/more/which-countries-use-the-us-dollar-heres-a-complete-list.

[316] Currently, the euro is the official currency in 20 EU Member States. See the European Union, 'Countries using the euro', available at european-union.europa.eu/institutions-law-budget/euro/countries-using-euro_en.

[317] 24.KG, 'Kyrgyzskiy som: Kak rodilas i menyalas natsionalnaya valyuta' ['The Kyrgyz Som: How the National Currency was Born and Changed'], available at 24.kg/spetsproekty/83648_kyirgyizskiy_som_kak_rodilas_imenyalas_natsionalnaya_valyuta/.

[318] Altyn Asyr, 'Turkmenskiy manat praznuyet godovshchinu' ['The Turkmen Manat Is Celebrating Its Anniversary'], 1 November 2021, available at turkmenistan.gov.tm/ru/post/58268/turkmenskij-manat-prazdnuet-godovshchinu.

[319] I Gumyrkina, '1993 god. Kak vvodili tenge' ['1993. How the Tenge Was Introduced'], 17 February 2023, available at vlast.kz/modern_history/53658-1993-god-kak-vvodili-tenge.html.

[320] E Sorochin, 'Evolyutsiya uzbekskogo suma' ['The Evolution of the Uzbek Soum'], 1 July 2022, available at www.gazeta.uz/ru/2022/07/01/money/.

[321] 'Valyuta v Tadjikistane' [Currency in Tajikistan], available at www.sravni.ru/text/valyuta-v-tadzhikistane/.

C. State Symbols

State symbols – namely the State flag,[322] emblem (coat of arms),[323] and anthem[324] – denote State sovereignty and serve practical functions under international law. State flags and emblems identify diplomatic[325] and consular[326] missions and may be displayed at the head of mission's residence and on official transport.[327] Special missions may also use the sending State's flag and emblem on their premises and transport when conducting official business.[328] Every State, whether coastal or landlocked, has the right to sail ships flying its flag on the high seas;[329] ships acquire the nationality of the State whose flag they are

[322] See Chapter 2 and Annex 1 to the Constitutional Law 'On the State Symbols of the Republic of Kazakhstan' of 4 June 2007 (as amended, in Russian, replacing the Constitutional Law 'On the State Symbols of the Republic of Kazakhstan' of 24 January 1996): online.zakon.kz/Document/?doc_id=30106150&pos=249;-43#pos=249;-43; Chapter II of the Law 'On the State Symbols of the Kyrgyz Republic' of 17 July 2004 (as amended, in Russian): cbd.minjust.gov.kg/1490/edition/955/ru; Law 'On the State Flag of the Kyrgyz Republic' of 17 July 2004 (as amended, in Russian): cbd.minjust.gov.kg/1490/edition/955/ru; Chapter 2 of the Law 'On the State Symbols of the Republic of Tajikistan' of 12 May 2007 (as amended, in Russian): ncz.tj/system/files/Legislation/254_ru.pdf; Law 'On the State Flag of Turkmenistan' of 24 January 2001 (as amended, in Russian): online.zakon.kz/Document/?doc_id=31337892; Law 'On the State Flag of the Republic of Uzbekistan' of 18 November 1991 (as amended, in Russian): www.lex.uz/acts/57181.

[323] See Chapter 3 and Annex 2 to the Constitutional Law 'On the State Symbols of the Republic of Kazakhstan' of 4 June 2007 (as amended, in Russian, replacing the Constitutional Law 'On the State Symbols of the Republic of Kazakhstan' of 24 January 1996): online.zakon.kz/Document/?doc_id=30106150&pos=249;-43#pos=249;-43; Chapter III of the Law 'On the State Symbols of the Kyrgyz Republic' of 17 July 2004 (as amended, in Russian): cbd.minjust.gov.kg/1490/edition/955/ru; Chapter 3 of the Law 'On the State Symbols of the Republic of Tajikistan' of 12 May 2007 (as amended, in Russian): ncz.tj/system/files/Legislation/254_ru.pdf; Law 'On the State Emblem of Turkmenistan' of 15 August 2003 (as amended, in Russian): online.zakon.kz/Document/?doc_id=31337878; Law 'On the State Emblem of the Republic of Uzbekistan' of 2 July 1992 (as amended, in Russian): lex.uz/acts/17771.

[324] See Chapter 4 and Annex 3 to the Constitutional Law 'On the State Symbols of the Republic of Kazakhstan' of 4 June 2007 (as amended, in Russian, replacing the Constitutional Law 'On the State Symbols of the Republic of Kazakhstan' of 24 January 1996): online.zakon.kz/Document/?doc_id=30106150&pos=249;-43#pos=249;-43; Chapter IV of the Law 'On the State Symbols of the Kyrgyz Republic' of 17 July 2004 (as amended, in Russian): cbd.minjust.gov.kg/1490/edition/955/ru; Chapter 4 of the Law 'On the State Symbols of the Republic of Tajikistan' of 12 May 2007 (as amended, in Russian): ncz.tj/system/files/Legislation/254_ru.pdf; Law 'On the State Anthem of Turkmenistan' of 5 December 2008 (as amended, in Russian, replacing the Law 'On the State Anthem of Turkmenistan' of 27 September 1996): online.zakon.kz/Document/?doc_id=31337831; Law 'On the State Anthem of the Republic of Uzbekistan' of 10 December 1992 (as amended, in Russian): www.lex.uz/acts/1780.

[325] See Art 20 of the Vienna Convention on Diplomatic Relations: legal.un.org/ilc/texts/instruments/english/conventions/9_1_1961.pdf.

[326] See Art 29 of the Vienna Convention on Consular Relations: legal.un.org/ilc/texts/instruments/english/conventions/9_2_1963.pdf.

[327] See n 323 above.

[328] See Art 19 of the 1969 Convention on Special Missions: legal.un.org/ilc/texts/instruments/english/conventions/9_3_1969.pdf.

[329] See Art 90 of the United Nations Convention on the Law of the Sea: www.un.org/depts/los/convention_agreements/texts/unclos/unclos_e.pdf.

authorised to fly.[330] In international aviation law, '[t]he concept of nationality for aircraft was adapted from maritime law where the national flag is used to indicate a ship's country of registration'.[331] The use of national flags also bears consequences in international responsibility, international humanitarian law (IHL),[332] and international criminal law (ICL).[333]

[330] See Art 91(1) (second sentence) of the United Nations Convention on the Law of the Sea.
[331] ICAO, 'Annex 7 – Aircraft Nationality and Registration Marks', available at applications.icao.int/postalhistory/annex_7_aircraft_nationality_and_registration_marks.htm.
[332] See Chapter 14 below.
[333] See Chapter 15 below.

3

International Organisations

I. LEGAL PERSONALITY OF INTERNATIONAL ORGANISATIONS

A. Introduction

INTERNATIONAL ORGANISATIONS ARE secondary actors – that is, they are established by primary actors (States) to attain their collective goals, and carry out functions entrusted to them by the primary actors.[1] In public international law, the notion 'international organisations' usually means 'intergovernmental' organisations of which States are members, whereas 'international non-governmental organisations' (international NGOs) whose membership includes individuals and their associations are non-State actors.[2] This chapter introduces the notion and key characteristics of international (intergovernmental) organisations, offers the Central Asian perspectives on the United Nations and its specialised agencies, and discusses a few regional organisations of which the States of Central Asia are members.

B. Membership of States

International organisations are established by States to offer joint responses to challenges, which States are not able – or not sufficiently able – to cope with on their own.[3] States contribute to international organisations their human and financial resources, experience, technologies and know-how, and distribute these in accordance with the needs of their members.[4] Intergovernmental organisations operate on the basis of sovereign equality of their members, whereas supranational organisations – such as the European Union (EU) – have

[1] HT Adilkariyev, *Mezhdunarodnoye pravo* [*International law*] (Tashkent, Tashkent State Law Institute, 2003), 95–97, 187–202; II Lukashuk and AH Saidov, *Hozirgi zamon xalqaro huquqi nazariyasi asoslari* [*The theoretical fundamentals of modern international law*] (Tashkent, Adolat, 2006), 92–93, 202–33.

[2] See Chapter 4, section II below.

[3] J Klabbers, *International Law*, 3rd edn (Cambridge, Cambridge University Press, 2021), 92.

[4] I Hurd, *International Organizations: Politics, Law, Practice*, 4th edn (Cambridge, Cambridge University Press, 2021), 1–3.

the capacity to directly affect the legal orders of their members.[5] The Eurasian Economic Union (EAEU) also has some elements of supranationality.[6] The rules of some international organisations also provide for admission of other international organisations as collective members – for example, the EU is a collective member of the World Trade Organisation (WTO).[7] Likewise, the EU is a member of the Hague Conference on Private International Law (HCCH), of which Kazakhstan and Uzbekistan are the current Central Asian members.[8]

C. Statutory Document

The structure, competence and functions of international organisations are laid down in their statutory documents – usually, treaties. Like with other treaties,[9] the formal titles of such statutory documents are without prejudice to their legal force: to give just a few examples, the United Nations (UN) and the Shanghai Cooperation Organisation (SCO) operate on the basis of Charters; the United Nations Educational, Scientific and Cultural Organization (UNESCO) and the World Health Organization (WHO) have Constitutions; the Commonwealth of Independent States (CIS) has a Statute; and the Eurasian Economic Union (EAEU) was established by a Treaty. The thematic competences of international organisations can be general and include multiple areas (eg, UN, CIS, SCO), or specific and cover a single theme or area of responsibility (eg, UNESCO, WHO, WTO, NATO, CSTO), whereas their geographic reach can be universal or regional.

D. Stable Structure

Unlike international conferences and other international organs, which meet periodically according to needs and may indeed be temporary,[10] international organisations have stable structures, and the powers and functions of their main and subsidiary organs are clearly defined in the statutory documents.[11] In some organs, all members are represented (eg, the UN General Assembly), whereas membership in other organs is limited (eg, the Security Council or the Economic and Social Council of the United Nations). Some organs operate continuously (usually, these are Secretariats located at the Headquarters), and others meet in

[5] ibid, 281–94. See also D Chalmers, G Davies and G Monti, *European Union Law*, 3rd edn (Cambridge, Cambridge University Press, 2014).

[6] See Chapter 12, section II below.

[7] See Chapter 12, section I below.

[8] HCCH, 'HCCH Members', available at www.hcch.net/en/states/hcch-members.

[9] See Chapter 6 below.

[10] For example, on the Conference on Security and Co-operation in Europe, see: www.osce.org/who/87.

[11] Klabbers (n 3), 93.

periodic sessions. Some organs make decisions binding on all members (eg, the UN Security Council), and others make recommendations (eg, the UN General Assembly). Finally, the functions of organs of international organisations can be quasi-legislative (eg the UN General Assembly, the Inter-Parliamentary Assembly of the CIS), executive (eg the Council of Heads of State, the Council of Heads of Government, or the Council of Ministers of Foreign Affairs of the CIS), and judicial or quasi-judicial (eg the International Court of Justice, the WTO Dispute Settlement Body, or the Court of the Eurasian Economic Union).

E. Seat

The seats of international organisations are usually where their Secretariats and, as the case may be, other main organs are located. Large international organisations like the UN are represented in several parts of the world.[12] Sometimes the main organs of an international organisation are located in different places – for example, the UN Headquarters is in New York, but the International Court of Justice is in The Hague where its predecessor – the Permanent Court of International Justice – was located.[13] Likewise, the Secretariat of the SCO is located in Beijing but Tashkent is home to its Regional Anti-terrorist Structure (RATS).[14]

F. Budget

The budget of international organisations is contributed to by their members, with due regard to the size of their populations, the relative strength of their economies, and other elements and criteria.[15] For the sake of fairness, international organisations may set the minimum and maximum assessment rates: for example, in the United Nations, a minimum assessment rate amounts to 0.001 per cent of the UN budget, whereas a maximum assessment rate for the least developed countries is 0.01 per cent.[16] The maximum assessment rate (currently applicable only to the United States) is 22 per cent.[17] In accordance with Article 19 of the UN Charter,

> [a] Member of the United Nations which is in arrears in the payment of its financial contributions to the Organization shall have no vote in the General Assembly if the amount of its arrears equals or exceeds the amount of the contributions due from it

[12] See section II.G below.
[13] See section II.F below.
[14] See section IV.E below.
[15] United Nations, 'Regular contributions and working capital fund', available at www.un.org/en/ga/contributions/budget.shtml.
[16] ibid.
[17] ibid.

> for the preceding two full years. The General Assembly may, nevertheless, permit such a Member to vote if it is satisfied that the failure to pay is due to conditions beyond the control of the Member.

As of June 2025, this rule affects four Members of the United Nations.[18]

Notably, international financial institutions – such as the World Bank, International Monetary Fund (IMF), International Finance Corporation (IFC), and others – use 'weighted voting', whereby 'Member countries are allocated votes at the time of membership and subsequently for additional subscriptions to capital. Votes are allocated differently in each organization'.[19] Obviously, under this system, larger contributors have more voting powers. For example, in the International Bank for Reconstruction and Development (IBRD), Kazakhstan has 5398 votes (0.19 per cent), Kyrgyzstan – 1932 votes (0.07 per cent), Tajikistan – 2029 votes (0.07 per cent), Turkmenistan – 1452 votes (0.05 per cent), and Uzbekistan – 5063 votes (0.18 per cent), compared to 439,300 votes (15.64 per cent) held by the US, or 200,710 votes (7.15 per cent) held by Japan.[20]

II. UNITED NATIONS (UN)

A. Introduction

The Charter of the United Nations (UN) was adopted at the San Francisco Conference on 26 June 1945, and entered into force on 24 October 1945.[21] Established by a coalition of victor nations of the Second World War,[22] in order to maintain international peace and security, develop friendly relations and cooperation between States, encourage respect for human rights and fundamental freedoms for all, and to pursue other Purposes in accordance with Article 1 of the UN Charter, the UN now has 193 Members.[23] All Central Asian nations became UN Members on 2 March 1992, soon after the dissolution of the Soviet Union.[24] This membership was essential for the consolidation of the newly independent States' sovereignty.[25] The contributions made by the Central Asian

[18] United Nations, 'Countries in arrears in the payment of their financial contributions under the terms of Article 19 of the UN Charter', available at www.un.org/en/ga/about/art19.shtml, currently Afghanistan, Bolivia, Sao Tome and Principe, and Venezuela.

[19] World Bank, 'Voting Powers', available at www.worldbank.org/en/about/leadership/votingpowers.

[20] IBRD, 'Subscriptions and Voting Power of Member Countries', available at thedocs.worldbank.org/en/doc/a16374a6cee037e274c5e932bf9f88c6-0330032021/original/IBRDCountryVotingTable.pdf.

[21] For the text of the UN Charter, see: www.un.org/en/about-us/un-charter/full-text.

[22] S Chesterman, I Johnstone and DP Malone, *Law and Practice of the United Nations: Documents and Commentary*, 2nd edn (Oxford, Oxford University Press, 2016), 3–4.

[23] United Nations, 'Member States', available at www.un.org/en/about-us/member-states.

[24] ibid. See also Chesterman, Johnstone and Malone (n 22), 213–16.

[25] S Sayapin, 'International Law in Central Asia: Practices and Doctrines' (2022) 47 *Review of Central and East European Law* 322, 336 (footnotes omitted): 'The early years of Tajikistan's independence were marked by a violent non-international armed conflict, and the UN's peacebuilding

nations to various UN organs and, more broadly, to the UN system are discussed below.

If Dag Hammarskjöld's famous statement about the raison d'être of the UN is any guide,[26] then the UN system might overall be regarded as a relatively successful project. Although the world has not got rid of wars, the prohibition of the use of force has now acquired the character of *jus cogens*, and recourse to military force is now regarded as an aberration from normality, and not a lawful means of settling international disputes.[27] Many deadly diseases have become a thing of the past. International transport and telecommunications networks are transcending distances and connecting the world. Progressive liberalisation of international trade is contributing to the improvement of the quality of life worldwide. States are working together to combat transnational organised crime. No State – however rich and powerful – would be able to cope with these challenges on its own. These and other achievements are to the credit of the UN system, and it is hoped that its prospective reform will enhance its overall efficiency.[28]

B. General Assembly

The General Assembly is the only main organ of the United Nations where all 193 UN Members are represented, each Member having not more than five representatives and only one vote.[29] The composition, functions and powers, voting and procedure of the General Assembly are laid down in Chapter IV of the UN Charter (Articles 9–22).[30] In accordance with Article 10, the General Assembly

> may discuss any questions or any matters within the scope of the … Charter or relating to the powers and functions of any organs provided for in the … Charter, and … may make recommendations to the Members of the United Nations or to the Security Council or to both on any such questions or matters.

In particular, the General Assembly discusses matters of international peace and security (Article 11), encourages the progressive development of international

efforts were important. In 1995, Turkmenistan had its permanent neutrality recognized by the UN General Assembly, and in 2007, the United Nations Regional Centre for Preventive Diplomacy for Central Asia (UNRCCA) was established'.

[26] 'It has been said that the United Nations was not created in order to bring us to heaven, but in order to save us from hell', Address by Secretary-General Dag Hammarskjöld at University of California Convocation, Berkeley, California, Thursday, 13 May 1954, at 10 am (Pacific Coast Time), available at digitallibrary.un.org/record/1291161?ln=en&v=pdf.

[27] See Chapter 10 below.

[28] United Nations, 'Pact for the Future, Global Digital Compact and Declaration on Future Generations', available at www.un.org/sites/un2.un.org/files/sotf-pact_for_the_future_adopted.pdf.

[29] UN General Assembly, available at www.un.org/en/ga/. See also MJ Peterson, 'General Assembly' in TG Weiss and S Daws (eds), *The Oxford Handbook on the United Nations* (Oxford, Oxford University Press, 2007).

[30] For the Rules of Procedure of the UN General Assembly, see: www.un.org/en/ga/about/ropga/.

law and its codification (Article 13(1)(a)), and assists in the realisation of human rights and fundamental freedoms (Article 13(1)(b)). It also receives and considers annual and special reports from the Security Council (Article 15(1)), and from the other organs of the United Nations (Article 15(2)).

Although most resolutions of the UN General Assembly are indeed recommendatory, some are binding – for example, those on the admission of new Members (Article 4(2)) or concerning the UN budget (Article 17(1)). It appears that resolutions adopted by consensus or without a vote,[31] and those codifying or reproducing rules of 'hard' international law are legally binding as well.[32] For example, the General Assembly resolutions of 12 December 1995, as well as of 3 June 2015 on the permanent neutrality of Turkmenistan were adopted without a vote,[33] and one may argue that the permanent neutrality of Turkmenistan derives its legal force from consensus among the UN Members, and is part of general international law.

The General Assembly makes most decisions by a simple majority of Members present and voting (Article 18(3)), whereas decisions on 'important' questions require 'a two-thirds majority of the members present and voting'. Article 18(2) stipulates that such 'important' questions include

> recommendations with respect to the maintenance of international peace and security, the election of the non-permanent members of the Security Council, the election of the members of the Economic and Social Council ... the admission of new Members to the United Nations, the suspension of the rights and privileges of membership, the expulsion of Members ... and budgetary questions.[34]

In accordance with Article 20 of the UN Charter, the General Assembly meets 'in regular annual sessions and in such special sessions as occasion may require'. The regular sessions take place each year in September–December.[35] Special sessions may be convened 'at the request of the Security Council, of a majority of Member States, or of one Member State if the majority of Members concur'.[36] In turn,

> [e]mergency special sessions may be called within 24 hours of a request by the Security Council on the vote of any nine Council members, or by a majority of UN Member States, or by one Member State if the majority of Members concur.[37]

[31] United Nations, 'How Decisions are Made at the UN', available at www.un.org/en/model-united-nations/how-decisions-are-made-un.

[32] S Sayapin, 'The United Nations General Assembly Resolution 68/262 in the Context of General International Law (2015 2 *Evropsky politicky a pravni diskurz* 19; S Sayapin, 'Territorialnaya tselostnost Ukrainy v svete Rezolyutsii 68/262 Generalnoy Assamblei OON' ['The Territorial Integrity of Ukraine in the Context of the UN General Assembly Resolution 68/262'] (2014) 1–2(5) *Journal of Constitutionalism and Human Rights* 66.

[33] See Chapter 5, section II.D below.

[34] Obviously, the General Assembly's functions pertaining to the trusteeship system and the Trusteeship Council are now largely outdated. See section II.G below.

[35] For an overview of sessions of the General Assembly, see: www.un.org/en/ga/sessions/.

[36] ibid.

[37] ibid.

So far, 11 emergency special sessions have taken place – most recently, on the occasion of Russia's full-scale invasion of Ukraine in February 2022.[38]

Article 22 empowers the General Assembly to 'establish such subsidiary organs as it deems necessary for the performance of its functions'. Such subsidiary organs include, for example, the International Law Commission (ILC), which works for the progressive development of international law and its codification, and consists of 34 academics and practitioners who are 'persons of recognized competence in international law'.[39] The ILC has not yet had any Central Asian members, and nominating competent experts from Central Asia for membership in the ILC would be a strategic move.[40]

C. Security Council

The Security Council bears the primary responsibility for the maintenance of international peace and security (Article 24(1) of the UN Charter), and is the only main organ of the United Nations, which functions continuously (Article 28(1)).[41] Pursuant to Article 29 of the Charter, the Security Council may establish such subsidiary organs as it deems necessary for the performance of its functions. Notable examples of such subsidiary organs include the International Criminal Tribunal for the Former Yugoslavia (ICTY, established in 1993), and the International Criminal Tribunal for Rwanda (ICTR, established in 1994).[42] The Council consists of 15 Members – that is, less than 10 per cent of the current total UN membership – whereby five Members are permanent, and 10 non-permanent Members are elected for a term of two years (Article 23(2)). In accordance with Article 23(1) of the Charter, the permanent Members of the Security Council are the Republic of China, France, the Union of Soviet Socialist Republics, the United Kingdom of Great Britain and Northern Ireland, and the United States of America. Clearly, this provision no longer corresponds to reality, and should be updated in the framework of the UN reform. Each Member of the Security Council has one vote. Decisions on procedural matters require nine affirmative votes, and those on all other matters are made by an affirmative vote of nine Members including the concurring votes of the permanent members.[43]

[38] See Eleventh Emergency Special Session, https://www.un.org/en/ga/sessions/emergency11th.shtml.

[39] cf Art 2(1) of the ILC Statute.

[40] Sayapin (n 25), 350.

[41] P Gaeta, JE Viñuales and S Zappalà, *Cassese's International Law*, 3rd edn (Oxford, Oxford University Press, 2020), 316–17; DM Malone, 'Security Council' in Weiss and Daws (n 29).

[42] Chesterman, Johnstone and Malone (n 22), 140–43; R Goldstone, 'International Criminal Court and Ad Hoc Tribunals' in Weiss and Daws (n 29).

[43] cf Art 27(3) of the UN Charter. In decisions under Chapter VI, and under paragraph 3 of Article 52, a party to a dispute should abstain from voting. For the Provisional Rules of Procedure of the UN Security Council, see: main.un.org/securitycouncil/en/content/provisional-rules-procedure.

As crucial as the Security Council is for the success of the United Nations, its efficiency has been limited for the most part of the UN's existence. Since 1946, the permanent Members have used their veto power at least 271 times,[44] with the USSR (and later Russia) accounting for more than 45 per cent of the vetoes.[45] After a period of 'revival' since the end of the Cold War, the Security Council has again been paralysed by disagreements over Russia's continued aggression against Ukraine from 2014 onward. Since the Security Council's responsibility for the maintenance of international peace and security is primary but not exclusive,[46] the lack of agreement in the Council has led the General Assembly to adopt a series of resolutions on various aspects of this conflict,[47] and the International Court of Justice to engage in the settlement of disputes between Ukraine and Russia.[48]

Since 1992, only one Central Asian nation – Kazakhstan – has been a non-permanent Member of the Security Council (2017–18).[49] Kazakhstan used this

> status to, among other things, promote its campaign against nuclear weapons, raise international awareness of the security situation in and around Afghanistan, and to consolidate its role in UN peacekeeping operations. For this purpose, the Almaty-based Peacekeeping Training Centre (Partnership for Peace) under the Ministry of Defense of the Republic of Kazakhstan [was] instrumental.[50]

In drawing international attention to these key issues, Kazakhstan advanced not only its own political agenda but, more broadly, the interests of the region as a whole. More recently, President of Kazakhstan stated at the session of the UN General Assembly in September 2023:

> Without comprehensive reform of the Security Council, we will not be able to cope with these challenges … I am deeply convinced that the voices of the 'middle powers' and all developing countries in the Council must be strengthened and clearly heard. Because the Security Council appears unable to break the deadlock, it must become

[44] United Nations, 'UN Security Council Meetings & Outcomes Tables', available at https://research.un.org/en/docs/sc/quick.

[45] ibid.

[46] S Sayapin, *The Crime of Aggression in International Criminal Law: Historical Development, Comparative Analysis and Present State* (The Hague, TMC Asser Press, 2014), 49–56.

[47] Security Council Report, 'UN Documents for Ukraine: General Assembly Documents', available at https://www.securitycouncilreport.org/un_documents_type/general-assembly-documents/?ctype=Ukraine&cbtype=ukraine.

[48] M Milanovic, 'ICJ Delivers Preliminary Objections Judgment in the Ukraine v. Russia Genocide Case, Ukraine Loses on the Most Important Aspects', EJIL:Talk!, 2 February 2024, available at https://www.ejiltalk.org/icj-delivers-preliminary-objections-judgment-in-the-ukraine-v-russia-genocide-case-ukraine-loses-on-the-most-important-aspects/.

[49] WA Sanchez, 'Analyzing Kazakhstan's First Tenure at the UN Security Council: As the first Central Asian state to sit on the UNSC, what did Kazakhstan achieve?', 22 March 2019, available at thediplomat.com/2019/03/analyzing-kazakhstans-first-tenure-at-the-un-security-council/.

[50] Sayapin (n 25), 336 (footnotes omitted).

more representative so that other countries, including Kazakhstan, can play a greater role in maintaining peace and security.[51]

D. Economic and Social Council

The Economic and Social Council (ECOSOC) consists of 54 UN Members elected by the General Assembly for a term of three years (Article 61 of the UN Charter). Kazakhstan's term on the ECOSOC ended in 2024, while Uzbekistan will be a member until 31 December 2027.[52] In accordance with Article 67 of the Charter, each member of the ECOSOC has one vote, and decisions are made by a majority of the UN Members present and voting. The Economic and Social Council focuses on three dimensions of sustainable development – economic, social, and environmental.[53] The ECOSOC provides 'overall guidance and coordination' to a network of UN organs and entities, including 'regional economic and social commissions, functional commissions facilitating intergovernmental discussions of major global issues, expert bodies establishing important global normative frameworks, and specialized agencies, programmes and funds at work around the world'.[54] It interacts with the UN specialised agencies,[55] and holds consultations with more than 6300 registered non-governmental organisations,[56] and other civil society actors within its areas of competence.[57]

E. Trusteeship Council

In accordance with Chapters XI–XIII of the UN Charter, the Trusteeship Council worked 'to promote the advancement of the inhabitants of Trust Territories and their progressive development towards self-government or independence'.[58] In fact, the Trusteeship Council may be regarded as the most successful main organ of the United Nations, since '[t]he aims of the Trusteeship System have been fulfilled to the extent that all Trust Territories

[51] Zakon.Kz, 'Tokayev o reformirovanii Sovbeza OON: Golosa razvivayushchihsya stran dolzhny byt uslyshany' ['Tokayev on Reforming the UN Security Council: The Voices of Developing Countries Must Be Heard'], 20 September 2023, www.zakon.kz/sobytiia/6407415-tokaev-o-reformirovanii-sovbeza-oon-golosa-razvivayushchikhsya-stran-dolzhny-byt-uslyshany.html.

[52] ECOSOC, 'Members', available at ecosoc.un.org/en/about-us/members.

[53] ECOSOC, 'About Us', www.un.org/ecosoc/en/content/about-us. See also G Rosenthal, 'Economic and Social Council' in Weiss and Daws (n 29).

[54] ibid. cf also Art 68 of the UN Charter.

[55] See Arts 57 and 70 of the UN Charter and section III below.

[56] cf Art 71 of the UN Charter.

[57] P Wapner, 'Civil Society' in Weiss and Daws (n 29).

[58] United Nations, 'Trusteeship Council', available at www.un.org/en/about-us/trusteeship-council.

have attained self-government or independence, either as separate States or by joining neighbouring independent countries'.[59] Central Asia was unaffected by the Trusteeship System, since the region was a part of the Soviet Union from 1945–91, and the newly independent Central Asian States were admitted to the UN on 2 March 1992. The Trusteeship Council suspended its operations on 1 November 1994 after the last remaining trust territory – Palau – had attained independence.[60] Now, the Council may be formally liquidated in the course of UN reform, or else its functions may be revised to include the protection of the environment and the global commons.[61]

F. International Court of Justice (ICJ)

The predecessor of the International Court of Justice (ICJ), the Permanent Court of International Justice (PCIJ), was established in 1922, and was dissolved on 31 January 1946.[62] The PCIJ was the world's first international tribunal with general jurisdiction. Between 1922 and 1940, it considered 29 disputes between States, and delivered 27 advisory opinions.[63] In 1945,

> the San Francisco Conference considered that a degree of continuity should be maintained … The Charter therefore clearly stated that the Statute of the International Court of Justice was based upon that of the PCIJ. At the same time, the necessary steps were taken to transfer as much of the PCIJ's jurisdiction as possible to the International Court of Justice.[64]

The ICJ thus continues a rich judicial tradition, but this also means it is a conservative organ probably requiring a degree of modernisation.

As the principal judicial organ of the United Nations,[65] the International Court of Justice performs two main functions. First, the Court considers contentious cases between States,[66] and, in accordance with Article 94(1) of the UN Charter, '[e]ach Member of the United Nations undertakes to comply with the decision of the International Court of Justice in any case to which it is a party'. Notably, none of the Central Asian States have recognised the compulsory

[59] ibid.
[60] ibid.
[61] R Wilde, 'Trusteeship Council' in Weiss and Daws (n 29).
[62] For a historical overview of the PCIJ, see: www.icj-cij.org/pcij.
[63] ibid.
[64] See: https://www.icj-cij.org/history.
[65] cf Art 92 of the UN Charter. See also J Crawford and T Grant, 'International Court of Justice' in Weiss and Daws (n 29); H Lauterpacht, *The Development of International Law by the International Court* (Cambridge, Grotius Publications Limited, 1982).
[66] See, for example, VP Kononenko, *Razresheniye territorialnyh sporov Mezhdunarodnym Sudom OON: teoriya i praktika* [*The Settlement of Territorial Disputes by the International Court of Justice: Theory and Practice*] (Odessa, Phoenix Press, 2017).

jurisdiction of the ICJ,[67] and none of them have appeared before the Court so far. The second function concerns advisory proceedings:[68]

> Advisory proceedings before the Court are only open to five organs of the United Nations and 16 specialized agencies of the United Nations family or affiliated organizations.
>
> The United Nations General Assembly and Security Council may request advisory opinions on 'any legal question'. Other United Nations organs and specialized agencies which have been authorized to seek advisory opinions can only do so with respect to 'legal questions arising within the scope of their activities' …
>
> Such opinions are essentially advisory; in other words, unlike the Court's judgments, they are not binding. The requesting organ, agency or organization remains free to give effect to the opinion as it sees fit, or not to do so at all. However, certain instruments or regulations provide that an advisory opinion by the Court does have binding force (e.g., the conventions on the privileges and immunities of the United Nations).[69]

In accordance with Article 3(1) of the ICJ Statute, the Court consists of 15 Judges, no two of whom may be nationals of the same State.[70] They must be 'persons of high moral character, who possess the qualifications required in their respective countries for appointment to the highest judicial offices, or are jurisconsults of recognized competence in international law' (Article 2 of the ICJ Statute). The Members of the Court are elected by the General Assembly and by the Security Council for a term of nine years, and may be re-elected (Articles 4(1) and 13(1) of the ICJ Statute). The ICJ has not had any Members from Central Asia so far, and the States of the region may consider nominating qualified candidates in the future.

G. Secretariat

In accordance with Article 97 of the UN Charter, the Secretariat comprises 'a Secretary-General and such staff as the Organization may require. The Secretary-General [is] appointed by the General Assembly upon the recommendation of the Security Council. He [is] the chief administrative officer of the Organization'.[71] In the early years of the United Nations, there were debates about whether the role of the Secretary-General should be more technical or

[67] See 'Declarations recognizing the jurisdiction of the Court as compulsory', available at https://www.icj-cij.org/declarations.

[68] See, for example, F Paddeu and M Jackson, 'State Responsibility in the ICJ's Advisory Opinion on Climate Change', EJIL:Talk!, 25 July 2025, available at www.ejiltalk.org/state-responsibility-in-the-icjs-advisory-opinion-on-climate-change/.

[69] For an overview of the Court's working modalities, including Advisory proceedings, see: www.icj-cij.org/how-the-court-works.

[70] For a list of the current Members of the ICJ, see: www.icj-cij.org/current-members. For the full text of the ICJ Statute, see: www.icj-cij.org/statute.

[71] JOC Jonah, 'Secretariat: Independence and Reform' in Weiss and Daws (n 29).

political. As a result, the doctrine of 'implied powers' has prevailed,[72] and all holders of the post were prominent diplomats (four from Europe, two from Asia, two from Africa, and one from Latin America).[73] António Guterres, the ninth Secretary-General, took office on 1 January 2017. Before his current appointment, he served as United Nations High Commissioner for Refugees (June 2005–December 2015), and prior to that, he spent more than two decades in government and public service.[74] Notably, despite the determination on the part of the United Nations 'to reaffirm faith … in the equal rights of men and women',[75] all Secretaries-General to date have been men, and it is hoped that a woman will be elected within the foreseeable future.

In 2011, Dr Kassym-Jomart Tokayev – at the time, Chair of the Senate of the Parliament of Kazakhstan – was appointed as the Director-General of the United Nations Office at Geneva (UNOG).[76] He was the first (and, so far, only) non-European holder of the post, which he occupied until 2013.

The Secretariat employs 'tens of thousands' of staff members at the UN Headquarters and in the field.[77] The Secretariat 'is organized along departmental lines, with each department or office having a distinct area of action and responsibility'.[78] The UN Headquarters is home to the Office of Legal Affairs, Department of Political and Peacebuilding Affairs, Office for Disarmament Affairs, Department of Peace Operations, and others.[79] The UN Offices outside the main Headquarters are located in Geneva,[80] Nairobi,[81] and Vienna.[82] The UN also has five Economic Commissions – for Africa (in Addis Ababa),[83] Asia and the Pacific (in Bangkok),[84] Europe (in Geneva),[85] Latin America and the Caribbean (in Santiago),[86] and Western Asia (in Beirut).[87] In Central Asia, the UN is represented in each capital as well as in Almaty.[88]

[72] R Lavalle, 'The "Inherent" Powers of the UN Secretary-General in the Political Sphere: A Legal Analysis' (1990) 37 *Netherlands International Law Review* 22.

[73] United Nations, 'Former Secretaries-General', available at www.un.org/sg/en/content/former-secretaries-general.

[74] UN Secretary-General, 'Biography', www.un.org/sg/en/content/sg/biography.

[75] cf the second preambular paragraph of the UN Charter.

[76] United Nations, 'Secretary-General Appoints Kassym-Jomart Tokayev of Kazakhstan as Director-General, United Nations Office at Geneva', 11 March 2011, available at press.un.org/en/2011/sga1281.doc.htm.

[77] United Nations, 'Secretariat', available at www.un.org/en/about-us/secretariat.

[78] ibid.

[79] ibid.

[80] See: www.ungeneva.org/en.

[81] See: www.unon.org/.

[82] See: www.unov.org/unov/en/.

[83] See: www.uneca.org/.

[84] See: www.unescap.org/.

[85] See: unece.org/.

[86] See: www.cepal.org/en.

[87] See: www.unescwa.org/.

[88] For an overview of the UN action in Central Asia, see: kazakhstan.un.org/en (Kazakhstan); kyrgyzstan.un.org/en (Kyrgyzstan); tajikistan.un.org/en (Tajikistan); turkmenistan.un.org/en (Turkmenistan); and uzbekistan.un.org/en (Uzbekistan).

H. Other UN Organs

In addition to the main organs, the United Nations has numerous other organs, which are subsidiary to the main ones.[89] They support the main organs' operation in the respective areas, and are responsible for specific topics or geographical regions. For example, the Human Rights Council was established by the General Assembly in 2006 to strengthen 'the promotion and protection of human rights around the globe'.[90] It consists of 47 UN Member States, which are elected by the General Assembly for three years, and may not be re-elected immediately after serving two consecutive terms. The current composition of the Human Rights Council includes Kyrgyzstan (until the end of 2025). Uzbekistan completed its term at the end of 2023, and Kazakhstan at the end of 2024.[91]

III. SPECIALISED AGENCIES OF THE UNITED NATIONS AND RELATED ORGANISATIONS

A. Introduction[92]

Specialised agencies are international organisations which coordinate their work with the United Nations on the basis of Article 57 of the UN Charter.[93] This section briefly discusses, in the alphabetic order, all specialised agencies and related organisations maintaining their liaison offices at the UN Headquarters.

B. Food and Agriculture Organization of the United Nations (FAO)

Established in 1945, the Food and Agriculture Organization (FAO) is a UN specialised agency leading 'international efforts to defeat hunger'.[94] At the time of writing, the FAO consisted of 194 Member Nations, one Member Organisation (European Union), and two Associate Members (Faroe Islands and Tokelau).[95] All Central Asian States are FAO Members.[96] The FAO Headquarters is in Rome, and a Regional Office for Europe and Central Asia is located in Budapest.[97]

[89] For a UN System Chart, see: unsdg.un.org/resources/un-system-chart.
[90] See: www.ohchr.org/en/hr-bodies/hrc/about-council.
[91] See: www.ohchr.org/en/hr-bodies/hrc/current-members.
[92] For a detailed overview of specialised agencies and related organisations, see: https://www.un.org/en/about-us/specialized-agencies.
[93] See: ask.un.org/faq/140935.
[94] See: www.fao.org/about/about-fao/en/.
[95] See: www.fao.org/legal-services/membership-of-fao/en/.
[96] ibid.
[97] See: www.fao.org/europe/en/.

C. International Atomic Energy Agency (IAEA)

The International Atomic Energy Agency (IAEA) was established in 1957 'in response to the deep fears and expectations generated by the discoveries and diverse uses of nuclear technology'.[98] As of 15 November 2024, the IAEA had 180 Members, including all Central Asian States.[99] The IAEA Headquarters is in Vienna, and two Liaison Offices are located in New York and Geneva.

D. International Civil Aviation Organization (ICAO)

Founded by the Convention on international Civil Aviation (Chicago Convention) of 7 December 1944, the International Civil Aviation Organization (ICAO) was established in 1947 'to help countries share their skies to their mutual benefit'.[100] In particular, the ICAO develops 'standards, practices, and policies for international civilian flight'.[101] The ICAO currently has 193 Member States, including all Central Asian nations,[102] and a few intergovernmental and non-governmental organisations may be 'invited to attend suitable ICAO meetings'.[103] The ICAO Headquarters is in Montreal.

E. International Criminal Court (ICC)

The International Criminal Court (ICC) was established in 2002 to prosecute individuals for genocide, crimes against humanity, war crimes, and the crime of aggression.[104] At the time of writing, the ICC Assembly of States Parties includes 125 States.[105] The ICC is located in The Hague. In Central Asia, so far, only Tajikistan has ratified the Rome Statute.[106] For more details on the ICC, see Chapter fifteen, section IV.L below.

F. International Fund for Agricultural Development (IFAD)

The International Fund for Agricultural Development (IFAD) was set up in 1977 as an international financial institution 'to finance agricultural development

[98] See: www.iaea.org/about/overview/history.
[99] See: www.iaea.org/about/governance/list-of-member-states.
[100] See: www.icao.int/about-icao/Pages/default.aspx.
[101] ibid.
[102] See: www.icao.int/about-icao/Pages/member-states.aspx.
[103] See: www.icao.int/about-icao/Pages/Invited-Organizations.aspx.
[104] See: www.icc-cpi.int/.
[105] See: asp.icc-cpi.int/.
[106] See: asp.icc-cpi.int/states-parties.

projects, primarily for food production in the developing countries'.[107] At the time of writing, the IFAD has 180 Members, including all Central Asian States except Turkmenistan.[108] The IFAD Headquarters is in Rome.

G. International Labour Organization (ILO)

Established in 1919, the International Labour Organization (ILO) is a unique tripartite international organisation uniting in its executive organs representatives of governments, employers and workers 'to set labour standards, develop policies and devise programmes promoting decent work for all women and men'.[109] The ILO currently has 187 Members, including all Central Asian States.[110] Its Headquarters is in Geneva.

H. International Maritime Organization (IMO)

The International Maritime Organization (IMO) met for the first time in January 1959. It is a UN specialised agency 'responsible for measures to improve the safety and security of international shipping and to prevent pollution from ships. It is also involved in legal matters, including liability and compensation issues and the facilitation of international maritime traffic'.[111] The IMO currently has 176 Member States, including Kazakhstan, Kyrgyzstan and Turkmenistan, and three Associate Members (Faroe Islands, Hong Kong, and Macao).[112] At the time of writing, 66 intergovernmental organisations have observer status with the IMO,[113] and consultative status has been granted to 88 non-governmental organisations.[114] The IMO Secretariat is in London (United Kingdom).

I. International Monetary Fund (IMF)

The International Monetary Fund (IMF) was established in 1994 to support 'economic policies that promote financial stability and monetary cooperation, which are essential to increase productivity, job creation, and economic

[107] See: www.ifad.org/en/history.
[108] See: webapps.ifad.org/members/member-states.
[109] See: www.ilo.org/global/about-the-ilo/lang--en/index.htm.
[110] See: www.ilo.org/global/about-the-ilo/how-the-ilo-works/member-states/lang--en/index.htm.
[111] See: www.imo.org/en/About/Pages/FAQs.aspx.
[112] See: www.imo.org/en/OurWork/ERO/Pages/MemberStates.aspx.
[113] See: www.imo.org/en/OurWork/ERO/Pages/IGOsWithObserverStatus.aspx.
[114] See: www.imo.org/en/OurWork/ERO/Pages/NGOsInConsultativeStatus.aspx.

well-being'.[115] The IMF currently has 191 Members, including all Central Asian States,[116] and is headquartered in Washington, DC.

J. International Organization for Migration (IOM)

Established in 1951, the International Organization for Migration (IOM)

> supports migrants across the world, developing effective responses to the shifting dynamics of migration and, as such, is a key source of advice on migration policy and practice. The organization works in emergency situations, developing the resilience of all people on the move, and particularly those in situations of vulnerability, as well as building capacity within governments to manage all forms and impacts of mobility.[117]

The IOM currently has 175 Members, including all Central Asian nations,[118] and eight Observer States.[119] The IOM Headquarters is in Geneva.

K. International Seabed Authority (ISA)

The International Seabed Authority (ISA) operates under the 1982 UN Convention on the Law of the Sea (UNCLOS) and the 1994 Agreement relating to the Implementation of Part XI of the United Nations Convention on the Law of the Sea. Through ISA,

> States Parties to UNCLOS organize and control all mineral-resources-related activities in the Area for the benefit of humankind as a whole. In so doing, ISA has the mandate to ensure the effective protection of the marine environment from harmful effects that may arise from deep-seabed-related activities.[120]

Since all States Parties to UNCLOS are ipso facto Members of ISA, ISA currently has 169 Members (168 States and the European Union). At the time of writing, UNCLOS has not been ratified by any Central Asian nation.[121] The ISA Headquarters is in Kingston (Jamaica).

L. International Telecommunication Union (ITU)

Established in 1865, the role of the International Telecommunication Union (ITU) is to

[115] See: www.imf.org/en/About/Factsheets/IMF-at-a-Glance.
[116] See: www.imf.org/en/About/executive-board/members-quotas.
[117] See: www.iom.int/mission.
[118] See: www.iom.int/member-states.
[119] See: www.iom.int/observer-states.
[120] See: www.isa.org.jm/about-isa/.
[121] See: www.isa.org.jm/member-states/.

> allocate global radio spectrum and satellite orbits, develop the technical standards that ensure networks and technologies seamlessly interconnect, and strive to improve access to ICTs to underserved communities worldwide. Every time you make a phone call via the mobile, access the Internet or send an email, you are benefitting from the work of ITU.[122]

Membership of ITU is mixed, and involves 194 States,[123] one Observer (Palestine), and over 900 companies and academic institutions, as well as international and regional organisations.[124] The ITU's Headquarters is in Geneva.

M. International Tribunal for the Law of the Sea (ITLOS)

The International Tribunal for the Law of the Sea (ITLOS) was established by the 1982 United Nations Convention on the Law of the Sea (UNCLOS). ITLOS

> has jurisdiction over any dispute concerning the interpretation or application of the Convention, and over all matters specifically provided for in any other agreement which confers jurisdiction on the Tribunal. Disputes relating to the Convention may concern the delimitation of maritime zones, navigation, conservation and management of the living resources of the sea, protection and preservation of the marine environment and marine scientific research.[125]

The Tribunal is composed of 21 independent Judges elected for nine years by States Parties to UNCLOS.[126] The seat of ITLOS is in Hamburg.

N. Preparatory Commission for the Comprehensive Nuclear Test-Ban Treaty Organization (CTBTO)

The Preparatory Commission for the Comprehensive Nuclear-Test-Ban Treaty Organization (CTBTO) was established in 1996. The Commission's

> main purpose is to carry out the necessary preparations for the effective implementation of the CTBT and to prepare for the first session of the Conference of States Parties to the Treaty, which will take place when the CTBT has entered into force.[127]

The Treaty will enter into force 180 days after it has been ratified by 44 States which participated in its negotiations in 1996, 'and possessed nuclear power or research reactors at the time'.[128] At the time of writing, the Treaty has 178 States

[122] See: www.itu.int/en/about/Pages/default.aspx.
[123] See: www.itu.int/hub/membership/our-members/directory/?myitu-members-states=true&request=countries.
[124] See: www.itu.int/hub/membership/our-members/.
[125] See: www.itlos.org/en/main/latest-news/.
[126] See: www.itlos.org/en/main/the-tribunal/members/.
[127] See: www.ctbto.org/our-mission/the-organization/the-preparatory-commission.
[128] ibid. For the list of these States, see: https://www.ctbto.org/our-mission/states-signatories?f%5B0%5D=annex_2_state%3A1.

Parties, including all Central Asian nations.[129] The seat of the Preparatory Commission is in Vienna.

O. United Nations Children's Fund (UNICEF)

The United Nations Children's Emergency Fund (UNICEF) was established in 1946 'to meet the emergency needs of children in post-war Europe and China'.[130] In 1950, its mandate 'was broadened to address the long-term needs of children and women in developing countries everywhere', and in 1953, its name 'was shortened to the United Nations Children's Fund'.[131] Now, UNICEF works in more than 190 countries and territories, including all States of Central Asia,[132] and focuses on 'child health and nutrition, safe water and sanitation, quality education and skill building, HIV prevention and treatment for mothers and babies, and the protection of children and adolescents from violence and exploitation'.[133] UNICEF is headquartered in New York.

P. United Nations Development Programme (UNDP)

The United Nations Development Programme (UNDP) was launched in 1966 by merging the United Nations Expanded Programme on Technical Assistance (created in 1949) and the United Nations Special Fund (founded in 1958). UNDP helps countries 'to develop policies, leadership skills, partnering abilities, institutional capabilities, and to build resilience to achieve the Sustainable Development Goals'.[134] UNDP priorities include sustainable development, democratic governance and peace building, and climate and disaster resilience.[135] UNDP has its Headquarters in New York but works primarily through its offices in about 170 countries and territories. UNDP is represented in all States of Central Asia.[136]

Q. United Nations Educational, Scientific and Cultural Organization (UNESCO)

The United Nations Educational, Scientific and Cultural Organization (UNESCO) contributes 'to peace and security by promoting international

[129] See: www.ctbto.org/our-mission/states-signatories.
[130] See: www.unicef.org/about-unicef/frequently-asked-questions#1.
[131] ibid.
[132] See: www.unicef.org/where-we-work.
[133] See: www.unicef.org/about-unicef/frequently-asked-questions#1.
[134] See: www.undp.org/about-us.
[135] ibid.
[136] See: www.undp.org/eurasia.

cooperation in education, sciences, culture, communication and information. UNESCO promotes knowledge sharing and the free flow of ideas to accelerate mutual understanding and a more perfect knowledge of each other's lives'.[137] It was established in 1946, and currently has 194 Members, including all Central Asian States, and 12 Associate Members.[138] The seat of UNESCO is in Paris.

R. United Nations Industrial Development Organization (UNIDO)

Established in 1966, the United Nations Industrial Development Organization (UNIDO) works 'to promote, dynamize and accelerate industrial development'.[139] Its current work is focused on three priorities – ending hunger, stopping climate breakdown, and supporting sustainable supply chains.[140] At the time of writing, UNIDO has 173 Member States, including all States of Central Asia.[141] UNIDO has its Headquarters in Vienna.

S. Universal Postal Union (UPU)

The Universal Postal Union (UPU) was founded in 1874, and hence is one of the oldest international organisations. The UPU is 'the primary forum for cooperation between postal sector players. It helps to ensure a truly universal network of up-to-date products and services'.[142] More specifically, it 'sets the rules for international mail exchanges and makes recommendations to stimulate growth in mail, parcel and financial services volumes and improve quality of service for customers'.[143] At the time of writing, the UPU has 192 Members, including all Central Asian States.[144] The UPU International Bureau is located in Berne.

T. World Bank Group

Established in 1944, the World Bank Group consists of five institutions – the International Bank for Reconstruction and Development (IBRD), the

[137] See: www.unesco.org/en/brief. See also A Akhmetkali, 'Joint UNESCO-EU Effort Brings Central Asian Heritage Sites Closer to Tourists', Astana Times, 10 July 2024, available at astanatimes.com/2024/07/joint-unesco-eu-effort-brings-central-asian-heritage-sites-closer-to-tourists/.

[138] See: www.unesco.org/en/countries. See also Fergana News, 'Komitet UNESCO sohranil Shahrisabz v Spiske pamyatnikov vsemirnogo naslediya' ['UNESCO Committee Keeps Shakhrisabz on the World Heritage List'], 23 July 2025, available at fergana.agency/news/139076/.

[139] See: www.unido.org/about-us/who-we-are.

[140] ibid.

[141] See: treaties.un.org/Pages/ViewDetails.aspx?src=TREATY&mtdsg_no=X-9&chapter=10&clang=_en.

[142] See: www.upu.int/en/Universal-Postal-Union.

[143] ibid.

[144] See: www.upu.int/en/Universal-Postal-Union/About-UPU/Member-Countries.

International Development Association (IDA), the International Finance Corporation (IFC), the Multilateral Investment Guarantee Agency (MIGA), and the International Centre for Settlement of Investment Disputes (ICSID). The World Bank consists of IBRD and IDA, which provide 'financing, policy advice, and technical assistance to governments of developing countries. IDA focuses on the world's poorest countries, while IBRD assists middle-income and creditworthy poorer countries'.[145] In turn, 'IFC, MIGA, and ICSID focus on strengthening the private sector in developing countries. Through these institutions, the World Bank Group provides financing, technical assistance, political risk insurance, and settlement of disputes to private enterprises, including financial institutions'.[146] Each organisation in the World Bank Group has a membership of its own. At the time of writing, IBRD has 189 Member States, including all Central Asian nations.[147] IDA currently has 175 Members, including all Central Asian nations except Turkmenistan.[148] 186 States, including all States of Central Asia, are Members of IFC.[149] MIGA involves 182 States, including all Central Asian nations.[150] ICSID involves 158 States, including Kazakhstan, Kyrgyzstan, Turkmenistan, and Uzbekistan.[151] The Headquarters of the World Bank Group is in Washington, DC.

U. World Health Organization (WHO)

The World Health Organization (WHO) was established in 1948 to 'coordinate the world's response to health emergencies, promote well-being, prevent disease and expand access to health care'.[152] Most recently, the WHO was instrumental in coordinating response to the COVID-19 pandemic.[153] The WHO currently has 194 Members, including all Central Asian States.[154] Its Headquarters is in Geneva.

V. World Intellectual Property Organization (WIPO)

Established in 1967, the World Intellectual Property Organization (WIPO) is 'the global forum for intellectual property (IP) services, policy, information and

[145] See: www.worldbank.org/en/who-we-are.
[146] ibid.
[147] See: www.worldbank.org/en/about/leadership/members#ibrd.
[148] See: www.worldbank.org/en/about/leadership/members#ida.
[149] See: www.worldbank.org/en/about/leadership/members#ifc.
[150] See: www.worldbank.org/en/about/leadership/members#miga.
[151] See: www.worldbank.org/en/about/leadership/members#icsid.
[152] See: www.who.int/about/who-we-are.
[153] N Hendel, 'World Health Organization (WHO)' in S Sayapin et al (eds), *International Conflict and Security Law: A Research Handbook* (The Hague, TMC Asser Press, 2022).
[154] See: www.who.int/countries.

cooperation'.[155] At the time of writing, WIPO consists of 193 Member States, including all States of Central Asia,[156] and about 250 intergovernmental and non-governmental organisations have observer status at WIPO meetings.[157] The WIPO Headquarters is in Geneva.

W. World Meteorological Organization (WMO)

The World Meteorological Organization (WMO) was established in 1950 to promote 'international cooperation and coordination on the state and behaviour of the Earth's atmosphere, its interaction with the land and oceans, the weather and climate it produces, and the resulting distribution of water resources'.[158] The WMO currently has 187 Member States, including all Central Asian nations, and six Member Territories.[159] It is headquartered in Geneva.

X. World Tourism Organization (UNWTO)

Founded in 1946, the World Tourism Organization (UNWTO) is 'responsible for the promotion of responsible, sustainable and universally accessible tourism'.[160] As such, 'UNWTO promotes tourism as a driver of economic growth, inclusive development and environmental sustainability and offers leadership and support to the sector in advancing knowledge and tourism policies worldwide'.[161] At the time of writing, UNWTO has 160 Member States (including all States of Central Asia), six Associate Members, and two Observers.[162] The UNWTO is headquartered in Madrid.

IV. REGIONAL ORGANISATIONS

A. Introduction

The Central Asian States are also members of a few regional organisations. Some of these serve to maintain and develop relations with other former Soviet nations, whereas others involve China, India, Türkiye and Central Asia's other

[155] See: www.wipo.int/about-wipo/en/.
[156] See: www.wipo.int/members/en/.
[157] See: www.wipo.int/about-wipo/en/observers/index.html.
[158] See: public.wmo.int/en/our-mandate/what-we-do.
[159] See: public.wmo.int/en/about-us/members.
[160] See: www.unwto.org/about-us.
[161] ibid.
[162] See: www.unwto.org/member-states.

neighbours beyond the post-Soviet space. The following subsections offer an overview of a few regional organisations of which the Central Asian States are Members, and recall a pending proposal for the establishment of a Central Asian Union.

B. Commonwealth of Independent States (CIS)[163]

The Commonwealth of Independent States (CIS) is a regional intergovernmental organisation founded on 8 December 1991 by the Republic of Belarus, the Russian Federation (RSFSR) and Ukraine, whereby they jointly declared that the Union of Soviet Socialist Republics (USSR) had 'ceased to exist as a subject of international law and a geopolitical reality' (cf the first preambular paragraph of the Agreement on the Establishment of the Commonwealth of Independent States). On 21 December 1991, the Heads of Azerbaijan, Armenia, Belarus, Kazakhstan, Kyrgyzstan, Moldova, the Russian Federation, Tajikistan, Turkmenistan, Uzbekistan and Ukraine signed a Protocol to that Agreement with the effect of establishing the CIS. The CIS Charter was adopted in Minsk on 22 January 1993. Georgia joined the CIS in 1993 and terminated its membership in 2008 (effective as of 2009), following an armed conflict with the Russian Federation in August 2008. Turkmenistan and Ukraine did not formally adhere to the Statute. Since 2005, Turkmenistan has been an Associate Member of the CIS, which enables its participation in some activities of the Commonwealth. As a result of Russia's continued use of force against Ukraine since February 2014, Ukraine terminated its participation in a number of CIS treaties and recalled its accredited representatives at the CIS statutory organs, in May 2018. The seat of the CIS Executive Committee is in Minsk.

In accordance with Article 2 of the Charter, the Purposes of the CIS are:

- implementation of cooperation in the political, economic, environmental, humanitarian, cultural and other fields;
- comprehensive and balanced economic and social development of member states within the framework of the common economic space, interstate cooperation and integration;
- ensuring human rights and fundamental freedoms in accordance with generally recognized principles and norms of international law and CSCE documents;
- cooperation between Member States in ensuring international peace and security, the implementation of effective measures to reduce arms and

[163] This section uses the author's material published in S Sayapin, 'Commonwealth of Independent States (CIS)' in S Lee et al (eds), *Encyclopedia of Public International Law in Asia, Vol III: Central & South Asia* (Leiden, Brill, 2021). Permission to use published material is gratefully acknowledged.

military spending, eliminate nuclear and other types of weapons of mass destruction, and achieve general and complete disarmament;
- assistance to citizens of Member States in free communication, contacts and movement in the Commonwealth;
- mutual legal assistance and cooperation in other areas of legal relations;
- peaceful resolution of disputes and conflicts between the States of the Commonwealth.

In accordance with Articles 21–32 of the Charter, the main statutory organs of the CIS are the Council of Heads of State, the Council of Heads of Government, the Council of Ministers of Foreign Affairs, the Economic Council, the Council of Ministers of Defence, the Council of Commanders of the Border Troops, and the Economic Court. Article 33 provides for a Human Rights Commission, and Article 34 provides a legal basis for some 70 thematic cooperation organs. The CIS Inter-Parliamentary Assembly operates on the basis of Articles 36–37 of the Charter. The working language of the CIS is Russian (cf Article 35 of the Charter).

Although the CIS maintained a fairly satisfactory degree of post-Soviet integration in such areas as regional trade, transport, cultural and humanitarian cooperation, it also attracted some criticism as an organisation dominated by the Russian Federation, and one perpetuating the Soviet political legacy. The disintegration of the USSR led to a number of conflicts in the post-Soviet space – such as the conflict between Armenia and Azerbaijan over the Nagorno-Karabakh (since 1988), in Transnistria (frozen since 1992), in Tajikistan (1992–97), between Russia and Georgia (2008), or between Russia and Ukraine (since 2014) – which Russia arguably used to reinforce, in particular, its military and economic influence over most of its post-Soviet neighbours. The CIS model of economic development still has some elements of planned economy: for instance, on 14 November 2008, the CIS Council of Heads of State approved an Economic Development Strategy of the Commonwealth of Independent States until 2020. Regional integration in the areas of military cooperation and trade is supplanted, respectively, by the Collective Security Treaty Organization (CSTO, founded in 2002 on the basis of the 1992 Collective Security Treaty), and the Eurasian Economic Union (EAEU, founded in 2015 as a successor to the Eurasian Economic Community (2001–14)).

C. Eurasian Economic Union (EAEU)

Established on 1 January 2015, the Eurasian Economic Union (EAEU) is a regional trade organisation of five post-Soviet nations: Armenia, Belarus, Kazakhstan, Kyrgyzstan, and the Russian Federation. For more details on the EAEU, see Chapter twelve, sections II–III below.

D. Collective Security Treaty Organization (CSTO)[164]

The Collective Security Treaty Organization (CSTO) grew out of a Collective Security Treaty of 15 May 1992, which was signed in Tashkent (Uzbekistan) on behalf of Armenia, Kazakhstan, Kyrgyzstan, the Russian Federation, Tajikistan and Uzbekistan. In 1993, Azerbaijan, Belarus and Georgia joined in. The treaty entered into force on 20 April 1994, and applied until 1999 when Azerbaijan, Georgia and Uzbekistan terminated their participation, and the other States Parties agreed to automatically extend the treaty's validity for subsequent five-year periods. On 14 May 2002, the treaty was transformed into an intergovernmental organisation whose Statute was approved on 7 October 2002, and registered at the UN Secretariat in 2003. In 2004, the CSTO was granted observer status at the UN General Assembly. The current CSTO membership includes Armenia, Belarus, Kazakhstan, Kyrgyzstan, Russia and Tajikistan (Uzbekistan renewed its membership in 2006 and suspended it in 2012).

Article 4 of the Collective Security Treaty corresponds to Chapter VIII of the UN Charter, and is fairly similar to analogous provisions in the statutory documents of other regional security arrangements (for instance, Article 5 of the North Atlantic Treaty):

> If one of the States Parties is subjected to aggression (an armed attack threatening security, stability, territorial integrity and sovereignty), then it will be considered by the States Parties as aggression (armed attack threatening security, stability, territorial integrity and sovereignty) against all States Parties to this Treaty.
>
> In the event of an aggression (an armed attack threatening security, stability, territorial integrity and sovereignty) against any of the States Parties, all other States Parties, at the request of that State Party, will immediately provide him with the necessary assistance, including military assistance, and will also provide support by means at their disposal in the exercise of the right to collective defence in accordance with Article 51 of the UN Charter.
>
> States Parties shall immediately notify the United Nations Security Council of measures taken pursuant to this article. In implementing these measures, States Parties will adhere to the relevant provisions of the UN Charter.

The supreme organ of the CSTO, consisting of Heads of the Member States, is the Collective Security Council (CSC). The CSC coordinates the CSTO's action and meets at least once a year. Between the sessions of the CSC, the CSTO is coordinated by a Permanent Council consisting of the Member States' permanent and plenipotentiary representatives. Thematic coordination in

[164] This section uses the author's material published in S Sayapin, 'Collective Security Treaty Organisation (CSTO)' in S Lee et al (eds), *Encyclopedia of Public International Law in Asia, Vol III: Central & South Asia* (Leiden, Brill, 2021). Permission to use published material is gratefully acknowledged.

the respective areas is carried out by the Council of Foreign Ministers, the Council of Ministers of Defence, and the Committee of Secretaries of Security Councils. The CSTO Joint Staff and Secretariat are seated in Moscow. The CSTO Secretary-General is appointed for a three-year term. Inter-parliamentary cooperation is carried out by the CSTO Parliamentary Assembly.

The CSTO employs an inclusive approach to regional security, based on three 'pillars': political cooperation, military cooperation, and responding to current challenges and threats. Political cooperation includes consultations and coordination of the CSTO Member States' foreign policies, interaction with other intergovernmental organisations, and crisis response. The CSTO military capacity includes Collective Rapid Reaction Forces (about 20,000 troops), the Russian-Belarusian and Russian-Armenian regional groupings, Collective Air Forces and Collective Peacekeeping Forces (about 3,000 troops and 600 police officers), combined (joint) military systems and military infrastructure facilities. Humanitarian dialogue is maintained with the International Committee of the Red Cross (ICRC), with a view to further integrating rules of international humanitarian law (IHL) in the CSTO Member States' relevant laws and practices. The third 'pillar' embraces, in particular, institutional responses to international terrorism and extremism, drug trafficking, illegal migration and human trafficking, and criminal activities in cyberspace. Still a relatively young organisation, the CSTO needs to accumulate more operational experience, especially given that quite a few security threats that the CSTO seeks to respond to originate within its Member States, and as such are subject to their domestic jurisdictions.

E. Shanghai Cooperation Organization (SCO)[165]

On 15 June 2001, Kazakhstan, China, Kyrgyzstan, Russia, Tajikistan, and Uzbekistan announced the establishment of the Shanghai Cooperation Organization (SCO). The SCO Charter was adopted in June 2002, and entered into force on 19 September 2003. As of 2025, the SCO has 10 Member States – Belarus (admitted in 2024), India (admitted in 2017), Iran (admitted in 2023), Kazakhstan, China, Kyrgyzstan, Pakistan (admitted in 2017), Russia, Tajikistan, and Uzbekistan – and thus is the largest regional intergovernmental organisation in terms of territory and population. Afghanistan and Mongolia have the status of Observer States, whereas Armenia, Azerbaijan, Bahrain, Cambodia, Egypt, Kuwait, the Maldives, Myanmar, Nepal, Qatar, Saudi Arabia, Sri Lanka, Türkiye, and the United Arab Emirates are the SCO dialogue partners.

[165] This section uses the author's material published in S Sayapin, 'Shanghai Cooperation Organisation (SCO)' in S Lee et al (eds), *Encyclopedia of Public International Law in Asia, Vol III: Central & South Asia* (Leiden, Brill, 2021). Permission to use published material is gratefully acknowledged.

In accordance with Article 3 of the SCO Charter, the Organization's main areas of cooperation include:

- maintenance of peace and enhancing security and confidence in the region;
- search of common positions on foreign policy issues of mutual interest, including issues arising within international organisations and international fora;
- development and implementation of measures aimed at jointly counteracting terrorism, separatism and extremism, illicit narcotics and arms trafficking and other types of criminal activity of a transnational character, and also illegal migration;
- coordination of efforts in the field of disarmament and arms control;
- support for, and promotion of regional economic cooperation in various forms, fostering favorable environment for trade and investments with a view to gradually achieving free flow of goods, capital, services and technologies;
- effective use of available transportation and communication infrastructure, improvement of transit capacity of the member States and development of energy systems;
- sound environmental management, including water resources management in the region, and implementation of specific joint environmental programs and projects;
- mutual assistance in preventing natural and man-made disasters and mitigation of their impacts;
- exchange of legal information in the interests of development of cooperation within SCO;
- expansion of interaction in such areas as science and technology, education, health care, culture, sports and tourism.
- Further areas of cooperation may be added by the Member States' mutual consent.

Articles 4–11 of the SCO Charter regulate the competence of the SCO organs: the Council of Heads of State; the Council of Heads of Government (Prime Ministers); the Council of Ministers of Foreign Affairs; Meetings of Heads of Ministries and/or Agencies; the Council of National Coordinators; the Regional Anti-terrorist Structure (RATS); and the Secretariat. The latter two organs operate on a permanent basis, and are situated, respectively, in Tashkent and Beijing. From 2025–27, the SCO Secretary-General is Mr Nurlan Yermekbayev (Kazakhstan). In accordance with Articles 16–17 of the Charter, decisions in the SCO organs are made by consensus, except for decisions on suspension of membership or expulsion from the organisation, and enforced by the Member States in accordance with their respective national legislations. The official working languages of the SCO are Chinese and Russian.

The SCO maintains cooperation with other international organisations. On 2 December 2004, it was granted observer status at the UN General Assembly, and subsequently established cooperation with a few institutions within the UN system. The SCO concluded Memoranda of Understanding with the Commonwealth of Independent States (CIS, 2005); the Association of Southeast Asian Nations (ASEAN, 2005); the Collective Security Treaty

Organization (CSTO, 2007); the Economic Cooperation Organization (ECO, 2007); the Conference on Interaction and Confidence-Building Measures in Asia (CICA, 2014); and the International Committee of the Red Cross (ICRC, 2017).

Although the SCO is arguably one of the most efficient integration projects in Asia, it has attracted some criticism by Western and regional human rights actors, in particular, for supposedly tolerating violations of the *non-refoulement* principle, judicial guarantees, freedom of information and religion, and minority rights within its Member States. The SCO is sure to continue gaining weight as an alternative to the West's global leadership, along with other regional integration formats led by Asian powers – such as the Belt and Road Initiative.

F. Organization for Security and Co-operation in Europe (OSCE)

The Organization for Security and Co-operation in Europe (OSCE) grew out of the Conference on Security and Co-operation in Europe (CSCE), which met in 1973–75, and adopted the Helsinki Final Act on 1 August 1975.[166] The 1990 Charter of Paris for a New Europe set the stage for the development of the CSCE after the end of the Cold War,[167] and on 1 January 1995, the CSCE became the OSCE. The OSCE currently has 57 participating States in Europe, Central Asia, and North America,[168] and 'maintains privileged relations with 11 Asian and Mediterranean Partners for Co-operation to better address shared security challenges'.[169] The Organization

> works for stability, peace and democracy for more than a billion people, through political dialogue about shared values and through practical work that contributes to sustainable progress. The OSCE's comprehensive concept of security covers the politico-military; the economic and environmental; and the human dimensions.[170]

OSCE decisions are made by consensus, and are politically binding.[171]

Kazakhstan has been the only Central Asian State to have chaired the OSCE so far (in 2010). In a speech delivered on 14 January 2010, the first President of Kazakhstan, Nursultan Nazarbayev, explained his vision for Kazakhstan's OSCE Chairmanship as follows:

> The motto of Kazakhstan's Chairmanship will be four Ts, namely, 'Trust', 'Tradition', 'Transparency' and 'Tolerance'. The first T refers to the trust that is necessary for all of us. The second one refers to our commitment to the fundamental principles and

[166] For the text of the Helsinki Final Act (in multiple languages), see: www.osce.org/helsinki-final-act.
[167] For the text of the Charter (in multiple languages), see: www.osce.org/mc/39516.
[168] For the OSCE's membership, see: www.osce.org/participating-states.
[169] See: www.osce.org/partners-for-cooperation.
[170] See: www.osce.org/what-we-do.
[171] See: www.osce.org/resources/csce-osce-key-documents.

> values of the OSCE. The third one conveys maximum openness and transparency in international relations, free from 'double standards' and 'dividing lines', as well as a focus on constructive co-operation in order to address challenges and threats to security.
>
> Finally, the fourth T reflects global trends towards a strengthening of intercultural and intercivilizational dialogue, which is gaining major importance in today's world.[172]

The outcomes of the 2010 OSCE summit in Astana received mixed reviews:

> The summit descended into disarray amid disagreements over the final declaration, with conflicts in the South Caucasus the chief stumbling block. The agreement was eventually watered down and the accompanying action plan discarded altogether.
>
> For Astana, though, the fact that it persuaded leaders to sign the declaration at all was a diplomatic victory – as was widespread praise at the summit for its smooth running of the chairmanship and its role in defusing last year's political crisis in Kyrgyzstan.
>
> Neighboring Uzbekistan, however, used the summit to attack the OSCE's reaction to June's ethnic clashes in southern Kyrgyzstan as ineffective, and ongoing delays in deploying a planned OSCE police mission there have also drawn fire.[173]

The OSCE is present in all Central Asian capitals.[174] The OSCE Academy in Kyrgyzstan's capital, Bishkek, was established in 2002, and is currently offering an undergraduate degree in economics, graduate programmes in politics and security, economic governance and development, and human rights and sustainability, as well as professional training.[175]

G. Organization of Turkic States

The Cooperation Council of Turkic-Speaking States (Turkic Council) was established on 3 October 2009 with the aim of promoting comprehensive cooperation among Turkic States. Its founding members and the original signatories of the Nakhchivan Agreement of 3 October 2009 are Azerbaijan, Kazakhstan, Kyrgyzstan, and Türkiye. In 2019, Uzbekistan joined as a full member. Hungary, Turkmenistan, Northern Cyprus, and the ECO have the status of observers. In November 2021, the Turkic Council was reformed into the Organization of Turkic States. The main organs of the Organization include the Council of Heads of State, the Council of Foreign Ministers, the Senior Officials Committee, the Council of Elders of Turkic-Speaking States, and a Secretariat with a seat in Istanbul. The latter two organs operate on a permanent basis.

[172] OSCE, 'Text of the video address by President Nursultan Nazarbayev on the occasion of Kazakhstan's assumption of the Chairmanship of the OSCE, January 2010', available at www.osce.org/files/f/documents/d/c/41121.pdf. See also S Sayapin (n 25), 332–33.

[173] J Lillis, 'Kazakhstan: Experts Give Astana Mixed Review on OSCE Chairmanship', 13 January 2011, available at eurasianet.org/kazakhstan-experts-give-astana-mixed-review-on-osce-chairmanship.

[174] See: www.osce.org/where-we-are.

[175] See: www.osce-academy.net/en/.

Pursuant to Article 2 of the Nakhchivan Agreement, the purposes of the Organization include

- strengthening mutual confidence and friendship among the Parties;
- maintaining peace and security in the region and worldwide;
- developing common positions on foreign policy issues;
- coordinating actions to combat international terrorism, separatism, extremism and cross-border crimes;
- promoting effective regional and bilateral cooperation in all areas of common interest;
- creating favorable conditions for trade and investment;
- aiming for comprehensive and balanced economic growth, social and cultural development;
- expanding interaction in the fields of science, technology, education, health, culture, sports and tourism;
- encouraging interaction of mass media and other means of communication; strengthening cooperation and integration between Member States;
- and promoting exchange of legal information and enhancing legal cooperation.[176]

On 3 November 2023, President Kassym-Jomart Tokayev of Kazakhstan announced at the 10th Meeting of the Council of Heads of State that during Kazakhstan's annual Chairmanship in the Organization, its priorities would be Traditions, Unification, Reforms, Knowledge, Trust, Investments, Mediation, and Energy (abbreviated as TURKTIME!).[177] Given Russia's attempts to reassert its influence in Central Asia against the background of its invasion of Ukraine, and the Central Asian States' growing concerns about their own security, the Organization of Turkic States could indeed become a counterweight to Russia, help neutralise some of the current security threats, reassert the international influence of Turkic-speaking nations, and enhance the welfare of their peoples.

H. Central Asian Integration[178]

The number and intensity of challenges currently facing the Central Asian region seem to require even closer regional integration. For many years, Uzbekistan had

[176] For the text of the Nakhchivan Agreement, see:https://www.turkicstates.org/u/d/basic-documents/nakhchivan-agreement-on-the-establishment-of-the-copperation-council-of-turkic-speaking-states-1-en.pdf.
[177] Fergana News, 'Tokayev obyavil "TURKTIME!"' ['Tokayev Announced "TURKTIME!"'], 3 November 2023, available at fergana.agency/news/131908/.
[178] This section uses the author's material published in Sayapin (n 25), 338–39 (selected footnotes omitted). Permission to use published material is gratefully acknowledged.

a visa regime with most of its Central Asian neighbours, and Turkmenistan's visa policy is still very strict, including with respect to nationals of Central Asian States. In April 2021 and September 2022, unresolved border issues led to armed conflicts between Tajikistan and Kyrgyzstan – and the fact that both States are members of the CSTO could not prevent the conflicts.[179] Crucially, a treaty on the delimitation of the Kyrgyz-Tajik border was signed on 13 March 2025, and ratified by the end of the month.[180] Water scarcity is another problem, which, if unresolved, will aggravate the situation in the future.[181] The Aral Sea environmental disaster has been affecting the region for decades. These and other problems could probably be resolved more effectively if all Central Asian States were to make more concerted efforts.

In as early as 2007, the first President of Kazakhstan, Nursultan Nazarbayev, suggested establishing a Central Asian Union, but so far this opportunity for integration has not been seized. However, in recent years, important steps were taken to intensify regional integration in Central Asia. On 21 July 2022, the Presidents of Kazakhstan, Kyrgyzstan, and Uzbekistan signed a 'Treaty of Friendship, Good Neighborliness and Cooperation for the Development of Central Asia in the 21st Century'. In August 2025. Tajikistan signed too. On 4 April 2025, the leaders of all Central Asian States and the European Union adopted a Joint Declaration following the First European Union – Central Asia Summit,[182] whereby relations between the European Union and Central Asia were upgraded to a strategic partnership (paragraph 1 of the Joint Declaration). No doubt, if the Central Asian Union ever materialises, it will contribute to its members' sustainable development, and to the prosperity of all Central Asian societies.

[179] See Chapter 10, section IX.D below.

[180] Fergana News, 'Dogovor o gosudarstvennoy granitse mezhdu Kyrgyzstanom i Tadjikistanom vstupil v silu' ['The Treaty on the State Border between Kyrgyzstan and Tajikistan Has Entered into Force'], 31 March 2025, available at fergana.agency/news/137213/. See also Fergana News, 'Prezidenty Kyrgyzstana, Tadjikistana i Uzbekistana podpisali dogovor o tochke styka treh granits' ['The Presidents of Kyrgyzstan, Tajikistan and Uzbekistan Signed an Agreement on the Junction Point of Three Borders'], 31 March 2025, available at fergana.agency/news/137220/.

[181] See Chapter 10, section IX.I below.

[182] For the text of the Joint Declaration, see: https://www.consilium.europa.eu/media/rdfjrb55/250403_eu-ca-summit_joint-declaration_final.pdf.

4

Non-State Actors

IN ADDITION TO States and international organisations, international law also affects the conduct of some non-State actors. While most of these actors do not create the rules of international law – since this remains the prerogative of States and international organisations – they nonetheless play a significant role in law-making processes through their subject-matter expertise and influence. This chapter discusses the respective roles of the International Committee of the Red Cross (ICRC), notable international non-governmental organisations (NGOs), the Vatican City State, multinational corporations (MNCs), individuals, non-State armed groups, and mass media.

I. INTERNATIONAL COMMITTEE OF THE RED CROSS (ICRC)

A. Introduction

The International Committee of the Red Cross (ICRC) is the world's oldest and conceivably the most experienced humanitarian organisation.[1] It was established on 17 February 1863 in Geneva, and now operates in more than 90 countries.[2] The ICRC is the founding member of the International Red Cross and Red Crescent Movement,[3] which also includes 191 Red Cross or Red Cresent Societies,[4] and their International Federation (founded in 1919).[5] Legally, the ICRC is an association under Articles 60 to 79 of the Swiss Civil Code, but its key functions are codified in the Geneva Conventions of 12 August 1949 and their Additional Protocols of 8 June 1977. In accordance with Article 7(1) of the ICRC Statutes,[6] its Assembly comprises between 15 and 25 members who

[1] See: www.icrc.org/en. See also J Kellenberger, 'The Role of the International Committee of the Red Cross' in A Clapham and P Gaeta, *The Oxford Handbook of International Law in Armed Conflict* (Oxford, Oxford University Press, 2014).

[2] See: www.icrc.org/en/we-are-international-committee-red-cross-icrc.

[3] For the Statutes of the Movement, see: www.ifrc.org/document/statutes-international-red-cross-and-red-crescent-movement.

[4] See: www.ifrc.org/who-we-are/international-red-cross-and-red-crescent-movement/about-national-societies.

[5] See: www.ifrc.org/.

[6] See: www.icrc.org/en/document/statutes-international-committee-red-cross-0.

are co-opted from among Swiss citizens.[7] The ICRC mission statement is as follows:[8]

> The ICRC is an impartial, neutral and independent organization whose exclusively humanitarian mission is to protect the lives and dignity of victims of armed conflict and other violence and to provide them with assistance.
>
> The ICRC also endeavours to prevent suffering by promoting and strengthening humanitarian law and universal humanitarian principles.
>
> Established in 1863, the ICRC is at the origin of the Geneva Conventions and the International Red Cross and Red Crescent Movement. During armed conflict and other violence, the ICRC directs and coordinates the international activities carried out by members of the Movement.

The ICRC Regional Delegation in Central Asia was established in 1992. It is located in Tashkent (Uzbekistan),[9] and works in coordination with the ICRC offices in Kazakhstan,[10] Kyrgyzstan,[11] Tajikistan,[12] and Turkmenistan.[13] Throughout Central Asia, the ICRC focuses on cooperation and prevention activities. It also does protection work (in Kyrgyzstan), and delivers assistance (in Kyrgyzstan and Tajikistan).

B. Protection

The ICRC protection activities are guided by the Protection Policy of 23 September 2008.[14] Such activities encompass humanitarian visits to prisoners of war, civilian internees and security detainees, the reestablishment of family links, and tracing missing persons.[15] In Central Asia, such work was carried out in Uzbekistan (from the early 2000s until the mid-2010s), and Kyrgyzstan.[16] The protection work is strictly confidential, and based on bilateral dialogue between the ICRC and the authorities of the respective States.

[7] For the current membership of the ICRC Assembly, see: www.icrc.org/en/members-international-committee-red-cross.

[8] See: www.icrc.org/en/our-mandate-and-mission.

[9] See: www.icrc.org/en/where-we-work/uzbekistan.

[10] See: www.icrc.org/en/where-we-work/kazakhstan.

[11] See: www.icrc.org/en/where-we-work/kyrgyzstan.

[12] See: www.icrc.org/en/where-we-work/tajikistan.

[13] See: www.icrc.org/en/where-we-work/turkmenistan.

[14] For the text of the Policy, see: international-review.icrc.org/sites/default/files/irrc-871-icrc-protection-policy.pdf.

[15] S Sayapin, 'Rethinking the Responsibility of the International Committee of the Red Cross: A *Sui Generis* Regime' in A Berkes, R Collins and R Deplano (eds), *Reassessing the Articles on the Responsibility of International Organizations: From Theory to Practice* (Cheltenham, Edward Elgar Publishing, 2024), 252.

[16] ICRC, 'Kyrgyzstan: Prison block offering lenient conditions for prisoners serving life sentences opens in Penal Colony 19', 25 December 2017, available at www.icrc.org/en/document/kyrgyzstan-prison-block-offering-lenient-conditions-prisoners-serving-life-sentences-opens.

C. Assistance

The ICRC Assistance Policy was adopted on 29 April 2004.[17] The concept of assistance includes three key areas: water and habitat (paragraph 5.3.1), economic security (paragraph 5.3.2), and health (paragraph 5.3.3).[18] Such work is essential in the aftermath of armed conflicts and other situations of violence. In Central Asia, the ICRC carried out large-scale assistance programmes in Kyrgyzstan and Tajikistan.[19]

D. Cooperation

In ICRC jargon, cooperation means interaction between the members of the International Red Cross and Red Crescent Movement.[20] The tasks and responsibilities of the Movement's members are now regulated by the Movement Coordination for Collective Impact Agreement (Seville Agreement 2.0),[21] which replaced the original 1997 Seville Agreement on the Organization of the International Activities of the Components of the International Red Cross and Red Crescent Movement,[22] and the 2005 Supplementary Measures to Enhance the Implementation of the Seville Agreement.[23] Throughout Central Asia, the ICRC contributes to enhancing the competence of the Red Crescent Societies, in particular, in the areas of conflict preparedness, reestablishment of family links, and dissemination of international humanitarian law (IHL).

E. Prevention

The ICRC Prevention Policy[24] stipulates that prevention complements the protection, assistance, and cooperation approaches,[25] and lays down that:

> [T]he ICRC seeks to avert human suffering by fostering an environment conducive to: (1) respect for the life and dignity of persons affected by armed conflict and other

[17] For a public version of the Policy, see: www.icrc.org/en/doc/assets/files/other/irrc_855_policy_ang.pdf.
[18] Sayapin (n 15), 253.
[19] ICRC, 'Tajikistan: ICRC provides medical supplies to Ishkashim District Hospital', 5 May 2017, available at www.icrc.org/en/document/tajikistan-icrc-provides-medical-supplies-ishkashim-district-hospital.
[20] See generally H Spieker, 'The International Red Cross and Red Crescent Movement' in S Sayapin et al (eds), *International Conflict and Security Law: A Research Handbook* (The Hague, TMC Asser Press, 2022); R Hakimov, *Mezhdunarodnoye gumanitarnoye pravo* [*International humanitarian law*] (Tashkent, Uzbekistan, 2007), 66–73.
[21] For the text, see: www.ifrc.org/sites/default/files/2022-10/Seville_Agreement_2.0_EN.pdf.
[22] For the text, see: https://www.ifrc.org/sites/default/files/Seville-Agreement_EN.pdf.
[23] Sayapin (n 15), 256.
[24] For the text of the Policy, see: https://www.icrc.org/en/doc/assets/files/publications/icrc-002-4019.pdf.
[25] ibid, 7.

> situations of violence; and (2) respect for the ICRC's work. This approach entails taking action to prevent suffering by influencing those who can determine – directly or indirectly – the fate of those affected and generally implies a medium- or long-term perspective. It encompasses efforts to communicate, develop, clarify and promote the implementation of IHL and other relevant bodies of law, as well as efforts to facilitate acceptance of the ICRC's work.[26]

The most typical prevention activities include contributing to the progressive development of international humanitarian law (IHL) and advising States on its domestic implementation, providing training on the law of armed conflict to members of the armed forces (as well as non-State armed groups), raising awareness of fundamental human rights among the police and security forces, the dissemination of IHL among students and academic staff at secondary and higher education institutions, and informing the general public about humanitarian law and action.[27] The ICRC carries out these activities throughout Central Asia.

II. INTERNATIONAL NON-GOVERNMENTAL ORGANISATIONS (NGOs)

A. Introduction

Modern international law would not be the same without competent and dedicated NGOs. They work worldwide to protect human rights, promote justice, improve the quality of education, raise awareness of environmental issues, and in many other areas. Indeed, they are helping to shape entire areas of international law – such as international human rights law,[28] or international criminal law – by maintaining dialogue with States, international organisations and domestic NGOs.[29] Some of the most prominent international NGOs are also active in Central Asia.

B. Amnesty International

Amnesty International was founded in 1961 in London. It is a 'global movement of more than 10 million people who are committed to creating a future where human rights are enjoyed by everyone'.[30] They monitor human rights developments and promote respect for human rights in more than

[26] ibid, 5.
[27] Sayapin (n 15), 258.
[28] D Weissbrodt, 'Roles and Responsibilities of Non-State Actors' in D Shelton (ed), *The Oxford Handbook of International Human Rights Law* (Oxford, Oxford University Press, 2013).
[29] See, for example, the Kazakhstan International Bureau for Human Rights and the Rule of Law, available at https://bureau.kz/en/.
[30] See: www.amnesty.org/en/about-us/.

150 countries, including all Central Asian nations.[31] Amnesty International publishes annual reports documenting human rights concerns worldwide,[32] ranging from economic, social and cultural rights, corporate responsibility and climate change, to arms control, police brutality, torture and enforced disappearances.[33]

C. Human Rights Watch (HRW)

Another prominent international human rights NGO is Human Rights Watch (HRW). Founded in 1978 as Helsinki Watch, HRW is headquartered in New York, and works 'to protect the most at risk, from vulnerable minorities and civilians in wartime, to refugees and children in need' by 'investigat[ing] and report[ing] on abuses happening in all corners of the world'.[34] HRW monitors human rights developments worldwide, including in Central Asia, and publishes thematic reports on a rolling basis as well as annual reports.[35]

D. Médecins Sans Frontières (MSF)

Médecins Sans Frontières (MSF, Doctors Without Borders) was founded in 1971 in Paris. Now, it is a worldwide movement consisting of 27 associations and uniting nearly 68,000 members who provide 'medical assistance to people affected by conflict, epidemics, disasters, or exclusion from healthcare'.[36] The associations define the strategic direction of 24 sections and 18 branch offices, and hold the sections accountable for their work.[37] In Central Asia, MSF is present in all countries, except Kazakhstan. In Kyrgyzstan, the current focus is on the early detection of cervical and breast cancers.[38] In Tajikistan, MSF works with the Ministry of Health and Social Protection to diagnose and treat children with drug-resistant tuberculosis (DR-TB).[39] In Turkmenistan, MSF offered a TB programme in 1999–2003, and provided medical care to children in Magdanly in 2004–2009.[40] In Uzbekistan, MSF is currently running a comprehensive care programme for drug-resistant and drug-sensitive tuberculosis in the republic

[31] See: www.amnesty.org/en/countries/.
[32] The 2024 report is available at www.amnesty.org/en/documents/pol10/7200/2024/en/.
[33] See: www.amnesty.org/en/what-we-do/.
[34] See: www.hrw.org/about/about-us.
[35] The 2024 report is available at www.hrw.org/world-report/2024. See also: 'Kazakhstan: New Law to Protect Women Improved, but Incomplete', Human Rights Watch, 23 April 2024, available at www.hrw.org/news/2024/04/23/kazakhstan-new-law-protect-women-improved-incomplete.
[36] See: www.msf.org/who-we-are.
[37] See: www.msf.org/how-we-are-run.
[38] See: www.msf.org/kyrgyzstan.
[39] See: www.msf.org/tajikistan.
[40] See: www.msf.org/turkmenistan.

of Karakalpakstan, and providing support for the diagnosis and treatment of people living with HIV and co-infections in Tashkent.[41]

E. International Commission of Jurists (ICJ)

The International Commission of Jurists (ICJ) was established in 1952, and is headquartered in Geneva. It is a standing group of 60 eminent judges and lawyers 'defending human rights and the rule of law worldwide'.[42] Among the ICJ Commissioners, there is currently one expert from Kyrgyzstan, and one from Uzbekistan.[43] The ICJ focuses on 23 countries, and has activities in 65 other nations.[44] The ICJ focus areas include global security and the rule of law, independence of judges and lawyers, business and human rights, sexual orientation and gender identity, and a few other areas.[45]

F. Learned International Law Associations

In Central Asia, there are two international law associations (in Kazakhstan and Uzbekistan), and a few Central Asian scholars are members of the American Society of International Law (ASIL),[46] European Society of International Law (ESIL),[47] and Asian Society of International Law (Asian SIL).[48] Two senior Central Asian international lawyers are members of the governing bodies of the Asian SIL.[49] On 24–25 May 2024, Narxoz University and KIMEP University (both located in Almaty) hosted an Intersessional Conference of the Asian SIL entitled 'Asia and International Law: Historical Legacy and Progressive Development'.[50] The Conference brought together 76 scholars from 26 countries in Asia, Europe, North America, and Australia. Academic events like this help Central Asian international law scholars to 'make their respective doctrines better known abroad, and … gradually integrate the Central Asian schools of international law into the international academic community'.[51]

[41] See: www.msf.org/uzbekistan.
[42] See: www.icj.org/about/.
[43] See: www.icj.org/commission/commissioners-from-europe-and-cis/.
[44] See: www.icj.org/about/where-we-work/.
[45] See: www.icj.org/themes/.
[46] See: www.asil.org/.
[47] See: esil-sedi.eu/.
[48] See: www.asiansil.org/.
[49] See: www.asiansil.org/about-us/governing-bodies/.
[50] See: en.narxoz.kz/callforpapers.
[51] S Sayapin, 'International Law in Central Asia: Practices and Doctrines' (2022) 47 *Review of Central and East European Law* 322, 351.

G. International Olympic Committee (IOC)

The International Olympic Committee (IOC) is an international not-for-profit organisation whose

> job is to encourage the promotion of Olympic values, to ensure the regular celebration of the Olympic Games and its legacy and to support all the organisations affiliated to the Olympic Movement. The IOC cultivates its success through a series of programmes and projects which give life to the Olympic values.[52]

The IOC is

> the supreme authority leading the Olympic Movement and the catalyst for all Olympic family members: National Olympic Committees, International, Federations, athletes, Organising Committees for the Olympic Games, TOP partners and broadcasters, plus United Nations agencies.[53]

The IOC was established in 1894, and is headquartered in Lausanne. The organisation, actions and functioning of the Olympic Movement are governed by the Olympic Charter.[54] At the time of writing, the IOC includes 109 Members and 39 Honorary Members.[55] As natural persons, the IOC Members are 'representatives of the IOC in their respective countries, and not their country's delegate within the IOC'.[56] The IOC has the sole authority to recognise a National Olympic Committee (NOC), of which there are currently 206.[57] The mission of the NOCs is 'to develop, promote and protect the Olympic Movement in their respective countries, in accordance with the Olympic Charter'.[58]

All Central Asian NOCs joined the Olympic Movement in 1993,[59] at the dawn of their respective nations' independence, and have been its active members ever since. The Central Asian athletes' performance at the 2024 Paris Olympics was sensational. The Uzbek team ranked 13th in the world by the overall number of medals (eight gold, two silver, and three bronze medals). Kazakhstan ranked 43rd with one gold, three silver, and three bronze medals. Kyrgyzstan's athletes won two silver, and four bronze medals (68th rank), and the Tajik team ranked 79th with three bronze medals.[60]

[52] See: olympics.com/ioc/faq/ioc-organisation/what-is-the-international-olympic-committee-ioc-and-what-is-its-mission.

[53] ibid.

[54] For the text of the Olympic Charter, see: olympics.com/ioc/olympic-charter.

[55] See: olympics.com/ioc/members.

[56] ibid.

[57] See: olympics.com/ioc/national-olympic-committees.

[58] ibid.

[59] See: olympics.com/ioc/kazakhstan; olympics.com/ioc/kyrgyzstan; olympics.com/ioc/tajikistan; olympics.com/ioc/turkmenistan; olympics.com/ioc/uzbekistan.

[60] Paris 2024, 'Medal Table', available at olympics.com/en/paris-2024/medals.

H. Other International NGOs

A few notable NGOs have been active in Central Asia's science and education sectors since the 1990s, to promote the learning of foreign languages, and support the academic efforts of Central Asian students and scholars. American Councils for International Education provide a range of educational opportunities in all Central Asian countries.[61] The Fulbright Programme is present throughout Central Asia, except Turkmenistan.[62] Chevening offers scholarships and fellowships in all Central Asian countries.[63] In the past, the German Academic Exchange Service (DAAD) was also present in Kazakhstan and Uzbekistan, and currently it maintains a presence in Kyrgyzstan[64] and Tajikistan.[65] The French Institute for Central Asian Studies (IFEAC) was located in Uzbekistan until 2010, and is now present in Kyrgyzstan.[66] The Open Society Foundations (formerly the Open Society Institute) announced the closure of its last office in Central Asia (Soros Foundation – Kyrgyzstan) on 15 April 2024.[67]

Notably, institutions supporting higher education and international research initiatives have also been established in some Central Asian countries. Since 1993, more than 10,000 high-performing students from Kazakhstan have been awarded the Bolashak International Scholarship to study abroad.[68] In Uzbekistan, 828 scholarships were awarded by the Umid Foundation (1997–2003), followed by 914 scholarships awarded by the Istedod Foundation (2003–18).[69] In 2018, the El-Yurt Umidi Foundation was established to further strengthen contacts with compatriots living abroad, and to coordinate doctoral, master's, internship, and in-service training scholarship programmes in education, science and research, healthcare, public administration, and emerging areas of the economy.[70]

In 2021, the International Institute for Central Asia was established in Tashkent, to 'promote peace and sustainable development through partnership, based on our shared values and common interests for [a] secure, prosperous and resilient Central Asia'.[71] In particular, the Institute strives to 'establish extensive partnerships with leading research organizations in Central Asia and

[61] See: www.americancouncils.org/where-we-work/south-and-central-asia.

[62] See: us.fulbrightonline.org/countries/south-and-central-asia.

[63] See: www.chevening.org/fellowships/find-a-programme/.

[64] See: www.daad-kyrgyzstan.org/en/.

[65] See: duschanbe.diplo.de/tj-de/willkommen-in-tadschikistan/daad-tadschikistan/1586270.

[66] See: ifeac.hypotheses.org/institut/structure-2.

[67] C Putz, 'Open Society Foundations Closes Down Kyrgyzstan Operation', 17 April 2024, available at thediplomat.com/2024/04/open-society-foundations-closes-down-kyrgyzstan-operation/.

[68] See: bolashak.gov.kz/en/o-stipendii.

[69] El-Yurt Umidi Foundation, 'Brief Historical Excursion', available at eyuf.uz/site/view-page?id=15.

[70] ibid.

[71] 'About the International Institute for Central Asia', 10 May 2023, available at iica.uz/en/page/o-mejdunarodnom-institute-tsentralnoy-azii.

beyond, as well as to maintain constant dialogue among scholars, researchers and experts focusing on Central Asian studies'.[72] The current Director of the Institute is Javlon Vakhabov, Uzbekistan's former Ambassador to the United States, Canada, and Brazil.

Nowadays, environmental action is almost synonymous with Greenpeace. Founded in 1971 in Canada, it is a 'global network comprised of 25 independent national/regional organisations in over 55 countries across Europe, the Americas, Africa, Asia and the Pacific, as well as a co-ordinating body, Greenpeace International'.[73] Greenpeace International is a foundation under the law of the Netherlands.[74] In its environmental action, Greenpeace focuses on climate and energy, biodiversity, and social and economic issues.[75] Greenpeace's annual reports since 1995 are available online.[76] Greenpeace is not present in Central Asia but some of its expertise may be useful, in particular, in the climate and energy sector.

III. *SUI GENERIS* INTERNATIONAL ACTORS

A. The Vatican City State

An absolute elective ecclesiastical monarchy, the Vatican City State is under 'the full ownership, exclusive dominion, and sovereign authority and jurisdiction of the Holy See'.[77] Established in 1929 by the Lateran Treaty between the Holy See and the Kingdom of Italy, formally, Vatican City meets all the criteria for statehood, with functional nuances. It has an area of 0.44 km^2 within the city of Rome.[78] Its population (as of 31 December 2024) comprises 882 persons.[79] The Vatican has 618 citizens of whom 246 reside within the State (including 104 members of the Swiss Guard).[80] 66 citizens are Cardinals (of whom 10 are resident within the State).[81] The State power is organised as follows:

> The legislative function, except in cases that the Supreme Pontiff intends to reserve for himself, is exercised by the Pontifical Commission for the State of the Vatican

[72] ibid.
[73] Greenpeace, 'How we're structured', available at www.greenpeace.org/international/about/structure/. For a list of Greenpeace organisations, see: www.greenpeace.org/international/about/worldwide/.
[74] ibid.
[75] Greenpeace, 'The issues we work on', available at www.greenpeace.org/international/explore/.
[76] For the annual reports since 1995, see: www.greenpeace.org/international/about/annual-report/.
[77] See Art 3, first paragraph of the Lateran Treaty of 11 February 1929. For the text of the Treaty, see: spcp.prf.cuni.cz/dokument/lateran.htm.
[78] See: www.vaticanstate.va/it/stato-governo/note-generali/geografia.html.
[79] See: www.vaticanstate.va/it/stato-governo/note-generali/popolazione.html.
[80] ibid.
[81] ibid.

> City, composed of Cardinals, including the President, and other members, appointed by the Supreme Pontiff for a five-year period.
>
> The executive function is exercised by the President of the Pontifical Commission who is the President of the Governorate and is assisted by the General Secretary and the Deputy General Secretary.
>
> The judicial function is exercised, in the name of the Supreme Pontiff, by the bodies established according to the judicial system and by other bodies to which the law confers competence for specific matters.[82]

International relations of the Holy See or the Vatican City State are extensive and diverse. They are parties to numerous treaties, including on human rights, international humanitarian law, law of the sea, diplomatic law, and in other areas.[83] The Vienna Convention on Diplomatic Relations of 18 May 1961 contains a provision on the precedence of representatives of the Holy See.[84] The Holy See is a member of or has observer status at numerous international organisations.[85] It also maintains diplomatic relations with most States in the world, including all Central Asian nations.[86]

B. Multinational Corporations (MNCs)

Multinational corporations (MNCs) – or transnational corporations (TNCs) – are business entities with a global presence. They are central actors in international investment law and international economic law in that they carry out their business activities worldwide and perform high-value transactions with private and public counterparts, including States.[87] Indeed, the annual revenue of top-performing companies such as Alibaba, Amazon, Apple, Coca Cola, Google, Meta, Samsung, Shell and the like is higher than the GDP of some States[88] – hence their influence on the world economy and also in the international legal domain. They bring claims against States before courts and arbitral tribunals, and are treated in such proceedings as subjects equal to States. They contribute to the development of international human

[82] See: www.vaticanstate.va/it/stato-governo/organi-stato/organi-dello-stato.html.

[83] See: www.vaticanstate.va/it/stato-governo/rapporti-internazionali/adesione-a-convenzioni-internazionali.html.

[84] cf Art 16(3) of the Vienna Convention on Diplomatic Relations.

[85] See: holyseemission.org/contents/mission/diplomatic-relations-of-the-holy-see.php.

[86] ibid.

[87] AV Sharma, 'Starlink and International Law: The Challenge of Corporate Sovereignty in Outer Space', EJIL: Talk!, 17 March 2025, available at www.ejiltalk.org/starlink-and-international-law-the-challenge-of-corporate-sovereignty-in-outer-space/.

[88] For example, in 2024, Alibaba's revenue was US$131.23, Google earned US$278.13 billion, and Apple earned US$381.62 billion. In comparison, in 2022, Kazakhstan's GDP was US$225.5 billion, and Uzbekistan's GDP amounted to US$80.39 billion.

rights – in particular, economic, social and cultural rights[89] – but also to combatting corruption, and to international humanitarian law.[90] For details, see relevant chapters in this book.

C. Individuals

In classical international law, there was no place for individuals, except in very limited settings. Now, it is commonly accepted that individuals are 'special subjects' of international law in that they have rights and bear obligations under international human rights law (IHRL), international humanitarian law (IHL), international criminal law (ICL), as well as diplomatic and consular law.[91] In particular, individuals are entitled to bring claims against States under universal human rights instruments and before one of the three regional human rights courts, depending on location. Fundamental human rights are also recognised and enforced in international and non-international armed conflicts under IHRL and IHL. Individuals who commit genocide, crimes against humanity, war crimes, and the crime of aggression are liable directly under ICL. Although diplomatic privileges and immunities are derived from State sovereignty, they are enjoyed by diplomatic agents – that is, individuals carrying out diplomatic functions. For details, see relevant chapters in this book.

D. Non-State Armed Groups

Non-State armed groups – who may be key actors especially in non-international armed conflicts – cannot formally become parties to treaties of international humanitarian law. However, it is not uncommon for such groups

[89] PM Sukhorolsky, 'Vplyv transnatsionalnyh IT-kompaniy na prava lyudyny ta problemy evolyutsii mizhnarodnogo prava' ['The Influence of Transnational IT Companies on Human Rights and Issues in the Evolution of International Law'] in V Repetsky and V Gutnyk (eds), *Current Problems of International Law* (Odessa, Phoenix Press, 2017); L Burnard and D Minogue, 'Can Companies Knowingly Profiting from Forced Labour "Buy" Their way out of Accountability?', OpinioJuris, 13 May 2024, available at opiniojuris.org/2024/05/13/world-uyghur-congress-v-national-crime-agency-court-of-appeal-hearing/.

[90] M Nirula, 'The Role of Business in War: A Different Defense to Corporate Complicity? Part I: The Old Offense', OpinioJuris, 7 April 2025, available at opiniojuris.org/2025/04/07/the-role-of-business-in-war-a-different-defense-to-corporate-complicity-part-i-the-old-offense/; M Nirula, 'The Role of Business in War: A Different Defense to Corporate Complicity? Part II: A Different Defense', OpinioJuris, 7 April 2025, available at opiniojuris.org/2025/04/07/the-role-of-business-in-war-a-different-defense-to-corporate-complicity-part-ii-a-different-defense/.

[91] G Gaja, 'The Position of Individuals in International Law: an ILC Perspective' (2010) 21 *European Journal of International Law*, 11; S Sayapin, 'K voprosu o mejdunarodnoy pravosub'yektnosti individov' ['The Question of Individuals' Personality in International Law'] (2005) (4) *Moscow Journal of International Law* 27.

to accept obligations under relevant IHL instruments.[92] There is also general agreement to the effect that non-State armed groups are bound by customary IHL rules, and accordingly, their members bear responsibility under domestic and international criminal law, among others, for violations of IHL and human rights law.[93]

E. Mass Media

The impact of mass media – both traditional and new – on international law (and vice versa) is multifaceted. Mass media report on daily developments in international relations and often discuss the significance of new agreements concluded between States or international organisations. They expose violations committed by States, international organisations, and individuals, and assist in holding them accountable. Notable trials are broadcast (on TV or online), to enable maximum coverage and ensure the quality of justice. International organisations and many States now have an official online presence. All of these are important aspects of the freedom 'to seek, receive and impart information and ideas through any media and regardless of frontiers'.[94] International law also sets professional standards for journalists,[95] and lays down rules for their protection.[96]

Especially online media are increasingly used to disseminate knowledge of international law, and to advance learned debate among international law academics and practitioners. The United Nations maintains an extensive audiovisual library on international law.[97] Experts produce online courses on international law.[98] International law blogs – such as *Opinio Juris*,[99] *EJIL: Talk!*,[100] *Völkerrechtsblog*,[101] *International Law Agendas*,[102]

[92] R Atadjanov, 'Ensuring Compliance of Non-State Actors with Rules of International Humanitarian Law on the Use of Weapons in NIAC: A Way to Follow?' (2008–2011) 4 *Asia-Pacific Yearbook of International Humanitarian Law* 140.

[93] JM Henckaerts and L Doswald-Beck, *Customary International Humanitarian Law, Volume I: Rules* (Cambridge, Cambridge University Press, 2005), 497–98, 536; C Castañeda, 'Victims' Perspective on the Development of Enforced Disappearances by Non-State Actors', *Völkerrechtsblog*, 17 June 2024, available at voelkerrechtsblog.org/victims-perspective-on-the-development-of-enforced-disappearances-by-non-state-actors/.

[94] cf Art 19 of the Universal Declaration of Human Rights.

[95] Article 19, 'International standards: Regulation of media workers', 4 April 2012, available at www.article19.org/resources/international-standards-regulation-media-workers/.

[96] UNESCO, 'Basic Texts Related to the Safety of Journalists', available at www.unesco.org/en/safety-journalists/basic-texts.

[97] UN Audiovisual Library on International Law, available at legal.un.org/avl/intro/welcome_avl.html.

[98] For example, this author's video course on international law (in Russian) is available at prg.kz/pravmedia/video_lectures/570-vvedenie-v-kurs-lekciy-po-mp.html.

[99] See: opiniojuris.org/.

[100] See: www.ejiltalk.org/.

[101] See: voelkerrechtsblog.org/.

[102] See: ila-brasil.org.br/blog/.

Afronomicslaw,[103] and *ASIANSIL Voices*[104] – publish analyses of and opinions on current developments, thematic symposia, and book review symposia. These and other international law textbooks will be particularly useful, if they are read in conjunction with quality online resources.

[103] See: www.afronomicslaw.org/.
[104] See: asiansilvoices.com/.

Part II

International Law-making Processes

5

International Law as a Source of Law in the Central Asian States

THE QUESTION OF how international law relates to domestic (or municipal) law is a matter of practical importance. It means, in effect, how States apply international law in their domestic legal systems, and to what extent various actors within domestic legal orders – individuals, legal entities, and State organs – may directly rely on various rules of international law to advance their interests. In other words, this question is about whether – and to what extent – international law is a source of domestic law. This chapter will recall the predominant perspectives on the interaction between international and municipal law, discuss how those perspectives are reflected in the Constitutions of the Central Asian States, and conclude by looking into some of the key policy documents guiding the approaches of the Central Asian States to international law.

I. THEORIES OF RELATIONSHIP BETWEEN INTERNATIONAL LAW AND DOMESTIC LAW

A. Dualism

The dualist approach rests on the premise that a State's domestic law governs all relations within its domestic legal order, whereas international law governs international relations.[1] It is assumed that domestic legal orders do not come in direct contact with processes occurring in the international arena, since they are confined within the borders of the individual States, and hence do not exercise any direct influence on international processes. Likewise, the latter have no direct effect on any dynamics within States since international relations 'stop' where the domestic jurisdiction of a State begins. Hence the only way to make feasible an interaction between the complex international legal order and numerous domestic legal orders is to implement the rules of international law through various legal techniques.[2]

[1] M Shaw, *International Law*, 9th edn (Cambridge, Cambridge University Press, 2021), 112.
[2] See Chapter 6, sections III.E – III.F below.

B. Monism

By contrast, the monist approach suggests that the rules of international and domestic law are all rules of law, although they are created by different actors and result from different processes, and as such form a single legal regime.[3] As a result, international law can apply directly within a domestic legal order. The monist approach involves dissimilar but equally solid theoretical cases. Sir Hersch Lauterpacht (1897–1960), for example,

> emphasized that individuals are the ultimate subjects of international law, representing both the justification and moral limit of the legal order … The state is disliked as an abstraction and distrusted as a vehicle for maintaining human rights. International law is seen as the best available moderator of human affairs, and also as a condition of the *legal* existence of states and therefore of the national legal systems.[4]

A strong counterargument against this perspective is that in most areas of international law, individuals act as organs of States,[5] and possess a legal personality directly under international law only in international human rights law, international humanitarian law, and international criminal law (see Chapter four, section III.C above). International law's dominant focus on States is still a fact.

Another powerful – in Alexander Orakhelashvili's words, indeed, 'radical'[6] – defence of monism was proposed by Hans Kelsen (1881–1973).[7] According to Kelsen, all law – domestic and international – derives from a fundamental rule (*Grundnorm*) of international law, which

> rationalizes the creation and existence of State legal orders and is therefore also ultimately responsible for the validity and legitimacy of national law. However, such unity of national and international systems does not entail the supremacy or primacy of international law. On the monist view, international law merely legitimizes the existence of national legal systems, but does not pre-determine, or set limits on, the validity or content of the rules that national systems enact.[8]

Kelsen's theory appears to be formally reflected in Article 4(1) of the Constitution of the Republic of Kazakhstan.[9]

The third approach claims that both international and domestic law are

[3] ibid.

[4] J Crawford, *Brownlie's Principles of Public International Law*, 9th edn (Oxford, Oxford University Press, 2019), 45–46 (footnotes omitted).

[5] S Sayapin, 'K voprosu o mejdunarodnoy pravosub'yektnosti individov' ['The Question of Individuals' Personality in International Law Revisited'] (2005) (4) *Moscow Journal of International Law* 27.

[6] A Orakhelashvili, *Akehurst's Modern Introduction to International Law*, 8th edn (Abingdon, Routledge, 2019), 57.

[7] H Kelsen, 'Die Einheit von Völkerrecht und staatlichem Recht' (1958) 41 *Zeitschrift für ausländisches öffentliches Recht und Völkerrecht* 234.

[8] Orakhelashvili (n 6), 57–58. See also H Kelsen, *General Theory of Law and State* (Cambridge MA, Harvard University Press, 1945), 371.

[9] See section II.A below.

> supreme in [their] own sphere, much as French law and English law are in France and England. And just as one cannot talk in terms of the supremacy of French law over English law, but only of two distinct legal systems each operating within its own field, so it is possible to treat international law and municipal law in the same way. They are both the legal element contained within the domestic and international systems respectively, and they exist within different juridical orders.[10]

This perspective appears to contain an element of dualism, for it accepts for a fact the existence of a multitude of (international and domestic) legal orders, although it treats all of them equally.

C. Primacy of Domestic Law

The next theoretical perspective accords primacy to municipal law where the latter conflicts with international law. It is known as 'international legal nihilism', for it effectively rejects the force of international law.[11] Fortunately enough, the practical application of this theory is still quite rare. States resort to this theory, for example, when they seek to limit the scope of their responsibility under international law. A recent example is the enactment, in 2020, of a new sentence in Article 79 of the Constitution of the Russian Federation: 'Decisions of interstate bodies adopted on the basis of the provisions of international treaties of the Russian Federation in their interpretation contrary to the Constitution of the Russian Federation shall not be enforceable in the Russian Federation'.

D. Primacy of International Law

Finally, States may decide to recognise the primacy of international law over domestic law. An obvious advantage of this perspective consists in the gradual harmonisation of a State's domestic laws and practices with foreign ones, through the medium of international law, with a view to amplifying the State's international cooperation in various thematic areas.[12] This approach should not be seen as a limitation on State sovereignty, as the decision to accord primacy to international law is itself an expression of that sovereignty. The paradigm is usually reflected in constitutional provisions, as well as in other domestic legal acts, to the effect that in cases of conflict between the rules of domestic laws with applicable rules of international law, the latter shall prevail. Let us now

[10] M Shaw, *International Law*, 8th edition (Cambridge, Cambridge University Press, 2017), 98–99.

[11] R Abu-Maneh et al, 'Jurisdictional Battleground in Disputes with Sanctioned Russian Persons', available at www.mayerbrown.com/en/insights/publications/2024/07/jurisdictional-battleground-in-disputes-with-sanctioned-russian-persons.

[12] II Lukashuk, *Mezhdunarodnoye pravo: Obshchaya chast* [*International Law: General Part*], 3rd edn (Moscow, Wolters Kluwer, 2008), 257.

consider how the respective paradigms operate in the domestic legal orders of the Central Asian States.

II. CONSTITUTIONAL APPROACHES TO INTERNATIONAL LAW

A. Kazakhstan

Article 4(1) of the Constitution of the Republic of Kazakhstan (1995) stipulates as follows:

> The provisions of the Constitution, the laws corresponding to it, other normative legal acts, international treaty-based and other obligations of the Republic, as well as normative regulations of the Constitutional Court and the Supreme Court of the Republic, shall be the functioning law in the Republic of Kazakhstan.[13]

Two conclusions may be drawn from this provision with respect to the place of international law in Kazakhstan's legal system.

First, Kazakhstan exercises a monist approach inasmuch as 'international treaty-based and other obligations of the Republic' are listed in the same constitutional provision along with other – domestic – sources of law. A literal interpretation of Article 4(1) suggests that it describes a totality of sources of the law of Kazakhstan, which include the Constitution, various sources of domestic law (laws corresponding to the Constitution, and other normative legal acts), as well as treaties and other international obligations of the Republic. Since the Constitutional Court of the Republic of Kazakhstan 'considers, before ratification, the treaties of the Republic for their compliance with the Constitution',[14] such compliance is presumed if Kazakhstan expresses its consent to a treaty. This inference is reinforced by Article 74(1) of the Constitution: 'Laws and treaties recognised as non-compliant with the Constitution of the Republic of Kazakhstan may not be signed or, respectively, ratified and enforced'.

Second, Kazakhstan recognises as a source of law not only treaties but also 'other [international] obligations'. Presumably, these include, at least, customary international law,[15] and legally binding acts of international institutions of which Kazakhstan is a member.[16] This supplement is important, because, as will be seen, the other Central Asian States' constitutional approaches to international law are more limited.

[13] For the text of the Constitution of the Republic of Kazakhstan (in Russian), see: www.akorda.kz/ru/official_documents/constitution.
[14] Article 72(1)(3) of the Constitution.
[15] See Chapter 7, section I below.
[16] See Chapter 7, section II.C.

As far as treaties, which are subject to ratification, are specifically concerned, Article 4(3) of the Constitution provides:

> Treaties ratified by the Republic shall have primacy over its laws. The legislation of the Republic shall determine the procedure and conditions of operation of treaties, to which Kazakhstan is a party, in the territory of the Republic of Kazakhstan.

The Law 'On Treaties of the Republic of Kazakhstan' was adopted on 30 May 2005.[17] Its Article 11 stipulates that nine categories of treaties are subject to ratification, namely treaties

> 1) the subject of which are the rights and freedoms of man and citizen;
> 2) the implementation of which requires a change in existing or adoption of new laws, as well as establishing other rules than those provided for by the laws of the Republic of Kazakhstan;
> 3) on the territorial delimitation of the Republic of Kazakhstan with other states, including international treaties on the passage of the state border of the Republic of Kazakhstan, as well as on the delimitation of the exclusive economic zone and the continental shelf of the Republic of Kazakhstan;
> 4) on the foundations of interstate relations, on issues of disarmament or international arms control, ensuring international peace and security, as well as international peace treaties and international treaties on collective security;
> 5) on the participation of the Republic of Kazakhstan in interstate associations and international organizations, if such international treaties provide for the transfer to them of the exercise of a part of the sovereign rights of the Republic of Kazakhstan or establish legally binding[ness] of decisions of their bodies for the Republic of Kazakhstan;
> 6) on state loans;
> 7) on the provision by the Republic of Kazakhstan of economic and other assistance, except humanitarian assistance and official development assistance;
> 8) at the signing of which the parties involved in the negotiations agreed on their subsequent ratification;
> 9) which provide that such consent is expressed by ratification.

On 10 July 2008, the Supreme Court of the Republic of Kazakhstan adopted Normative Regulation No 1 'On the application of rules of treaties of the Republic of Kazakhstan'.[18] Its second preambular paragraph stipulates that

> [t]reaties play a significant role in ensuring judicial protection of the rights, freedoms and legitimate interests of citizens and organisations, therefore, in necessary cases, the courts are obliged, within the jurisdiction of the Republic of Kazakhstan, to be guided by the norms of international law.

[17] See Chapter 6, section VII.B below.

[18] For the text of the Normative Regulation (in Russian), see: https://zakonpravo.kz/en/on-the-application-of-the-norms-of-international-treaties-of-the-republic-of-kazakhstan.

A more detailed analysis of Kazakhstan's Law on treaties and the Normative Regulation is offered in Chapter six.

Notably, Article 8 of the Constitution stipulates that

> [t]he Republic of Kazakhstan shall respect the principles and norms of international law, pursue a policy of cooperation and good neighbourly relations between states, their equality and non-interference in each other's internal affairs, the peaceful resolution of international disputes, and renounce the first use of military armed force.

Unlike some other Central Asian Constitutions (see below), this provision does not single out 'generally recognised' principles and norms of international law but implies, in a monist way, all principles and rules of international law. Similarly, Article 12(4) provides that all individuals – citizens of Kazakhstan, foreigners and stateless persons – enjoy equal rights and bear equal obligations, subject to specific exceptions:

> Foreigners and stateless persons in the Republic shall enjoy the rights and freedoms, as well as bear the obligations established for citizens, unless otherwise provided by the Constitution, laws and international treaties.

For an overview of human rights in Kazakhstan, see Chapter thirteen, section III.A below.

B. Kyrgyzstan

Since 1991, three Constitutions have been successively enacted in Kyrgyzstan – in 1993, 2010, and 2021. The most recent Constitution was adopted by a referendum of 11 April 2021, and enacted on 5 May 2021.[19] Its Article 6(3) formulates the monist perspective as follows:

> The generally recognized principles and norms of international law, as well as treaties that have entered into force in accordance with the legislation of the Kyrgyz Republic, are an integral part of the legal system of the Kyrgyz Republic.
>
> The procedure and conditions for the application of international treaties and generally recognized principles and norms of international law shall be determined by law.

It is quite interesting that in these two paragraphs, the 'generally recognised principles and norms of international law' and 'treaties' are listed in different sequences. In the first paragraph, the generally recognised principles and norms are mentioned before treaties, which might suggest that these principles and norms are primary, or superior, with respect to treaties. The fact that 'treaties' are mentioned after the conjunction 'as well as' reinforces this first impression. The concept of 'generally recognised principles and norms

[19] For the text of the Constitution of the Kyrgyz Republic (in Russian), see: cbd.minjust.gov.kg/1-2/edition/1202952/ru.

of international law' is widespread in the post-Soviet doctrine of international law but its precise content allows for at least four interpretations. First, the concept could mean 'general international law' – that is, in the words of Grigoriy Tunkin (1906–93), 'law recognised by all States and regulating relations between them'.[20] Second, it could mean international custom 'as evidence of a general practice accepted as law', in the language of Article 38(1)(b) of the Statute of the International Court of Justice. Third, in the words of Igor Lukashuk (1926–2007), the concept refers to the 'main principles of international law'[21] as 'the most general norms of international law, which determine its main content and characteristic features, [and] possess the supreme political, moral, and legal authority'.[22] These 'main principles' include those listed in Article 2 of the UN Charter, the 1970 Friendly Relations Declaration,[23] and the Declaration of Principles in the 1975 Helsinki Final Act.[24] Finally, the concept could well mean the peremptory norms of general international law (*jus cogens*) in the sense of the second sentence of Article 53 of the Vienna Convention on the Law of Treaties.[25] It appears that the relative vagueness of the concept might complicate its practical application.

In the second paragraph of Article 6(3) of the current Constitution of the Kyrgyz Republic, quoted above, treaties precede the 'generally recognised principles and norms of international law', and rightly so, since the 'procedure and conditions for the application of treaties' are much easier to lay down in a law than those for 'generally recognised principles and norms of general international law', especially given that the content of the latter concept allows for multiple interpretations. The Law 'On Treaties of the Kyrgyz Republic' was adopted on 24 April 2014.[26] As for the rest of the second paragraph of Article 6(3), it probably implies that the application of individual 'generally recognised principles and norms of international law' is regulated by relevant domestic legislation (for example, the Criminal Code, relevant laws on human rights, use of force, etc).

Significantly, the new Constitution of the Kyrgyz Republic contains many direct references to international human rights law (IHRL). The third paragraph of Article 24(1) stipulates that '[s]pecial measures established by law and aimed at ensuring equal opportunities for various social groups in accordance with

[20] G Tunkin, *Teoriya mezhdunarodnogo prava* [*Theory of International Law*] (Moscow, Zertsalo, 2000), 16.

[21] cf Cassese's concept of 'the fundamental principles of international relations', as explained in P Gaeta, JE Viñuales and S Zappalà, *Cassese's International Law*, 3rd edn (Oxford, Oxford University Press, 2020), 45–76.

[22] Lukashuk (n 12), 296.

[23] For the text of the Friendly Relations Declaration, see: www.jus.uio.no/english/services/library/treaties/01/1-01/friendly-relations.html.

[24] For the text of the Helsinki Final Act, see: www.osce.org/files/f/documents/5/c/39501.pdf.

[25] See Chapter 6, section V.H and Chapter 7 section II.B below.

[26] See Chapter 6, section VII.C below.

international obligations do not constitute discrimination'. Further, the second sentence of Article 51(2) provides that '[p]ersons who are citizens of the Kyrgyz Republic shall be recognised as belonging to the citizenship of another state in accordance with the laws and treaties to which the Kyrgyz Republic is a party'. Article 52(1) is fairly similar to Article 12(4) of the Constitution of Kazakhstan in that it reads as follows:

> In the Kyrgyz Republic, foreign citizens and stateless persons have rights and obligations on an equal footing with citizens of the Kyrgyz Republic, except for cases established by laws or treaties that have entered into force in accordance with the procedure established by law, to which the Kyrgyz Republic is a party.

In turn, pursuant to Article 52(2), '[t]he Kyrgyz Republic, in accordance with its international obligations, shall provide political asylum to foreign citizens and stateless persons persecuted for political reasons, as well as for violations of human rights and freedoms'.

Article 55 provides further that

> [i]n the Kyrgyz Republic, human and civil rights and freedoms are recognised and guaranteed in accordance with the generally recognised principles and norms of international law, as well as treaties that have entered into force in the manner prescribed by law, to which the Kyrgyz Republic is a party.

Importantly, Article 58(5) of Kyrgyzstan's Constitution is unique in Central Asia in that it rules that '[e]very person has the right to apply for the protection of their violated rights and freedoms to international human rights bodies in accordance with international treaties that have entered into force in the manner prescribed by law'. Last but not least, domestic remedies are guaranteed by Article 61(1): 'Everyone shall be guaranteed judicial protection of his rights and freedoms provided for by the Constitution, laws, treaties to which the Kyrgyz Republic is a party, and generally recognised principles and norms of international law'. An overview of the human rights developments in Kyrgyzstan is offered in Chapter thirteen, section III.B below.

C. Tajikistan

The Constitution of the Republic of Tajikistan was adopted on 6 November 1994.[27] The third paragraph of Article 10 of the Constitution provides:

> International legal acts recognised by Tajikistan are an integral part of the legal system of the republic. In case of non-compliance of the laws of the republic with recognised international legal acts, the norms of international legal acts shall be applied.

[27] For the text of the Constitution of the Republic of Tajikistan (in Russian), see: mfa.tj/ru/main/tadzhikistan/konstitutsiya.

It appears from this provision that Tajikistan accords weight to positive international law but not to international custom or other unwritten sources of international law. Although the phrase 'international legal acts' could in theory encompass, for example, unilateral acts of States (see Chapter seven, section II.D below), in practical terms, it is likely to be limited to treaties and, at most, legally binding acts of international organisations.[28] The most recent edition of the Law 'On Treaties of the Republic of Tajikistan' was adopted on 23 July 2016.[29]

Article 11 appears to reflect a dualist perspective:

> Tajikistan, pursuing a peaceful policy, respects the sovereignty and independence of other states, determines its foreign policy on the basis of international norms.
>
> Propaganda for war is prohibited.
>
> Tajikistan, guided by the highest interests of the people, can enter into commonwealths and other international organisations, as well as withdraw from them, and establish relations with foreign countries.
>
> The State shall cooperate with foreign compatriots.

The Constitution contains two more references to international law in the context of human rights. The first paragraph of Article 14 stipulates that '[t]he rights and freedoms of man and citizen are regulated and protected by the Constitution, laws of the republic, [and] international legal acts recognised by Tajikistan'. The first paragraph of Article 15 provides further:

> A citizen of Tajikistan is a person who, on the day the Constitution was adopted, was a citizen of the Republic of Tajikistan, or, in accordance with the legislation of the Republic of Tajikistan, or treaties of Tajikistan, acquired citizenship of the Republic of Tajikistan.

Some of the current human rights issues in Tajikistan are discussed in Chapter thirteen, section III.C below.

D. Turkmenistan

The most recent amendments to the Constitution of Turkmenistan (1992) were enacted on 21 January 2023.[30] The Constitution is unique in Central Asia in that it makes a direct mention of the United Nations, to reaffirm Turkmenistan's status as a permanently neutral State. Article 2 of the Constitution of Turkmenistan stipulates:

> Turkmenistan has the status of permanent neutrality, recognised by the world community and secured by law.

[28] See Chapter 7, section II.C below.
[29] See Chapter 6, section VII.D below.
[30] For the text of the Constitution of Turkmenistan (in Russian), see: online.zakon.kz/Document/?doc_id=31337929.

> The United Nations in the Resolutions of the General Assembly 'Permanent Neutrality of Turkmenistan' of 12 December 1995, as well as of 3 June 2015, recognises and supports the status of permanent neutrality proclaimed by Turkmenistan, calls on the Member States of the United Nations to respect and support this status of Turkmenistan, respecting also its independence, sovereignty and territorial integrity.
>
> The permanent neutrality of Turkmenistan is the basis of its domestic and foreign policy.

Given that resolutions adopted by the UN General Assembly are normally not binding,[31] one may wonder about the legal force of the respective resolutions of 12 December 1995[32] and 3 June 2015.[33] It should be recalled that both resolutions were adopted without a vote, which means they reflect a consensus among *all* UN Members.[34] It may therefore be argued that the permanent neutrality of Turkmenistan derives its legal force from this consensus, and is part of general international law.

The role of international law in the legal system of Turkmenistan is regulated by Article 9 of the Constitution:

> Turkmenistan, being a fully-fledged subject of the world community, adheres in foreign policy to the principles of permanent neutrality, non-interference in the domestic affairs of other countries, refusal to use force and to participate in military blocs and alliances, and promoting the development of peaceful, friendly and mutually beneficial relations with the countries of the region and all states of the world.
>
> Turkmenistan recognises the priority of generally recognised norms of international law.

The first paragraph of Article 9 is undoubtedly dualist in that it emphasises the role of the specified principles in Turkmenistan's foreign policy only. The principles mentioned in the paragraph (non-interference, prohibition of the use of force, and the promotion of friendly relations) were selectively implemented from Articles 1 and 2 of the UN Charter. In turn, the principle of permanent neutrality is the basis of both the domestic and foreign policy of Turkmenistan (cf the third paragraph of Article 2 of the Constitution).

Further, the second paragraph of Article 9 reads that 'Turkmenistan recognises the priority of generally recognised norms of international law'. This

[31] cf Arts 10–14 of the UN Charter. However, some resolutions of the UN General Assembly may codify legally binding rules, see: S Sayapin, 'The United Nations General Assembly Resolution 68/262 in the Context of General International Law (2015 2 *Evropsky politicky a pravni diskurz* 19; S Sayapin, 'Territorialnaya tselostnost Ukrainy v svete Rezolyutsii 68/262 Generalnoy Assamblei OON' ['The Territorial Integrity of Ukraine in the Light of the UN General Assembly Resolution 68/262'] (2014) 1–2(5) *Journal of Constitutionalism and Human Rights* 66.

[32] UN GA resolution A/RES/50/80A, available at digitallibrary.un.org/record/284240?ln=en.

[33] UN GA resolution A/RES/69/285, available at digitallibrary.un.org/record/795445?ln=ru&v=pdf.

[34] See: 'How Decisions are Made at the UN', available at www.un.org/en/model-united-nations/how-decisions-are-made-un.

provision does not specify that this priority extends to the domestic legal order. It should therefore be concluded from the context of Article 9 that its second paragraph is also meant to apply only in the context of international relations. Besides, unlike Article 6(3) of the Constitution of Kyrgyzstan,[35] the second paragraph of Article 9 of the Constitution of Turkmenistan makes no mention of 'principles' but only refers to generally recognised 'norms' of international law. It may be assumed that the superior status of 'principles' is accorded only to the rules specifically listed in the first paragraph of Article 9, whereas all other rules of international law are meant to be simple 'norms', even if they are 'generally recognised'. The Law 'On Treaties of Turkmenistan' was adopted on 10 May 2010.[36]

Article 11 pertains to the legal status of foreigners in Turkmenistan:

> Foreign citizens and stateless persons enjoy rights and freedoms, and perform duties in the same way as citizens of Turkmenistan, in accordance with the laws and treaties of Turkmenistan.
>
> Turkmenistan, in accordance with the generally recognised norms of international law, provides asylum to foreign citizens and stateless persons in the manner prescribed by law.

Notably, Articles 15 and 16 of this Law emphasise the significance of international cooperation in two areas. According to the third paragraph of Article 15, '[t]he state promotes the development of international cooperation in the field of culture, education, sports and tourism'. In turn, the first paragraph of Article 16 provides '[t]he state promotes the development of science, engineering and technology, and also supports international cooperation in these areas'. Finally, Article 25 stipulates that '[i]n Turkmenistan, the rights and freedoms of man and citizen are recognised in accordance with the generally recognised norms of international law and are guaranteed by this Constitution and laws'. For an overview of the human rights situation in Turkmenistan, see Chapter thirteen, section III.D below.

E. Uzbekistan

The first edition of the Constitution of Uzbekistan was adopted on 8 December 1992, and the new edition was adopted by a referendum held on 30 April 2023.[37] The fifth preambular paragraph of the Constitution reaffirms the 'priority of generally recognised norms of international law'.[38] International

[35] See section II.B above.
[36] See Chapter 6, section VII.E below.
[37] For the text of the Constitution of the Republic of Uzbekistan (in Russian), see: constitution.uz/ru.
[38] For comments on this concept, see section II.B above.

law is further mentioned in Chapter IV of the Constitution entitled 'Foreign Policy':

> Article 17
>
> The Republic of Uzbekistan is a fully-fledged subject of international relations.
>
> Its foreign policy is based on the principles of sovereign equality of States, non-use of force or threat of force, inviolability of frontiers, territorial integrity of States, peaceful settlement of disputes, non-interference in the internal affairs of other States and other generally recognised principles and norms of international law.
>
> Article 18
>
> The Republic of Uzbekistan pursues a peaceful foreign policy aimed at the comprehensive development of bilateral and multilateral relations with States and international organisations.
>
> The Republic can establish alliances, enter into commonwealths and other interstate formations, as well as withdraw from them, based on the highest interests of the State, the people, its welfare and security.

The fact that Articles 17 and 18 relate only to foreign policy leads one to conclude that Uzbekistan's approach to international law is dualist as a matter of principle. Article 6 of Uzbekistan's new Law 'On Normative Legal Acts' does not mention treaties among normative legal acts.[39] The fact that the primacy of international law is recognised in some domestic legal acts[40] could be interpreted as a technique of implementing international law in specific and selected legal areas. A new edition of the Law 'On Treaties of the Republic of Uzbekistan' was promulgated on 6 February 2019.[41]

Notably, the third paragraph of Article 23 of the Constitution stipulates that '[t]he State, in accordance with the norms of international law, takes care to maintain and develop ties with compatriots living abroad', and Article 24 mentions international law in the context of human rights of foreigners and stateless persons, in line with the dualist perspective:

> Foreign citizens and stateless persons who are on the territory of the Republic of Uzbekistan are provided with rights and freedoms in accordance with the norms of international law. They bear obligations established by the Constitution, laws and treaties of the Republic of Uzbekistan.

The constitutional rights and obligations (mostly pertaining to nationals of Uzbekistan, unless it follows from a specific provision that it applies to all persons) are laid down in Chapters VII–XI of the Constitution. For an overview of human rights in Uzbekistan, see Chapter thirteen, section III.E below.

[39] For the text of the Law (in Russian), see: lex.uz/docs/5378968.
[40] See, for example, Art 7 of the Civil Code of the Republic of Uzbekistan.
[41] See Chapter 6, section VII.F below.

III. LEGAL POLICY DOCUMENTS

At least four States of Central Asia have enacted legal policy documents dealing, among other things, with the role of international law in their respective domestic legal orders. Such a policy document for Turkmenistan does not seem to be publicly available. The following subsections highlight some of the key ideas in the legal policy documents, and offer some general observations.

A. Kazakhstan: Legal Policy Concept Until 2030

The Legal Policy Concept of the Republic of Kazakhstan until 2030 was promulgated by the President's Decree No 674 of 15 October 2021.[42] In accordance with its inaugural paragraph, the Concept 'is a document of the State Planning System, which determines the priority areas for the development of national law, law enforcement and judicial systems, foreign policy and foreign economic activity, as well as legal education and legal propaganda'.[43] The Concept consists of eight sections, whereby section 6 is devoted to the legal support of foreign policy and foreign economic activity. Notably, this is the only section in the Concept which explicitly mentions international law (although some other sections also occasionally refer to 'international experience', 'international standards', 'international and non-governmental organisations'. The fact that section 6 relates only to foreign policy and foreign economic activity is somewhat surprising, given the presence of the monist perspective in the Constitution.[44] The section is very concise (less than one page). It starts with a statement of purpose:

> The international legal aspects of the legal policy of the state in modern conditions are aimed at stabilising international relations and overcoming new global threats and challenges. In this regard, one of the main directions of policy is the legal support of the foreign policy and foreign economic activity of the state, taking into account the protection of its national interests.[45]

The 'national interests' are the section's key idea, and they are mentioned explicitly on two more occasions. On another occasion, the 'interests of the State' are referred to. The fourth paragraph in section 6 stipulates that

> it is important to take measures aimed at improving the quality of protection of the national interests in the process of drafting international legal documents and decisions within the framework of integration associations, as well as the quality component in the implementation of such obligations at the level of national legislation.

[42] For the text of the Concept (in Russian), see: adilet.zan.kz/rus/docs/U2100000674.
[43] ibid, section 1, first paragraph.
[44] See section II.A above.
[45] Concept (n 42), section 6, first paragraph.

The sixth paragraph stipulates further:

> In the course of planning and at subsequent stages of concluding treaties, it is important to proceed from the national interests of the Republic of Kazakhstan, carefully assess their sectoral expediency, and predict possible socio-economic and political consequences. High-quality assessment of the conclusion of treaties directly affects the level of protection of the interests of the state in the international arena.

Treaties and international legal obligations are further key ideas in section 6. Importantly, the third paragraph provides that 'a significant component of the national legislation will continue to be formed under the influence of the international legal obligations of the Republic of Kazakhstan'. The fifth paragraph reinforces this idea: 'In the future, it [will be] necessary to focus on improving the quality of law enforcement practice. First of all, the legislation in the field of treaties [must be] strictly observe[d]'. The final paragraph reaffirms that

> [i]t is necessary to ensure the mandatory and conscientious implementation of existing treaties of the Republic of Kazakhstan. In this regard, it is necessary to improve the quality of systematic monitoring of treaties. High-quality monitoring will allow timely development of adequate response measures in case of detection of instances of non-compliance with their obligations by international partners.

It appears from the general tone of section 6 that Kazakhstan will be moving towards dualism as a matter of practice, and that opportunities for a direct application of international law in the domestic legal system may, over time, be reduced.

B. Legal Policy Concept of the Kyrgyz Republic for 2023–26

The Legal Policy Concept of the Kyrgyz Republic for 2023–26 was approved by the President's Decree No 146 of 31 May 2023.[46] Unlike the 2021–25 Draft Concept previously developed by the Ministry of Justice,[47] the final approved version is notably concise and includes only a few brief references to international law. Thus, paragraph 6 in section 2 ('Improving the Rule-Making Processes') provides for an increasing role of justice authorities:

> – in the creation of an effective system of legal protection of the interests of the Kyrgyz Republic in international and foreign organisations, mechanisms for widely informing the international community and foreign investors about the legal reforms being carried out in the country …

[46] For the text of the Concept (in Russian), see: cbd.minjust.gov.kg/30-162/edition/1259268/ru.

[47] *Kaktus Media*, 'Minyust razrabotal proyekt Kontseptsii pravovoy politiki na 2021–2025 gody' ['The Ministry of Justice Has Developed a Draft Concept of Legal Policy for 2021–2025'], 10 September 2020, available at kaktus.media/doc/420615_minust_razrabotal_proekt_koncepcii_pravovoy_politiki_na_2021_2025_gody.html.

- in ensuring the conduct of fundamental legal research into legal factors that impede the improvement of the position of the Kyrgyz Republic in international rankings and indices on the rule of law.

Further, paragraph 7 in section 2 calls for organising

> close cooperation with the national human rights institute by obtaining relevant opinions on the development or improvement of legislation affecting the sphere of human rights and freedoms, in order to apply international standards for the protection of human rights, and strengthen legal protection and respect for the rights of citizens.

C. Legal Policy Concept of the Republic of Tajikistan for 2018–28

The Legal Policy Concept of the Republic of Tajikistan for 2018–28 was enacted by the President's Decree No 1005 of 6 February 2018.[48] The Concept contains numerous references to international law.[49] After a general observation on the effect of Tajikistan's 'active participation in various international organisations, in international economic, social, political and cultural relations' (paragraph 9), the Concept makes a key statement on the relationship between international and domestic law (in paragraph 12):

> Along with the inclusion of international normative legal acts in the national legal system, the most important problem is their correlation and alignment. The correct resolution is determined with due regard to the actual relationship between them in the course of applying international and national legal norms … At the same time, the adoption of international normative legal acts without their full analysis can lead to contradictions, inconsistencies and shortcomings in the legislation and, as a result, have a negative impact on the quality of laws … Since the legislation of the Republic of Tajikistan as a national legal system is in interaction with and under the influence of other legal systems. This situation requires their convergence, including coordination, unification and implementation of the norms of one legal system into the norms of another legal system.

Among the priority areas of domestic law requiring further development in accordance with Tajikistan's commitments under international law, the Concept specifically mentions international trade and taxation (paragraph 20), customs law (paragraph 22), criminal law (paragraph 26), criminal procedure (paragraph 29), energy law (paragraph 38), tourism (paragraphs 47–48), civil procedure (paragraph 53), and fair trial standards (paragraph 57). For this, Tajikistan intends to train

[48] For the text of the Decree (in Russian), see: portali-huquqi.tj/publicadliya/view_qonunhoview.php?showdetail=&asosi_id=20685.

[49] For the text of the Concept (in Russian), see: portali-huquqi.tj/publicadliya/view_qonunhoview.php?showdetail=&asosi_id=20686.

> highly qualified legal personnel ready for legal activities in the context of expanding and intensifying international relations, improv[e] educational policy in the field of training legal personnel; increas[e] the level of study of international law, taking into account the prospect of resolving legal disputes in international courts, [enable] advanced training after receiving a higher professional legal education [paragraph 60].

Section 6 of the Concept is entitled 'International Legal Policy', and reflects, in a detailed manner, Tajikistan's approaches to the role of international law as a foreign policy tool. Paragraph 70 singles out the following 'national goals and interests':

- protection and strengthening of the State independence of Tajikistan and ensuring its national security at the international level;
- creation of a zone of security and good neighborliness along the borders of the country;
- development of trusting relations, friendship and cooperation with all countries of the world on the basis of mutual interests;
- creation of favorable conditions for economic, social, cultural development and gradual improvement of people's living standards, ensuring the economic security of the country;
- ensuring the energy security of Tajikistan, achieving food security and leading the country out of the communication impasse through the establishment of international cooperation;
- ensuring and protecting the rights and freedoms, esteem and interests of citizens of Tajikistan abroad;
- strengthening the external image of Tajikistan in the world as a democratic, legal and secular State;
- assistance to the cultural and legal activities of the societies of Tajiks and compatriots in other countries.

Paragraph 73 emphasises further that '[t]he foreign policy of Tajikistan is based on unconditional respect for international law and is aimed at achieving [the above] goals and national interests'. Paragraph 74 recognises that,

> [d]iscrepancies between the norms of national law and international law, economic and social threats, international conflicts, proliferation of nuclear, chemical and biological weapons, international terrorism, extremism, separatism, transnational organised crimes, imperfect guarantees of world and regional security, mismatch of interests of superpowers, non-settlement of conflicts between countries, the clash of civilisations, the unresolved disputes related to water in the region and the world, disrespect for democracy and the infringement of human rights negatively affect the effectiveness of international legal policy.

In fairness, it appears that 'discrepancies between the norms of national law and international law' do not pose the same level of danger as the other factors listed in paragraph 74. In fact, international law – duly implemented within the domestic legal order – is capable of contributing to mitigating those other threats, provided that the following comprehensive measures are taken (paragraph 75):

- determine the real situation of national legislation in accordance with the process of development of relations between international public and private law;

- constantly, accurately analyse and eliminate contradictions between national legislation and acts of international law recognised by Tajikistan;
- make wider use of the right to express reservations and their forms in the process of giving consent to the conclusion of multilateral international treaties, in particular in the economic, social and cultural spheres;
- create a healthy competitive environment for national companies in the implementation of foreign economic activity by organising transnational companies of Tajikistan in the fields of energy and drinking water supply;
- expand international legal relations, taking into account the interests and risks of the merger of the world economy in conjunction with regional and interregional cooperation, the strong preservation of identity, national consciousness and self-knowledge;
- expand bilateral and multilateral mutually beneficial cooperation in the use of water resources, including the implementation of the provisions of the resolution of the United Nations General Assembly on the International Decade for Action 'Water for Sustainable Development 2018–2028';
- promote the creation of and entry into new economic unions in order to create a single market, free movement of people, free delivery of goods, works and services;
- expand bilateral and multilateral international legal cooperation in combating international offences, including international terrorism, extremism, separatism, transnational organised crime, etc.;
- improve the activities of consular offices in foreign countries, including the consular agency at airports and railway stations of countries in which or in the neighbourhood of which armed conflicts occur, in order to prevent the entry of citizens of the country into extremist groups;
- expand international legal cooperation with the International Nuclear Energy Agency, the European Union and other international organisations and institutions in order to solve environmental problems, including the neutralisation and destruction of radioactive waste in the country;
- intensify bilateral and multilateral international legal cooperation on climate change issues, including preventing the melting of the country's glaciers;
- expand international legal cooperation in the field of labour migration, with due regard to the protection of the rights of Tajik migrants in foreign countries.

D. Uzbekistan: Presidential Decree 'On Measures to Further Improve the Activities of Bodies and Institutions of Justice in the Implementation of State Legal Policy'

On 19 May 2020, the President of Uzbekistan promulgated Decree UP-5007 'On Measures to Further Improve the Activities of Bodies and Institutions of Justice in the Implementation of State Legal Policy'.[50] The broad aim of the Decree is

[50] For the text of the Decree (in Russian), see: lex.uz/ru/docs/4820075.

> further improvement of the activities of the bodies and institutions of justice for the qualitative organisation of a unified state legal policy, including rule-making activities, the formation of consistent and uniform law enforcement practice, ensuring the effectiveness of the public administration system, improving the legal culture of the population, providing qualified legal assistance to citizens, as well as for the purpose of extensive implementation of digital technologies in the field.[51]

The attached Concept deals with numerous aspects of international law. Thus, paragraph 4 stresses the importance of:

> [e]nsuring the implementation of tasks to fulfil obligations under treaties in the field of intellectual property, to which the Republic of Uzbekistan has acceded.
>
> [s]tudying the issues of accession of the Republic of Uzbekistan to other treaties in the field of intellectual property and preparing proposals for joining them in the future.

Further, paragraph 7 explicitly refers to '[t]aking measures for a phased introduction of international standards in the field of human rights protection'. As noted in section II.E above, the Constitution of Uzbekistan does not currently provide for direct application of international human rights standards for everyone, and the proposed reform is therefore groundbreaking. Importantly, paragraph 8, entitled 'Development and further strengthening of international legal cooperation, ensuring legal protection of the interests of the Republic of Uzbekistan in international and foreign organisations' lists pragmatic measures related to international law and cooperation in every sentence:

- Activation of cooperation with representative offices of international organisations in the Republic of Uzbekistan and relations with foreign donors through the implementation of joint projects.
- Strengthening work on organising foreign internship, seminars and training courses for employees of bodies and institutions of justice, with the participation of international experts.
- Studying the issue of expanding the legal base of the Ministry with the relevant authorities of foreign countries and establishing cooperation with international legal organisations.
- Taking measures for the timely, efficient and high-quality consideration of appeals and requests for international legal assistance with the definition of the competence of authorised bodies.
- Intensification of work to increase the level of legal awareness of the international community about ongoing reforms in all spheres of public and state life, and positive trends in the protection of human rights and freedoms.
- Establishing close and constructive cooperation with international ranking agencies, in particular ranking agencies in the legal field.
- Establishing strong partnerships with international ranking and index organisations assigned to the Ministry, such as the World Bank Development Research Group, The World Justice Project, and The Economist Intelligence Unit (UK).

[51] ibid.

- Establishing the practice of evaluating legal acts in terms of their impact on the position of the Republic of Uzbekistan in international rankings and indices.
- Implementation of international standards (in particular, ISO 37001 (anti-bribery management system) and others) in the areas of activity of the Ministry in order to strengthen international prestige and trust.
- Establishing the practice of periodic advanced training of employees of the Ministry involved in the process of considering citizens' complaints about violations of their rights and freedoms received from international organisations, including the UN Human Rights Committee …
- Use, in the process of developing agreements (contracts) aimed at attracting investments, of alternative mechanisms for resolving disputes in pre-trial order, including ensuring measures for the enforcement of obligations in accordance with the Uniform Rules for Demand Guarantees (URDG) of the International Chamber of Commerce, as well as achieving dispute resolution through the institution of mediation.
- Expansion of the scale of international legal forums held in the country, in particular the International Legal Forum '*Tashkent Law Spring*', increasing their prestige and attractiveness.
- Assistance in the formation of a new generation of experts, capable of objectively assessing the progress and results of the reforms being implemented in the country.
- Establishment of a unified procedure for organising activities to protect the interests of Uzbekistan in international arbitrations and courts of foreign states.

The Concept also discusses, in paragraph 9, ways to improve the quality of secondary and higher education in the area of law, among other things, by developing and publishing quality textbooks, involving local and foreign law practitioners in the process of education, strengthening the potential of local law schools, and establishing branches of foreign ones. The ambitious character of the proposed measures is truly impressive. Their outcomes may already be seen from a medium-term perspective.

IV. FOREIGN POLICY DOCUMENTS

All Central Asian States have also enacted Foreign Policy Concepts where the role of international law specifically in foreign policy is discussed. In the case of Uzbekistan, the Concept, although enacted in 2012, does not seem to be publicly available, so a few general observations are offered on the basis of open sources.

A. Foreign Policy Concept of Kazakhstan for 2020–30

The President of Kazakhstan approved a Foreign Policy Concept for 2020–30 by his Decree No 280 of 6 March 2020.[52] The Concept discusses, in a

[52] For the text of the Concept (in Russian), see: adilet.zan.kz/rus/docs/U2000000280.

comprehensive manner, Kazakhstan's prospective approaches to modern challenges such as:

> a crisis of confidence and an increase in conflict, including as a result of a decrease in the functionality of multilateral institutions for security and dialogue, the low effectiveness of preventive diplomacy and conflict resolution mechanisms;
>
> erosion of the fundamental principles of international law, a clash on a global scale of two main trends – globalism and nationalism, which creates serious risks for medium and small states;
>
> exacerbation of traditional challenges and threats to security, such as terrorism, extremism, the arms race, including missiles, nuclear weapons and space, climate change and a number of others;
>
> the emergence of new factors of influence on geopolitics and geoeconomics, including those related to the development of information and communication technologies, the phenomena of hybrid and cyber warfare;
>
> erosion of the modern model of globalization and the international trading system, an increase in the gap in economic and technological development between countries and regions, the vulnerability of the global financial system, the tightening of trade and currency wars, and sanctions confrontation.[53]

In view of the above challenges, Kazakhstan's foreign policy priorities are grouped into four thematic areas (Chapter 5 of the Concept).

To contribute to the maintenance of international peace and security, Kazakhstan focuses, inter alia, on the promotion of the Principles and Purposes of the United Nations (paragraph 1.1), nuclear disarmament (paragraph 1.3), arms control (paragraph 1.4), combating international terrorism and extremism (paragraph 1.6), and addressing cyberthreats (paragraph 1.7).

In the area of economic diplomacy, priorities include a structural transformation of the national economy (paragraph 2.1), attracting foreign investments (paragraph 2.2), the digitalisation of the economy (paragraph 2.3), the 'green economy' (paragraph 2.4), and contributing to an efficient functioning of the international trade system (paragraph 2.12).

In the area of human rights, humanitarian diplomacy and protection of the environment, Kazakhstan is determined to combat illegal migration and human trafficking (paragraph 3.4), to continue concluding bilateral agreements on mutual legal aid (paragraph 3.6), to improve the legal regulation of the use of transboundary water resources (paragraph 3.17), and to respond to the consequences of the desertification of the Aral Sea (paragraph 3.18).

As far as priorities in the area of regional and multilateral diplomacy are concerned, these include enhancing cooperation, in appropriate formats, with the Russian Federation, China, the United States, the States of Central Asia, the European Union (EU) and its individual Members (paragraph 4.2), and the

[53] See chapter 1 of the Concept.

Commonwealth of Independent States (paragraph 4.4); ensuring compliance with the Convention on the Legal Status of the Caspian Sea (paragraph 4.6); reinforcing relations with the nations of East, Southeast, and Southeast Asia, Near and Middle East, North Africa (paragraph 4.8), North and South America, and the Caribbean and Africa (paragraph 4.9); and developing interaction with international and regional economic and financial institutions (paragraph 4.10).

Obviously, the role of international law in the realisation of these priorities will be crucial, and although formally external to the country, these processes will also have profound effects on the situation within the country.

B. Foreign Policy Concept of Kyrgyzstan

The current Foreign Policy Concept of the Kyrgyz Republic was enacted by the President's Decree UP No 37 of 11 March 2019.[54] Fairly concise, the Concept is 'a fundamental political document in the field of foreign policy of the Kyrgyz Republic, which contains a system of views on the content, principles and main directions of the foreign policy of the state, [and] determines its key priorities'.[55] The foreign policy of Kyrgyzstan rests upon

> the Constitution of the Kyrgyz Republic, generally recognised principles and norms of international law, the Law of the Kyrgyz Republic 'On the Interaction of State Bodies in the Field of Foreign Policy of the Kyrgyz Republic', the National Development Strategy of the Kyrgyz Republic for 2018–2040 and other regulatory legal acts of the Kyrgyz Republic, as well as treaties that have entered into force in accordance with the procedure established by law, to which the Kyrgyz Republic is a party.[56]

Chapter 2 of the Concept lays down the principles of Kyrgyzstan's foreign policy as follows:

> The Kyrgyz Republic pursues a pragmatic, balanced, open, multi-vector and consistent foreign policy.
>
> A pragmatic foreign policy is focused on creating favourable external conditions and opportunities for achieving the strategic goals of the State's development.
>
> The Kyrgyz Republic maintains a reasonable balance in interaction with external partners, taking into account national interests, and consistently implements its inalienable right to development.
>
> Building an open multi-vector foreign policy, the Kyrgyz Republic develops cooperation with all member states of the United Nations and international organisations on the basis of goodwill, mutual understanding and mutual respect of interests.

[54] For the text of the Concept (in Russian), see: cbd.minjust.gov.kg/430045/edition/949067/ru.
[55] ibid, first paragraph.
[56] ibid, second paragraph.

> Pursuing a consistent foreign policy, the Kyrgyz Republic stands for the conscientious fulfilment of the obligations assumed by all subjects of international law.
>
> International cooperation is carried out on the basis of generally recognised principles and norms of international law, enshrined in the Charter of the United Nations and other international documents to which the Kyrgyz Republic is a party, including the sovereign equality of states, non-use of force and threat of force, non-interference in internal affairs, respect for territorial integrity and the settlement of international disputes by peaceful means.
>
> The Kyrgyz Republic stands for strengthening international cooperation based on the principles of multipolarity, ensuring equal rights and opportunities for all United Nations Member States in the areas of international politics, security, economics, trade and other areas.

The specific priorities of Kyrgyzstan's foreign policy are listed under three headings. With respect to the political area, the Concept states, in particular, that

> in the context of globalisation, the importance of close cooperation of the Kyrgyz Republic with world and regional powers, associations and active players in the international arena is increasing. The foreign policy of the Kyrgyz Republic is aimed at broad, multifaceted and mutually beneficial cooperation with the main centres of international politics on the principles of mutual understanding and respect for interests and the maximum use of the achievements and resources of the world economy.[57]

Further, a timely and constructive observation with respect to the United Nations is offered:

> The United Nations, as the only global universal organisation, plays a key role in ensuring peace and international security. In order to strengthen the consolidating role of the United Nations and adapt its activities to modern realities, the Kyrgyz Republic stands for taking the necessary measures to improve the United Nations Security Council, which will take into account the interests of the vast majority of the world's states and be based on the principles of universality, efficiency and broad geographical representation.[58]

The Concept also emphasises the role of universal and regional international organisations:

> In order to promote national interests, assist in ensuring national and regional security and solve socio-economic problems, the Kyrgyz Republic actively cooperates within the framework of the United Nations, the Eurasian Economic Union, the Collective Security Treaty Organization, the Shanghai Cooperation Organization, the Commonwealth of Independent States, the Organization for Security and Cooperation in Europe, the Organization for Islamic Cooperation, the Cooperation

[57] ibid, section 4.
[58] ibid.

> Council of Turkic-Speaking States, the Economic Cooperation Organization and other international organizations.[59]

In the area of finance, economy, and ecology, '[t]aking into account national interests, the Kyrgyz Republic follows the strategic course of regional and international economic integration for the sustainable development of the country and improving the living standards of the population'.[60] The Concept calls, among other things, for a modernisation of the national economy, further liberalisation of international trade, further integration of the international transport and communication networks, ensuring the nation's food security and its commitment to a 'green economy'.[61] The protection of the environment is another important priority:

> In order to ensure environmental safety, preserve biodiversity and a favourable environment, the Kyrgyz Republic cooperates with foreign States and international organisations to take effective measures to adapt to climate change and mitigate its consequences. The environmental security of the country also includes the preservation of the zone of formation of water resources, the solution of the problems of uranium tailings on its territory, and the prevention and elimination of emergency situations, natural and man-made disasters.
>
> Ensuring the country's water and energy security is a priority in foreign policy. Water and energy diplomacy of the Kyrgyz Republic is aimed at promoting dialogue, forming an international legal framework and developing a mutually beneficial economic mechanism for the integrated and rational use of water and energy resources in the region.[62]

In the cultural and humanitarian arena, the Kyrgyz Republic makes it a priority 'to make full use of international cooperation to strengthen cultural, educational, scientific and human potential, to improve the healthcare system, and the quality of medical services, as well as to develop high technologies and innovations'.[63] Kyrgyzstan is proud of its nomadic heritage: 'The Kyrgyz Republic, being the founder of the World Nomad Games, will continue to contribute to the revival and preservation of the culture, identity and way of life of the nomadic peoples of the world'.[64] Kyrgyzstan also intends to capitalise on the diversity of its education market: 'One of the most important foreign policy priorities of the Kyrgyz Republic is positioning the country as a regional educational centre on the Eurasian continent'.[65] For more details on higher education in Kyrgyzstan, see Chapter thirteen, section III.B below.

[59] ibid.
[60] ibid.
[61] ibid.
[62] ibid.
[63] ibid.
[64] ibid.
[65] ibid.

C. Foreign Policy Concept of Tajikistan

The Foreign Policy Concept of the Republic of Tajikistan was approved by the President's Decree No 332 of 27 January 2015.[66] In accordance with paragraph 1.1, the Concept is 'a political document defining and regulating the basic principles, goals and objectives and priority areas of the foreign policy of the Republic of Tajikistan, with due regard to the long-term national interests of the country'. Pursuant to paragraph 1.3,

> [t]he legal basis of the Concept is constituted by the Constitution of the Republic of Tajikistan, laws and regulations governing the activities of state bodies of the country in the field of foreign policy, international legal acts recognised by the Republic of Tajikistan.

Paragraph 1.4 lists the principles of Tajikistan's foreign policy:

- recognition of equality, respect for the sovereignty and territorial integrity of states, inviolability of borders, non-use of force and threat of force in international relations, commitment to the peaceful settlement of disputes and conflicts, non-interference in each other's internal affairs;
- respect for human rights and fundamental freedoms;
- fulfilment of obligations arising from international law;
- observance of the principle of the supremacy of international law in international relations;
- de-ideologization of interstate relations, the establishment and development of equal and mutually beneficial relations with all countries of the world community;
- rejection in international practice of any form of violation of rights.[67]

Like Article 11 of the Constitution of Tajikistan,[68] paragraph 1.4 of the Foreign Policy Concept unmistakably reflects a dualist approach. This conclusion is confirmed by paragraph 2.8: 'The foreign policy of the Republic of Tajikistan is a transparent and predictable policy and proceeds from the principle of recognition and commitment by the country to interstate treaties and generally recognised norms of international law'.[69] The foreign policy priorities of Tajikistan include bilateral diplomacy (that is, bilateral cooperation with States in all parts of the world – paragraph 3.1), multilateral diplomacy (cooperation with universal and regional international organisations – paragraph 3.2), economic diplomacy (further expansion of bilateral and multilateral foreign economic relations – paragraph 3.3), diplomacy of water cooperation in Central Asia (paragraph 3.4), cultural and humanitarian diplomacy (paragraph 3.5),

[66] For the text of the Concept (in Russian), see: mfa.tj/ru/main/view/988/kontseptsiya-vneshnei-politiki-respubliki-tadzhikistan.

[67] ibid.

[68] See section II.C above.

[69] Concept (n 66).

and information diplomacy (paragraph 3.6). Importantly, 'The Republic of Tajikistan is a supporter of the development of a set of international legal and ethical norms aimed at ensuring information security and full compliance with them in the global information space'.[70]

D. Foreign Policy Concept of Turkmenistan as a Neutral State

On 27 December 1997, the Halq Maslahaty (Parliament) of Turkmenistan adopted the Foreign Policy Concept of Turkmenistan as a Neutral State.[71] Remarkably, the Concept's second preambular paragraph confirms the unity of the internal and external policy of Turkmenistan:

> The foreign policy of Turkmenistan is a logical continuation of the domestic policy and is determined by the international legal status of permanent positive neutrality assumed by Turkmenistan voluntarily, as part of the implementation of the inalienable rights of a sovereign State.

The main objectives of Turkmenistan's foreign policy are:

- preservation and strengthening of the State sovereignty of Turkmenistan, the growth of its role and importance in the system of international relations;
- creation of the most favourable foreign policy conditions for the internal development of the State;
- defending and realising the national interests of Turkmenistan by all forms of diplomatic contacts established in international practice;
- ensuring the security of Turkmenistan by political or diplomatic means;
- development of constructive mutually beneficial cooperation with all foreign partners on the basis of equality and mutual respect;
- ensuring full compliance of foreign policy actions of Turkmenistan with international law and the UN Charter.[72]

Probably because of the State's permanent neutrality, the above provisions are worded in a very general way, as are the Concept's guidelines on bilateral and multilateral cooperation:

> When shaping the Concept of its foreign policy, Turkmenistan proceeds from the objective fact that Turkmenistan develops civilised relations with all States without exception, it does not have hostile relations with any of the foreign States, does not make territorial claims against anyone and no one makes territorial claims against it. The implementation of Turkmenistan's foreign policy tasks may not in any way infringe on the interests of other States or threaten their security.

[70] cf the position of the Russian Federation discussed in S Sayapin, 'Russian Approaches to International Law and Cyberspace' in N Tsagourias and R Buchan (eds), *Research Handbook on International Law and Cyberspace*, 2nd edn (Cheltenham, Edward Elgar Publishing, 2021).

[71] For the text of the Concept (in Russian), see: ir.rudn.ru/books/b1/p5/66.pdf.

[72] ibid.

> Turkmenistan is open to all forms of constructive international cooperation.
>
> Turkmenistan, as a member state of the UN, recognises its priority in resolving any issues within its competence. The adoption by Turkmenistan of the status of permanent neutrality does not affect the fulfilment of its obligations arising from the UN Charter and will contribute to the achievement of the goals of the United Nations.
>
> Based on the understanding of the special international legal status of Turkmenistan as a neutral state, this Concept confirms its international obligations in this capacity and determines the political, economic and humanitarian aspects of their implementation.[73]

The Concept includes a Declaration on the International Obligations of Neutral Turkmenistan in the Area of Human Rights. The Declaration formally reflects the letter and spirit of the key tenets of international human rights law:[74]

> Turkmenistan provides every person with the rights and freedoms enshrined in the Constitution, laws and generally recognised norms of international law, without any distinction whatsoever, as regards race, gender, language, religion, place of residence, political and other beliefs, national or social origin, property, official or other status.
>
> Human rights in Turkmenistan are inviolable, inalienable, guaranteed by the State and protected by law. No one can be deprived of any rights and freedoms or limited in rights except in accordance with the Constitution and laws.
>
> All people in Turkmenistan are equal before the law and are entitled, without any distinction, to the equal protection of the law. All people have the right to equal protection against any kind of discrimination that infringes on their rights.
>
> Every person has the right to have their rights restored by the competent State authorities in cases of violation of their rights granted by the Constitution and laws, enjoy equal access to effective remedies.
>
> Turkmenistan provides the political, economic, legal and other conditions necessary for the full realisation of human rights and freedoms, promotes the free development of the individual.
>
> To this end, a system of democratic institutions and procedures for the free expression of the will of citizens is being created in Turkmenistan, the equal existence of various forms of ownership and economic activity is being ensured, and national legislation is being formed that meets international human rights standards.
>
> Turkmenistan fulfils the obligations in the field of human rights arising from treaties to which it is a party. Turkmenistan is making the necessary efforts to regulate its relations with other States on issues related to the observance of human rights, including through the conclusion of bilateral and multilateral treaties and agreements.

[73] ibid.

[74] For an overview of the human rights situation in Turkmenistan, see Chapter 13, section III.D below.

Turkmenistan will regularly take part in the discussion of the problems of human rights and freedoms at the international level.

Turkmenistan guarantees the exact and strict observance of the provisions of this Declaration and considers it as the basis for the consistent democratisation of society and the State.[75]

E. Law 'On the Concept of the Foreign Political Activity of the Republic of Uzbekistan'

The Law ZRU-330 'On the Concept of the Foreign Political Activity of the Republic of Uzbekistan' was promulgated by the first President of Uzbekistan on 10 September 2012. In 2021, it was proposed to amend the Concept 'for the purpose of consistently implementing an open and pragmatic foreign policy of Uzbekistan and ensuring an accelerated implementation of the set strategic plans'.[76] At the time of writing, the Law is not displayed in the National legislation database Lex.Uz. As was reported in 2012, the main tenets of the Concept are as follows:

1) Uzbekistan reserves the right to enter into alliances, join commonwealths and other interstate formations, as well as withdraw from them, guided by the highest interests of the State, people, their welfare and security, priority areas for the modernisation of the country, current national legislation and accepted international obligations;
2) Uzbekistan pursues a peaceful policy and does not take part in military-political blocs, reserves the right to withdraw from any interstate entity in the event of its transformation into a military-political bloc;
3) Uzbekistan takes political, economic and other measures to prevent its involvement in armed conflicts and hotbeds of tension in neighboring states, and also does not allow the deployment of foreign military bases and facilities on its territory;
4) In accordance with the Constitution, the Law 'On Defence', the Military Doctrine, the Armed Forces of Uzbekistan are created solely to protect the state sovereignty and territorial integrity of the country, the peaceful life and security of its population and do not take part in peacekeeping operations abroad.[77]

In line with this policy, Uzbekistan suspended its membership in the Collective Security Treaty Organization (CSTO) in 2012.[78] It participates pragmatically in the activities of the Commonwealth of Independent States (CIS),[79] and has

[75] See n 71 above.

[76] Gazeta.Uz, 'V Kontseptsiyu vneshnepolitcheskoy deyatelnosti planiruyetsya vnesti izmeneniya' ['It is Planned to Make Changes to the Concept of Foreign Policy Activity'], 19 January 2021, available at www.gazeta.uz/ru/2021/01/19/foreign-policy/.

[77] ibid.

[78] See Chapter 3, section IV.D above.

[79] See Chapter 3, section IV.B above.

been an observer State in the Eurasian Economic Union (EAEU) since December 2020.[80] Negotiations on Uzbekistan's accession to the World Trade Organization (WTO) are progressing.[81] In recent years, Uzbekistan took measures to notably improve relations with its Central Asian neighbours, and is consistently emphasising the importance of regional cooperation.[82] It is hoped that steps such as these will help consolidate Uzbekistan's regional leadership role, and have a positive impact on the quality of life of its people.

[80] See Chapter 12, section II below.
[81] See Chapter 12, section I below.
[82] See Chapter 3, section IV.H above.

6

Law of Treaties

INTERNATIONAL LAW IS essentially about treaties.[1] The earliest known treaties date back to the fourth millennium BCE,[2] and throughout most of the history of international law, not only were treaties regarded as its foundation but they were indeed seen as an embodiment of 'sanctity'.[3] Modern international law is predominantly the written law of treaties and operates on the basis of the *pacta sunt servanda* rule.[4] This chapter lays out the fundamentals of the law of treaties – that is, how bilateral and multilateral treaties are negotiated, concluded, applied, amended or modified, suspended and terminated – and discusses how these rules are implemented in relevant domestic laws of the Central Asian States.

I. LEGAL FRAMEWORKS

A. The 1969 Vienna Convention on the Law of Treaties (VCLT)

The key document on the law of treaties is the Vienna Convention on the Law of Treaties of 23 May 1969 (in force since 27 January 1980).[5] Itself a treaty, the 1969 Vienna Convention lays down rules and procedures for States to follow in the process of making and applying treaties. The Convention serves as a basis for all Central Asian domestic laws on treaties.[6]

[1] HT Adilkariyev, *Mezhdunarodnoye pravo [International law]* (Tashkent, Tashkent State Law Institute, 2003), 59–61, 167–186; II Lukashuk and AH Saidov, *Hozirgi zamon xalqaro huquqi nazariyasi asoslari [The theoretical fundamentals of modern international law]* (Tashkent, Adolat, 2006), 179–201.

[2] AI Dmitriyev and WE Butler (eds), *Istoriya mezhdunarodnogo prava [History of International Law]* (Odessa, Phoenix Press, 2013), 72. See also O Butkevych, *U istokov mezhdunarodnogo prava [At the Origins of International Law]* (St Petersburg, Yuridicheskiy Tsentr Press, 2008), 253.

[3] cf Art 227 of the Versailles Treaty. See also M Sarsembayev, *Mezhdunarodnoye pravo v istorii Kazakhstana i Sredney Azii [International law in the history of Central Asia]* (Astana, Foliant, 2011), 31–51.

[4] Art 2(2) of the UN Charter: 'All Members, in order to ensure to all of them the rights and benefits resulting from membership, shall fulfill in good faith the obligations assumed by them in accordance with the present Charter'.

[5] For the text of the 1969 Vienna Convention, see: legal.un.org/ilc/texts/instruments/english/conventions/1_1_1969.pdf.

[6] See section VII below.

B. The 1986 Vienna Convention on the Law of Treaties between States and International Organizations or between International Organizations

The Vienna Convention on the Law of Treaties Between States and International Organizations or Between International Organizations was adopted at Vienna on 21 March 1986.[7] It is not yet in force. Its purpose was to adapt the 1969 Vienna Convention to the needs of international organisations, given that international organisations often engage in treaty-making. Some rules of the 1986 Vienna Convention have been implemented in the Central Asian domestic laws on treaties.[8]

C. The 1978 Vienna Convention on Succession of States in Respect of Treaties

The Vienna Convention on Succession of States in Respect of Treaties was adopted at Vienna on 23 August 1978 (in force since 6 November 1996). Its rules were pertinent soon after the Central Asian States gained independence in 1991 but are not reflected in the current domestic laws on treaties.[9] The Central Asian States may consider implementing some of these rules when they amend their domestic laws on treaties in the future.

II. CONCLUSION OF TREATIES

A. Definition of a Treaty

According to Article 2(1)(a) of the 1969 Vienna Convention, a treaty is 'an international agreement concluded between States in written form and governed by international law, whether embodied in a single instrument or in two or more related instruments and whatever its particular designation'. It follows from this definition and other related provisions that:

(1) treaties may be concluded between States but also between States and international organisations,[10] between such organisations,[11] or between other subjects of international law;[12]

[7] For the text of the 1986 Vienna Convention, see: legal.un.org/ilc/texts/instruments/english/conventions/1_2_1986.pdf.

[8] See section VII below.

[9] R Hakimov, *Problemy pravopreemstva gosudarstv v mezhdunarodnom prave* [*Issues of state succession in international law*] (Tashkent, Fan, 2008). See section VII below.

[10] Art 1(a) of the 1986 Vienna Convention.

[11] Art 1(b) of the 1986 Vienna Convention.

[12] cf the introductory sentence of Art 2 of the 1969 Vienna Convention.

(2) the written form of treaties is now preferred (and, indeed, standard) but the conclusion of treaties other than in writing is not excluded as a matter of principle;[13]
(3) unlike contracts between States and natural persons or legal entities, which are governed by commercial law or other areas of private law, treaties are governed by international law – that is, their subject-matter is covered by public international law,[14] and not private law;
(4) a treaty may consist of one or more related instruments;[15] and
(5) their particular designations do not affect their legal force – that is, all treaties are equally binding irrespective of their specific title (eg convention, covenant, statute, agreement, protocol, etc.). Only one treaty – the Charter of the United Nations – prevails over other treaties in the event of a conflict between the obligations of the UN Members under the Charter and their obligations under any other international agreement.[16]

As will be seen below, this definition's essential elements are duly reflected in relevant provisions of the Central Asian States' domestic laws on treaties.

Depending on the number of parties, treaties can be bilateral or multilateral. Bilateral treaties involve only two parties, whereas multilateral treaties involve three or more parties. Bilateral treaties regulate relations affecting only two parties, to the exclusion of any other parties. Indeed, some treaties can only be bilateral by their very nature – for example, treaties delimiting borders between States. In turn, multilateral treaties can be open to all States, or alternatively accession of new parties may be conditional upon the consent of existing parties.[17]

B. Authority to Conclude Treaties

Treaty-making is a sovereign function of States as primary subjects of international law.[18] States may also delegate this capacity to international organisations,[19] and recognise it on the part of prominent non-State actors.[20] The sovereign character of the treaty-making capacity is reflected, for instance, in Article 7 of Uzbekistan's law on treaties: 'The right to conclude treaties of the Republic of Uzbekistan belongs to

[13] II Lukashuk, *Sovremennoye pravo mezhdunarodnyh dogovorov [Modern Law of Treaties*], vol 1 (Moscow, Wolters Kluwer, 2004), 533–43; MN Shaw, *International Law*, 9th edn (Cambridge, Cambridge University Press, 2021), 789.

[14] ibid, 78.

[15] cf, for example, the Marrakesh Agreement establishing the World Trade Organization and its Annexes, which are accepted by WTO Members as an integral whole (see Chapter 11 below).

[16] cf Art 103 of the UN Charter.

[17] This is typical for some treaties establishing international organisations. See, for example, Art 10 of the North Atlantic Treaty of 4 April 1949.

[18] Art 6 of the 1969 Vienna Convention.

[19] Art 6 of the 1986 Vienna Convention: 'The capacity of an international organization to conclude treaties is governed by the rules of that organization'.

[20] Lukashuk (n 13), 103–23.

the State'. Similarly, Article 2(2) of Kazakhstan's law on treaties stipulates: 'It is not permitted to conclude treaties which do not correspond to the national interests of the Republic of Kazakhstan, [or] which can harm national security or lead to the loss of independence of the Republic of Kazakhstan'.

C. Full Powers

By default, a person or persons designated to represent a State or an international organisation for negotiating, adopting or authenticating the text of a treaty, for expressing the consent of the State or of the organisation to be bound by a treaty, or for accomplishing any other act with respect to a treaty require a document conferring full powers.[21] Such persons are expected to produce full powers, unless it appears from practice or from other circumstances that it was the intention of the States or international organisations concerned to consider those persons as representing them for such purposes without having to produce full powers.[22] In accordance with established practice, in virtue of their functions, the following officials are not required to produce full powers:[23]

(a) Heads of State, Heads of Government and Ministers for Foreign Affairs, for the purpose of performing all acts relating to the conclusion of a treaty between one or more States and one or more international organizations;
(b) heads of diplomatic missions, for the purpose of adopting the text of a treaty between the accrediting State and the State to which they are accredited;
(c) representatives accredited by States to an international conference, for the purpose of adopting the text of a treaty between States and international organizations;
(d) representatives accredited by States to an international organization or one of its organs, for the purpose of adopting the text of a treaty in that organization or organ;
(e) heads of permanent missions to an international organisation, for the purpose of adopting the text of a treaty between the accrediting States and that organization.

These rules are duly reflected in all Central Asian domestic laws on treaties,[24] with reasonable variations. Importantly, an act relating to the conclusion of a treaty performed by a person who cannot be considered authorised to represent

[21] Art 2(1)(c) of the 1969 Vienna Convention, Art 2(1)(c) of the 1986 Vienna Convention.

[22] Art 7(1) of the 1969 Vienna Convention, Art 7(1) of the 1986 Vienna Convention. See also Lukashuk (n 13), 378–88.

[23] Art 7(2) of the 1969 Vienna Convention [(a)–(c)], Art 7(2) of the 1986 Vienna Convention [(a)–(d)].

[24] Arts 9–10 of Kazakhstan's law on treaties, Arts 9–10 of Kyrgyzstan's law on treaties, Arts 7–8 of Tajikistan's law on treaties, Arts 7–8 of Turkmenistan's law on treaties, and Arts 15–16 of Uzbekistan's law on treaties.

a State or an international organisation for that purpose is without legal effect unless subsequently confirmed by that State or that organisation.[25]

D. Negotiating a Treaty

The texts of bilateral treaties are negotiated directly by representatives of States, international organisations or non-State actors with treaty-making capacity. Multilateral (regional and universal) treaties are usually negotiated at international conferences. The negotiation of a treaty results in the adoption and authentication of its text. The adoption of the text of a treaty takes place by the consent of all the States and international organisations or, as the case may be, all international organisations participating in its drawing up.[26] The adoption of the text of a treaty at an international conference takes place in accordance with the procedure agreed upon by the participants in that conference. If no agreement is reached on any such procedure, the adoption of the text takes place by the vote of two thirds of the participants present and voting unless by the same majority they decide to apply a different rule.[27] The twelfth paragraph of Article 4 of Uzbekistan's law on treaties defines adoption as 'a sequence of procedures for forming the content of a treaty, accepting its text and expressing the consent of the Republic of Uzbekistan to be bound by the treaty'.

> The text of a treaty between States or between States and international organizations is established as authentic and definitive:
>
> (a) by such procedure as may be provided for in the text or agreed upon by the States participating in its drawing up; or
> (b) failing such procedure, by the signature, signature *ad referendum* or initialling by the representatives of those States of the text of the treaty or of the Final Act of a conference incorporating the text.[28]

In turn, the text of a treaty between international organisations is established as authentic and definitive:

> (a) by such procedure as may be provided for in the text or agreed upon by the organizations participating in its drawing up; or
> (b) failing such procedure, by the signature, signature *ad referendum* or initialling by the representatives of those States and those organizations of the text of the treaty or of the Final Act of a conference incorporating the text.[29]

[25] Art 8 of the 1969 Vienna Convention, Art 8 of the 1986 Vienna Convention.
[26] Art 9(1) of the 1969 Vienna Convention, Art 9(1) of the 1986 Vienna Convention.
[27] Art 9(2) of the 1969 Vienna Convention, Art 9(2) of the 1986 Vienna Convention. See also Lukashuk (n 13), 300–362.
[28] Art 10 of the 1969 Vienna Convention, Art 10(1) of the 1986 Vienna Convention.
[29] Art 10(2) of the 1986 Vienna Convention.

These rules and key notions have been implemented in the Central Asian laws on treaties.[30] Thus, the third paragraph of Article 2 of Kyrgyzstan's law on treaties provides that signature 'depending on the case, means establishing the authenticity of the text of a treaty (establishing the final form and content of a treaty) or a method of expressing consent to be bound by a treaty'. The third paragraph of Article 2 of Tajikistan's law on treaties defines initialling as

> preliminary signing of the agreed draft treaty or its individual norms, indicating the initials of the representatives of the parties participating in the negotiations, as a sign of consent to the text of the draft treaty, or one of the ways to establish the authenticity of the text of the draft treaty.

E. Consent to be Bound by a Treaty

There are several ways for States and international organisations to express their consent to be bound by a treaty, with due regard to the political level at which a treaty is concluded, and its subject-matter. In general terms, the consent of a State to be bound by a treaty may be expressed by signature, exchange of instruments constituting a treaty, ratification, acceptance, approval or accession, or by any other means if so agreed.[31] The consent of an international organisation to be bound by a treaty may be expressed by signature, exchange of instruments constituting a treaty, act of formal confirmation, acceptance, approval or accession, or by any other means if so agreed.[32]

More specific rules on the expression of consent to be bound by a treaty are found in Articles 12–17 of the 1969 Vienna Convention, and in Articles 12–17 of the 1986 Vienna Convention. In turn, Article 1(8) of Kazakhstan's law on treaties provides that consent to be bound by a treaty is expressed by means of signature

> in the event that the treaty provides that the signature has such force, or the agreement between the Republic of Kazakhstan and other parties participating in the negotiations is otherwise established that the signature should have such force, or the intention of the Republic of Kazakhstan to give the signature such force follows from the full powers of its representative, and (or) was expressed during negotiations.

If a treaty is subject to ratification, act of formal confirmation, acceptance or approval, signature may be withheld until those acts have taken place. However,

[30] See Art 8 of Kazakhstan's law on treaties, Art 9 of Kyrgyzstan's law on treaties, Art 7 of Tajikistan's law on treaties, Art 6 of Turkmenistan's law on treaties, and Art 16 of Uzbekistan's law on treaties.

[31] Art 11 of the 1969 Vienna Convention, Art 11(1) of the 1986 Vienna Convention. On the expression of consent to be bound by a treaty through referendum, see European Union, 'Lisbon Treaty Post-Referendum Survey Ireland 2009', available at europa.eu/eurobarometer/surveys/detail/834. See also Lukashuk (n 13), 401–33; Shaw (n 13), 793–97.

[32] Art 11(2) of the 1986 Vienna Convention.

a contracting State or international organisation is obliged to refrain from acts which would defeat the object and purpose of a treaty until that State or that organisation has made its intention clear not to become a party to the treaty, or until it has expressed its consent to be bound by the treaty.[33]

The laws on treaties explicitly list the categories of treaties which are subject to ratification by Parliaments.[34] Treaties that are not subject to ratification are accepted or approved by the top executive organs.[35] Accession is defined in the tenth paragraph of Article 2 of Tajikistan's law on treaties as 'a means of expressing the consent of the Republic of Tajikistan to a treaty, which has entered into force, [and was not originally] signed by its authorised representative'. Provisions on accession are found in Article 17 of Kazakhstan's law on treaties, Articles 16–17 of Kyrgyzstan's law on treaties, Articles 14–15 of Tajikistan's law on treaties, Article 16 of Turkmenistan's law on treaties, and Article 23 of Uzbekistan's law on treaties.

F. Reservations

A reservation is a unilateral statement, however phrased or named, made by a State or by an international organisation when signing, ratifying, formally confirming, accepting, approving or acceding to a treaty, whereby it purports to exclude or to modify the legal effect of certain provisions of the treaty in their application to that State or to that organisation.[36] Although the 1969 and 1986 Vienna Conventions do not stipulate it expressly, reservations can only be made to multilateral treaties. A reservation may be formulated unless:

(a) the reservation is prohibited by the treaty;
(b) the treaty provides that only specified reservations, which do not include the reservation in question, may be made; or
(c) in cases not falling under subparagraphs (a) and (b), the reservation is incompatible with the object and purpose of the treaty.[37]

Both Vienna Conventions further specify that a reservation expressly authorised by a treaty does not require any subsequent acceptance by the contracting States and contracting organisations or, as the case may be, by the contracting organisations

[33] Art 18 of the 1969 Vienna Convention, Art 18 of the 1986 Vienna Convention.
[34] Arts 11–14 of Kazakhstan's law on treaties, Arts 11–15 of Kyrgyzstan's law on treaties, Arts 11–12 of Tajikistan's law on treaties, Arts 11–14, of Turkmenistan's law on treaties, and Arts 18–21 of Uzbekistan's law on treaties.
[35] Art 15 of Kazakhstan's law on treaties, Art 18 of Kyrgyzstan's law on treaties, Art 13 of Tajikistan's law on treaties, Art 15 of Turkmenistan's law on treaties, and Art 22 of Uzbekistan's law on treaties.
[36] Art 2(1)(d) of the 1969 Vienna Convention, Art 2(1)(d) of the 1986 Vienna Convention. See also Lukashuk (n 13), 433–53; Shaw (n 13), 797–806.
[37] Art 19 of the 1969 Vienna Convention, Art 19 of the 1986 Vienna Convention.

unless the treaty so provides.[38] When it appears from the limited number of the negotiating States or negotiating organisations and the object and purpose of a treaty that the application of the treaty in its entirety between all the parties is an essential condition of the consent of each one to be bound by the treaty, a reservation requires acceptance by all the parties.[39] When a treaty is a constituent instrument of an international organisation and unless it otherwise provides, a reservation requires the acceptance of the competent organ of that organisation.[40] As a rule, reservations and objections to reservations may be withdrawn at any time.[41] Provisions on reservations are found in Article 19 of Kazakhstan's law on treaties, Article 25 of Kyrgyzstan's law on treaties, Article 17 of Tajikistan's law on treaties, and Article 26 of Uzbekistan's law on treaties. Turkmenistan's law on treaties does not contain any express rules on reservations.

G. Entry into Force

As a rule, a treaty enters into force in such manner and upon such date as it may provide or as the negotiating States or international organisations may agree.[42] For example, parties to a treaty may agree that it will enter into force after an agreed number of ratifications has been achieved,[43] or after a specified period of time has lapsed since the deposit of a certain minimum number of instruments of ratification.[44] Failing any such provision or agreement, a treaty enters into force as soon as consent to be bound by the treaty has been established for all the negotiating States and international organisations.[45] These regulations are duly reflected in all Central Asian domestic laws on treaties.[46] The laws of Tajikistan, Turkmenistan, and Uzbekistan specify additionally that treaties may enter into force in accordance with the laws themselves.

H. Registration and Publication

In accordance with both Vienna Conventions, treaties should, after their entry into force, be transmitted to the Secretariat of the United Nations for registration

[38] Art 20(1) of the 1969 Vienna Convention, Art 20(1) of the 1986 Vienna Convention.
[39] Art 20(2) of the 1969 Vienna Convention, Art 20(2) of the 1986 Vienna Convention.
[40] Art 20(3) of the 1969 Vienna Convention, Art 20(3) of the 1986 Vienna Convention.
[41] Art 22 of the 1969 Vienna Convention, Art 22 of the 1986 Vienna Convention.
[42] Art 24(1) of the 1969 Vienna Convention, Art 24(1) of the 1986 Vienna Convention. See also Lukashuk (n 13), 462–66; Shaw (n 13), 807.
[43] Art 110(3) of the UN Charter.
[44] Art 49(1) of the International Covenant on Civil and Political Rights.
[45] Art 24(2) of the 1969 Vienna Convention, Art 24(2) of the 1986 Vienna Convention.
[46] Art 23 of Kazakhstan's law on treaties, Art 18^1 of Kyrgyzstan's law on treaties, Art 20 of Tajikistan's law on treaties, Art 23 of Turkmenistan's law on treaties, and Art 25 of Uzbekistan's law on treaties.

or filing and recording, as the case may be, and for publication.[47] Where a depositary has been designated, these acts should be performed by the depositary.[48] In accordance with domestic laws, treaties are also published in official printed collections and digital databases.[49] The domestic laws on treaties also assign the depositary functions to the Ministries of Foreign Affairs and other relevant State organs.[50]

III. APPLICATION OF TREATIES

A. Performance in Good Faith

Pacta sunt servanda is an existential and system-building principle of international law.[51] Indeed, it is this rule that enables '[a]lmost all nations [to] observe almost all principles of international law and almost all of their obligations almost all the time'.[52] The rule stipulating that '[e]very treaty in force is binding upon the parties to it and must be performed by them in good faith' has been implemented in all Central Asian domestic laws on treaties, with reasonable variations. Article 20(1) of Kazakhstan's law on treaties reads that '[e]very treaty in force for the Republic of Kazakhstan shall be complied with by the Republic of Kazakhstan mandatorily and in good faith'. Article 31(1) of Kyrgyzstan's law on treaties provides similarly: 'Treaties of the Kyrgyz Republic are subject to strict compliance by the Kyrgyz Republic in accordance with the norms of international law and regulatory legal acts of the Kyrgyz Republic'. Article 18(1) of Tajikistan's law stipulates: 'A treaty is subject to compliance by the Republic of Tajikistan mandatorily and in good faith'. The singular noun used in this provision ('a treaty') should be interpreted as 'every treaty'. Article 17(1) of Turkmenistan's law on treaties provides: 'Treaties of Turkmenistan are subject to strict compliance by Turkmenistan represented by its State organs in accordance with the norms of international law'. Finally, the first paragraph of Article 33 of Uzbekistan's law on treaties reads: 'Treaties of the Republic of Uzbekistan

[47] Art 80(1) of the 1969 Vienna Convention, Art 81(1) of the 1986 Vienna Convention.

[48] Art 80(2) of the 1969 Vienna Convention, Art 81(2) of the 1986 Vienna Convention. For the functions of depositaries, see Art 77 of the 1969 Vienna Convention, Art 78 of the 1986 Vienna Convention.

[49] Arts 24–25 of Kazakhstan's law on treaties, Arts 26–29 of Kyrgyzstan's law on treaties, Arts 21–22 of Tajikistan's law on treaties, Arts 24–25 of Turkmenistan's law on treaties, and Arts 29–31 of Uzbekistan's law on treaties.

[50] Art 26 of Kazakhstan's law on treaties, Art 30 of Kyrgyzstan's law on treaties, Art 23 of Tajikistan's law on treaties, Art 25(2) of Turkmenistan's law on treaties, and Art 32 of Uzbekistan's law on treaties.

[51] Art 26 of the 1969 Vienna Convention, Art 26 of the 1986 Vienna Convention. See also II Lukashuk, *Sovremennoye pravo mezhdunarodnyh dogovorov [Modern Law of Treaties]*, vol 2 (Moscow, Wolters Kluwer, 2004), 1–29.

[52] L Henkin, *How Nations Behave* (New York, Columbia University Press, 1979), 47.

are subject to strict and mandatory execution by the Republic of Uzbekistan in accordance with the norms of international law'.

Importantly, a State party to a treaty may not invoke the provisions of its internal law as justification for its failure to comply with a treaty.[53] Likewise, an international organisation may not invoke its own rules as justification for its failure to comply with a treaty.[54] States or international organisations so invoking their law bear responsibility in accordance with applicable secondary rules of international law.[55]

B. Territorial Application

As a rule, treaties apply in respect of the entire territory of a State, including land, internal waters and, where applicable, territorial sea, airspace, and subsoil.[56] The jurisdiction of a State also extends to its warships, military aircraft and military bases located abroad, as well as to its civilian vessels and aircraft, respectively, in international waters and airspace, subject to more specific provisions of domestic laws.[57] Where a State's jurisdiction over (a part of) its territory is limited as a matter of fact – for example, in the situation of military occupation – its ability to enforce treaties in the territory beyond its control is restricted accordingly.

C. Temporal Application

As a rule, treaties do not apply retroactively – that is, in accordance with Article 28 common to the 1969 and 1986 Vienna Conventions,

> [u]nless a different intention appears from the treaty or is otherwise established, its provisions do not bind a party in relation to any act or fact which took place or any situation which ceased to exist before the date of the entry into force of the treaty with respect to that party.

Unless a treaty is concluded for a specific term (with or without the possibility of prolongation) or its termination is made conditional upon a specific circumstance scheduled (or expected) to emerge in the future, its term of application is indefinite.

[53] Art 27 of the 1969 Vienna Convention, Art 27(1) of the 1986 Vienna Convention.
[54] Art 27(2) of the 1986 Vienna Convention.
[55] See Chapter 9 below.
[56] Art 29 of the 1969 Vienna Convention, Art 29 of the 1986 Vienna Convention. See also Lukashuk (n 51), 46–47.
[57] S Sayapin, 'Transnational and International Criminal Law' in S Sayapin et al (eds), *International Conflict and Security Law: A Research Handbook* (The Hague, TMC Asser Press, 2022), 472.

A treaty (or a part thereof) may be applied provisionally pending its entry into force if the treaty itself so provides, or the negotiating States or international organisations have agreed to this effect.[58] This rule has been implemented in Article 18 of Kazakhstan's law on treaties, Article 22 of Kyrgyzstan's law on treaties, Article 16 of Tajikistan's law on treaties, and Article 24 of Uzbekistan's law on treaties. Turkmenistan's law contains no rules on the provisional application of treaties. The provisional application of a treaty (or a part thereof) is terminated if a State or international organisation notifies its counterpart(s) of its intention not to become a party to the treaty.[59]

D. Application of Successive Treaties Relating to the Same Subject-Matter

The application of successive treaties relating to the same subject-matter is regulated by Article 30 of the 1969 Vienna Convention and Article 30 of the 1986 Vienna Convention.[60] The core rules of both provisions are identical:

> 2. When a treaty specifies that it is subject to, or that it is not to be considered as incompatible with, an earlier or later treaty, the provisions of that other treaty prevail.
>
> 3. When all the parties to the earlier treaty are parties also to the later treaty but the earlier treaty is not terminated or suspended in operation …, the earlier treaty applies to the extent that its provisions are compatible with those of the later treaty.
>
> 4. When the parties to the later treaty do not include all the parties to the earlier one:
>
> (a) as between two parties, each of which is a party to both treaties, the same rule applies as in paragraph 3;
>
> (b) as between a party to both treaties and a party to only one of the treaties, the treaty to which both are parties governs their mutual rights and obligations.

Importantly, paragraph 1 of Article 30 of the 1969 Vienna Convention is subject to, and paragraph 6 of Article 30 of the 1986 Vienna Convention explicitly restates the rule contained in Article 103 of the Charter of the United Nations to the effect that in the event of a conflict between obligations under the Charter of the United Nations and obligations under a treaty, the obligations under the Charter shall prevail.

Notably, these rules have not been implemented in the Central Asian domestic rules on treaties but they certainly apply as customary international

[58] Art 25(1) of the 1969 Vienna Convention, Art 25(1) of the 1986 Vienna Convention.
[59] Art 25(2) of the 1969 Vienna Convention, Art 25(2) of the 1986 Vienna Convention.
[60] Lukashuk (n 51), 47–60.

law. For example, the Minsk Convention on Legal Assistance and Legal Relations in Civil, Family, and Criminal Matters of 22 January 1993 was ratified by Armenia, Azerbaijan, Belarus, Georgia, Kazakhstan, Kyrgyzstan, Moldova, Russia, Tajikistan, Turkmenistan, Ukraine, and Uzbekistan. In turn, the Chisinau Convention on Legal Assistance and Legal Relations in Civil, Family, and Criminal Matters of 7 October 2002 was ratified by Armenia, Azerbaijan, Belarus, Kazakhstan, Kyrgyzstan, Russia, Tajikistan, and Uzbekistan. Therefore, their mutual relations with respect to legal assistance are now regulated by the 2002 Chisinau Convention but their relations with Georgia, Moldova, Turkmenistan, and Ukraine are still regulated by the 1993 Minsk Convention.

E. Self-executing Treaties

Depending on their effect on domestic legal systems, treaties can be self-executing or non-self-executing. Self-executing treaties apply directly, and do not require any implementing legislation to be adopted. In other words, executive or judicial organs within a State can base their decisions directly on self-executing treaties, as the position of such treaties within the respective legal order is determined. For example, Article 20-1 of Kazakhstan's law on treaties provides that treaties that have been ratified by the Republic of Kazakhstan and are in force take precedence over its laws and apply directly, except where a treaty's application requires the adoption of a law. Importantly, Article 3 of Uzbekistan's law on treaties stipulates that '[t]reaties of the Republic of Uzbekistan, along with generally recognised principles and norms of international law, are an integral part of the legal system of the Republic of Uzbekistan'. However, Article 3 does not specify the exact place of treaties in the hierarchy of normative legal acts. Article 6 of the Law of the Republic of Uzbekistan 'On Normative Legal Acts' of 20 April 2021 does not list treaties in the hierarchy of normative legal acts either.[61] The second paragraph of Article 33 of Uzbekistan's law on treaties does *imply* that some treaties are self-executing but does not offer any definite criteria:

> In cases where, in order to implement a treaty of the Republic of Uzbekistan, it is necessary to adopt an act of legislation of the Republic of Uzbekistan, interested government organs, in agreement with the Ministry of Foreign Affairs and the Ministry of Justice of the Republic of Uzbekistan, shall submit proposals for the adoption of an appropriate act on the implementation of the norms of the treaty of the Republic of Uzbekistan.

[61] For the text of the Law (in Russian), see lex.uz/docs/5378968#5383294.

The other Central Asian countries' laws on treaties do not contain any similar provisions, which means that in most cases, treaties are non-self-executing, and require domestic implementation.

F. Domestic Implementation of Treaties

Domestic implementation is the process of integrating rules of treaties in domestic legal acts, in order to give effect to the rules of treaties within domestic legal orders. For example, Article 32(2) of Kyrgyzstan's law on treaties lays down that

> the Government shall develop and carry out measures for the implementation of treaties of the Kyrgyz Republic and assign ministries, state committees, administrative departments and officials who are responsible for the fulfilment of obligations under treaties of the Kyrgyz Republic.

Article 18(2) of Tajikistan's law on treaties provides that 'the President of the Republic of Tajikistan or the Government of the Republic of Tajikistan shall take measures to ensure the implementation of treaties and assign the official or agency responsible for monitoring the implementation of treaties'. Article 18 of Turkmenistan's law on treaties is similar: 'The President of Turkmenistan and the Cabinet of Ministers of Turkmenistan shall take measures to ensure the implementation of treaties of Turkmenistan'. The designated State organs implement the rules of treaties in laws, regulations, orders, instructions, and other normative legal acts within their competence.

Technically, implementation occurs in three main ways. First, where appropriate, a State organ may incorporate a treaty rule into a domestic normative act verbatim. Second, the rule may be rephrased, in order for it to become compatible with the domestic legal technique. This method is known as transformation. Transformation does not change the substance of a rule but only its form. Third, a domestic legal act may simply refer to a treaty, without reproducing its substantive rules. A distinct advantage of this method is brevity but the resulting implementing legislation most certainly will require additional clarifications.

G. Treaties and Third States

As a rule, treaties do not create either obligations or rights for a third State or a third international organisation without the consent of that State or that organisation.[62] Exceptional situations whereby obligations or rights are created

[62] Art 34 of the 1969 Vienna Convention, Art 34 of the 1986 Vienna Convention.

by treaties for a third State are governed by Section 4 in Part III of the 1969 Vienna Convention, and Section 4 in Part III of the 1986 Vienna Convention. These rules are not found in the Central Asian domestic laws on treaties but they certainly apply as customary international law.

IV. INTERPRETATION OF TREATIES

In order for States, international organisations, and other subjects with treaty-making capacity to apply treaties properly, treaties should be understood correctly and uniformly by all parties. This may be especially challenging where a treaty was concluded in multiple languages. The law of treaties offers three main methods of treaty interpretation, which are used to establish the intended meaning of treaty provisions and terms used in treaties.[63] These methods have not been expressly implemented in any of the Central Asian countries' laws on treaties. An indirect indication relating to interpretation is found in the first paragraph of Article 33 of Kyrgyzstan's law on treaties, which states that interpretation of treaties 'shall be carried out in accordance with norms of international law'.

A. Language(s) of a Treaty

The 1969 and 1986 Vienna Conventions do not contain any explicit rules on the use of languages by negotiating States or international organisations.[64] The Central Asian States' domestic laws on treaties are more specific in this regard.

Article 7(1) of Kazakhstan's law provides that *bilateral* treaties with foreign States are concluded in the State language of the Republic of Kazakhstan and other languages by agreement of the parties, whereas bilateral treaties with international organisations are concluded in languages determined by agreement of the parties participating in the negotiations. In accordance with Article 7(2) of the same law, *multilateral* treaties are concluded in languages determined by agreement of the parties participating in the negotiations. Article 7(3) lays down that amendments to treaties are drawn up in the languages of their conclusion.

The first paragraph of Article 4(1) of Kyrgyzstan's law on treaties lays down that treaties are concluded in the State language of the Kyrgyz Republic, and in some cases, in the official language of the Kyrgyz Republic and (or) in the language

[63] Lukashuk (n 13), 629–42; Shaw (n 13), 813–18.
[64] Lukashuk (n 13), 531–33.

of the other party(ies) to the treaty.[65] In accordance with the third paragraph of the same article, by agreement of the parties to a treaty, another language may also be determined as the language of the treaty. The fourth paragraph specifies that the language in which the text of a treaty is drawn up is indicated in the text of that treaty. The fifth paragraph of the same article stipulates:

> If a treaty is concluded within the framework of an international organisation, the Kyrgyz Republic shall conclude such a treaty in the working language of this international organisation or in a language agreed upon by the parties [*sic*!] to the international organisation.

According to Article 6(1) of Tajikistan's law on treaties, '[b]ilateral treaties are concluded in the State languages of the parties participating in the negotiations. By agreement of the parties, other languages may be chosen as the languages of treaties'. Article 6(2) of the same law provides that multilateral treaties are concluded in languages determined by agreement of the parties participating in the negotiations. Article 6(3) lays down that amendments to treaties are introduced in the languages of their conclusion.

According to Article 10(1) of Turkmenistan's law on treaties, bilateral treaties of Turkmenistan are drawn up in two copies in the languages of the contracting parties, and both texts are recognised as legally equivalent (authentic).[66] By agreement of the parties, a treaty can be drawn up additionally in another language or only in one language. Article 10(2) of the same law lays down that multilateral treaties with the participation of Turkmenistan are drawn up either in the languages of the contracting parties, or, by agreement, in one language.

In accordance with the first paragraph of Article 5 of Uzbekistan's law on treaties, the languages of a treaty of the Republic of Uzbekistan are the State language of the Republic of Uzbekistan and the language of the other contracting party. The second paragraph of the same Article lays down that by agreement with the other contracting party, another language may be chosen as the language of a treaty of the Republic of Uzbekistan. The language in which the text of a treaty is drawn up is indicated in the text of this treaty, where its authenticity and officiality are determined.

B. Literal Interpretation

A treaty should be interpreted in good faith in accordance with the ordinary meaning to be given to its terms.[67] This method is fairly objective in that it involves

[65] The official language in Kyrgyzstan is Russian.
[66] For rules on the interpretation of treaties authenticated in two or more languages, see Art 33 of the 1969 Vienna Convention, Art 33 of the 1986 Vienna Convention.
[67] Art 31(1) of the 1969 Vienna Convention, Art 31(1) of the 1986 Vienna Convention.

analysis of the treaty content expressed in words, with due regard to their juridical meaning (as opposed to more general, or colloquial, meaning).[68]

C. Contextual Interpretation

Article 31(1) common to the 1969 Vienna Convention and the 1986 Vienna Convention mentions 'context' as the first subjective factor in the interpretation of treaties. According to paragraphs 2 and 3 of the same article, the wider context of a treaty includes the following elements:

> 2. The context for the purpose of the interpretation of a treaty shall comprise, in addition to the text, including its preamble and annexes:
>
> (a) any agreement relating to the treaty which was made between all the parties in connection with the conclusion of the treaty;
>
> (b) any instrument which was made by one or more parties in connection with the conclusion of the treaty and accepted by the other parties as an instrument related to the treaty.
>
> 3. There shall be taken into account, together with the context:
>
> (a) any subsequent agreement between the parties regarding the interpretation of the treaty or the application of its provisions;
>
> (b) any subsequent practice in the application of the treaty which establishes the agreement of the parties regarding its interpretation;
>
> (c) any relevant rules of international law applicable in the relations between the parties.

Although paragraphs 2 and 3 of Article 31 focus on rules of international law contained in treaties and other related agreements or instruments and the practice of their application, it is also helpful to consider non-legal factors – political, historical, economic, ideological, religious, and others – in the determination and analysis of intentions of parties to a treaty within specific contexts.[69]

D. Teleological Interpretation

The second subjective factor referred to in Article 31(1) common to the 1969 Vienna Convention and the 1986 Vienna Convention is the object and purpose of a treaty. This means that any interpretation leading to a conclusion conflicting with the object and purpose of a specific treaty is inadmissible. For example, given that the 1984 Convention against Torture prohibits torture in all circumstances, interpretations of the Convention resulting in the justification of torture in any circumstances, however limited, are unacceptable.

[68] Art 31(4) of the 1969 Vienna Convention, Art 31(4) of the 1986 Vienna Convention.
[69] Lukashuk (n 13), 634–639.

E. Supplementary Means of Interpretation

In accordance with Article 32 common to the 1969 Vienna Convention and the 1986 Vienna Convention, in addition to the three main methods of interpretation discussed above:

> Recourse may be had to supplementary means of interpretation, including the preparatory work of the treaty and the circumstances of its conclusion, in order to confirm the meaning resulting from the application of article 31, or to determine the meaning when the interpretation according to article 31:
>
> (a) leaves the meaning ambiguous or obscure; or
> (b) leads to a result which is manifestly absurd or unreasonable.

The preparatory work (*travaux préparatoires*) of a treaty includes 'the documentary evidence of the negotiation, discussions, and drafting of a final treaty text'.[70] More particularly, such evidence comprises official statements by representatives of States and international organisations made in the course of negotiations, diplomatic correspondence, draft treaty texts, and the like.

V. INVALIDITY OF TREATIES

The 1969 Vienna Convention and the 1986 Vienna Convention lay down, respectively, in Articles 46–53 eight grounds for the invalidity of treaties.[71] The first five grounds are relative,[72] whereas the last three ones are absolute.[73] These rules have been explicitly implemented (by reference to 'norms of international law') in Article 36 of Kyrgyzstan's law on treaties, and Article 39 of Uzbekistan's law on treaties.

A. Provisions of Internal Law and Rules of an International Organisation Regarding Competence to Conclude Treaties

States, international organisations and non-State actors with treaty-making capacity are entitled to presume that their counterparts act in conformity with their respective domestic laws and internal rules regarding competence to conclude treaties. Such competence is formalised by valid full powers of their representatives, or derives from the leadership status of such representatives within States or international organisations, which enables them to negotiate and conclude treaties

[70] Dag Hammarskjöld Library, 'What are travaux préparatoires and how can I find them?', available at ask.un.org/faq/14541.

[71] The consequences of the invalidity of a treaty are laid down in Art 69 of the 1969 Vienna Convention and Art 69 of the 1986 Vienna Convention.

[72] Lukashuk (n 51), 103–28.

[73] ibid, 128–57.

without producing full powers.[74] Consequently, provisions of a State's internal law or rules of an international organisation regarding competence to conclude treaties may only rarely be invoked as a ground for the invalidity of a treaty:

> 1. A State may not invoke the fact that its consent to be bound by a treaty has been expressed in violation of a provision of its internal law regarding competence to conclude treaties as invalidating its consent unless that violation was manifest and concerned a rule of its internal law of fundamental importance.
> 2. A violation is manifest if it would be objectively evident to any State conducting itself in the matter in accordance with normal practice and in good faith.[75]

Article 46 of the 1986 Vienna Convention contains a similar provision with respect to treaties concluded between States and international organisations or between international organisations. This ground for the invalidity of a treaty might be invoked, for example, where a representative of a State or an international organisation acted ultra vires but this excess of authority were related to a nuance in the domestic law or internal rules of the organisation that would not be obvious to a reasonable observer.

B. Specific Restrictions on Authority to Express Consent of a State or an International Organisation

In accordance with Article 47 of the 1969 Vienna Convention, if the authority of a representative to express the consent of a State to be bound by a particular treaty has been made subject to a specific restriction, his omission to observe that restriction may not be invoked as invalidating the consent expressed by him unless the restriction was notified to the other negotiating States prior to his expressing such consent. A similar provision is found in Article 47 of the 1986 Vienna Convention.[76] Such restrictions ought to be specifically mentioned in the full powers. This ground may be invoked, for example, in the unlikely situation where a State or international organisation meant to include the restriction in their representative's full powers but failed to do so by oversight.

C. Error

Pursuant to Article 48(1) of the 1969 Vienna Convention, a State may invoke an error in a treaty as invalidating its consent to be bound by the treaty if the error relates to a fact or situation which was assumed by that State to exist at the time when the treaty was concluded and formed an essential basis of its consent to be

[74] See section II.C above.
[75] Art 46 of the 1969 Vienna Convention.
[76] Lukashuk (n 51), 117–18.

bound by the treaty. A similar provision is found in Article 48(1) of the 1986 Vienna Convention with respect to international organisations.[77] Crucially, these rules do not relate to errors 'relating only to the wording of the text of a treaty'.[78] They pertain to essential facts or situations – that is, objective circumstances – whose correct assessment would have rendered the conclusion of the treaty unnecessary. Such errors include (but are not limited to) reliance on incorrect scientific or statistical data which forms the basis for the conclusion of a treaty.

D. Fraud

If a State, international organisation, or a non-State actor with treaty-making capacity was induced to conclude a treaty by the fraudulent conduct of its counterpart(s), it may invoke the fraud as invalidating its consent to be bound by the treaty.[79]

E. Corruption of a Representative of a State or of an International Organisation

Direct or indirect corruption is the last relative ground for the invalidity of treaties.[80] Article 50 of the 1969 Vienna Convention provides that if the expression of a State's consent to be bound by a treaty has been procured through the corruption of its representative directly or indirectly by another negotiating State, the consenting State may invoke such corruption as invalidating its consent to be bound by the treaty. Article 50 of the 1986 Vienna Convention contains a similar provision.

F. Coercion of a Representative of a State or of an International Organisation

Physical or psychological coercion of a representative of a State or an international organisation is the first absolute ground for the invalidity of a treaty.[81] Article 51 of the 1969 Vienna Convention provides that the expression of a State's consent to be bound by a treaty which has been procured by the coercion of its representative through acts or threats directed against him shall be without any legal effect, and Article 51 of the 1986 Vienna Convention provides the same with respect to the coercion of representatives of international organisations.

[77] ibid, 118–23; Shaw (n 13), 821.

[78] Art 48(3) of the 1969 Vienna Convention, Art 48(3) of the 1986 Vienna Convention. See also Lukashuk (n 51), 123–24; Shaw (n 13), 821.

[79] Art 49 of the 1969 Vienna Convention, Art 49 of the 1986 Vienna Convention.

[80] Lukashuk (n 51), 124–28; Shaw (n 13), 821.

[81] Lukashuk (n 51), 128–31; Shaw (n 13), 821–22.

G. Coercion of a State or of an International Organisation by the Threat or Use of Force

As the threat or use of force is outlawed by Article 2(4) of the UN Charter,[82] coercion of a State or international organisation by the threat or use of force is another absolute ground for the invalidity of a treaty.[83] Article 52 common to the 1969 Vienna Convention and the 1986 Vienna Convention stipulates that a treaty is void if its conclusion has been procured by the threat or use of force in violation of the principles of international law embodied in the Charter of the United Nations.

H. Treaties Conflicting with a Peremptory Norm of General International Law

Last but not least, in accordance with Article 53 common to the 1969 Vienna Convention and the 1986 Vienna Convention, a treaty is void if, at the time of its conclusion, it conflicts with a peremptory norm of general international law.[84] For a discussion of the *jus cogens* concept, see Chapter seven, section II.B below. Here, it suffices to say that a treaty concluded to legalise, for example, torture, slavery, genocide, aggression, or conflicting with any other peremptory norm of general international law would be void.[85]

VI. SUSPENSION AND TERMINATION: GROUNDS COVERED BY THE 1969 AND 1986 VIENNA CONVENTIONS

Freedom to conclude treaties generally also implies freedom to voluntarily terminate them,[86] or to suspend their operation if circumstances so require.[87] More specific rules on the suspension and termination of treaties are included in Section 3 of Part V of the 1969 Vienna Convention, and in Section 3 of Part V of the 1986 Vienna Convention. The relevant procedures have been generally implemented in Articles 28–30 of Kazakhstan's law on treaties, Articles 37–41 of Kyrgyzstan's law on treaties, Articles 25–27 of Tajikistan's law

[82] See Chapter 10, section II below.

[83] Lukashuk (n 51), 131–43; Shaw (n 13), 822–23; R Frau, 'The Law of Treaties and Ukraine's Resource Curse', *Völkerrechtsblog*, 11 March 2025, available at voelkerrechtsblog.org/the-law-of-treaties-and-ukraines-resource-curse/.

[84] Lukashuk (n 51), 143–57; Shaw (n 13), 823.

[85] The consequences of the invalidity of a treaty under Art 53 are laid down in Art 71(1) common to the 1969 Vienna Convention and the 1986 Vienna Convention.

[86] The consequences of the termination of a treaty are laid down in Art 70 of the 1969 Vienna Convention and Art 70 of the 1986 Vienna Convention.

[87] The consequences of the suspension of the operation of a treaty are laid down in Art 72 of the 1969 Vienna Convention and Art 72 of the 1986 Vienna Convention.

on treaties, Articles 26–27 of Turkmenistan's law on treaties, and Articles 40–50 of Uzbekistan's law on treaties.

A. Termination of or Withdrawal from a Treaty under its Provisions or by Consent of the Parties

The thirteenth paragraph of Article 2 of Kyrgyzstan's law on treaties defines the termination of or withdrawal from a treaty as 'discontinuing the application of a treaty in relation to a party to the treaty in accordance with international law'. Relatedly, Article 1(5) of Kazakhstan's law on treaties defines denunciation as 'a duly executed withdrawal of the Republic of Kazakhstan from a treaty concluded by it and one of the ways to terminate the validity of a treaty of the Republic of Kazakhstan'. The fourth paragraph of Article 4 of Uzbekistan's law on treaties contains an analogous definition applicable to treaties concluded by the Republic of Uzbekistan.

Article 54 common to the 1969 Vienna Convention and the 1986 Vienna Convention underlying the above provisions contains a general rule to the effect that:

> The termination of a treaty or the withdrawal of a party may take place:
>
> (a) in conformity with the provisions of the treaty; or
>
> (b) at any time by consent of all the parties after consultation with the other contracting States.[88]

Treaties allowing for withdrawal usually contain provisions specifying the period after which they will cease to have effect. For example, Article 127(1) of the Rome Statute of the International Criminal Court provides that

> [a] State Party may, by written notification addressed to the Secretary-General of the United Nations, withdraw from this Statute. The withdrawal shall take effect one year after the date of receipt of the notification, unless the notification specifies a later date.

B. Reduction of the Parties to a Multilateral Treaty below the Number Necessary for its Entry into Force

In accordance with Article 55 common to the 1969 Vienna Convention and the 1986 Vienna Convention, unless the treaty otherwise provides, a multilateral treaty does *not* terminate by reason only of the fact that the number of the parties falls below the number necessary for its entry into force.[89] For example, if a treaty requires 20 ratifications to enter into force (and enters into

[88] Lukashuk (n 51), 158–69.
[89] Lukashuk (n 51), 169–71.

force accordingly) but the number of parties subsequently drops below 20 as a result of one or more withdrawals, the treaty will remain in force for the remaining parties, unless they decide otherwise.

C. Denunciation or Withdrawal not Expressly Stipulated by the Treaty

As a rule, a treaty which contains no provision regarding its termination and which does not provide for denunciation or withdrawal, may not be denounced or withdrawn from, unless it is established that the parties intended to admit the possibility of denunciation or withdrawal, or a right of denunciation or withdrawal may be implied by the nature of the treaty.[90] In such cases, a party shall give not less than 12 months' notice of its intention to denounce or withdraw from a treaty.[91] Notable examples of treaties not containing any provisions on termination include the International Covenant on Civil and Political Rights and the International Covenant on Economic, Social and Cultural Rights, which is explicable by their nature: both Covenants are intended to protect the respective categories of human rights indefinitely.

D. Suspension of the Operation of a Treaty under its Provisions or by Consent of the Parties

Article 57 common to the 1969 Vienna Convention and the 1986 Vienna Convention contains a general rule with respect to the suspension of treaties:

> The operation of a treaty in regard to all the parties or to a particular party may be suspended:
>
> (a) in conformity with the provisions of the treaty; or
>
> (b) at any time by consent of all the parties after consultation with the other contracting States.[92]

This provision is reproduced verbatim in Article 40 of Uzbekistan's law on treaties. In turn, Article 37 of Kyrgyzstan's law on treaties provides that the suspension of a treaty of the Kyrgyz Republic is possible 'in accordance with norms of international law'. Article 26(1) of Tajikistan's law on treaties specifies that treaties are suspended in accordance with their own provisions, the norms of international law, and the provisions of the law on treaties. Article 29(1) of Kazakhstan's law on treaties is more specific in that it provides that treaties or their specific provisions

[90] Art 56(1) of the 1969 Vienna Convention, Art 56(1) of the 1986 Vienna Convention. See also Lukashuk (n 51), 171–75.

[91] Art 56(2) of the 1969 Vienna Convention, Art 56(2) of the 1986 Vienna Convention.

[92] Lukashuk (n 51), 175–76.

may be suspended 'in the course of the Republic of Kazakhstan taking retaliatory measures (countermeasures)'. The same provision stipulates that the application of treaties, or compliance with treaties or their specific provisions may be resumed after suspension in accordance with the treaty provisions, the norms of international law, and the provisions of the law on treaties.

E. Suspension of the Operation of a Multilateral Treaty by Agreement between Certain of the Parties Only

Article 58 common to the 1969 Vienna Convention and the 1986 Vienna Convention pertains to a specific scenario whereby the operation of a multilateral treaty is suspended by two or more parties thereto:

> 1. Two or more parties to a multilateral treaty may conclude an agreement to suspend the operation of provisions of the treaty, temporarily and as between themselves alone, if:
>   (a) the possibility of such a suspension is provided for by the treaty; or
>   (b) the suspension in question is not prohibited by the treaty and:
>   (i) does not affect the enjoyment by the other parties of their rights under the treaty or the performance of their obligations;
>   (ii) is not incompatible with the object and purpose of the treaty.[93]
> 2. Unless in a case falling under paragraph 1 (a) the treaty otherwise provides, the parties in question shall notify the other parties of their intention to conclude the agreement and of those provisions of the treaty the operation of which they intend to suspend.

This scenario is not specifically provided for in the Central Asian laws on treaties but since all of them contain general references to 'norms of international law', Article 58 common to the 1969 and 1986 Vienna Conventions may be resorted to in appropriate situations.

F. Termination or Suspension of the Operation of a Treaty Implied by Conclusion of a Later Treaty

In accordance with Article 59(1) common to the 1969 Vienna Convention and the 1986 Vienna Convention, a treaty is considered terminated if all the parties to it conclude a later treaty relating to the same subject-matter and it appears from the later treaty or is otherwise established that the parties intended that the matter should be governed by that treaty, or the provisions of the later treaty are so far incompatible with those of the earlier one that the two treaties are not

[93] ibid, 176–78.

capable of being applied at the same time.[94] Pursuant to Article 59(2) common to both Conventions, the earlier treaty is considered only suspended in operation if it appears from the later treaty or is otherwise established that such was the intention of the parties.

G. Termination or Suspension of the Operation of a Treaty as a Consequence of its Breach

Article 60 of the 1969 Vienna Convention and Article 60 of the 1986 Vienna Convention lay down rules on the termination or suspension of the operation of bilateral and multilateral treaties as a consequence of their material breach.[95] Article 60(1) common to both Vienna Conventions provides that a material breach of a bilateral treaty by one of the parties entitles the other to invoke the breach as a ground for terminating the treaty or suspending its operation in whole or in part. In turn, Article 60(2) of the 1969 Vienna Convention applies to multilateral treaties and stipulates as follows:

> 2. A material breach of a multilateral treaty by one of the parties entitles:
>
> (a) the other parties by unanimous agreement to suspend the operation of the treaty in whole or in part or to terminate it either:
>
> (i) in the relations between themselves and the defaulting State; or
>
> (ii) as between all the parties;
>
> (b) a party specially affected by the breach to invoke it as a ground for suspending the operation of the treaty in whole or in part in the relations between itself and the defaulting State;
>
> (c) any party other than the defaulting State to invoke the breach as a ground for suspending the operation of the treaty in whole or in part with respect to itself if the treaty is of such a character that a material breach of its provisions by one party radically changes the position of every party with respect to the further performance of its obligations under the treaty.[96]

Importantly, not just any breach may be invoked by a State or an international organisation as a ground to terminate a treaty or suspend its operation under these provisions, but only a material one. In accordance with Article 60(3) common to both Vienna Conventions, a material breach of a treaty consists in a repudiation of the treaty not sanctioned by the respective rules of the 1969 or 1986 Vienna Conventions, or the violation of a provision essential to the accomplishment of the object or purpose of the treaty. Minor breaches thus

[94] ibid, 178–82.

[95] ibid, 182–99; Shaw (n 13), 826–28.

[96] Art 60(2) of the 1986 Vienna Convention reproduces essentially the same rules with respect to treaties concluded between States and international organisations or between international organisations.

do not qualify as sufficient grounds for terminating a treaty or suspending its operation.

It follows from Article 60(4) common to both Vienna Conventions that a treaty may contain more specific provisions applicable in the event of a breach. If such provisions are present, they should prevail over the general regulations contained in the Conventions. Finally, Article 60(5) common to both Conventions provides that the foregoing rules 'do not apply to provisions relating to the protection of the human person contained in treaties of a humanitarian character, in particular to provisions prohibiting any form of reprisals against persons protected by such treaties'. Given that treaties of international humanitarian law were designed to apply in armed conflicts – that is, in the circumstances of extreme gravity – the restriction imposed by Article 60(5) is fully justified.[97]

H. Supervening Impossibility of Performance

In accordance with the first sentence of Article 61(1) common to the 1969 Vienna Convention and the 1986 Vienna Convention, 'a party may invoke the impossibility of performing a treaty as a ground for terminating or withdrawing from it if the impossibility results from the permanent disappearance or destruction of an object indispensable for the execution of the treaty'.[98] This rule may be invoked, for instance, where an endangered species becomes extinct, or where a unique work of art is destroyed. The second sentence of Article 61(1) stipulates that 'if the impossibility is temporary, it may be invoked only as a ground for suspending the operation of the treaty'.

In turn, Article 61(2) common to both Conventions provides that a party to a treaty may not invoke the impossibility of performance as a ground for terminating, withdrawing from or suspending the operation of a treaty 'if the impossibility is the result of a breach by that party either of an obligation under the treaty or of any other international obligation owed to any other party to the treaty'. This rule is in line with the customary maxim *ex injuria jus non oritur* ('A legal right does not arise from an unlawful act').

I. Fundamental Change of Circumstances

A fundamental change of circumstances (*rebus sic stantibus*), in the sense of Article 62(1) common to the 1969 Vienna Convention and the 1986 Vienna Convention, is another customary ground for terminating or withdrawing from

[97] On international humanitarian law, see Chapter 14 below.
[98] Lukashuk (n 51), 199–202; Shaw (n 13), 828.

a treaty.[99] However, with a view to preventing abuse of this doctrine by States or international organisations, Article 62(1) is worded in rigid terms:

> 1. A fundamental change of circumstances which has occurred with regard to those existing at the time of the conclusion of a treaty, and which was not foreseen by the parties, may not be invoked as a ground for terminating or withdrawing from the treaty unless:
>
> (a) the existence of those circumstances constituted an essential basis of the consent of the parties to be bound by the treaty; and
>
> (b) the effect of the change is radically to transform the extent of obligations still to be performed under the treaty.

Thus, in order to successfully invoke Article 62(1), a party to a treaty must show the cumulative existence of three conditions: (1) the change of circumstances was unforeseen – that is, sudden and not reasonably predictable in advance; (2) the change of circumstances was fundamental – that is, if the new set of circumstances had existed at the time of conclusion of the treaty, the treaty would not have been concluded; and (3) if the treaty remained in force for the party in question, it would radically transform the extent of its obligations under the treaty.

Importantly, with due regard to the principle of the inviolability of frontiers,[100] both Conventions provide that a party may not invoke a fundamental change of circumstances as a ground for terminating or withdrawing from the treaty if it establishes a boundary.[101] Likewise, in line with the customary maxim *ex injuria jus non oritur*, the fundamental change of circumstances may not be invoked if it is the result of a breach by the party invoking it either of an obligation under the treaty or of any other international obligation owed to any other party to the treaty.[102]

J. Severance of Diplomatic or Consular Relations

The severance of diplomatic or consular relations does not automatically lead to the termination or suspension of the operation of treaties in force between States, or between States and international organisations.[103] More specifically, Article 63 of the 1969 Vienna Convention stipulates that the severance of diplomatic or consular relations between parties to a treaty does not affect the legal relations established between them by the treaty except insofar as the existence of diplomatic or consular relations is indispensable for the application of the treaty.[104]

[99] Lukashuk (n 51), 202–29; Shaw (n 13), 828–31.

[100] See the 1975 Helsinki Final Act, Declaration on Principles Guiding Relations between Participating States, section III.

[101] Art 62(2)(a) of the 1969 Vienna Convention, Art 62(2) of the 1986 Vienna Convention.

[102] Art 62(2)(b) of the 1969 Vienna Convention, Art 62(3) of the 1986 Vienna Convention.

[103] Lukashuk (n 51), 229–34.

[104] Art 63 of the 1986 Vienna Convention contains a similar provision.

K. Conflict with an Emerging Peremptory Norm of General International Law

In accordance with Article 64 common to the 1969 Vienna Convention and the 1986 Vienna Convention, if a new peremptory norm of general international law emerges, any existing treaty which is in conflict with that norm becomes void and terminates.[105]

VII. DOMESTIC LAWS ON TREATIES IN CENTRAL ASIA

A. Overview

All Central Asian States have acceded to the 1969 Vienna Convention on the Law of Treaties,[106] and have adopted domestic laws implementing the Convention. Notably, the States of Central Asia have not formally acceded to the 1986 Vienna Convention on the Law of Treaties between States and International Organizations or between International Organizations,[107] or the 1978 Vienna Convention on Succession of States in Respect of Treaties[108] but the key provisions of the former have also been implemented in the domestic laws on treaties. This subsection offers a brief overview of the Central Asian laws on treaties and discusses, from a comparative legal perspective,[109] some of the most notable differences between the five laws. It thus highlights the Central Asian States' distinct approaches towards making and applying treaties, and singles out a few curious developments in the regional customary international law on the subject.

B. Kazakhstan

The Law 'On Treaties of the Republic of Kazakhstan' was adopted on 30 May 2005,[110] and replaced the legislative Decree by the President of Kazakhstan 'On the Order of Conclusion, Application, and Denunciation

[105] The consequences of the invalidity of a treaty under Art 64 are laid down in Art 71(2) common to the 1969 Vienna Convention and the 1986 Vienna Convention. See also Lukashuk (n 51), 234–35.

[106] For the ratification status of the 1969 Vienna Convention on the Law of Treaties, see: treaties.un.org/Pages/ViewDetailsIII.aspx?src=TREATY&mtdsg_no=XXIII-1&chapter=23&Temp=mtdsg3&clang=_en.

[107] For the ratification status of the 1986 Convention, see: treaties.un.org/Pages/ViewDetails.aspx?src=IND&mtdsg_no=XXIII-3&chapter=23&clang=_en.

[108] For the ratification status of the 1978 Convention, see: treaties.un.org/Pages/ViewDetails.aspx?src=TREATY&mtdsg_no=XXIII-2&chapter=23&clang=_en.

[109] More generally, on the development and place of international law in the Central Asian States' legal systems, see S Sayapin, 'International Law in Central Asia: Practices and Doctrines' (2022) 47 *Review of Central and East European Law* 322.

[110] For the text of the Law (in Russian), see: online.zakon.kz/Document/?doc_id=30012948&pos=420;-54#pos=420;-54.

of Treaties of the Republic of Kazakhstan' of 12 December 1995. The Law is usefully supplemented by the Supreme Court's Normative Regulation No 1 'On the Application of the Rules of Treaties of the Republic of Kazakhstan' of 10 July 2008.[111] The Law generally implements the 1969 Vienna Convention, and regulates the conclusion (chapter 2), application (chapter 3), publication, registration and storage (chapter 4), as well as modification, termination and suspension (chapter 5) of treaties. Since 2005, the Law has been amended on a few occasions, and it is these amendments that merit particular attention.

Article 2-1, introduced on 30 January 2014, provides for planning the conclusion of treaties. The Ministry of Foreign Affairs of the Republic of Kazakhstan produces current (for one year) and prospective (for three years) treaty-making plans, which are subject to approval by an Interministerial Commission on Issues of Treaties of the Republic of Kazakhstan under the Government of the Republic of Kazakhstan, in coordination with the President of the Republic of Kazakhstan. Article 2-2, introduced on the same day, further provides that a central administrative organ proposing to conclude a treaty in the area of its competence should develop a relevant treaty-making concept, and suggest it to the Ministry of Foreign Affairs. The Ministry uses the concept to decide on the expediency of concluding the treaty in the context of the foreign policy of the country.

Article 4-1, introduced on 29 October 2015, provides that draft treaties and treaties affecting the interests of private entrepreneurs are subject to mandatory approval by the National Chamber of Entrepreneurs of the Republic of Kazakhstan, and by members of the Expert Council on Matters of Private Entrepreneurship. This Expert Council operates under the Agency of the Republic of Kazakhstan for the Protection and Development of Competition, and contributes to the removal of administrative barriers in business, and to the development of business law.[112]

Article 20-1, introduced on 13 March 2021, builds on Article 4(3) of the Constitution of Kazakhstan, and provides that treaties that have been ratified by the Republic of Kazakhstan and are in force take precedence over its laws and apply directly, except where it follows from a treaty that its application requires the adoption of a law. This provision is crucial for the consolidation of the position of ratified treaties into the legal system of Kazakhstan.

Finally, Article 31-1, introduced on 30 January 2014, stipulates that '[v]iolation of the legislation of the Republic of Kazakhstan on the procedure for concluding, applying, amending and accepting treaties of the Republic of Kazakhstan shall entail responsibility in accordance with the laws of the Republic of Kazakhstan'. The Criminal Code does not contain explicit

[111] For the text of the Normative Regulation (in Russian), see: online.zakon.kz/Document/?doc_id=30197893.

[112] For the text of the Regulation on the Agency (in Russian), see: www.gov.kz/uploads/2020/11/27/7c34ecd6d44b6f4b7b8984f2e7cc1e0d_original.2156186.pdf.

provisions with respect to violation of treaties but relevant rules applicable to State officials include, for example, such corruption-related offences as abuse of authority (Article 361), excess of authority (Article 362), misappropriation of authority (Article 363), and offences related to bribery (Articles 366–368). In turn, Article 418 criminalises the issuance of a knowingly unlawful verdict, decision or another judicial act. For example, this provision would entail the criminal responsibility of a judge who was obliged to apply a human rights treaty ratified by Kazakhstan but knowingly failed to do so, and their judicial decision adversely affected the lawful interests of a natural or legal person. Here, State responsibility would also be invoked, as the State would be obliged to pay compensation to the victim(s) of the miscarriage of justice.

C. Kyrgyzstan

The current Law 'On Treaties of the Kyrgyz Republic' was adopted on 24 April 2014,[113] and replaced the previous law on the subject adopted on 21 July 1999. The very first sentence of the Law stipulates that '[t]reaties of the Kyrgyz Republic are the legal foundation of international relations of the Kyrgyz Republic', and thus emphasises Kyrgyzstan's dualist approach towards treaties. This understanding is reinforced by the definition of a treaty (in Article 2) as an 'agreement of the Kyrgyz Republic with one or several States, international organisations, or with other subjects of international law regarding [their] rights and obligations in the field of international relations'. The law generally implements the 1969 Vienna Convention, with a few variations, and contains numerous references to 'norms of international law' (that is, presumably, to the 1969 Vienna Convention). It regulates the conclusion and entry into force of treaties (chapter 2), their publication, registration and storage (chapter 3), compliance and fulfilment (chapter 4) as well as invalidity, suspension and denunciation (chapter 5). With 42 articles, including introductory and concluding provisions, it is the second-longest domestic law on treaties in Central Asia.

In addition to inter-State, intergovernmental, and interministerial treaties, which are also referred to in the laws on treaties of the Republic of Kazakhstan,[114] Turkmenistan,[115] and the Republic of Uzbekistan,[116] Article 3(3) specifically provides for the right of the *Jogorku Kenesh* (Parliament) of the Kyrgyz Republic to conclude inter-parliamentary treaties. In accordance with Article 11(3), such treaties, as well as interministerial treaties, are not subject to ratification.

[113] For the text of the Law (in Russian), see: cbd.minjust.gov.kg/205286/edition/1029753/ru.
[114] See Art 2.
[115] See Art 2(2).
[116] See Art 7.

Given Kyrgyzstan's dualist approach towards treaties, Article 32, regulating compliance with obligations under treaties, is key. In accordance with its paragraph 3, '[a]t the proposal of the Government, responsibility for the fulfilment of obligations under treaties of the Kyrgyz Republic is assigned to other relevant State bodies of the Kyrgyz Republic, whose competence includes issues regulated by such treaties'. Paragraph 4 stipulates further that

> Ministries, State committees and administrative agencies, other relevant State organs of the Kyrgyz Republic, whose competence includes issues regulated by treaties of the Kyrgyz Republic, ensure the fulfilment of obligations assumed under such treaties on the part of the Kyrgyz Republic, implement the rights belonging to the Kyrgyz Republic arising from these treaties, as well as monitor the compliance and fulfilment by other parties to these treaties of their obligations.

It is presumed that all State organs are empowered to enact implementing legislation within the limits of their competence.

Unlike the laws on treaties of Kazakhstan, Tajikistan, and Uzbekistan, the Law 'On Treaties of the Kyrgyz Republic' does not explicitly provide for responsibility for its violations. However, it is understood that the conduct of all relevant actors is subject, in particular, to provisions entailing responsibility, in particular, under constitutional, administrative, and criminal law.

D. Tajikistan

The current Law 'On Treaties of the Republic of Tajikistan' was adopted on 23 July 2016,[117] and replaced the previous law on the subject, of 11 December 1999. The law generally implements the 1969 Vienna Convention but its scope of application is limited to non-economic treaties: the law does not apply to 'investment, concession, and other agreements of a private legal character',[118] which are regulated by separate legislative acts (Article 1(2)). Like the law on treaties of the Kyrgyz Republic, the law contains numerous references to 'norms of international law'. It regulates the conclusion of treaties (chapter 2), ratification, approval and accession (chapter 3), compliance (chapter 4), publication, registration and storage (chapter 5) as well as amendments, termination and suspension (chapter 6). With 31 articles, it is the second-shortest domestic law on treaties in Central Asia.

The structure of the Law raises no questions, except with respect to Article 28 ('Commission of international acts through which the Republic of Tajikistan expresses its consent to be bound by a treaty or its intention to

[117] For the text of the Law (in Russian), see: mfa.tj/ru/main/view/126/zakon-respubliki-tadzhikistan-o-mezhdunarodnykh-dogovorakh-respubliki-tadzhikistan.

[118] Given the mixed nature of international investment law, its attribution to the private law sphere is questionable. See M Sornarajah, *The International Law on Foreign Investment*, 4th edn (Cambridge, Cambridge University Press, 2017), 98–101.

suspend or terminate the operation of a treaty'), which is included in chapter 7 ('Concluding Provisions'), together with the rules on responsibility and entry into force of the Law. Article 28 essentially relates to procedures which are regulated by chapters 3 and 6 of the Law, and would be better placed in (one of) those chapters.[119]

Like the relevant provisions in the laws on treaties of Kazakhstan and Uzbekistan, Article 29 provides for responsibility for violations. Notably, it specifically mentions the responsibility of natural persons and legal entities. Since Tajikistan's criminal law does not provide for criminal responsibility of legal entities, their responsibility appears to be limited to administrative and civil law.

E. Turkmenistan

With 28 articles grouped into six chapters, the Law 'On Treaties of Turkmenistan', adopted on 10 May 2010, is Central Asia's shortest domestic law on treaties.[120] The Law replaced the Law 'On the Procedure for Concluding, Application and Denunciation of Treaties of Turkmenistan' of 15 June 1995. Chapter II of the current Law regulates the conclusion of treaties, chapter III relates to compliance, chapter IV regulates the publication, registration, and storage of treaties, and chapter V pertains to the termination and suspension of treaties. Turkmenistan's Law generally implements customary international law on the subject, and, like the other Central Asian domestic laws on treaties, it refers to 'norms of international law' in multiple provisions. It is the only law on treaties in the region that does not contain a provision defining the key concepts and terms of the law of treaties.

Interestingly, Article 2(1) stipulates that treaties of Turkmenistan are concluded with foreign States and international organisations with respect to 'various issues of their mutual and international relations'. This provision apparently implies Turkmenistan's dualist approach towards the application of treaties.[121] It also follows from the context that 'mutual' most likely means 'bilateral', whereas 'international relations' mean 'multilateral relations' here.

It is notable that Article 8, which pertains to negotiating and signing treaties without full powers, explicitly mentions the President of Turkmenistan, Minister of Foreign Affairs as well as Heads of diplomatic missions and missions to international organisations but does not mention the Head of Government. The answer is found in the second sentence of Article 91 of the Constitution: the Cabinet of Ministers of Turkmenistan is chaired by the President of Turkmenistan.

[119] The same observation applies to Art 31 of Kazakhstan's law on treaties.
[120] For the text of the Law (in Russian), see: mejlis.gov.tm/single-law/249?lang=ru.
[121] Art 22 of the Law regulates the relevant implementation procedures.

Article 25(2) specifies that the Cabinet of Ministers of Turkmenistan acts as the depositary of inter-State and *intergovernmental* treaties, whereas the Ministry of Foreign Affairs acts as the depositary of *interministerial* treaties. This is a variation of the regional practice whereby in the other Central Asian States, treaties are deposited with the Ministry of Foreign Affairs,[122] or with other State organs on whose behalf the treaties were concluded.[123]

Like Kyrgyzstan's law on treaties, Turkmenistan's law does not plainly provide for responsibility for its violations. However, it is understood that rules on responsibility are found in other relevant normative legal acts.

F. Uzbekistan

The current Law 'On Treaties of the Republic of Uzbekistan' of 6 February 2019[124] replaced the Law 'On the Procedure for Concluding and Denouncing International Loan and Guarantee Agreements and Agreements between the Republic of Uzbekistan and International Financial Institutions' of 7 May 1993, and the Law 'On Treaties of the Republic of Uzbekistan' of 22 December 1995. With 56 articles grouped into six chapters, it is Central Asia's longest domestic law on treaties. The Law generally reflects customary international law in that chapter 2 regulates the conclusion of treaties, chapter 3 lays down rules for the publication, registration and storage of treaties, chapter 4 regulates compliance with treaties, and chapter 5 lays down conditions for invalidity, suspension or termination of treaties. Like the other Central Asian domestic laws on treaties, the Law refers to 'norms of international law' in multiple provisions.

In addition to the legal expertise of (draft) treaties provided for under Article 11,[125] Article 12 also provides for other types of expertise (eg economic, financial, scientific, ecological, linguistic, and others).[126] In accordance with the third paragraph of Article 12, '[e]xpert opinions are advisory in nature and are subject to consideration by a government organ whose competence includes issues regulated by a treaty'.

With respect to negotiating and signing treaties without full powers, the fifth paragraph of Article 16 stipulates, in addition to customary rules, that '[t]he head of a State organ, within their competence, has the right to negotiate and sign interdepartmental agreements without the need to present full powers'.

[122] Art 26(1) of Kazakhstan's law on treaties, Art 30 of Kyrgyzstan's law on treaties, Art 23(1) of Tajikistan's law on treaties, Art 32 (first paragraph) of Uzbekistan's law on treaties.

[123] Art 26(2) of Kazakhstan's law on treaties, Art 23(2) of Tajikistan's law on treaties, Art 32 (second paragraph) of Uzbekistan's law on treaties.

[124] For the text of the Law (in Russian), see: lex.uz/docs/4193763.

[125] Analogous provisions are contained in Art 3 of Kazakhstan's law on treaties, and Art 4 of Tajikistan's law on treaties. The law on treaties of Kyrgyzstan and Turkmenistan do not mention any expert procedures.

[126] Art 4 of Kazakhstan's law on treaties contains an analogous provision.

With respect to reservations, Article 26 fails to specify that reservations can only be made to multilateral treaties.[127] It is understood, with due regard to Articles 19–23 of the 1969 Vienna Convention, that reservations only make sense in the context of multilateral treaties.

Unlike any other Central Asian domestic laws on treaties, Uzbekistan's Law explicitly provides, in Article 28, for the possibility of prolongation: 'Treaties of the Republic of Uzbekistan can be prolonged (extended) in accordance with the conditions determined by the treaties of the Republic of Uzbekistan themselves, or by agreement between their parties'.

Article 30 provides that treaties of the Republic of Uzbekistan are registered at the Secretariat of the United Nations and the relevant organs of other international organisations by the Ministry of Foreign Affairs,[128] or by other State organs in coordination with the Ministry of Foreign Affairs. The laws on treaties of Kazakhstan, Kyrgyzstan, and Tajikistan do not single out the Secretariat of the United Nations, and more generally refer to 'international organisations' or their 'relevant organs'.

Articles 36 and 37 make a distinction, respectively, between the monitoring and inventory of treaties. The difference between the two procedures is based on their purposes. According to Article 36, based on the results of monitoring, the Ministry of Foreign Affairs 'assesses the effectiveness of the state of compliance with treaties of the Republic of Uzbekistan', and 'prepares proposals for proper enforcement of treaties of the Republic of Uzbekistan'. In turn, in accordance with Article 37,

> [b]ased on the results of the inventory of treaties of the Republic of Uzbekistan, proposals on recognising treaties of the Republic of Uzbekistan as valid or invalid, on their prolongation (extension) and revision are submitted by the Ministry of Foreign Affairs of the Republic of Uzbekistan to the Cabinet of Ministers of the Republic of Uzbekistan, and in some cases, to the President of the Republic of Uzbekistan.

In accordance with Article 50 of the Law, official notifications on the suspension, termination or denunciation of a treaty of the Republic of Uzbekistan are published in the National Database of Legislation of the Republic of Uzbekistan and in other sources, including on the official websites of relevant government organs. Similar rules are found in Article 30(3) of Kazakhstan's law on treaties, and Article 40 of Kyrgyzstan's law on treaties. Notably, the laws on treaties of Tajikistan and Turkmenistan do not explicitly require such notifications to be issued but their issuance is presumed as a matter of practice.

Interestingly, Article 51 contains useful rules on international acts of the Republic of Uzbekistan that are not treaties. Its first paragraph stipulates that

[127] Art 19 of Kazakhstan's law on treaties, Art 25 of Kyrgyzstan's law on treaties, and Art 17 of Tajikistan's law on treaties. Turkmenistan's law on treaties does not mention reservations.

[128] Art 25(1) of Turkmenistan's law on treaties contains a similar provision (it refers to 'the UN Secretariat *or* relevant organs of other international organisations' (emphasis added)).

> [i]nternational acts of the Republic of Uzbekistan that are not treaties must not contain legally binding provisions and contradict treaties, the Constitution and other acts of legislation of the Republic of Uzbekistan. At the same time, such international acts may refer to obligations arising from treaties of the Republic of Uzbekistan.

The second paragraph of Article 51 specifies that '[i]nternational acts of the Republic of Uzbekistan that are not international treaties are adopted, as a rule, in the form of declarations, statements, communiqués, memorandums of understanding, protocols of intent, plans and cooperation programmes'. These provisions are unique to Uzbekistan's law on treaties, and the other Central Asian laws on treaties do not contain similar rules.

Like the laws on treaties of Kazakhstan and Tajikistan, Uzbekistan's law provides, in Article 52, for 'responsibility in the established order' of 'persons guilty of violating the legislation on treaties of the Republic of Uzbekistan'. The conduct of relevant actors is subject, in particular, to provisions entailing responsibility, particularly those under constitutional, administrative, and criminal law.

G. Concluding Remarks

Now, a few more general comments applicable to all Central Asian domestic laws on treaties will be in order. First, it is obvious that none of these laws contain any provisions with respect to State succession. The formal legal reason for this is clear: the Central Asian States are not parties to the 1978 Vienna Convention on Succession of States in Respect of Treaties, and hence are not obliged to implement its rules. However, one should bear in mind that in Central Asia, land swaps may be an appropriate solution to solve some existing territorial disputes,[129] and State succession in respect of treaties will be relevant there.

It is also notable that Central Asian domestic laws on treaties lack provisions on the settlement of disputes, including at international judicial organs. Again, formal reasons for this are clear: none of the States of Central Asia have recognised as compulsory the jurisdiction of the International Court of Justice (ICJ),[130] and procedures for settling disputes under treaties are usually laid down in the treaties themselves. However, there are multilateral treaties providing for compulsory jurisdiction of the ICJ,[131] and domestic legislation on treaties ought to provide for such litigation, and the enforcement of relevant judicial decisions.

[129] Asia-Plus, 'V Kyrgyzstane ne isklychili obmen territoriyami pri reshenii voprosa granitsy s Tajikistanom' ['Kyrgyzstan has not ruled out an exchange of territories when resolving the border issue with Tajikistan'], 3 May 2024, available at asiaplustj.info/ru/news/tajikistan/politics/20240503/v-kirgizstane-ne-isklyuchili-obmen-territoriyami-pri-reshenii-voprosa-granitsi-s-tadzhikistanom.

[130] See 'Declarations recognizing the jurisdiction of the Court as compulsory', available at https://www.icj-cij.org/declarations.

[131] See, for example, Art IX of the Convention on the Prevention and Punishment of the Crime of Genocide, or Art 22 of the International Convention on the Elimination of All Forms of Racial Discrimination.

Another crucial omission (partly noted above) are very limited provisions on responsibility. The domestic laws on treaties of Kyrgyzstan and Turkmenistan do not contain such provisions at all, and responsibility under the laws of Kazakhstan and Uzbekistan appears to be limited to natural persons, and in Tajikistan, to natural persons and legal entities. Yet, treaties create obligations for States, and States bear the primary responsibility for their violations. The laws on treaties ought to contain clear rules on this, including with respect to applicable procedures under constitutional, administrative, and civil law. International remedies – including human rights monitoring organs and dispute settlement mechanisms available at international organisations – should also be cited.

Last but not least, modern technological developments and global challenges such as the recent COVID-19 pandemic suggest that workable mechanisms for concluding treaties online could be put in place. Such mechanisms are already employed in business transactions,[132] and there is hardly any reason not to extend this practice, gradually, to relations between subjects of international law. Especially in situations where face-to-face communication is impossible or severely limited (such as pandemics), effective cooperation between States, international organisations and other international actors is required in order to respond to global challenges by mutual efforts. It is suggested that modern technologies (such as blockchain) could be progressively employed for the purpose of treaty-making,[133] and domestic laws should reflect that trend in the future.

[132] Britannica Money, 'How smart contracts work with blockchain: A step-by-step guide', available at www.britannica.com/money/how-smart-contracts-work.

[133] M Rangeley and J Mignano, 'The Potential of Smart Treaties', *RAND*, 8 April 2024, available at www.rand.org/pubs/commentary/2024/04/the-potential-of-smart-treaties.html.

7

Other Sources of International Law

THE EXAMINATION OF sources of international law often starts with a reference to Article 38(1) of the Statute of the International Court of Justice (ICJ).[1] Indeed, that provision is regarded as a standard list of sources where rules of international law are to be found:

> The Court, whose function is to decide in accordance with international law such disputes as are submitted to it, shall apply:
>
> a. international conventions, whether general or particular, establishing rules expressly recognized by the contesting states;
> b. international custom, as evidence of a general practice accepted as law;
> c. the general principles of law recognized by civilized nations;
> d. subject to the provisions of Article 59, judicial decisions and the teachings of the most highly qualified publicists of the various nations, as subsidiary means for the determination of rules of law.[2]

However, as will be seen below, the range of sources of international law is now broader than it was in 1922 when the above provision was originally enacted.[3] In addition to treaties, international custom, and the general principles of law, rules of international law are also found in binding acts of international organisations and unilateral acts of States. A number of fundamental rules are embraced by the *jus cogens* concept. Some 'soft law' rules, over time, develop into 'hard' international law. This chapter examines these traditional and more novel sources of international law, and thus complements the extensive discussion on the law of treaties in Chapter six.

I. INTERNATIONAL CUSTOM

Article 38(1)(b) of the ICJ Statute defines international custom as 'evidence of a general practice accepted as law'. International custom is a major phenomenon

[1] A Orakhelashvili, *Akehurst's Modern Introduction to International Law*, 9th edn (Abingdon, Routledge, 2022), 33; MN Shaw, *International Law*, 9th edn (Cambridge, Cambridge University Press, 2021), 59; J Crawford, *Brownlie's Principles of Public International Law*, 9th edn (Oxford, Oxford University Press, 2019, 19–20.

[2] For the text of the ICJ Statute, see: www.icj-cij.org/statute (last visited 29 May 2025). 'Publicists' in this context indicates legal academic experts.

[3] cf Chapter 3, section II.F above.

in international law.[4] For millennia, such key areas as diplomatic and consular law,[5] law of the sea, or international humanitarian law were evolving as customary international law, and were codified as treaties only relatively recently. At present, some multilateral treaties and 'soft law' rules also give rise to international custom, and in such cases, analogous customary rules apply alongside treaty rules. Importantly, peremptory norms of general international law (*jus cogens*) often originate in rules of customary international law.[6] The following subsections will consider the significance and constituent elements of customary international law in more detail.

A. State Practice

The first essential constituent element of international custom is the 'general practice' of States (and, where relevant, international organisations).[7] Such practice 'should include the conduct of all [S]tates, which can participate in the formulation of the rule or the interests of which are specially affected'.[8] Importantly, 'general practice does not require the unanimous practice of all [S]tates or other international subjects'.[9] If a rule of customary international law does not affect a State (or group of States), or affects it less than others, the practice of such State(s) in the relevant area is less significant than that of States that have taken an active part in the shaping and application of the rule.[10] Thus, for example, the practice of Central Asian States is more instrumental in the

[4] HT Adilkariyev, *Mezhdunarodnoye pravo* [*International law*] (Tashkent, Tashkent State Law Institute, 2003), 62–64, 359–82; RB Baker, 'Customary International Law in the 21st Century: Old Challenges and New Debates' (2010) 21 *European Journal of International Law* 173; R Bernhardt, 'Ungeschriebenes Völkerrecht' (1976) 36 *Zeitschrift für ausländisches öffentliches Recht und Völkerrecht* 50; JB Bing, 'The Relations between Treaties and Custom' (2010) 9 *Chinese Journal of International Law* 81; I Brownlie, *International Law and the Use of Force by States* (Oxford, Clarendon Press, 1968), 4–11; A D'Amato, 'The Concept of Special Custom in International Law' (1969) 63 *American Journal of International Law* 211; JL Kunz, 'The Nature of Customary International Law' (1953) 47 *American Journal of International Law* 662; G Norman and JP Trachtman, 'The Customary International Law Game' (2005) 99 *American Journal of International Law* 541–80; AE Roberts, 'Traditional and Modern Approaches to Customary International Law: a Reconciliation' (2001) 95 *American Journal of International Law* 757; M Sarsembayev, *Mezhdunarodnoye pravo v istorii Kazakhstana i Sredney Azii* [*International law in the history of Central Asia*] (Astana, Foliant, 2011), 29–31; H Strebel, 'Quellen des Volkerrechts als Rechtsordnung' (1976) 36 *Zeitschrift für ausländisches öffentliches Recht und Völkerrecht* 301.

[5] Sarsembayev (n 4), 52–80; II Lukashuk and AH Saidov, *Hozirgi zamon xalqaro huquqi nazariyasi asoslari* [*The theoretical fundamentals of modern international law*] (Tashkent, Adolat, 2006), 154–78.

[6] See section II.B below.

[7] N Blokker, 'International Organizations and Customary International Law: Is the International Law Commission Taking International Organizations Seriously?' (2017) 14 *International Organizations Law Review* 1.

[8] P Malanczuk, *Akehurst's Modern Introduction to International Law*, 7th revised edn (London, Routledge, 1997), 42.

[9] ibid, 42–43.

[10] ibid, 42.

international movement against nuclear weapons than in the development of the law of the sea.

The more specific criteria laid down in the *ICRC Study on Customary International Humanitarian Law* are useful in identifying the practice of States (and, where appropriate, of international organisations) that contributes to the formation of customary international law:

(i) Both physical and verbal acts of States constitute practice that contributes to the creation of customary international law. Physical acts include, for example, battlefield behaviour, the use of certain weapons and the treatment provided to different categories of persons. Verbal acts include military manuals, national legislation, national case-law, instructions to armed and security forces, military communiqués during war, diplomatic protests, opinions of official legal advisers, comments by governments on draft treaties, executive decisions and regulations, pleadings before international tribunals, statements in international organisations and at international conferences and government positions taken with respect to resolutions of international organisations …[11]

(ii) The practice of the executive, legislative and judicial organs of a State can contribute to the formation of customary international law … In case of conflict between the positions of various organs of a State, the practice is considered internally inconsistent and does not contribute to the formation of customary law.[12]

(iii) Acts do not contribute to the formation of customary international law if they are never disclosed … In order to count, practice has to be public or communicated to some extent …[13]

(iv) Although decisions of international courts are subsidiary sources of international law, they do not constitute State practice. This is because, unlike national courts, international courts are not State organs …[14]

(v) International organisations have international legal personality and can participate in international relations in their own capacity, independently of their member States. In this respect, their practice can contribute to the formation of customary international law …[15]

(vi) The negotiation and adoption of resolutions by international organisations or conferences, together with the explanations of vote, are acts of the States involved. With a few exceptions, it is recognised that resolutions are normally not binding in themselves and therefore the value accorded to any particular resolution depends on its content, its degree of acceptance and the consistency of State practice outside it …[16]

[11] J-M Henckaerts and L Doswald-Beck (eds), *Customary International Humanitarian Law*, Volume I: Rules (Cambridge, Cambridge University Press, 2005), xxxii, available at https://www.icrc.org/sites/default/files/external/doc/en/assets/files/other/customary-international-humanitarian-law-i-icrc-eng.pdf.

[12] ibid, xxxiv.

[13] ibid.

[14] ibid, footnotes omitted. Strictly speaking, judicial decisions are not 'subsidiary sources of international law' but evidence of the law. See s II.G below and Crawford (n 1), 35.

[15] ibid, xxxv (footnotes omitted).

[16] ibid, xxxv–xxxvi (footnotes omitted).

(vii) The practice of armed opposition groups, such as codes of conduct, commitments made to observe certain rules of international ... law and other statements, does not constitute State practice as such ...[17]

Further, in order to qualify as customary international law, State practice must be sufficiently uniform, extensive, and representative:

(i) The first requirement for State practice to create a rule of customary international law is that it must be *virtually uniform*. Different States must not have engaged in substantially different conduct, some doing one thing and some another ...[18]

(ii) The second requirement for a rule of general customary international law to come into existence is that the State practice concerned must be both *extensive and representative*. It does not, however, need to be universal; a 'general' practice suffices. No precise number or percentage of States is required. One reason why it is impossible to put a precise figure on the extent of participation required is that the criterion is in a sense *qualitative* rather than quantitative. That is to say, it is not simply a question of how many States participate in the practice but also *which* States ...[19]

(iii) The third requirement is related to the time necessary to form a rule of customary international law through the adoption of virtually uniform, extensive and representative practice ... [W]hile some time will normally elapse before there is sufficient practice to satisfy these criteria, there is no specific time requirement. It is all a question of accumulating a practice of sufficient density, in terms of uniformity, extent and representativeness.[20]

Customary international law must be distinguished from other types of State practice, which are not legally binding – such as international usage,[21] or *comitas gentium*.[22] These are important in international relations but, unlike breaches of customary international law, their violations do not amount to internationally wrongful acts, and do not entail responsibility under international law.[23] Further, the third (temporal) criterion is waived with respect to 'instant customary international law', whereby limited State practice is given less weight, and more importance is attributed to *opinio juris*.[24] According to some views, 'it is not custom but some other (new) source of international law'.[25]

[17] ibid, xxxvi.
[18] ibid.
[19] ibid, xxxiii (footnotes omitted).
[20] ibid, xxxix (footnotes omitted).
[21] II Lukashuk, *Mezhdunarodnoye pravo: Obshchaya chast* [*International Law: General Part*], 3rd edn (Moscow, Wolters Kluwer, 2008), 115.
[22] ibid, 197–99.
[23] On responsibility under international law, see Chapter 9 below.
[24] Orakhelashvili (n 1), 42–44.
[25] Malanczuk (n 8), 46.

B. *Opinio Juris*

The second constituent element of international custom is *opinio juris sive necessitatis* (or simply, *opinio juris*) – that is, belief (or conviction) that specific practice is in conformity with, or indeed required by, international law.[26] According to Henckaerts and Doswald-Beck, the particular forms in which 'this legal conviction needs to be expressed may well differ depending on whether the rule involved contains a prohibition, an obligation or merely a right to behave in a certain manner'.[27] Where a prohibition is involved, 'statements that [specific] behaviour is prohibited and condemnations of instances where the prohibited behaviour did take place, possibly combined with justifications or excuses from the criticised State, but also physical practice abstaining from the prohibited behaviour' are relevant.[28] In turn, an obligation may be inferred primarily from State conduct 'in conformity with' the relevant requirement.[29] Notably,

> [t]he fact that it is a legal requirement, rather than one reflecting courtesy or mere comity, can be found by either an expression of the need for such behaviour, or by criticism by other States in the absence of such behaviour.[30]

Lastly, practice establishing the existence of permissive rules

> can be found in acts that recognise the right to behave in [a specific] way without actually requiring such behaviour. This will typically take the form of States undertaking such action, together with the absence of protests by other States.[31]

C. Persistent Objector Doctrine

The persistent objector doctrine holds that a State not wishing to be bound by an emerging rule of customary international law will not be bound by the rule when it takes final shape if the State persistently and consistently objected to its content. This doctrine is a reflection of State sovereignty in that States can reject rules of customary international law that are not acceptable to them.[32] The doctrine is limited to customary international law only, and does not apply to *jus cogens*.[33]

[26] T Weatherall, *Jus Cogens: International Law and Social Contract* (Cambridge, Cambridge University Press, 2015), 136–44.
[27] Henckaerts and Doswald-Beck (n 11), xxxix.
[28] ibid.
[29] ibid, xl.
[30] ibid.
[31] ibid.
[32] Crawford (n 1), 26.
[33] See section II.B below.

II. OTHER SOURCES

A. General Principles of Law

In accordance with Article 38(1)(c) of the ICJ Statute, the general principles of law are the third traditional source of international law. At present, the qualification 'recognised by the civilized nations' still featuring in the provision may be regarded as outdated.[34] The general principles of law are fundamental ideas about (domestic and international) law, which are shared by the main legal systems of the world.[35] Such ideas include equality before the law, equity, respect for human dignity and rights, justice, non-retroactivity of criminal law, and other fundamental notions shared across various legal systems.[36]

In 2017, the International Law Commission included the topic in its long-term programme of work,[37] and in 2023, the ILC Drafting Committee provisionally adopted the Draft conclusions on general principles of law as a source of international law.[38] According to Draft conclusion 3, general principles of law may be derived from national legal systems (subparagraph (a)), or formed within the international legal system (subparagraph (b)). The existence of general principles of law common to the various legal systems of the world is determined through a comparative analysis of national legal systems (Draft conclusion 5(1)). Such principles may be transposed to the international legal system in so far as they are compatible with that system (Draft conclusion 6). In turn, in order to determine the existence and content of a general principle of law that may be formed within the international legal system, it is necessary to ascertain that the community of nations has recognised the principle as intrinsic to the international legal system (Draft conclusion 7(1)). Decisions of international (and, as appropriate, national) courts and tribunals as well as teachings of the most highly qualified publicists of the various nations concerning the existence and content of general principles of law may serve as subsidiary means for the determination of such principles (Draft conclusions 8 and 9).

In accordance with Draft conclusion 10, general principles of law have two primary functions. First, they are mainly resorted to when other rules of international law do not resolve a particular issue in whole or in part. Thus, they fill existing gaps in the international legal regulation.[39] Second, they contribute to the coherence of the international legal system. They may serve, among

[34] On general principles of law, see Lukashuk (n 21), 160–62.
[35] ibid.
[36] ibid. See also Orakhelashvili (n 1), 48–49; Shaw (n 1), 82–88.
[37] International Law Commission, 'Summaries of the Work of the International Law Commission', available at legal.un.org/ilc/summaries/1_15.shtml.
[38] International Law Commission, 'General principles of law', Text of the draft conclusions provisionally adopted by the Drafting Committee on first reading, Doc. A/CN.4/L.982 (12 May 2023), available at documents.un.org/doc/undoc/ltd/g23/100/48/pdf/g2310048.pdf.
[39] Orakhelashvili (n 1), 49.

other things, (a) to interpret and complement other rules of international law,[40] and (b) as a basis for primary rights and obligations, as well as for secondary and procedural rules.[41] Notably, general principles of law 'are not in a hierarchical relationship with treaties and customary international law' (Draft conclusion 11(1)). Since international law interacts with domestic legal systems,[42] a general principle of law may exist in parallel with a rule of the same or similar content in a treaty or customary international law (Draft conclusion 11(2)). Finally, any conflict between a general principle of law and a rule in a treaty or customary international law is to be resolved by applying the generally accepted techniques of interpretation and conflict resolution in international law (Draft conclusion 11(3)).

B. *Jus Cogens*

The other sources of international law are not listed in Article 38(1) of the ICJ Statute, as they are more novel. The first of these are peremptory norms of general international law (*jus cogens*) referred to in Article 53 common to the 1969 Vienna Convention on the Law of Treaties and the 1986 Vienna Convention Between States and International Organizations or Between International Organizations.[43] Article 53 defines a peremptory norm of general international law as

> a norm accepted and recognized by the international community of States as a whole as a norm from which no derogation is permitted and which can be modified only by a subsequent norm of general international law having the same character.

The same definition features in Conclusion 3 of the International Law Commission's Draft Conclusions on Identification and Legal Consequences of Peremptory Norms of General International Law (*Jus Cogens*), adopted in 2022.[44]

Crucially, peremptory norms of general international law 'reflect and protect fundamental values of the international community', and 'are universally applicable and are hierarchically superior to other rules of international law' (Conclusion 2).[45] In the International Law Commission's view, a non-exhaustive list of such norms includes (a) the prohibition of aggression; (b) the prohibition of genocide; (c) the prohibition of crimes against humanity; (d) the basic rules of international humanitarian law; (e) the prohibition of racial discrimination

[40] Shaw (n 1), 82.
[41] Lukashuk (n 21), 163–66.
[42] cf Chapter 5 above.
[43] cf Chapter 6, section V.H above.
[44] For the text of the Draft Conclusions, see: legal.un.org/ilc/texts/instruments/english/draft_articles/1_14_2022.pdf.
[45] On *jus cogens*, see Orakhelashvili (n 1), 55–58; Shaw (n 1), 105–9.

and apartheid; (f) the prohibition of slavery; (g) the prohibition of torture; (h) and the right of self-determination (Conclusion 23 and Annex). The *jus cogens* norms give rise to obligations owed to the international community as a whole (obligations *erga omnes*), in relation to which all States have a legal interest (Conclusion 17(1)). Any State is entitled to invoke the responsibility of another State for a breach of *jus cogens*, in accordance with the rules on the responsibility of States for internationally wrongful acts (Conclusion 17(2)).

Customary international law is 'the most common basis for peremptory norms of general international law' (Conclusion 5(1)). Their bases may also be found in treaty provisions and general principles of law (Conclusion 5(2)).[46] To identify a norm as a peremptory norm of general international law,

> there must be evidence that such a norm is accepted and recognized by the international community of States as a whole as a norm from which no derogation is permitted and which can only be modified by a subsequent norm of general international law having the same character [Conclusion 6(2)].

Conclusion 7(2) specifies that acceptance and recognition 'by a very large and representative majority of States is required for the identification of a norm as a peremptory norm of general international law'. The same Conclusion stipulates that 'acceptance and recognition by all States is not required'.

Conclusion 7(3) emphasises the primary role of States in the formation of peremptory norms of general international law:

> While the positions of other actors may be relevant in providing context and for assessing acceptance and recognition by the international community of States as a whole, these positions cannot, in and of themselves, form part of such acceptance and recognition.

States may show acceptance and recognition of *jus cogens* in a variety of ways: in accordance with Conclusion 8(2),

> [f]orms of evidence include, but are not limited to: public statements made on behalf of States; official publications; government legal opinions; diplomatic correspondence; constitutional provisions; legislative and administrative acts; decisions of national courts; treaty provisions; resolutions adopted by an international organization or at an intergovernmental conference; and other conduct of States.

Conclusion 9(1) further stipulates that

> [d]ecisions of international courts and tribunals, in particular of the International Court of Justice, are a subsidiary means for determining the peremptory character of norms of general international law. Regard may also be had, as appropriate, to decisions of national courts.[47]

[46] Orakhelashvili (n 1), 56.
[47] Orakhelashvili (n 1), 57.

According to Conclusion 9(2),

> [t]he works of expert bodies established by States or international organizations and the teachings of the most highly qualified publicists of the various nations may also serve as subsidiary means for determining the peremptory character of norms of general international law.[48]

Peremptory norms of general international law entail a wide range of significant legal effects. Treaties conflicting with such norms are void (Conclusions 10–12).[49] Reservations to treaties must be compatible with *jus cogens* (Conclusion 13).[50] Rules of customary international law do not take shape if they would conflict with an existing peremptory norm of general international law (Conclusion 14(1)), and will cease to exist if and to the extent that they conflict with a new peremptory norm of general international law (Conclusion 14(2)).[51] The persistent objector rule does not apply to *jus cogens* (Conclusion 14(3)).[52] Unilateral acts of States manifesting their intention to be bound by obligations under international law that would be in conflict with *jus cogens* do not create such obligations (Conclusion 15(1)), and obligations under international law created by unilateral acts of States cease to exist if and to the extent that they conflict with a new peremptory norm of general international law (Conclusion 15(2)).[53] Resolutions, decisions or other acts of international organisations that would otherwise have binding effect do not create obligations under international law if and to the extent that they conflict with *jus cogens* (Conclusion 16).[54] Finally, no circumstance precluding wrongfulness under the rules on the responsibility of States for internationally wrongful acts may be invoked with regard to any act of a State that is not in conformity with an obligation arising under a peremptory norm of general international law (Conclusion 18).[55]

C. Legally Binding Acts of International Organisations

Some acts adopted by authorised organs within international organisations are legally binding – that is, they create legal rights and obligations for affected actors. For example, in accordance with Article 25 of the UN Charter, '[t]he Members of the United Nations agree to accept and carry out the decisions of the Security Council in accordance with the present Charter'. Article 39 of

[48] See section II.H below.
[49] See Chapter 6, section V.H above.
[50] See Chapter 6, section II.F above.
[51] See sections I.A–I.B above.
[52] See section I.C above.
[53] See section II.D below.
[54] See section II.C below.
[55] See Chapter 9, section X below.

the Charter further provides that the Security Council 'decide[s] what measures shall be taken in accordance with Articles 41 and 42, to maintain or restore international peace and security'. The words 'decisions' and 'decide' used in Articles 25 and 39 clearly suggest that the measures in questions are legally binding. It is also understood that decisions made by consensus are meant to be binding. Within the Eurasian Economic Union (EAEU), decisions of the Supreme Eurasian Economic Council,[56] the Eurasian Intergovernmental Council,[57] and the Eurasian Economic Commission[58] are legally binding, with due regard to the rank of the respective organ in the EAEU structure: thus, pursuant to Article 6(4) of the EAEU Treaty, decisions of the Supreme Eurasian Economic Council prevail over decisions of the Eurasian Intergovernmental Council and the Eurasian Economic Commission, and decisions of the Eurasian Intergovernmental Council prevail over decisions of the Eurasian Economic Commission.

D. Unilateral Acts of States

Some rights and obligations under international law arise from unilateral acts of States. According to Melnik, a unilateral act of State is 'a unilateral expression of a State's will with the intention of entailing legal consequences'.[59] Most often, 'such acts are proclaimed in the form of declarations, statements, letters, speeches by State leaders, etc. Sometimes unilateral acts can take the form of [assurances] or guarantees … [Important forms of] unilateral acts [include] diplomatic (verbal) note[s] or memorand[a]'.[60] The most common types of unilateral acts of States are promise, recognition, renunciation (waiver), and protest.[61]

A promise takes place when a written or oral statement is addressed on behalf of a State to one or more international actors, or *erga omnes*, to the effect that the State issuing the statement undertakes to behave in a specific manner with respect to a situation or other international actors.[62]

Recognition is an implicit or explicit act, individual or collective, whereby the existence of a factual or legal situation is acknowledged, and the recognising State(s) undertake(s) to treat the situation in a specific way.[63] Notably,

[56] See Chapter 12, section II.A below.
[57] See Chapter 12, section II.B below.
[58] See Chapter 12, section II.C below.
[59] SA Melnik, *Odnostoronniye akty gosudarstv v sovremennom mezhdunarodnom prave* [*Unilateral Acts of States in Modern International Law*] (Odessa, Phoenix Press, 2011), 73. See also Lukashuk (n 21), 123–28.
[60] Melnik (n 59), 77 (footnotes omitted).
[61] ibid, 78.
[62] ibid, 115–16.
[63] ibid, 137.

the addressee(s) of an act of recognition may subsequently demand that the author(s) of recognition comply with their unilateral obligations.[64] Likewise, in accordance with the doctrine of estoppel,[65] the author(s) of recognition that have acknowledged a particular situation are precluded from later disputing that same situation.[66]

Renunciations – whereby States waive their rights under international law – are relatively rare.[67]

By contrast, protest – that is, 'a formal objection by one subject of international law to a particular situation, stated claim, or conduct of another subject of international law'[68] – is very common, and may include 'any actions of a State constituting a negative reaction to specific actions of a third party, which, in its view, are illegal'.[69] The purpose of protest is exactly opposite to that of recognition: instead of accepting obligations, a protesting State reaffirms its rights or legal claims.[70] For example, in December 2002, Uzbekistan lodged an official protest with Turkmenistan over the raid on Uzbekistan's Embassy and the Ambassador's residence in Ashgabat.[71]

E. 'Soft Law'

'Soft law' consists of instruments which are not legally binding but nonetheless possess political, moral or ideological authority.[72] States and international institutions enact such instruments not out of a sense of legal obligation (because there is none at the relevant moment) but because they feel it is important to place a specific topic on the international agenda and start raising international awareness of it. Over time, provisions of some 'soft law' instruments may crystallise into rules of customary international law,[73] or may be codified in treaties.[74] For example, many rules of the Universal Declaration of Human Rights of 10 December 1948 are now regarded as customary international law,[75] and the Declaration served as a basis for the 1966 International Covenants and

[64] ibid, 138.
[65] On estoppel, see RA Kalamkaryan and YI Migachev, *Mezhdunarodnoye pravo* [*International Law*] (Moscow, Eksmo Education, 2005), 664–726.
[66] Melnik (n 59), 138.
[67] ibid, 148.
[68] ibid, 149.
[69] ibid, 169.
[70] ibid, 171.
[71] RadioFreeEurope/ RadioLiberty, 'Turkmenistan: Uzbekistan Protests Raid On Its Embassy', 17 December 2002, available at https://www.rferl.org/a/1101698.html.
[72] Lukashuk (n 21), 138–41.
[73] See section I above.
[74] See Chapter 6 above.
[75] RKM Smith, *International Human Rights Law*, 9th edn (Oxford, Oxford University Press, 2020), 57–58.

other universal human rights treaties as well as for binding regional human rights instruments (see Chapter thirteen below).

Notably, some 'soft law' instruments – for example, resolutions adopted by the UN General Assembly – reproduce binding rules of international law, and to that extent are legally binding. For example, such are the UN General Assembly resolutions supporting the territorial integrity of Ukraine since 2014 and reproducing the principles of territorial integrity, inviolability of frontiers, and the prohibition of aggression.[76]

F. A Hierarchy of Sources?

The hierarchical relationship between the various sources of international law is both interesting and significant in practical terms. All treaties, except the Charter of the United Nations, possess equal legal force.[77] Over time, treaties may give rise to international custom, and in turn, rules of customary international law may be codified in treaties.[78] Identical or similar rules may co-exist in treaty form and as customary international law.[79] General principles of law are meant to fill existing gaps in the legal regulatory landscape formed by treaty rules and customary international law. Finally, treaties, international custom, unilateral acts of States, and acts of international organisations may not conflict with any peremptory norms of general international law (*jus cogens*).[80]

III. JUDICIAL DECISIONS

Article 38(1)(d) of the ICJ Statute refers to judicial decisions as a subsidiary means for the determination of the rules of law. Significantly, international judicial organs do not create new rules of international law but only clarify their content and interpret them – and therefore, advisory opinions and judicial decisions in disputes between States are not sources of international law.[81] Since the Central Asian States have not recognised the jurisdiction of the ICJ as

[76] See S Sayapin, 'The United Nations General Assembly Resolution 68/262 in the Context of General International Law' (2015) 2 *Evropsky politicky a pravni diskurz* 19; S Sayapin, 'Territorialnaya tselostnost Ukrainy v svete Rezolyutsii 68/262 Generalnoy Assamblei OON' ['The Territorial Integrity of Ukraine in the Light of the UN General Assembly Resolution 68/262'] (2014) 1–2(5) *Journal of Constitutionalism and Human Rights* 66.

[77] See Chapter 6, II.A above, n 12.

[78] H Thirlway, *The Sources of International Law* (Oxford, Oxford University Press, 2014), 129–32.

[79] ibid, 132–41.

[80] See s II.B above.

[81] Thirlway (n 78), 122. See also H Lauterpacht, *The Development of International Law by the International Court* (Cambridge, Grotius Publications Limited, 1982), 20–22.

compulsory,[82] and generally maintain a reserved attitude towards international courts, the case law of international arbitral institutions[83] and quasi-judicial expert organs – such as the United Nations human rights monitoring bodies – is more relevant in the region. The case law of the Court of the Eurasian Economic Union (EAEU Court) is relevant to the Central Asian nations, which are EAEU Members.[84]

IV. TEACHINGS OF THE MOST HIGHLY QUALIFIED PUBLICISTS OF THE VARIOUS NATIONS

Article 38(1)(d) of the ICJ Statute also mentions teachings of the most highly qualified 'publicists' of the various nations as another subsidiary means for the determination of the rules of law. Again, such teachings – books, academic articles, expert reports, etc – do not as such create any new rules of international law (and therefore, are not sources of international law) but serve as their authoritative interpretations. Since the early 1990s, the Central Asian international law doctrines have been developing along two main tracks:

> The first generation of Central Asia's international lawyers were trained in the Soviet Union (mainly in Russia), and still maintain close working relations with Russian counterparts. Like a significant number of senior scholars of international law in the Russian Federation, many, if not most, senior Central Asian international lawyers lack knowledge of English and other foreign languages, and thus belong to a 'separate epistemological community' of Russian-speaking scholars of international law, 'tied together by a common language, history, and geographical space in the former USSR'.[85] This probably suggests the persistence of postcolonial trends in Central Asian doctrines of international law. The second and third generations of Central Asian international lawyers, in contrast, were trained in sovereign Central Asian states ... Usually well versed in several foreign languages, as well as their mother tongues and Russian, and therefore exposed to a variety of scholarly doctrines, skilled junior international lawyers from Central Asia are increasingly gaining authority in the academic community, both within the region and internationally. Some hold academic and administrative posts at leading international law schools in Central Asia ... South Korea, Finland, Germany, and the United Kingdom, and others work for international intergovernmental and non-governmental organizations, consultancies, and private law practices.[86]

[82] See ICJ, 'Declarations recognizing the jurisdiction of the Court as compulsory', available at https://www.icj-cij.org/declarations.

[83] See Chapter 8, sections II.D–II.F below.

[84] See Chapter 8, section II.A below.

[85] L Mälksoo, *Russian Approaches to International Law* (Oxford, Oxford University Press, 2015), 87.

[86] S Sayapin, 'International Law in Central Asia: Practices and Doctrines' (2022) 47 *Review of Central and East European Law* 322, 328 (footnotes in the original).

Since 1991, Central Asian scholars have contributed to the academic doctrine in various areas of international law:[87]

> In addition to several textbooks and manuals on international law,[88] Central Asian authors have produced studies dealing with the history of international law,[89] international legal personality and statehood,[90] state succession,[91] regional security,[92] human rights,[93] international humanitarian law,[94] and international criminal law.[95] Important monographs on regional integration,[96] international economic law,[97]

[87] ibid, 329–30 (footnotes in the original).

[88] HT Adilkariyev, *Mezhdunarodnoye pravo* [*International law*] (Tashkent, Tashkent State Law Institute, 2003); SZ Aidarbayev, *Mezhdunarodnoye publichnoye pravo* [*Public international law*] (Almaty, Zhety Zhargy, 2019); II Lukashuk and AH Saidov, *Hozirgi zamon xalqaro huquqi nazariyasi asoslari* [*The theoretical fundamentals of modern international law*] (Tashkent, Adolat, 2006); MA Sarsembayev and KM Sarsembayev, *Mezhdunarodnoye pravo* [International law] (Almaty, Zhety Zhargy, 2009).

[89] Sarsembayev (n 4); R Hakimov, *Mezhdunarodnoye pravo (Bibliografiya 1895–2012 gg)* [*International law (A Bibliography 1895–2012)*] (Tashkent, Yangi asr avlodi, 2013).

[90] UA Mansurov, *Mezhdunarodnaya pravosubyektnost Respubliki Tadjikistan, Chast 1: Pravo na chlenstvo v mezhdunarodnyh organizatsiyah* [*The international legal personality of the Republic of Tajikistan, Part 1: The right to membership in international organisations*] (Dushanbe, Russian-Tajik (Slavonic) University, 2019); RT Hakimov, *Mezhdunarodnaya pravosubyektnost: voprosy istorii, teorii i praktiki* [*International legal personality: Issues of history, theory, and practice*] (Tashkent, Yangi asr avlodi, 2012).

[91] R Hakimov, *Problemy pravopreemstva gosudarstv v mezhdunarodnom prave* [*Issues of state succession in international law*] (Tashkent, Fan, 2008).

[92] AS Rahmonov, OV Kravchenko, DS Naskov and DA Rahmonzoda, *Pravovye osnovy obespecheniya natsionalnoy bezopasnosti, protivodeystviya ekstremizmu i terrorizmu Rossiyskoy Federatsii* [*The legal foundations of reinforcing national security, countering terrorism and extremism of the Russian Federation*] (Dushanbe, Russian-Tajik (Slavonic) University, 2018).

[93] R Hakimov, *Detstvo: problemy i perspektivy* [*Childhood: Problems and Prospects*] (Tashkent, O'zbekiston, 2006).

[94] SA Rajabov, *Implementatsiya norm mezhdunarodnogo gumanitarnogo prava v Respublike Tadjikistan: problem teorii i praktiki* [*The implementation of rules of international humanitarian law in the Republic of Tajikistan: Issues of theory and practice*] (Dushanbe, Institute of State and Law under the Academy of Sciences of the Republic of Tajikistan, 2006); R Hakimov, *Mezhdunarodnoye gumanitarnoye pravo* [*International humanitarian law*] (Tashkent, O'zbekiston, 2007).

[95] AS Rahmonov, OV Kravchenko, DS Naskov, DA Rahmonzoda and EA Holikov, *Osnovy protivodeystviya terrorizmu i ekstremizmu po zakonodatelstvu Rossiyskoy Federatsii i Respubliki Tadjikistan* [*The foundations of countering terrorism and extremism in the legislation of the Russian Federation and the Republic of Tajikistan*] (Dushanbe, Russian-Tajik (Slavonic) University, 2017); N Sandibayev and R Hakimov, *Xalqaro jinoyat sudi* [*International Criminal Court*] (Tashkent, Yangi ast avlodi, 2013).

[96] Z Kembayev, *Legal Aspects of the Regional Integration Processes in the Post-Soviet Area* (Berlin, Springer, 2009).

[97] M Daulenov, *Przeplyw osob, uslug, towarow i kapitalu w umowach miedzynarodowych Unii Europejskiej* (Toruń, Adam Marszalek, 2016); A Rasulov and J Haskell (eds), *International Economic Law: New Voices, New Perspectives. Series: European Yearbook of International Economic Law* (Springer Nature Switzerland, 2020); D Saidov, *Conformity of Goods and Documents: The Vienna Sales Convention* (Oxford, Hart Publishing, 2015); D Saidov, *The Law of Damages in International Sales: The CISG and other International Instruments* (Oxford, Hart Publishing, 2008); D Saidov, *The Law of Damages in International Sales: The CISG and other International Instruments*, 2nd edition (Oxford, Hart Publishing, 2021); S Shadikhodjaev, *Industrial Policy and the World Trade Organization: Between Legal Constraints and Flexibilities* (Cambridge, Cambridge University Press, 2018); S Shadikhodjaev, *Retaliation in the WTO Dispute Settlement System* (Alphen aan den Rijn, Kluwer Law International, 2009).

> international criminal law,[98] and international conflict and security law[99] have been released by leading international law publishers. In 2022, [the inaugural volume of] an English-language *Central Asian Yearbook of International and Comparative Law and International Relations* [was] published.

It would be useful for the Central Asian States to benefit from such a wealth of academic expertise, for example, by setting up consultative expert organs like the International Law Council under the Ministry of Foreign Affairs of the Republic of Kazakhstan (established in 2024). The States would thus 'benefit from academic expertise, and academics could enrich their teaching with empirical data'.[100] As a strategic step, the Central Asian States might also consider nominating competent national academics for membership of the International Law Commission.[101]

[98] See R Atadjanov, *Humanness as a Protected Legal Interest of Crimes against Humanity: Conceptual and Normative Aspects* (The Hague, TMC Asser Press, 2019); S Sayapin, *The Crime of Aggression in International Criminal Law: Historical Development, Comparative Analysis and Present State* (The Hague, TMC Asser Press, 2014).

[99] See S Sayapin and E Tsybulenko (eds), *The Use of Force against Ukraine and International Law: Jus Ad Bellum, Jus in Bello, Jus Post Bellum* (The Hague, TMC Asser Press, 2018); S Sayapin et al (eds), *International Conflict and Security Law: A Research Handbook* (The Hague, TMC Asser Press, 2022).

[100] Sayapin (n 86), 350.

[101] ibid.

Part III

International Disputes and Responsibility

8

Peaceful Settlement of Disputes

Pursuant to Article 33(1) of the Charter of the United Nations,

> [t]he parties to any dispute, the continuance of which is likely to endanger the maintenance of international peace and security, shall, first of all, seek a solution by negotiation, enquiry, mediation, conciliation, arbitration, judicial settlement, resort to regional agencies or arrangements, or other peaceful means of their own choice.

This provision is of paramount importance. It adds practical details to the principle that States should settle their international disputes by peaceful means in such a manner that international peace and security and justice are not endangered.[1] The 1970 Friendly Relations Declaration places this principle in the context of other Principles and Purposes of the United Nations:

> Every State shall settle its international disputes with other States by peaceful means in such a manner that international peace and security and justice are not endangered.
>
> States shall accordingly seek early and just settlement of their international disputes by negotiation, inquiry, mediation, conciliation, arbitration, judicial settlement, resort to regional agencies or arrangements or other peaceful means of their choice. In seeking such a settlement the parties shall agree upon such peaceful means as may be appropriate to the circumstances and nature of the dispute.
>
> The parties to a dispute have the duty, in the event of failure to reach a solution by any one of the above peaceful means, to continue to seek a settlement of the dispute by other peaceful means agreed upon by them.
>
> States parties to an international dispute, as well as other States shall refrain from any action which may aggravate the situation so as to endanger the maintenance of international peace and security, and shall act in accordance with the purposes and principles of the United Nations.
>
> International disputes shall be settled on the basis of the sovereign equality of States and in accordance with the principle of free choice of means. Recourse to, or acceptance of, a settlement procedure freely agreed to by States with regard to existing or future disputes to which they are parties shall not be regarded as incompatible with sovereign equality.

[1] See Article 2(3) of the UN Charter. See also the 1975 Helsinki Final Act, Declaration on Principles Guiding Relations between Participating States, Section V.

> Nothing in the foregoing paragraphs prejudices or derogates from the applicable provisions of the Charter, in particular those relating to the pacific settlement of international disputes.[2]

In this context, the notion of 'dispute' is key. In order for a dispute to exist, the two sides must '"hold clearly opposite views concerning the question of the performance or non-performance of certain" international obligations'.[3] This helpful formula contains a few elements essential to the definition of a dispute:

(1) there must be two sides, each comprising one or more international actors (States, international organisations, or non-State entities with international procedural capacity);
(2) the two sides must be bound by an international legal relationship of obligation – that is, one side must be obliged to the other side, by virtue of a rule of international law, to act (or refrain from acting) in a specific way, and the other side must have a legal right to demand that the former perform the obligation;
(3) the international legal obligation must be certain – that is, its content must be discernible from an applicable treaty-based, customary or another rule of international law binding on the sides;
(4) the performance or non-performance of the specific obligation must raise a question; and
(5) the sides' views concerning the question must be clearly opposite.

Logically, in accordance with the law of (non-)contradiction,[4] both sides to a dispute holding opposing views about the mooted question cannot be right. At least one side is wrong, in any case to some extent, and the dispute settlement procedure(s) chosen by the sides determine(s) who is wrong (in absolute or relative terms), and what the specific effects of such wrongfulness will be.[5]

Importantly, disputes must be settled by peaceful means.[6] The principle is worded in imperative terms,[7] and States must comply with it by virtue of the

[2] For the text of the Friendly Relations Declaration, see: www.jus.uio.no/english/services/library/treaties/01/1-01/friendly-relations.html.

[3] *Alleged Violations of Sovereign Rights and Maritime Spaces in the Caribbean Sea (Nicaragua v. Colombia)*, Preliminary Objections, Judgment, [2016] ICJ Rep p 3, (III), para 50, citing *Interpretation of Peace Treaties with Bulgaria, Hungary and Romania*, First Phase, Advisory Opinion, [1950] ICJ Rep p 74.

[4] See Britannica, 'Laws of thought', available at www.britannica.com/topic/laws-of-thought#ref180925.

[5] cf Chapter 9 on international responsibility in this book.

[6] II Lukashuk and AH Saidov, *Hozirgi zamon xalqaro huquqi nazariyasi asoslari* [*The theoretical fundamentals of modern international law*] (Tashkent, Adolat, 2006), 311–22.

[7] cf relevant passages in the Friendly Relations Declaration: 'Every State *shall* settle its international disputes with other States by peaceful means'; 'States *shall* accordingly seek early and just settlement of their international disputes'; '[t]he parties to a dispute have the *duty*', etc. (emphasis added).

superior legal force of the UN Charter.[8] If a dispute cannot be resolved by peaceful means initially resorted to by the parties, they have the duty to continue to seek a settlement of the dispute by another peaceful means of their choice. In no case are the parties to a dispute allowed to settle it by military force, in contravention of the overarching prohibition of the threat or use of force enshrined in Article 2(4) of the UN Charter,[9] or to resort to any action which may aggravate the situation so as to endanger the maintenance of international peace and security.[10] This understanding was explicitly confirmed by the UN General Assembly,[11] Security Council,[12] and the International Court of Justice.[13]

This chapter explains the modalities of diplomatic, judicial, and arbitral means for settlement of international disputes, and discusses their relevance in the Central Asian context. A few notable examples of dispute settlement within the region as well as between Central Asian and external actors are also explored.

I. DIPLOMATIC MEANS

Essentially political disputes are commonly settled by diplomatic means. Such means allow for more flexibility and involve fewer procedural prerequisites than judicial or arbitral proceedings, which are considered below. In practice, it may not be easy to make a precise distinction between the diplomatic methods of dispute settlement, since some methods contain elements of others.

A. Negotiation

Negotiation is the standard means for parties to a dispute to engage in dialogue, understand the views of their opponent(s), and, ultimately, to find a mutually acceptable solution. Some treaties encourage the parties to a dispute to engage in negotiations before resorting to other means.[14] Negotiation involves direct

[8] See Art 103 of the UN Charter: 'In the event of a conflict between the obligations of the Members of the United Nations under the present Charter and their obligations under any other international agreement, their obligations under the present Charter shall prevail'.

[9] On the prohibition of the use of force, see Chapter 10, section II below.

[10] *Allegations of Genocide under the Convention on the Prevention and Punishment of the Crime of Genocide (Ukraine v. Russian Federation), Provisional Measures*, Order of 16 March 2022, [2022] ICJ Reports p 211, para 86(3).

[11] Friendly Relations Declaration (n 2).

[12] United Nations, 'Pacific Settlement of Disputes (Chapter VI of UN Charter)', available at https://main.un.org/securitycouncil/en/content/pacific-settlement-disputes-chapter-vi-un-charter.

[13] C Gray, 'The International Court of Justice and the Use of Force' in CJ Tams and J Sloan (eds), *The Development of International Law by the International Court of Justice* (Oxford, Oxford University Press, 2013).

[14] See, for example, Art IX of the Convention on the Prevention and Punishment of the Crime of Genocide, or Art 22 of the International Convention on the Elimination of All Forms of Racial Discrimination.

contact between the parties to a dispute and is the only format of dispute settlement where no third party is involved. The clear advantages of negotiation include (1) direct dialogue between expert communicators, which reduces the risk of misunderstanding or misinterpretation of the opponent's viewpoints; (2) first-hand knowledge of relevant circumstances; (3) confidentiality of dialogue; and (4) full control over the progress of negotiations.[15] The success of negotiations ultimately depends on the goodwill of the parties involved. For example, as a result of successful negotiations held after 2016, commercial flights between Uzbekistan and Tajikistan were reintroduced,[16] and the visa rules between Uzbekistan, on the one hand, and Kyrgyzstan and Tajikistan, on the other hand, were eased.[17] Conversely, the inability to solve border disputes between Kyrgyzstan and Tajikistan resulted, in 2021 and 2022, in armed conflicts (see Chapter ten, section IX.D below).

B. Enquiry (Inquiry)

Enquiry (inquiry) means fact-finding by a trustworthy external actor, with a view to establishing the facts which have led to the dispute in question.[18] Given the sensitivity of this mechanism, its use in practice is extremely rare.[19] For example, Article 90(2)(c) of the First Additional Protocol to the 1949 Geneva Conventions codifies an optional competence of the International Humanitarian Fact-Finding Commission (IHFFC) to 'enquire into any facts alleged to be a grave breach as defined in the Conventions and this Protocol or other serious violation of the Conventions or of this Protocol'.[20] The IHFFC was established in 1991 but its first mission took place only in 2017.

In May 2017, the Commission was asked by the Organization for Security and Co-operation in Europe (OSCE) to lead an independent forensic investigation in relation to an incident that occurred in Eastern Ukraine and caused the death of a paramedic and the injury of two monitors of its Special Monitoring Mission to Ukraine (SMM). The aim of the investigation was to establish the facts of the incident, which involved an armoured vehicle and an incendiary device, by conducting a post-blast scene forensic investigation and technical assessment against the background of international humanitarian law. The

[15] On negotiation, see S Blake, J Browne and S Sime, *A Practical Approach to Alternative Dispute Resolution*, 5th edn (Oxford, Oxford University Press, 2018), 169–223.

[16] Gazeta.Uz, 'Uzbekistan i Tadzhikistan vozobnovili regularnye aviareysy' ['Uzbekistan and Tajikistan Resume Regular Flights'], 16 January 2021, available at https://www.gazeta.uz/ru/2021/01/16/uzb-taj/.

[17] Dialog.Tj, 'Kto vyigrayet ot otmeny viz mezhdu Uzbekistanom i Tadzhikistanom' ['Who Will Benefit from Visa Abolition between Uzbekistan and Tajikistan'], 17 January 2018, available at https://dialog.tj/kto-vyigraet-ot-otmeny-viz-mezhdu-uzbekistanom-i-tadzhikistanom/.

[18] MN Shaw, *International Law*, 9th edn (Cambridge, Cambridge University Press, 2021), 887–90.

[19] ibid, 888.

[20] On the IHFFC, see: https://www.ihffc.org/index.asp?page=home.

mission was carried out successfully and the Commission's report was presented to the Permanent Council of the OSCE on 7 September 2017. An executive summary of the report can be found on the website of the OSCE.[21]

With respect to Central Asia, civil society was calling for an international enquiry into the circumstances of the Andijan protest of 13 May 2005.[22] Similar calls were also voiced after the January 2022 events in Kazakhstan.[23] On both occasions, the respective governments did not authorise international enquiries.

C. Mediation

Mediation is a method of alternative dispute resolution (ADR) whereby a third person who is trusted by all parties to a dispute (mediator) is invited 'to assist the parties in negotiating [a] jointly acceptable resolution of issues in conflict'.[24] Importantly,

> [t]he mediator is neutral in that he … does not stand to personally benefit from the terms of the settlement, and is impartial in that he … does not have a preconceived bias about how the conflict should be resolved.[25]

The mediator actively facilitates the negotiating process between the parties, and 'has an active and vital function to perform in seeking to cajole the disputing parties into accepting what are often his own proposals. It is his responsibility to reconcile the different claims and improve the atmosphere pervading the discussions'.[26]

As a result of Soviet mediation between India and Pakistan, the Tashkent Declaration was signed on 10 January 1966 to resolve the Second India–Pakistan War (August–September 1965).[27] In December 2014, the first President of Kazakhstan N Nazarbayev expressed readiness to act as an 'honest mediator' between Russia and Ukraine.[28] On 1 March 2022, President Tokayev confirmed

[21] *International Humanitarian Fact-Finding Commission (IHFFC): What is the International Humanitarian Fact-Finding Commission and what is its role in armed conflict situations?*, 15, available at https://www.osce.org/files/f/documents/1/e/338361.pdf.

[22] M Rittman, '20 Years Since Andijan, Remembering Past Abuses in Uzbekistan', Human Rights Watch, 14 May 2025, available at https://www.hrw.org/news/2025/05/14/20-years-andijan-remembering-past-abuses-uzbekistan.

[23] International Partnership for Human Rights, 'Civil society groups call on Kazakhstan to establish a fully independent investigation into the January 2022 events', 29 July 2022, available at iphronline.org/articles/civil-society-groups-call-on-kazakhstan-to-establish-a-fully-independent-investigation-into-the-january-2022-events/.

[24] Office of Civil Rights, 'What is mediation?', available at www.commerce.gov/cr/reports-and-resources/eeo-mediation-guide/what-mediation. See also Blake, Browne and Sime (n 15), 224–343.

[25] Office of Civil Rights (n 24).

[26] Shaw (n 18), 770.

[27] Britannica, 'Tashkent Declaration', available at https://www.britannica.com/event/Tashkent-Agreement.

[28] RadioFreeEurope/RadioLiberty, 'Nazarbaev Ready To "Mediate" In Ukraine', 22 December 2014, available at www.rferl.org/a/ukraine-russia-kazakhstan-nazarbaev/26755966.html.

that Kazakhstan was 'ready to provide all possible assistance, including mediation services if necessary' to help resolve the conflict between Russia and Ukraine.[29] In 2017–23, Astana was hosting talks between Russia, Türkiye and Iran regarding the situation in Syria.[30] It was agreed that afterwards, 'the Astana template would … continue outside the Kazakh capital'.[31]

D. Conciliation

Conciliation is a composite method of dispute settlement involving elements of mediation and enquiry in that '[t]he conciliator, who is appointed by agreement between the parties, investigates the facts of the dispute and suggests the terms of a settlement'.[32] Conciliation was defined by the Institut de Droit International as follows:

> A method for the settlement of international disputes of any nature according to which a Commission set up by the Parties, either on a permanent basis or an *ad hoc* basis to deal with a dispute, proceeds to the impartial examination of the dispute and attempts to define the terms of a settlement susceptible of being accepted by them or of affording the Parties, with a view to its settlement, such aid as they may have requested.[33]

As a rule, conciliation is performed by a group of conciliators, although individual conciliators may be appointed as well. In practice, conciliation and mediation may appear similar '[b]ut conciliation is more formal and less flexible than mediation; if a mediator's proposals are not accepted, he can go on formulating new proposals, whereas a conciliator usually only issues a single report'.[34]

It appears that conciliation has yet been underexploited in Central Asia. In 1992, the Convention on Conciliation and Arbitration within the OSCE was adopted, and entered into force in 1994.[35] The Convention has been ratified by

[29] The Times of Central Asia, 'Who Should Mediate between Russia and Ukraine? Kazakhstan Could Be the Best Option', 7 April 2022, available at timesca.com/who-should-mediate-between-russia-and-ukraine-kazakhstan-could-be-the-best-option/.

[30] FA Mohamad, 'The Astana Process Six Years On: Peace or Deadlock in Syria?, 1 August 2023, available at carnegieendowment.org/sada/2023/08/the-astana-process-six-years-on-peace-or-deadlock-in-syria?lang=en.

[31] ibid. More generally on mediation in Central Asia, see MA Birken and K O'Sullivan, 'The Evolution of Mediation in Central Asia: The Perspective of the European Bank for Reconstruction and Development' in P Quayle and X Gau (eds), *International Organizations and the Promotion of Effective Dispute Resolution* (Leiden, Brill, 2019).

[32] P Malanczuk, *Akehurst's Modern Introduction to International Law*, 7th revised edn (London, Routledge, 1997), 279.

[33] ibid.

[34] ibid, 279.

[35] For the text of the Convention, see: www.osce.org/files/f/documents/a/0/111409_2.pdf.

34 OSCE Members, including Tajikistan and Uzbekistan.[36] In accordance with the Convention, the Court of Conciliation and Arbitration within the OSCE was established, with a seat in Geneva. The Court is composed of conciliators (two per State party) and arbitrators (one per State party), each serving a renewable term of six years:[37]

> This mechanism can be activated unilaterally by any State party to the Convention for a dispute between it and one or more other States parties. At the conclusion of the proceedings, the conciliation commission presents a report and recommendations to the Parties. The Parties then have thirty days to decide whether they accept those or not. If there is no agreement within that period, and if the parties have agreed to submit to arbitration, an ad hoc arbitral tribunal may be set up whose ruling will be legally binding on the Parties. Arbitral proceedings may also be initiated by agreement between States parties concerned.[38]

The Court has not yet heard any cases. The Court's annual reports are available online.[39]

E. Good Offices

Good offices are about facilitating the start of negotiations between the parties to a dispute. Good offices may be undertaken by States or international officials such as the UN Secretary-General or his authorised representatives.[40] Officials of regional organisations or the International Committee of the Red Cross can also lend good offices to the parties.[41]

F. Resort to Regional Agencies or Arrangements

Regional organisations can be very useful in dispute settlement. They have fewer Members than global organisations, and their decision-making processes are therefore potentially quicker. By default, they have a better comprehension of regional issues than external actors, and their solutions and recommendations are better tailored to specific contexts.[42] Thus, in January 2022, the Collective

[36] For the ratification status of the Convention, see: www.osce.org/files/f/documents/8/2/40119_2.pdf.

[37] For the list of appointed members and alternate members of the Court, see: www.osce.org/files/f/documents/c/0/25460_26.pdf.

[38] OSCE, 'Court of Conciliation and Arbitration', available at www.osce.org/cca.

[39] For the annual reports of the Court, see ibid.

[40] Shaw (n 18), 885–87.

[41] THY Nguyen, 'Beyond Good Offices? The Role of Regional Organizations in Conflict Resolution' (2002) 55 *Journal of International Affairs* 463.

[42] RKM Smith, *International Human Rights Law*, 9th edn (Oxford, Oxford University Press, 2020), 73–74.

Security Treaty Organization (CSTO) was helpful in restoring security in Kazakhstan (although it is not entirely clear to what extent the CSTO is mandated to deal with security threats within States).[43] Conversely, in May 2021 and September 2022, the CSTO reaction with respect to the conflict between Armenia and Azerbaijan was not as resolute.[44]

II. JUDICIAL SETTLEMENT AND INTERNATIONAL ARBITRATION

Unless parties agree on a different means, essentially legal disputes are usually submitted for settlement to international courts or permanent or ad hoc arbitral organs. The following subsections consider the competence of selected international judicial and arbitral institutions with respect to Central Asian States.

A. Court of the Eurasian Economic Union (EAEU)[45]

In accordance with Article 19(1) of the Treaty on the Eurasian Economic Union of 29 May 2014 (EAEU Treaty),[46] the Court of the Eurasian Economic Union is a permanent judicial organ of the EAEU.[47] The status, composition, and jurisdiction of the Court are regulated by its Statute annexed to the EAEU Treaty (Article 19(2)). The Court includes two Judges from each Member State (paragraph 7 of the Statute). The Judges are appointed by the EAEU Supreme Council for nine years (paragraphs 8, 10 of the Statute). In accordance with paragraph 9 of the Statute, '[a]ll judges shall be of high moral character, highly qualified in the field of international and domestic law, and shall usually meet the requirements applicable to judges of the highest judicial authorities of the Member States'.[48] The seat of the Court is at Minsk (Belarus).[49]

The jurisdiction of the EAEU Court may be triggered at the request of a Member State (paragraph 39(1) of the Statute), or at the request of an economic

[43] F Kriener and L Brassat, 'Quashing protests abroad: The CSTO's intervention in Kazakhstan' (2023) 10 *Journal on the Use of Force and International Law* 271.

[44] Asbarez, 'CSTO Wants Armenia-Azerbaijan Peace Treaty to be Signed Soon', 19 May 2025, available at https://asbarez.com/csto-wants-armenia-azerbaijan-peace-treaty-to-be-signed-soon/.

[45] Section II.A uses the author's material published in S Sayapin, 'The Eurasian Economic Union (EAEU)' in A van Aaken, P d'Argent, L Mälksoo and JJ Vasel (eds), *The Oxford Handbook of International Law in Europe* (Oxford, Oxford University Press, 2023). Permission to use published material is gratefully acknowledged.

[46] For the text of the EAEU Treaty (in English), see: www.un.org/en/ga/sixth/70/docs/treaty_on_eeu.pdf.

[47] On the EAEU, see Chapter 11, section II below.

[48] For the current composition of the EAEU Court, see: courteurasian.org/about_the_court/judges/.

[49] See the website of the EAEU Court: courteurasian.org/.

entity (paragraph 39(2)).[50] The jurisdiction is not automatic, and may only be triggered

> following a prior appeal of an applicant to a Member State or the [Eurasian Economic] Commission to address the issue in the pretrial order through consultation, negotiation or other means provided for by the [EAEU] Treaty and international treaties within the Union, except as expressly provided for by the [EAEU] Treaty [paragraph 43].

At the time of writing, the EAEU Court has considered 101 cases,[51] in addition to 22 cases considered by the Court's predecessor – the Court of the Eurasian Economic Community (2001–14).[52] In addition to the sources of the EAEU law listed in Article 6(1) of the EAEU Treaty,[53] the Court may also apply 'the generally recognised principles and norms of international law' (paragraph 50(1) of the Statute), and 'international custom as evidence of the general practice accepted as law' (paragraph 50(4)). In contrast to Article 38 of the Statute of the International Court of Justice (ICJ), paragraph 50 of the Statute of the EAEU Court makes no mention of the general principles of law,[54] or judicial decisions and the teachings of the most highly qualified publicists of the various nations,[55] as subsidiary means for the determination of rules of law.

B. International Criminal Court (ICC)

The International Criminal Court (ICC) was established on 1 July 2002 to try individuals for genocide, crimes against humanity, war crimes, and the crime of aggression.[56] Pursuant to Article 34 of the Rome Statute, the ICC consists of (a) the Presidency, (b) an Appeals Division, a Trial Division and a Pre-Trial Division, (c) the Office of the Prosecutor, and (d) the Registry.[57] There are 18 Judges (Article 36(1)) 'chosen from among persons of high moral character, impartiality and integrity who possess the qualifications required in their

[50] For the purpose of the Statute (Annex 2 to the Treaty), economic entities include legal entities registered under the law of the Member States or third States, or natural persons registered as individual entrepreneurs registered under the law of the Member States or third States (see the concluding provision in para 39 of the Statute).

[51] For the case law of the EAEU Court (in Russian), see: courteurasian.org/court_cases/eaeu/.

[52] For the case law of the Court of the Eurasian Economic Community (in Russian), see: courteurasian.org/court_cases/eurazes/.

[53] These include the EAEU Treaty; other treaties concluded within the Union; treaties of the Union with a third party; decisions and dispositions of the Supreme Eurasian Economic Council, the Eurasian Intergovernmental Council, and the Eurasian Economic Commission adopted within the powers provided for by the EAEU Treaty and treaties concluded within the Union.

[54] Art 38(1)(c) of the ICJ Statute.

[55] Art 38(1)(d) of the ICJ Statute.

[56] For more details, see Chapter 15, sections IV.B–IV.F, IV.L below.

[57] C Safferling, *Internationales Strafrecht: Strafanwendungsrecht – Völkerstrafrecht – Europäisches Strafrecht* (Berlin, Springer, 2011), 272–75.

respective States for appointment to the highest judicial offices' (Article 36(3)(a)). They should have 'established competence', respectively, in criminal law and procedure (Article 36(3)(b)(i)), and 'in relevant areas of international law such as international humanitarian law and the law of human rights' (Article 36(3)(b)(ii)). Judges are elected from among nationals of the States Parties to the ICC Statute.[58] In turn, the ICC Prosecutor and Deputy Prosecutors should be

> persons of high moral character, be highly competent in and have extensive practical experience in the prosecution or trial of criminal cases. They [should] have an excellent knowledge of and be fluent in at least one of the working languages of the Court [Article 42(3)].[59]

Finally, the Registry is 'responsible for the non-judicial aspects of the administration and servicing of the Court' (Article 43(1)), and is headed by a Registrar (Article 43(2)). The Registrar and the Deputy Registrar should be 'persons of high moral character, be highly competent and have an excellent knowledge of and be fluent in at least one of the working languages of the Court' (Article 43(3)).[60] Article 44(1) provides that the Prosecutor and the Registrar 'appoint such qualified staff as may be required to their respective offices. In the case of the Prosecutor, this [includes] the appointment of investigators'. Now, the ICC has over 900 staff members from about 100 States.[61]

In Central Asia, the ICC has jurisdiction with respect to crimes within its jurisdiction committed only on the territory of Tajikistan, or by its nationals.[62] This enabled, in June 2021, a group of

> Kyrgyz academics together with multiple NGOs and CSOs [to send] a communication to the International Criminal Court asking to initiate an investigation into alleged war crimes committed by Tajik governmental officials … This initiative, however, did not receive support from the Kyrgyz president, who stated that all disputes between the two states should be resolved via other channels.[63]

On 26 August 2002, Tajikistan and the United States signed the Agreement Regarding the Surrender of Persons to the International Criminal Court.[64] Pursuant to Articles 1 and 2 of the Agreement, current or former government officials, employees (including contractors), or military personnel or nationals of one Party present in the territory of the other shall not, absent the expressed consent of the first Party, be surrendered or transferred by any means to the

[58] For a list of current ICC Judges, see: https://www.icc-cpi.int/judges/judges-who-s-who.

[59] For the current leadership of the ICC Office of the Prosecutor (OTP), see: https://www.icc-cpi.int/about/otp.

[60] For an overview of the ICC Registry, see: https://www.icc-cpi.int/about/registry/default.

[61] ICC, 'About the Court', available at https://www.icc-cpi.int/about/the-court.

[62] See Chapter 15, section IV.L.

[63] J Emtseva, 'Small conflicts with big impact: The Tajik-Kyrgyz war no one talks about', EJIL:Talk!, 11 October 2022: www.ejiltalk.org/small-conflicts-with-big-impact-the-tajik-kyrgyz-war-no-one-talks-about/.

[64] For the text of the Agreement, see: www.state.gov/03-623.

ICC for any purpose, or be surrendered or transferred by any means to any other entity or third country, or expelled to a third country, for any purpose of surrender to or transfer to the ICC. It now remains to be seen whether Russia will seek to conclude a similar treaty with Tajikistan, to prevent prosecutions of its nationals by the ICC,[65] or whether it expects to achieve the same outcome by informal means.

C. International Court of Justice (ICJ)

In accordance with Article 92 of the UN Charter, the International Court of Justice (ICJ) is the principal judicial organ of the United Nations. For details on the composition and competence of the ICJ, see Chapter three, section II.F above. No Central Asian State has recognised the jurisdiction of the ICJ as compulsory.[66] However, there are multilateral treaties providing for its compulsory jurisdiction,[67] and litigation on the basis of such treaties cannot be excluded altogether.

D. International Arbitration

International arbitration is defined as

> a method of dispute resolution whereby the parties agree to have their disputes resolved by one or more private individuals, i.e. the arbitrators rather than by a court of law. It requires the agreement of the parties, which is usually given via an arbitration clause that is inserted into the contract or agreement. The decision of the arbitrator(s) is final and binding on the parties on the basis of their initial agreement to arbitrate.[68]

A generic notion, international arbitration covers three categories of processes: (1) inter-State arbitration, whereby a dispute between States is settled through arbitration; (2) investor–State arbitration (or investor–State dispute settlement, ISDS) whereby an investor – that is, a private actor – brings a claim against a State whose actions have aggrieved the investor; and (3) international commercial arbitration, which occurs between private parties based in different jurisdictions.[69] The Central Asian States have not been involved in any

[65] See: mid.ru/ru/foreign_policy/legal_problems_of-international_cooperation/1949021/.
[66] See 'Declarations recognizing the jurisdiction of the Court as compulsory', available at https://www.icj-cij.org/declarations.
[67] See n 14 above.
[68] See Peace Palace Library, 'International Arbitration': peacepalacelibrary.nl/research-guide/international-arbitration#:~:text=International%20(Commercial)%20Arbitration%20is%20a,by%20a%20court%20of%20law. See also Blake, Browne and Sime, n 15 above, 481–500.
[69] Blake, Browne and Sime (n 15), 454–80.

inter-State arbitrations. By contrast, investor–State arbitrations and international commercial arbitrations are now commonplace in the region.

Arbitration has a number of advantages in comparison with litigation.[70] First, as a rule, litigation is public (with exceptions provided for in applicable laws), whereas arbitrations are usually private – in that 'third parties who are not a party to the arbitration agreement cannot attend any hearings or play any part in the arbitration proceedings'[71] – and, depending on applicable rules, also confidential.[72] Second, arbitrators are experts in specific areas – such as construction law, pharmaceutical law, banking, oil and gas, etc – whereas judges, as generalists with competence in criminal, civil, administrative, or labour law, may not readily have specific subject-matter expertise. Third, parties to arbitral proceedings participate in the appointment of arbitrators, whereas in courts of law, parties have no control over the appointment of the judges who will be hearing their case. Fourth, given that conditions for challenging arbitral awards are limited, and in turn, judicial decisions may be appealed in higher courts, arbitral proceedings may be relatively quicker than litigation (and therefore, potentially, less expensive).

Investor–State arbitration and international commercial arbitration are regulated by multilateral and bilateral treaties governing the enforcement of arbitral awards[73] as well as by implementing domestic legislation. The Convention on the Settlement of Investment Disputes between States and Nationals of Other States (ICSID Convention) of 14 October 1966 has been ratified by 166 States, including Kazakhstan, Kyrgyzstan, Turkmenistan, and Uzbekistan. At the time of writing, Tajikistan is not a signatory State.[74] Pursuant to Article 2 of the ICSID Convention, the seat of the International Centre for Settlement of Investment Disputes (ICSID) is at the principal office of the International Bank for Reconstruction and Development. Chapter I of the ICSID Convention (Articles 1–24) regulates the structure, status, financing, immunities and privileges of the Centre. Chapter II (Articles 25–27) describes its jurisdiction. Chapter III (Articles 28–35) is devoted to conciliation proceedings. Chapter IV (Articles 36–55) regulates arbitration proceedings. Chapter V (Articles 46–58) lays down conditions for the disqualification of conciliators and arbitrators. Chapter VI (Articles 59–61) contains regulations on the cost of proceedings, and chapter VII (Articles 62–63) regulates the place of proceedings. Chapter VIII (Article 64) pertains to disputes between contracting States. Chapter IX (Articles 65–66) is about the amendment procedure, and chapter X (Articles 67–75) contains final provisions.

[70] ibid, 424.

[71] R Smellie, 'Is arbitration confidential?' (May 2013): https://www.fenwickelliott.com/sites/default/files/richard_smellie_-_is_arbitration_confidential.pdf.

[72] ibid.

[73] See: guides.law.columbia.edu/c.php?g=1143492&p=8594689.

[74] The Database of ICSID Member States is available at icsid.worldbank.org/about/member-states/database-of-member-states. For the text of the ICSID Convention, Regulations and Rules, see: icsid.worldbank.org/sites/default/files/ICSID%20Convention%20English.pdf.

According to UN Trade and Development (UNCTAD), Kazakhstan has been a respondent in no fewer than 20 investor–State dispute settlement (ISDS) arbitral proceedings,[75] Kyrgyzstan in 18 such proceedings,[76] Turkmenistan in 17,[77] Tajikistan in two,[78] and Uzbekistan in nine.[79] Given Central Asia's considerable investment potential,[80] and that there will be more such proceedings in the future, domestic commercial lawyers ought to be trained in international commercial arbitration. To achieve this, leading Central Asian law schools ought to introduce undergraduate and postgraduate courses on international commercial arbitration, in cooperation with leading law firms as well as international and domestic arbitral institutions.[81]

In turn, all Central Asian States have acceded to the New York Convention on the Recognition and Enforcement of Foreign Arbitral Awards of 10 June 1958 (usually referred to as the New York Convention). At the time of writing, the New York Convention has 173 parties.[82] Article I defines the scope of application of the Convention. Article II obliges Contracting States to recognise written arbitral clauses or arbitration agreements. Article III codifies the Convention's central idea that States must recognise arbitral awards as binding and enforce them in accordance with the rules of procedure of the territory where the award is relied upon, under the conditions laid down in the subsequent provisions. Article IV lays down a straightforward procedure to the effect that the party applying for recognition and enforcement of an arbitral award should, at the time of the application, supply (a) the duly authenticated original award or a duly certified copy thereof, and (b) the original agreement referred to in Article II or a duly certified copy thereof as well as duly certified translations of these documents, if applicable. Correspondingly, Article V contains an exhaustive list of narrowly defined grounds for refusing recognition and enforcement of an award. Article VI stipulates the course of action for situations where an application for the setting aside or suspension of the award

[75] UNCTAD, 'Kazakhstan', available at investmentpolicy.unctad.org/investment-dispute-settlement/country/107/kazakhstan.

[76] UNCTAD, 'Kyrgyzstan', available at investmentpolicy.unctad.org/investment-dispute-settlement/country/113/kyrgyzstan.

[77] UNCTAD, 'Turkmenistan', available at investmentpolicy.unctad.org/investment-dispute-settlement/country/215/turkmenistan.

[78] UNCTAD, 'Tajikistan', available at investmentpolicy.unctad.org/country-navigator/213/tajikistan.

[79] UNCTAD, 'Uzbekistan', available at investmentpolicy.unctad.org/investment-dispute-settlement/country/226/uzbekistan.

[80] A Pecoraro, 'MFN in BITs: The Deconstruction of State Consent to Dispute Settlement' in S Sayapin and R Burnashev (eds), *Central Asian Yearbook of International Law and International Relations 2022* (The Hague, Eleven, 2022).

[81] S Sayapin, 'International Law in Central Asia: Practices and Doctrines' (2022) 47 *Review of Central and East European Law* 322, 349.

[82] The list of Contracting States of the 1958 New York Convention is available at www.newyorkconvention.org/countries. For the text of the New York Convention, see: www.newyorkconvention.org/text.

has been made to a competent authority referred to in Article V(1)(e). Article VII regulates the relationship between the New York Convention and other multilateral or bilateral treaties applicable to the recognition and enforcement of arbitral awards as well as relevant domestic laws. Article VII(2) provides that the Geneva Protocol on Arbitration Clauses of 1923 and the Geneva Convention on the Execution of Foreign Arbitral Awards of 1927 cease to have effect between parties to the New York Convention. Articles VIII–XVI are technical.

International arbitrations may be ad hoc or institutional. Ad hoc arbitrations lack the support of an arbitral institution, and thus are usually less expensive,

> as there is no need to pay institutional fees. The main disadvantage of ad hoc arbitrations is that they could be derailed by uncooperative parties. For instance, a counterparty may refuse to appoint its own arbitrator or fail to agree with you on the selection of the arbitral seat, which can lead to a procedural deadlock.[83]

In turn, '[t]he advantage of institutional arbitrations is that they do not depend on the parties' cooperation to be effective. Institutional rules have been designed and refined through decades of practice to avoid procedural breakdowns when parties are unwilling to arbitrate'.[84] Among the most reputable international arbitral institutions are the Permanent Court of Arbitration (PCA),[85] International Chamber of Commerce (ICC),[86] Stockholm Chamber of Commerce Arbitration Institute (SCC),[87] Hong Kong International Arbitration Centre (HKIAC),[88] Singapore International Arbitration Centre (SIAC),[89] and Dubai International Arbitration Centre.[90]

[83] See Cooley, 'The Main Institutions of International Arbitration', 31 July 2023: www.cooley.com/news/insight/2023/2023-07-31-the-main-institutions-of-international-arbitration.

[84] ibid.

[85] See: pca-cpa.org/home/.

[86] See: iccwbo.org/.

[87] See: sccarbitrationinstitute.se/en. On 19 December 2013, the SCC rendered an award in *Stati and others v Kazakhstan* (SCC Case No 116/2010). On the *Stati* case, see UNCTAD, 'Investment Policy Hub', available at investmentpolicy.unctad.org/investment-dispute-settlement/cases/379/stati-and-others-v-kazakhstan. The SCC found breaches of the fair and equitable treatment/minimum standard of treatment, including denial of justice claims, and awarded the investor US$497 million. The arbitral award was subject to judicial review by the Svea Court of Appeal and was upheld on 9 December 2016. After years of follow-up proceedings, the Ministry of Justice of Kazakhstan stated on 16 July 2024 that the Government of Kazakhstan, the National Bank of Kazakhstan and the claimants had entered into a 'legally binding framework agreement for peace and a mutually acceptable resolution of the ongoing dispute over oil and gas assets in Kazakhstan'. According to the statement, 'the parties are pleased to have reached an agreement on mutually favorable terms, which will result in the cessation of all legal proceedings and the suspension of pending claims in all jurisdictions. The specific terms of the agreement are confidential'. See Y Akhmetova, 'Pravitelstvo Kazakhstana i biznesmeny Stati uregulirovali spor' ['The Government of Kazakhstan and the Stati Businessmen Have Settled the Dispute'], 16 July 2024: forbes.kz/articles/pravitelstvo-kazahstana-i-biznesmeny-stati-uregulirovali-spor-a493ea.

[88] See: www.hkiac.org/.

[89] See: siac.org.sg/.

[90] See: www.diac.com/en/home/.

Domestic laws on international arbitration are in place in all Central Asian States.[91] In particular, they define the key notions pertaining to arbitration[92] and types of arbitral institutions,[93] lay down the principles of arbitration,[94] requirements for the arbitration clause,[95] and arbitration procedure,[96] and contain rules on the arbitral awards,[97] their recognition and enforcement.[98] Further rules on the recognition and enforcement of arbitral awards are found in the respective Civil Procedure Codes.[99] The Central Asian States are home to a few arbitral institutions such as the Kazakhstan International Arbitrage (KIA),[100] International Arbitration Court (IAC),[101] and the International Court of Arbitration in Affiliation with the Chamber of Commerce and Industry of the Kyrgyz Republic.[102]

E. International Arbitration Centre (IAC) of the Astana International Financial Centre (AIFC)

On 7 December 2015, Kazakhstan adopted the Constitutional Law 'On the Astana International Financial Centre' (usually abbreviated as the AIFC).[103]

[91] The Law 'On Arbitration Courts in the Kyrgyz Republic' was adopted on 30 July 2002, available at cbd.minjust.gov.kg/1092/edition/1241014/ru. Turkmenistan's Law 'On International Commercial Arbitration' was adopted on 16 August 2014, available at turkmenistan.gov.tm/ru/post/22591/zakon-turkmenistana-%3Cbr%3Eo-mezhdunarodnom-kommercheskom-arbitrazhe. Tajikistan adopted the Law 'On International Commercial Arbitration' on 18 March 2015, available at tpp.tj/kommercheskij-arbitrazh/o-mezhdunarodnom-kommercheskom-arbitrazhe/. Kazakhstan's current Law 'On Arbitration' was adopted on 8 April 2016, available at online.zakon.kz/Document/?doc_id=35110250. Uzbekistan's Law 'On International Commercial Arbitration' was adopted by the Legislative Chamber on 5 August 2020, and approved by the Senate on 11 September 2020, available at //lex.uz/docs/5294087.

[92] Art 2 of Kazakhstan's law, Art 2 of Kyrgyzstan's law, Art 2 of Tajikistan's law, Art 2 of Turkmenistan's law, and Art 5 of Uzbekistan's law.

[93] Art 4 of Kazakhstan's law, Art 3 of Kyrgyzstan's law, and Arts 5–10 of Tajikistan's law.

[94] Art 5 of Kazakhstan's law, Art 4 of Tajikistan's law, and Arts 6–7 of Uzbekistan's law.

[95] Art 9 of Kazakhstan's law, Art 7 of Kyrgyzstan's law, Art 11 of Tajikistan's law, Art 7 of Turkmenistan's law, and Art 12 of Uzbekistan's law.

[96] Arts 20–40 of Kazakhstan's law, Arts 14–27 of Kyrgyzstan's law, Arts 25–42 of Tajikistan's law, Arts 28–37 of Turkmenistan's law, and Arts 33–43 of Uzbekistan's law.

[97] Arts 44–53 of Kazakhstan's law, Arts 28–37 of Kyrgyzstan's law, Arts 43–51 of Tajikistan's law, Arts 38–45 of Turkmenistan's law, and Arts 44–50 of Uzbekistan's law.

[98] Arts 54–57 of Kazakhstan's law, Arts 40–44 of Kyrgyzstan's law, Arts 52–54 of Tajikistan's law, Arts 46–47 of Turkmenistan's law, and Arts 51–52 of Uzbekistan's law.

[99] See Chapters 20 and 56 of Kazakhstan's Civil Procedure Code, Chapter 48 and Arts 438–439 of Kyrgyzstan's Civil Procedure Code, Chapter 44 of Tajikistan's Civil Procedure Code, Regulations on the Court of Arbitration (Annex 1 to the Civil Procedure Code of Turkmenistan), Chapters 39 and 40 of the Civil Procedure Code of Uzbekistan.

[100] See: arbitrage.kz/en.

[101] See: www.arbitration.kz/main?lang=en.

[102] See: www.arbitr.kg/web/index.php.

[103] For the text of the Constitutional Law (in Russian), see: online.zakon.kz/Document/?doc_id=39635390. For an English translation, see: aifc.kz/files/legals/7/file/constitutional-statute-with-amendments-as-of-30-december-2019.pdf. On the AIFC, see M Kenzhaliyev, 'Perspectives

The Constitutional Law defines the AIFC as 'a territory within the limits of the city of Astana with precisely defined boundaries determined by the President of the Republic of Kazakhstan, in which a special legal regime in the financial sphere operates' (Article 1(1)). Article 2(2) of the Constitutional Law sets out the objectives of the Centre as follows:

1) Assistance in attracting investments into the economy of the Republic of Kazakhstan by creating an attractive environment for investment in the field of financial services;
2) Development of the securities market of the Republic of Kazakhstan, ensuring its integration with international capital markets;
3) Development in the Republic of Kazakhstan of the market for insurance, banking services, Islamic finance, financial technologies, digital assets, e-commerce and innovative projects;
4) Development of financial and professional services based on the best international practices;
5) Achieving international recognition as a financial centre.

Pursuant to Article 4(1) of the Constitutional Law, the functioning law of the Centre is based on the Constitution of the Republic of Kazakhstan and consists of (1) the Constitutional Law itself, (2) acts of the Centre that do not contradict the Constitutional Law, which may be based on the principles, norms and precedents of the law of England and Wales and (or) standards of the world's leading financial centres, adopted by the organs of the Centre within the powers granted by the Constitutional Law, and (3) functioning law of the Republic of Kazakhstan, which applies to the extent not regulated by the Constitutional Law and acts of the Centre.

Article 9(1)(5) of the Constitutional Law lists the International Arbitration Centre (IAC) among the organs of the Centre.[104] Arbitrations may be administered at the IAC in accordance with the IAC Arbitration and Mediation Rules,[105] UNCITRAL Arbitration Rules,[106] or ad hoc rules. The IAC panel includes highly qualified arbitrators from Asia, Europe, and North America.[107] Article 14(3) of the Constitutional Law stipulates that IAC awards are to be recognised and enforced in the Republic of Kazakhstan in the same way, and on the same terms, as arbitration awards issued by arbitral institutions in the Republic of Kazakhstan. The translation of IAC awards into Kazakh or Russian is ensured in accordance with the procedure laid down by the acts of the Centre. In turn, pursuant to Article 14(4), arbitral awards are recognised and enforced

of the Court of the Astana International Financial Centre: Potential to Transform the Central Asian Legal Landscape' (2024) 19 *Asian Journal of Comparative Law* 160.

[104] IAC, 'About us', available at https://iac.aifc.kz/en/about-the-iac.

[105] For the IAC Arbitration and Mediation Rules, see: iac.aifc.kz/uploads/AIFC%20Court%20and%20IAC/iac-rules-no-cover.pdf.

[106] For the text of UNCITRAL Arbitration Rules, see: https://uncitral.un.org/en/texts/arbitration/contractualtexts/arbitration.

[107] IAC, 'Who we are', available at https://iac.aifc.kz/en/who-we-are.

in the territory of the Centre in accordance with legislation of the Republic of Kazakhstan. The official language of the Centre is English (Article 15).

As of December 2023, the AIFC had reportedly 'attracted over USD 10,9 billion to the country's economy through AIFC, comprising USD 4,6 billion on AIX and USD 6,3 billion in investments from participants. This accomplishment aligns with the development strategy set for the [C]entre until 2025'.[108] Despite this progress, the AIFC has been criticised for the alleged incompatibility of its legal basis with the Constitution of Kazakhstan.[109] A comprehensive scholarly commentary on the AIFC Constitutional Law would probably help overcome such criticisms.

F. Arbitration Court of the Tashkent International Arbitration Centre (TIAC)

On 5 November 2018, the President of Uzbekistan signed a Decree establishing the Tashkent International Arbitration Centre (TIAC).[110] According to the TIAC website,

> [t]he TIAC Court of Arbitration is a fully autonomous organ within the TIAC ('Centre') and is the only body within the Centre's structure that administers disputes according to the TIAC Rules of Arbitration in complete independence from the Centre, its founders, the Director or any other entities.[111]

The current TIAC Rules of Arbitration were enacted in 2021.[112] The TIAC Panel of Arbitrators includes excellent practitioners from various parts of the world.[113] Notably, TIAC has a dedicated panel of arbitrators for sports disputes.[114] Over time, the TIAC is likely to become a viable alternative to the AIFC, depending on the development of the business climate in both countries.

[108] AIFC, 'Astana International Financial Centre has unveiled its achievements for the year 2023', 26 December 2023, available at aifc.kz/news/astana-international-financial-centre-has-unveiled-its-achievements-for-the-year-2023/.

[109] A Shaikenov and V Shaikenov, 'Konstitutsionen li MFCA i pomogut li popravki v Konstitutsiyu?' ['Is the AIFC Constitutional, and Will Amendments to the Constitution Help?'], 7 March 2017, available at forbes.kz//process/expertise/konstitutsionen_li_mftsa_i_pomogut_li_popravki_v_konstitutsiyu/?.

[110] For the text of the Decree (in Russian), see: https://lex.uz/docs/4039518.

[111] TIAC, 'About TIAC', available at www.tiac.uz/about-tiac-court-of-arbitration.

[112] For the current TIAC Rules of Arbitration, see: static1.squarespace.com/static/5c02f6d29772ae05d0a897a8/t/6352b96baa109a5a2a49bd9d/1666365808793/TIAC+RULES++OF+ARBITRATION+2021+.pdf.

[113] For the list of TIAC Panel of Arbitrators and TIAC Reserve Panel of Arbitrators, see: www.tiac.uz/arbitrators.

[114] For the list of TIAC arbitrators for sports disputes, see: www.tiac.uz/arbitrators-for-sports-disputes.

9

Responsibility under International Law

IN ACCORDANCE WITH the general theory of law, the relationship of legal responsibility presupposes the occurrence of negative consequences for an offender for their violation of at least one rule established by a source of law.[1] Accordingly, responsibility under international law presupposes a violation by an international actor (usually a State or an international organisation) of at least one rule of international law, and the occurrence of negative consequences for such international actor established by international law.[2] The legal rules on State responsibility under international law are codified in the 2001 Articles on the Responsibility of States for Internationally Wrongful Acts (the ARSIWA).[3] In turn, the 2011 Articles on the Responsibility of International Organizations (ARIO) adapted the relevant rules to the institutional settings of international

[1] MN Marchenko, *Problemy teorii gosudarstva i prava* [*Issues of the Theory of State and Law*] (Moscow, Prospect, 2013), 709.

[2] A Aust, *Handbook of International Law* (Cambridge, Cambridge University Press, 2005), 407–29; E Brown Weiss, 'Invoking State Responsibility in the Twenty-first Century' (2002) 96 *American Journal of International Law* 798; DD Caron, 'The ILC Articles on State Responsibility: the Paradoxical Relationship between Form and Authority' (2002) 96 *American Journal of International Law* 857; L Condorelli, 'Le règlement des différends en matière de responsabilité internationale des Etats: quelques remarques candides sur le débat á la C.D.I.' (1994) 5 *European Journal of International Law* 106; J Crawford, *State Responsibility: General Part* (Cambridge, Cambridge University Press, 2013), 49–51; HT Adilkariyev, *Mezhdunarodnoye pravo* [*International law*] (Tashkent, Tashkent State Law Institute, 2003), 241–65; II Lukashuk and AH Saidov, *Hozirgi zamon xalqaro huquqi nazariyasi asoslari* [*The theoretical fundamentals of modern international law*] (Tashkent, Adolat, 2006), 146–52; SD Murphy, 'U.S. Comments on ILC Draft Articles on State Responsibility' (2001) 95 *American Journal of International Law* 626; G Nolte, 'From Dionisio Anzilotti to Robert Ago: the Classical Law of State Responsibility and the Traditional Primacy of a Bilateral Conception of Inter-State Relations' (2002) *European Journal of International Law* 1083; ME O'Connell, 'Debating the Law of Sanctions' (2002) 13 *European Journal of International Law* 63; R Rosenstock, 'The ILC and State Responsibility' (2002) 96 *American Journal of International Law* 792; CJ Tams, 'Do Serious Breaches Give Rise to any Specific Obligations of the Responsible State?' (2002) 13 *European Journal of International Law* 1161. cf VF Antipenko, *Teoriya ugulovnoy otvetstvennosti gosudarstva* [*The Theory of the Criminal Responsibility of a State*] (Odessa, Phoenix Press, 2016); J Vazhna, *Konsteptsiya kriminalnoy vidpovidalnosti derzhavy: mozhlivist realizatsii v suchasnomu mizharodnomu pravi* [*The Concept of Criminal Responsibility of a State: The Feasibility of Its Realisation in Modern International Law*] (Kyiv, Lira–K, 2017).

[3] See Draft Articles on Responsibility of States for Internationally Wrongful Acts, with commentaries (ARSIWA Commentary): legal.un.org/ilc/texts/instruments/english/commentaries/9_6_2001.pdf.

organisations.[4] The chapter's focus is on the ARSIWA but references are also made to the ARIO where appropriate.

Drafted by the International Law Commission and adopted by the UN General Assembly, the ARSIWA and ARIO are authoritative doctrinal codifications of customary international law – that is, they codify the respective practices of States and international organisations accepted as law concerning their responsibility for breaches of obligations under international law. In general, the combined presence of three circumstances is required for the implementation of responsibility under international law: (1) an internationally wrongful act; (2) attribution of an internationally wrongful act to a specific international actor (that is, a State or an international organisation); and (3) the absence of circumstances excluding the responsibility of that international actor under international law.[5] The following sections examine these and other substantive and procedural rules in greater detail, in the light of developments in Central Asia and more globally.

I. GENERAL PROVISIONS

A. *Lex Specialis*

The ARSIWA and ARIO are the *lex generalis* in matters of responsibility under international law.[6] In accordance with Article 55 of the ARSIWA, the articles 'do not apply where and to the extent that the conditions for the existence of an internationally wrongful act or the content or implementation of the international responsibility of a State are governed by special rules of international law'. For example, pursuant to Article 2 of the 1974 Definition of Aggression,

> the Security Council may, in conformity with the [UN] Charter, conclude that a determination that an act of aggression has been committed would not be justified in the light of other relevant circumstances, including the fact that the acts concerned or their consequences are not of sufficient gravity.[7]

Similarly, Article 64 of the ARIO provides that the ARIO do not apply where the conduct of an international organisation, or of a State in connection with the conduct of an international organisation, is governed by special rules of international law. In particular, Article 64 provides that '[s]uch special rules of international law may be contained in the rules of the organization applicable

[4] See Draft Articles on the Responsibility of International Organizations, with commentaries (ARIO Commentary): legal.un.org/ilc/texts/instruments/english/commentaries/9_11_2011.pdf.

[5] II Lukashuk, *Pravo mezhdunarodnoy otvetstvennosti* [*Law of International Responsibility*] (Moscow, Wolters Kluwer, 2004), 80–84.

[6] Crawford (n 2), 48.

[7] On the UN General Assembly Resolution 3314(XXIX) 1974 Definition of Aggression, see Chapter 10, section III below.

to the relations between an international organization and its members'. For example, the WTO rules on dispute settlement should prevail over the ARIO as far as the responsibility of WTO members is concerned.[8] The rules of the International Court of Justice, those of the European Court of Human Rights and other regional human rights courts, as well as of other international judicial institutions also establish special legal regimes (*lex specialis*). The responsibility of the International Committee of the Red Cross (ICRC) is a special case too, given its *sui generis* nature.[9]

B. Questions of Responsibility not Regulated by the ARSIWA or ARIO

Article 56 of the ARSIWA and Article 65 of the ARIO provide that the applicable rules of international law continue to govern questions concerning the responsibility of a State or an international organisation for an internationally wrongful act to the extent that they are not regulated by the ARSIWA or ARIO. They complement the *lex specialis* principle (see section I.A above).[10] The International Law Commission's Commentary on the ARSIWA also makes it clear that:

> the present articles are not concerned with any legal effects of a breach of an international obligation which do not flow from the rules of State responsibility, but stem from the law of treaties or other areas of law. Examples include the invalidity of a treaty procured by an unlawful use of force, the exclusion of reliance on a fundamental change of circumstances where the change in question results from a breach of an international obligation of the invoking State to any other State party, or the termination of the international obligation violated in the case of a material breach of a bilateral treaty.[11]

On matters of obligations arising from the law of treaties, see Chapter six, sections V–VI above.

C. Responsibility of an International Organisation

Article 57 of the ARSIWA provides explicitly that '[t]hese articles are without prejudice to any question of the responsibility under international law of an

[8] On the WTO dispute settlement, see P Van den Bossche and W Zdouc, *The Law and Policy of the World Trade Organization*, 3rd edn (Cambridge, Cambridge University Press, 2013), 156–314; S Lester, B Mercurio, A Davies, *World Trade Law: Text, Materials and Commentary*, 2nd edn (Oxford, Hart Publishing, 2012), 149–220.

[9] S. Sayapin, 'Rethinking the Responsibility of the International Committee of the Red Cross: A *Sui Generis* Regime' in A Berkes, R Collins and R Deplano (eds), *Reassessing the Articles on the Responsibility of International Organizations: From Theory to Practice* (Cheltenham, Edward Elgar Publishing, 2024) 246.

[10] ARSIWA Commentary (n 3), 141.

[11] ibid.

international organization, or of any State for the conduct of an international organization'. Consequently, the ARIO constitute a *lex specialis* with respect to the ARSIWA.[12] The International Law Commission noted in its Commentary on the ARIO as follows:

> While the present draft articles are in many respects similar to the articles on State responsibility, they represent an autonomous text. Each issue has been considered from the specific perspective of the responsibility of international organizations. Some provisions address questions that are peculiar to international organizations. When, in the study of the responsibility of international organizations, the conclusion is reached that an identical or similar solution to the one expressed in the articles on State responsibility should apply with respect to international organizations, this is based on appropriate reasons and not on a general presumption that the same principles apply.[13]

D. Individual Responsibility

The ARSIWA and ARIO do not cover the responsibility of *individuals* under international criminal law (ICL),[14] or other appropriate fields of international law.[15] According to the International Law Commission, individual responsibility 'refers to the responsibility of individual persons, including State officials, under certain rules of international law for conduct such as genocide, war crimes and crimes against humanity'.[16] Article 58 of the ARSIWA stipulates explicitly that '[t]hese articles are without prejudice to any question of the individual responsibility under international law of any person acting on behalf of a State', and Article 66 of the ARIO contains a similar provision. Individual responsibility under international law is invoked and enforced through specific universal, regional, and domestic mechanisms, and may be implemented in parallel with the responsibility of States or international organisations.[17]

E. Charter of the United Nations

Article 59 of the ARSIWA and Article 67 of the ARIO stipulate that both sets of articles 'are without prejudice to the Charter of the United Nations'. The International Law Commission's Commentaries on these provisions recall Article 103 of the UN Charter to the effect that '[i]n the event of a conflict

[12] On the ARIO, see generally Berkes, Collins and Deplano (n 9).

[13] ARIO Commentary (n 4), 46.

[14] On international criminal law, see Chapter 15 below.

[15] On international human rights law (IHRL) and international humanitarian law (IHL), see Chapters 13 and 14 below.

[16] ARSIWA Commentary (n 3), 143.

[17] ibid, 142–43.

between the obligations of the Members of the United Nations under the present Charter and their obligations under any other international agreement, their obligations under the present Charter shall prevail'. Although the ARSIWA and ARIO are not 'international agreements' – that is, treaties – there is little doubt that they 'are *in all respects* to be interpreted in conformity with the Charter'.[18] In particular, the ILC Commentary on the ARIO states explicitly that

> [t]he reference to the Charter of the United Nations includes obligations that are directly stated therein as well as those flowing from binding decisions of the Security Council, which, according to the International Court of Justice, similarly prevail over other obligations under international law on the basis of Article 103 of the Charter of the United Nations.[19]

The same Commentary notes that 'the Charter of the United Nations has a prevailing effect also with regard to international organizations',[20] although international organisations are not Members of the United Nations as such. In particular, 'the Security Council does not distinguish [in some of its resolutions] between States and international organizations'.[21]

II. THE INTERNATIONALLY WRONGFUL ACT

Article 1 of the ARSIWA stipulates that '[e]very internationally wrongful act of a State entails the international responsibility of that State'. Article 1 of the ARIO contains an analogous provision with respect to international organisations. Generally, an internationally wrongful act is a breach of any obligation under any rule of international law in force for a State or an international organisation at the time of its commission.[22] An internationally wrongful act

> may consist in one or more actions or omissions or a combination of both. Whether there has been an internationally wrongful act depends, first, on the requirements of the obligation which is said to have been breached and, secondly, on the framework conditions for such an act.[23]

These framework conditions are found in Part One of the ARSIWA and Part Two of the ARIO. The International Law Commission notes that

> [n]either for States nor for international organizations is the legal relationship arising out of an internationally wrongful act necessarily bilateral. The breach of the

[18] ibid, 143 (emphasis added).
[19] ARIO Commentary (n 4), 104.
[20] ibid.
[21] ibid, 104–105.
[22] Lukashuk (n 5), 85–108.
[23] ARSIWA Commentary (n 3), 32.

> obligation may well affect more than one subject of international law or the international community as a whole.[24]

Therefore, depending on the circumstances, the relationship of international responsibility may be bilateral or multilateral.[25]

The International Law Commission did not define the meaning of 'international responsibility' either in the ARSIWA or in the ARIO.[26] Instead,

> the consequences of an internationally wrongful act are dealt with in Part Two [of the ARSIWA], which concerns the 'content of the international responsibility of a State'. [In the ARIO,] the content of international responsibility is addressed in [Part Three].[27]

Article 2 of the ARSIWA stipulates that:

> There is an internationally wrongful act of a State when conduct consisting of an action or omission:
>
> (*a*) is attributable to the State under international law; and
> (*b*) constitutes a breach of an international obligation of the State.

Article 4 of the ARIO adapts this provision to the context of international organisations. The International Law Commission notes that '[t]he element of attribution has sometimes been described as "subjective" and the element of breach as "objective", but [the ARSIWA] avoid such terminology'.[28] The term 'conduct' covers both acts and omissions,[29] and the relevant obligations may result from a treaty binding on the State or the international organisation whose responsibility is invoked, or from any other applicable source of international law.[30] For example, in the context of international economic law, an internationally unlawful act could be a State's unilateral increase of customs tariffs, and an internationally unlawful omission could be a State's failure to inform the WTO in due course about legislative or administrative measures taken to implement the WTO law in its domestic legislation.

In accordance with Article 3 of the ARSIWA and Article 5 of the ARIO, the characterisation of an act as internationally wrongful is governed by international law, and (in the case of States) is not affected by the characterisation of the same act as lawful by internal law. The International Law Commission notes that this provision has two dimensions:

> First, an act of a State cannot be characterized as internationally wrongful unless it constitutes a breach of an international obligation, even if it violates a provision of

[24] ARIO Commentary (n 4), 53.
[25] ARSIWA Commentary (n 3), 33; ARIO Commentary (n 4), 53.
[26] ARIO Commentary (n 4), 53.
[27] ibid, 53 (footnotes omitted).
[28] ARSIWA Commentary (n 3), 34 (footnotes omitted).
[29] ARIO Commentary (n 4), 53.
[30] ibid, 53.

> the State's own law. Secondly and most importantly, a State cannot, by pleading that its conduct conforms to the provisions of its internal law, escape the characterization of that conduct as wrongful by international law. An act of a State must be characterized as internationally wrongful if it constitutes a breach of an international obligation, even if the act does not contravene the State's internal law – even if, under that law, the State was actually bound to act in that way.[31]

For example, since 2014, the Russian Federation included Crimea and four regions of Ukraine in its Constitution and regards these as its own regions.[32] However, the UN Charter's prohibition of the use of force against the territorial integrity or political independence of other States makes these measures internationally wrongful,[33] and necessitates international sanctions.[34]

III. ATTRIBUTION OF CONDUCT TO A STATE OR AN INTERNATIONAL ORGANISATION

The International Law Commission observes that '[i]n theory, the conduct of all human beings, corporations or collectivities linked to the State by nationality, habitual residence or incorporation might be attributed to the State, whether or not they have any connection to the Government'.[35] However, in the practice of international law,

> such an approach is avoided, both with a view to limiting responsibility to conduct which engages the State as an organization, and also so as to recognize the autonomy of persons acting on their own account and not at the instigation of a public authority.[36]

Therefore, the fundamental rule is that 'the only conduct attributed to the State at the international level is that of its organs of government, or of others who have acted under the direction, instigation or control of those organs, i.e. as agents of the State'.[37] Depending on the circumstances, the conduct may be attributed to one or more international actors:

> Although it may not frequently occur in practice, dual or even multiple attribution of conduct cannot be excluded. Thus, attribution of a certain conduct to an international organization does not imply that the same conduct cannot be attributed to a State, nor does attribution of conduct to a State rule out attribution of the same conduct to an international organization. One could also envisage conduct being

[31] ARSIWA Commentary (n 3), 36.
[32] See Art 65(1) of the Constitution of the Russian Federation.
[33] See Chapter 10, sections II.A–II.F below.
[34] Russia Sanctions Dashboard, available at https://www.castellum.ai/russia-sanctions-dashboard.
[35] ARSIWA Commentary (n 3), 38.
[36] ibid.
[37] ibid (footnote omitted).

simultaneously attributed to two or more international organizations, for instance when they establish a joint organ and act through that organ.[38]

A. Conduct of Organs of a State or an International Organisation

First of all, an internationally wrongful act is attributed to a State by virtue of the delinquent conduct of any organ of that State (Article 4 of the ARSIWA):[39]

1. The conduct of any State organ shall be considered an act of that State under international law, whether the organ exercises legislative, executive, judicial or any other functions, whatever position it holds in the organization of the State, and whatever its character as an organ of the central Government or of a territorial unit of the State.
2. An organ includes any person or entity which has that status in accordance with the internal law of the State.

Consequently, a State commits an internationally unlawful act every time any of its central or local organs in the legislative, executive or judicial branches breach an obligation of this State under any rule of international law. Examples may include the adoption of a normative legal act in contravention of international law in force for the State;[40] arbitrary conduct on the part of law enforcement agents (such as torture or other cruel, inhuman or degrading treatment or punishment[41]) or other executive organs;[42] issuing judicial decisions in violation of international law (most notably, internationally recognised human rights, including the right to a fair trial);[43] or lack of transparency when introducing domestic regulatory measures in the economic sphere.[44] In order to avoid (or at least, reduce the number of) breaches of international law by State organs, States ought to take measures to improve the qualifications of their civil servants, law enforcement officers, and judges at all levels by organising courses, training, and workshops on relevant topics of international law.[45]

[38] ARIO Commentary (n 4), 54.

[39] Article 6 of the ARIO contains a similar provision with respect to international organisations. See also SS Andreychenko, *Kontseptsiya attributsii povedinky derzhavi v mizhnarodnomu pravi* [*The Concept of Attribution of State Conduct in International Law*] (Odessa, Phoenix Press, 2015), 179–207.

[40] Andreychenko (n 39), 207–25.

[41] On the Ruzakhunov case, see 24.KG, 'Vikram Ruzahunov demands 61 million tenge in compensation from Kazakh police', 14 December 2024, available at https://24.kg/english/314215_Vikram_Ruzahunov_demands_61_million_tenge_in_compensation_from_Kazakh_police/.

[42] Andreychenko (n 39), 225–46.

[43] See *Vladislav Chelakh v Kazakhstan* (CCPR/C/121/D/2645/2015), available at https://juris.ohchr.org/casedetails/2359/en-US. See also Andreychenko (n 39), 247–70.

[44] Van den Bossche and Zdouc (n 8), 498–502, 532–33.

[45] S Sayapin, 'International Law in Central Asia: Practices and Doctrines' (2022) 47 *Review of Central and East European Law* 322, 350.

B. Conduct of Persons or Entities Exercising Elements of Governmental Authority

The responsibility of a State under international law also arises in the event of a breach of an international obligation of that State by a person or entity that is not an organ of the State but is nonetheless authorised to exercise elements of governmental authority:

> The conduct of a person or entity which is not an organ of the State under article 4 but which is empowered by the law of that State to exercise elements of the governmental authority shall be considered an act of the State under international law, provided the person or entity is acting in that capacity in the particular instance [ARSIWA, Article 5].

This provision relates, first of all, to State-owned (or, in the language of the International Law Commission, 'parastatal'[46]) entities managing natural (in particular, energy) resources, first tier banks, national transport companies (air and rail carriers), trade missions and other legal entities carrying out economic activities and functions delegated by the State.[47] It is understood that such legal entities act in the economic interests of the State and on its behalf, and therefore, these entities' acts, which result in breaches of the respective States' obligations under international law, give rise to the international responsibility of the States themselves.

C. Conduct of Organs Placed at the Disposal of a State or an International Organisation

Article 6 of the ARSIWA pertains to the 'limited and precise situation in which an organ of a State is effectively put at the disposal of another State so that the organ may temporarily act for its benefit and under its authority':[48]

> The conduct of an organ placed at the disposal of a State by another State shall be considered an act of the former State under international law if the organ is acting in the exercise of elements of the governmental authority of the State at whose disposal it is placed [ARSIWA Article 6].

In order for Article 6 to apply, two criteria must be explicitly met: 'First, the organ in question must possess the status of an organ of the sending State; and secondly its conduct must involve the exercise of elements of the governmental authority of the receiving State'.[49] According to the International Law Commission, examples covered by this provision include situations whereby

[46] ARSIWA Commentary (n 4), 42.
[47] Crawford (n 2), 126–32.
[48] ARSIWA Commentary (n 3), 44; Andreychenko (n 39), 271–90.
[49] ARSIWA Commentary (n 3), 44.

> a section of the health service or some other unit placed under the orders of another country to assist in overcoming an epidemic or natural disaster, or judges appointed in particular cases to act as judicial organs of another State.[50]

Thus, the conduct of North Korean troops aiding the Russian Federation in its war against Ukraine since 2024 is not attributable solely to Russia as long as they remain under their own command.[51]

Article 7 of the ARIO pertains to the responsibility of an international organisation when an organ is seconded to it by a State or another international organisation:

> The conduct of an organ of a State or an organ or agent of an international organization that is placed at the disposal of another international organization shall be considered under international law an act of the latter organization if the organization exercises effective control over that conduct.

In Central Asia, Kazakhstan is particularly active in the UN peace operations where Article 7 of the ARIO is highly relevant.[52] The provision covers situations

> in which the seconded organ or agent still acts to a certain extent as organ of the seconding State or as organ or agent of the seconding organization. This occurs for instance in the case of military contingents that a State places at the disposal of the United Nations for a peacekeeping operation, since the State retains disciplinary powers and criminal jurisdiction over the members of the national contingent.[53]

On Kazakhstan's contribution to the UN peace operations, see Chapter ten, sections VI.D and VI.E below.

D. Excess of Authority of Contravention of Instructions

In accordance with Article 7 of the ARSIWA, the conduct of a State organ or an entity exercising elements of governmental authority is attributable to the relevant State, even if the organ or entity in question exceeds its authority (that is, acts ultra vires) or contravenes instructions:

> The conduct of an organ of a State or of a person or entity empowered to exercise elements of the governmental authority shall be considered an act of the State under

[50] ibid. See also Crawford (n 2), 161–65.

[51] M Santora and H Cooper, 'Fighting Alongside Russia, North Koreans Wage Their Own War', New York Times, 22 January 2025, available at www.nytimes.com/2025/01/22/world/europe/north-korea-soldiers-ukraine.html; M Milanovic, 'North Korea's Troop Deployment in the Russian War of Aggression against Ukraine: The DPRK as a Principal or as an Accomplice?', EJIL:Talk!, 4 November 2024, available at www.ejiltalk.org/north-koreas-troop-deployment-in-the-russian-war-of-aggression-against-ukraine-the-dprk-as-a-principal-or-as-an-accomplice/.

[52] A Assaniyaz, 'Kazakhstan's First Independent Peacekeeping Mission Reaches Golan Heights', The Astana Times, 16 March 2024, available at astanatimes.com/2024/03/kazakhstans-first-independent-peacekeeping-mission-reaches-golan-heights/.

[53] ARIO Commentary (n 4), 56.

> international law if the organ, person or entity acts in that capacity, even if it exceeds its authority or contravenes instructions.

This rule was included in the ARSIWA in order not to enable the State to

> take refuge behind the notion that, according to the provisions of its internal law or to instructions which may have been given to its organs or agents, their actions or omissions ought not to have occurred or ought to have taken a different form.[54]

Thus, nuclear threats by Deputy Chairman of Russia's Security Council, Dmitry Medvedev, are still attributable to the Russian Federation, despite the fact that his foreign policy statements do not allegedly 'represent the official position of the country's leadership'.[55] Article 8 of the ARIO contains a similar provision with respect to international organisations. The International Law Commission notes that

> '*[u]ltra vires* conduct may be within the competence of the organization, but exceed the authority of the acting organ or agent. It also may exceed the competence of the organization, in which case it will also exceed the authority of the organ or of the agent who performed it'.[56]

Thus, the ICRC invokes selected civil, economic and social rights in its humanitarian action but it would be acting ultra vires if it ever invoked a political right, as it would be against its own principle of neutrality.[57]

E. Conduct Directed or Controlled by a State

As a rule, the conduct of private individuals or legal entities is not attributable to their State under international law.[58] However, the opposite may be true in two situations: 'The first involves private persons acting on the instructions of the State in carrying out the wrongful conduct. The second deals with a more general situation where private persons act under the State's direction or control':[59]

[54] ARSIWA Commentary (n 3), 45; Andreychenko (n 39), 291–309.

[55] The Moscow Times, 'Posol Rossii v Velikobritanii nazval vneshnepoliticheskiye zayavleniya Medvedeva ego chastnym mneniyem' ['The Russian Ambassador to the UK Called Medvedev's Foreign Policy Statements his Private Opinion']: 19 November 2024, available at: www.moscowtimes.ru/2024/11/19/posol-rossii-vvelikobritanii-nazval-vneshnepoliticheskie-zayavleniya-medvedeva-ego-chastnim-mneniem-a148014.

[56] ARIO Commentary (n 4), 60 (footnotes omitted).

[57] S Sayapin, 'The International Committee of the Red Cross and International Human Rights Law' (2009) 9 *Human Rights Law Review* 95; S Sayapin, 'International Committee of the Red Cross and the Use of International Human Rights Law' in D Rogers (ed), *Human Rights in War* (Singapore, Springer, 2022).

[58] Check Point, 'Cyber Espionage on Afghanistan, Kyrgyzstan and Uzbekistan by Chinese-speaking Hacker Group', 1 July 2021, available at blog.checkpoint.com/security/cyber-espionage-on-afghanistan-kyrgyzstan-and-uzbekistan-by-chinese-speaking-hacker-group/.

[59] ARSIWA Commentary (n 3), 47; Andreychenko (n 39), 348–77.

> The conduct of a person or group of persons shall be considered an act of a State under international law if the person or group of persons is in fact acting on the instructions of, or under the direction or control of, that State in carrying out the conduct [ARSIWA Article 8].

The difference between the two scenarios consists in the strength of the nexus between the State and the non-State actor(s).[60] In the first scenario, 'State organs supplement their own action by recruiting or instigating private persons or groups who act as "auxiliaries" while remaining outside the official structure of the State'.[61] This scenario covers the involvement of private military companies such as Wagner, Academi (Blackwater), etc.[62] In the second one, conduct is 'attributable to the State … if it directed or controlled the specific operation and the conduct complained of was an integral part of that operation'.[63] The rule covers, for example, the role of the so-called Donetsk and Luhansk People's Republics in advancing Russia's goals in its war against Ukraine since 2014.[64]

F. Conduct Carried Out in the Absence or Default of the Official Authorities

Article 9 of the ARSIWA covers exceptional situations 'such as during revolution, armed conflict or foreign occupation, where the regular authorities dissolve, are disintegrating, have been suppressed or are for the time being inoperative'.[65] It also extends to 'cases where lawful authority is being gradually restored, e.g. after foreign occupation':[66]

> The conduct of a person or group of persons shall be considered an act of a State under international law if the person or group of persons is in fact exercising elements of the governmental authority in the absence or default of the official authorities and in circumstances such as to call for the exercise of those elements of authority [ARSIWA Article 9].

Article 9 establishes three cumulative conditions for conduct to be attributable to a State:

> [F]irst, the conduct must effectively relate to the exercise of elements of the governmental authority, secondly, the conduct must have been carried out in the absence or

[60] Crawford (n 2), 141–61.
[61] ARSIWA Commentary (n 3), 47.
[62] J Aparac, G Rona and S Shameem, 'Regulating Private Military and Security Companies: What's in it for States?', EJIL:Talk!, 7 April 2025, available at www.ejiltalk.org/regulating-private-military-and-security-companies-whats-in-it-for-states/.
[63] ARSIWA Commentary (n 3), 47.
[64] T Korotkyi and N Hendel, 'The Legal Status of the Donetsk and Luhansk "Peoples' Republics"' in S Sayapin and E Tsybulenko (eds), *The Use of Force against Ukraine and International Law: Jus Ad Bellum, Jus In Bello, Jus Post Bellum* (The Hague, TMC Asser Press / Springer, 2018).
[65] ARSIWA Commentary (n 3), 49.
[66] ibid.

> default of the official authorities, and thirdly, the circumstances must have been such as to call for the exercise of those elements of authority.[67]

The criteria were probably met during the civil war in Tajikistan (1992–97),[68] and during the situation of violence in the south of Kyrgyzstan in the summer of 2010.[69]

G. Conduct of an Insurrectional or Other Movement

Article 10 of ARSIWA is additional to the rules contained in Articles 4–9, and, according to the International Law Commission, 'deals with the special case of attribution to a State of conduct of an insurrectional or other movement which subsequently becomes the new Government of the State or succeeds in establishing a new State':[70]

> 1. The conduct of an insurrectional movement which becomes the new Government of a State shall be considered an act of that State under international law.
> 2. The conduct of a movement, insurrectional or other, which succeeds in establishing a new State in part of the territory of a pre-existing State or in a territory under its administration shall be considered an act of the new State under international law.
> 3. This article is without prejudice to the attribution to a State of any conduct, however related to that of the movement concerned, which is to be considered an act of that State by virtue of articles 4 to 9 [ARSIWA Article 10].

Most notably, these rules are applicable to current developments in Afghanistan, and their effects on the neighbouring and other nations. Since 'the conduct of an insurrectional or other movement is not attributable to the [pre-existing] State',[71] it is understood that the Taliban are responsible under international law for whatever they have undertaken since regaining political power in 2021 – including for measures affecting the rights of minorities and women, such as their rights to non-discrimination, education, work, and others.[72]

[67] ibid.
[68] See Chapter 10, section IX.A below.
[69] See Chapter 10, section IX.C below.
[70] ARSIWA Commentary (n 3), 50.
[71] ibid; Andreychenko (n 39), 377–410.
[72] Human Rights Watch, 'Afghanistan: Events of 2024', available at https://www.hrw.org/world-report/2025/country-chapters/afghanistan; Fergana News, 'Taliby v Kandagare potrebovali ot rabotayushchih zhenshchin oformit "mahram-karty"' ['Taliban in Kandahar Demand Working Women Get "Mahram Cards"'], 25 July 2025, available at fergana.agency/news/139101/; Fergana News, 'Genassambleya OON odobrila rezolyutsiyu o rezkom osuzhdenii politiki talibov v Afganistane' ['UN General Assembly Approves Resolution Strongly Condemning Taliban Policies in Afghanistan'], 8 July 2025, available at fergana.agency/news/138807/.

H. Conduct Acknowledged and Adopted by a State or an International Organisation as its Own

The International Law Commission noted with respect to Article 11 of the ARSIWA that unlike all other bases for attribution, except the conduct of insurrectional or other movements under Article 10, Article 11 'provides for the attribution to a State of conduct that was not or may not have been attributable to it at the time of commission, but which is subsequently acknowledged and adopted by the State as its own':[73]

> Conduct which is not attributable to a State under the preceding articles shall nevertheless be considered an act of that State under international law if and to the extent that the State acknowledges and adopts the conduct in question as its own [ARSIWA Article 11].

In the post-Soviet space, an obvious example of conduct covered by Article 11 of ARSIWA was Vladimir Putin's acknowledgment of Russian military presence in Eastern Ukraine made in December 2015:

> Following repeated denials of Russian involvement in Ukraine's Donetsk and Luhansk regions, President Putin finally admitted in a press conference on December 17, 2015, that Russia 'never said there [in Eastern Ukraine] were not people there who carried out certain tasks including in the military sphere'. For the purpose of international law, it is immaterial that President Putin 'insisted this was not the same as regular Russian troops', because under subparagraph (g) of Article 3 of the 1974 Definition of Aggression, aggression is also constituted by a State's substantial involvement in '[t]he sending by or on behalf of a State of armed bands, groups, irregulars or mercenaries, which carry out acts of armed force against another State'. It is submitted that Russia's 'substantial involvement' in the commission of aggression against Ukraine under sub-paragraph (g) of Article 3 of the 1974 Definition of Aggression consisted of Russia, on May 5, 2014, effectively decriminalizing Russian nationals' participation in military units in the territory of a foreign State, which are not provided for in the legislation of that State, where the aims of such participation would not contradict the interests of the Russian Federation, and thus legitimized, under Russia's domestic law, the involvement of thousands of Russian 'volunteers' in the armed conflict in Eastern Ukraine. Since this protracted involvement amounts to aggression in the sense of applicable international law, there is a ground for invoking Russia's responsibility under international law.[74]

[73] ARSIWA Commentary (n 3), 52; Andreychenko (n 39), 410–27. According to the International Law Commission, Art 9 of the ARIO 'is identically worded but for the reference to a State instead of an international organization', see ARIO Commentary (n 4), 62.

[74] S Sayapin, 'International Law on the Use of Force: Current Challenges' in LN Sadat (ed), *Seeking Accountability for the Illegal Use of Force: Challenges and Future Prospects* (Cambridge, Cambridge University Press, 2018), 280–81 (footnotes omitted).

IV. BREACH OF AN INTERNATIONAL OBLIGATION

Chapter III in Part One of the ARSIWA and Chapter III in Part Two of the ARIO offer a few criteria to define what a breach of an international obligation is, and how it may extend in time. Article 12 of the ARSIWA and Article 10(1) of the ARIO stipulate that there is a breach of an international obligation, respectively, by a State or an international organisation when an act of that State or international organisation is not in conformity with what is required of it by that obligation, regardless of its origin or character.[75] In other words, international obligations stem from any rules of 'hard' international law,[76] and any breach thereof entails international responsibility. Article 10(2) of the ARIO lays down more specifically that Article 10(1) covers breaches of any international obligations that may arise for an international organisation towards its members under the rules of the organisation.

A. International Obligation in Force for a State or an International Organisation

Further, Article 13 of the ARSIWA and Article 11 of the ARIO provide that in order for an act of a State or an international organisation to constitute a breach of an international obligation, the State or the international organisation must be bound by the obligation in question at the time the act occurs.[77] That is, treaties do not give rise to obligations before they enter into force, and a State persistently objecting to an emerging rule of customary international law is not bound by that rule.[78] The persistent objector rule does not apply to peremptory norms of general international law (*jus cogens*).[79]

B. Single, Continuing, and Composite Breaches

Breaches of international obligations can be instantaneous,[80] continuing,[81] or composite.[82] The more controversial notion of 'complex' breaches was not

[75] ARSIWA Commentary (n 3), 54; ARIO Commentary (n 4), 63.
[76] See Chapter 6 and Chapter 7, sections I, II.A–II.D.
[77] ARSIWA Commentary (n 3), 57; ARIO Commentary (n 4), 64.
[78] See Chapter 6, section II.G and Chapter 7, section I.C.
[79] See Chapter 7, section II.B. See also Art 26 of the ARSIWA ('Compliance with peremptory norms'): 'Nothing in this chapter precludes the wrongfulness of any act of a State which is not in conformity with an obligation arising under a peremptory norm of general international law'. A similar rule features in Art 26 of the ARIO.
[80] Art 14(1) of the ARSIWA, Art 12(1) of the ARIO. See also Crawford (n 2), 254–58.
[81] Art 14(2) of the ARSIWA, Art 12(2) of the ARIO. See also Crawford (n 2), 258–65.
[82] Art 15 of the ARSIWA, Art 13 of the ARIO. See also Crawford (n 2), 265–69.

included in the final version of the ARSIWA.[83] An instantaneous breach of an international obligation, by an act of a State or an international organisation, not having a continuing character occurs at the moment when the act is performed, even if its effects continue – for example, when the armed forces of a State commit a war crime.[84] In turn, the breach of an international obligation having a continuing character extends over the entire period during which the act continues and remains not in conformity with the international obligation. Typically, foreign occupation is a continuing breach until it comes to an end.[85] Next, the breach of an international obligation requiring a State or an international organisation to prevent a given event occurs when the event occurs, and extends over the entire period during which the event continues and remains not in conformity with that obligation.[86] For example, as noted by the International Law Commission, 'the obligation to prevent transboundary damage by air pollution, dealt with in the *Trail Smelter* arbitration, was breached for as long as the pollution continued to be emitted'.[87] Last but not least, Article 15 of the ARSIWA and Article 13 of the ARIO lay down rules on responsibility for composite acts. A composite act is 'a series of actions or omissions defined in aggregate as wrongful', which, 'taken with the other actions or omissions, is sufficient to constitute the wrongful act' (Article 15(1) of the ARSIWA). In the International Law Commission's view, genocide is an obvious example of 'an accumulation of acts of killing, causing harm, etc., committed with the relevant intent'.[88] Composite acts extend 'over the entire period starting with the first of the actions or omissions of the series and lasts for as long as these actions or omissions are repeated and remain not in conformity with the international obligation'.[89]

V. ONE STATE OR INTERNATIONAL ORGANISATION'S RESPONSIBILITY IN CONNECTION WITH ANOTHER'S ACT

Chapter IV in Part One of the ARSIWA and Chapter IV in Part Two of the ARIO regulate international responsibility of a State or an international organisation in connection with the act of another State or international organisation. The International Law Commission notes that 'internationally wrongful conduct often results from the collaboration of several States rather than of one State acting alone'.[90] Therefore, 'Articles 16 to 18 on the

[83] Crawford (n 2), 269–73.
[84] On war crimes, see Chapter 15, section IV.E.
[85] On occupation, see generally A Gross, *The Writing on the Wall: Rethinking the International Law of Occupation* (Cambridge, Cambridge University Press, 2017).
[86] Art 14(3) of the ARSIWA, Art 12(3) of the ARIO.
[87] ARSIWA Commentary (n 3), 62 (footnotes omitted).
[88] ARSIWA Commentary (n 3), 62.
[89] Art 15(2) of the ARSIWA, Art 13(2) of the ARIO.
[90] ARSIWA Commentary (n 3), 64.

responsibility of States for internationally wrongful acts cover the cases in which a State aids or assists, directs and controls, or coerces another State in the commission of an internationally wrongful act'.[91] In particular, according to Article 16 of the ARSIWA:[92]

> A State which aids or assists another State in the commission of an internationally wrongful act by the latter is internationally responsible for doing so if:
>
> (*a*) that State does so with knowledge of the circumstances of the internationally wrongful act; and
>
> (*b*) the act would be internationally wrongful if committed by that State.

The International Law Commission comments that

> [s]uch situations arise where a State voluntarily assists or aids another State in carrying out conduct which violates the international obligations of the latter, for example, by knowingly providing an essential facility or financing the activity in question. Other examples include providing means for the closing of an international waterway, facilitating the abduction of persons on foreign soil, or assisting in the destruction of property belonging to nationals of a third country. The State primarily responsible in each case is the acting State, and the assisting State has only a supporting role.[93]

A recent telling example is the support provided by Belarus to Russia since the beginning of the full-scale invasion of Ukraine.[94]

In turn, according to Article 17 of the ARSIWA:[95]

> A State which directs and controls another State in the commission of an internationally wrongful act by the latter is internationally responsible for that act if:
>
> (*a*) that State does so with knowledge of the circumstances of the internationally wrongful act; and
>
> (*b*) the act would be internationally wrongful if committed by that State.

In such a scenario, 'a State which directs and controls another in the commission of an internationally wrongful act is responsible for the act itself, since it controlled and directed the act in its entirety'.[96] Most notably, in international armed conflict, 'the occupying State is responsible for acts of the occupied State which it directs and controls'.[97] Last but not least, Article 18 of ARSIWA covers

[91] ARIO Commentary (n 4), 65 (footnotes omitted).

[92] See also Art 14 of the ARIO.

[93] ARSIWA Commentary (n 3), 66.

[94] J Rankin, 'Lukashenko says he has "no regrets" about Belarus helping Russia to invade Ukraine', 27 January 2025, available at https://www.theguardian.com/world/2025/jan/26/lukashenko-says-he-has-no-regrets-about-belarus-helping-russia-to-invade-ukraine.

[95] See also Art 15 of the ARIO.

[96] ARSIWA Commentary (n 3), 68.

[97] ibid.

situations where a State coerces another State to commit an internationally wrongful act:[98]

> A State which coerces another State to commit an act is internationally responsible for that act if:
>
> (*a*) the act would, but for the coercion, be an internationally wrongful act of the coerced State; and
>
> (*b*) the coercing State does so with knowledge of the circumstances of the act.

The International Law Commission clarifies that '[i]n such cases the responsibility of the coercing State with respect to the third State derives not from its act of coercion, but rather from the wrongful conduct resulting from the action of the coerced State'.[99] Coercion can range from serious economic pressure to a threat or use of force contrary to the UN Charter.[100] Since coercion under Article 18 is essentially equated to force majeure under Article 23,[101] 'the responsibility of the coerced State [is] precluded *vis-à-vis* the injured third State'.[102] Finally, Article 19 of the ARSIWA leaves unprejudiced 'the international responsibility, under other provisions of these articles, of the State which commits the act in question, or of any other State'.[103] In other words, it 'recognizes that the attribution of international responsibility to an assisting, directing or coercing State does not preclude the responsibility of the assisted, directed or coerced State',[104] and implies that the specific responsibilities of the coercing and coerced States depend on the particular circumstances of the case.

VI. CONTENT OF THE INTERNATIONAL RESPONSIBILITY OF A STATE

Part Two of the ARSIWA and Part Three of the ARIO lay down the respective rules on the content of the international responsibility of States and international organisations. Article 28 of the ARSIWA stipulates generally that '[t]he international responsibility of a State which is entailed by an internationally wrongful act in accordance with the provisions of part one involves legal consequences as set out in this part'.[105] Importantly, reparation for injury does not exclude the continued duty of performance under Article 29 of the ARSIWA:[106] 'The legal consequences of an internationally wrongful act under this part do not affect the continued duty of the responsible State to perform the obligation breached'.

[98] See also Art 16 of the ARIO.
[99] ARSIWA Commentary (n 3), 69.
[100] ibid, 70.
[101] See section X.D below.
[102] ARSIWA Commentary (n 3), 70.
[103] See also Art 19 of the ARIO.
[104] ARSIWA Commentary (n 3), 70.
[105] See also Art 28 of the ARIO.
[106] See also Art 29 of the ARIO.

International responsibility for an internationally wrongful act

> does not mean that the pre-existing legal relation established by the primary obligation disappears. Even if the responsible State complies with its obligations [under Articles 30[107] and 31[108] of the ARSIWA] to cease the wrongful conduct and to make full reparation for the injury caused, it is not relieved thereby of the duty to perform the obligation breached[109]

as long as the underlying rule of international law remains in force for the State.

Article 32 of the ARSIWA reinforces the rule contained in Article 3 of the ARSIWA regarding the irrelevance of internal law:[110] 'The responsible State may not rely on the provisions of its internal law as justification for failure to comply with its obligations under this part'. According to Article 33(1) of the ARSIWA, the obligations in question 'may be owed to another State, to several States, or to the international community as a whole, depending in particular on the character and content of the international obligation and on the circumstances of the breach'.[111] In turn, Article 33(2) of the ARSIWA makes it clear that '[t]he articles do not deal with the possibility of the invocation of responsibility by persons or entities other than States':[112] 'This part is without prejudice to any right, arising from the international responsibility of a State, which may accrue directly to any person or entity other than a State'. For such scenarios, special procedures – such as universal and regional mechanisms for the protection of human rights – are in place.

VII. REPARATION FOR INJURY

Chapter II in Part Two of the ARSIWA and Chapter II in Part Three of the ARIO are central in that they define the notion of reparation and its forms and lay down rules on interest and contribution to injury.

A. Forms of Reparation

Article 34 of the ARSIWA stipulates that '[f]ull reparation for the injury caused by the internationally wrongful act shall take the form of restitution,

[107] See Art 30 of the ARSIWA ('Cessation and non-repetition'): 'The State responsible for the internationally wrongful act is under an obligation: (*a*) to cease that act, if it is continuing; (*b*) to offer appropriate assurances and guarantees of non-repetition, if circumstances so require'. See also Art 30 of the ARIO.

[108] See Art 31 of the ARSIWA ('Reparation'): '1. The responsible State is under an obligation to make full reparation for the injury caused by the internationally wrongful act. 2. Injury includes any damage, whether material or moral, caused by the internationally wrongful act of a State'. See also Art 31 of the ARIO.

[109] ARSIWA Commentary (n 3), 88.

[110] See also Art 32 of the ARIO.

[111] See also Art 33(1) of the ARIO.

[112] ARSIWA Commentary (n 3), 95. See also Art 33(2) of the ARIO.

compensation and satisfaction, either singly or in combination, in accordance with the provisions of this chapter'.[113] This general provision is subject to more specific conditions laid down in the subsequent provisions.

B. Restitution

In accordance with Article 35 of the ARSIWA, restitution is the primary form of reparation 'to the extent that any changes that have occurred [since an internationally wrongful act] may be traced to that act':[114]

> A State responsible for an internationally wrongful act is under an obligation to make restitution, that is, to re-establish the situation which existed before the wrongful act was committed, provided and to the extent that restitution:
> (*a*) is not materially impossible;
> (*b*) does not involve a burden out of all proportion to the benefit deriving from restitution instead of compensation.

The International Law Commission explains that '[i]n its simplest form, this involves such conduct as the release of persons wrongly detained or the return of property wrongly seized'.[115] Thus, for example, Russia is bound to return to Kazakhstan the skull of the last Kazakh Khan, Kenesary, who led the national liberation movement of the Kazakhs in 1837–47 for independence from the Russian Empire.[116]

C. Compensation

Article 36 of the ARSIWA lays down rules for compensation to the extent that material or moral damage caused by an internationally wrongful act is not made good by restitution:[117]

> 1. The State responsible for an internationally wrongful act is under an obligation to compensate for the damage caused thereby, insofar as such damage is not made good by restitution.

[113] See also Art 34 of the ARIO and Crawford (n 2), 480–505.
[114] ARSIWA Commentary (n 3), 96. See also Art 35 of the ARIO.
[115] ARSIWA Commentary (n 3), 96. See also Crawford (n 2), 510–16.
[116] Sputnik Kazakhstan, 'Sushchestvuyet li golova Kenesary hana i vernut li ee Kazahstanu, otvetili v MID' ['Does the Head of Kenesary Khan Exist and Will It Be Returned to Kazakhstan, the Foreign Ministry Responded'], 14 August 2023, available at ru.sputnik.kz/20230814/suschestvuet-li-golova-kenesary-khana-i-vernut-li-ee-kazakhstanu-otvetili-v-mid-37668498.html.
[117] See also Art 36 of the ARIO and Crawford (n 2), 516–26; C Tomuschat, 'State Responsibility and the Individual Right of Compensation Before National Courts' in A Clapham and P Gaeta, *The Oxford Handbook of International Law in Armed Conflict* (Oxford, Oxford University Press, 2014).

2. The compensation shall cover any financially assessable damage including loss of profits insofar as it is established.

The International Law Commission explains that

> [f]inancially assessable damage encompasses both damage suffered by the State itself (to its property or personnel or in respect of expenditures reasonably incurred to remedy or mitigate damage flowing from an internationally wrongful act) as well as damage suffered by nationals, whether persons or companies, on whose behalf the State is claiming within the framework of diplomatic protection.[118]

In line with this reasoning, the first preparatory meeting regarding a Claims Commission for Ukraine took place in The Hague on 9–10 July 2024.[119] Where applicable, interest must be paid in addition to the principal sum, in accordance with Article 38 of the ARSIWA.[120] In turn, Article 36(2) of the ARSIWA implies that some damage is not 'financially assessable' and therefore 'is the subject matter of satisfaction, dealt with in article 37 [of the ARSIWA]'.[121]

D. Satisfaction

Restitution and compensation being the economic forms of reparation, satisfaction in the sense of Article 37 of the ARSIWA is available for 'non-material injury':[122]

1. The State responsible for an internationally wrongful act is under an obligation to give satisfaction for the injury caused by that act insofar as it cannot be made good by restitution or compensation.
2. Satisfaction may consist in an acknowledgement of the breach, an expression of regret, a formal apology or another appropriate modality.
3. Satisfaction shall not be out of proportion to the injury and may not take a form humiliating to the responsible State.

The International Law Commission explains that '[t]he forms of satisfaction listed in [Article 37(2)] are no more than examples. The appropriate form of satisfaction will depend on the circumstances and cannot be prescribed in

[118] ARSIWA Commentary (n 3), 99.
[119] Register of Damage for Ukraine, 'First Preparatory Meeting on an International Instrument to establish a Claims Commission for Ukraine', 12 July 2024, available at: rd4u.coe.int/en/-/first-preparatory-meeting-on-an-international-instrument-to-establish-a-claims-commission-for-ukraine.
[120] See Art 38 of the ARSIWA ('Interest'): '1. Interest on any principal sum due under this chapter shall be payable when necessary in order to ensure full reparation. The interest rate and mode of calculation shall be set so as to achieve that result. 2. Interest runs from the date when the principal sum should have been paid until the date the obligation to pay is fulfilled'. See also Art 38 of the ARIO and Crawford (n 2), 531–38.
[121] ARSIWA Commentary (n 3), 99.
[122] ARSIWA Commentary (n 3), 106 (footnotes omitted). See also Art 37 of the ARIO and Crawford (n 2), 527–31.

advance'.[123] According to the ILC, some of the most common modalities of satisfaction include 'a declaration of the wrongfulness of the act by a competent court or tribunal',[124] and apology.[125] Formal apologies are still expected for such unpunished crimes of the past as deportations of peoples to Central Asia, the man-made famine in Kazakhstan (1928–34),[126] and the desertification of the Aral Sea.[127]

E. Contribution to the Injury

Injured States, persons, or entities sometimes materially contribute to the injury by their own wilful or negligent conduct. Article 39 of the ARSIWA stipulates accordingly that '[i]n the determination of reparation, account shall be taken of the contribution to the injury by wilful or negligent action or omission of the injured State or any person or entity in relation to whom reparation is sought'.[128] The International Law Commission notes that such questions

> arise most frequently in the context of compensation [but] the principle may also be relevant to other forms of reparation. For example, if a State-owned ship is unlawfully detained by another State and while under detention sustains damage attributable to the negligence of the captain, the responsible State may be required merely to return the ship in its damaged condition.[129]

VIII. INVOKING THE RESPONSIBILITY OF A STATE OR INTERNATIONAL ORGANISATION

The implementation of international responsibility is regulated, respectively, by Part Three of the ARSIWA and Part Four of the ARIO. The International Law Commission highlights that

> [c]entral to the invocation of responsibility is the concept of the injured State. This is the State whose individual right has been denied or impaired by the internationally wrongful act or which has otherwise been particularly affected by that act.[130]

[123] ARSIWA Commentary (n 3), 106 (footnotes omitted).
[124] ibid.
[125] ibid, 107.
[126] V Polovinko, 'Asharshylyq: 90 let Golodomoru v Kazahstane, ubivshemu ne menee milliona kazahov. Vina SSSR i Stalina neosporima. Kak za eto budet otvechat Rossiya?' ['Asharshylyq: 90 Years of the Holodomor in Kazakhstan, which Killed at Least a Million Kazakhs. The Guilt of the USSR and Stalin is Undeniable. How will Russia be Responsible for This?'], 31 May 2021, available at novayagazeta.ru/articles/2021/05/31/asharshylyk.
[127] See Chapter 2, section IV.G.
[128] See also Art 39 of the ARIO.
[129] ARSIWA Commentary (n 3), 110.
[130] ibid, 116.

As a rule, responsibility under international law is invoked by an injured State or international organisation, but exceptions are possible where the obligation breached is owed to a group of States and is established for the protection of a collective interest of the group, or where the obligation breached is owed to the international community as a whole.[131] According to Article 42 of the ARSIWA:[132]

> A State is entitled as an injured State to invoke the responsibility of another State if the obligation breached is owed to:
>
> (*a*) that State individually; or
>
> (*b*) a group of States including that State, or the international community as a whole, and the breach of the obligation:
>
> (i) specially affects that State; or
>
> (ii) is of such a character as radically to change the position of all the other States to which the obligation is owed with respect to the further performance of the obligation.

For the purpose of Article 42, 'invocation should be understood as taking measures of a relatively formal character, for example, the raising or presentation of a claim against another State or the commencement of proceedings before an international court or tribunal'.[133] A mere protest is not sufficient to invoke the responsibility under international law.[134] Article 43 of the ARSIWA specifies that the responsible State must be given a formal notice of claim:[135]

> 1. An injured State which invokes the responsibility of another State shall give notice of its claim to that State.
> 2. The injured State may specify in particular:
>
> (*a*) the conduct that the responsible State should take in order to cease the wrongful act, if it is continuing;
>
> (*b*) what form reparation should take in accordance with the provisions of part two.

In appropriate circumstances, a notice of claim may be given *by* a plurality of injured States or international organisations,[136] or *to* a plurality of responsible States or international organisations.[137] Under Article 44 of the ARSIWA, a

[131] See Art 48(1) of the ARSIWA and Art 49 of the ARIO.

[132] See also Art 43 of the ARIO.

[133] ARSIWA Commentary (n 3), 117.

[134] ibid.

[135] See also Art 44 of the ARIO.

[136] See Art 46 of the ARSIWA ('Plurality of injured States'): 'Where several States are injured by the same internationally wrongful act, each injured State may separately invoke the responsibility of the State which has committed the internationally wrongful act'. See also Art 47 of the ARIO.

[137] See Art 47 of the ARSIWA ('Plurality of responsible States'): '1. Where several States are responsible for the same internationally wrongful act, the responsibility of each State may be invoked in relation to that act. 2. Paragraph 1: (*a*) does not permit any injured State to recover, by way of compensation, more than the damage it has suffered; (*b*) is without prejudice to any right of recourse against the other responsible States'. See also Art 48 of the ARIO.

claim is inadmissible if it is 'not brought in accordance with any applicable rule relating to the nationality of claims', or it is 'one to which the rule of exhaustion of local remedies applies and any available and effective local remedy has not been exhausted'.[138] These rules pertain especially to diplomatic protection and the international protection of human rights.[139]

Pursuant to Article 45 of the ARSIWA, an injured State loses its right to invoke responsibility if the injured State has validly waived the claim, or if the injured State is to be considered as having, by reason of its conduct, validly acquiesced in the lapse of the claim. The International Law Commission stresses with respect to the first scenario that

> waiver is only effective if it is validly given. As with other manifestations of State consent, questions of validity can arise with respect to a waiver, for example, possible coercion of the State or its representative, or a material error as to the facts of the matter, arising perhaps from a misrepresentation of those facts by the responsible State.[140]

The question of consent was central in the trial of Ukraine's ex-President Yanukovych for his role in facilitating Russia's use of force against Ukraine.[141] The second scenario

> deals with the case where an injured State is to be considered as having, by reason of its conduct, validly acquiesced in the lapse of the claim. The article emphasizes *conduct* of the State, which could include, where applicable, unreasonable delay, as the determining criterion for the lapse of the claim.[142]

In this regard, the International Law Commission quoted an ICJ ruling to the effect that 'international law does not lay down any specific time limit in that regard. It is therefore for the Court to determine in the light of the circumstances of each case whether the passage of time renders an application inadmissible'.[143]

IX. SERIOUS BREACHES OF OBLIGATIONS UNDER PEREMPTORY NORMS OF GENERAL INTERNATIONAL LAW

Chapter III in Part Two of the ARSIWA contains particular rules on international responsibility for serious breaches of obligations arising under peremptory norms of general international law.[144] The International Law Commission's Draft

[138] ARSIWA Commentary (n 3), 120–21.
[139] Crawford (n 2), 567–87.
[140] ARSIWA Commentary (n 3), 122.
[141] S Sayapin, 'The *Yanukovych* Trial in Ukraine: A Revival of the Crime of Aggression?' (2020) 50 *Israel Yearbook on Human Rights* 63.
[142] ARSIWA Commentary (n 3), 122.
[143] ibid (footnotes omitted).
[144] On such norms, see generally A Orakhelashvili, *Peremptory Norms in International Law* (Oxford, Oxford University Press, 2006). See also I Brownlie, *Principles of Public International Law*, 5th edn (Oxford, Clarendon Press, 1998), 511–19; T Christakis, 'L'obligation de non-reconnaissance des situations créées par le recours illicite à la force ou d'autres actes enfreignant

Conclusions on Identification and Legal Consequences of Peremptory Norms of General International Law contain a non-exhaustive list of such superior rules of international law, including the prohibition of aggression, genocide,[145] crimes against humanity, and a few other rules. Article 40(2) of the ARSIWA lays down that '[a] breach of such an obligation is serious if it involves a gross or systematic failure by the responsible State to fulfil the obligation'. Under Article 41 of the ARSIWA:

1. States shall cooperate to bring to an end through lawful means any serious breach within the meaning of article 40.
2. No State shall recognize as lawful a situation created by a serious breach within the meaning of article 40, nor render aid or assistance in maintaining that situation.
3. This article is without prejudice to the other consequences referred to in this part and to such further consequences that a breach to which this chapter applies may entail under international law.

Russia's aggression against Ukraine has entailed an unprecedented number and intensity of international sanctions. Since 2022, Russia is the most sanctioned country in history.[146] The Central Asian nations have not formally introduced or joined any sanctions, given their strong bonds with Russia, but they officially declare compliance with international sanctions,[147] in

des règles fondamentales' in C Tomuschat and JM Thouvenin (eds), *The Fundamental Rules of the International Legal Order: Jus Cogens and Obligations Erga Omnes* (Leiden, Martinus Nijhoff Publishers, 2006) 127; A Orakhelashvili, 'The Impact of Peremptory Norms on the Interpretation and Application of United Nations Security Council Resolutions' (2005) 16 *European Journal of International Law* 59; JAC Salcedo, 'Reflections on the Existence of a Hierarchy of Norms in International Law' (1997) 8 *European Journal of International Law* 583; E Schwelb, 'Some Aspects of International *Jus Cogens* as Formulated by the International Law Commission' (1967) 61 *American Journal of International Law* 946; I Scobbie, 'The Invocation of Responsibility for the Breach of "Obligations under Peremptory Norms of General International Law"' (2002) 13 *European Journal of International Law* 1201; D Shelton, 'Normative Hierarchy in International Law' (2006) 100 *American Journal of International Law* 291; LA Sicilianos, 'The Classification of Obligations and the Multilateral Dimension of the Relations of International Responsibility' (2002) 13 *European Journal of International Law* 1127; S Talmon, 'The Duty not to "Recognize as Lawful" a Situation Created by the Illegal Use of Force or Other Serious Breaches of a *Jus Cogens* Obligation: an Obligation without Real Substance?' in C Tomuschat and JM Thouvenin (eds), *The Fundamental Rules of the International Legal Order: Jus Cogens and Obligations Erga Omnes* (Leiden, Martinus Nijhoff Publishers, 2006) 99–125; A Von Verdross, '*Jus Dispositivum* and *Jus Cogens* in International Law' (1966) 60 *American Journal of International Law* 55; E Vranes, 'The Definition of "Norm Conflict" in International Law and Legal Theory' (2006) 17 *European Journal of International Law* 395; JHH Weiler and AL Paulus, 'The Structure of Change in International Law or Is There a Hierarchy of Norms in International Law?' (1997) 8 *European Journal of International Law* 545; E Wyler, 'From "State Crime" to Responsibility for "Serious Breaches of Obligations under Peremptory Norms of General International Law"' (2002) 13 *European Journal of International Law* 1147.

[145] E Carli, 'On State Responsibility for Complicity in Genocide: Will South Africa's "All-In Strategy" Be Effective?', EJIL:Talk!, 5 March 2024, available at www.ejiltalk.org/on-state-responsibility-for-complicity-in-genocide-will-south-africas-all-in-strategy-be-effective/.

[146] Forbes, 'The Most Sanctioned Countries', available at forbes.ge/en/the-most-sanctioned-countries/.

[147] A Satubaldina, 'EU Sanctions Envoy Commends Cooperation with Kazakhstan', The Astana Times, 30 January 2025, available at https://astanatimes.com/2025/01/eu-sanctions-envoy-commends-cooperation-with-kazakhstan/.

an effort not to become subject to secondary sanctions. In December 2022, the European Union created the post of International Special Envoy for the Implementation of EU Sanctions 'to ensure continuous, high-level discussions with third countries to avoid the evasion or even the circumvention of the unprecedented restrictive measures that have been imposed on Russia since the start of its war against Ukraine'.[148]

X. CIRCUMSTANCES PRECLUDING WRONGFULNESS

The circumstances precluding the wrongfulness of an act under international law are listed in Chapter V of Part One of the ARSIWA and Chapter V of Part Two of the ARIO. As noted by the International Law Commission, these circumstances are 'different in nature but are brought together by their common effect':[149] they exempt States and international organisations from responsibility under international law. By and large,

> they apply to any internationally wrongful act whether it involves the breach by a State of an obligation arising under a rule of general international law, a treaty, a unilateral act or from any other source. They do not annul or terminate the obligation; rather they provide a justification or excuse for non-performance while the circumstance in question subsists.[150]

The six circumstances are considered below.

A. Consent

According to Article 20 of the ARSIWA,

> [v]alid consent by a State to the commission of a given act by another State precludes the wrongfulness of that act in relation to the former State to the extent that the act remains within the limits of that consent.[151]

The International Law Commission recalls that

> consent by a State to particular conduct by another State precludes the wrongfulness of that act in relation to the consenting State, provided the consent is valid and to the extent that the conduct remains within the limits of the consent given.[152]

[148] European Commission, 'EU appoints David O'Sullivan as International Special Envoy for the Implementation of EU Sanctions', 13 December 2022, available at ireland.representation.ec.europa.eu/news-and-events/news/eu-appoints-david-osullivan-international-special-envoy-implementation-eu-sanctions-2022-12-13_en.
[149] ARIO Commentary (n 4), 70.
[150] ARSIWA Commentary (n 3), 71.
[151] See also Art 20 of the ARIO and Crawford (n 2), 283–89.
[152] ARSIWA Commentary (n 3), 73.

It is a daily business for States to consent, for example, to the transit of foreign commercial aircraft through their airspace. The key questions about the validity of consent are 'whether the agent or person who gave the consent was authorized to do so on behalf of the State … or whether the consent was vitiated by coercion or some other factor'.[153] The consent is valid as long as the organ or agent acting on behalf of a State or an international organisation does so in accordance with applicable (domestic or institutional) law, and acts freely. Thus, in the past, Kyrgyzstan, Tajikistan and Uzbekistan gave valid consents to the presence of foreign military bases in their territories. In November 2005, the US vacated the Karshi–Khanabad (K2) military base in Uzbekistan, and in June 2014, the US Transit Center at Manas International Airport was closed.[154]

B. Self-defence

Pursuant to Article 21 of the ARSIWA, '[t]he wrongfulness of an act of a State is precluded if the act constitutes a lawful measure of self-defence taken in conformity with the Charter of the United Nations'.[155] On self-defence, see Chapter ten, section V below. In Central Asia, Kyrgyzstan and Tajikistan accused each other of aggression and invoked self-defence in the context of armed conflicts in 2021 and 2022.[156]

C. Countermeasures

Article 22 of the ARSIWA stipulates that '[t]he wrongfulness of an act of a State not in conformity with an international obligation towards another State is precluded if and to the extent that the act constitutes a countermeasure taken against the latter State'.[157] Injured States or international organisations use countermeasures as a tool of 'self-help' but other States and international organisations may as well rely on them in appropriate circumstances.[158] The most typical types of countermeasures are reprisals and retorsions. A reprisal is a formally unlawful

[153] ARSIWA Commentary, 73.

[154] A Cooley and E Larson, 'Military Base Timeline of Central Asia', available at https://harriman.columbia.edu/central-asia-military-base-timeline/.

[155] See also Art 21 of the ARIO and Crawford (n 2), 289–92.

[156] See Chapter 10, section IX.D below.

[157] See also Art 22 of the ARIO and Crawford (n 2), 292–95.

[158] See Art 54 of the ARSIWA ('Measures taken by States other than an injured State'): 'This chapter does not prejudice the right of any State, entitled under article 48, paragraph 1, to invoke the responsibility of another State, to take lawful measures against that State to ensure cessation of the breach and reparation in the interest of the injured State or of the beneficiaries of the obligation breached'. See also Art 57 of the ARIO, and M Jackson and F Paddeu, 'Assistance to a Countermeasure in International Law', EJIL:Talk!, 17 July 2024, available at www.ejiltalk.org/assistance-to-a-countermeasure-in-international-law/.

act, which is rendered lawful by the illegality of the prior act by a State or an international organisation, to which the reprisal constitutes a reaction. For example, if a State unilaterally increases a customs tariff, the State that is affected by this measure usually will be allowed to increase the tariff on the same or other goods originating in the first State.[159] In turn, a retorsion is a formally lawful but unfriendly countermeasure, such as declaring a foreign diplomat *persona non grata* in accordance with Article 9(1) of the Vienna Convention on Diplomatic Relations.[160]

Countermeasures are more specifically regulated by Articles 49–54 of the ARSIWA and Articles 51–57 of the ARIO. Article 49 explains the object and limits of countermeasures:[161]

1. An injured State may only take countermeasures against a State which is responsible for an internationally wrongful act in order to induce that State to comply with its obligations under part two.
2. Countermeasures are limited to the non-performance for the time being of international obligations of the State taking the measures towards the responsible State.
3. Countermeasures shall, as far as possible, be taken in such a way as to permit the resumption of performance of the obligations in question.

In accordance with Article 50 of the ARSIWA, the scope of countermeasures is not unlimited.[162] In particular, countermeasures are not permitted to affect the obligation to refrain from the threat or use of force as embodied in the Charter of the United Nations, obligations for the protection of fundamental human rights, obligations of a humanitarian character prohibiting reprisals, and other obligations under peremptory norms of general international law.[163] Importantly, a State taking countermeasures is not relieved of its obligations under any dispute settlement procedure applicable between it and the responsible State (Article 50(2)(a) of the ARSIWA), and to respect the inviolability of diplomatic or consular agents, premises, archives and documents (Article 50(2)(b) of the ARSIWA).[164] Countermeasures must be commensurate with the injury suffered, taking into account the gravity of the internationally wrongful act and the rights in question (Article 51 of the ARSIWA).[165] Thus, when Russian police broke into a Kyrgyz diplomat's apartment in Moscow in April 2024,[166]

[159] Van den Bossche and Zdouc (n 8), 449–53.
[160] For the text of the Vienna Convention on Diplomatic Relations, see: legal.un.org/ilc/texts/instruments/english/conventions/9_1_1961.pdf.
[161] See also Art 51 of the ARIO.
[162] See also Art 53 of the ARIO.
[163] Lukashuk (n 5), 335–39.
[164] ibid, 338.
[165] See also Art 54 of the ARIO.
[166] Radio Liberty, 'V Moskve politsiya vorvalas v kvartiru kirgizskogo diplomata' ['In Moscow, Police Broke into the Apartment of a Kyrgyz Diplomat'], 12 April 2024, available at www.svoboda.org/a/v-moskve-politsiya-vorvalasj-v-kvartiru-kirgizskogo-diplomata/32902865.html. See also *Diplomaticheskoye i konsulskoye pravo* [*Diplomatic and Consular Law*] (Moscow, Prospect, 2024), 93–96.

they clearly acted in a manner out of proportion to the situation. Article 52 of the ARSIWA lays down conditions relating to resort to countermeasures as such and especially to such urgent countermeasures as are necessary to preserve the rights of the injured State.[167] Article 53 provides that countermeasures must be terminated 'as soon as the responsible State has complied with its obligations … in relation to the internationally wrongful act'.[168] Unjustifiably prolonged countermeasures would themselves become internationally unlawful.[169]

D. Force Majeure

The concept of force majeure under international law is akin to that in the civil law doctrine.[170] Indeed, it may constitute a general principle of law.[171] It means an irresistible force, which a State is 'unable to avoid or oppose by its own means',[172] and which makes it materially impossible in the circumstances to perform an obligation. Pursuant to Article 23 of the ARSIWA:[173]

> 1. The wrongfulness of an act of a State not in conformity with an international obligation of that State is precluded if the act is due to force majeure, that is the occurrence of an irresistible force or of an unforeseen event, beyond the control of the State, making it materially impossible in the circumstances to perform the obligation.
> 2. Paragraph 1 does not apply if:
>
>   (*a*) the situation of force majeure is due, either alone or in combination with other factors, to the conduct of the State invoking it; or
>   (*b*) the State has assumed the risk of that situation occurring.

[167] See Art 52 of the ARSIWA ('Conditions relating to resort to countermeasures'): '1. Before taking countermeasures, an injured State shall: (*a*) call upon the responsible State, in accordance with article 43, to fulfil its obligations under part two; (*b*) notify the responsible State of any decision to take countermeasures and offer to negotiate with that State.

2. Notwithstanding paragraph 1 (*b*), the injured State may take such urgent countermeasures as are necessary to preserve its rights.

3. Countermeasures may not be taken, and if already taken must be suspended without undue delay if:

(*a*) the internationally wrongful act has ceased; and (*b*) the dispute is pending before a court or tribunal which has the authority to make decisions binding on the parties.

4. Paragraph 3 does not apply if the responsible State fails to implement the dispute settlement procedures in good faith'. See also Art 55 of the ARIO.

[168] See also Art 56 of the ARIO.

[169] Lukashuk (n 5), 335–39.

[170] cf AP Sergeyev and YK Tolstoy, *Grazhdanskoye pravo* [*Civil Law*], 6th edn, Vol 1 (Moscow, Prospect, 2006), 681–82.

[171] ARSIWA Commentary (n 3), 78.

[172] ARSIWA Commentary (n 3), 76.

[173] See also Art 23 of the ARIO and Crawford (n 2), 295–301.

The International Law Commission explains that three criteria must be met, in order for a State to invoke force majeure:

> (*a*) the act in question must be brought about by an irresistible force or an unforeseen event; (*b*) which is beyond the control of the State concerned; and (*c*) which makes it materially impossible in the circumstances to perform the obligation.[174]

These criteria also apply to international organisations.[175] Some of the most typical examples of force majeure include natural disasters, international or non-international armed conflicts, or pandemics.[176] Thus, during the COVID-19 pandemic, numerous human rights were affected – most notably, the freedom of movement, the rights to education, access to information, and fair trial.[177] A State or an international organisation may not invoke force majeure if it has 'caused or induced the situation in question'.[178] Now that the US Congress has reported that the coronavirus 'likely emerged because of a laboratory or research related accident' in Wuhan,[179] it remains to be seen whether the US will invoke China's responsibility.

E. Distress

Article 24 of the ARSIWA 'deals with the specific case where an individual whose acts are attributable to the State is in a situation of peril, either personally or in relation to persons under his or her care':[180]

> 1. The wrongfulness of an act of a State not in conformity with an international obligation of that State is precluded if the author of the act in question has no other reasonable way, in a situation of distress, of saving the author's life or the lives of other persons entrusted to the author's care.
> 2. Paragraph 1 does not apply if:
>   (*a*) the situation of distress is due, either alone or in combination with other factors, to the conduct of the State invoking it; or
>   (*b*) the act in question is likely to create a comparable or greater peril.

The International Law Commission points out that Article 24 'is limited to cases where human life is at stake'.[181] In practical terms, 'cases of distress have mostly

[174] ARSIWA Commentary (n 3), 76.
[175] ARIO Commentary (n 4), 73.
[176] Sergeyev and Tolstoy (n 170). See also K De Vriese, 'COVID-19 and "War" Clauses in Investment Treaties: A Breach through the Wall of State Sovereignty?', EJIL:Talk!, 10 June 2020, available at www.ejiltalk.org/covid-19-and-war-clauses-in-investment-treaties-a-breach-through-the-wall-of-state-sovereignty/.
[177] See Chapter 13, section III below.
[178] ARSIWA Commentary (n 3), 78.
[179] Al Jazeera, 'COVID-19 likely came from a lab, US committee finds', 3 December 2024: https://www.aljazeera.com/news/2024/12/3/us-lawmakers-back-covid-lab-leak-theory-after-two-year-probe.
[180] ARSIWA Commentary, 78. See also Art 24 of the ARIO and Crawford (n 2), 301–5.
[181] ARSIWA Commentary, 79.

involved aircraft or ships entering [foreign] territory under stress of weather or following mechanical or navigational failure'.[182] Article 24 also applies to emergency landings, an increasing number of which are expected to occur in the light of international sanctions against Russian airlines.[183]

F. Necessity

Whereas the concept of force majeure is closely related to an analogous civil law notion (see section X.D), the logic behind the concept of necessity appears close to the criminal law doctrine.[184] According to the International Law Commission,

> [t]he term 'necessity' (*état de nécessité*) is used to denote those exceptional cases where the only way a State can safeguard an essential interest threatened by a grave and imminent peril is, for the time being, not to perform some other international obligation of lesser weight or urgency.[185]

Article 25 of ARSIWA reads:

> 1. Necessity may not be invoked by a State as a ground for precluding the wrongfulness of an act not in conformity with an international obligation of that State unless the act:
>   (*a*) is the only way for the State to safeguard an essential interest against a grave and imminent peril; and
>   (*b*) does not seriously impair an essential interest of the State or States towards which the obligation exists, or of the international community as a whole.
> 2. In any case, necessity may not be invoked by a State as a ground for precluding wrongfulness if:
>   (*a*) the international obligation in question excludes the possibility of invoking necessity; or
>   (*b*) the State has contributed to the situation of necessity.

Necessity is exceptional and fundamentally different from all other circumstances precluding wrongfulness in that:

> Unlike consent (art. 20), self-defence (art. 21) or countermeasures (art. 22), it is not dependent on the prior conduct of the injured State. Unlike *force majeure* (art. 23), it does not involve conduct which is involuntary or coerced. Unlike distress (art. 24), necessity consists not in danger to the lives of individuals in the charge of a State

[182] ibid, 78.

[183] A Tuguzov, 'Rossiyskiy samolet sovershil avariynuyu posadku v Aktobe' ['Russian Plane Made an Emergency Landing in Aktobe'], 18 September 2023, available at 365info.kz/2023/09/rossijskij-samolet-sovershil-avarijnuyu-posadku-v-aktobe.

[184] W Wilson, *Criminal Law*, 5th edn (Harlow, Pearson, 2014), 258–70; II Rogov and KZ Baltabayev (eds), *Ugolovnoye pravo Respubliki Kazakhstan: Obshchaya chast* [*Criminal Law of the Republic of Kazakhstan: General Part*] (Almaty, Zhety Zhargy, 2016), 216–20.

[185] ARSIWA Commentary (n 3), 80. See also Art 25 of the ARIO and Crawford (n 2), 305–15.

> official but in a grave danger either to the essential interests of the State or of the international community as a whole. It arises where there is an irreconcilable conflict between an essential interest on the one hand and an obligation of the State invoking necessity on the other.[186]

It is impossible to produce a complete list of essential interests protected by the concept of necessity. The range of such interests is so broad as to include 'safeguarding the environment, preserving the very existence of the State and its people in time of public emergency, or ensuring the safety of a civilian population'.[187] To be viable, a plea of necessity 'must be the "only way" available to safeguard' an essential interest.[188] Thus, for example, WTO law permits States to introduce general, security, and other exceptions to give effect to some superior values such as human life and health, environment, culture and religion, and others.[189]

G. Consequences of Invoking a Circumstance Precluding Wrongfulness

Article 27 of the ARSIWA serves two purposes:

> First, it makes it clear that circumstances precluding wrongfulness do not as such affect the underlying obligation, so that if the circumstance no longer exists the obligation regains full force and effect. Secondly, it refers to the possibility of compensation in certain cases.[190]

Article 27 reads:

> The invocation of a circumstance precluding wrongfulness in accordance with this chapter is without prejudice to:
>
> (*a*) compliance with the obligation in question, if and to the extent that the circumstance precluding wrongfulness no longer exists;
>
> (*b*) the question of compensation for any material loss caused by the act in question.

Thus, for example, if a State invokes an economic emergency to restore the viability of a specific sector within its economy, it is expected to resume 'business as usual' once the economic emergency is over.[191] As far as compensation is concerned, subparagraph (b) of Article 27 does not contain any detailed regulations: it is assumed that '[i]t will be for the State invoking a circumstance precluding wrongfulness to agree with any affected States on the possibility

[186] ARSIWA Commentary (n 3), 80.
[187] ibid, 83.
[188] ibid.
[189] Van den Bossche and W Zdouc (n 8), 543–672.
[190] ARSIWA Commentary (n 3), 86. See also Art 27 of the ARIO.
[191] Van den Bossche and W Zdouc (n 8), 624–25.

and extent of compensation payable in a given case'.[192] Notably, compensation under Article 27(b) is meant 'to make good any material loss suffered by any State directly affected',[193] and in this sense, it is different from compensation under Article 34 of the ARSIWA, which is meant as a form of reparation for wrongful conduct.[194]

[192] ARSIWA Commentary (n 3), 86.
[193] ibid.
[194] See section VII.C above.

Part IV

Current Challenges

10

*International Peace and Security**

AT THE HEART of the international legal order lies the imperative to maintain international peace and security, a goal fundamentally shaped and constrained by the rules governing the use of force. Beginning with a discussion of the core rules of *jus contra bellum*,[1] this chapter proceeds to explore how Central Asian States have addressed critical peace and security concerns in regional and global contexts. Sections I to VIII examine the overarching prohibition of the threat or use of force under Article 2(4) of the UN Charter, along with Charter-based, Charter-related, and extra-Charter exceptions. Given their global relevance, these topics are addressed from a broader perspective, beyond Central Asia, drawing on global practices and doctrines. Section IX examines the legal dimensions of the non-international armed conflict in Tajikistan (1992–97), the Kyrgyzstan–Tajikistan border clashes (2021 and 2022), and other situations of violence in the region since 2000. It also explores Central Asian perspectives on ongoing conflicts elsewhere, the Central Asian Nuclear-Weapon-Free Zone (CANWFZ), and the legal and political implications of regional water scarcity. The concluding section underscores the progressive development of a culture of peace.

I. INTRODUCTION

A principal aim of the modern international legal order, grounded in the United Nations Charter, is the maintenance of international peace and security. Article 2(4) of the Charter establishes a fundamental restriction on the use of force in international relations – an obligation intended to hold superior legal authority.[2] It is now widely recognised as part of customary international law[3]

* Sections I–VIII of this chapter are a revised and updated version of the author's material previously published in S Sayapin, *The Crime of Aggression in International Criminal Law: Historical Development, Comparative Analysis and Present* State (The Hague, TMC Asser Press, 2014), 75–133. Permission to use published content is gratefully acknowledged.

[1] II Lukashuk and AH Saidov, *Hozirgi zamon xalqaro huquqi nazariyasi asoslari* [*The theoretical fundamentals of modern international law*] (Tashkent, Adolat, 2006), 323–32.

[2] cf Charter of the United Nations, Art 103: 'In the event of a conflict between the obligations of the Members of the United Nations under the present Charter and their obligations under any other international agreement, their obligations under the present Charter shall prevail'.

[3] See Chapter 7, section I above.

and even as a norm of *jus cogens*.[4] Malanczuk notably argued that this rule was binding even on the few States that are not UN Members.[5]

Permitted uses of force are addressed through various provisions of the Charter, beginning with the seventh preambular paragraph: '[T]o ensure … that armed force shall not be used, save in the common interest'. While the Preamble is not legally binding,[6] it reflects the spirit guiding the Charter's substantive provisions. Consistently with the 'common interest' clause, Article 1(1) identifies among the UN's purposes the use of 'effective collective measures for the prevention and removal of threats to peace, and for the suppression of acts of aggression or other breaches of peace' (on collective measures, see section VI below). At least two main UN organs – the General Assembly (Article 12) and the Security Council (Articles 24(1) and 39) – are empowered to respond, albeit differently, to threats to peace, breaches of the peace, and acts of aggression.[7] Chapters VII ('Action with Respect to Threats to the Peace, Breaches of the Peace, and Acts of Aggression') and VIII ('Regional Arrangements') are fully devoted to maintaining international peace and security through collective action by the United Nations or regional mechanisms. More specifically, Article 42 authorises the Security Council to 'take such action by air, sea or land forces as may be necessary to maintain or restore international peace and security'. Article 43 was intended to establish a framework for agreements between the Security Council and UN Member States contributing to peace and security efforts, while Article 44 addresses the Council's relations with Member States not on the Council but involved in such operations. Article 51 affirms the inherent right of Member States to self-defence against armed attacks. Lastly, the now outdated Articles 53 and 107 concern the use of force, if necessary, against former enemies from the Second World War.[8]

[4] See Chapter 7, section II.B above.

[5] P Malanczuk, *Akehurst's Modern Introduction to International Law*, 7th revised edn (London, Routledge, 1997), 309. In turn, Randelzhofer specifies that States which are not members of the United Nations 'are protected, though not bound' by Article 2(4). See A Randelzhofer, 'Article 2(4)' in B Simma (ed), *The Charter of the United Nations: A Commentary* (Oxford, Oxford University Press, 1994), 115.

[6] II Lukashuk, *Sovremennoye pravo mezhdunarodnyh dogovorov* [*Modern Law of Treaties*], vol 1 (Moscow, Wolters Kluwer, 2004), 585.

[7] On the role of the International Court of Justice in this domain, see sections II.C(ii)–II.G below.

[8] With the admission of Italy (1955), Japan (1956) and Germany (1973) as 'peace-loving States' (in the language of Article 4 of the Charter) to the United Nations, these provisions became obsolete and were recommended for deletion from the Charter. See: 'A More Secure World: Our Shared Responsibility, Report of the High-level Panel on Threats, Challenges and Change', UN Doc. A/59/565 (2004), para 298, available at www.un.org/secureworld/; and 'In Larger Freedom: Towards Development, Security and Human Rights for All', Report of the Secretary-General, UN Doc. A/59/2005 (2005), para 217, available at www.un.org/largerfreedom/. See also M Odello, 'Commentary on the United Nations' High-Level Panel on Threats, Challenges and Change' (2005) 10 *Journal of Conflict and Security Law* 231.

Since the 1999 NATO operation in Kosovo[9] – especially in connection with the US-led *Operation Enduring Freedom* (Afghanistan)[10] and *Operation Iraqi Freedom* (Iraq) – several novel doctrines have been proposed to justify these uses of force. This represents a potentially significant development in a field of international law as conservative as the post-1945 *jus contra bellum*,[11] as some of these doctrines purported to modify the Charter's rules on the use of force. By contrast, this chapter argues that Article 2(4) and related international legal norms should not be interpreted too broadly, and that any use of force in inter-State relations incompatible with the overarching prohibition in Article 2(4) constitutes a breach of the Charter.[12]

II. PROHIBITION OF THE THREAT OR USE OF FORCE

A. Article 2(4) of the UN Charter

As the Covenant of the League of Nations and the Kellogg-Briand Pact failed to prevent the Second World War, the drafters of the United Nations Charter aimed to address the shortcomings of both instruments.[13] Their ambitious reform was unprecedented, seeking to transform the traditional *jus ad bellum* – which allowed States to use force to advance foreign policy goals – into a novel *jus contra bellum* that not only outlawed war as a legitimate means of resolving disputes but also prohibited most uses of military force short of war, as well as threats of force in international relations.[14] The following sections examine Article 2(4) of the Charter as conventional law, customary international law, and *jus cogens*.

[9] CG Badescu, *Humanitarian Intervention and the Responsibility to Protect: Security and Human Rights* (Abingdon, Routledge, 2001), 1: 'In March 1999, the North Atlantic Treaty Organisation (NATO) started a bombing campaign against the Former Federal Republic of Yugoslavia to protect the Albanian population in Kosovo from being ethnically cleansed … NATO's actions were morally justified yet violated international law, as the UN Security Council had not authorized the military intervention'.

[10] R Schmidt-Radefeldt, 'Enduring Freedom – Antiterrorkrieg für immer? – Ein Beitrag zum *Jus Post Bellum* in Afghanistan' (2005) 19 *Humanitäres Völkerrecht – Informationsschriften* 245.

[11] As Müllerson so candidly noted, 'the legal texts concerning use of force have indeed undergone little, if any, change since the adoption of the UN Charter in 1845. Even General Assembly resolutions on the issue have not contained anything that could be even remotely defined as "progressive development of international law"'. See R Müllerson, 'Jus ad Bellum: Plus ça change (le monde) plus c'est la meme chose (le droit)' (2002) 7 *Journal of Conflict and Security Law* 149, 150–51.

[12] N Schrijver, 'Challenges to the Prohibition to Use Force: Does the Straitjacket of Article 2(4) UN Charter Begin to Gall Too Much?' in N Blokker and N Schrijver (eds), *The Security Council and the Use of Force: Theory and Reality – a Need for Change?* (Leiden, Martinus Nijhoff Publishers, 2005), 36–37.

[13] Y Dinstein, *War, Aggression and Self-Defence*, 3rd edn (Cambridge, Cambridge University Press, 2001), 80.

[14] Randelzhofer (n 5), 111.

B. Treaty Obligation under Article 2(4)

Article 2(4) is a provision of paramount importance, often described as 'the cornerstone of peace in the Charter', 'the heart of the United Nations Charter', or the 'basic rule of contemporary public international law'.[15] It is undoubtedly more precisely worded than Article 1 of the Kellogg-Briand Pact, as it prohibits not only war but the use of force in general, including threats of force. Moreover, in conjunction with related provisions, it establishes – at least theoretically, as Randelzhofer notes – an institutional UN system of collective sanctions against any offender (Articles 39–51).[16] As adopted at the San Francisco Conference, Article 2(4) reads:

> All Members shall refrain in their international relations from the threat or use of force against the territorial integrity or political independence of any state, or in any other manner inconsistent with the Purposes of the United Nations.

Article 2(4) of the UN Charter raises several foundational questions concerning its scope, beneficiaries, and normative content. First, while formally imposing obligations only on UN Members, the provision in practice protects both Members and non-Members ('any State').[17] Second, it identifies two categories of objects safeguarded from unlawful threats or use of force. On one hand, it explicitly protects States' territorial integrity and political independence. On the other, it prohibits threats or force used 'in any other manner inconsistent with the Purposes of the United Nations'. These Purposes are listed separately in Article 1 of the Charter and include:

- the maintenance of 'international peace and security' and related undertakings to that end (Article 1(1));
- developing 'friendly relations among nations based on respect for the principle of equal rights and self-determination of peoples', and taking 'other appropriate measures to strengthen universal peace' (Article 1(2));
- developing 'international co-operation in solving international problems of an economic, social, cultural, or humanitarian character, and in promoting and encouraging respect for human rights and for fundamental freedoms for all without distinction as to race, sex, language, or religion' (Article 1(3));
- and being 'a centre for harmonizing the actions of nations in the attainment of these common ends' (Article 1(4)).

Since both parts of the provision must be read together, it follows that the Purposes of the United Nations, as protected objects under Article 2(4), hold equal value to States' territorial integrity and political independence. Notably, an inverse reading

[15] ibid.

[16] ibid. See also MC Waxman MC, 'Regulating Resort to Force: Form and Substance of the UN Charter Regime' (2013) 24 *European Journal of International Law* 151.

[17] Malanczuk (n 5), 309.

of Article 2(4) suggests that UN Members may lawfully threaten or use force in international relations to preserve their own territorial integrity or political independence, or, in appropriate cases, that of other States, provided such actions align with the Purposes of the United Nations. The foremost exceptions to the prohibition in Article 2(4) are discussed in sections IV–VII below.

C. The Meaning of 'Force'

Understanding the notion of 'force' in Article 2(4) is essential. It is generally accepted that the provision primarily refers to the threat or use of armed or military force – that is, the deployment by a State of its regular armed forces[18] (in the broad sense currently accepted in international law[19]), irregular armed groups,[20] or means and methods of warfare as defined in international humanitarian law, against another State, its nationals, or its public or private property. Although Article 2(4) does not qualify the term 'force', this interpretation is supported by related Charter provisions (eg, Articles 41 and 46, which explicitly refer to *military* force), the 1970 Friendly Relations Declaration, and the Charter's *travaux préparatoires*. Notably, Brazil's proposal at the San Francisco Conference on 6 May 1945 to extend the prohibition to *economic* coercion was explicitly – and rightly – rejected.[21] As Randelzhofer observes, broadening Article 2(4) to include other forms of force would leave States with virtually no lawful means of exerting pressure upon States that violate international law.[22] Accordingly, the first Principle of the 1970 Friendly Relations Declaration, which interprets Article 2(4), addressed only military force,[23] while economic, political, and other forms of coercion were treated under the principle of non-intervention.[24]

The following subsections briefly examine two specific types of force – so-called 'physical' force and 'indirect' force – which, though distinct from armed force, may in certain circumstances produce similar effects, particularly in triggering a State's right to self-defence.

[18] Gray refers to 'an invasion by the regular armed forces of one state into the territory of another state' as '[t]he paradigm case' of an armed attack. See C Gray, *International Law and the Use of Force*, 3rd edn (Oxford, Oxford University Press, 2008), 128.

[19] For a current definition of armed forces under international law, see Art 43 of the First Additional Protocol to the 1949 Geneva Conventions, of 8 June 1977.

[20] It is understood that the activities of those groups must be attributable to the State concerned in accordance with international law. See Gray (n 18), 132–40.

[21] Randelzhofer (n 5), 112.

[22] ibid.

[23] For the text of the Declaration, see: https://digitallibrary.un.org/record/202170?ln=en.

[24] ibid, Principle 3, para 2.

(i) *Physical (Non-military) Force*

States may be affected by forcible measures of a natural or technical kind that do not involve military force in the strict sense – manifestations of so-called 'physical' force – whose effects can at times be as severe as those of armed force.[25] A contemporary and highly relevant example of such non-military physical force that effectively produced the consequences of an armed attack were the terrorist attacks of 11 September 2001 in New York, Washington, DC., and Pennsylvania.[26] Their unprecedented scale prompted the UN Security Council, in Resolution 1368 (2001), to declare that 'such acts, like any act of international terrorism, [were] a threat to international peace and security', and to stress 'that those responsible for aiding, supporting or harbouring the perpetrators, organizers and sponsors of these acts [should] be held accountable'.[27] These provisions call for at least two related observations. First, the Security Council regarded 'any act of international terrorism' – including those of 11 September 2001 – as a threat to international peace and security serious enough to justify a victim State's invocation of its 'inherent right of individual or collective self-defence in accordance with the Charter',[28] ie an act comparable to an 'armed attack' under Article 51. Yet, the 9/11 attacks were not *stricto sensu* 'armed', unless one analogises the hijacked civilian airplanes as 'weapons'. While the planes were used to cause massive destruction, their primary function is not to kill or destroy, and they should not be classified as 'weapons' or 'means of warfare' under applicable

[25] Randelzhofer (n 5), 112. cf VM Kulagin (2006) *Mejdunarodnaya bezopasnost* [*International Security*] (Moscow, Aspect Press, 2006), 79–103.

[26] For insightful comments on the impact of the 9/11 attacks on international law, see G Abi-Saab, 'The Proper Role of International Law in Combating Terrorism' (2002) 1 *Chinese Journal of International Law* 305; A Cassese, 'Terrorism is Also Disrupting Some Crucial Legal Categories of International Law' (2001) 12 *European Journal of International Law* 993; J Fitzpatrick, 'Speaking Law to Power: the War against Terrorism and Human Rights' (2003) 14 *European Journal of International Law* 241; TM Franck, 'Terrorism and the Right of Self-defense' (2001) 95 *American Journal of International Law* 839; E McWhinney, 'International Law-based Responses to the September 11 International Terrorist Attacks' (2002) 1 *Chinese Journal of International Law* 280; J Pejic, 'Terrorist Acts and Groups: a Role for International Law?' (2005) 76 *British Yearbook of International Law* 71; A Pellet and V Tzankov, 'Can a State Victim of a Terror Act have Recourse to Armed Force?' (2004) 17 *Humanitäres Völkerrecht – Informationsschriften* 68; SR Ratner, '*Jus ad Bellum* and *Jus in Bello* after September 11' (2002) 96 *American Journal of International Law* 905; WM Reisman, 'Assessing Claims to Revise the Laws of War' (2003) 97 *American Journal of International Law* 82; AE Roberts, 'Righting Wrongs or Wronging Rights? The United States and Human Rights Post-September 11' (2004) 15 *European Journal of International Law* 721; T Ruys and S Verhoeven, 'Attacks by Private Actors and the Right of Self-defence' (2005) 19 *Journal of Conflict and Security Law* 289; M Sassóli, 'Terrorism and War' (2006) 4 *Journal of International Criminal Justice* 959; CJ Tams, 'The Use of Force against Terrorists' (2009) 20 *European Journal of International Law* 359; S Von Schorlemer, 'Human Rights: Substantive and Institutional Implications of the War against Terrorism' (2003) 14 *European Journal of International Law* 265; S Yee, 'The Potential Impact of the Possible US Responses to the 9–11 Atrocities on the Law Regarding the Use of Force and Self-defence' (2002) 1 *Chinese Journal of International Law* 287.

[27] Resolution 1368, adopted by the Security Council at its 4370th meeting, on 12 September 2001, paras 1 and 3.

[28] ibid, 3rd preambular paragraph.

international law. The Security Council's reference to Article 51 was justified by the scale and effects of the 9/11 attacks, which were comparable to an armed attack, though not by their military nature.

Secondly, the 11 September 2001 attack was carried out not by a State or on its own behalf, but by a non-State actor. Notably, Article 51 of the UN Charter does not stipulate that an armed attack triggering a State's right to individual or collective self-defence must be committed by a State. It affirms that '[n]othing in the present Charter shall impair the inherent right of individual or collective self-defence, if an armed attack occurs against a Member of the United Nations', without identifying the source of the attack. A literal reading thus suggests that every UN Member has an inherent right to self-defence against any armed attack, whether by a State or a non-State entity.

(ii) 'Indirect Force'

As discussed above at section II.C, the scope of Article 2(4) is limited to the prohibition of armed force, but importantly, this also encompasses the concept of 'indirect force'. This term generally refers to a State's technical or organisational involvement in an international armed conflict between other States or in a non-international armed conflict within another State[29] – for instance, by sending armed bands, groups, irregulars, or mercenaries. The UN General Assembly addressed the prohibition of indirect force in the 1970 Friendly Relations Declaration as follows:

> Every State has the duty to refrain from organising or encouraging the organization of irregular forces or armed bands, including mercenaries, for incursion into the territory of another State.
>
> Every State has the duty to refrain from organizing, instigating, assisting or participating in acts of civil strife or terrorist acts in another State or acquiescing in organized activities within its territory directed towards the commission of such acts, when the acts referred to in the present paragraph involve a threat or use of force.[30]

As Randelzhofer observes, both prohibited forms of conduct – the organisation or encouragement of irregular forces or armed bands, and the prohibition of participation in civil strife or terrorist acts – are formulated so broadly that nearly any technical or organisational support by a State could fall under 'organising', 'encouraging', 'instigating', 'assisting', or 'participating.' This would risk blurring the meaning of 'armed force' under international law.[31] To avoid such overreach, the International Court of Justice rightly noted in the *Nicaragua*

[29] Gray (n 18), 105–10.
[30] Friendly Relations Declaration (n 23), paras 8 and 9.
[31] Randelzhofer (n 5), 113.

Judgment that not every act of assistance amounts to a use of force.[32] However, the Court did not establish clear criteria for identifying which acts of assistance constitute an internationally wrongful threat or use of force under Article 2(4) of the Charter.[33] A possible criterion may lie in evaluating the legality of the threat or use of force itself, with the use of 'indirect force' deriving its (il)legality from the principal action. In other words, assistance rendered in support of a lawful use of force should be considered lawful, while employing 'indirect force' to support a threat or use of force in violation of Article 2(4) would itself constitute a breach. It is proposed that the International Law Commission be tasked with drafting Articles on the Use of Force by States, and its expert opinion on 'indirect force' could help clarify the normative ambiguity left unresolved by the *Nicaragua* Judgment.

D. Obligation under Customary International Law[34]

Beyond its conventional status, some jurists also consider Article 2(4) of the Charter to form part of customary international law.[35] However, this view is only partially accurate. In the *Nicaragua* Judgment, the ICJ held that the use of force is governed not only by the Charter's treaty provisions but also by customary international law, the content of which does not necessarily mirror that of the Charter:

> As regards the suggestion that the areas covered by the two sources of law are identical, the Court observes that the United Nations Charter … by no means covers the whole area of the regulation of the use of force in international relations.[36]

The ICJ explicitly held that the Charter's operation neither 'subsumes' nor 'supervenes' applicable customary international law,[37] noting that 'the areas governed by the two sources of law [did] not exactly overlap, and the substantive rules in which they are framed [were] not identical in content'.[38] Furthermore,

[32] *Case Concerning Military and Paramilitary Activities in and against Nicaragua (Nicaragua v United States of America)* (*Nicaragua* Judgment), [1986] I.C.J. Reports p 14, para 116.

[33] ibid, paras 95, 97, 107, 110.

[34] cf Chapter 7, section I above.

[35] Gazzini's view is notable: '[T]he norms on the use of force embodied in the Charter and those existing under international law are substantially identical because of the interaction between the Charter and customary international law, on the one hand, and the virtual universality of the UN, on the other hand'. See T Gazzini, 'The Rules on the Use of Force at the Beginning of the XXI Century' (2006) 11 *Journal of Conflict and Security Law* 319, 320.

[36] *Nicaragua* Judgment (n 32), para 176. For a contrary position, see *The Legality of United States Participation in the Defense of Viet-Nam*, 4 March 1966, where the United States affirmed that 'it should be recognized that much of the substantive law of the Charter has become part of the general law of nations through a very wide acceptance by nations the world over. This is particularly true of the Charter provisions on the use of force', quoted in R Falk (ed), *The Vietnam War and International Law* (Princeton, Princeton University Press, 1968), 585.

[37] *Nicaragua* Judgment (n 32), para 174.

[38] ibid, para 175.

the Court affirmed that even when a treaty norm and a customary norm share identical content, this does not preclude the parallel applicability of the relevant customary rule.[39]

E. Prohibition under Customary International Law

The *Nicaragua* Judgment has, in fact, shown some inconsistencies on key points. While the ICJ acknowledged the primacy of the UN Charter in regulating the use of force, it nonetheless found it appropriate to 'supplant' the Charter's rules with customary international law applicable to the case.[40] Although the Court claimed to identify such rules, it merely concluded that State practice must 'in general, be consistent' with them,[41] without thoroughly analysing that practice. Moreover, in assessing *opinio juris*, the ICJ inaccurately relied on a few non-binding ('soft law') sources as evidence of States' legal belief regarding the prohibition of the use of force.[42]

As noted above at section II.D, the Court began with the premise that the legal regulation of the use of force in international relations is not confined to the UN Charter but also encompasses customary international law.[43] To illustrate the continued relevance of customary rules alongside the Charter, the Court cited Article 51 – the inherent right of individual or collective self-defence.[44] Reaffirming that 'nothing [in the present Charter] shall impair' this right in the event of an armed attack, the Court concluded that Article 51 would be meaningful only if the right it refers to were of customary origin, even if its current formulation is confirmed and shaped by the Charter.[45]

Nor does the Charter regulate all aspects of the right of self-defence or its implementation. For instance, it lacks any provision requiring that individual

[39] ibid.

[40] In Gazzini's words, the Court concluded 'that the rules on the use of force cannot be construed on the basis of postulates established through the inclusion of these rules in the Charter and their reiteration in subsequent documents. Rather, it has to be determined through the analysis of the practice regarding the interpretation and application of these norms by the subjects to which these are addressed'. See Gazzini (n 35), 321.

[41] *Nicaragua* Judgment (n 32), para 186.

[42] ibid, paras 191–92.

[43] A passage in the Separate Opinion of the Court's President, Judge Singh, on the interrelation between the rules of customary and conventional law on the use of force is remarkable: 'If an issue was raised whether the concepts of the principle of non-use of force and the exception to it in the form of use of force for self-defence are to be characterized as either part of customary international law or that of conventional law, the answer would appear to be that both the concepts are inherently based in customary international law in their origins, but have been developed further by treaty-law. In any search to determine whether these concepts belong to customary or conventional international law it would appear to be a fallacy to try to split any concept to ascertain what part or percentage of it belongs to customary law and what fraction belongs to conventional law. There is no need to try to separate the inseparable': See Separate Opinion of President Nagendra Singh, 152.

[44] *Nicaragua* Judgment (n 32), para 24.

[45] ibid, para 176.

or collective self-defence measures be proportionate to the armed attack and necessary for an effective response – a requirement well established in customary international law.[46] The ICJ similarly noted that the concept of 'armed attack', which triggers the exercise of self-defence, is neither defined in the Charter nor addressed in general or particular treaty law.[47] Given this absence of detailed treaty regulation, the Court reasonably declined to find that Article 51 'subsume[d] and supervene[d]' relevant customary law. Instead, it concluded that customary law continues to operate alongside treaty law in governing the use of force in inter-State relations, with the two legal sources not 'overlapping exactly'.[48]

F. Customary International Law on the Use of Force: The State Practice

Significant problems arose when the Court sought to identify the core rules of customary international law governing the use of force in inter-State relations. Although it acknowledged a substantial degree of agreement between Nicaragua and the United States on the applicable customary rules,[49] the Court nevertheless asserted its readiness to address the issue:

> This concurrence of [the Parties'] views does not however dispense the Court from having itself to ascertain what rules of customary international law are applicable. The mere fact that States declare their recognition of certain rules is not sufficient for the Court to consider these as being part of customary international law, and as applicable as such to those States. Bound as it is by Article 38 of its Statute to apply, *inter alia*, international custom 'as evidence of a general practice accepted as law', the Court may not disregard the essential role played by general practice. Where two States agree to incorporate a particular rule in a treaty, their agreement suffices to make that rule a legal one, binding upon them; but in the field of customary international law, the shared view of the Parties as to the content of what they regard as the rule is not enough. The Court must satisfy itself that the existence of the rule in the *opinio juris* of States is confirmed by practice.[50]

The Court did not require

> that in the practice of States the application of the rules in question should have been perfect, in the sense that States should have refrained, with complete consistency, from the use of force or from intervention in each other's internal affairs.[51]

In its view, Article 2(4) and related Charter rules could still be considered customary even if State practice did not perfectly align. What mattered was that

[46] ibid.
[47] ibid.
[48] ibid.
[49] ibid, para 187.
[50] ibid, para 184.
[51] ibid, para 186.

State practice[52] was generally consistent with the rules, and that deviations were treated as breaches – not as evidence of a new legal norm:

> If a State acts in a way *prima facie* incompatible with a recognised rule, but defends its conduct by appealing to exceptions or justifications contained within the rule itself, then whether or not the State's conduct is in fact justifiable on that basis, the significance of that attitude is to confirm rather than to weaken the rule.[53]

According to Tsagourias, the ICJ committed a methodological flaw by focusing primarily on *opinio juris*, inferring from it the consistency of State practice, while largely avoiding a substantive analysis of actual State behaviour regarding the prohibition of inter-State force.[54] In such a critical and sensitive area, State practice warrants closer scrutiny, as it remains insufficiently measurable. Glennon notes that, according to the 2004 Report of the High-Level Panel on Threats, Challenges and Change,[55] 'from 1945 to 1989, states used military force numerous times in interstate disputes. By one count, force was employed 200 times, and by another, 680 times'.[56] The panel, he adds,

> does not tell us who is right; indeed, it does not seem to care who is right. Apparently, it would not matter whether the rules had been violated 200 or 680 or 6800 times – the panel seems to suppose the number of violations is irrelevant.[57]

However, Glennon argues, the frequency of violations matters, for at least two reasons:

> First … the report rejects humanitarian intervention by states. The reason, the report says, is that humanitarian intervention by states would pose a fatal risk to the stability of the global order. Yet, how can we know how great the threat would be to the stability of the global order unless we know how stable that order really is – unless we know how effective the current rules actually have been in preventing the use of force?
>
> Second, after the number of violations exceeds a certain point, it is reasonable to conclude that states no longer consent to the rule and that the rule is no longer binding – that it has fallen into desuetude. Without examining the extent of non-compliance,

[52] On the content of State practice, see Chapter 7, section I.A above.

[53] *Nicaragua* Judgment (n 32), para 186.

[54] As Tsagourias points out, it would have been more accurate to derive the *opinio juris*, as evidence of States' conviction that their behaviour is in conformity with binding rules of international law, from their practice (in the first place, physical but also verbal acts), whereas the inverse methodology is not as convincing. See N Tsagourias, 'The *Nicaragua* Case and the Use of Force: the Theoretical Construction of the Decision and its Deconstruction' (1996) 1 *Journal of Conflict and Security Law* 81, 85. Besides, in practices contrary to established rules of customary international law there is, in fact, an inherent risk that these contrary practices can, over time, 'shake' the rules and weaken them. See Gazzini (n 35), 321.

[55] See n 8 above.

[56] Quoted in MJ Glennon, 'The Emerging Use-of-Force Paradigm' (2006) 11 *Journal of Conflict and Security Law* 309, 310. See also A Bleckmann, 'Völkergewohnheitsrecht trotz widersprüchlicher Praxis?' (1976) 36 *Zeitschrift für ausländisches öffentliches Recht und Völkerrecht* 374; A Bleckmann, 'Zur Verbindlichkeit des allgemeinen Völkerrechts für internationale Organisationen' (1977) 37 *Zeitschrift für ausländisches öffentliches Recht und Völkerrecht* 107.

[57] Glennon (n 56), 311.

> however, it is impossible to know whether the rule is still a good law. Why does the panel assume that the law *is* what it believes the law *should be*?[58]

G. *Opinio Juris* on the Use of Force

From the Parties' submissions, it was clear that both regarded Article 2(4) as generally reflective of customary international law and did not dispute the obligation to 'refrain in their international relations from the threat or use of force against the territorial integrity or political independence of any State, or in any other manner inconsistent with the purposes of the United Nations'.[59] Nonetheless, the Court felt compelled to go beyond the parties' positions and verify the existence of a broader *opinio juris* affirming the rule's mandatory character under customary law. In the Court's view, such *opinio juris* could be inferred from, among other sources, the attitude of the parties and other UN Members toward relevant General Assembly resolutions, particularly the 1970 Friendly Relations Declaration:

> The effect of consent to the text of such resolutions cannot be understood as merely that of a 'reiteration or elucidation' of the treaty commitment undertaken in the Charter. On the contrary, it may be understood as an acceptance of the validity of the rule or set of rules declared by the resolution by themselves. The principle of non-use of force, for example, may thus be regarded as a principle of customary international law[60]

As regards the United States in particular, its stance on the prohibition of the use of force was said to be reflected in certain early verbal acts, such as its approval of a resolution condemning aggression at the Sixth International Conference of American States on 18 February 1928,[61] and its ratification of the Montevideo Convention on Rights and Duties of States, whose Article 11 obliged States Parties not to recognise territorial acquisitions or special advantages obtained by force.[62] In the same spirit, the US acceptance of the prohibition of the use of force, as articulated in the 1975 Conference on Security and Co-operation in Europe (CSCE) Final Act's Declaration of Principles – whereby participating States undertook to 'refrain in their mutual relations, as well as in their international relations in general' from the threat or use of force – was also cited as evidence of its official position.[63] Without examining actual State practice, the International Court of Justice nonetheless held that acceptance of such

[58] ibid.
[59] *Nicaragua* Judgment (n 32), para 188.
[60] ibid.
[61] ibid, para 189.
[62] For the text of the Montevideo Convention on the Rights and Duties of States of 26 December 1933, see: www.jus.uio.no/english/services/library/treaties/01/1-02/rights-duties-states.xml.
[63] See Conference on Security and Co-operation in Europe, Final Act, 1 August 1975, Principle II ('Refraining from the threat or use of force'), available at www.osce.org/mc/39501.

non-binding declarations and resolutions, most of which were framed in political rather than legal terms, sufficiently demonstrated the existence of an *opinio juris* prohibiting the use of force in international relations.[64]

This conclusion was highly questionable, as the Court relied on the Parties' verbal acts rather than on actual State practice to establish customary international law. In reality, General Assembly resolutions do not inherently possess *opinio juris* – the psychological belief that their provisions reflect binding international law. As Tsagourias noted, drawing on Hart, States may support rules due to popular 'criticism and pressure' or because the rules in question are 'not mandatory'.[65] In Tsagourias' view, General Assembly resolutions, beyond lacking binding force under the UN Charter,[66] are shaped by policy deals, concessions, and political bargaining over national interests.[67] He also aptly cited Thirlway's view that a General Assembly resolution may be considered evidence of *opinio juris* only where 'a sufficient body of state practice for the usage element of the alleged custom [is] established without reference to the resolution'.[68] Moreover, the inconsistency of State behaviour with resolutions they supported suggests that States often vote for what they believe international law '*ought* to be' – or *might* become – rather than what it 'actually *is*' at the time.[69]

H. *Jus Cogens* Obligation

While the treaty-based and customary nature of Article 2(4) has been considered above, it is worth examining whether this provision – or at least some of its elements – also constitutes a peremptory norm of general international law (*jus cogens*).[70] If so, the legal consequences of its violation would be more severe than those arising from breaches of 'ordinary' conventional or customary rules.[71] *Jus cogens* norms entail *erga omnes* obligations,[72] meaning their violation affects not just individual States but the international community as a whole.[73] This

[64] *Nicaragua* Judgment (n 32), paras 186 and 189.
[65] Quoted in Tsagourias (n 54), 86 and 92, fn 42.
[66] cf UN Charter, Art 14.
[67] Tsagourias (n 54), 86.
[68] ibid, 87, 93, fn 45.
[69] ibid, 87.
[70] See the Vienna Convention on the Law of Treaties, Article 53 and Chapter 6, section V.H and Chapter 7, section II.B above. See also U Scheuner, 'Conflict of Treaty Provisions with a Peremptory Norm of General International Law and its Consequences: Comments on Articles 50, 61 and 67 of the ILC's 1966 Draft Articles on the Law of Treaties' (1967) 27 *Zeitschrift für ausländisches öffentliches Recht und Völkerrecht* 520; U Scheuner, 'Conflict of Treaty Provisions with a Peremptory Norm of General International Law' (1969) 29 *Zeitschrift für ausländisches öffentliches Recht und Völkerrecht* 28.
[71] See Chapter 9, section IX above.
[72] II Lukashuk, *Pravo mezhdunarodnoy otvetstvennosti* [*Law of International Responsibility*] (Moscow, Wolters Kluwer, 2004), 252.
[73] ibid.

implies that international law should equip States with more robust mechanisms to respond to such breaches, in proportion to their exceptional gravity.

The 2001 Articles on Responsibility of States for Internationally Wrongful Acts (ARSIWA) suggest,[74] in Articles 40 and 41, several important consequences if a State's use of force in violation of Article 2(4) of the UN Charter is deemed a breach of a peremptory norm of general international law. Most notably, States are required ('shall cooperate') – not merely permitted or encouraged – to bring an end, by joint efforts, to any serious breach under Article 40. Under current international law, lawful means for suppressing acts of aggression and other serious violations of Article 2(4) include suspension of rights and privileges under the UN Charter (Article 5), expulsion from UN membership (Article 6), individual or collective self-defence (Article 51), enforcement action by the Security Council (Chapter VII), recourse to regional arrangements (Chapter VIII), and economic or other countermeasures.

Second, States are obliged to refrain from recognising as lawful any situations resulting from serious breaches of *jus cogens*, and from providing aid or assistance in maintaining such situations. Acts of aggression produce unlawful outcomes, often affecting the territorial integrity or political independence of the victim State. On numerous occasions, States and international institutions have indeed declined to recognise the legal validity of outcomes stemming from unlawful uses of force or violations of the principle of self-determination,[75] likely reflecting the *jus cogens* status of the underlying rules.

Finally, Article 41(3) notes that serious breaches of obligations under *jus cogens* norms may entail 'further consequences' under international law. If Article 2(4) is indeed *jus cogens*, such consequences could include the direct[76] or indirect[77] enforcement of individual criminal responsibility for natural persons involved in the planning, preparation, initiation, or execution of a State's act of aggression.

I. Acceptance and Recognition by the International Community of States as a Whole

Article 2(4) is broadly accepted and recognised by the international community of States. As a UN Principle, it is binding on all Member States and offers protection to non-Members, even if not formally binding upon them. It has been invoked in numerous acts of international organs and institutions – such as the

[74] UN General Assembly resolution A/RES/56/589, 12 December 2001. On the ARSIWA, see Chapter 9 above.
[75] See section VII.B below.
[76] See Chapter 15, section IV.L below.
[77] See Chapter 15, section IV.M below.

UN General Assembly[78] and the CSCE / OSCE[79] – as well as in decisions of the International Court of Justice.[80] However, since 1945, its application has not always aligned with such formal recognition. States have breached the prohibition, directly or indirectly, often invoking the right to individual or collective self-defence – explicitly referred to in Article 51 of the Charter as an exception to the prohibition of the use of force.[81] As noted above,[82] Article 51 does not regulate the exercise of this inherent right in detail and relies on customary international law – leaving room for (sometimes self-serving) interpretation.

J. Non-derogable Character

Turning to the second criterion, one must ask whether specific (normative or practical) standards exist to distinguish legitimate uses of force from 'derogations' from Article 2(4) – which are impermissible if the rule constitutes *jus cogens*. The assertion of legal title over territory by (armed) force is clearly one such standard. According to Orakhelashvili, since 1945, the prohibition on acquiring legal title through illegal force or breaches of self-determination has attained *jus cogens* status.[83] In his important treatise, he cites Jennings' view that force cannot confer title if condemned as illegal,[84] and De Visscher's view that benefits from force cannot be lawful if force itself is absolutely outlawed.[85] Orakhelashvili further noted that several territorial changes were declared null and void due to conflicts with *jus cogens*: for instance, 'Jordan's occupation of East Jerusalem since 1948 was a violation of Article 2(4) of the UN Charter, and consequently Jordan was unable to acquire sovereignty over that area',[86] and '[t]he Israeli Occupation of the West Bank and East Jerusalem was similarly void for an identical reason'.[87] He concluded that these occupations were not only illegal but null and void – producing no legal effect *ab initio*.[88] Hence, despite the passage of time, the territories are still referred to as occupied, and Israel as the occupying power.[89]

[78] See Chapter 3, section II.B above.
[79] See Chapter 3, section IV.F above.
[80] See Chapter 3, section II.F above.
[81] See section V below.
[82] See section II.D above.
[83] A Orakhelashvili, *Peremptory Norms in International Law* (Oxford, Oxford University Press, 2006), 218–19.
[84] ibid, 218.
[85] ibid. See also J Vidmar, 'Greenland and Territorial Acquisition under International Law', EJIL:Talk!, available at www.ejiltalk.org/greenland-and-territorial-acquisition-under-international-law/.
[86] Orakhelashvili (n 83), 220.
[87] ibid.
[88] ibid.
[89] ibid. See also M Milanovic, 'ICJ Delivers Advisory Opinion on the Legality of Israel's Occupation of Palestinian Territories', EJIL:Talk!, 20 July 2024, available at www.ejiltalk.org/icj-delivers-advisory-opinion-on-the-legality-of-israels-occupation-of-palestinian-territories/.

To conclude on the second criterion, one may suggest, by analogy, that if the prohibition of armed force against the territorial integrity or political independence of States and the principle of self-determination of peoples have been recognised – by both the International Court of Justice and leading legal experts – as peremptory norms of general international law (*jus cogens*), there is little reason to oppose extending similar protection to other fundamental values enshrined in Article 2(4). These include 'international co-operation in solving international problems of an economic, social, cultural, or humanitarian character, and in promoting and encouraging respect for human rights and for fundamental freedoms for all without distinction as to race, sex, language, or religion',[90] along with other UN Purposes. If this reasoning holds, the case for the legitimacy of 'humanitarian intervention' – an international military response to large-scale human rights violations – may be considerably strengthened.[91]

K. Normative Stability

Regarding the final criterion – that a *jus cogens* norm may only be modified by a subsequent norm of the same character – it presents little difficulty. As noted above,[92] the conservative legal framework governing the use of force has remained virtually unchanged since the UN Charter's adoption, and significant revision is unlikely given the complexity of amending such a foundational treaty.[93] While customary international law may evolve through State practice, a *jus cogens* norm cannot be altered by inconsistent practice, as such conduct would constitute a breach of the norm itself. There is broad consensus that Article 2(4) of the UN Charter qualifies as a peremptory norm of general international law, and that aggression constitutes a serious breach, triggering both the responsibility of the violating State and the individual criminal responsibility of its authors, in accordance with Article 41(3) of the 2001 Articles on Responsibility of States for Internationally Wrongful Acts.[94]

III. ELEMENTS OF AN ACT OF AGGRESSION UNDER THE 1974 DEFINITION OF AGGRESSION

General Assembly resolution 3314 (XXIX), adopted on 14 December 1974, offered an interpretation of Article 2(4) of the UN Charter, with a Definition of Aggression annexed.[95] Substantially based on the draft definition proposed

[90] cf Art 1(3) of the UN Charter.
[91] Igor Lukashuk seems to share this supposition. See Lukashuk (n 72), 249–50, and section VIII.A below.
[92] See n 11.
[93] cf Art 109 of the UN Charter.
[94] See Chapter 9, section IX above.
[95] UN GA Res. 3314 (XXIX), *GAOR* 29th Sess., Supp. No. 31 (1974).

by the Soviet Union in 1933 and alternative drafts from the USSR and various Western and developing States during the 1950s and 1960s,[96] the definition was adopted nearly 30 years after the Charter's entry into force. It was intended as a guideline for the Security Council's determination of acts of aggression[97] and gained general (though not universal) recognition.[98]

A. 'Chapeau' of the Definition

The 1974 Definition includes a general part followed by a non-exhaustive list of examples of acts of aggression. Its general provision (Article 1) states:

> Aggression is the use of armed force by a State against the sovereignty, territorial integrity or political independence of another State, or in any other manner inconsistent with the Charter of the United Nations, as set out in this Definition.

Dinstein identified six key distinctions between this formulation and the primary rule set out in Article 2(4) of the UN Charter:

> (i) the mere threat of force is excluded; (ii) the adjective 'armed' is interposed before the noun 'force'; (iii) 'sovereignty' is mentioned together with the territorial integrity and the political independence of the victim State; (iv) the victim is described as 'another' (rather than 'any') State; (v) the use of force is proscribed whenever it is inconsistent with the UN Charter as a whole, and not only with the Purposes of the United Nations; (vi) a linkage is created with the rest of the Definition.[99]

It has been suggested that the inclusion of additional elements in the definition of aggression aimed to raise the threshold for assessment, thereby preventing incidents such as 'a few stray bullets across a boundary' from qualifying as acts of aggression.[100] However, the normative and practical impact of this progressive development in international law could have been more substantial. Its more precise language, compared to Article 2(4) of the Charter, might have rendered the Definition a more effective instrument for protecting State sovereignty and upholding international peace and security – thereby reinforcing Article 2(4) itself. The main limitation lay in its recommendatory nature as an annex to a

[96] BB Ferencz, 'Defining Aggression: Where It Stands and Where It's Going' (1972) 66 *American Journal of International Law* 491, 495.

[97] JI Garvey, 'The UN Definition of "Aggression": Law and Illusion in the Context of Collective Security' (1976–1977) 17 *Vanderbilt Journal of International Law* 177, 193–94.

[98] J Stone, 'Hopes and Loopholes in the 1974 Definition of Aggression' (1977) 71 *American Journal of International Law* 224.

[99] Dinstein (n 13), 116.

[100] Article 2 of the Definition stipulates that alleged acts of aggression, or their consequences, must be of 'sufficient gravity' to qualify as aggression. Accordingly, minor incidents involving the use of armed force may not meet the threshold, subject to the Security Council's assessment in accordance with the Charter. cf Dinstein (n 13), 116.

General Assembly resolution.[101] Had it been given stronger legal force – such as through approval by the Security Council, whose decisions are binding on all UN Members – it might have become a 'harder' source of international law, demanding more consistent State compliance.

B. Examples of Acts of Aggression

Building on the general part, Article 3 of the Definition provides examples of acts of aggression, whether or not accompanied by a declaration of war:

(a) The invasion or attack by the armed forces of a State of the territory of another State, or any military occupation, however temporary, resulting from such invasion or attack, or any annexation by the use of force of the territory of another State or part thereof;

(b) Bombardment by the armed forces of a State against the territory of another State or the use of any weapons by a State against the territory of another State;

(c) The blockade of the ports or coasts of a State by the armed forces of another State;

(d) An attack by the armed forces of a State on the land, sea or air forces, or marine and air fleets of another State;

(e) The use of armed forces of one State which are within the territory of another State with the agreement of the receiving State, in contravention of the conditions provided for in the agreement or any extension of their presence in such territory beyond the termination of the agreement;

(f) The action of a State in allowing its territory, which it has placed at the disposal of another State, to be used by that other State for perpetrating an act of aggression against a third State;

(g) The sending by or on behalf of a State of armed bands, groups, irregulars or mercenaries, which carry out acts of armed force against another State of such gravity as to amount to the acts listed above, or its substantial involvement therein.

Of these, only the final subparagraph was explicitly recognised by the International Court of Justice as declaratory of customary international law.[102] Dinstein, however, argued that other parts of Article 3 of the 1974 Definition might also reflect 'harder' rules of international law than General Assembly resolutions typically do.[103] In fact, the *Nicaragua* case is not an appropriate reference for assessing the ICJ's position on this issue, as the Court did not

[101] cf UN Charter, Art 11.
[102] *Nicaragua* Judgment (n 32), paras 106 et seq.
[103] Dinstein (n 13), 118.

examine whether subparagraphs (a)–(f) reflected customary law, given that the case's factual basis was limited to subparagraph (g).[104]

C. The Problem of the 'First Use' of Force

According to Article 2 of the 1974 Definition, the first use of armed force by a State in contravention of the UN Charter constitutes prima facie evidence of an act of aggression. However, the Security Council may, in line with the Charter, determine that such a conclusion is unwarranted in light of other relevant circumstances, including the insufficient gravity of the acts or their consequences.[105] The reference to the first use of force must be understood alongside the key condition that it be 'in contravention of the Charter'. For instance, a State may initiate a minor use of force, but if the target State responds disproportionately, it may itself violate the Charter and thus bear responsibility for aggression.[106]

D. The Discretionary Power of the UN Security Council

Another issue concerning the legal value of the 1974 Definition is that Article 3 is not exhaustive; the UN Security Council may determine other uses of force that constitute aggression.[107] Under the Charter, the Security Council holds primary authority in determining the existence of acts of aggression. Yet in numerous instances, even overtly hostile conduct was not characterised as such. This restrictive application was likely driven by political, not purely legal, considerations. As a political organ, the Council reflects the interests of its members – particularly the permanent ones[108] – and cannot be expected to apply international law with the impartiality required of judicial bodies like the International Court of Justice or the International Criminal Court.[109] By contrast, these provisions may prove more workable in the ICC's future practice. Although Article 8 bis(2) of the Rome Statute draws directly from Article 3 of the 1974 Definition – and perhaps unnecessarily cites General Assembly resolution 3314 (XXIX) – its

[104] ibid.

[105] ibid, Art 2 (first sentence): 'The first use of armed force by a State in contravention of the Charter shall constitute *prima facie* evidence of an act of aggression'.

[106] Dinstein (n 13), 117.

[107] See n 95 above, Annex, Art 4.

[108] A Chauprade, *Géopolitique: constantes et changements dans l'histoire* (Paris, Ellipses, 2003), 767.

[109] R Higgins, 'The Place of International Law in the Settlement of Disputes by the Security Council' (1970) 64 *American Journal of International Law* 1; I Johnstone, 'Security Council Deliberations: The Power of the Better Argument' (2003) 14 *European Journal of International Law* 437.

verbatim inclusion elevates the definition from 'soft law' to binding treaty law for the growing number of States Parties. The Security Council should not disregard this development.

IV. CHARTER-BASED EXCEPTIONS TO PROHIBITION ON USE OF FORCE

Sections V and VI below examine the Charter-based exceptions to the prohibition of the threat or use of force. The UN Charter explicitly provides two such exceptions: the inherent right of individual or collective self-defence under Article 51, and collective security measures.

V. RIGHT TO INDIVIDUAL OR COLLECTIVE SELF-DEFENCE

A. Introduction

As Schachter observed, two principal schools of thought underlie the concept of States' inherent right of self-defence:[110] the natural law school, represented inter alia by Hugo Grotius (1583–1645), and the *realpolitik* school, exemplified by figures such as US Secretary of State Dean Gooderham Acheson (1893–1971).[111] The natural law school views the right of self-defence as intrinsic to statehood and applicable in a wide range of scenarios – from 'an extreme circumstance of self-defence' to less urgent, routine situations.[112] In contrast, Eduardo Jiménez de Aréchaga (1918–94) argued that self-defence is 'not a legal concept but merely a political excuse for the use of force'.[113] The *realpolitik* approach sees self-defence more as a function of power than of legal principle.[114] Yet, invoking self-defence as a right under international law would be meaningless if a State using force were unwilling or unable to justify its actions in legal terms.[115]

[110] On the right of self-defence, see generally Dinstein (n 13), 157–245; TD Gill, 'The Temporal Dimension of Self-defence: Anticipation, Pre-emption, Prevention and Immediacy' (2006) 11 *Journal of Conflict and Security Law* 361; D Kretzmer, 'The Inherent Right to Self-defence and Proportionality in *Jus ad Bellum*' (2013) 24 *European Journal of International Law* 235; JL Kunz, 'Individual and Collective Self-defense in Article 51 of the Charter of the United Nations' (1947) 41 *American Journal of International Law* 872–79; K Okimoto, 'The Cumulative Requirements of *Jus ad Bellum* and *Jus in Bello* in the Context of Self-defense' (2011) 10 *Chinese Journal of International Law* 45; NA Shah, 'Self-defence, Anticipatory Self-defence and Pre-emption: International Law's Response to Terrorism' (2007) 12 *Journal of Conflict and Security Law* 95.

[111] O Schachter, 'Self-defense and the Rule of Law' (1989) 83 *American Journal of International Law* 259, 259–60.

[112] *Legality of the Threat or Use of Nuclear Weapons, Advisory Opinion*, [1996] ICJ Reports, para 97.

[113] Quoted in Dinstein (n 13), 160.

[114] H Kissinger, *Diplomacy* (New York, Simon & Schuster Paperbacks, 1994), 804–36.

[115] M Weller, 'Does the ICJ have the Legal Authority to Pronounce itself on the Right to Self-Defence?', EJIL:Talk!, 10 January 2024, available at www.ejiltalk.org/does-the-icj-have-the-legal-authority-to-pronounce-itself-on-the-right-to-self-defence/.

B. Article 51 of the UN Charter

Under conventional international law, the general conditions for States to resort to force in self-defence are set out in Article 51 of the UN Charter:

> Nothing in the present Charter shall impair the inherent right of individual or collective self-defence if an armed attack occurs against a Member of the United Nations, until the Security Council has taken measures necessary to maintain international peace and security.

While Article 51 does not exhaustively regulate the right of self-defence under modern international law, it provides a suitable overarching conventional framework, complemented – but not replaced – by customary elements.[116]

(i) 'Nothing in the Present Charter shall Impair the Inherent Right …'

The opening language of Article 51 affirms the inviolability of a State's right of self-defence as a matter of principle. Described as 'inherent' – in line with the natural law tradition discussed above – this right is framed in relatively superior terms to other Charter provisions ('Nothing in the present Charter shall impair …'), suggesting that, if exercised in good faith, self-defence may take precedence over other Charter rules.[117]

(ii) '… Of Individual or Collective Self-defence …'

The term 'self-defence' in Article 51 is generally understood to imply recourse to armed or military force,[118] and does not directly encompass non-military measures (eg diplomatic or economic), which may nonetheless serve as subsidiary tools to restore the security of a State under attack.[119] A State may exercise this right individually or collectively, with collective self-defence taking more or less formalised forms – either through regional security organisations (eg NATO, CSTO) or ad hoc international coalitions established for specific operations.[120]

(iii) '[I]f an Armed Attack Occurs against a Member of the United Nations …'

At first glance, Article 51 appears to protect only UN Members. However, the 'inherent' nature of the right of self-defence, along with the broader applicability

[116] See sections II.F–II.I above.

[117] According to Lukashuk, '[s]uch a right is an indispensable institution of any legal system'. See II Lukashuk, *Mejdunarodnoe pravo: Osobennaya chast* [*International Law: Special Part*], 3rd edn (Moscow, Wolters Kluwer, 2008), 290.

[118] ibid, 289.

[119] ibid, 407–10.

[120] ibid, 296–97.

of the Charter's provisions on the use of force to all States – including non-Members[121] – supports the conclusion that the Charter, in practice, recognises *every* State's right of self-defence against armed attacks.

(iv) '[U]ntil the Security Council has Taken Measures Necessary to Maintain International Peace and Security'

The concluding clause of Article 51 provides that the Security Council must take measures to maintain international peace and security following an armed attack against a UN Member.[122] While the language may suggest that the right of self-defence ends once the Council takes action,[123] in practice, a State may continue to exercise this right until peace and security are fully restored – consistently with its 'inherent' and thus inalienable character.

C. Preventive Self-defence

Since the end of the Second World War, there has been limited State practice supporting the legitimacy of preventive self-defence.[124] Wiefelspütz defined it as 'repelling an attack, which is not immediately challenging or threatening, or repelling a danger, which is not at hand'.[125] A notable case – cited by Kinacioglu[126] – was Israel's 1981 attack on an Iraqi nuclear reactor under construction, allegedly intended to produce material for weapons that Iraq might use against Israel.[127] The Security Council reviewed the case[128] and unanimously condemned the Israeli action.[129] However, Council members were divided on the broader legitimacy of preventive self-defence.[130]

[121] See section I above.

[122] See section VI below.

[123] Lukashuk (n 117), 290.

[124] On preventive self-defence, see H Fischer, 'Zwischen autorisierter Gewaltanwendung und Praventivkrieg: Der völkerrechtliche Kern der Debatte um ein militärisches Eingreifen gegen den Irak' (2003) 16 *Humanitäres Völkerrecht – Informationsschriften* 4; V Kroning, 'Prävention oder Präemption?' (2003) 16 *Humanitäres Völkerrecht – Informationsschriften* 82; D Wiefelspütz, 'Die Zulassigkeit präemptiver oder präventiver Anwendung militärischer Gewalt' (2006) 19 *Humanitäres Völkerrecht – Informationsschriften* 103.

[125] Wiefelspütz (n 124), 103.

[126] M Kinacioglu, 'A Response to Amos Guiora: Reassessing the Parameters of Use of Force in the Age of Terrorism' (2008) 13 *Journal of Conflict and Security Law* 33, 39.

[127] The Israeli and US strikes on Iran in June 2025 followed a similar rationale. See M Milanovic, 'Is Israel's Use of Force Against Iran Justified by Self-Defence?', EJIL:Talk!, 13 June 2025, available at www.ejiltalk.org/is-israels-use-of-force-against-iran-justified-by-self-defence/.

[128] Kinacioglu (n 126), with references to documents UN Doc. S/PV. 2280 (1981), at 16; UN Doc. S/PV.2283 (1981), at 56; UN Doc. S/PV.2282 (1981), at 42; and UN Doc. S/PV.2288 (1981), at 14.

[129] Security Council Resolution 487 (1981), quoted in Kinacioglu (n 126), 39.

[130] Kinacioglu (n 126), 39.

D. Pre-emptive Self-defence

Since 11 September 2001, the United States has emerged as the leading advocate of pre-emptive self-defence.[131] In the 2002 *National Security Strategy to Combat Weapons of Mass Destruction*, President George W Bush stated:

> United States military force and appropriate civilian agencies must have the capability to defend against a weapons of mass destruction-armed adversary, including in appropriate cases through pre-emptive measures. This requires capabilities to detect and destroy an adversary's weapons of mass destruction assets before their weapons are used … The primary objective of a response is to disrupt an imminent attack or an attack in progress, and eliminate the threat of future attacks.[132]

The statement received limited support from international lawyers, partly because it conflated three distinct legal regimes – interceptive, pre-emptive, and preventive self-defence – under a single umbrella. Notably, even the United States' closest ally in the 'global war against terror', the United Kingdom, voiced reservations. The British Foreign Secretary commented as follows:

> The issue of pre or post-pre-emption in respect of Iraq, I do not quite see the relevance. The issue is that here you have a regime which is in clear breach of an endless number of Security Council Resolutions requiring them to do certain things under Chapter VII.[133]

Pre-emptive self-defence refers to a State's military action against a potential adversary in anticipation of a hypothetical armed attack.[134] It differs from both preventive and interceptive self-defence in that, while politically aimed at a

[131] As such, the claim was not unprecedented in United States foreign policy. More than 15 years before the issuance of the 'Bush Doctrine' cited in the text, President Reagan stated in his *Address to the Nation on the Air Strikes against Libya* on 13 April 1986 (Public Papers of the United States Presidents, 1986, vol I, 468–69): 'We believe that this pre-emptive action against the terrorist installations will not only diminish Colonel Qadhafi's capacity to export terror, it will provide him with incentives and reasons to alter his criminal behavior'.

[132] United States President, *National Security Strategy to Combat Weapons of Mass Destruction*, 17 September 2002, 3.

[133] United Kingdom, House of Commons, Foreign Affairs Committee, 2nd Report, Session 2002–2003, para 150.

[134] On pre-emptive self-defence, see M Bothe, 'Terrorism and the Legality of Pre-emptive Force' (2003) 14 *European Journal of International Law* 227; B Ching, 'Pre-emptive or Similar Type of Self-defense in the Territory of Foreign States' (2013) 12 *Chinese Journal of International Law* 1; T Gazzini, 'A Response to Amos Guiora: Pre-emptive Self-defence against Non-State Actors?' (2008) 13 *Journal of Conflict and Security Law* 25; C Gray, 'The Bush Doctrine Revisited: the 2006 National Security Strategy of the USA' (2005) 4 *Chinese Journal of International Law* 555; C Henderson, 'The Bush Doctrine: From Theory to Practice' (2004) 9 *Journal of Conflict and Security Law* 3; WM Reisman and A Armstrong, 'The Past and Future of the Claim of Preemptive Self-defense' (2006) 100 *American Journal of International Law* 525; M Sapiro, 'Iraq: The Shifting Sands of Preemptive Self-defense' (2003) 97 *American Journal of International Law* 599; AD Sofaer, 'On the Necessity of Pre-emption' (2003) 14 *European Journal of International Law* 209; R Wedgwood, 'The Fall of Saddam Hussein: Security Council Mandates and Preemptive Self-defense' (2003) 97 *American Journal of International Law* 576.

somewhat defined potential threat, the military response lacks a clear, prima facie defensive character. Proponents of pre-emptive self-defence typically justify it by pointing to flaws in the Security Council's decision-making process, which effectively shields permanent members and their allies from enforcement measures.

E. Interceptive Self-defence

Unlike anticipatory self-defence, interceptive self-defence is invoked when the threat of an armed attack is grave, imminent, and unmistakable. Dinstein provided an illustrative explanation of its nature:

> Let us assume hypothetically that the Japanese carrier striking force, *en route* to the point from which it mounted the notorious attack on Pearl Harbor in December 1941, had been intercepted and sunk by the US Pacific Fleet prior to reaching its destination and before a single Japanese naval aircraft got anywhere near Hawaii. If that were to have happened, and the Americans had succeeded in aborting an onslaught which in one fell swoop managed to change the balance of military power in the Pacific, it would have been preposterous to look upon the United States as answerable for inflicting an armed attack upon Japan …
>
> Had the Japanese striking force been destroyed on its way to Pearl Harbor, this would have constituted not an act of preventive war but a miraculously early use of counter-force. To put it in another way, the self-defence exercised by the United States (in response to an incipient armed attack) would have been not anticipatory but interceptive in nature. Interceptive, unlike anticipatory, self-defence takes place after the other side has committed itself to an armed attack in an ostensibly irrevocable way. Whereas a preventive strike anticipates an armed attack that is merely 'foreseeable' (or even just 'conceivable'), an interceptive strike counters an armed attack which is 'imminent' and practically 'unavoidable'. It is the opinion of the present writer that interceptive, as distinct from anticipatory, self-defence is legitimate even under Article 51 of the Charter.[135]

In such circumstances, it would be unwise for a potential victim State to await a fatal blow that could cripple its defensive capabilities. Where the totality of facts leaves no doubt about an impending attack,[136] the State should be entitled – under Article 51 of the Charter – to intercept it through a targeted and proportionate military response. Crucially, '[t]he invocation of the right to self-defence

[135] Dinstein (n 13), 171–72 (footnotes omitted).

[136] Dinstein offered the following practical example of a comprehensive assessment of the circumstances warranting interceptive self-defence: '[I]n the "Six Days War" of June 1967, Israel was the first to open fire. Nevertheless, a careful analysis of the events surrounding the actual outbreak of the hostilities … would lead to the conclusion that the Israeli campaign amounted to an interceptive self-defence, in response to an incipient armed attack by Egypt (joined by Jordan and Syria). True, no single Egyptian step, evaluated alone, may have qualified as an armed attack. But when all of the measures taken by Egypt … were assessed in the aggregate, it seemed to be crystal clear that Egypt was bent on an armed attack, and the sole question was not whether war would materialize but when'. See Dinstein (n 13), 173.

must be weighed on the ground of the information available (and reasonably interpreted) at the moment of action, without the benefit of *post factum* wisdom'.[137]

VI. COLLECTIVE SECURITY MEASURES UNDER UN CHARTER, CHAPTER VII

Unlike individual or collective self-defence, which counters external aggression, the collective security mechanism is, in Dinstein's words, 'introverted', as it targets aggressors within the system.[138] The key distinction lies in the fact that self-defence is exercised at the discretion of the State(s) subjected to armed, physical, or indirect force, whereas collective security relies on the centralised authority of the United Nations Security Council.[139]

A. Functions of the UN Security Council under Article 39 of the Charter

The United Nations' collective security system is outlined in Chapter VII of the Charter (Articles 39–51). Article 39 makes clear that the Security Council's role in this area is both preventive and restorative.[140] As Dinstein noted:

> The notion of maintaining international peace and security has a preemptive thrust. The purpose is to ensure, before it is too late, that no breach of the peace will in fact occur. Measures taken by the Council to forestall a breach of international peace and security have deterrence and prevention as their goals. Once a breach of international peace and security occurs (notwithstanding any prophylactic measures that may have been taken), the situation changes dramatically. At this point, the Council's mission is to restore the peace. It has to take steps calculated to re-establish international law and order.[141]

Under Article 39, the Security Council may issue non-binding recommendations or adopt binding decisions to prompt action by UN Member States. A grammatical interpretation of Article 39 indicates that the non-military and military measures listed in Articles 41 and 42 are linked to binding decisions rather than recommendations.[142]

[137] ibid.
[138] ibid, 246.
[139] ibid. See also DD Caron, 'The Legitimacy of the Collective Authority of the Security Council' (1993) 87 *American Journal of International Law* 552.
[140] UN Charter, Art 39: 'The Security Council shall determine the existence of any threat to the peace, breach of the peace, or act of aggression and shall make recommendations, or decide what measures shall be taken in accordance with Articles 41 and 42, to maintain or restore international peace and security'.
[141] Dinstein (n 13), 248.
[142] ibid.

B. Non-military Measures

Article 41 of the Charter addresses non-military measures and provides:

> The Security Council may decide what measures not involving the use of armed force are to be employed to give effect to its decisions, and it may call upon the Members of the United Nations to apply such measures. These may include complete or partial interruption of economic relations and of rail, sea, air, postal, telegraphic, radio, and other means of communication, and the severance of diplomatic relations.

Notably, this list is not exhaustive ('[the measures] may include …'), and the Security Council may determine which additional measures not involving the use of force may be employed.[143]

C. Military Measures

After the Cold War, the Security Council became significantly more active in maintaining international peace and security. It invoked Chapter VII of the Charter in full or cited specific Articles in numerous resolutions.[144] However, Article 42 – the chapter's key provision – was not applied due to the lack of special agreements required under Article 43. The same disagreements among permanent members that blocked these agreements also rendered Article 106 ineffective and left the Military Staff Committee under Article 47 inoperative. As a result, two main alternative mechanisms emerged: peacekeeping and non-Article 42 peace enforcement

D. Peacekeeping

The concept of peacekeeping originates from former UN Secretary-General Boutros Boutros-Ghali's report *An Agenda for Peace: Preventive Diplomacy, Peacemaking and Peace-keeping*.[145] Paragraph 15 states that the UN aims 'through peace-keeping, to work to preserve peace, however fragile, where fighting has been halted and to assist in implementing agreements achieved by the peacemakers'. Additionally, paragraph 20 offers the following definition of peacekeeping:

> Peace-keeping is the deployment of a United Nations presence in the field, hitherto with the consent of all parties concerned, normally involving United Nations

[143] ibid, 249. See also B Conforti, 'Non-coercive Sanctions in the United Nations Charter: Some Lessons from the Gulf War' (1991) 2(2) *European Journal of International Law* 110.

[144] Dinstein (n 13), 256–63.

[145] B Boutros-Ghali, *An Agenda for Peace: Preventive Diplomacy, Peacemaking and Peace-keeping* (New York, United Nations, 1992), available at digitallibrary.un.org/record/145749?ln=en&v=pdf. See also MW Doyle and N Sambanis, 'Peacekeeping Operations' in TG Weiss and S Daws (eds), *The Oxford Handbook on the United Nations* (Oxford, Oxford University Press, 2007).

military and / or police personnel and frequently civilians as well. Peace-keeping is a technique that expands the possibilities for both the prevention of conflict and the making of peace.

According to UN Peacekeeping:

> Although each UN peace operation is different, there is a considerable degree of consistency in the types of mandated tasks assigned by the Security Council. Depending on their mandate, peace operations may be required to:
>
> – Deploy to prevent the outbreak of conflict or the spill-over of conflict across borders;
> – Stabilize conflict situations after a ceasefire, to create an environment for the parties to reach a lasting peace agreement;
> – Assist in implementing comprehensive peace agreements;
> – Lead states or territories through a transition to stable government, based on democratic principles, good governance and economic development.
>
> Depending on the specific set of challenges, UN peacekeepers are often mandated to play a catalytic role in the following essentially peacebuilding activities:
>
> – Disarmament, demobilization and reintegration of ex-combatants;
> – Mine action;
> – Security sector reform and other rule of law-related activities;
> – Protection and promotion of human rights;
> – Electoral assistance;
> – Support for the restoration and extension of State authority;
> – Promotion of social and economic recovery and development.[146]

Kazakhstan has been notably active in UN peacekeeping operations.[147] On 15 June 2015, it enacted the Law 'On the Peacekeeping Action of the Republic of Kazakhstan',[148] which sets out the principles, purposes, and tasks of its peacekeeping efforts. Article 4 of the Law outlines the following basic principles:

– legality;
– compliance with norms of international law;
– impartiality and neutrality;
– respect for customs and traditions of the local population;
– non-participation in hostilities, except in peace enforcement operations.

According to Article 5, the purposes of Kazakhstan's peacekeeping action are: (1) supporting a foreign State or States in preventing, containing, or ending

[146] UN Peacekeeping, 'Mandates and the Legal Basis for Peacekeeping', available at peacekeeping.un.org/en/mandates-and-legal-basis-peacekeeping.

[147] See generally S Sayapin, *Pravovye aspekty operatsiy po podderjaniyu mira* [*Legal Aspects of Peace Support Operations*] (Astana–Tashkent, Ministry of Defence of the Republic of Kazakhstan, ICRC Regional Delegation in Central Asia, 2016).

[148] For the text of the Law (in Russian, as amended), see: online.zakon.kz/Document/?doc_id=39843849&pos=248;-51#pos=248;-51.

armed conflicts between or within States; and (2) providing humanitarian aid in line with Kazakhstan's international obligations. These aims fully align with the UN's vision of peacekeeping. Under Article 6, the more specific tasks of peacekeeping action are:

- preventing disagreements between parties, not allowing conflicts to escalate, limiting the scale of a conflict;
- contributing, by diplomatic means and methods, to the ceasing of hostilities;
- military personnel's participation in joint international enforcement actions in accordance with the UN Charter;
- protecting territories and (or) populations in the peacekeeping operation's area from armed attacks;
- ensuring compliance with ceasefire conditions;
- setting the conflicting parties apart, disarmament and dismantling of units;
- contributing to solving the problems of refugees and internally displaced persons;
- providing humanitarian aid;
- restoring infrastructure in the peacekeeping operation's area;
- ensuring law and order, the population's safety, respect for human rights;
- fulfilling other tasks provided for in a peacekeeping operation's mandate.

These are not typical duties of military personnel,[149] and, as B Boutros-Ghali noted, 'peace-keeping can rightly be called the invention of the United Nations'.[150] As peacekeeping evolved, the UN developed a set of conditions essential for the success of such missions:

> The nature of peace-keeping operations has evolved rapidly in recent years. The established principles and practices of peace-keeping have responded flexibly to new demands of recent years, and the basic conditions for success remain unchanged: a clear and practicable mandate; the cooperation of the parties in implementing that mandate; the continuing support of the Security Council; the readiness of Member States to contribute the military, police and civilian personnel, including specialists, required; effective United Nations command at Headquarters and in the field; and adequate financial and logistic support.[151]

Under Article 11(1) of the Law 'On the Peacekeeping Action of the Republic of Kazakhstan', the legal basis for deploying Kazakhstan's national peacekeeping contingent may be twofold: (1) a decision of an international organisation; and/or (2) a treaty ratified by Kazakhstan. Such decisions may be adopted by the UN Security Council or regional security organisations of which Kazakhstan is a member, such as the Collective Security Treaty Organization.

[149] See *passim* General Sir R Smith, *The Utility of Force: The Art of War in the Modern World* (London, Vintage, 2008).
[150] Boutros-Ghali (n 145), para 46.
[151] ibid, para 50.

Peacekeeping forces are established and maintained with the consent of all parties involved and are generally not authorised to use force, except in self-defence.[152] They typically consist of national contingents provided by UN Member States[153] and possess a dual legal status:

> [T]he commander of the United Nations force is head in the chain of command and is answerable to the United Nations. The functions of the force as a whole are international. But its individual component forces have their own national duty and discipline and remain in their own national service.[154]

It should also be noted that UN peacekeeping personnel must comply with the fundamental principles and rules of international humanitarian law when using force in self-defence.[155]

E. Peace-enforcement

Peace-enforcement has served as a practical workaround to Article 42 of the Charter, given the absence of special agreements under Article 43.[156] Since the 1990s, the Security Council has authorised – rather than required – individual or collective military actions by UN Member States to enforce its resolutions.[157] *Operation Desert Storm* (1990) is widely seen as a 'revolutionary development' and 'the catalyst for fundamental change in the international regulation of the use of force'.[158] Subsequent operations in Somalia (1992), Rwanda (1994), the former Yugoslavia (1994–95),[159] Haiti

[152] Dinstein (n 13), 263.
[153] ibid, 268.
[154] ibid.
[155] See UN document ST/SGB/1999/13 (Secretary-General's Bulletin 'Observance by United Nations forces of international humanitarian law'). See also J Abrisketa, 'Blue Helmets and International Humanitarian Law: How They Come Together' (2009) 22 *Humanitäres Völkerrecht – Informationsschriften* 85; N Tsagourias, 'Consent, Neutrality / Impartiality and the Use of Force in Peacekeeping: Their Constitutional Dimension' (2006) 11 *Journal of Conflict and Security Law* 465.
[156] Dinstein (n 13), 268; M Pugh, 'Peace Enforcement' in Weiss and Daws (n 145).
[157] M Byers, 'The Shifting Foundations of International Law: A Decade of Forceful Measures against Iraq' (2002) 13 *European Journal of International Law* 21; P Van Walsum, 'The Security Council and the Use of Force: Kosovo, East Timor and Iraq' in Blokker and Schrijver (n 12).
[158] Gray (n 18), 327; C Dominicé, 'La securite collective et la crise du Golfe' (1991) 2 *European Journal of International Law* 85; WM Reisman, 'The Raid on Baghdad: Some Reflections on its Lawfulness and Implications' (1994) 5 *European Journal of International Law* 120; P Tavernier, 'Le caractère obligatoire de la résolution 598 (1987) du Conseil de Sécurité relative à la guerre du Golfe' (1990) 1(1) *European Journal of International Law* 278.
[159] M Cox, 'The Dayton Agreement in Bosnia and Herzegovina: A Study of Implementation Strategies' (1999) 70 *British Yearbook of International Law* 201; C Gray, 'Bosnia and Herzegovina: Civil War or Inter-State Conflict? Characterization and Consequences' (1997) 68 *British Yearbook of International Law* 155; P Gaeta, 'The Dayton Agreements and International Law' (1996) 7 *European Journal of International Law* 147; T Gazzini, 'NATO Coercive Military Activities in the Yugoslav Crisis (1992–1999)' (2001) 12 *European Journal of International Law* 391.

(1994[160] and 2004), Albania (1997),[161] the Central African Republic (1997), East Timor (1999),[162] Liberia, the Democratic Republic of the Congo,[163] Côte d'Ivoire (2003), Kosovo (1999), Afghanistan (2001–21), Iraq (2003–11),[164] Chad (2007), and others followed this trend. In mandating such operations, the Security Council largely relied on regional arrangements under Chapter VIII of the Charter (Articles 52–54).[165] The success of these operations has been uneven, and, as Gray noted, the use of regional arrangements[166] may not always be devoid of ulterior motives:

> There is ... a danger that interested states operating under UN authorization would gain legitimacy to further their own interests. The early tradition of not using the forces of permanent members of the Security Council or of those states with geographical or historical interests in the state concerned has been further

[160] O Corten, 'La résolution 940 du Conseil de Sécurité autorisant une intervention militaire en Haïti: L'émergence d'un principe de légitimité démocratique en droit international?' (1995) 6 *European Journal of International Law* 116.

[161] C Kreß, 'Die Rettungsoperation der Bundeswehr in Albanien am 14. Marz 1997 aus völker- und verfassungsrechtlicher Sicht' (1997) 57 *Zeitschrift für ausländisches öffentliches Recht und Völkerrecht* 329.

[162] C Drew, 'The East Timor Story: International Law on Trial' (2001) 12 *European Journal of International Law* 651; MC Maffei, 'The Case of East Timor before the International Court of Justice – Some Tentative Comments' (1993) 4 *European Journal of International Law* 223.

[163] PN Okowa, 'Congo's War: The Legal Dimension of a Protracted Conflict' (2007) 78 *British Yearbook of International Law* 203.

[164] R Buchan, 'International Community and the Occupation of Iraq' (2007) 12 *Journal of Conflict and Security Law* 37; B Fassbender, 'Uncertain Steps into a Post-Cold War World: The Role and Functioning of the UN Security Council after a Decade of Measures against Iraq' (2002) 13 *European Journal of International Law* 273; TM Franck, 'What Happens Now? The United Nations after Iraq' (2003) 97 *American Journal of International Law* 607; C Gray, 'From Unity to Polarization: International Law and the Use of Force against Iraq' (2002) 13 *European Journal of International Law* 1; HJ Heintze, 'Zerfällt der Irak unter amerikanischen Bomben?' (2003) 16 *Humanitäres Völkerrecht – Informationsschriften* 16; V Lowe, 'The Iraq Crisis: What Now?' (2003) 52 *The International and Comparative Law Quarterly* 859; J Yoo, 'International Law and the War in Iraq' (2003) 97 *American Journal of International Law* 563.

[165] Dinstein (n 13), 269.

[166] A Abass, 'The New Collective Security Mechanism of ECOWAS: Innovations and Problems' (2000) 5 *Journal of Conflict and Security Law* 211; M Al-Qahtani, 'The Shanghai Cooperation Organization and the Law of International Organizations' (2006) 5 *Chinese Journal of International Law* 129; G Bebr, 'Regional Organizations: A United Nations Problem' (1955) 49 *American Journal of International Law* 166; R Dolzer, 'Enforcement of International Obligations through Regional Arrangements: Structures and Experience of the OAS' (1987) 47 *Zeitschrift für ausländisches öffentliches Recht und Völkerrecht* 113; T Gazzini, 'NATO's Role in the Collective Security System' (2003) 8 *Journal of Conflict and Security Law* 231; M Khadduri, 'The Arab League as a Regional Arrangement' (1946) 40 *American Journal of International Law* 756; EN Van Kleffens, 'Regionalism and Political Pacts' (1949) 43 *American Journal of International Law* 666; GKA Ofosu-Amaah, 'Regional Enforcement of International Obligations: Africa' (1987) 47 *Zeitschrift für ausländisches öffentliches Recht und Völkerrecht* 80; B Simma, 'NATO, the UN and the Use of Force: Legal Aspects' (1999) 10 *European Journal of International Law* 1; R Wolfrum, 'Der Beitrag regionaler Abmachumgen zur Friedenssicherung: Möglichkeiten und Grenzen' (1993) 53 *Zeitschrift für ausländisches öffentliches Recht und Völkerrecht* 576; M Zwanenburg, 'Regional Organisations and the Maintenance of International Peace and Security: Three Recent Regional African Peace Operations' (2006) 11 *Journal of Conflict and Security Law* 483.

circumvented through this type of operation. Thus it was the USA that led the 1994 and 2004 operations in Haiti, France in Rwanda and the Central African Republic (1997), Italy in Albania, and Australia in East Timor. There was some suspicion of the motives of these states. In Rwanda *Operation Turquoise* was criticized for providing a safe haven for the perpetrators of genocide ... There were newspaper reports that the use of the EU in the DRC was interpreted by some as evidence of foreign state support for the incumbent President in the elections. And Chad seems to have regarded an EU force led by its former colonial power and current supporter, France, as more acceptable than a UN force.[167]

VII. CHARTER-RELATED EXCEPTIONS TO PROHIBITION ON USE OF FORCE

The second category of exceptions to the prohibition on the use of force under Article 2(4) of the UN Charter is not explicitly stated in the Charter but can be inferred from its programmatic and operative provisions. Key examples include General Assembly resolution 377 A (V) ('Uniting for Peace') of 3 November 1950, the use of force to uphold the right of peoples to self-determination, and the 2005 Responsibility to Protect doctrine.

A. 'Uniting for Peace'

During the General Assembly's debate on the draft resolution 'Uniting for Peace',[168] numerous arguments – grounded in both positive international law and legal scholarship – were advanced for and against its adoption.[169] It was already evident that the Security Council's procedure for maintaining international peace and security was imperfect, and the resolution aimed to address this shortcoming through the General Assembly. The first operative paragraph read as follows:

> The General Assembly ...
>
> 1. *Resolves* that if the Security Council, because of lack of unanimity of the permanent members, fails to exercise its primary responsibility for the maintenance of international peace and security in any case where there appears to be a threat to the peace, breach of the peace, or act of aggression, the General Assembly shall consider the matter immediately with a view to making appropriate recommendations to Members for collective measures, including in the case of a breach of the peace or act of aggression the use of armed force when necessary, to maintain or

[167] Gray (n 18), 334 (footnotes omitted).

[168] UN General Assembly resolution 377 (V), 3 November 1950.

[169] J Andrassy, 'Uniting for Peace' (1956) 50 *American Journal of International Law* 563; LH Woolsey, 'The "Uniting for Peace" Resolution of the United Nations' (1951) 45 *American Journal of International Law* 129.

> restore international peace and security. If not in session at the time, the General Assembly may meet in emergency special session within twenty-four hours of the request therefor. Such emergency special session shall be called if requested by the Security Council on the vote of any seven members, or by a majority of the Members of the United Nations.

The main argument against the resolution was that it violated the UN Charter by assigning to the General Assembly a role properly belonging to the Security Council, thus undermining a core principle of the UN: the unanimity of the permanent Security Council members as a prerequisite for effectively maintaining international peace and security.[170] Opponents argued that the resolution was inconsistent with the Charter and, in effect, amounted to an illicit amendment, contrary to Articles 108 and 109.[171]

Although the Charter's drafters intended a clear division of roles between the General Assembly and the Security Council, this was only partially achieved.[172] Under Article 24(1), the Security Council holds 'primary responsibility' for maintaining international peace and security.[173] However, as Andrassy observed, a literal reading implies a 'subsidiary' or 'supplementary' responsibility, which proponents of the resolution argued belonged to the General Assembly.[174] Article 10 authorises the General Assembly to discuss any matter within the UN's competence, including those related to peace and security, despite the Council's primary responsibility.[175] Article 11(2) outlines three possible General Assembly responses: (1) discussion, (2) recommendations, and (3) recognition of the need for enforcement action.[176] Since 1956, 11 emergency special sessions have been convened under the resolution.[177] Six concerned the Middle East (1956, 1958, 1967), Palestine (1980–82), the occupied Arab territories (1982), and East Jerusalem and the wider Occupied Palestinian Territory (since 1997).[178] The other five addressed Hungary (1956), Congo (1960), Afghanistan (1980), Namibia (1981), and Ukraine (since 2023).[179]

[170] Andrassy (n 169), 563.
[171] ibid.
[172] ibid, 563–64; N Greenwood Onuf, 'Professor Falk on the Quasi-legislative Competence of the General Assembly' (1970) 64 *American Journal of International Law* 349.
[173] J Brunnee, 'The Security Council and Self-defence: Which Way to Global Security?' in Blokker and Schrijver (n 12), 107–32.
[174] Andrassy (n 169), 564.
[175] ibid, 565.
[176] ibid, 566.
[177] See: http://www.un.org/en/ga/sessions/emergency.shtml.
[178] cf E Cannizzaro, 'A Humanitarian Action by the UN General Assembly in Gaza?', EJIL:Talk!, 17 June 2025, available at www.ejiltalk.org/a-humanitarian-action-by-the-un-general-assembly-in-gaza/.
[179] cf F Kriener and A Peters, 'Legal Limits for UNSC Action on Peace in Ukraine', EJIL:Talk!, 8 April 2025, available at www.ejiltalk.org/legal-limits-for-unsc-action-on-peace-in-ukraine/.

B. The Use of Force in Pursuit of Peoples' Right to Self-determination

The question of whether national liberation movements may use force to pursue peoples' right to self-determination[180] – and whether supportive States may assist them[181] – has been debated among international lawyers since the Second World War. With the UN Charter's entry into force, including Articles 73 and 74 on non-self-governing territories, many former colonies began seeking independence, sometimes through armed struggle. As Gray recalls, early examples included violent independence movements in Tunisia, Morocco, and Algeria against France; in Malaya, Kenya, and Cyprus against the UK; in Indonesia against the Netherlands; and in Goa against Portuguese rule.[182] As decolonisation advanced, some former colonies and socialist States increasingly supported the right of liberation movements to use force – and of third States to aid them – a stance firmly opposed by Western States.[183] The key document on decolonisation – the 1960 Declaration on the Granting of Independence to Colonial Countries and Peoples[184] – did not explicitly address the use of force. However, subsequent resolutions used language that could be interpreted as supporting it in certain cases.[185] For example, resolution A/RES/2105 (XX) 'recognise[d] the legitimacy of the *struggle* by the peoples under colonial rule to exercise their right to self-determination and independence and invite[d] all states to provide material and moral assistance to the national liberation movements in colonial territories'.[186] As Gray observes, it remained unclear whether 'struggle' in this context referred to armed or peaceful means,[187] though its common usage suggests force was at least implied. Similarly, the 1970 Friendly Relations Declaration did not explicitly authorise the use of force by national liberation movements, but did call upon States:

> [t]o refrain from any forcible action which deprives peoples … of their right to self-determination and freedom and independence. In their actions against, and resistance to, such forcible action in pursuit of the exercise of the right to self-determination,

[180] I Brownlie, *Principles of Public International Law*, 5th edn (Oxford, Clarendon Press, 1998), 599–602; T Van Boven, 'Human Rights and Rights of Peoples' (1995) 6 *European Journal of International Law* 461; B Kashnikov, 'Self-determination of Peoples' in S Sayapin et al (eds), *International Conflict and Security Law: A Research Handbook* (The Hague, TMC Asser Press, 2022); M Weller, 'Settling Self-determination Conflicts: Recent Developments' (2009) 20 *European Journal of International Law* 111.

[181] Malanczuk (n 5), 326–37.

[182] Gray (n 18), 59.

[183] ibid. cf also Article 1(4) of the First Additional Protocol to the 1949 Geneva Conventions.

[184] See UN General Assembly resolution 1514 (XV) of 14 December 1960, available at: www.un.org/ga/search/view_doc.asp?symbol=A/RES/1514(XV).

[185] Gray (n 18), 60.

[186] UN General Assembly resolution A/RES/2105 (XX), 20 December 1965, quoted in Gray (n 18), 60 (emphasis added).

[187] Gray (n 18), 60.

> such peoples are entitled to seek and to receive support in accordance with the purposes and principles of the Charter.[188]

A similar approach appears in Article 7 of General Assembly resolution 3314 (XXIX):[189]

> Nothing in this Definition … could in any way prejudice the right to self-determination, freedom and independence, as derived from the Charter, of peoples forcibly deprived of that right and referred to in the Declaration on Principles of International Law concerning Friendly Relations and Co-operation among States in accordance with the Charter of the United Nations, particularly peoples under colonial and racist regimes or other forms of alien domination; nor the right of these peoples to struggle to that end and to seek and receive support, in accordance with the principles of the Charter and in conformity with the above-mentioned Declaration.

Since the use of force in pursuit of self-determination remains relevant only in the residual context of Palestine and the Israeli occupation of the West Bank and Gaza,[190] it may be assumed that the gradual recognition of Palestine's statehood will ultimately render this issue a matter of history.[191] Claims by ethnic groups to secede from existing States on self-determination grounds are generally not supported by States.[192]

C. Responsibility to Protect (R2P)

According to the United Nations, '[t]he responsibility to protect embodies a political commitment to end the worst forms of violence and persecution'.[193] The concept 'emerged in response to the failure of the international community to adequately respond to mass atrocities committed in Rwanda and the former

[188] Friendly Relations Declaration, Principle 5, para 5, quoted in Gray (n 18), 61.

[189] On this resolution, see section III above.

[190] FA Boyle, 'The Creation of the State of Palestine' (1990) 1 *European Journal of International Law*, 301–6; A Cassese, 'The Israel – PLO Agreement and Self-determination' (1993) 4 *European Journal of International Law* 564; J Crawford, 'The Creation of the State of Palestine: Too Much Too Soon?' (1990) 1 *European Journal of International Law* 307; AM Husain, 'Who is the Legitimate Representative of the Palestinian People?' (2003) 2 *Chinese Journal of International Law* 207; P Malanczuk, 'Some Basic Aspects of the Agreements between Israel and the PLO from the Perspective of International Law' (1996) 7 *European Journal of International Law* 485; J Vidmar, 'Palestine and the Conceptual Problem of Implicit Statehood' (2013) 12 *Chinese Journal of International Law* 19.

[191] See section IX.G below.

[192] Gray (n 18), 64; A Aust, *Handbook of International Law* (Cambridge, Cambridge University Press, 2005), 85–117; HJ Heintze, 'Indigenous Peoples and the Right of Self-determination – Is the Claim to Self-determination a Trap?' (2008) 21 *Humanitäres Völkerrecht – Informationsschriften* 238; WG Werner, 'Self-determination and Civil War' (2001) 6 *Journal of Conflict and Security Law* 171.

[193] United Nations, Office on Genocide Prevention and the Responsibility to Protect, 'About the Responsibility to Protect', available at www.un.org/en/genocide-prevention/responsibility-protect/about.

Yugoslavia during the 1990s',[194] and was unanimously endorsed at the 2005 UN World Summit. It is articulated in paragraphs 138–139 of the World Summit Outcome Document:[195]

> 138. Each individual State has the responsibility to protect its populations from genocide, war crimes, ethnic cleansing and crimes against humanity. This responsibility entails the prevention of such crimes, including their incitement, through appropriate and necessary means. We accept that responsibility and will act in accordance with it. The international community should, as appropriate, encourage and help States to exercise this responsibility and support the United Nations in establishing an early warning capability.

Paragraph 139 further states that R2P may involve 'diplomatic, humanitarian and other peaceful means' as well as 'collective [enforcement] action … through the Security Council, in accordance with the Charter, including Chapter VII'. Notably, R2P action may be carried out 'in cooperation with relevant regional organizations as appropriate'.[196] Since 2005:

> R2P has been invoked in more than 95 UN Security Council resolutions concerning crises in Central African Republic, Côte d'Ivoire, Democratic Republic of the Congo, Liberia, Libya, Mali, Somalia, South Sudan, Syria, and Yemen, as well as thematic resolutions concerning the prevention of genocide, prevention of armed conflict and restricting the trade of small arms and light weapons among other topics. The Responsibility to Protect has also been invoked in more than 80 Human Rights Council resolutions and 40 General Assembly resolutions.[197]

Yet, according to critics, 'R2P was set up to fail'.[198] Lee maintains that '[a]fter all the optimistic talk in 2005, by 2009 there had been little progress in implementing R2P'.[199] Further,

> [b]y 2018, fighting in Syria had been underway for eight years, and the UN reported the conflict had led to 400,000 dead, 5.6 million refugees and 6.6 million internally displaced people. Yet Russia and China still refused to invoke R2P. Russia and China also vetoed UN attempts to refer Syria and the perpetrators of war crimes to the International Criminal Court.[200]

[194] Global Centre for the Responsibility to Protect, 'What is R2P?', available at www.globalr2p.org/what-is-r2p/.

[195] For the text of the World Summit Outcome Document, see: 24 October 2005, www.globalr2p.org/resources/2005-world-summit-outcome-a-60-l-1/.

[196] ibid.

[197] Global Centre for the Responsibility to Protect (n 194).

[198] P Lee, 'Ukraine: the UN's "responsibility to protect" doctrine is a hollow promise for civilians under fire', *The Conversation*, 7 March 2022, available at theconversation.com/ukraine-the-uns-responsibility-to-protect-doctrine-is-a-hollow-promise-for-civilians-under-fire-178661.

[199] ibid.

[200] ibid. See also D Akande, 'The Legality of Military Action in Syria: Humanitarian Intervention and Responsibility to Protect', EJIL:Talk!, 28 August 2013, available at www.ejiltalk.org/humanitarian-intervention-responsibility-to-protect-and-the-legality-of-military-action-in-syria/.

More recently, the UN has failed to invoke the R2P doctrine in response to Russia's war against Ukraine,[201] and the worsening situation of women and other vulnerable groups in Afghanistan.[202]

VIII. OTHER FORMS OF UNILATERAL MILITARY INTERVENTION

Extra-Charter exceptions to the prohibition of the use of force are particularly problematic, as they lack a basis in the UN Charter and stem from external sources of international law. Since these rules are not codified, their content remains vague. They are thus best described as 'purported' or, at most, 'emerging' exceptions. The three most notable examples are 'humanitarian intervention', the forcible protection of nationals abroad, and 'pro-democratic intervention'.

A. 'Humanitarian Intervention'

The legal aspects of 'humanitarian intervention' are among the most complex in modern *jus contra bellum*.[203] Murphy defines it as 'the threat or use of force by a State, group of States, or international organization primarily for the purpose of protecting the nationals of the target state from widespread deprivations of internationally recognized human rights'.[204] The central, and exceptionally

[201] Lee (n 198): 'But the real priority is not protecting Ukrainian civilians but to avoid a third world war by preventing a clash between Russia and the west. Plus, protecting Ukrainian civilians by intervening with massive military power would be costly – politically, financially and in terms of military lives lost'.

[202] Global Centre for the Responsibility to Protect, 'Afghanistan', available at www.globalr2p.org/countries/afghanistan/.

[203] cf the UN Secretary-General's Press Release SG/SM/7136 (20 September 1999), in which Kofi Annan remarked that humanitarian intervention would pose a 'core challenge to the Security Council and the United Nations as a whole in the next century'. See also N Berman, 'Intervention in a "Divided World": Axes of Legitimacy' (2006) 17 *European Journal of International Law* 743; A Cassese, 'A Follow-up: Forcible Humanitarian Countermeasures and *Opinio Necessitatis*' (1999) 10 *European Journal of International Law* 791–99; S Chesterman, *Just War or Just Peace? Humanitarian Intervention and International Law* (Oxford, Oxford University Press, 2001); P Hilpold, 'Humanitarian Intervention: Is There a Need for a Legal Reappraisal?' (2001) 12 *European Journal of International Law* 437; WM Reisman, 'Unilateral Action and the Transformations of the World Constitutive Process: The Special Problem of Humanitarian Intervention' (2000) 11 *European Journal of International Law* 3; R Thakur, 'Humanitarian Intervention' in Weiss and Daws (n 145); A Zwitter, 'Menschliche Sicherheit, Humanitäre Intervention und ihre völkerrechtlichen Perspektiven' (2007) 20 *Humanitäres Völkerrecht – Informationsschriften* 231.

[204] SD Murphy, *Humanitarian Intervention: The United Nations in an Evolving World Order* (Philadelphia PA, University of Pennsylvania Press, 1996), 11–12. Badescu's definition is similar: 'The definition of humanitarian intervention … is the use of armed force by either a state, a group of states, or an international organization to address widespread suffering or death among civilians in another state affected by grave violations of human rights', see CG Badescu, *Humanitarian Intervention and the Responsibility to Protect: Security and Human Rights* (London, Routledge, 2001), 8 (footnotes omitted).

difficult, question is whether international law permits States to intervene militarily – without Security Council authorisation – to stop genocide or atrocities of similar scale.

In the early twenty-first century, the issue gained prominence due to international coalitions' interventions in Kosovo (1999)[205] and Iraq (2003), as well as the failure to intervene in Sudan. The principal concern regarding the legitimacy of 'humanitarian intervention' lies in the risk that, if legalised, States might misuse it as a pretext to wage wars in pursuit of selfish national interests.[206] This policy dilemma was already recognised by Grotius and subsequent European classics of international law. The doctrine of 'humanitarian intervention' held considerable sway in the early twentieth century,[207] before the League of Nations established the first legal constraints on the inter-State use of force following the First World War. After the UN Charter entered into force, international political[208] and scholarly[209] opinion shifted firmly against 'humanitarian intervention'. Notably, even States that undertook such interventions without Security Council authorisation generally refrained from invoking a legal right to do so, instead presenting them as ad hoc responses.[210]

Although contrary views have occasionally been voiced,[211] it is widely accepted that international law prohibits States from unilaterally using force, even for the purpose of rescuing victims of humanitarian catastrophes.[212] The principal treaty governing the use of force, the Charter of the United Nations, does

[205] JI Charney, 'Anticipatory Humanitarian Intervention in Kosovo' (1999) 93 *American Journal of International Law* 834; CM Chinkin, 'Kosovo: A "Good" or "Bad" War?' (1999) 93 *American Journal of International Law* 841; L Henkin, 'Kosovo and the Law of Humanitarian Intervention' (1999) 93 *American Journal of International Law* 824; DH Joyner, 'The Kosovo Intervention: Legal Analysis and a More Persuasive Paradigm' (2002) 13 *European Journal of International Law* 597; A Orford, 'Muscular Humanitarianism: Reading the Narratives of new Interventionism' (1999) 10 *European Journal of International Law* 679; S Wheatley, 'The Foreign Affairs Select Committee Report on Kosovo: NATO Action and Humanitarian Intervention' (2000) 5 *Journal of Conflict and Security Law* 261–73; ND White, 'The Legality of Bombing in the Name of Humanity' (2000) 5 *Journal of Conflict and Security Law* 27.

[206] R Goodman, 'Humanitarian Intervention and Pretexts for War' (2006) 100 *American Journal of International Law* 107.

[207] I Brownlie, *International Law and the Use of Force by States* (Oxford, Clarendon Press, 1968), 338.

[208] Within five years of the 1999 intervention in Kosovo, more than 130 States, representing approximately 80 per cent of the world's population, issued policy statements rejecting the legality of humanitarian intervention. See, for example, UN Doc S/PV.4011 (10 June 1999) documenting China's opinion that humanitarian intervention 'promote[s] hegemonism under the pretext of human rights'.

[209] See, for example, R Bilder, 'Kosovo and the "New Interventionism": Promise or Peril?' (1999) 9 *Journal of Transnational Law and Policy* 153, 161; O Schachter, 'The Right of States to Use Armed Force' (1984) 82 *Michigan Law Review* 1620, 1629.

[210] See, for example, United Kingdom Foreign Office, Policy Document No 148, reprinted in (1986) 57 *British Yearbook of International Law* 614, 619.

[211] For a persuasive discussion in favour of the lawfulness of humanitarian intervention, see C Greenwood, 'Humanitarian Intervention: The Case of Kosovo' (1999) 10 *Finnish Yearbook of International Law* 141.

[212] Badescu (n 204), 48–73.

not list 'humanitarian intervention' among the lawful exceptions to Article 2(4), and relevant General Assembly resolutions affirm this overarching norm.[213] The International Court of Justice has likewise confirmed the prohibition,[214] and leading treatises recognise that 'humanitarian intervention' is barred under both treaty and customary international law, despite some inconsistent State practice in recent years.[215]

It may be assumed, however, that the legal regulation of humanitarian intervention could evolve to some extent. Following ECOWAS interventions in Liberia (1990) and Sierra Leone (1997), and NATO's intervention in Kosovo (1999), some scholars proposed that new rules permitting an exception to the Article 2(4) prohibition on the use of force might be emerging.[216] In 2009, the possibility of codifying the law of 'humanitarian intervention' was even raised in academic discourse.[217] Whether customary international law on this issue will further develop remains to be seen.

B. Forcible Protection of Nationals Abroad

The political and scholarly debate on the legitimacy of the so-called 'forcible protection of nationals abroad' has continued for decades. Its substantive basis lies in military interventions by certain States in other States, without Security Council authorisation, to rescue or evacuate their nationals threatened by a collapse of law and order or other life-threatening dangers in the target States.[218] Customary international law on this issue, as it currently stands, does not define either the exceptional circumstances justifying such use of force or its permissible extent. These operations are sometimes classified as a sub-type of 'humanitarian intervention' since both (1) occur outside the intervening State's territory, (2) involve inter-State military force under Article 2(4) of the Charter, and

[213] cf Definition of Aggression, GA Res 3314 (XXIX) (14 December 1974); Declaration on Principles of International Law Concerning Friendly Relations and Cooperation Among States in Accordance with the Charter of the United Nations, GA Res 2625 (XXV) (24 October 1970); Declaration on the Inadmissibility of Intervention and Interference in the Internal Affairs of States, GA Res 36/103 (9 December 1981).

[214] *Nicaragua* Judgment (n 32), para 268: '[W]hile the United States might form its own appraisal of the situation as to respect for human rights in Nicaragua, the use of force could not be the appropriate method to monitor or ensure such respect … The Court concludes that the argument derived from the preservation of human rights in Nicaragua cannot afford a legal justification for the conduct of the United States'.

[215] A Cassese, *International Law*, 2nd edn (Oxford, Oxford University Press, 2005), 373–74; Brownlie (n 180), 710–12; Malanczuk (n 5), 221.

[216] Gray (n 18), 99.

[217] C Henke, 'Vorschlag für ein Übereinkommen über die Regelung der völkerrechtlichen Voraussetzungen einer humanitären Intervention' (2009) 22 *Humanitäres Völkerrecht – Informationsschriften* 15.

[218] T Gazzini, *The Changing Rules on the Use of Force in International Law* (Manchester, Manchester University Press, 2005), 170–71; Gray (n 18), 156.

(3) aim to prevent harm to identifiable persons or groups in the target State.[219] Nevertheless, there is broad agreement that the two must be distinguished under international law.[220] The key difference lies in their ratione personae: 'humanitarian intervention' protects the target State's population from mass or grave human rights violations, whereas operations to protect nationals aim to defend the intervening State's own citizens facing imminent threats abroad.

States and legal scholars generally justify the 'forcible protection of nationals' by invoking three cumulative conditions: (1) an imminent threat of physical harm to a State's nationals; (2) the territorial sovereign is unwilling or unable to protect them; and (3) the intervening State's military action must not exceed the objective of protecting its nationals from the identified threat.[221] It is undisputed that such interventions were accepted before 1945.[222] Similarly, they are considered consistent with the UN Charter when the host State consents. However, whether military operations conducted without such consent – or where the host State's authority is uncertain, such as during a high-intensity non-international armed conflict – comply with international law remains a core issue in contemporary *jus ad bellum*.[223]

Proponents of the 'forcible protection of nationals' doctrine offer several justifications.[224] One group of jurists argues, plausibly, that such operations do not violate the Charter's Article 2(4) prohibition on the use of force, as they do not compromise a State's 'territorial integrity or political independence'; their sole purpose is to rescue foreign nationals from imminent danger that the host State is unwilling or unable to avert.[225] Another mainstream view holds that such operations constitute a form of self-defence under Article 51 of the UN Charter.[226] A two-tiered argument is advanced to support this position. First, it is argued that the Charter recognises an inherent right of self-defence, which

[219] U Beyerlin, 'Die israelische Befreiungsaktion in Entebbe in völkerrechtlicher Sicht' (1977) *Zeitschrift für ausländisches öffentliches Recht und Völkerrecht* 213; KE Eichensehr, 'Defending Nationals Abroad: Assessing the Lawfulness of Forcible Hostage Rescues' (2008) 48 *Virginia Journal of International Law* 462; T Ruys, 'The "Protection of Nationals" Doctrine Revisited' (2008) 13 *Journal of Conflict and Security Law* 233.

[220] Eichensehr (n 219), 461–63.

[221] CHM Waldock, 'The Regulation of the Use of Force by Individual States in International Law' (1952) 81 *Recueil des Cours* 467.

[222] Brownlie (n 207), 289.

[223] L Doswald-Beck, 'The Legal Validity of Military Intervention by Invitation of the Government' (1985) 56 *British Yearbook of International Law* 189; N Ronzitti, *Rescuing Nationals Abroad Through Military Coercion and Intervention on Grounds of Humanity* (Dordrecht, Martinus Nijhoff Publishers, 1985), 1–88.

[224] RJ Zedalis, 'Protection of Nationals Abroad: Is Consent the Basis of Legal Obligation?' (1990) 25 *Texas Journal of International Law* 221.

[225] JJ Paust, 'Entebbe and Self-Help: The Israeli Response to Terrorism' (1978) 2 *Fletcher Forum* 89; R Higgins, *Problems and Process: International Law and How We Use It* (Oxford, Oxford University Press, 1994), 220–21.

[226] A Gerard, 'L'opération Stanleyville-Paulis devant le Parlement belge et les Nations Unies' (1967) 3 *Revue belge de droit international* 242, 254–55; O Schachter, 'In Defense of International Rules on the Use of Force' (1986) 53 *University of Chicago Law Review* 113, 139.

should be interpreted broadly in light of pre-existing customary international law – under which States had the right to protect their nationals abroad. Second, it is suggested that nationals temporarily abroad remain part of the State's population and thus represent a fundamental attribute of statehood;[227] a deliberate attack against them may therefore be equated with an attack on the State itself, justifying self-defence under Article 51. Other justifications – such as appeals to a 'state of necessity'[228] or to 'humanitarian considerations' and fundamental rights[229] – have also been proposed but remain less widely accepted. Another group of jurists has argued, perhaps more convincingly, that the right to protect nationals abroad should be seen as a novel, essentially customary and self-standing exception to Article 2(4), as it does not fit neatly within the existing legal framework.[230]

C. 'Pro-democratic Intervention'

The transition of Iraq's regime from dictatorship to democracy was the declared political objective of *Operation Iraqi Freedom*,[231] reflecting President George W Bush's dual ambition to eliminate threats from 'rogue' States and to promote democracy. This ambition appears to have influenced UN Security Council practice significantly, at least during Bush's presidency. As Taft and Buchwald noted, *Operation Iraqi Freedom* was justified on a specific interpretation of Security Council resolutions 678 (1991), 687 (1991), and 1441 (2002), whereby Iraq's 'material breach' of disarmament obligations under resolution 687 (1991) revived the authorisation to use force under resolution 678 (1991).[232] A related question is whether Security Council resolutions 1483 (2003), 1511 (2003), and 1546 (2004) – adopted after the intervention – served to consolidate the new regime.

Iraq's 'forced democratisation' appears inconsistent with current international law. Under Article 43 of the Regulations annexed to the 1907 Hague Convention (IV) on the Laws and Customs of War on Land, an occupying

[227] Lukashuk (n 117), 25.

[228] J Raby, 'The State of Necessity and the Use of Force to Protect Nationals' (1988) 26 *Canadian Yearbook of International Law* 253.

[229] DJ Gordon, 'Use of Force for the Protection of Nationals Abroad: The Entebbe Incident' (1977) 9 *Case Western Reserve Journal of International Law* 117, 132; T Schweisfurth, 'Operations to Rescue Nationals in Third States Involving the Use of Force in Relation to the Protection of Human Rights' (1980) 23 *German Yearbook of International Law* 159, 161.

[230] N Ronzitti, 'The Expanding Law of Self-defence' (2006) 11 *Journal of Conflict and Security Law* 343, 354.

[231] Agence France Presse, 'The leaders' two declarations: "We uphold a vision of international security"', New York Times, 17 March 2003.

[232] WH Taft IV and TF Buchwald, 'Preemption, Iraq, and International Law' (2003) 97 *American Journal of International Law* 557; K Bennoune, '"Sovereignty vs. Suffering"? Re-examining Sovereignty and Human Rights through the Lens of Iraq' (2002) 13 *European Journal of International Law* 243.

power must respect, 'unless absolutely prevented', the laws in force in the occupied country. As Article 43 reflects customary international law,[233] the imposition of political reforms in occupied territories would generally be prohibited. However, this conclusion is incomplete when considered alongside Articles 24(1) and 103 of the UN Charter: if Charter obligations prevail over other treaty commitments (including the 1907 Hague Convention), and the Security Council acts on behalf of Member States in maintaining international peace and security, then Chapter VII resolutions may supersede both treaty and customary law, including the Hague Regulations. In practice, post hoc criticism of the US-led coalition's intervention and regime change carries limited weight when Security Council members enabled the adoption of relevant resolutions by not using their veto. Ultimately, the Council's ambiguous stance on Iraq – and later on Libya – set critical precedents whose long-term consequences remain uncertain.[234]

IX. CENTRAL ASIAN PERSPECTIVES ON INTERNATIONAL PEACE AND SECURITY

Since 1991, Central Asia has witnessed a non-international armed conflict in Tajikistan (1992–97), two armed conflicts between Kyrgyzstan and Tajikistan (in 2021 and 2022), and several incidents of violence in Kazakhstan, Kyrgyzstan, and Uzbekistan. The Central Asian States have also taken official positions on other conflicts – most notably in Afghanistan, the Russia–Ukraine war, and more recently, on the use of force by Hamas and Iran against Israel – and jointly established one of the world's five Nuclear-Weapon-Free Zones (NWFZs). The following subsections briefly examine these developments, and the chapter concludes with reflections on the imperative to promote a culture of peace.

A. Armed Conflict in Tajikistan (1992–97)

In early 1992, Tajikistan faced profound economic, political, and social instability. Regional divisions within society, compounded by high levels of religiosity, further deepened internal tensions. A brutal civil war erupted on 5 May 1992, involving, on one side, regular government forces and the pro-government People's Front of Tajikistan – supported by Russia and Uzbekistan – and, on the other, a coalition of secular and religious opposition groups, including the United Tajik Opposition (UTO), the Democratic Party, the People's Unity Party

[233] cf Chapter 7, section I above.

[234] R Müllerson, 'Promoting Democracy without Starting a New Cold War?' (2008) 7 *Chinese Journal of International Law* 1.

of Tajikistan, Lali Badakhshan, the Islamic Revival Party (IRP) of Tajikistan, the Islamic Movement of Uzbekistan, the Taliban, and others.[235]

Tensions escalated in spring 1992 when opposition members protested in Dushanbe, disputing the results of the November 1991 presidential election. As a result, President Nabiyev was forced to resign. In the second phase, the war expanded from Dushanbe to the country's southern regions, with most fighting concentrated in southern Tajikistan and incursions from Afghanistan. Government forces received support from around 25,000 Russian troops. In the third stage, opposition forces advanced from Afghanistan into Tajikistan's eastern and central areas. In December 1996, President Rakhmonov reached a peace agreement with Sayed Abdullo Nuri, leader of the IRP, and initiated dialogue with the UTO to enable reintegration of political and military elements. Sporadic clashes continued into spring 1997. A final peace accord was signed on 27 June 1997.

As Atadjanov notes, official reports estimate that the five-year conflict resulted in over 60,000 casualties, whereas most independent sources place the actual toll between 100,000 and 150,000.[236] Thousands remain unaccounted for, and the identities of the occupants of more than 40 mass graves have yet to be established. Approximately 1.2 million people were displaced, seeking refuge internally and in Afghanistan, Uzbekistan, Russia, and Kyrgyzstan.[237]

B. Violence in Andijan (2005)

According to a report issued by the OSCE Office for Democratic Institutions and Human Rights,

> [t]he violent events on 13 May 2005 in the Uzbek city of Andijan were closely linked to a trial of 23 popular local businessmen.[238] These 23 businessmen had been arrested during the summer of 2004 and charged with 'extremism, fundamentalism and separatism'. The trial had started on 10 February 2005 in Andijan and lasted for three months (five days a week).[239]

The verdict was scheduled to be announced on 11 May 2005 but its announcement of the verdict was postponed to an unknown date.[240] On 11–12 May 2005,

[235] SA Rajabov, *Implementatsiya norm mezhdunarodnogo gumanitarnogo prava v Respublike Tadjikistan: problem teorii i praktiki* [*The implementation of rules of international humanitarian law in the Republic of Tajikistan: Issues of theory and practice*] (Dushanbe, Institute of State and Law under the Academy of Sciences of the Republic of Tajikistan, 2006), 72–79.

[236] See Chapter 2, section I.C above and R Atadjanov, 'Non-International Armed Conflict in Tajikistan' in S Lee et al (eds), *Encyclopedia of Public International Law in Asia*, Volume III: Central & South Asia (Leiden, Brill, 2021), 208.

[237] Atadjanov (n 236).

[238] ODIHR, 'Preliminary Findings on the Events in Andijan, Uzbekistan, 13 May 2005', p 6 (footnotes omitted), available at www.osce.org/files/f/documents/1/1/15653.pdf.

[239] ibid.

[240] ibid.

the National Security Service (SNB) detained and questioned a few male relatives of the defendants, and '[a]nother group of 13 Andijan businessmen had been arrested on similar charges in the beginning of 2005, but their trial had not yet started'.[241]

On 13 May 2005, 'unidentified persons stormed Andijan Prison and freed the detainees, including the businessmen on trial, from their cells. The attackers informed the detainees that a meeting was being organized on Babur Square. Many freed detainees proceeded to the square'.[242] During the day,

> members of the crowd took a number of hostages (at least 20) and held them inside the Hokimiyat [Regional Administration] building until the crowd left the square in the evening, taking some hostages with them. The hostages included the Head of the Prosecutors Office and the Chief of the Tax Inspection Authority.[243]

At 17:00–18:00, 'there were an estimated 10,000–15,000 protesters on the square. At this point security forces launched a major offensive on the square, attacking simultaneously from different sides'.[244] Official and independent reports of the numbers of casualties differed dramatically:

> According to the Uzbek government, 187 people were killed, most of them soldiers and insurrectionists. Civilian deaths, only about 60 according to the Prosecutor-General's Office, were attributed to the insurrectionists
>
> But eyewitness accounts pointed to a civilian casualty figure that was many times higher, with some estimates putting the figure well over 1,000 killed, with reports of mass graves being dug and bodies being flown to Russia. International calls for an independent investigation were rejected.[245]

In the subsequent years, numerous individuals were subjected to repeated police interrogations, arbitrary detention and ill-treatment in custody, threats to have their homes confiscated, and other forms of pressure.[246] Human Rights Watch has reported that '[b]etween September 2005 and July 2006, at least 303 people were convicted and sentenced to lengthy prison terms in 22 trials, all but one closed to the public',[247] and that '[n]o one has been held accountable for the killings in Andijan'.[248] The disproportionate use of force was not admitted by Uzbekistan's authorities until 7 February 2020 when Deputy Prosecutor-General Svetlana Artykova gave an interview to

[241] ibid.
[242] ibid.
[243] ibid.
[244] ibid, p 7.
[245] B Pannier, '"We Made Mistakes": In Uzbekistan, A Rare Admission Over Andijon Killings', RadioFreeEurope/RadioLiberty, 18 February 2020, available at www.rferl.org/a/uzbekistan-andijon-assacre-officials-willingness-talk-analysis/30442215.html.
[246] Human Rights Watch, 'Uzbekistan: Stop Persecuting Andijan Refugees' Families', 4 May 2010, available at www.hrw.org/news/2010/05/04/uzbekistan-stop-persecuting-andijan-refugees-families.
[247] ibid.
[248] ibid.

the Uzbek news agency *Qalampir*, and said that '"innocent" people were shot' on 13 May 2005.[249] She explained that 'communications were bad, the commanding officer either didn't hear the orders in time or misunderstood them; there were no proper preparations … we made mistakes'.[250] In the same interview, Artykova emphasised 'that Uzbekistan had changed' since 2016: 'Now it is a new Uzbekistan. Now there is a new style of politics. Now there is a new political will'.[251]

C. Kyrgyzstan (2010)

On 10 June 2010, violence erupted in the southern Kyrgyz cities of Osh and Jalal-Abad. After five days of brutality, '[o]ver 400 people were killed and nearly two thousand homes were destroyed'.[252] About 400,000 persons were displaced, and 80,000 persons – mostly, ethnic Uzbeks – sought refuge in the neighbouring Uzbekistan.[253] UN assessments estimate that approximately 1 million people were affected by the violence. The UN announced a US$ 71 million appeal, and the ICRC requested 10 million Swiss francs from donors, in order to assist the victims. The level of violence may have reached that of crimes against humanity.[254] At least three counts of crimes against humanity appear to be valid in this context: murder,[255] rape,[256] and 'persecution against any identifiable group or collectivity on … ethnic, cultural, … gender … or other grounds'.[257] According to Human Rights Watch, 'most criminal investigations into crimes committed during the violence, nearly 4,000 of over 5,000 cases, according to government data published in 2017, have been suspended because the accused could not be identified or could not be found'.[258] Notably, '[t]he Kyrgyz government has not acknowledged that ethnic Uzbeks disproportionately were the victims of attacks or that attacks on ethnic Uzbek neighborhoods were systematic'.[259] Human Rights Watch

[249] Pannier (n 245).
[250] ibid.
[251] ibid.
[252] Human Rights Watch, 'Kyrgyzstan: Justice Elusive 10 Years On', 9 June 2020, available at www.hrw.org/news/2020/06/09/kyrgyzstan-justice-elusive-10-years.
[253] Global Centre for the Responsibility to Protect, 'Kyrgyzstan', available at www.globalr2p.org/countries/kyrgyzstan/.
[254] Human Rights Watch, 'Where is the Justice? Interethnic Violence in Southern Kyrgyzstan and its Aftermath', 16 August 2010, available at https://www.hrw.org/report/2010/08/16/where-justice/interethnic-violence-southern-kyrgyzstan-and-its-aftermath.
[255] ICC Statute, Art 7(1)(a).
[256] ICC Statute, Art 7(1)(g).
[257] ICC Statute, Art 7(1)(h).
[258] Human Rights Watch (n 252).
[259] ibid.

> also documented that the profoundly flawed criminal investigations and trials, mainly affecting the ethnic Uzbek minority, were marred by widespread arbitrary arrests and ill-treatment, including torture. Prosecutorial authorities refused to investigate torture allegations, and frequent physical attacks against defendants and their lawyers marred courtroom proceedings.[260]

The 2011 Report of the Independent International Commission of Inquiry into the Events in Southern Kyrgyzstan in June 2010 contained similar findings.[261] No one had been prosecuted specifically for alleged crimes against humanity, because the concept was introduced in Kyrgyzstan's criminal law only in 2019.[262]

D. Armed Conflicts between Kyrgyzstan and Tajikistan (2021, 2022)[263]

Although both are members of the Collective Security Treaty Organization (CSTO), Kyrgyzstan and Tajikistan used military force against each other from 28 April to 1 May 2021. The clashes reportedly stemmed from a dispute over a water supply facility, leaving at least 55 dead on both sides,[264] and prompting the evacuation of over 33,000 local residents.[265] Both States launched criminal proceedings on charges of crimes against peace,[266] and allegations of war crimes were also raised.[267]

Kyrgyzstan and Tajikistan again used military force against each other in September 2022:

> [A] four-day border clash between Kyrgyz and Tajik border guards injured 206 people and killed at least 62 people, including a 15-year-old girl who was reportedly hit by a shell fragment. At least one school was attacked and burned by Tajik-affiliated forces.[268]

[260] ibid.

[261] ibid.

[262] See Chapter 15, section IV.D below.

[263] This section reproduces the author's material published in S Sayapin, 'State Practice of Asian Countries in International Law: Central Asia' (2021) 27 *Asian Yearbook of International Law* 152–54; S Sayapin, 'State Practice of Asian Countries in International Law: Central Asia' (2022) 28 *Asian Yearbook of International Law* 203–6. Permissions to use published content are gratefully acknowledged.

[264] B Abdülkerimov, 'Death toll rises to 55 from Kyrgyz-Tajik border clashes', 5 May 2021, available at www.aa.com.tr/en/asia-pacific/death-toll-rises-to-55-from-kyrgyz-tajik-border-clashes/2230340.

[265] Trend News Agency, '33,388 Kyrgyzstanis evacuated from conflict zone in Batken', 2 May 2021, available at en.trend.az/casia/kyrgyzstan/3418071.html.

[266] J Emtseva, 'Small conflicts with big impact: The Tajik-Kyrgyz war no one talks about', EJIL:Talk!, 11 October 2022, available at www.ejiltalk.org/small-conflicts-with-big-impact-the-tajik-kyrgyz-war-no-one-talks-about/.

[267] J Pedneault and S Sultanalieva, 'Civilians Harmed in Kyrgyzstan, Tajikistan Border Clashes: Both Sides Should Abide by Laws of War', 30 April 2021, available at www.hrw.org/news/2021/04/30/civilians-harmed-kyrgyzstan-tajikistan-border-clashes.

[268] Human Rights Watch, 'Kyrgyzstan: Events of 2022', available at www.hrw.org/world-report/2023/country-chapters/kyrgyzstan.

Moreover,

> [a]uthorities reported scores of civilian homes had been burned, however, no reports were available on how many people may have been internally displaced. Tajik authorities also claimed that Kyrgyz forces allegedly fired on an ambulance traveling not far from Isfara, near the Kyrgyz border, killing five members of a family, including two children, who were inside the vehicle.[269]

Following these clashes, 'bilateral relations remained tense, although negotiations continued in 2023 on demarcation and other border-related issues'.[270] Reportedly, in May 2023, 'both governments committed to end the use of military drones to patrol the border. The use of such drones in the conflict led to civilian deaths'.[271]

E. Kazakhstan (2022)

On 2 January 2022, protests began in Zhanaozen, a town in Western Kazakhstan, 'over a sharp increase in gas prices'.[272] By 4 January 2022, thousands of protesters 'in other parts of the country had joined in, demanding economic and political reforms'.[273] According to eyewitnesses,

> new groups – unidentified men belonging to criminal gangs, radical Islamic groups, as well as armed groups close to the local or regional elites – joined the peaceful demonstrations and resorted to violence against the security forces, attacking members of the security forces, looting shops, and storming and burning government buildings.[274]

According to official data, at least 238 people lost their lives, including 19 law enforcement officers.[275] The Office of the General Prosecutor 'has said that 149 of those killed were "engaged in attacks on government buildings" while only 20 "accidentally" came under fire. Local human rights defenders say that numbers of those "accidently" killed are higher'.[276] Human Rights Watch has documented

[269] Human Rights Watch, 'Tajikistan: Events of 2022', available at www.hrw.org/world-report/2023/country-chapters/tajikistan.

[270] Human Rights Watch, 'Kyrgyzstan: Events of 2023', available at www.hrw.org/world-report/2024/country-chapters/kyrgyzstan#750cd3.

[271] ibid.

[272] Human Rights Watch, 'Kazakhstan: Killings, Excessive Use of Force in Almaty', 26 January 2022, available at www.hrw.org/news/2022/01/26/kazakhstan-killings-excessive-use-force-almaty.

[273] ibid.

[274] International Federation for Human Rights, 'Kazakhstan: Still no real investigation into the violence against protesters, two years after the January 2022 Events', 8 February 2024, available at www.fidh.org/en/region/europe-central-asia/kazakhstan/kazakhstan-still-no-real-investigation-into-the-violence-on.

[275] ibid.

[276] Human Rights Watch, '"New Kazakhstan" Needs Independent Inquiry on January Events', 18 March 2022, available at www.hrw.org/news/2022/03/18/new-kazakhstan-needs-independent-inquiry-january-events.

> that Kazakh security forces arbitrarily arrested peaceful protesters and others, and ill-treated and tortured some detainees, including with beatings with batons and electric shocks. According to official figures, 8 people detained in connection with the January events have died in pretrial detention centers and 234 criminal cases have been initiated on allegations of torture. [President Tokayev] acknowledged the use of torture during the January events and condemned it as a barbaric practice.[277]

Following the events, the United Nations and several governments urged Kazakhstan 'to establish an independent investigation'.[278] In particular, on 7 March 2022, the UN High Commissioner for Human Rights, Michelle Bachelet, stated that an investigation should 'be thoroughly and independently conducted, delivering accountability'.[279] In turn, the European Union expressed concern 'about the violence in Kazakhstan last January and commend[ed] the commitment to investigate the situation',[280] Switzerland called for an 'independent inquiry to be put in place to examine alleged violations of human rights',[281] and Luxemburg 'strongly condemn[ed] the disproportionate use of force against peaceful protesters in Kazakhstan'.[282] Such calls were firmly rejected.[283] As of 2024, some 30 law enforcement officers have been found guilty of abuses committed in January 2022.[284] In turn, 'almost 1,400 people have been convicted of "taking part in the riots"'.[285]

F. Karakalpakstan (2022)

On 25 June 2022, draft constitutional amendments were published in Uzbekistan,[286] proposing, among other changes, 'to remove the right of Karakalpaks to vote on independence in a referendum and the reference to the sovereign status of the Republic of Karakalpakstan from Uzbekistan's Constitution'.[287]

[277] ibid.
[278] ibid.
[279] Office of the UN High Commissioner for Human Rights, 'Global Update: Bachelet urges inclusion to combat "sharply escalating misery and fear"', 7 March 2022, available at www.ohchr.org/en/speeches/2022/03/global-update-bachelet-urges-inclusion-combat-sharply-escalating-misery-and-fear?LangID=E&NewsID=28225.
[280] Human Rights Watch (n 276).
[281] ibid.
[282] ibid.
[283] EURACTIV, 'Kazakh leader rejects international probe into deadly unrest', 29 January 2022, available at www.euractiv.com/section/global-europe/news/kazakh-leader-rejects-international-probe-into-deadly-unrest/.
[284] International Federation for Human Rights (n 274).
[285] E Collet, 'Victims of Kazakhstan's "Bloody January" long for justice', 24 June 2024, available at www.lemonde.fr/en/international/article/2024/06/24/victims-of-kazkhstan-s-bloody-january-long-for-justice_6675593_4.html.
[286] For the text (in Uzbek and Russian), see: www.gazeta.uz/ru/2022/06/25/doc/.
[287] Human Rights Watch, 'Uzbekistan: Police Abuses in Autonomous Region Protests', 7 November 2022, available at www.hrw.org/news/2022/11/07/uzbekistan-police-abuses-autonomous-region-protests.

Popular protests against the proposed amendments occurred in Karakalpakstan on 1–2 July 2022. There were

> incidents in which protesters threw stones and other objects at security officers and buildings, attacked an armored personnel carrier, and surrounded security force officers who had been stripped of their armor. However, Human Rights Watch research indicates that most protesters remained peaceful.[288]

Reportedly, Uzbek security forces' responses 'included the inappropriate use of small arms and various types of grenades, weapons that can cause severe injuries and death when used recklessly. At least 21 people died, including 4 law enforcement officers, and over 270 were injured'.[289] The state of emergency in Karakalpakstan lasted from 3 until 21 July 2022.[290]

The draft amendments to the Constitution affecting the status of Karakalpakstan were withdrawn but, according to Human Rights Watch, the authorities

> arrested more than 500 people in the immediate aftermath of the protests, and in two high-profile criminal trials, prosecuted a total of 61 people, including lawyers, bloggers, activists, and journalists, for their alleged involvement. Dauletmurat Tazhimuratov, a blogger and lawyer who first called for peaceful protests, was sentenced to 16 years in prison. Police and the courts ignored his allegations of ill-treatment and torture.[291]

Only

> [t]hree police officers have been prosecuted for 'illegal actions' during the protests. The Kagan City Court on August 4, 2023, sentenced two of them to seven years in prison for torture, and another to three years in prison for perjury and leaving a person in danger resulting in his death in connection with the Karakalpakstan events. But information about the prosecutions was only made public after sentencing, and little is known about the cases, including the specific crimes.[292]

On 22 February 2024,

> Uzbekistan's Supreme Court ruled that Alga Karakalpakstan, an opposition group in Karakalpakstan, is 'extremist' and banned its activities in Uzbekistan. The movement's leader, Aman Sagidullaev, a Karakalpak activist who has political asylum in Norway, was prosecuted in absentia in connection with the July 2022 protests and sentenced to 18 years in prison.[293]

[288] ibid.
[289] ibid.
[290] ibid.
[291] Human Rights Watch, 'Uzbekistan: 2 Years on, No Justice in Autonomous Republic', 1 July 2024, available at www.hrw.org/news/2024/07/01/uzbekistan-2-years-no-justice-autonomous-republic.
[292] ibid.
[293] ibid.

An 'independent parliamentary commission tasked in July 2022 with investigating human rights violations committed during and after the events has yet to publish its findings'.[294]

G. Attitudes to Other Conflicts

In recent years, Central Asian States have expressed official positions on several ongoing conflicts. On 14 July 2021, Uzbekistan's Ministry of Foreign Affairs stated that 'Uzbekistan [was] interested in the establishment of Afghanistan as an independent and sovereign State. In relation to Afghanistan, Uzbekistan is pursuing a friendly policy based on the principles of good neighborliness, mutual respect and equality'.[295] The same statement emphasised that 'Uzbekistan remain[ed] committed to the fundamental principle that the political process in Afghanistan should be carried out only by Afghans themselves and under the leadership of the people of Afghanistan'.[296] On 19 August 2021, Kazakhstan's Ministry of Foreign Affairs stated:

> Kazakhstan calls on all parties involved to ensure the peaceful transition of power as the main prerequisite for internal stabilisation. We support the UN Security Council statement on creating an inclusive and representative government, respecting the rights of national minorities and women, preventing the presence of groups that pose a threat to other states, and respecting international law.[297]

Despite these calls, developments in Afghanistan since 2021 concerning human rights – especially women's rights – remain troubling.

Regarding the armed conflict between Russia and Ukraine since 2014, Central Asian States have generally abstained from voting on related General Assembly resolutions. While not joining Western sanctions against Russia, they have taken steps – particularly in the banking sector – to prevent their circumvention.[298] These actions have caused irritation in Russian official circles,[299] and Central Asian officials occasionally signal quiet disapproval to

[294] ibid.

[295] Government Portal of the Republic of Uzbekistan, 'Glava MID Uzbekistana prinyal uchastiye v zasedanii kontaktnoy gruppy "SHOS – Afghanistan"' ['The Head of the Ministry of Foreign Affairs of Uzbekistan Took Part in a Meeting of the "SCO – Afghanistan" Contact Group'], 14 July 2021, available at old.gov.uz/ru/news/view/31493.

[296] ibid.

[297] Ministry of Foreign Affairs of the Republic of Kazakhstan, 'Zayavleniye MID RK po situatsii v Afganistane' ['Statement by the MFA of the Republic of Kazakhstan on the Situation in Afghanistan'], 19 August 2021, available at www.gov.kz/memleket/entities/mfa/press/news/details/243962?lang=ru.

[298] See Chapter 9, section IX above, especially n 144 and accompanying text.

[299] See Chapter 3 above, n 3 and accompanying text.

Moscow.[300] Thus, in March 2022, Kyrgyzstan's Minister of Foreign Affairs, Ruslan Kazakbayev, made a statement in favour of de-escalation, and warned of an impending 'catastrophe, and possibly a third world war'.[301] Likewise, in March 2022, Uzbekistan's Minister of Foreign Affairs, Abdulaziz Komilov, emphasised that 'Uzbekistan recognise[d] the independence, sovereignty and territorial integrity of Ukraine. We did not recognise the Luhansk and Donetsk People's Republics'.[302] In April 2023, Kazakhstan's Deputy Minister of Foreign Affairs, Roman Vassilenko, recalled that 'Kazakhstan has clearly defined its position regarding conflict between Russia and Ukraine. This position consists in the necessity to respect the territorial integrity of all States, including Ukraine, on the basis of the UN Charter'.[303] In September 2024, Mr Vassilenko stated: 'Kazakhstan … offered its services as a possible mediator or venue for negotiations between the two warring parties. This position has not changed'.[304] It was reported in February 2023 that '[n]either during diplomatic contacts nor in official statements throughout the year did the leaders of Turkmenistan say anything about the war in Ukraine. The Turkmen press does not publish news about the war'.[305]

Central Asian States adopt a cautious stance toward the Middle East conflict. All maintain diplomatic relations with Israel,[306] and on 17 October 2023, Kazakhstan condemned 'Hamas attacks on Israeli civilians and taking hostages, including

[300] Fergana News, 'Zaverbovannogo v ryady CHVK "Wagner" iz tyurmy uzbekistantsa na rodine osudili za nayomnichestvo' ['Uzbek Recruited from Prison to Wagner PMC Convicted of Mercenarism in His Home Country'], 17 July 2025, available at fergana.agency/news/138995/; Fergana News, 'V Uzbekistane dvum uchastnikam SVO naznachili tyuremnye sroki za nayomnichestvo' ['In Uzbekistan, Two Participants of the Special Military Operation Were Sentenced to Prison Terms for Mercenarism'], 7 July 2025, available at fergana.agency/news/138777/.

[301] Deutsche Welle, 'Glava MID Kyrgyzstana o konflikte Rossii s Ukrainoy' ['The Head of the Ministry of Foreign Affairs of Kyrgyzstan on the Conflict between Russia and Ukraine'], 29 March 2022, available at www.dw.com/ru/glava-mid-kyrgyzstana-o-konflikte-rossii-s-ukrainoj-trudovoj-migracii-i-otnoseniah-s-kazahstanom-29032022/video-61297354.

[302] Gazeta.Uz, '"My ne priznali Luganskuyu i Donetskuyu narodnye respubliki" – glava MID Uzbekistana' ['"We Did Not Recognise the Luhansk and Donetsk People's Republics" – Head of the Ministry of Foreign Affairs of Uzbekistan'], 17 March 2022, available at www.gazeta.uz/ru/2022/03/17/ukraine/.

[303] Kapital.Kz, 'Pozitsiya Kazahstana v otnoshenii Rossii i Ukrainy osnovana na natsionalnyh interesah – MID' ['The Position of Kazakhstan Towards Russia and Ukraine is Based on National Interests – MFA'], 3 April 2023, available at kapital.kz/gosudarstvo/114425/pozitsiya-kazakhstana-v-otnoshenii-rossii-i-ukrainy-osnovana-na-natsional-nykh-interesakh-mid.html.

[304] Gazeta.Ru, 'Kazahstan vnov vyrazil gotovnost stat posrednikom v peregovorah RF I Ukrainy' ['Kazakhstan Again Expressed its Readiness to Become a Mediator in Negotiations between the Russian Federation and Ukraine'], 15 September 2024, available at www.gazeta.ru/politics/news/2024/09/15/23927257.shtml.

[305] Radio Azatlyk, 'Pozitsiya Turkmenistana ne izmenilas za god voyny' ['Turkmenistan's Position Has Not Changed During the Year of War'], 24 February 2023, available at rus.azathabar.com/a/32284743.html.

[306] See 'Diplomatic Relations of Israel around the World', available at embassies.gov.il/MFA/AboutIsrael/Maps/Pages/Diplomatic-Relations-of-Israel-around-the-World.aspx.

foreigners'.[307] In the same statement, Kazakhstan called 'on Israel to refrain from the disproportionate use of force, leading to numerous civilian casualties in the Gaza Strip and the destruction of civilian infrastructure',[308] and recalled that

> [i]n this situation, it is extremely important to comply with international law, as well as follow the relevant UN Security Council resolutions providing for the legitimate rights of the Palestinian people. Violence begets counter-violence and will inevitably lead to tragic consequences for the Middle East and the entire world.[309]

Similarly, in April 2024, Kazakhstan's Ministry of Foreign Affairs (MFA) called upon Iran and Israel to resolve their conflict peacefully.[310] In the same context, Uzbekistan's MFA warned that '[a] further increase in tension in the region could lead to more serious consequences and widespread military confrontation'.[311] In October 2023, Kyrgyzstan's MFA emphasised the relevance of international humanitarian law in the conflict between Hamas and Israel,[312] and in early October 2024, called 'on the conflicting parties to comply with the fundamental principles and norms of international law, including to refrain from actions leading to an escalation of the situation in the region'.[313] On 9 October 2023, the Ministry of Foreign Affairs of Tajikistan, 'strongly condemning the acts of violence, call[ed] on the parties to immediately put an end to the violence and begin a dialogue to normalise the situation'.[314] In early June 2024, Uzbekistan called 'on all parties to exercise restraint, respect international law, and prevent

[307] Ministry of Foreign Affairs of the Republic of Kazakhstan, 'Zayavleniye Ministerstva inostrannyh del Respubliki Kazahstan po vooruzhennomu stolknoveiyu Hamas i Izrailya' ['Statement by the Ministry of Foreign Affairs of the Republic of Kazakhstan on the Armed Clash between Hamas and Israel'], 17 October 2023, available at www.gov.kz/memleket/entities/mfa/press/news/details/637460?lang=ru. See also G Ulfstein, 'Does Israel have the right to self-defence – and what are the restrictions?', EJIL:Talk!, 8 May 2024, available at www.ejiltalk.org/does-israel-have-the-right-to-self-defence-and-what-are-the-restrictions/.

[308] Ministry of Foreign Affairs of the Republic of Kazakhstan (n 307).

[309] ibid.

[310] Zakon.Kz, 'MID RK prizval Iran i Izrail reshit konflikt mirnym putem' ['The Ministry of Foreign Affairs of the Republic of Kazakhstan Called on Iran and Israel to Resolve the Conflict Peacefully'], 14 April 2024, available at www.zakon.kz/sobytiia/6430824-mid-rk-prizval-iran-i-izrail-reshit-konflikt-mirnym-putem.html.

[311] Gazeta.Uz, '"Rost napryazhennosti na Blizhnem Vostoke mozhet privesti k shirokoy voyennoy konfrontatsii" – MID Uzbekistana' ['"Increasing Tension in the Middle East Could lead to Widespread Military Confrontation" – Uzbekistan Foreign Ministry'], 15 April 2024, available at www.gazeta.uz/ru/2024/04/15/mfa/.

[312] Radio Ozodi, 'Bishkek prizval k rassledovaniyu narusheniya mezhdunarodnogo gumanitarnogo prava v Gaze' ['Bishkek Calls for Investigation into Violations of International Humanitarian Law in Gaza'], 18 October 2023, available at rus.ozodi.org/a/32643197.html.

[313] Kaktus Media, 'MID Kyrgyzstana vystupil s zayavleniyem po situatsii na Blizhnem Vostoke' ['The Ministry of Foreign Affairs of Kyrgyzstan Issued a Statement on the Situation in the Middle East'], 2 October 2024, available at kaktus.media/doc/510458_mid_kyrgyzstana_vystypil_s_zaiavleniem_po_sityacii_na_blijnem_vostoke.html.

[314] Asia-Plus, 'MID Tadzhikistana vystupil s zayavleniyem po situatsii na Blizhnem Vostoke' ['The Ministry of Foreign Affairs of Tajikistan Issued a Statement on the Situation in the Middle East'], 9 October 2023, available at www.asiaplustj.info/ru/news/tajikistan/politics/20231009/mid-tadzhikistana-vistupil-s-zayavleniem-o-situatsii-na-blizhnem-vostoke.

violence and a further increase in the number of civilian casualties'.[315] In November 2024, President Mirziyoyev made an explicit statement to the effect that 'Palestinian people have every right to establish an independent state with East Jerusalem as its capital within the 1967 borders'.[316]

H. The Central Asian Nuclear-Weapon-Free Zone (CANWFZ)

The Central Asian States consistently oppose nuclear weapons and their proliferation. In August 1991, Kazakhstan shut down the Soviet nuclear test site in Semey (Semipalatinsk), and in 1997, Uzbekistan hosted an international conference titled 'Central Asia – a zone free of nuclear weapons'. The Central Asian Nuclear-Weapon-Free Zone (CANWFZ) treaty was signed on 8 September 2006 and, after ratification by all Central Asian States, entered into force on 21 March 2009.[317] Under Article 3(1)(a), each party undertakes '[n]ot to conduct research on, develop, manufacture, stockpile or otherwise acquire, possess or have control over any nuclear weapon or other nuclear explosive device by any means anywhere'. This general obligation is reinforced by provisions on transit of foreign ships, aircraft, and ground transport (Article 4); nuclear weapons testing (Article 5); environmental security (Article 6); peaceful use of nuclear energy (Article 7); and protection of nuclear material and equipment (Article 9). Procedural clauses address cooperation with the IAEA and consultative meetings (Articles 8 and 10). Central Asia is currently one of five Nuclear-Weapon-Free Zones (NWFZs) worldwide.[318]

I. Water Scarcity[319]

Water scarcity poses a major security threat in Central Asia.[320] In June 2023, it was reported that by 2030, Kazakhstan's fresh water supply 'may be reduced by

[315] Kun.Uz, 'MID Uzbekistana vyrazil obespokoyennost v svyazi s situatsiyey v Gaze' ['The MFA of Uzbekistan Expressed Concern about the Situation in Gaza'], available at kun.uz/ru/18739828.

[316] Kun.Uz, 'Mirziyoyev vystupil za nezavisimuyu Palestinu so stolitsey v Vostochnom Ierusalime' ['Mirziyoyev Spoke in Favour of an Independent Palestine with its Capital in East Jerusalem'], 11 November 2024, available at kun.uz/ru/news/2024/11/11/mirziyoyev-vystupil-za-nezavisimuyu-palestinu-so-stolitsey-v-vostochnom-iyerusalime. See also E Cannizzaro, 'The strange story of the "conditional" admission of the State of Palestine to the United Nations', EJIL:Talk!, 11 June 2024, available at www.ejiltalk.org/the-strange-story-of-the-conditional-admission-of-the-state-of-palestine-to-the-united-nations/.

[317] The original English text and ratification status of the Treaty is available at treaties.unoda.org/t/canwfz.

[318] United Nations Platform for Nuclear-Free Zones, 'Overview of Nuclear-Weapon-Free Zones,' available at www.un.org/nwfz/content/overview-nuclear-weapon-free-zones.

[319] This section uses the author's material published in S Sayapin, 'The Aral Sea' in S Lee et al (eds), *Encyclopedia of Public International Law in Asia*, Volume III: Central & South Asia (Leiden, Brill, 2021). Permission to use published material is gratefully acknowledged.

[320] See Chapter 2, sections IV.F–IV.G above.

five times to 23 km^3, which is comparable to the annual consumption rate'.[321] In Kyrgyzstan, more than 300 villages

> have never had a drinking water supply system. In another 600, there is no clean water due to the deterioration of water pipes or the stoppage of work on installing water pipes … About a million Kyrgyzstanis need help with access to clean drinking water. Currently, 40% of the country's population drinks water from ditches, rivers, canals, and springs and uses imported water.[322]

Uzbekistan is among 27 countries facing high water scarcity.[323] By 2030, the population of Uzbekistan will

> increase to almost 40 million people, which will cause a reduction in available water resources by 7–8 km^3. Under these conditions, the shortage of water resources will increase by 2030 from the current 13–14 % to 44–46 %, which will slow down the development of agriculture and other industries.[324]

According to the Eurasian Development Bank,

> [t]he challenges of the Central Asian water and energy complex cannot be tackled by the countries of the region independently. Historically, the five countries of the region have been closely linked by the two largest transboundary rivers, [the Amudaryo and the Syrdaryo]. They form the Aral Sea basin that is home to 80% of the region's population. This is where the close intersectoral relationship (i.e. nexus) between water, energy and food becomes particularly evident.[325]

Central Asian States have recognised the challenge of water scarcity since the early years of independence. In February 1992, the Agreement on Cooperation in Joint Management and Protection of Interstate Water Resources was signed in Almaty, establishing the Interstate Commission for Water Coordination (ICWC). At a summit in Tashkent on 4 January 1993, Central Asian leaders agreed to create the International Foundation for Saving the Aral Sea (IFAS) to

> raise awareness of the international community about the disastrous situation in the Aral Sea, organize financing for environmental, applied science and practical projects and programs aimed at environmental rehabilitation of the affected areas, as well as at addressing socio-economic issues in the region, using the funds of the Central Asian States and international organizations.[326]

[321] B Chynybaeva, 'The water crisis in Central Asia – how to find solutions?', Climate Action Network, 17 June 2023, available at caneecca.org/en/the-water-crisis-in-central-asia-how-to-find-solutions/.

[322] ibid.

[323] ibid.

[324] ibid.

[325] Eurasian Development Bank, 'Water Crisis in Central Asia: from Diagnostic Assessment to Decisive Action', 9 July 2024, available at eabr.org/en/press/news/water-crisis-in-central-asia-from-diagnostic-assessment-to-decisive-action/.

[326] Quoted in Sayapin (n 319), 198.

On 26 March 1993, the Agreement on Joint Action to Address the Problems of the Aral Sea and Surroundings was signed, and the IFAS Statute was adopted. Since 1994, three Aral Sea Basin Programmes (ASBP) have been implemented with financial support from Central Asian and other States, UNDP, the World Bank, USAID, the Asian Development Bank, and other donors. UNESCO has also supported scientific projects aimed at policy recommendations and capacity-building in the Aral Sea basin.

According to IFAS,

> [t]he dry bed of the Aral Sea has become a source of powerful dust storms. The dust is blown and spread in the radius of 150–500 km. Just the former south-eastern coast of the Aral Sea alone produces 15–75 million tons of dust annually. The dust contains toxic sulfate and chloride salts and sets on hundreds of thousands square kilometers, harming the generative and vegetative organs of plants, reducing pasture productivity and crop yields … [T]he levels of morbidity and mortality in the region increased significantly, especially among children. The incidence of typhoid, cholelithiasis, chronic gastritis, kidney disease, esophageal cancer, and tuberculosis rose dramatically.[327]

Between 2003 and 2005, the Dike Kokaral (Kok-Aral Dam) was built with World Bank support to separate the North Aral Sea ('Small Sea') from the South Aral Sea ('Large Sea') and raise the water level of the former. This led to reduced salinity, microclimate improvements, and a revival of the fishing industry in the North Aral Sea. Amid the continuing desiccation of the South Aral Sea, proposals emerged to construct an artificial delta of the Syrdaryo river.[328]

X. TOWARDS A CULTURE OF PEACE

'Peace' is a central concept in the UN Charter, which contains at least 35 direct references to it as a value protected by international law,[329] with related terms (eg, 'peaceful', 'pacific', 'peace-loving') appearing in at least nine additional Articles.[330] While the UN Security Council holds primary responsibility for maintaining international peace and security,[331] all UN organs and international institutions contribute to peace through their thematic roles – such as education, science, human rights,[332] and dispute resolution. For instance, the UNESCO

[327] ibid.

[328] ibid, 199.

[329] UN Charter, Preamble, paras 5, 6, Arts 1(1), (2), 2(3), (6), 11(1)–(3), 12(2), 15(1), 18(1), 23(1), 24(1), 26, 33(1), 34, 37(2), 39, 42, 43(1), 47(1), 48(1), 51, 52(1), 54, 73, 76, 84, 99, 106.

[330] ibid, Arts 1(1), 2(3), 4(1), 14, 33(1), 35(2), 38, 52(2), (3), 55.

[331] cf Art 24(1) of the UN Charter.

[332] E Pribytkova, 'The Right to Peace: From Proclamation to Human Right', Centre for International Law/ National University of Singapore, available at cil.nus.edu.sg/blogs/the-right-to-peace-from-proclamation-to-human-right/.

Constitution opens with the idea that 'wars begin in the minds of men so it is in the minds of men that the defences of peace must be constructed'.[333]

Peace is not a static condition achieved once and for all; it is a dynamic process involving States, international institutions, and non-State actors. In 1981, the UN General Assembly designated 21 September as the International Day of Peace, to 'commemorat[e] and strengthe[n] the ideals of peace both within and among all nations and peoples'.[334] The fourth preambular paragraph of the Declaration and Programme of Action on a Culture of Peace, adopted on 6 October 1999, notably affirms that 'peace not only is the absence of conflict, but also requires a positive, dynamic participatory process where dialogue is encouraged and conflicts are solved in a spirit of mutual understanding and cooperation'.[335] Article 1 of the same resolution defines a culture of peace as a multifaceted set of values, attitudes, traditions, behaviours, and ways of life based on:

> (*a*) Respect for life, ending of violence and promotion and practice of non-violence through education, dialogue and cooperation;
> (*b*) Full respect for the principles of sovereignty, territorial integrity and political independence of States and non-intervention in matters which are essentially within the domestic jurisdiction of any State, in accordance with the Charter of the United Nations and international law;
> (*c*) Full respect for and promotion of all human rights and fundamental freedoms;
> (*d*) Commitment to peaceful settlement of conflicts;
> (*e*) Efforts to meet the developmental and environmental needs of present and future generations;
> (*f*) Respect for and promotion of the right to development;
> (*g*) Respect for and promotion of equal rights and opportunities for women and men;
> (*h*) Respect for and promotion of the right of everyone to freedom of expression, opinion and information;
> (*i*) Adherence to the principles of freedom, justice, democracy, tolerance, solidarity, cooperation, pluralism, cultural diversity, dialogue and understanding at all levels of society and among nations;
>
> and fostered by an enabling national and international environment conducive to peace.

Article 2 of the resolution states that '[p]rogress in the fuller development of a culture of peace comes about through values, attitudes, modes of behaviour and ways of life conducive to the promotion of peace among individuals, groups and nations'. Such progress can only be achieved through a combination of legal,

[333] UNESCO Constitution, available at www.unesco.org/en/legal-affairs/constitution.
[334] See document A/RES/36/67, available at docs.un.org/en/A/RES/36/67.
[335] For the text of the Declaration and Programme of Action, see: digitallibrary.un.org/record/285677?ln=en&_gl=1*10yfemm*_ga*MTQzNDI5NTIxMy4xNzE4MDEwMzg2*_ga_TK9BQL5X7Z*MTczMTY2MTEyNC4yOC4wLjE3MzE2NjExMjcuMC4wLjA.&v=pdf.

political, economic, cultural, and other constructive approaches (Article 3, footnotes omitted):

> The fuller development of a culture of peace is integrally linked to:
>
> (*a*) Promoting peaceful settlement of conflicts, mutual respect and understanding and international cooperation;
> (*b*) Complying with international obligations under the Charter of the United Nations and international law;
> (*c*) Promoting democracy, development and universal respect for and observance of all human rights and fundamental freedoms;
> (*d*) Enabling people at all levels to develop skills of dialogue, negotiation, consensus-building and peaceful resolution of differences;
> (*e*) Strengthening democratic institutions and ensuring full participation in the development process;
> (*f*) Eradicating poverty and illiteracy and reducing inequalities within and among nations;
> (*g*) Promoting sustainable economic and social development;
> (*h*) Eliminating all forms of discrimination against women through their empowerment and equal representation at all levels of decision-making;
> (*i*) Ensuring respect for and promotion and protection of the rights of children;
> (*j*) Ensuring free flow of information at all levels and enhancing access thereto;
> (*k*) Increasing transparency and accountability in governance;
> (*l*) Eliminating all forms of racism, racial discrimination, xenophobia and related intolerance;
> (*m*) Advancing understanding, tolerance and solidarity among all civilizations, peoples and cultures, including towards ethnic, religious and linguistic minorities;
> (*n*) Realizing fully the right of all peoples, including those living under colonial or other forms of alien domination or foreign occupation, to self-determination enshrined in the Charter of the United Nations and embodied in the International Covenants on Human Rights, as well as in the Declaration on the Granting of Independence to Colonial Countries and Peoples contained in General Assembly resolution 1514 (XV) of 14 December 1960.

Article 4 of the resolution underscores the vital role of education in fostering a culture of peace: 'Education at all levels is one of the principal means to build a culture of peace. In this context, human rights education is of particular importance'. Strengthening peace education in Central Asia's secondary and higher education institutions – across subjects such as history, international relations, law, journalism, and social studies – would be highly appropriate, with due regard to the region's rich cultural heritage. Governments, international institutions, civil society, and the media must collaborate to promote a culture of peace (cf Articles 5–7 of the resolution). In particular, the legal prohibitions on propaganda for war and discrimination must be strictly upheld. Central Asia has recently faced episodes of violence and retains significant conflict potential, requiring political wisdom and a strong commitment to the rule of law. At the same time, Central Asian States should modernise their Armed Forces to counter current and emerging external threats. Article 8 identifies key actors essential to peacebuilding:

> A key role in the promotion of a culture of peace belongs to parents, teachers, politicians, journalists, religious bodies and groups, intellectuals, those engaged in scientific, philosophical and creative and artistic activities, health and humanitarian workers, social workers, managers at various levels as well as to non-governmental organizations.

For such collective action to be effective, it must be continuous and pursued in good faith. Finally, under Article 9, '[t]he United Nations should continue to play a critical role in the promotion and strengthening of a culture of peace worldwide'. The newly adopted UN 'Pact for the Future' will be central to this effort.[336]

[336] See document A/RES/79/1, available at docs.un.org/en/A/RES/79/1.

11

International Trade Law

INTERNATIONAL TRADE LAW, often referred to as international economic law, world trade law, international trade regulation, global trade law, or the law governing the World Trade Organization (WTO),[1] is essential for the regulation of global and regional trade in goods and services, as well as for promoting the free movement of capital and labour. This legal framework seeks to reduce trade barriers,[2] promote equitable competition, and address disputes between States and private entities, thereby contributing to a stable and predictable environment for global trade.[3] By establishing clear and transparent regulations, it mitigates protectionist tendencies, facilitates market access, and supports the integration of developing nations into the global economy. This chapter offers an overview of the WTO, examines the achievements and challenges faced by the Eurasian Economic Union (EAEU), and provides a brief analysis of the bilateral free trade and investment agreements concluded by the Central Asian States.

I. WORLD TRADE ORGANIZATION (WTO)

The World Trade Organization (WTO) was established on 1 January 1995 to 'use trade as a means to improve people's living standards, create better jobs and promote sustainable development'.[4] It is regarded as (one of) the most efficient international organisation(s).[5] The WTO facilitates economic cooperation

[1] S Lester, B Mercurio and A Davies, *World Trade Law: Text, Materials and Commentary*, 2nd edn (Oxford, Hart Publishing, 2012), 3; HT Adilkariyev, *Mezhdunarodnoye pravo* [*International law*] (Tashkent, Tashkent State Law Institute, 2003), 463–87; II Lukashuk and AH Saidov, *Hozirgi zamon xalqaro huquqi nazariyasi asoslari* [*The theoretical fundamentals of modern international law*] (Tashkent, Adolat, 2006), 255–76; VA Belov, *Mezhdunarodnoye torgovoye pravo i pravo VTO* [*International Trade Law and WTO Law*], vol 1 (Moscow, Urait, 2015), 21–22.

[2] On the imposition of tariffs by the second Trump administration, see N Lamp, 'What President Trump's "Reciprocal" Tariffs Mean for International (Trade) Law', EJIL:Talk!, 30 April 2025, available at www.ejiltalk.org/what-president-trumps-reciprocal-tariffs-mean-for-international-trade-law/.

[3] P Van den Bossche and W Zdouc, *The Law and Policy of the World Trade Organization*, 3rd edn (Cambridge, Cambridge University Press, 2013), 26–30.

[4] WTO, 'What is the WTO?', available at www.wto.org/english/thewto_e/whatis_e/whatis_e.htm.

[5] Van den Bossche and Zdouc (n 3), 74. See also B Dhar, 'The future of the World Trade Organization' in R Baldwin, M Kawai and G Wignaraja (eds), *A World Trade Organization for the 21st Century: The Asian Perspective* (Cheltenham, Eldward Elgar Publishing, 2014).

among its 166 Members, which are responsible for 98 per cent of global trade, by providing a platform for trade negotiations, establishing trade-related regulations, and resolving disputes.[6] In Central Asia, Kyrgyzstan, Tajikistan, and Kazakhstan are WTO Members (in chronological order), while Turkmenistan and Uzbekistan hold Observer State status.[7] The WTO actively monitors national trade policies to ensure adherence to established commitments, thereby fostering transparency and compliance among its Members. Additionally, the WTO offers technical assistance and capacity-building programmes aimed at developing and supporting least-developed nations, thereby strengthening their ability to participate effectively in the global trading system.

A. WTO Structure

The WTO organs make most decisions by consensus.[8] The highest decision-making body is the Ministerial Conference, which meets at least once every two years. Comprising Ministers of Trade (or Ministers with equivalent competence) from all Member States, it has the authority to take decisions on any trade-related matter and adopt amendments to WTO agreements.[9] The General Council operates as the central governing body in the periods between Ministerial Conferences. It is composed of Ambassadors or delegates from Member countries and fulfils multiple roles. As the Dispute Settlement Body, it oversees the dispute resolution process, while as the Trade Policy Review Body, it monitors Members' trade policies to ensure transparency and adherence to WTO rules.[10] Below the General Council are specialised Councils, including the Council for Trade in Goods, the Council for Trade in Services, and the Council for Trade-Related Aspects of Intellectual Property Rights (TRIPS).[11] These bodies administer specific agreements and provide forums for addressing sector-specific trade issues. The WTO Secretariat, headed by the Director-General, provides administrative and technical support, facilitates negotiations, and delivers capacity-building programmes.[12]

B. WTO Principles

Two cornerstone rules of the WTO aimed at promoting fairness and non-discrimination in international trade are the Most-Favoured Nation (MFN)

[6] WTO, 'Members and Observers', available at www.wto.org/english/thewto_e/whatis_e/whatis_e.htm.
[7] ibid.
[8] Marrakesh Agreement (WTO Agreement), Art IX:1. See also Van den Bossche and Zdouc (n 3), 136–38.
[9] Van den Bossche and Zdouc (n 3), 121–22.
[10] ibid, 122–24.
[11] ibid, 125–27.
[12] ibid, 130–36.

principle and the National Treatment (NT) rule. They are enshrined in the General Agreement on Tariffs and Trade (GATT 1994),[13] the General Agreement on Trade in Services (GATS),[14] and other WTO agreements. The MFN principle, outlined in Article I:1 of the GATT and Article II:1 of the GATS, mandates that any trade advantage, such as reduced tariffs or improved market access, granted by a Member to one trading partner must be extended to all WTO Members. For example, if a country reduces import tariffs for a specific nation, it must offer the same concession to all other WTO Members. This principle ensures equal treatment among Members, prevents trade discrimination, and fosters a predictable trading environment.[15] Exceptions to MFN include preferential treatment under free trade agreements,[16] or for developing countries under the Generalized System of Preferences.[17]

In turn, the National Treatment rule, codified in Article III of the GATT, requires that imported goods, once they have entered a Member's market, be treated no less favorably than domestically produced goods. This rule applies not only to tariffs but also to internal taxes, regulations, and other measures.[18] For instance, a country cannot impose higher taxes or stricter regulations on foreign goods than on comparable domestic goods. Similar provisions exist under the GATS and the Agreement on Trade-Related Aspects of Intellectual Property Rights (TRIPS) for services and intellectual property, respectively.[19] Together, the MFN and NT principles promote fairness, reduce protectionism, and ensure that trade liberalisation benefits are shared equitably among Members.

C. WTO Law

The WTO law consists of the Marrakesh Agreement Establishing the World Trade Organization of 15 April 1994,[20] and its four Annexes. The Marrakesh Agreement sets out the WTO organisational framework, its objectives, functions, and core principles, including trade liberalisation, non-discrimination, and transparency. The Annexes encompass multilateral agreements, which are binding on all Members, and plurilateral agreements, which apply only among their States Parties. Multilateral agreements include foundational texts

[13] For the text of the GATT 1994, see: www.wto.org/english/docs_e/legal_e/06-gatt_e.htm.

[14] For the text of the GATS, see: www.wto.org/english/docs_e/legal_e/26-gats_01_e.htm.

[15] Van den Bossche and Zdouc (n 3), 315–48; Lester, Mercurio and Davies (n 1), 309–26.

[16] Van den Bossche and Zdouc (n 3), 648–72. On the Eurasian Economic Union (EAEU), see Chapter 12, section II below.

[17] Lester, Mercurio and Davies (n 1), 813–49.

[18] Van den Bossche and Zdouc (n 3), 349–417; Lester, Mercurio and Davies (n 1), 265–308.

[19] Van den Bossche and Zdouc (n 3), 962–68.

[20] For the text of the Marrakesh Agreement, see: www.wto.org/English/docs_e/legal_e/04-wto_e.htm.

such as the GATT 1994 (Annex 1A),[21] the GATS (Annex 1B),[22] and the TRIPS (Annex 1C).[23] In addition to these core texts, Annex 1 also includes specialised agreements covering trade-related areas such as dumping,[24] subsidies and countervailing measures,[25] technical barriers to trade,[26] sanitary and phytosanitary measures,[27] foreign direct investment,[28] and others. These agreements aim to address sector-specific challenges while maintaining consistency with broader WTO principles. In contrast, plurilateral agreements (Annex 4), involve only some WTO members and focus on specific issues, such as trade in civil aircraft[29] and government procurement.[30] While these agreements do not bind non-signatory Members, they are integral to advancing cooperation in areas where consensus among all Members is challenging.[31] The Dispute Settlement Mechanism (regulated by Annex 2)[32] and the Trade Policy Review Mechanism (regulated by Annex 3)[33] are critical components of the WTO, ensuring compliance and fostering transparency.

D. Exceptions to the WTO Principles

The WTO allows Members to deviate from their trade obligations under specific exceptions, balancing trade liberalisation with other legitimate objectives. These exceptions are primarily outlined in Articles XX (General Exceptions) and XXI (Security Exceptions) of the GATT 1994, and parallel provisions in other WTO agreements. General exceptions permit trade-restrictive measures necessary to

[21] See n 13 above. See also Lester, Mercurio and Davies (n 1), 635–68.

[22] See n 14 above. See also DCK Chow and TJ Schoenbaum, *International Trade Law: Problems, Cases, and Materials*, 4th edn (New York, Wolters Kluwer Law & Business, 2022), 531–66.

[23] For the text of the TRIPS, see: www.wto.org/english/docs_e/legal_e/27-trips_01_e.htm. See also VA Belov, *Mezhdunarodnoye torgovoye pravo i pravo VTO* [*International Trade Law and WTO Law*], vol 2 (Moscow, Urait, 2015), 524–33.

[24] In international trade law, dumping refers to the practice of exporting goods at a price lower than their normal value – usually the domestic market price or cost of production – in order to gain an unfair competitive advantage in the importing country. See Van den Bossche and Zdouc (n 3), 673–743; Belov (n 23), 563–71.

[25] Van den Bossche and Zdouc (n 3), 744–849.

[26] ibid, 850–93.

[27] ibid, 894–950.

[28] Chow and Schoenbaum (n 22), 567–86. See also Y Zhang and R Wang, 'The role of foreign direct investment flows and a possible multilateral agreement' in Baldwin, Kawai and Wignaraja (n 5).

[29] For the text of the Agreement on Trade in Civil Aircraft, see: www.wto.org/english/docs_e/legal_e/tca_e.htm.

[30] For the text of the Agreement on Government Procurement, see: www.wto.org/english/tratop_e/gproc_e/gp_gpa_e.htm. See also Lester, Mercurio and Davies (n 1), 697–737.

[31] M Nakatomi, 'Plurilateral agreements: a viable alternative to the World Trade Organization?' in Baldwin, Kawai and Wignaraja (n 5). See also Belov (n 1), 571–83.

[32] Van den Bossche and Zdouc (n 3), 156–314; Chow and Schoenbaum (n 22), 63–94.

[33] Van den Bossche and Zdouc (n 3), 124.

protect public morals, human, animal, or plant life, or to conserve exhaustible natural resources, provided such measures do not constitute disguised protectionism.[34] Next, security exceptions allow Members to act in ways deemed necessary for national security, such as during armed conflict or to safeguard essential security interests.[35] In turn, economic emergency exceptions (or safeguards) allow temporary measures like tariffs to protect domestic industries from serious injury caused by surges in imports.[36] Other permissible exceptions address specific contexts, including regional trade agreements[37] and special treatment for developing countries.[38] Overall, these provisions ensure flexibility within the multilateral trading system, balancing rules with national interests.

E. Achievements and Criticisms of the WTO

The WTO is playing a pivotal role in fostering trade liberalisation and economic integration globally, including in Central Asia. One of the WTO's key achievements in Central Asia is its role in promoting trade reforms. For instance, Kazakhstan's 2015 accession marked significant progress in aligning its trade policies with international standards, boosting foreign investment and export diversification.[39] Similarly, Kyrgyzstan, the first Central Asian State to join the WTO, on 20 December 1998, has benefited from increased access to global markets, particularly for its agricultural products.[40] Despite these successes, criticisms persist. A major challenge lies in some Central Asian States' limited institutional capacity to fully implement WTO agreements.[41] In particular, compliance with complex rules on intellectual property, subsidies, and trade facilitation often strains administrative resources. Furthermore, the anticipated economic benefits of WTO membership, such as increased exports and industrial growth, have been uneven. For instance, smaller economies like Tajikistan and Kyrgyzstan have struggled to compete in global markets, facing domestic

[34] ibid, 543–94; Lester, Mercurio and Davies (n 1), 363–417; PV Parwani, 'XX (b), (g) and Everything in Between: A Case Comment on WTO Panel EU-Palm Oil's (Mis) Interpretation of GATT Article XX (b) and (g)', Völkerrechtsblog, 27 January 2025, available at voelkerrechtsblog.org/xx-b-g-and-everything-in-between/.

[35] Van den Bossche and Zdouc (n 3), 594–600.

[36] Van den Bossche and Zdouc (n 3), 606–47; Chow and Schoenbaum (n 22), 373–401.

[37] See n 15 above. See also M Kawai and G Wignaraja, 'Policy challenges posed by Asian free trade agreements: a review of the evidence' in Baldwin, Kawai and Wignaraja (n 5).

[38] See n 17 above.

[39] A Kourmanova, 'Kazakhstan and the WTO: A New Era', 2 July 2015, available at www.csis.org/analysis/kazakhstan-and-wto-new-era.

[40] 24.KG, 'WTO Reference Center opened in Kyrgyzstan', 27 April 2015, available at 24.kg/archive/en/bigtiraj/175491-news24.html/.

[41] WTO, 'Second Central Asia Trade Policy Forum: Economic integration through WTO accession and membership', June 2024, available at www.wto.org/english/thewto_e/acc_e/acc_0306202409_e/acc_0306202409_e.htm.

constraints and external trade barriers.[42] Critics also point to the WTO's limited capacity to address regional challenges unique to Central Asia, such as landlocked geography, infrastructure deficits, and dependence on primary commodities.[43] Besides, the slow progress of Turkmenistan and Uzbekistan in WTO accession highlights broader concerns about the organisation's ability to encourage timely and inclusive economic integration.[44]

II. EURASIAN ECONOMIC UNION (EAEU)

The Eurasian Economic Union (EAEU), established on 1 January 2015, is a regional trade organisation bringing together five post-Soviet States: Armenia, Belarus, Kazakhstan, Kyrgyzstan, and the Russian Federation. Three other nations – Cuba, Moldova, and Uzbekistan – currently possess Observer State status within the EAEU. According to Article 8 of the EAEU Treaty, the EAEU consists of four main organs: the Supreme Eurasian Economic Council, the Eurasian Intergovernmental Council, the Eurasian Economic Commission, and the Court of the Eurasian Economic Union. Simultaneous chairmanship of the Supreme Council, the Intergovernmental Council, and the Commission rotates annually in accordance with the Russian alphabetical order, with each term lasting one calendar year and without the possibility of extension, as stipulated in Article 8(4) of the EAEU Treaty.

A. Supreme Eurasian Economic Council

The Supreme Eurasian Economic Council, commonly known as the Supreme Council, is the supreme organ of the EAEU. It appears to have been largely modelled after the European Council. However, a key distinction lies in the composition of the EAEU Supreme Council, which is exclusively formed by the Heads of State of the EAEU Member States, in accordance with Article 10 of the EAEU Treaty. In contrast, the European Council comprises 'the heads of state or government of the 27 EU member states, the European Council President and the President of the European Commission'.[45]

The Supreme Council convenes at least once annually for regular sessions, with the possibility of extraordinary meetings being called to address pressing matters, as outlined in Article 11(1) of the EAEU Treaty. The agenda for

[42] A Temirgaliyeva, 'Kyrgyzstan, Tajikistan to boost trade turnover to $500mln', Qazinform, 4 March 2025, available at qazinform.com/news/kyrgyzstan-tajikistan-to-boost-trade-turnover-to-500mln-4dd59c.

[43] WTO, 'Economic integration through WTO accession and membership', 3 June 2024, available at www.wto.org/english/news_e/spno_e/spno46_e.htm.

[44] ibid.

[45] European Union, 'European Council', www.consilium.europa.eu/en/european-council/.

these sessions is prepared by the Commission, taking into account suggestions from the Member States (Article 11(3), third paragraph). The Supreme Council considers significant issues related to the Union's operations, establishing strategic directions and prospects for integration, and making decisions that facilitate the Union's objectives (Article 12(1)).

Article 12(2) enumerates 22 essential functions of the Supreme Council, which encompass aspects such as staffing, budgetary considerations, procedural matters, and the overall governance of the Union, and provides that the Council exercises 'other powers provided for by this Treaty and treaties concluded within the Union'. Decisions and dispositions made by the Supreme Council are reached by consensus, with the exception of matters concerning the termination of membership. In such cases, the Member State intending to withdraw must abstain from voting, as specified in Article 13(2).

B. Eurasian Intergovernmental Council

The Eurasian Intergovernmental Council, also referred to as the Intergovernmental Council, is composed of the Heads of Governments from all Member States, as stipulated in Article 14 of the EAEU Treaty. Its structure and roles differ significantly from those of the Council of the European Union, which 'meets in 10 different configurations, each corresponding to the policy area being discussed. Depending on the configuration, each country sends their minister responsible for that policy area'.[46] In contrast, the EAEU Intergovernmental Council meets as required, with a minimum of two sessions annually (Article 15(1) of the EAEU Treaty). The agenda for these meetings is prepared by the Commission, incorporating suggestions from the Member States (Article 15(3), third paragraph). Article 16 delineates nine primary functions of the Intergovernmental Council, which include enforcing EAEU law, supporting the Supreme Council, and issuing directives to the Commission, thereby serving as an intermediary organ between the Supreme Council and the Commission. Decisions and dispositions made by the Intergovernmental Council are reached by consensus, as outlined in Article 17(2) of the EAEU Treaty.

C. Eurasian Economic Commission

The Eurasian Economic Commission, also known as the Commission, serves as the permanent governing organ of the EAEU. It comprises a Council and a Board, in accordance with Article 18(1) of the EAEU Treaty. The Council makes its

[46] European Union, 'Council of the European Union', https://european-union.europa.eu/institutions-law-budget/institutions-and-bodies/institutions-and-bodies-profiles/council-european-union_en.

decisions, dispositions, and recommendations by consensus, whereas decisions, dispositions and recommendations of the Board are made by a qualified majority, requiring two-thirds of its members, or by consensus (Article 18(2)). The Commission's status, responsibilities, structure, functions, powers and procedures are detailed in Annex 1 of the EAEU Treaty. The seat of the Commission is in Moscow (Russian Federation).

D. Court of the Eurasian Economic Union

The Court of the Eurasian Economic Union is a permanent judicial organ of the EAEU. For more details on the Court of the Union, see Chapter eight, section II.A above.

E. EAEU Law[47]

The scope of the EAEU law is determined by Article 6 of the EAEU Treaty. In accordance with Article 6(1), the EAEU law includes:

- the EAEU Treaty;
- other treaties concluded within the Union;
- treaties of the Union with a third party;
- decisions and dispositions of the Supreme Eurasian Economic Council, the Eurasian Intergovernmental Council, and the Eurasian Economic Commission adopted within the powers provided for by the EAEU Treaty and treaties concluded within the Union.

The EAEU Treaty was concluded in Astana (Kazakhstan) on 29 May 2014. It is a comprehensive document consisting of 118 articles grouped into four parts and 28 sections, with 33 annexes. Part One (Articles 1–22) contains general and structural provisions pertaining to the establishment of the EAEU. Part Two (Articles 23–61) lays down the legal regime of the EAEU Customs Union, and largely builds on the law of the WTO. Part Three (Articles 62–98) is devoted to the EAEU Common Economic Space,[48] and includes specific regulations on macroeconomic policy; monetary policy; trade in services, incorporations, activities and investments; financial markets; taxes and taxation; competition; natural monopolies; energy industry; transport; public procurement; intellectual

[47] Chapter 12, sections II.E and III use the author's material published in S Sayapin, 'The Eurasian Economic Union (EAEU)' in A van Aaken et al (eds), *The Oxford Handbook of International Law in Europe* (Oxford, Oxford University Press, 2023), doi: 10.1093/oxfordhb/9780198865315.013.26, with selected footnotes omitted. Reproduced by permission of Oxford University Press.
[48] See Chapter 13, section III below.

property; manufacturing industry; agriculture; labour migration; and other matters. Part Four (Articles 99–118) contains transitional and final provisions.

In accordance with Article 6(3) of the EAEU Treaty, the Treaty has superior legal force in the Union. The Treaty prevails in case of its conflict with other treaties concluded within the Union. Decisions and dispositions of the Union may not be inconsistent with the Treaty (Article 6(3)). Article 6(2) emphasises that the EAEU treaties with a third party may not contradict the main objectives,[49] principles and rules of the Union.[50]

Decisions of the Supreme Eurasian Economic Council and Eurasian Intergovernmental Council are enforceable by the Member States in accordance with the procedures provided for by their national legislation.[51] The legal force of the EAEU organs is determined by their respective rank in the EAEU structure: Article 6(4) of the EAEU Treaty provides that decisions of the Supreme Eurasian Economic Council prevail over decisions of the Eurasian Intergovernmental Council and the Eurasian Economic Commission, and decisions of the Eurasian Intergovernmental Council prevail over decisions of the Eurasian Economic Commission.

III. EAEU COMMON ECONOMIC SPACE

Part Three of the EAEU Treaty lays down regulations for a few key parameters of the EAEU Common Economic Space. In fact, the overall success of the EAEU may be assessed by these very parameters.

A. Macroeconomic Policy

In accordance with Annex 14 to the EAEU Treaty, the Commission carries out coordination of the implementation of an agreed macroeconomic policy, for the purpose of achieving the Member States' 'balanced economic development'.[52] Article 62(3) further stipulates the main directions of the agreed macroeconomic policy:

1) ensuring sustainable development of the economies of the Member States using the integration potential of the Union and competitive advantages of each Member State;
2) establishing common operation principles for the economies of the Member States and ensuring their effective interaction;

[49] Art 4 of the EAEU Treaty.
[50] Art 3 of the EAEU Treaty.
[51] Art 6(1) of the EAEU Treaty, second paragraph.
[52] cf Art 62(1) of the EAEU Treaty.

3) creating conditions to increase internal sustainability of the economies of the Member States, including their macroeconomic stability and resistance to external influences;
4) development of common principles and guidelines to predict social and economic development of the Member States.

These principles appear to be somewhat internally inconsistent. The first principle contradicts the second in that it may be difficult to exploit the Member States' individual competitive advantages while establishing 'common' operating principles for their economies. In turn, 'resistance to external influences' in the third principle sounds quite isolationist, and the development of 'common principles and guidelines' for the purpose of 'predict[ing] social and economic development' in the fourth principle sounds reminiscent of planned economies. Finally, 'common principles and guidelines' may be detrimental to the Member States' competitive advantages, which are individual to each EAEU Member State, and are conditioned by such objective factors as geography, size, population, and resources.

B. Monetary Policy

According to Article 64(1) of the EAEU Treaty, the coordinated monetary policy of the EAEU is guided by five primary objectives: (1) to enhance economic integration among the Member States, (2) to foster collaboration in the monetary domain, (3) to ensure free movement of goods, services, and capital within the territories of the Member States, (4) to strengthen the prominence of national currencies in foreign trade and investment activities, and (5) to guarantee the mutual convertibility of these currencies. However, in practical terms, the EAEU monetary policy has led to adverse consequences since 2015. The predominance of the Russian ruble in the EAEU financial landscape has meant that international sanctions imposed on the Russian Federation and its banking sector since 2014 – and particularly since 2022[53] – have had significant spillover effects on the other currencies within the EAEU. For instance, in August 2015, the Kazakh tenge (KZT) experienced a dramatic devaluation of approximately 23 per cent in a single day,[54] and fluctuations in the KZT were notably pronounced in 2022. Other currencies within the EAEU have similarly faced comparable challenges.

[53] Russia Briefing, 'Eurasian Economic Union Dedollarizes: Emphasis Now On Increasing Use Of Mutual Currencies & China Yuan Trade', 29 August 2022, available at https://meatcommerce.com/news/eurasian-economic-union-dedollarizes-emphasis-now-439348.

[54] AE Kramer, 'Kazakhstan's Currency Plunges', available at New York Times, 21 August 2015, www.nytimes.com/2015/08/21/business/international/kazakhstans-currency-plunges.html.

C. Energy Industry

Article 79(1) of the EAEU Treaty provides that

> [i]n order to effectively utilise the potential of the fuel and energy complex of the Member States, as well as to provide national economies with the main types of energy resources (electricity, gas, oil and petroleum products), the Member States shall develop long-term mutually beneficial cooperation in the energy sphere, conduct coordinated energy policy and gradually create common energy markets … with due account for ensuring energy security.

It appears that the qualification 'gradually' is key in this context, since it is repeated in Articles 81(1) (on a common electric power market), 83(1) (on a common gas market), and 84(1) (on common markets of oil and petroleum products). Whereas it *does* make sense that relevant developments depend, to a decisive extent, on the 'existing technical capabilities',[55] and on the conclusion of treaties regulating the markets in question,[56] one may call into question whether some decisions pertaining to the EAEU energy market were made in good faith. For example, on 19 June 2022, just two days after the President of Kazakhstan, Kassym-Jomart Tokayev, had stated at the 2022 St Petersburg Economic Forum that Kazakhstan would not recognise the so-called Donetsk and Luhansk 'People's Republics',[57] Russia stopped the transit of oil from Kazakhstan via the Novorossiysk port, the official reason being 'mines from the Second World War, which were suddenly discovered in the port waters'.[58] After a brief resumption, the transit was blocked again on 5 July 2022, after the President of Kazakhstan, on 4 July 2022, in a discussion with the President of the European Council, Charles Michel, expressed his readiness to help Europe overcome the energy crisis.[59]

D. Transport

Article 86(1) of the EAEU Treaty stipulates that the coordinated transport policy of the EAEU aims at 'ensuring economic integration, consistent and

[55] Arts 83(4) and 84(4) of the EAEU Treaty.

[56] Arts 81(3), 83(3) and 84(3) of the EAEU Treaty.

[57] Radio Liberty, 'Tokayev: Kazakhstan ne priznayet "kvazigosudarstvennye" "DNR" i "LNR"' ['Tokayev: Kazakhstan does not recognise the "quasi-State" "DPR" and "LPR"'], 18 June 2022, available at rus.azattyq.org/a/tokaev-o-priznanii-lnr-i-dnr/31903400.html.

[58] See EurAsia Daily, 'Rossiya priostanovila otgruzku kazakhstanskoy nefti iz Novorossiyska' ['Russia suspended the shipment of Kazakh oil from Novorossiysk'], 19 June 2022, available at eadaily.com/ru/news/2022/06/19/rossiya-priostanovila-otgruzku-kazahstanskoy-nefti-iz-novorossiyska.

[59] See O Pavlysh, 'Otvet na shag Moskvy: Kazakhstan hochet transportirovat neft v Evropu v obkhod RF' ['Response to Moscow's move: Kazakhstan wants to transport oil to Europe bypassing the Russian Federation'], European Pravda, 7 July 2022, available at www.epravda.com.ua/rus/news/2022/07/7/688954/.

gradual formation of a common transport space based on the principles of competition, transparency, security, reliability, availability and sustainability'. The types of transport covered by the EAEU Treaty and its Annex 24 are road, air, water and rail transport (Article 87(1) of the EAEU Treaty). In the years preceding 2022, there were some notable developments relative to the construction and renovation of roads, the role of the Caspian Sea in the international transport networks,[60] or the ambitious Belt and Road Initiative (BRI). According to Nurlanova and Kaliyeva, modernisation of the transport system was 'one of the main goals', because the transport infrastructure was seen as a 'catalyst for [the] social and economic development of Kazakhstan' in the long term.[61] However, in 2022, as a result of new sanctions introduced in response to Russia's invasion of Ukraine, a few threats to the integrity of the EAEU transport system became apparent.

For example, China is now seeking alternative rail routes to the West through the territories of Kyrgyzstan and Uzbekistan, so that the territory of Russia could be bypassed.[62] Also, the sanctions affected more than 500 aircraft – mostly, Boeing and Airbus – used by Russian airlines in that the aircraft are no longer allowed to use the airspace of most countries in Europe and North America, and they may not, at this time, land abroad except in a few 'friendly nations' where there is currently no threat of their impending arrest on the ground of termination of lease agreements. The need for Western spare parts is also becoming acute.

E. Intellectual Property

The legal basis for the protection of intellectual property (IP) in the EAEU is Article 89(1) of the EAEU Treaty, which provides that '[t]he Member States shall cooperate in the sphere of protection and enforcement of intellectual property rights and ensure in their territories the protection and safeguarding of these rights in accordance with international law, international treaties and acts constituting the law of the Union and the legislation of the Member States', and Annex 26 to the EAEU Treaty. Article 90(1) further stipulates that citizens of EAEU Member States are entitled to national treatment concerning IP protection. Article 90(3) lists the key treaties on the international protection of IP rights and explicitly states that 'Member States, which are not parties to

[60] See Chapter 12 below.

[61] NK Nurlanova and AB Kaliyeva, 'The Eurasian Economic Community is a New Opportunity to Develop Transit Potential of Kazakhstan' (2015) 70(2) *KazNU Bulletin. International relations and international law series* 207.

[62] Oilprice.Com, 'China Signs Major Railroad Deal With Uzbekistan And Kyrgyzstan, Bypassing Russia', available at oilprice.com/Geopolitics/International/China-Signs-Major-Railroad-Deal-With-Uzbekistan-And-Kyrgyzstan-Bypassing-Russia.html; Fergana News, 'KNR otpravila pervyy poyezd iz provintsii Hubei po marshrutu "Kitay–Kyrgyzstan–Uzbekistan"' ['China Sends First Train from Hubei Province on "China–Kyrgyzstan–Uzbekistan" Route'], 18 July 2025, available at fergana.agency/news/139010/.

these agreements, shall be obliged to accede thereto'. Domestic laws governing the protection of IP rights are also in place.[63] Nevertheless, in 2022, Russia implemented extensive measures that contravened its commitments under international IP law, ostensibly to navigate restrictive measures impacting various sectors of its economy and to mitigate the adverse consequences of such measures. For instance, while initiatives labelled as 'import replacement' by Russian authorities were not inherently unlawful, the actions taken to legitimise 'parallel imports' of goods and technologies subject to sanctions most certainly were,[64] and the holders of respective IP rights might contemplate remedial action.

F. Manufacturing Industry

In contrast to most sectors of the EAEU economy that necessitate coordinated efforts, Article 92(1) of the EAEU Treaty stipulates that national industrial development programmes and other industrial policy measures are to be formulated by the Member States 'independently'. While coordination through the Commission and, when applicable, the Intergovernmental Council is encouraged,[65] this independence likely stems from the varying industrial capabilities of the EAEU Member States. Further, unlike the WTO regulations, which typically discourage the use of subsidies, Article 93 of the EAEU Treaty establishes 'common rules for granting subsidies for industrial goods', subject to Annex 28 of the EAEU Treaty. Following the imposition of increased sanctions against Russia, there has been a notable rise in businesses' dependence on State subsidies.[66] In 2022, following the exit of numerous foreign companies from the Russian market, some began negotiating potential relocation with the governments of Kazakhstan and Uzbekistan.[67]

G. Labour Migration

The free movement of workforce, both internally and externally, plays a crucial role in the functioning of national economies. It is therefore commendable

[63] At the domestic level, IP rights are regulated in the EAEU Member States by the Civil Codes and IP laws.

[64] D Khabarov, Y Yakhin, A Bychkov and V Efremov, 'Russia partially legalizes parallel imports', 6 May 2022, available at sanctionsnews.bakermckenzie.com/russia-partially-legalizes-parallel-imports/.

[65] cf Annex 27 of the EAEU Treaty.

[66] See 'Na kakuyu podderzhku mohet rasschityvat malyy i sredniy biznes v period sanktsiy?' ['What kind of support can small and medium businesses count on during the sanctions period?'], 29 September 2023, available at fincult.info/article/na-kakuyu-podderzhku-mozhet-rasschityvat-malyy-i-sredniy-biznes-v-period-sanktsiy/.

[67] See, for example, 'Relotsirovat biznes iz Rossii v Kazakhstan gotovy 56 mezhdunarodnyh kompaniy – Smailov' ['56 international companies are ready to relocate business from Russia to Kazakhstan'], Vlast, 19 October 2022, available at vlast.kz/novosti/52184-relocirovat-biznes-iz-rossii-v-kazahstan-gotovy-56-mezdunarodnyh-kompanij-smailov.html.

that, in accordance with the second sentence of Article 97(1) of the EAEU Treaty, nationals of the Member States are not required to secure work permits in the State where they seek employment. Furthermore, Article 97(3) specifies that educational qualifications obtained from institutions within the Member States are to be automatically recognised, with the exception of fields such as teaching, law, medicine, and pharmacy, which require adherence to standard recognition procedures as established by law. Additionally, Article 97(6) provides that nationals from Member States who enter another Member State for employment, along with their family members, are not obligated to register with migration authorities within 30 days of their arrival. A detailed enumeration of the rights and obligations of workers is included in Article 98 of the EAEU Treaty.

H. Concluding Observations

After 10 years in existence, the EAEU seems to be at a crossroads. On the one hand, contemporary realities do beg for closer economic integration in the post-Soviet space, if the experience of some of the most successful economic integration projects elsewhere – such as the EU, NAFTA / United States–Mexico–Canada Agreement, ASEAN, and others – is any guide. Objectively, the individual EAEU economies are not among the strongest, and more intensive economic cooperation with neighbours, with due regard to the international distribution of resources, and division of labour, should help improve the quality of life in the EAEU Member States. On the other hand, regional economic organisations are still part of the world economic system, and a regional project will be successful only if it is properly integrated with the other components of the overall network.

It appears that currently, the EAEU is lacking the necessary external outlook. The EAEU approach to energy focuses predominantly on non-renewable sources, and the concept of 'green energy' does not at all feature in the EAEU Treaty. The Energy Charter Treaty (ECT) is of limited significance within the EAEU, since it is secondary to the EAEU law.[68] Besides, on 20 August 2009, Russia informed the ECT depositary of its decision not to ratify the ECT.[69] Developments since 2022 – triggered by Russia's full-scale invasion of Ukraine – have shown that the traditional consumers of the EAEU energy resources – such as the EU – are working with alternative suppliers, and the perception of the EU dependence on Russian oil and gas was significantly exaggerated. The EAEU should therefore urgently reconsider its energy strategy, and contemplate ways to increase the role of 'green energy'.

[68] See Chapter 12, section II.E above.

[69] See T Voon and AD Mitchell, 'Ending International Investment Agreements: Russia's Withdrawal from Participation in the Energy Charter Treaty' (2017) 111 *AJIL Unbound* 461, 463.

Notably, ecology does not feature prominently in the EAEU documentation. The concept is explicitly mentioned only once in the EAEU Treaty (in Article 86(1), in connection with the transport policy), and is referred to only on two occasions in Annex 20 to the EAEU Treaty.[70] 'Environment' is mentioned in the EAEU Treaty no more than four times.[71] Given the impact of the Aral Sea disaster on the economies and livelihoods especially in Central Asia,[72] and the ever-growing climate change concerns, much more attention should now be paid to the EAEU environmental policies.[73]

Corruption is another major issue in all EAEU Member States.[74] Unless genuine and sufficient efforts are made to combat it, chances for real progress in the economy and other areas are very low. Among other things, the digitalisation of State services is a major factor in reducing corruption-related risks. The EAEU Member States should invest, as a matter of urgency, in developing efficient and transparent digital platforms for the provision of State services with a minimum involvement of the human factor. The experience of Kazakhstan may be useful in this regard.[75]

Importantly, the rule of law and the quality of justice will be important factors for the future sustainability of the EAEU. The independence of domestic judges,[76] and the quality of their understanding of the EAEU law and international law, will be crucial for the protection of lawful interests of domestic and international economic actors, and the role of arbitration in the protection of investments will be key. Measures should therefore be taken to provide regular in-service training on international law to judges in the EAEU Member States,[77] and to continue building local expertise in international investment arbitration.[78]

Overall, the EAEU is not likely to live up to its full potential without a genuine democratisation of its Member States' political systems,[79] embracing

[70] Paras 9(6) and 20(4) in Annex 20 (Protocol on Common Regulation Principles and Rules for Activities of Natural Monopoly Entities).

[71] Arts 29(1)(3), 52(1), 68(5) and 86(2)(7) of the EAEU Treaty.

[72] See Chapter 2, section IV.G above.

[73] Fergana News, 'Kitayskaya kompaniya postroit v Kyrgyzstane solnechnuyu i vetrovuyu elektrostantsii' ['Chinese Company to Build Solar and Wind Power Plants in Kyrgyzstan'], 8 July 2025, available at fergana.agency/news/138794/.

[74] See Transparency International's Corruption Perception Index 2024: https://www.transparency.org/en/cpi/2024.

[75] For the Electronic government of the Republic of Kazakhstan, see: https://egov.kz/cms/en.

[76] S Sayapin, '"Critical Analysis, Strict Discipline and Personal Responsibility": Some Reflections on Strengthening the Independence of the Judiciary in Central Asia' (2019) 84(3) *Law and State* 18; S Sayapin, 'Réflexions sur le renforcement de l'indépendance de la magistrature en Asie centrale' ['Reflections on the Reinforcement of the Independence of the Judiciary in Central Asia'] (2019) 14 *Les Cahiers de la justice* 655.

[77] S Sayapin, 'Mezhdunarodnoye pravo v Tsentralnoy Azii: teoriya i praktika' [International Law in Central Asia: Theory and Practice] (2022) 95(2) *Law and State* 31, 46.

[78] ibid, 46–47. See also S Sayapin, 'International Law in Central Asia: Practices and Doctrines' (2022) 47 *Review of Central and East European Law* 322, 349.

[79] See J Wouters, 'Democracy and International Law' (2003) 34 *Netherlands Yearbook of International Law* 139; EA Vázquez, 'In defense of a human right to democracy: Reflections on

freedom,[80] and respect for the rule of law,[81] including international law beyond the EAEU legal framework. Sustainable economic prosperity is impossible where economies are State-centric, investors have little faith in their counterparts, courts are not independent, and where the leading economy in the Union is under a comprehensive regime of international sanctions for waging a war of aggression. The EAEU is in urgent need of internal reform, if its progress is to be meaningful.

IV. BILATERAL FREE TRADE AND INVESTMENT TREATIES

In addition to joining the WTO and the EAEU, the Central Asian nations have concluded bilateral trade agreements to diversify their economies, boost trade, and attract foreign investment. A notable example are sectoral agreements between Kazakhstan and China,[82] which emphasise energy cooperation and cross-border trade facilitation. Kazakhstan's strategic location along the BRI corridor noticeably enhances its role as a trade hub connecting East Asia and Europe. Similarly, Uzbekistan and Türkiye have engaged in negotiations to establish preferential trade agreements, bolstering Uzbekistan's export of textiles, chemicals, and agricultural products while benefiting from Türkiye's industrial goods.[83] While these FTAs certainly offer economic benefits, challenges persist. Limited infrastructure, overlapping trade blocs, and complex political dynamics hinder full implementation of trade commitments.[84] Additionally, concerns about dependency on larger economies, particularly China, have raised debates over threats to economic sovereignty.[85]

Bilateral investment treaties (BITs) have also become essential for Central Asian States seeking to attract foreign direct investment (FDI). Such treaties establish a legal framework to protect foreign investors, reduce investment risks,

the pending Advisory Opinion before the Inter-American Court of Human Rights', EJIL:Talk!, 11 July 2025, available at www.ejiltalk.org/in-defense-of-a-human-right-to-democracy-reflections-on-the-pending-advisory-opinion-before-the-inter-american-court-of-human-rights/.

[80] See Freedom House's annual Freedom in the World Report at: freedomhouse.org/countries/freedom-world/scores.

[81] See The 2024 World Justice Project Rule of Law Index at: worldjusticeproject.org/rule-of-law-index/.

[82] D Omirgazy, 'Kazakhstan, China Deepen Strategic Partnership, Sign 24 Agreements', Astana Times, 16 June 2025, available at astanatimes.com/2025/06/kazakhstan-china-deepen-strategic-partnership-sign-24-agreements/.

[83] International Trade Administration, 'Uzbekistan Country Commercial Guide', available at www.trade.gov/country-commercial-guides/uzbekistan-trade-agreements.

[84] K Karymshakov and B Sulaimanova, 'Trade Facilitation, Infrastructure, and International Trade in Central Asian Countries', ADB East Asia Working Paper No. 58, February 2023, available at www.adb.org/publications/trade-facilitation-infrastructure-central-asian-countries.

[85] T Umarov, 'What Does Xi Jinping Want From Central Asia?', July 2024, available at carnegieendowment.org/posts/2024/07/what-does-xi-jinping-want-from-central-asia?lang=en; Fergana News, 'Kitay vpervye stal krupneyshim torgovym partnerom Tadzhikistana' ['China Becomes Tajikistan's Largest Trading Partner for the First Time'], 15 July 2025, available at fergana.agency/news/138934/.

and promote economic cooperation.[86] Kazakhstan has entered into at least 53 BITs with key economies in Asia, Europe, and North America, including China, Germany, Qatar, Singapore, and the United States.[87] The Kazakhstan–Germany BIT has been instrumental in fostering investment in Kazakhstan's energy and industrial sectors.[88] Similarly, the Kazakhstan–China BIT supports infrastructure and energy projects aligned with the BRI, underscoring Kazakhstan's strategic geographic position.[89] Among Kyrgyzstan's 39 BITs, those with China and Türkiye have played a key role in attracting investment in mining, energy, and infrastructure, thereby deepening the country's economic integration with its regional partners.[90] Tajikistan's 44 BITs have particularly supported investment in hydropower projects – a vital sector of the national economy.[91] Turkmenistan's 30 BITs have encouraged investments in its natural gas industry.[92] Uzbekistan has concluded at least 58 BITs to attract investments as part of its economic liberalisation efforts.[93] For example, the Uzbekistan–Japan BIT has facilitated Japanese investment, in particular, in automotive manufacturing and telecommunications.[94] Uzbekistan's BITs with South Korea and Türkiye have bolstered investments in textiles, mining, and technology.[95]

[86] See also A Lieser, 'Bilateral Investment Treaties as a Tool for Global Climate Governance? Bridging the Tension Between International Investment Law and International Climate Change Law by Redesigning Bilateral Investment Treaties', Völkerrechtsblog, 11 September 2024, available at voelkerrechtsblog.org/bilateral-investment-treaties-as-a-tool-for-global-climate-governance/.

[87] UNCTAD, 'Kazakhstan', available at investmentpolicy.unctad.org/international-investment-agreements/countries/107/kazakhstan.

[88] ibid.

[89] ibid. See also Fergana News, 'Vtoruyu i tretyu AES v Kazahstane postriot Kitay' ['China to Build Second and Third Nuclear Power Plants in Kazakhstan'], 31 July 2025, available at fergana.agency/news/139213/.

[90] UNCTAD, 'Kyrgyzstan', available at investmentpolicy.unctad.org/international-investment-agreements/countries/113/kyrgyzstan.

[91] UNCTAD, 'Tajikistan', available at investmentpolicy.unctad.org/international-investment-agreements/countries/206/tajikistan.

[92] UNCTAD, 'Turkmenistan', available at investmentpolicy.unctad.org/international-investment-agreements/countries/215/turkmenistan.

[93] UNCTAD, 'Uzbekistan', available at investmentpolicy.unctad.org/international-investment-agreements/countries/226/uzbekistan.

[94] ibid.

[95] ibid.

12

*The Legal Status of the Caspian Sea**

I. BACKGROUND

THE CASPIAN SEA is the world's largest natural inland reservoir of salt water.[1] With a length of almost 1200 km from north to south and the average width of about 320 km, the Caspian Sea covers an area of approximately 386,400 km^2, and contains about 78,200 km^3 of water.[2] It is home to some 850 animal and more than 500 plant species.[3] The Caspian Sea's energy resources in onshore and offshore fields are massive: an estimated 48 billion barrels of oil are four times as much as Europe's reserves, and 8.26 trillion cubic metres of natural gas are more than South and Central America's gas reserves.[4]

Until the dissolution of the Soviet Union, the exploitation of the Caspian Sea was governed by treaties between Iran and Russia (and subsequently, the Soviet Union) – in particular, the Treaties of Saint Petersburg (1723), Resht (1732), Golestan (1813), Turkmenchai (1828), the 1921 Treaty of Friendship, and the 1931, 1935, and 1940 Treaties of Commerce.[5] Janusz-Pawletta (as quoted by Masoudi Lamraski) cites nearly 25 treaties pertaining to the Caspian Sea since the eighteenth century.[6] The emergence of new sovereign post-Soviet nations in 1991 – and the related needs to delimit their borders and assert sovereignty over their natural resources – called for revisiting (and consolidation of) the legal regime of the Caspian Sea.

According to Masoudi Lamraski, after 1991, the Caspian States proposed five approaches to the regulation of the Sea:

> (1) condominium status applying to both the surface and the seabed; (2) division based on UNCLOS; (3) equal division of 20% of the sea, and the seabed to each

* This chapter uses the author's material published in S Sayapin, 'Convention on the Legal Status of the Caspian Sea' in S Lee et al (eds), *Encyclopedia of Public International Law in Asia, Vol III: Central & South Asia* (Leiden, Brill, 2021). Permission to use published material is gratefully acknowledged.

[1] Britannica, 'Caspian Sea', available at www.britannica.com/place/Caspian-Sea.

[2] ibid.

[3] ibid.

[4] A Masoudi Lamraski, 'Aktau Convention on the Legal Status of the Caspian Sea' in KW Gray (ed), *Global Encyclopedia of Territorial Rights* (Springer Nature Switzerland, 2023), 1.

[5] ibid.

[6] ibid, 2.

littoral State; (4) division based on the Soviet maps; and (5) division of the seabed based on UNCLOS and the surface with condominium status.[7]

This multiplicity of legal views and the fact that in parallel with negotiations of the framework Convention on the Legal Status of the Caspian Sea, the post-Soviet Caspian States concluded among themselves several treaties known as the 'North Caspian Agreements' (all of which were contested by Iran)[8] show the degree of lack of consensus at the time. During the same period, a few thematic treaties were concluded to respond to some pressing challenges – in particular, on environmental matters, disaster warning and relief,[9] and security matters.[10] The fact that at the time of writing, Iran has not yet ratified the Convention on the Legal Status of the Caspian Sea demonstrates that the lack of consensus persists.

II. CONVENTION ON THE LEGAL STATUS OF THE CASPIAN SEA

A. Introduction

The Convention on the Legal Status of the Caspian Sea (also known as the Aktau Convention) was concluded at the Fifth Caspian Summit at Aktau (Kazakhstan) on 12 August 2018, on behalf of the Republic of Azerbaijan, the Islamic Republic of Iran, the Republic of Kazakhstan, the Russian Federation and Turkmenistan.[11] The Convention was the result of negotiations among the contracting States since 1996 with a view to 'facilitat[ing] the development and strengthening of cooperation among the Parties, and promot[ing] the use of the Caspian Sea for peaceful purposes and rational management of its resources, as well as exploration, protection and conservation of its environment'.[12] The Convention will enter into force on the date of the receipt by the Republic of Kazakhstan acting as the depositary of the Convention of the fifth (that is, Iran's) instrument of ratification (Article 22).[13] The Convention was concluded in the Azerbaijani, Farsi, Kazakh, Russian, Turkmen and English languages, all

[7] ibid, 2–3.
[8] ibid. See also n 18 below.
[9] See section II.E below.
[10] See section II.F below.
[11] For the English text of the Aktau Convention, see: tehranconvention.org/system/files/web/convention_on_the_legal_status_of_the_caspian_sea_en.pdf.
[12] cf the 9th preambular para of the Convention.
[13] Allegedly, '[t]he main reason why the Iranian government has still not sent the … Convention for ratification relates to ongoing expert and technical negotiations related to determining the "baselines" of the Caspian Sea', see V Kaleji, 'Iran Balks at Definition of Offshore Territorial Baselines in Caspian Sea', 3 June 2021, Eurasia Daily Monitor, jamestown.org/program/iran-balks-at-definition-of-offshore-territorial-baselines-in-caspian-sea/.

texts being equally authentic. In case of any disagreement, the Parties should refer to the English text (Article 24).

In accordance with Article 2(2), the Convention defines and regulates 'the rights and obligations of the Parties in respect of the use of the Caspian Sea, including its waters, seabed, subsoil, natural resources and the airspace over the Sea'. Article 4 provides that the Parties' activities in the Caspian Sea should conform to the Convention, other agreements between the Parties consistent with the Convention, and their domestic legislation. After the Convention enters into force, those other agreements will remain in force to the extent they are consistent with the Convention.

B. Spaces

The water area of the Caspian Sea is divided into internal waters,[14] territorial waters,[15] fishery zones[16] and the common maritime space[17] (Article 5). The internal waters and territorial waters (not exceeding 15 nautical miles), as well as the seabed and subsoil thereof, and the airspace over it, are subject to the sovereignty of the respective Parties (Articles 6 and 7(1)). In accordance with the first paragraph of Article 7(2), the outer limit of the territorial waters is the line every point of which is located at a distance from the nearest point of the baseline equal to the breadth of the territorial waters. The third paragraph of the same article lays down that the outer limit of the territorial waters is the State border.

Article 8(1) specifies that the

> [d]elimitation of the Caspian Sea seabed and subsoil into sectors shall be effected by agreement between States with adjacent and opposite coasts, with due regard to the generally recognized principles and norms of international law, to enable those States to exercise their sovereign rights to the subsoil exploitation and other legitimate economic activities related to the development of resources of the seabed and subsoil.

In the absence of such a comprehensive agreement, bilateral treaties concluded between some Caspian States apply at this time.[18]

[14] Internal waters are 'waters on the landward side of the baseline', see para 7 of Art 1 of the Aktau Convention.

[15] Territorial waters are 'a belt of sea to which the sovereignty of a coastal State extends', see para 8 of Art 1 of the Aktau Convention.

[16] A fishery zone is 'a belt of sea where a coastal State holds an exclusive right to harvest aquatic biological resources', see para 9 of Art 1 of the Aktau Convention.

[17] The common maritime space is 'a water area located outside the outer limits of fishery zones and open for use by all the Parties', see para 10 of Art 1 of the Aktau Convention.

[18] See, for example, the Agreement between the Russian Federation and the Republic of Kazakhstan on Delimitation of the Deep Seabed of the Northern Part of the Caspian Sea for the Purpose of the

In accordance with the first sentence of Article 8(2), '[w]ithin its sector, a coastal State shall have the exclusive right to construct, as well as to authorize and regulate the construction, operation and use of artificial islands, installations and structures'. Kazakhstan has been constructing artificial islands 'for oil drilling activities' since the early 2000s.[19] In 2024, Azerbaijan announced its plans to construct several artificial islands 'in the next few decades', to implement some wind and solar energy projects.[20] The second sentence of Article 8(2) provides that

> [a] coastal State may, where deemed necessary, establish safety zones around artificial islands, installations and structures to ensure the safety of navigation and of the artificial islands, installations and structures. The breadth of the safety zones shall not exceed a distance of 500 meters around them, measured from each point of the outer edge of such artificial islands, installations and structures.

All ships must respect those safety zones (Article 8(3)).

The Caspian Sea is home to more than 120 fish species, including sturgeon, herring, pike, perch, sprat, and many others.[21] Reportedly, '[s]ome 90 percent of the world's caviar comes from the Caspian Sea'.[22] The Aktau Convention acknowledges the Caspian littoral States' exclusive rights to their respective fishery zones but also emphasises the importance of responsible fishing. In accordance with Article 9,

> [e]ach Party shall establish a 10 nautical miles-wide fishery zone adjacent to the territorial waters … In its fishery zone, each Party shall have the exclusive right to harvest aquatic biological resources in accordance with this Convention, separate agreements concluded by the Parties on the basis of the Convention and its national legislation.

The same article stipulates that, as a rule, the harvesting of aquatic biological resources should be carried out within the limits of determined national quotas, and that '[t]erms and procedures for harvesting shared aquatic biological resources in the Caspian Sea shall be determined by the separate agreement concluded by all Parties'.

Exercise of Sovereign Rights to Subsoil Management of 6 July 1998, or the Agreement between the Russian Federation and the Republic of Azerbaijan on the Delimitation of the Contiguous Areas of Seabed of the Caspian Sea of 23 September 2002.

[19] Kashagan Oil Field Development, available at www.kasktas.com.tr/en/portfolio-item/kashagan-oil-field-development/.

[20] A Aydinli, 'Can Azerbaijan benefit from artificial islands in Caspian?', 8 May 2024, News.AZ, available at news.az/news/-can-azerbaijan-benefit-from-artificial-islands-in-caspian-. An earlier ambitious project to construct 55 artificial islands for tourism was reported to be on hold, see A Scotto Di Santolo, 'The incredible abandoned £80bn mega-project to build 55 new islands in landlocked country', Express, 11 May 2024, available at www.express.co.uk/news/world/1896221/eurasia-azerbaijan-mega-project-Kazar-islands.

[21] Britannica (n 1).

[22] Reuters, 'U.N. lifts ban on caviar exports from Caspian', 9 August 2007, available at www.reuters.com/article/business/environment/un-lifts-ban-on-caviar-exports-from-caspian-idUSL02934641/.

C. Freedoms of Navigation and Transit

Freedom of navigation beyond the outer limits of the territorial waters for ships flying the flags of the Parties is reaffirmed in Article 10.[23] In particular, according to Article 10(2),

> [e]ach Party shall grant ships flying the flags of other Parties that carry goods, or passengers and baggage, or perform towing or rescue operations the same treatment as to its national ships with regard to free access to its ports in the Caspian Sea, their use for loading and unloading goods, boarding or disembarking passengers, payment of tonnage and other port dues, use of navigation services and performance of regular commercial activities.

To make possible 'free access from the Caspian Sea to other seas and the Ocean, and back', freedom of transit for the Parties' means of transport through the territories of transit Parties is recognised in Article 10(4). Article 11 regulates civilian and military vessels' navigation through the Parties' territorial waters.

According to Parkhomchik, the merchant marine fleets on the Caspian Sea include bulk carriers, oil tankers, barges, road and rail ferries, and most ships are mixed river–sea navigation vessels with relatively small tonnage (3–5 thousand tonnes).[24] However,

> low-tonnage ships could not provide [an] appropriate level of oil cargo transportation, which is the most profitable part of commercial shipment in the Caspian Sea [Therefore] each regional actor tries to replenish its national merchant marine fleet with … vessels with deadweight up to 12–13 thousand [tonnes].[25]

After 2022, many Russian and Iranian vessels were reportedly used to circumvent international sanctions introduced in response to Russia's aggression against Ukraine. Thus, in May 2023,

> 138 Russian-flagged ships sailing on the Caspian produced 657 gaps in their [Automatic Identification Systems]. In June, there were 625 such gaps involving 160 vessels, and in July there were at least 630 involving 157 vessels … That's four times as many AIS gaps as during May, June, and July last year, when Russia-flagged ships on the Caspian Sea went dark 159, 135, and 138 times, respectively.[26]

In turn, in May 2023,

> 48 Iranian-flagged vessels had 199 AIS gaps; in June, 48 Iranian vessels had 218 gaps, and in July 47 vessels had 192 gaps. That's a few more vessels per month than during

[23] B Janusz-Pawletta, *The Legal Status of the Caspian Sea: Current Challenges and Prospects for Future Development* (Berlin, Springer, 2021), 127–45.

[24] L Parkhomchik, 'Shipping in the Caspian Sea: Case of Kazakhstan', January 2015: eurasian-research.org/wp-content/uploads/2020/06/Weekly-e-bulletin-06-01-2015-12-01-2015-No-2.pdf.

[25] ibid.

[26] E Braw, 'The Caspian Sea Is a Sanctions-Busting Paradise', Foreign Policy, 14 August 2023, available at: foreignpolicy.com/2023/08/14/russia-iran-caspian-sea-sanctions-busting-paradise/. Braw explains that the Automatic Identification System (AIS) is a 'system, which virtually all commercial vessels are obliged to use; AIS gaps are the periods of time when a vessel's system stops transmitting'.

> the same time last year – and about twice as many AIS gaps. A significant number of the AIS-gap vessels were traveling between Russian and Iranian ports.[27]

The Caspian Policy Center (CPC) claims unequivocally that these vessels are used to deliver 'weapons from Iran to fuel the Kremlin's war machine'.[28] By contrast, according to Braw,

> Azerbaijani, Kazakh, and Turkmen ships traveling in the Caspian Sea had very few AIS gaps. They seem to be following the rules – for now. But if they decided they wanted to obscure their activities, it would be hard to stop them.[29]

All Caspian States have military presence on the Caspian Sea. With 28 warships,[30] 'the Russian Caspian flotilla is the largest and most powerful naval unit in the Caspian Sea'.[31] Gorgemans notes that Russia's 'Caspian Flotilla has been transformed into a small but effective fleet capable of projecting power well beyond Russia's Caspian shores'.[32] Notably, it is 'located within striking distance of hotspots in Syria to the southwest and Crimea to the northwest'.[33] The reinforcement of the Caspian flotilla with an additional 32 amphibious armoured personnel vehicles in May 2018 – according to Gorgemans, 'a strategic move that increased the flotilla's ability to conduct landings anywhere along the Caspian shoreline' – may be interpreted as 'a message intended to keep the former Soviet states in Russia's sphere of influence'.[34]

D. Jurisdiction

Article 12 reaffirms each Party's jurisdiction over the ships flying its flag in the Caspian Sea, and, within its sector, over artificial islands, installations, structures, its submarine cables and pipelines. Marine scientific research in the Parties' territorial waters is regulated by Article 13. Article 14 regulates the laying of submarine cables and pipelines on the seabed.

The Caspian States have established research institutions to conduct marine scientific research on the Caspian Sea. For example, the Caspian Scientific Research Center at Azerbaijan's Western Caspian University (established in 2019) carries out fundamental and applied scientific research 'focused on gaining new

[27] ibid.

[28] H Nelson, 'Dark Deals on the Caspian: How Iran Ships Drones to Russia', Caspian Policy Center, 21 August 2023, available at: www.caspianpolicy.org/research/security-and-politics-program-spp/dark-deals-on-the-caspian-how-iran-ships-drones-to-russia.

[29] ibid.

[30] B Gorgemans, 'The Caspian Flotilla: Russia's Offensive Reinvention', August 2021, available at: www.usni.org/magazines/proceedings/2021/august/caspian-flotilla-russias-offensive-reinvention.

[31] Eurasian Research Institute, 'The Russian Navy in the Caspian Sea: A New Chapter', April 2018, available at: www.eurasian-research.org/publication/the-russian-navy-in-the-caspian-sea-a-new-chapter/.

[32] Gorgemans (n 30).

[33] ibid.

[34] ibid.

knowledge of the biology and ecology of the Caspian Sea and inland waters'.[35] In 1992, the Ministry of Energy of Iran established the National Center for Caspian Sea Relevant Studies and Research.[36] Likewise, the Iranian National Institute for Oceanography and Atmospheric Science runs the Caspian Sea Oceanography Center.[37] On 26 January 2024, the Government of Kazakhstan approved a resolution to establish the Caspian Sea Research Institute. The Institute will

> study environmental issues of the Caspian Sea, the problem of declining water levels, the causes of mass mortalities of seals and fish, and the preservation of the Caspian seal population, marine life, and coastal areas. It will also be engaged in activities to foster close collaboration with other Caspian states.[38]

On 9 August 2019, the Institute of the Caspian Sea was established by the President of Turkmenistan.[39] In August 2023, Turkmenistan

> hosted the scientific and practical conference [entitled] 'The Caspian Sea – the Sea of Peace and Friendship', timed to coincide with the International Day of the Caspian Sea, which is celebrated on August 12. The forum discussed topical issues … [such as] the interaction of coastal countries in the political, economic, scientific, environmental and other fields.[40]

In Russia, the Caspian Marine Scientific Research Center has been in place since 1995 as a research institution of the Russian Federal Service for Hydrometeorology and Environmental Monitoring (Roshydromet).[41]

The Caspian States are working on integrating their data and energy systems with those of their neighbours via submarine cables. Thus, in early May 2024, the Ministers of Energy of Azerbaijan, Kazakhstan, and Uzbekistan signed a Memorandum of Cooperation to 'implement the most efficient energy trade through technical and economic support, including laying high-voltage cables at the bottom of the Caspian Sea and other countries' territories, to facilitate the connection of energy systems'.[42] In June 2024, the Kazakh and Azerbaijani telecom operators announced the Digital Silk Road project, involving

[35] See: wcu.edu.az/en/page/caspian-sea-problems-research-center.

[36] See: www.wri.ac.ir/en/national-center-for-caspian-sea-relevant-studies-and-research/.

[37] See: inio.ac.ir/en/node/108.

[38] The Astana Times, 'Kazakh Government to Establish Caspian Sea Research Institute', 27 January 2024, available at: astanatimes.com/2024/01/kazakh-government-to-establish-caspian-sea-research-institute/.

[39] Ministry of Foreign Affairs of Turkmenistan, 'The Institute of the Caspian Sea is established in Turkmenistan', 10 August 2019, available at: www.mfa.gov.tm/en/news/1538.

[40] TURKMENPORTAL, 'Turkmenistan calls for scientific cooperation on the Caspian', 13 August 2023, available at: turkmenportal.com/en/blog/65680/turkmenistan-calls-for-scientific-cooperation-on-the-caspian.

[41] See: www.caspianmonitoring.ru/en/glavnaya-stranica/.

[42] CEEnergy News, 'Kazakhstan, Azerbaijan and Uzbekistan agree on energy cable project', 7 May 2024, available at: ceenergynews.com/electricity/kazakhstan-azerbaijan-and-uzbekistan-agree-on-energy-cable-project/.

> the construction of a 370-kilometer underwater fiber-optic cable from the Kazakh port of Aktau to the Azerbaijani city of Sumgayit. The maximum capacity of the cable will reach 400 Tbps, allowing for the efficient transmission of large volumes of data between the regions.[43]

The project will 'significantly improve communication between Central Asia and Azerbaijan, promote economic development, and integrate the regions into the global digital community'.[44]

In 2023, Turkmenistan and Azerbaijan revived the Trans-Caspian Gas Pipeline project.[45] The new pipeline 'would run beneath the Caspian Sea to connect with an existing terminal in Turkey',[46] and thus bypass both Russia and Iran. The project has been approved to receive public financing from the European Union.[47]

E. Protection and Preservation of Ecological System

Article 15 relates to the protection and preservation of the Caspian Sea's ecological system. It specifies, in particular, that any activity damaging the biological diversity of the Caspian Sea should be prohibited, and that responsibility for any damage caused to the ecological system of the Caspian Sea should be borne in accordance with international law.

According to the United Nations Environment Programme (UNEP),

> [t]he Caspian region is rich in biological resources and serves as the world's largest spawning ground for sturgeon. Although the Caspian Sea has relatively small biological diversity, it boasts high-level endemism, with over 130 fish species and rare lotus fields. Additionally, it is home to more than 100 species of wetland birds that use the area for nesting and migration. The Caspian Seal, the only marine mammal living in the Sea, is also endemic to this region.[48]

In order to protect the unique ecosystem of the Caspian Sea, the littoral States adopted, on 4 November 2003, the Framework Convention for the Protection of the Marine Environment of the Caspian Sea (the Tehran Convention).[49] The Tehran Convention and its Aktau and Moscow Protocols have been ratified by all Caspian States. The Protocol Concerning Regional Preparedness, Response

[43] S Alizade, 'How Kazakhstan and Azerbaijan connect Europe and Asia with a submarine cable', News.AS, 20 June 2024, available at: news.az/news/how-kazakhstan-and-azerbaijan-connect-europe-and-asia-with-a-submarine-cable.

[44] ibid.

[45] D Onyango, 'Turkmenistan Revives Trans-Caspian Gas Pipeline Prospect to Send Gas to Europe', 1 November 2023, available at: www.pipeline-journal.net/news/turkmenistan-revives-trans-caspian-gas-pipeline-prospect-send-gas-europe.

[46] ibid.

[47] See: ec.europa.eu/energy/maps/pci_fiches/PciFiche_7.1.1.pdf.

[48] UNEP, 'The Tehran Convention', available at www.unep.org/tehran-convention.

[49] For the text of the Convention, see tehranconvention.org/en/tc.

and Co-operation in Combating Oil Pollution Incidents (Aktau Protocol) was adopted on 12 August 2011.[50] The Protocol for the Protection of the Caspian Sea against Pollution from Land-Based Sources and Activities (Moscow Protocol) was adopted on 12 December 2012.[51] The Protocol for the Conservation of Biological Diversity (Ashgabat Protocol) was adopted on 30 May 2014, and ratified by Iran, Kazakhstan, and Turkmenistan.[52] The Protocol on Environmental Impact Assessment in a Transboundary Context was adopted on 20 July 2018, and ratified by all Caspian States except Iran.[53] The Protocol on Monitoring, Assessment and Information Exchange is currently being negotiated by the Parties to the Tehran Convention.[54] Regular consultations are held to address environmental crimes in the Caspian Sea region.[55]

F. Cooperation

In accordance with Article 16, the Parties' cooperation with natural and legal persons of third States, and with international organisations, should conform to the Convention. Article 17 provides for the Parties' cooperation 'in combating international terrorism and financing thereof, trafficking in arms, drugs, psychotropic substances and their precursors, as well as poaching, and in preventing and suppressing smuggling of migrants by sea and other crimes in the Caspian Sea'.

On 18 November 2010, the Caspian States concluded the Agreement on Cooperation in the Field of Security in the Caspian Sea, and on 12 August 2018, the Protocol on Cooperation in Combating Organized Crime in the Caspian Sea was concluded.[56] Article 3 of the Protocol lists five priority areas for cooperation between the Parties:

(1) combating crimes against persons, including against human life and health;
(2) crimes related to trafficking in persons, especially women and children, and removal of human organs or tissues for transplantation and illegal migration;
(3) trafficking in firearms, ammunition, explosive devices and explosive and toxic substances;
(4) crimes in the sphere of economic activity, including those related to the legalisation (laundering) of revenues, including proceeds of crime;

[50] For the texts of the Protocols, see tehranconvention.org/en/tc/protocols.
[51] ibid.
[52] ibid.
[53] ibid.
[54] ibid.
[55] Tehran Times, 'Caspian states hold meeting to address environmental crimes', 14 April 2024, available at: www.tehrantimes.com/news/497109/Caspian-states-hold-meeting-to-address-environmental-crimes.
[56] For the text of the Protocol, see mid.ru/ru/foreign_policy/mnogostoronnie-struktury-i-forumy/vzaimodeystvie_v_regione_kaspiyskogo_morya/1574920/?lang=en.

(5) manufacturing and sale of counterfeit currency notes, documents, securities, as well as credit or debit cards and other payment and valuable documents.

According to the Geneva Centre for Security Policy, the security measures taken so far are comprehensive but not yet sufficient:

> The Caspian states undoubtedly consider cooperation in dealing with serious regional challenges to be in their strategic interests ... Still, the absence of a unified Caspian Sea regional organization, with the participation of all littoral states, is a serious impediment to cooperation and regional security ... The creation of such a multilateral forum would be a huge step forward in establishing common strategies among the littoral states in responding to new challenges, including fighting terrorism, drug trafficking, WMD proliferation, and avian flu. It would also strengthen trade, economic, and scientific relations ... External actors that would benefit from enhanced regional cooperation and integration should encourage the creation of such an organization. Until that happens, bilateral cooperation will continue to be the only effective means of dealing with regional challenges.[57]

G. Settlement of Disputes

In accordance with Article 19,

> [t]o ensure effective implementation of the Convention and to review cooperation in the Caspian Sea, the Parties shall establish a mechanism of five-party regular high-level consultations under the auspices of their Ministries of Foreign Affairs to be held at least once a year, on a rotation basis, in one of the coastal States, in accordance with the agreed rules of procedure.

Disputes related to the implementation of the Convention should be settled through consultations and negotiations or, at the discretion of the Parties, through other peaceful means provided for by international law (Article 21). The Convention does not provide for a compulsory jurisdiction of the International Court of Justice (ICJ).

[57] K Shadrina, 'GCSP Policy Brief No. 9 – Security in the Caspian Sea Region: Challenges and Opportunities in a Globalized World', 28 September 2006, available at www.files.ethz.ch/isn/26528/Brief-9.pdf (footnotes omitted).

13

International Human Rights Law

I. BACKGROUND

A. Introduction

INTERNATIONAL HUMAN RIGHTS law (IHRL) is somewhat easier to define than 'human rights' as such. In general terms, IHRL may be defined as rules of international law enacted to safeguard the rights and fundamental freedoms of individuals and groups within national jurisdictions.[1] Rights and freedoms certainly go along with corresponding duties vis-à-vis society and the State. But the content of human rights is more complex than this. The phrase 'human rights' implies that these rights are distinct from the rights of other actors under international law – for example, States. It is worth recalling that in international law, the rights and duties of States had been codified way earlier than human rights were.[2] The concept may also imply that other living beings – such as animals – might have rights as well.[3] Last but not least, it may suggest that 'human rights' derive from human nature, and States simply acknowledge their existence but do not 'grant' them to individuals as an act of sovereignty, favour, or mercy.[4] The latter approach appears to be predominant in the modern human rights discourse.

Modern IHRL derives from the Charter of the United Nations, and is a normative reaction to the mass atrocities of the Second World War.[5] The

[1] P Alston and R Goodman, *International Human Rights: The Successor to International Human Rights in Context* (Oxford, Oxford University Press, 2013); I Bantekas and L Oette, *International Human Rights Law and Practice*, 3rd edn (Cambridge, Cambridge University Press, 2020); O De Schutter, *International Human Rights Law: Cases, Materials, and Commentary*, 3rd edn (Cambridge, Cambridge University Press, 2019); RKM Smith, *International Human Rights Law*, 9th edn (Oxford, Oxford University Press, 2020); HT Adilkariyev, Mezhdunarodnoye pravo [*International law*] (Tashkent, Tashkent State Law Institute, 2003), 326–41; II Lukashuk and AH Saidov, *Hozirgi zamon xalqaro huquqi nazariyasi asoslari* [*The theoretical fundamentals of modern international law*] (Tashkent, Adolat, 2006), 234–37.

[2] See Chapter 2, section II above.

[3] RN Fasel and SC Butler, *Animal Rights Law* (Oxford, Hart Publishing, 2023); F Dalpane and M Baideldinova (eds), *Animal Law Worldwide: Key Issues and Main Trends Across 27 Jurisdictions* (The Hague, TMC Asser Press, 2024).

[4] Alston and Goodman (n 1), 3–17.

[5] Bantekas and Oette (n 1), 14–15. See also W Osiatyński, 'The historical development of human rights' in S Sheeran and N Rodley (eds), *Routledge Handbook of International Human Rights Law* (London, Routledge, 2013).

second preambular paragraph of the Charter recalls that the Peoples of the United Nations are determined 'to reaffirm faith in fundamental human rights, in the dignity and worth of the human person, in the equal rights of men and women and of nations large and small'.[6] Article 1(2) recalls further that the development of friendly relations among nations should be based on the principle of equal rights and self-determination of peoples, and Article 1(3) reaffirms 'respect for human rights and for fundamental freedoms for all without distinction as to race, sex, language, or religion'. Article 13(2) emphasises the role of the General Assembly in the 'realization of human rights and fundamental freedoms for all'. Articles 62(2) and 68 deal with the role of the Economic and Social Council in the same respect. Although Article 76(3) is obsolete now, it stressed the significance of human rights and fundamental freedoms in the UN trusteeship system, with a particular emphasis on 'recognition of the interdependence of the peoples of the world'. Finally, Article 80(1) provides that nothing in the Charter should be 'construed in or of itself to alter in any manner the rights whatsoever of … any peoples or the terms of existing international instruments to which Members of the United Nations may respectively be parties'.

In furtherance of these provisions, and in order to give effect to them, a set of interrelated universal human rights instruments was developed under the auspices of the United Nations. On 10 December 1948, the General Assembly adopted the Universal Declaration of Human Rights (UDHR).[7] Although not legally binding as such,[8] and intended to be 'a common standard of achievement for all peoples and all nations',[9] the UDHR became, over time, the most widely translated international law document in history,[10] and its key provisions are now widely regarded as customary international law.[11] The UDHR includes provisions on civil and political rights (Articles 3–15, 18–21), economic, social and cultural rights (Articles 16–17, 22–27), collective rights (Article 28) as well as individual and collective duties (Articles 29–30). This attests to the Declaration's fundamental and programmatic character. On 16 December 1966, two International Covenants were adopted to give legally binding effect to two groups of rights provided for in the UDHR. The International Covenant on Civil and Political Rights (ICCPR) entered into force on 23 March 1976, and currently has 174 States Parties.[12] The ICCPR has two Optional Protocols.

[6] For the text of the UN Charter, see: www.un.org/en/about-us/un-charter/full-text.

[7] Smith (n 1), 56–70.

[8] ibid, 57–58.

[9] cf the last preambular paragraph of the UDHR.

[10] See: https://www.ohchr.org/en/search?f%5B0%5D=event_type_taxonomy_term_name%3A Universal%20Declaration%20of%20Human%20Rights.

[11] Smith (n 1), 58–59; Bantekas and Oette (n 1), 15–19, 63–64. See also E Grant, 'Customary law and human rights' in Sheeran and Rodley (n 5).

[12] For the ratification status of the ICCPR, see: treaties.un.org/pages/viewdetails.aspx?chapter=4&clang=_en&mtdsg_no=iv-4&src=ind.

The First Optional Protocol (1966) enables the Human Rights Committee – an expert organ established to monitor compliance with the ICCPR – to receive and consider individual communications.[13] The Second Optional Protocol (1989) aims at the abolition of the death penalty.[14] The International Covenant on Economic, Social and Cultural Rights (ICESCR) entered into force on 3 January 1976, and currently has 173 States Parties.[15] The UDHR, two International Covenants, and two Optional Protocols to the ICCPR together make up the International Bill of Human Rights.[16]

In addition to these 'umbrella' texts, the United Nations has also initiated the adoption of seven thematic human rights instruments – aimed, respectively, against all forms of racial discrimination, all forms of discrimination against women, torture and other inhuman or degrading treatment or punishment, and enforced disappearance, and specifically codifying the rights of children, migrant workers and their families, and persons with disabilities.[17] Both International Covenants and all thematic instruments have their own expert mechanisms for monitoring compliance.[18] The Central Asian States have ratified the key human rights instruments,[19] and show varying degrees of compliance.[20]

So far, the States of Central Asia have not accepted the jurisdiction of any regional human rights mechanisms[21] – although Kazakhstan might, theoretically, accede to the European Convention on Human Rights,[22] and accept the jurisdiction of the European Court of Human Rights.[23] In 1995, the post-Soviet States, as members of the Commonwealth of Independent States (CIS), adopted a Convention on Human Rights and Fundamental Freedoms, which included, along with civil and political rights, a broad catalogue of economic and social

[13] For the ratification status of the First Optional Protocol to the ICCPR, see: treaties.un.org/pages/viewdetails.aspx?src=treaty&mtdsg_no=iv-5&chapter=4&clang=_en.

[14] For the ratification status of the Second Optional Protocol to the ICCPR, see: treaties.un.org/pages/ViewDetails.aspx?src=TREATY&mtdsg_no=IV-12&chapter=4.

[15] For the ratification status of the ICESCR, see: treaties.un.org/Pages/ViewDetails.aspx?src=IND&mtdsg_no=IV-3&chapter=4.

[16] Smith (n 1), 56–71.

[17] Office of the UN High Commissioner for Human Rights, 'The Core International Human Rights Instruments and their monitoring bodies', available at www.ohchr.org/en/core-international-human-rights-instruments-and-their-monitoring-bodies.

[18] Office of the UN High Commissioner for Human Rights, 'Treaty Bodies', available at www.ohchr.org/en/treaty-bodies. See also Bantekas and Oette (n 1), 214–37; De Schutter (n 1), 869–932; N Bernaz, 'Continuing evolution of the United Nations treaty bodies system' in Sheeran and Rodley (n 5); NS Rodley, 'The Role and Impact of Treaty Bodies' in D Shelton (ed), *The Oxford Handbook of International Human Rights Law* (Oxford, Oxford University Press, 2013).

[19] UN Treaty Body Database, available at https://tbinternet.ohchr.org/_layouts/15/TreatyBodyExternal/treaty.aspx.

[20] See section III below.

[21] C Heyns and M Killander, 'Universality and the Growth of Regional Systems' in Shelton (n 18).

[22] P Leach, 'The European system and approach' in Sheeran and Rodley (n 5).

[23] S Sayapin, 'Sleduyet li Kazakhstanu ratifitsirovat Evropeyskuyu konventsiyu o zashchite prav cheloveka?' ['Should Kazakhstan ratify the European Convention on Human Rights?'], 25 March 2016, available at online.zakon.kz/Document/?doc_id=35064919.

rights.[24] In 1993, the CIS established a Human Rights Commission with a mandate to consider inter-State communications as well as communications from individuals and NGOs. However, the Commission has not been very active as a matter of practice.[25] It is suggested that the States of the region contemplate the establishment of a Central Asian Court of Human Rights.[26] The idea of a Central Asian Union has been in the air for a few years now,[27] and if it ever materialises, the new integration project should most definitely provide for a Central Asian human rights mechanism.

B. Islamic Origins of Human Rights

Human rights are traditionally regarded as a product of Western civilisation. However, this approach is not quite accurate in historical terms. As early as in the seventh century CE, more than a millennium before the French and American Revolutions, the Islamic civilisation – of which Central Asia was later an important centre[28] – produced ideas and practices that could be regarded as reflective of human rights in their modern understanding. The Holy Quran – of which some 500 *ayats* (verses) contain rules of law – regulates, in particular, some marriage and family matters, inheritance, and includes a number of criminal law rules.[29] After the Holy Quran, the Sunnah of the Prophet Muhammad (570–632) is the second most important source of Islamic Law. Edited by some of the learned authorities of the early age of Islam, the Sunnah are authoritative collections of the Prophet's verbal statements and acts (*hadiths*) pertaining to various aspects of the Islamic faith.[30] Among the six most influential collections of *hadiths* compiled by the Sunni scholars, two were produced in Central Asia – by Imam Al-Bukhari (810–70), and Imam Al-Termizi (824–92). On this account, Central Asia is rightfully regarded as one of the world's centres of medieval knowledge – in particular, Islamic law.

[24] For the text of the Convention (in Russian), see: eccis.org/page/11326/konvencii-sodruzestva-nezavisimyh-gosudarstv-o-pravah-i-osnovnyh-svobodah-celoveka-26-maa-1995-g-minsk.

[25] See: e-cis.info/cooperation/3850/.

[26] S Sayapin, 'Rethinking Humanitarian and Human Rights Institutions for Asia' in V Popovski and A Malhotra (eds), *Reimagining the International Legal Order* (Abingdon, Routledge, 2024).

[27] See Chapter 3, section IV.H above.

[28] See SF Starr, *Utrachennoye prosveshcheniye: Zolotoy vek Tsentralnoy Azii ot arabskogo zavoyevaniya do vremen Tamerlana* [*Lost Enlightenment: Central Asia's Golden Age from the Arab Conquest to Tamerlane*] (Moscow, Alpina Publisher, 2019).

[29] M Sarsembayev, *Mezhdunarodnoye pravo v istorii Kazakhstana i Sredney Azii* [*International law in the history of Central Asia*] (Astana, Foliant, 2011), 28–29.

[30] M Rohe, *Islamskoye pravo: istoriya i sovremennost* [*Islamic Law: History and Contemporaneity*] (Moscow, Medina, 2019), 73. The Sunni Muslims also recognise the veracity of *hadiths* attributable to the Rashidun (or the four Rightly Guided Caliphs), whereas the Shia Muslims only acknowledge the *hadiths* deriving from the fourth Caliph, ibid, 74.

The human rights rules reflected in the *hadiths* are strikingly progressive even by modern standards. For example, some of them describe life as a superior value:

> The sins of the first order include: reverence with Allah on an equal footing with another deity; disobedience towards parents; depriving a person of life, and perjury (in court).[31]

It is confirmed elsewhere that murder is the most abhorrent crime:

> The cases that [on the Day of Judgment] will be dealt with in the first place are cases related to bloodshed.[32]

Judges are called upon to administer justice without undue emotion – that is, objectively and neutrally:

> No judge shall judge two opponents while in a state of anger.[33]

Another *hadith* pertains to consumers' rights:

> Whoever sells a thing, knowing that it has a defect, and does not inform the customer about this defect, will forever remain under the wrath of Allah.[34]

This *hadith* is very explicit in protecting one's dwelling and privacy:

> If someone sneaks into your house and you throw a stone at him, damaging his eyesight, you will not have sinned.[35]

And this one obviously seeks to protect women's rights in the family:

> According to faith in God, the best of believers is the one who best follows the rules of good manners and is kindest to his wife.[36]

The following *hadith* noticeably resonates with the right to self-determination codified in Article 1 common to both International Covenants of 1966:

> The people of each country jointly own drinking springs, forests and pastures, and energy reserves.[37]

And this one calls for the consolidation of social solidarity and, more generally, peace:

> The most hated by Allah is the one who most gives rise to quarrels with opponents.[38]

[31] Reported by Al-Bukhari, quoted in *Hadisy Proroka, perevod i kommentarii Iman Valerii Porokhovoy* [*The Hadiths of the Prophet, Translation and Comments by Iman Valeriya Porokhova*] (Moscow, Ripol Classic, 2006), 102.
[32] ibid, 153.
[33] ibid, 119.
[34] ibid, 121.
[35] ibid, 188.
[36] ibid, 195.
[37] ibid, 167.
[38] ibid, 173.

These and other examples allow one to draw clear parallels with modern rules of IHRL, and to make a few important conclusions. First, not only is the idea of human rights not at all alien to Islamic Law, but in historical terms, it even precedes analogous European concepts by several centuries. Second, the fact that two of the most authoritative collections of the *hadiths* were compiled and edited by Central Asian scholars emphasises the historical role of the region in the development of human rights ideas. Third, this role was not accidental – although the editors of the *hadiths* had to travel long distances in order to get hold of the teachings and verify them,[39] the recording and preservation of the *hadiths* would not have been possible without Central Asia's sophisticated urban culture (and libraries) along the Great Silk Road. In the centuries that followed, the nomadic neighbours of Central Asia's sedentary nations developed a distinct legal culture, which also merits an account.

C. Human Rights in the Sources of Kazakh Nomadic Law

The Kazakh Khanate produced a notable corpus of Turkic customary law.[40] In the early sixteenth century, Qassym Khan (1445/55–1521) promulgated the earliest code, *The Light Way of Qassym Khan*, which, like Genghis Khan's *Yassa* (1206) consisted of five sections – property law, criminal law, military law, ambassadorial custom, and public law.[41] About a century later, Yessim Khan (1565–1628) enacted amendments to Qassym Khan's code, and promulgated *The Ancient Way of Yessim Khan*: 'The [new] law was widely accepted by the people, whereby the norms of *adat* were more acceptable than Sharia Law due to cattle breeding'.[42] Finally, towards the end of the seventeenth century, Tauke Khan (1635–1718) ordered another revision of Kazakhs' customary law, which resulted in the adoption of *Zhety Zhargy* ('Seven Regulations'), with contributions by the Three Great Biys (Judges) – Tole Bi (1663–1756), Qazybek Bi (1667–1763), and Aiteke Bi (1682–1766).

According to *Qazaqstan Taryhy*,

> [t]he main principles, based on which Tauke wanted to unite the Kazakhs, were the principles of strict subordination of the younger to the elders (children – to parents, wife – to her husband, subordinate – to the ruler); [and] the principle of collective responsibility ([of] a person before the clan, [or] the clan for each of its members). Criminal punishment was based on the principle of talion (blood for blood) but the death penalty (4 types) could always be replaced by a ransom (kun).[43]

[39] Starr (n 28), 168.
[40] On the Kazakh Khanate, see Chapter 2, section I.A above.
[41] Qazaqstan Tarihy, 'Pervye zakony Stepi' ['The First Laws of the Steppe'], 29 August 2014, available at e-history.kz/ru/news/show/6277/.
[42] ibid.
[43] ibid.

Some of *Zhety Zhargy*'s more specific rules were as follows:

- blood for blood, therefore, for the murder of a person, a ransom is due (for a man – 1000 rams; for a woman – 500 rams);
- for theft, robbery, violence, the death penalty is applied; punishment can be mitigated by paying a ransom;
- for the injury, a ransom is paid, commensurate with the damage caused (for a thumb – 100 rams; for the little finger – 20 rams);
- for the murder of her husband by a woman, the death penalty is applied (when the relatives of the murdered person forgive her guilt, the death penalty is replaced by a ransom; when such a crime is committed by a pregnant woman, she is exempted from retribution);
- violence against a woman is equated with the murder of a person. For such a crime, the woman's husband or the girl's parents are paid a ransom. If the perpetrator pays a ransom and marries the raped girl, he is released from punishment.[44]

The rules limiting the application of the death penalty were evidently progressive in that they were aimed at saving lives in the demanding conditions of the Great Steppe. Although the Turkic customary law included some elements of the Sharia Law, most of its rules were authentic and specifically designed to apply among the nomadic peoples of Central Asia. Now, it will be curious to see how these rules fit within the broader mosaic of the universal rules of modern IHRL.

II. INTERNATIONAL HUMAN RIGHTS

A. Civil and Political Rights

Civil and political rights are codified in Articles 3–15, 18–21 of the UDHR and Articles 6–27 of the ICCPR, and are reaffirmed in all thematic human rights instruments. Civil rights are the most fundamental rights inherent in the human person. Given their essential character, they are often referred to as the 'first generation' of internationally recognised human rights.[45] They find their intellectual origins in core values deriving from various philosophical, ethical, and religious paradigms. Civil rights include, for example, the right to life,[46] prohibition of torture and other ill-treatment,[47] freedom from discrimination,[48] and the right to liberty and security of person.[49] In turn, political rights enable individuals – as social and political actors – to participate meaningfully in the

[44] Qazaqstan Tarihy, 'Sem faktov o "Zhety Zhargy"' ['Seven Facts about "Zhety Zhargy"'], 20 April 2015, available at e-history.kz/ru/projects/show/23217. Notably, the latter rule survives, as a matter of practice, to this day and exists parallel to statutory provisions on rape.

[45] Alston and Goodman (n 1), 157–276; Bantekas and Oette (n 1), 350–410.

[46] Smith (n 1), 238–56. See also N Rodley, *The Treatment of Prisoners under International Law* (Oxford, Oxford University Press, 1999), 177–242.

[47] Smith (n 1), 312–29; Rodley (n 46), 18–176.

[48] Smith (n 1), 185–209.

[49] bid, 257–73; Rodley (n 46), 243–353.

life of their communities, society and the government of the State. The 'first generation' of human rights is characteristically traced back to the *Magna Carta* (1215),[50] the United States' Declaration of Independence (1776)[51] and its Constitution (in force since 1789),[52] and the French Declaration of the Rights of Man and the Citizen (1789).[53] Such understanding of civil, and especially political, rights is clearly Eurocentric, and fails to take account of the human rights legacy offered by non-Western legal traditions.[54]

It is often said that in order for civil and political rights to be respected, negative obligations on the part of States – that is, obligations to refrain from interference with such rights – must be fulfilled. This approach is certainly correct in that States may not deprive human beings of their lives arbitrarily, torture or deprive them of their status as persons before the law, among other things. But at the same time, it is a simplification. As Bantekas and Oette observe, the

> implementation [of human rights standards] requires certain structures without which it is unlikely that core civil and political rights can be effectively protected. The rule of law, the administration of justice and democratic institutions are key components in this regard.[55]

In addition to structures, compliance with civil and political rights also entails significant active efforts on the part of States: for example, law enforcement officials and judges must be trained properly, so that lethal force is not used excessively, due process rights are respected, and torture is prevented. Similarly, in order to reduce the infant mortality rate and thus protect the right to life, States should invest in training qualified medical personnel and equipping hospitals. More generally, in order to advance a culture of respect for human rights, consistent efforts must be applied through the State education systems, in collaboration with civil society.[56]

B. Non-derogable Human Rights

The COVID-19 pandemic compelled the Central Asian States – and, in fact, virtually all States – to derogate from their obligations under the

[50] Britannica, 'Marna Carta', available at www.britannica.com/topic/Magna-Carta.

[51] For the text of the Declaration, see: www.archives.gov/founding-docs/declaration-transcript.

[52] For the text of the US Constitution, see: https://www.archives.gov/founding-docs/constitution-transcript.

[53] For the text of the Declaration, see: https://www.elysee.fr/en/french-presidency/the-declaration-of-the-rights-of-man-and-of-the-citizen. From a modern perspective, the title of the Declaration is clearly sexist.

[54] See sections I.B–I.C above.

[55] Bantekas and Oette (n 1), 350–51.

[56] Smith (n 1), 398–402.

ICCPR to various extents. Article 4(1) of the ICCPR stipulates in this regard that:

> [i]n time of public emergency which threatens the life of the nation and the existence of which is officially proclaimed, the States Parties to the present Covenant may take measures derogating from their obligations under the present Covenant to the extent strictly required by the exigencies of the situation, provided that such measures are not inconsistent with their other obligations under international law and do not involve discrimination solely on the ground of race, colour, sex, language, religion or social origin.

In other words, the validity of derogations is made conditional on States' compliance with the requirements of legitimate authority, proportionality, limited duration, consistency with other obligations under international law, and non-discrimination.[57] Article 4(2) provides further that there is a 'core' of civil and political rights, from which no derogation may be made under Article 4(1). These include the right to life (Article 6); the prohibition of torture or inhuman or degrading treatment or punishment (Article 7); the prohibition of slavery, the slave trade, and servitude (Article 8(1), (2)); the prohibition of imprisonment merely on the ground of one's inability to fulfil a contractual obligation (Article 11); non-retroactivity of criminal law (Article 15); the right to recognition everywhere as a person before the law (Article 16); and the right to freedom of thought, conscience and religion (Article 18). In Central Asia, the importance of these rules is underscored by a history of excessive use of force, torture in detention, forced labour, due process violations, and pressure on certain religious groups.[58]

C. Economic, Social and Cultural Rights

Economic, social and cultural (ESC) rights are known as the 'second generation' of human rights.[59] They are codified in Articles 16–17, 22–27 of the UDHR and Articles 6–15 of the ICESCR, and, like civil and political rights, are reaffirmed in some thematic human rights instruments – dealing, in particular, with the rights of women[60] and children,[61] migrant workers and members of their families,[62]

[57] De Schutter (n 1), 607–54.

[58] See section III for more details.

[59] Bantekas and Oette (n 1), 412–61; P Hunt, J Bueno, J-Y Lee and S-A Way, 'Implementation of economic, social and cultural rights' in Sheeran and Rodley (n 5).

[60] A Byrnes, 'Gender challenges for international human rights' in Sheeran and Rodley (n 5); C Bunch, 'Women and Gender' in TG Weiss and S Daws (eds), *The Oxford Handbook on the United Nations* (Oxford, Oxford University Press, 2007).

[61] Y Beigbeder, 'Children' in Weiss and Daws (n 60).

[62] IOM, 'The Human Rights of Migrants', available at https://publications.iom.int/system/files/pdf/migrants_human_rights.pdf.

and persons with disabilities.[63] This 'generation' of human rights dates back to industrialisation in the second half of the nineteenth century, and was, in the twentieth century, actively promoted by the Soviet Union and its allies in the developing world.

It should be noted that the characterisation of ESC rights as the 'second generation' does not mean that they are 'secondary'. Indeed, some authors argue that 'many' civil and political rights are

> meaningless without ESC rights. By way of illustration, the right to life is to some degree dependent on adequate food and water, decent housing and health care. Equally, a decent education is a good platform for an informed exercise of the freedom of expression.[64]

Indeed, the very fact that the UDHR listed both groups of human rights, and that both International Covenants were adopted at the same time suggests that all human rights should be treated as indivisible and interdependent.

The catalogue of rights in the ICESCR is extensive: the right to work (Article 6); the enjoyment of just and favourable conditions of work (Article 7);[65] the right to form and join trade unions (Article 8); the right to social security, including social insurance (Article 9); the protection of, and assistance to, the family, mothers, children and young persons (Article 10); the right to an adequate standard of living, including adequate food, clothing and housing, and to the continuous improvement of living conditions (Article 11); the right to the enjoyment of the highest attainable standard of physical and mental health (Article 12); the right to education (Article 13);[66] and the right of everyone to take part in cultural life, to enjoy the benefits of scientific progress and its applications, and to benefit from the protection of the moral and material interests resulting from any scientific, literary or artistic production of which he or she is the author (Article 14). Most ESC rights have been implemented in the Central Asian States' Constitutions and relevant domestic laws (eg the Labour, Housing and Family Codes, laws on education, intellectual property, healthcare and others). Yet, since ESC rights entail positive obligations on the part of States – that is, they require States to continuously allocate resources for their progressive realisation – more work needs to be accomplished throughout the region. Access to high-quality primary and secondary education should be improved, especially in rural areas. Poverty remains a problem.[67] Especially in light of the

[63] Human Rights Watch, 'Disability Rights', available at https://www.hrw.org/topic/disability-rights.

[64] Bantekas and Oette (n 1), 413.

[65] Smith (n 1), 296–311.

[66] LM Nevara, 'Mizhnarodno-pravova osnova prava na osvitu v sistemi prav lyudyny' ['The International Legal Foundation of the Right to Education in the Human Rights System'] in V Repetsky and V Gutnyk (eds), *Current Problems of International Law* (Odessa, Phoenix Press, 2017).

[67] U Baxi, 'International development, global impoverishment and human rights' in Sheeran and Rodley (n 5).

recent COVID-19 pandemic, the Central Asian states should make concerted efforts to improve their healthcare systems. Crucially, urgent measures must be taken to raise the prestige of the medical and pedagogical professions.[68]

D. Collective Rights

Whereas most human rights are individual – that is, they are due to each and every person, without discrimination, and are individually justiciable and enforceable before the courts – some other rights make sense in groups.[69] Important entitlements such as the right of peoples to self-determination (cf Article 1 of the ICCPR and ICESCR),[70] the emerging right to peace,[71] or the rights of minorities[72] or indigenous peoples[73] hold little meaning when considered solely in individual terms. A single person simply cannot form or govern a State and, in that sense, claim to be an individual subject of the right to self-determination. It therefore makes full sense that the Constitutions of all Central Asian States stipulate, in their respective provisions, that the respective 'peoples' as a whole are the only source of State power.[74] Given that all Central Asian societies are polyethnic and representative of multiple religious, the maintenance of inclusivity with due regard to the rights of minorities is crucial.

Notably, in the developing world, the role of local communities and other collectivities in the shaping and development of individual personalities has always been prominent. One may recall provisions on solidarity rights featuring in the African Charter on Human and Peoples' Rights (ACHPR)[75] – for example, on the right to continued existence (Article 20), the right to development (Article 22), or the right to a generally satisfactory environment (Article 24). Obviously, these rights also make sense in the Central Asian – and, for that matter, many other – country contexts.[76] Collectivism is a strong factor in

[68] See section III for more details.

[69] Bantekas and Oette (n 1), 464–66.

[70] Smith (n 1), 330–47; Bantekas and Oette (n 1), 466–78.

[71] On the emerging culture of peace, see Chapter 10, section X above.

[72] Bantekas and Oette (n 1), 478–90; Smith (n 1), 349–64.

[73] Bantekas and Oette (n 1), 490–506; Smith (n 1), 364–74; M Genovese, 'Legal Pluralism in Practice: Colombia's New Framework for Indigenous Territorial Self-Government', EJIL:Talk!, 3 July 2025, available at www.ejiltalk.org/legal-pluralism-in-practice-colombias-new-framework-for-indigenous-territorial-self-government/.

[74] Constitution of Kazakhstan, Art 3(1); Constitution of Kyrgyzstan, Art 1(4); Constitution of Tajikistan, Art 6, first para; Constitution of Turkmenistan, Art 3, first para; Constitution of Uzbekistan, Art 7, first para.

[75] F Viljoen, 'The impact and influence of the African regional system on domestic law' in Sheeran and Rodley (n 5).

[76] M Namanya, 'The Inter-American Court's Advisory Opinion on the Climate Emergency and Human Rights: A Win for Climate-Displaced Persons?', EJIL:Talk!, 29 July 2025, available at www.ejiltalk.org/the-inter-american-courts-advisory-opinion-on-the-climate-emergency-and-human-

all Central Asian societies, as are various local and regional affiliations. This can lead to adverse effects – such as conflicts between clans, nepotism and corruption – but can also result in remarkable institutional developments such as the traditional *mahalla* network in Uzbekistan, which has a role to play in matters ranging from marriage, family, and divorce, to the maintenance of communal territories, to local self-governance and public safety. It is observable (and perfectly acceptable) that some Central Asian perspectives on human rights are different from Western ones. However, the reasonable argument of 'cultural relativism' should not be taken so far as to render essential human rights protections meaningless.[77] The current stigmatisation of some groups – for example, sexual minorities – at times reaches the level of denial of their right to be recognised as persons before the law,[78] which is unacceptable in States claiming to be law-governed.

E. 'New' Rights

Industrial and technological developments in the twentieth and twenty-first centuries have brought about dramatic changes, which were difficult, if not impossible, to imagine in the early decades of modern IHRL. These include, in particular, climate change,[79] globalisation, and the emergence of cyberspace. In Central Asia, the former challenge manifested itself, above all, in a catastrophic desertification of the Aral Sea, and other environmental issues.[80] The new environmental reality has given rise to new dimensions in the human rights discourse. The Aral Sea catastrophe has resulted in the loss of human and animal life, the deterioration of the economic and social quality of life, and widespread physical and mental health issues. Now that the catastrophe seems to be physically

rights-a-win-for-climate-displaced-persons/; J Auz, 'The Inter-American Court of Human Rights' Advisory Opinion on the Climate Emergency: A Global South Contribution to Climate Governance', EJIL:Talk!, 18 July 2025, available at www.ejiltalk.org/the-inter-american-court-of-human-rights-advisory-opinion-on-the-climate-emergency-a-global-south-contribution-to-climate-governance/.

[77] M Freeman, 'Universalism of human rights and cultural relativism' in Sheeran and Rodley (n 5); VV Mitsyk, 'Kontseptsii universalnosti i kulturnogo relyativizma prav cheloveka v mezhdunarodnom prave' ['The Concepts of Universality and Cultural Relativism of Human Rights in International Law'] in A Melnyk, S Melnyk and T Korotkyi (eds), *Mezhdunarodnoye pravo kak osnova sovremennogo miroporyadka* [*International Law as the Foundation of Modern World Order*] (Odessa, Phoenix Press, 2012).

[78] RadioFreeEurope / RadioLiberty, 'Sexual Minorities In Kazakhstan Hide Who They Are To Avoid Abuse', 19 June 2021, available at https://www.rferl.org/a/kazakhstan-lgbt-hide-from-abuse/31316186.html.

[79] Alston and Goodman (n 1), 1516–46; K Hulme, 'International environmental law and human rights' in Sheeran and Rodley (n 5); P Rundel, 'Is It Time? On the Recognition of the Human Right to a Healthy Environment in Europe', Völkerrrechtsblog, 10 September 2024, available at voelkerrechtsblog.org/is-it-time/.

[80] Fergana News, 'VB: 65 tysyach ezhegodnyh rannih smertey v Tsentralnoy Azii svyazany s zagryazneniyem vozduha' ['World Bank: 65,000 Annual Early Deaths in Central Asia are Linked to Air Pollution'], 24 June 2025, available at fergana.agency/news/138572/.

irreversible, the Central Asian States ought to devise, in a cooperative way, workable and human rights-compliant policies aimed at mitigating the adverse effects.[81] Such national and regional policies should encompass economic, medical and social dimensions, and may involve compensations, medical treatment and rehabilitation, and, as the case may be, resettlement of affected populations.

Globalisation provides enormous economic opportunities but also brings along notable threats.[82] In Central Asia, in the past 30 years, the income gap has visibly widened, and even in Kazakhstan, the leading Central Asian economy, in 2021, about 8.5 per cent of the population were living in poverty.[83] According to the Asian Development Bank, in 2024, 8.9 per cent of Uzbekistan's population were living below the national poverty line.[84] For decades, millions of citizens, especially of Tajikistan, Uzbekistan, and Kyrgyzstan, were seeking seasonal employment abroad, chiefly in the Russian Federation, at the risk of humiliation, extortion and mistreatment by police, involvement in illegal activities, and human trafficking. Until 2016, the government of Uzbekistan largely ignored the problem of labour migration. In the past few years, the situation started changing for the better, and the authorities of Uzbekistan are making efforts to legalise the labour migration processes and protect the rights of labour migrants, by concluding agreements on the regulation of labour migration with foreign States, opening consultation centres for prospective migrants, and, probably most importantly, improving the situation on the local labour market by creating new workplaces.

Finally, access to the Internet is a matter of concern in many Central Asian contexts.[85] On the one hand, such access is now indispensable for quality education (including, but not only, in the context of the pandemic) and academic research, business, and communication. On the other hand, cyberspace is increasingly used for financial and other cybercrime, transnational organised crime, and recruitment into ISIS and other terrorist groups, and States should certainly take effective measures to respond to cyberthreats. However, such responses must be proportionate to the threats, and if States introduce restrictions on access to the Internet, these must be prescribed by law and necessary, with due regard to Article 19(3) of the ICCPR. Excessive restrictions – such as in Turkmenistan, or the blocking of independent media outlets – are hard to justify.

[81] See Chapter 2, section IV.G above.

[82] Bantekas and Oette (n 1), 878–900.

[83] World Bank Group, 'Kazakhstan: Poverty and Equity Assessment 2024', Executive Summary p 10, available at https://documents1.worldbank.org/curated/en/099121024150515312/pdf/P501104-791e5cc5-12d2-4e7c-9b3d-6b0aecd7cc53.pdf.

[84] Asian Development Bank, 'Poverty Data: Uzbekistan', available at https://www.adb.org/where-we-work/uzbekistan/poverty.

[85] Human Rights Watch, 'How are the Authorities in Central Asia Trying to Control the Internet?', 18 November 2021, available at https://www.hrw.org/news/2021/11/18/how-are-authorities-central-asia-trying-control-internet.

III. HUMAN RIGHTS DYNAMICS IN CENTRAL ASIA[86]

A. Kazakhstan

An economic leader in the region, Kazakhstan also positions itself as a regional political power with a multi-vector foreign policy. Since 1991, it has been trying to balance its development priorities with other commitments, including under IHRL, with varying degrees of success. In 1993, the Bolashak scholarship was instituted, to let talented Kazakhstani youth obtain world-class higher education abroad. In the same year, a highly efficient human rights NGO – the Kazakhstan International Bureau for Human Rights and Rule of Law – was established.

A moratorium on the death penalty has been in place since 1 January 2004, and in 2020, Kazakhstan acceded to the Second Optional Protocol to the International Covenant on Civil and Political Rights (ICCPR), and abolished the death penalty in accordance with its provisions. In 2013, a National Preventive Mechanism (NPM) was put in place to reinforce combatting torture and other ill-treatment.[87] Since the Russian annexation of Crimea in 2014, the State has introduced a programme of ethnic Kazakhs' voluntary resettlement to the north of the country, and several nationals of Kazakhstan were sentenced under Article 172 of the Criminal Code for taking part in the ongoing armed conflict in eastern Ukraine. Anti-corruption reforms have included the establishment of an efficient system of e-government (Egov), and a network of public service centres (TSON). Legislation on trade unions was amended in 2020.

On the other hand, quite a few issues have attracted the attention of domestic and international human rights monitors. As of this writing, one individual complaint has been considered under the Optional Protocol to the Convention on the Elimination of All Forms of Discrimination against Women, 17 individual complaints have been submitted under the Convention against Torture, and 85 individual complaints considered under the First Optional Protocol to the ICCPR.[88] On 16–17 December 2011, police used force against protesters in Zhanaozen,

[86] This section uses the author's material published in S Sayapin, 'Human Rights in Post-Soviet Central Asia' in L Leontiev and P Amarasinghe (eds), *Thirty Years Looking Back: State-Building, Rule of Law, Good Governance and Human Rights in the Post-Soviet Space* (Abingdon, Routledge, 2022), and in the State Report sections of the *Asian Yearbook of International Law* (2021–23), with selected footnotes omitted. Permissions to use published material are gratefully acknowledged.

[87] Fergana News, 'Eks-glavu sluzhby spetsprokurorov Kazahstana Keksel zapodozriki v pytkah–vo vtoroy raz' ['Former Head of Kazakhstan's Special Prosecutors Service Keksel Suspected of Torture – for the Second Time'], 14 July 2025, available at fergana.agency/news/138918/; Fergana News, 'Byvshego glavu kazahstanskogo Antikora zaderzhali po delu o pytkah' ['Former Head of Kazakhstan's Anticorruption Agency Detained in Torture Case'], 4 July 2025, available at fergana.agency/news/138766/.

[88] See data at: tbinternet.ohchr.org/_layouts/15/TreatyBodyExternal/Countries.aspx?CountryCode=KAZ&Lang=EN.

as a result of which 17 persons were killed, and more than 100 were wounded, according to official data.[89] Domestic violence remains widespread, and sexual violence – including against children – continues to be a serious concern. In 2019 and 2020, criminal responsibility for sexual crimes was reinforced.[90] In 2025, criminal responsibility for bride kidnapping was introduced.[91]

After the First President of Kazakhstan, Nursultan Nazarbayev, resigned on 19 March 2019, Dr Kassym-Jomart Tokayev was elected President on 9 June 2019, and heralded a number of human rights reforms. In particular, the concept of a 'hearing State' was announced, with a view to improving the quality of dialogue with civil society; legislation on peaceful assemblies was revised; and, in 2021, a reform of electoral law took place. On 29 December 2021, the Law 'On the Legal Status of Foreigners' was amended. In particular, Article 18 of the Law, as amended, reads that '[f]oreigners in Kazakhstan shall have the right to appeal to the courts, the Commissioner for Human Rights in Kazakhstan and other public authorities for the protection of their property and personal non-property rights'.

As a result of the January 2022 tragic events,[92] far-reaching reforms to the country's political system were announced. In particular, 'President Tokayev proposed a series of reforms aimed at building what he has termed as "New Kazakhstan" or "Just and Fair Kazakhstan". This included amendments to the country's laws, including the Constitution, as approved by the nationwide referendum'.[93] However, the implementation of these initiatives has been inconsistent. In October 2023, Kazakhstan's Parliamentarian Zharkynbek Zharkynbekov sparked controversy by suggesting that women who are victims of domestic violence should be held accountable for their abuse. In the same month, Human Rights Watch and eight other organisations called on Kazakhstan to abolish its 'foreign funding register', a publicly accessible list of individuals and entities receiving foreign financial support.[94] Critics argued that the register stigmatised civil society actors and human rights defenders, potentially exposing them to harassment and retaliation.

[89] Radio Azattyq, 'Zhanaozen. Nezazhivayushaya rana' ['Zhanaozen – an Unhealing Wound'], 16 December 2020, rus.azattyq.org/a/kazakhstan-zhanaozen-2011-documentary-azattyq-12162020/31002595.html.

[90] See Arts 120–124 of the Criminal Code.

[91] Sputnik Kazakhstan, 'Za pohishcheniye nevesty mogut posadit na 10 let: v chem sut podpisannyh Tokayevm popravok' ['Kidnapping a Bride Can Lead to 10 Years in Prison: What is the Essence of the Amendments Signed by Tokayev'], 16 July 2025, available at ru.sputnik.kz/20250716/za-pokhischenie-nevesty-mogut-posadit-na-10-let-v-chem-sut-podpisannykh-tokaevym-popravok-55682438.html.

[92] See Chapter 10, section IX.E above.

[93] Euraktiv Events, 'Kazakhstan in 2022 – A Seismic Year of Change and Unprecedented Regional Geopolitics', 28 November 2022, available at events.euractiv.com/event/info/kazakhstan-a-new-geopolitical-role-in-central-asia.

[94] Human Rights Watch, 'Kazakhstan: Abolish the "Foreign Funding" Register', 20 October 2023, available at hrw.org/news/2023/10/20/kazakhstan-abolish-foreign-funding-register.

B. Kyrgyzstan

Kyrgyzstan is a paradoxical nation. Often referred to as Central Asia's 'island of democracy',[95] Kyrgyzstan experienced two revolutions (in 2005 and 2010), which suggests that the political system's ability for peaceful power transition is limited, albeit in a way that is different from its neighbours. The country's political landscape has been dominated by competition for power between the 'North' and the 'South' ever since 1991. Organised crime remains a major concern. Kyrgyzstan retains a strong Soviet legacy: the statues of Lenin, Marx, and Engels are standing in the centre of Bishkek, and the Party of Kyrgyzstan's Communists is active. Russia's influence in politics, the economy, military affairs, and higher education is strong: Kyrgyzstan has been a member of the Eurasian Economic Union (EAEU, since 2015), it hosts a Joint Russian military base, and the Kyrgyz–Russian Slavonic University (KRSU) was established in 1992.[96] At the same time, Kyrgyzstan's higher education market hosts the American University of Central Asia (AUCA, founded in 1993), and the OSCE Academy in Bishkek (founded in 2002). Until 2021, non-governmental organisations, including local and international human rights NGOs, could operate relatively freely.

As of the time of writing, one individual complaint has been submitted against Kyrgyzstan under the Optional Protocol to the Convention on the Elimination of All Forms of Discrimination against Women, and the Human Rights Committee has considered no fewer than 66 individual complaints under the First Optional Protocol to the ICCPR.[97] Violence against women and girls is frequent. Although explicitly proscribed by Article 175 of the Criminal Code, bride kidnapping remains a pressing issue. Massive inter-ethnic violence, which erupted in the south of the country in June 2010, and likely amounted to crimes against humanity,[98] has not been fully investigated,[99] and a prominent human rights defender, ethnic Uzbek Azimjon Askarov, who had been given a life sentence, died in prison on 25 July 2020.

Since 1991, Kyrgyzstan has enacted three Constitutions – in 1993, 2010, and, most recently, in 2021. The 1993 Constitution was amended on several occasions with a view to reinforcing the authority of the President. After Presidents Askar

[95] J Anderson, *Kyrgyzstan: Central Asia's Island of Democracy?* (Abingdon, Routledge, 1999).

[96] Fergana News, 'Putin utverdil vydeleniye 15 mlrd rubley na stroitelstvo novogo kampusa RTSU pod Bishkekom' ['Putin Approved the Allocation of 15 Billion Rubles for the Construction of a New KRSU Campus Near Bishkek'], 27 June 2025, available at fergana.agency/news/138643/.

[97] See data at: tbinternet.ohchr.org/_layouts/15/TreatyBodyExternal/Countries.aspx?CountryCode=KGZ&Lang=EN.

[98] Amnesty International, 'Kyrgyzstan Must Deliver Justice to Victims of Crimes against Humanity', 10 May 2011, www.amnestyusa.org/press-releases/kyrgyzstan-must-deliver-justice-to-victims-of-crimes-against-humanity-2-2/.

[99] Kyrgyzstan introduced the concept of crimes against humanity in its Criminal Code in 2016, and is the only Central Asian State to have done so. See S Sayapin, 'Why a Crimes against Humanity Convention from a Perspective of Post-Soviet States?' (2020) 6 *African Journal of International Criminal Justice* 125, 130–34.

Akayev and Kurmanbek Bakiyev had been ousted from office, inter alia, on the grounds of corruption and abuse of power, the 2010 Constitution replaced the presidential republic with a parliamentary one. The most recent Constitution was enacted on 5 May 2021. It consolidated the power of the President in that it transferred

> power from the parliament to the president to appoint members of the cabinet, and appoint and dismiss judges, the prosecutor general, the chairman of the National Bank and of the Accounting Chamber, as well as nominate and dismiss half of the Central Election Committee, undermining their independence from the executive.[100]

The new Constitution also placed restrictions on the rights to freedom of expression, assembly, and association, and introduced new regulations for NGOs and political parties.

In 2022, there were growing concerns over human rights developments in the country. More specifically,

> [i]n June, the UN special rapporteur on extreme poverty urged the authorities to invest more in pre-primary education, improve the quality of schools, and strengthen its social protection system for persons in poverty, as well as tackle the problem of corruption.[101]

The 2023 Human Rights Report for the Kyrgyz Republic, released by the US Department of State, indicated no significant changes in the human rights situation during the year. Credible reports detailed issues such as torture by law enforcement officers, harsh prison conditions, arbitrary arrests, judicial independence problems, restrictions on freedom of expression and media, government corruption, gender-based violence, and significant restrictions on workers' freedom of association.[102]

C. Tajikistan

Complicated by religion, competition for power among regional clans, social traditions, and the enduring legacy of a violent non-international armed conflict of 1992–97, the human rights situation in Tajikistan is quite tense. Domestic violence is widespread, and early marriages occur. Arbitrary detentions of opposition supporters and attacks against journalists have been recorded. The situation is exacerbated by the weakness of Tajikistan's economy: in 2019,

[100] Human Rights Watch, 'Kyrgyzstan: Withdraw Problematic Draft Constitution', 5 March 2021, available at www.hrw.org/news/2021/03/05/kyrgyzstan-withdraw-problematic-draft-constitution.

[101] Human Rights Watch, 'Kyrgyzstan: Events of 2022', available at www.hrw.org/world-report/2023/country-chapters/kyrgyzstan.

[102] US Embassy to the Kyrgyz Republic, 'Kyrgyz Republic 2023 Human Rights Report', Executive Summary, available at kg.usembassy.gov/wp-content/uploads/sites/139/2024/05/528267_KYRGYZ-REPUBLIC-2023-HUMAN-RIGHTS-REPORT-1-1.pdf.

personal remittances received by families of Tajik labour migrants working abroad (primarily, in the Russian Federation) constituted 28.6 per cent of the overall GDP.[103] Like in Kyrgyzstan, Russia's influence in the politics, military affairs, and education space of Tajikistan is extensive. Tajikistan hosts Russia's 201st military base, is a member of the Collective Security Treaty Organization (CSTO), and the Tajik President Emomali Rakhmon – who had been in power since 1994 and appointed his elder son as mayor of Tajikistan's capital Dushanbe in 2017 – was the only foreign Head of State present at the annual Victory Parade in Moscow in 2021. The Russian-Tajik Slavonic University (RTSU) was founded in 1996, and is among the most popular higher education institutions in Tajikistan. In 2020–21, Russia invested up to US$30 million in the construction of Russian schools in Tajikistan. According to Article 2 of the Constitution of Tajikistan, Russian is the 'language of inter-ethnic communication'. With all these factors in place, Russian influence is likely to stay for decades to come.

As of the time of writing, the Human Rights Committee considered no fewer than 33 individual complaints under the First Optional Protocol to the ICCPR.[104] The COVID-19 pandemic posed a serious challenge to Tajikistan, as it did to the other Central Asian States, including regarding respect for human rights. Tajikistan did not acknowledge the existence of COVID-19 cases on its territory until 30 April 2020. According to Human Rights Watch, 'Tajik authorities have provided some information about how to prevent the spread of Covid-19 on government ministry websites, and have visited some schools, universities, and army bases to inform people about the disease'.[105] Still, 'they have not imposed a quarantine or encouraged social distancing in any meaningful way. The government did not cancel Nowruz, or New Year, festivities in late March, and schools, businesses, and most public spaces remain[ed] open'.[106] Obviously, apart from the right to the highest attainable standard of health, the COVID-19 pandemic also affected throughout Central Asia, inter alia, the right to education at all levels, access to justice, as well as the rights to freedom of movement, expression, and assembly.

As reported by Human Rights Watch, '[b]etween November 2021 and June 2022, at least 40 people were killed as a result of actions by security forces in [the Gorno Badakshan Autonomous Oblast (GBAO)] to quash protests by the region's population over perceived harassment and persecution'.[107]

[103] World Bank, 'Personal remittances, received (% of GDP) – Tajikistan', available at data.worldbank.org/indicator/BX.TRF.PWKR.DT.GD.ZS?locations=TJ.

[104] See data at: tbinternet.ohchr.org/_layouts/15/TreatyBodyExternal/Countries.aspx?CountryCode=TJK&Lang=EN.

[105] Human Rights Watch, 'Central Asia: Respect Rights in Covid-19 Responses', 23 April 2020, available at www.hrw.org/news/2020/04/23/central-asia-respect-rights-covid-19-responses.

[106] ibid.

[107] Human Rights Watch, 'Tajikistan: Events of 2022', available at www.hrw.org/world-report/2023/country-chapters/tajikistan.

On 4 April 2023, Human Rights Watch called for the immediate release of Manuchehr Kholiqnazarov, a prominent human rights lawyer from GBAO. He was sentenced to 16 years in prison in December 2022 for 'participation in a criminal association' and 'participating in the activities of a banned organisation due to its extremist activities'.[108] Human Rights Watch considered his detention a retaliation for his human rights advocacy and involvement in investigating the 2021 killing of Gulbiddin Ziyobekov, a Pamiri man whose death had sparked protests in GBAO.

D. Turkmenistan

Turkmenistan is the most complex Central Asian context. The authoritarian political system is rigidly controlled by the President, and independent human rights scrutiny is very difficult. In 1985, Mr Saparmurat Niyazov became First Secretary of the Turkmen Communist Party, and remained in power as the first President of Turkmenistan (*Türkmenbaşy* – 'Head of the Turkmen') until his death in December 2006. Turkmenistan became a permanently neutral State in 1995, and maintains conscription-based armed forces. During Mr Niyazov's time in power, opera, ballet, and circuses were banned (in 2001), the months of the year and weekdays were renamed (in 2002), and his two-volume book, *Ruhnama*, became mandatory reading at all schools, higher education institutions, and government agencies. Knowledge of its contents was required to qualify for a driving licence, and quotes from *Ruhnama*, along with those from the Quran, were built into the walls of the Türkmenbaşy Ruhy Mosque in Turkmenistan's capital city Ashgabat. Niyazov's successor, Gurbanguly Berdimuhamedow, also had sweeping powers in the largely isolated political system, and held the title of *Arkadag* ('Protector'). Berdimuhamedow published no fewer than 55 books on various subjects,[109] some of which people 'worship like bread or The Quran, kissing them upon receipt and applying the coveted tome to their foreheads'.[110] Meanwhile, the mass media are strictly censored, access to the Internet is limited, and political dissent is suppressed. Gurbanguly Berdimuhamedow's only son Serdar was a member of Parliament, held a few posts in the executive, was appointed Deputy Chairman of the Cabinet of Ministers on 11 February 2021, and was elected third President of Turkmenistan on 12 March 2022.

[108] Human Rights Watch, 'Tajikistan: Free Autonomous Region Rights Defender', 4 April 2023, available at www.hrw.org/news/2023/04/04/tajikistan-free-autonomous-region-rights-defender.

[109] Hronika Turkmenistana, 'Berdimuhamedow napisal knigu pro neytralitet Turkmenistana' ['Berdimuhamedow Wrote a Book about the Neutrality of Turkmenistan'], 5 December 2020, available at www.hronikatm.com/2020/12/neutrality-book/.

[110] V Polovinko, 'Arkadag i Okeaniya' ['Arkadag and Oceania'], 7 August 2020, available at novayagazeta.ru/articles/2020/08/07/86567-argadag-i-okeaniya.

The social and economic situation in the country is difficult. Turkmenistan did not report a single COVID-19 case up until June 2021[111] but already in July 2020, the World Health Organisation (WHO) was advising the Turkmen authorities to take 'critical public health measures … as if COVID-19 was circulating'.[112] On 3 June 2021, the Union Cycliste Internationale (UCI) announced that the 2021 Tissot UCI Track Cycling World Championships, which were scheduled to take place in Ashgabat on 13–17 October 2021 in Ashgabat, 'have been cancelled in their initial format, at the request of their organisers, as the health constraints and restrictions linked to the Covid-19 pandemic make it impossible to stage the event in the country'.[113] Earlier in 2021, food queues were banned, 'in order not to discredit the President'.[114] In 2022, according to Amnesty International:

> [s]erious human rights violations continued unabated across the board, including arbitrary detentions and politically motivated convictions of anyone daring to criticize or challenge official policy. The authorities continued to exercise strict control over the flow of information and all media. Turkmenistan failed to take meaningful action to address climate change. Women and girls saw their rights and freedoms, including bodily autonomy, restricted further. Abortion was effectively banned. Consensual sex between men remained a criminal offence.[115]

In 2023 and later, Turkmenistan's human rights record continued to reflect a closed society where fundamental freedoms were systematically suppressed. While some activists were released, many remain imprisoned on politically motivated charges, and enforced disappearances, torture, and ill-treatment persisted. Restrictions on civil society, media, and internet access continued, with persecution of activists and their families both within and outside the country. Forced labour in the cotton fields remained widespread, and citizens faced barriers to freedom of movement, including arbitrary denials of international travel.[116] As of the time of writing, one individual complaint has been submitted against Turkmenistan under the Optional Protocol to the Convention on the Elimination of All Forms of Discrimination against Women, and the Human Rights Committee has considered no fewer than 26 individual complaints under

[111] Fergana News, 'Ashhabad otkazalsya prinyat chempinat mira-2021 po velotreku' ['Ashgabat Refuses to Host the 2021 Track Cycling Championship'], 4 June 2021, available at fergana.agency/news/122194/.

[112] Reuters, 'WHO urges Turkmenistan to take steps "as if COVID-19 was circulating"', 15 July 2020, available at www.reuters.com/article/us-health-coronavirus-turkmenistan-idUSKCN24G276.

[113] See the UCI statement concerning the 2021 Tissot UCI Track Cycling World Championships, 3 June 2021, https://www.uci.org/pressrelease/uci-statement-concerning-the-2021-tissot-uci-track-cycling-world-championships/5U1rK2ytZT8RVLOMuznrO5.

[114] Radio Azattyq, 'V Turkmenistane zapretili ocheredi za produktami, chtoby ne diskreditirovat prezidenta' ['Turkmenistan Banned Food Queues in Order not to Discredit the President'], 28 April 2021, available at rus.azattyq.org/a/31227843.html.

[115] Amnesty International, 'Turkmenistan 2022', available at www.amnesty.org/en/location/europe-and-central-asia/eastern-europe-and-central-asia/turkmenistan/report-turkmenistan/.

[116] Human Rights Watch, 'Turkmenistan: Events of 2023', available at www.hrw.org/world-report/2024/country-chapters/turkmenistan.

the First Optional Protocol to the ICCPR.[117] The fact that these statistics are lower than those of the other Central Asian countries' is almost certainly due to practical obstacles in communicating the Turkmen cases to the Human Rights Committee and other human rights bodies.

E. Uzbekistan

Although the Universal Declaration of Human Rights was the first international legal instrument ratified by Uzbekistan after proclaiming its independence on 31 August 1991,[118] until 2016, the human rights record of the post-Soviet Uzbekistan was consistently problematic – indeed, Human Rights Watch called it 'abysmal'.[119] The powers of the Ministry of Interior and the National Security Service were sweeping, and it was not until 2016 that a Law on Internal Affairs Bodies was adopted, and in 2018 the National Security Service was reorganised into the State Security Service. As at the time of writing, one individual complaint has been submitted against Uzbekistan under the Convention against Torture, and the Human Rights Committee has considered no fewer than 61 individual complaints under the First Optional Protocol to the ICCPR.[120] According to the former UN Special Rapporteur on Torture, Theo van Boven, torture in Uzbek places of detention was 'systematic' at the time of his visit to the country in 2002.[121] The name of Zhaslyk – a detention facility in the West of the country – became synonymous with ill-treatment. The second President of Uzbekistan, Shavkat Mirziyoyev, ordered Zhaslyk's closure in 2019. According to the International Labour Organization (ILO), the use of forced labour, including child labour, in the cotton harvest was 'systematic and systemic' in the country, until a report issued in early 2021 confirmed that '[s]ystematic child labour has been eradicated and child labour [was] no longer a major concern'.[122] According to the same report,

> [t]he Uzbek government has significantly increased wages since 2017 and introduced a differentiated pay scale so that pickers are paid more per kilogramme of

[117] See data at: tbinternet.ohchr.org/_layouts/15/TreatyBodyExternal/Countries.aspx?CountryCode=TKM&Lang=EN.

[118] The Universal Declaration of Human Rights is not a treaty but the sovereign Uzbekistan did formally ratify the Declaration on 30 September 1991. See: Mustaqilliq, 'Respublika Uzbekistan ratifitsirovala vseobshuyu deklaratsiyu prav cheloveka' ['The Republic of Uzbekistan Ratified the Universal Declaration of Human Rights'], 30 September 1991, available at mustaqillik.uz/ru/events/view/83.

[119] Human Rights Watch, 'Uzbekistan', available at www.hrw.org/europe/central-asia/uzbekistan.

[120] See data at: tbinternet.ohchr.org/_layouts/15/TreatyBodyExternal/Countries.aspx?CountryCode=UZB&Lang=EN.

[121] Z Eshanova, 'Uzbekistan: UN Rapporteur Says Use Of Torture "Systematic"', 9 December 2002, available at www.rferl.org/a/1101615.html.

[122] International Labour Organization, 'Systemic forced labour and child labour has come to an end in Uzbek cotton', 29 January 2021, available at https://www.ilo.org/resource/news/systemic-forced-labour-and-child-labour-has-come-end-uzbek-cotton.

> cotton towards the end of the harvest, when conditions are less favourable and there is less cotton to pick. This has led to a significant drop in the prevalence of forced labour.[123]

The government has also recognised the issue of labour migration, and started taking measures to improve the situation of labour migrants abroad.

Progressive reforms carried out in Uzbekistan since 2016 are yielding fruit. The number of acquittals in criminal cases has increased significantly since 2017.[124] In 2018, President Mirziyoyev mandated a revision of the Criminal and Criminal Procedure Codes of Uzbekistan, among other things, with a view to filling 'gaps in criminal law and procedure resulting in inadequate protection of human rights and freedoms'.[125] Although the draft of a new edition of Uzbekistan's Criminal Code *does* contain a few notable improvements, it has also attracted some criticism on the part of international human rights experts, in particular, in the context of offences relative to the exercise of the freedom of association, domestic violence, LGBT rights, and criticism of public figures.[126] In early 2020, Uzbekistan announced the completion of landmine clearance along its border with Tajikistan. Given that over the previous 20 years, a total of 374 citizens of Tajikistan were killed by anti-personnel landmines, and another 485 Tajik nationals were injured,[127] the humanitarian significance of this development was outstanding. On 22 June 2020, the President of Uzbekistan approved a National Human Rights Strategy of the Republic of Uzbekistan,[128] which expounds, across 66 pages, the functions of various national authorities with respect to the implementation of international human rights law, and recommends measures on human rights education.

On 10 August 2022, Uzbekistan's Embassy in the Russian Federation cautioned the citizens of Uzbekistan living or working in Russia 'against creating

[123] ibid.

[124] See S Sayapin, 'Critical Analysis, Strict Discipline and Personal Responsibility": Some Reflections on Strengthening the Independence of the Judiciary in Central Asia' (2019) 84(3) *Law and State* 18, 22; S Sayapin, 'Réflexions sur le renforcement de l'indépendance de la magistrature en Asie centrale' ['Reflections on the Reinforcement of the Independence of the Judiciary in Central Asia'] (2019) (4) *Les Cahiers de la justice* 655, 662.

[125] S Sayapin, 'Crimes against the Peace and Security of Mankind in the Revised Edition of the Criminal Code of the Republic of Uzbekistan' (2020) 45 *Review of Central and East European Law* 36, 37.

[126] Human Rights Watch, 'Uzbekistan: Draft Criminal Code Offers Little Meaningful Reform', 10 March 2021, available at www.hrw.org/news/2021/03/10/uzbekistan-draft-criminal-code-offers-little-meaningful-reform.

[127] The Tashkent Times, 'Uzbekistan completes mine clearance of its border with Tajikistan', 4 January 2021, available at tashkenttimes.uz/national/4816-uzbekistan-completes-mine-clearance-of-its-border-with-tajikistan.

[128] See Decree No UP-6012 'On Approval of the National Strategy of the Republic of Uzbekistan on Human Rights' of 22 June 2020 (in Russian) at: lex.uz/ru/docs/4872357.

"volunteer battalions" or participating in "hostilities on the territory of foreign states"'.[129] The Embassy's press release 'pointed to Article 154 of Uzbekistan's Criminal Code as explicitly outlawing the participation of Uzbeks in armed conflicts in foreign countries, with up to 10 years in jail as punishment for violating the law'.[130] For more details on transnational and international criminal law, see Chapter fifteen below.

On 1 December 2023, the Shaykhontohur District Court in Tashkent fined a cafe owner for gender discrimination, marking the first such case under Uzbekistan's newly enacted law prohibiting gender-based discrimination.[131] The incident occurred on 18 November 2023, when journalist Inobat Akhatova and a friend were denied entry to the Sahil Street Food café after 10:30 pm, based on the establishment's internal policy that prohibited women from entering at that time. Akhatova reported the incident to the authorities, leading to the café owner being fined 6.6 million Uzbek sums (approximately US$ 537.00). Both the owner and an employee acknowledged their wrongdoing and issued public apologies.

F. Concluding Remarks

Almost 35 years after the dissolution of the Soviet Union, Central Asian States are still learning to apply international human rights law, and to communicate about it with external and internal audiences. More recently, the COVID-19 pandemic exposed numerous practical human rights issues in Central Asia, and not only with respect to healthcare as such. During the pandemic, access to information was not always consistent, statistical methods employed were at times contradictory, the legal status of regulations issued by the Chief Sanitary Doctors was uncertain, and the legal challenges posed by the state of emergency regime were plentiful. The transfer of education online was not a satisfactory solution, in terms of quality, for families with many children where there was not enough hardware to let children attend classes simultaneously. Defence lawyers reported that online – civil but, especially, administrative and criminal – trials via WhatsApp were not a good solution either, among other things, due to the limited number of possible participants in a session, and difficulties related to

[129] C Putz, 'Uzbek Government Warns Citizens in Russia Against Joining Ukraine War', The Diplomat, 12 August 2022, available at thediplomat.com/2022/08/uzbek-government-warns-citizens-in-russia-against-joining-ukraine-war/.

[130] ibid.

[131] Current Time, 'V Tashkente upravlyuayusshchego kafe oshtrafovali za gendernuyu diskimi-natsiyu. Eto pervoye podobnoye delo v Uzbekistane' ['Tashkent cafe manager fined for gender discrimination. First such case in Uzbekistan'], 1 December 2023, available at www.currenttime.tv/a/tashkent-shtraf-za-gendernuyu-diskriminatsiyu/32709899.html.

the examination of evidence.[132] The consequences of these ad hoc solutions are yet to be seen. But there are also useful lessons to be learnt.

The Central Asian States should invest, as a matter of urgency, in the digitalisation of administrative procedures and other State services.[133] Doing so will increase the efficiency and speed of such procedures, significantly reduce corruption risks,[134] and visibly improve the quality of dialogue between governments and civil society. Instead of introducing new rules, regulatory barriers should be taken down, wherever possible, especially in the economy. Greater transparency and accountability should be achieved in political decision-making. As a result of such reforms, economic and political systems will be modernised, and the quality of life will grow.

The political tradition in the region is such that workable reforms will only originate at the top of the political systems. This means, in effect, that governments should realise that compliance with international human rights law is not 'harmful' to the State, and will, in the end, contribute to 'further strengthening the country's authority in the international arena, in particular, [to] improving the position [of the State] in economic, political and legal rankings and indices'.[135] International human rights are closely linked with all areas of life, and respect for human rights is an important indicator both for international investors and policy-makers,[136] for it testifies to the stability, predictability, and trustworthiness of a State's judiciary and law enforcement system. Judges – especially those dealing with criminal and administrative cases – and law enforcement agents should be trained on the application of domestic and international human rights law, and States should genuinely align their law enforcement practices with their obligations under applicable human rights instruments. Importantly, international human rights treaties and constitutional provisions on human rights

[132] Informburo.Kz, 'V Kazahstane sudy prohodyat onlain. Ne narushayet li eto zakon i prava kazahstantsev?' ['In Kazakhstan, Trials are Held Online. Does this not Violate the Law and the Rights of Kazakhstanis?'], 15 June 2020, available at informburo.kz/stati/v-kazahstane-sudy-prohodyat-onlayn-ne-narushaet-li-eto-zakon-i-prava-kazahstancev.html. See also J Fraser and A Mbogoh, 'The Right to Access to Justice is Denied to Some Two Thirds of the World's Population. How Can We Close the Global Justice Gap?', OpinioJuris, 29 July 2025, available at opiniojuris.org/2025/07/29/the-right-to-access-to-justice-is-denied-to-some-two-thirds-of-the-worlds-population-how-can-we-close-the-global-justice-gap/.

[133] Fergana News, 'Prezident Uzbekistana poruchil chinovnikam zanyatsya sodaniyem "Tsifrovogo pravitelstva"' ['Uzbek President Instructs Officials to Create a "Digital Government"'], 2 July 2025, available at fergana.agency/news/138709/.

[134] R Khakimov, *Korruptsiya – globalnaya problema* [*Corruption as a Global Problem*] (Tashkent, Falsafa va huquq, 2006); Fergana News, 'Byvshego glavu Minyusta Kazahstana prigovorili k 9 godam tyurmy' ['Former Head of Kazakhstan's Ministry of Justice Sentenced to 9 Years in Prison'], 30 June 2025, available at fergana.agency/news/138673/.

[135] See n 128 above, 4th preambular paragraph.

[136] For instance, the Enhanced Partnership and Cooperation Agreement between the European Union and its Member States, of the one part, and the Republic of Kazakhstan, of the other part, of 21 December 2015, explicitly mentions 'human rights' on at least 20 occasions. For the text of the Agreement, see: eur-lex.europa.eu/legal-content/EN/TXT/PDF/?uri=CELEX:22016A0204(01)&from=EN.

should be directly applicable in domestic legal systems. Resolute measures must be taken to combat torture and other forms of ill-treatment. The legal status and influence of national human rights institutions should be elevated,[137] and they should be staffed by individuals with professional knowledge of international human rights law, international humanitarian law, and international criminal law. Regular dialogue with the UN human rights organs, international and domestic human rights NGOs will be helpful. The cumulative effect of such measures will benefit individuals, society, and the State alike.

[137] Office of the UN High Commissioner on Human Rights, 'UN Human Rights and NHRIs', available at www.ohchr.org/en/countries/nhri/pages/nhrimain.aspx.

14

International Humanitarian Law

I. INTRODUCTION TO INTERNATIONAL HUMANITARIAN LAW (IHL)

INTERNATIONAL HUMANITARIAN LAW (IHL)[1] is also known as the laws and customs of war,[2] the law of armed conflict (LoAC),[3] *jus in bello*,[4] the law of war,[5] or human rights in armed conflicts.[6] The choice of specific terminology largely depends on who is using a term, on the context, or the nuanced meaning one wishes to convey. Since warfare is a very ancient human activity,[7] the laws and customs of war are similarly ancient. In Central Asia, their authoritative reflections could be found, for example, in such sources as *Institutes of Temur*,[8] or the Kyrgyz epic *Manas*.[9] Having originated as a matter of practice, the laws and customs of war were occasionally codified – the Lieber Code of 24 April 1863 being a prime example – until they took treaty form in the second half of the nineteenth century. Since then, the relevant rules have developed

[1] D Fleck, *The Handbook of International Humanitarian Law*, 3rd edn (Oxford, Oxford University Press, 2013); N Tsagourias and A Morrison, *International Humanitarian Law: Cases, Materials and Commentary*, 2nd edn (Cambridge, Cambridge University Press, 2023); HT Adilkariyev, *Mezhdunarodnoye pravo* [*International law*] (Tashkent, Tashkent State Law Institute, 2003), 305–25; R Hakimov, *Mezhdunarodnoye gumanitarnoye pravo* [*International humanitarian law*] (Tashkent, O'zbekiston, 2007); II Lukashuk and AH Saidov, *Hozirgi zamon xalqaro huquqi nazariyasi asoslari* [*The theoretical fundamentals of modern international law*] (Tashkent, Adolat, 2006), 298–310; M Sarsembayev, *Mezhdunarodnoye pravo v istorii Kazakhstana i Sredney Azii* [*International law in the history of Central Asia*] (Astana, Foliant, 2011), 81–89.

[2] cf Convention (IV) respecting the Laws and Customs of War on Land and its annex: Regulations concerning the Laws and Customs of War on Land. The Hague, 18 October 1907, available at ihl-databases.icrc.org/en/ihl-treaties/hague-conv-iv-1907.

[3] E David, *Printsipy prava vooruzhennyh konfliktov* [*Principles of the Law of Armed Conflicts*], 2nd edn (Moscow, ICRC, 2011). See also A Gurmendi, 'The IHL / LOAC Divide Does Not Exist: On the Myth of the Two Cultures Problem in a Postcolonial World', OpinioJuris, 22 July 2025, available at opiniojuris.org/2025/07/22/the-ihl-loac-divide-does-not-exist-on-the-myth-of-the-two-cultures-problem-in-a-postcolonial-world/.

[4] LC Green, *The Contemporary Law of Armed Conflict* (Manchester, Manchester University Press, 1993), 14.

[5] *Department of Defense Law of War Manual*, 2nd edn (Maplewood NJ, Lieber & Sons, 2016).

[6] D Jinks, 'International Human Rights Law in Time of Armed Conflict' in A Clapham and P Gaeta (eds), *The Oxford Handbook of International Law in Armed Conflict* (Oxford, Oxford University Press, 2014); A Clapham, *Human Rights Obligations of Non-State Actors* (Oxford, Oxford University Press, 2006), 271–316.

[7] A Clapham, *War* (Oxford, Oxford University Press, 2021), 10–19.

[8] *Temur Tuzuklari / Institutes of Temur / Les Instituts de Temour* (Tashkent, G'afur G'ulom nomidagi adabiyot va san'at nashriyoti, 1996).

[9] *Manas*, Parts I–II (Bishkek, Rarity, 2004).

along two main (and mutually complementary) tracks – the Law of Geneva (or IHL *stricto sensu*), which protects certain categories of persons and objects in armed conflicts, and Hague Law (or LoAC *stricto sensu*), which prohibits certain means and methods of warfare, and regulates others. Notably, elements of the law of war are also present in the sources of the law of peace – for example, in rules on the effects of war on treaties,[10] or international trade.[11] In turn, the fundamental rules of the law of peace – such as the *jus cogens* norms or the non-derogable human rights – continue to apply in armed conflicts.[12]

A. Origins of the Law of Geneva

The Law of Geneva is historically connected with the International Committee of the Red Cross (ICRC) and other components of the International Red Cross and Red Crescent Movement.[13] Both the Movement and the Law of Geneva resulted from Henry Dunant's book *A Memory of Solferino* (1862), depicting the suffering of wounded soldiers during the Second Italian War of Independence, and the ICRC has been playing the role of the 'guardian' of IHL ever since. The Convention for the Amelioration of the Condition of the Wounded in Armies in the Field – known as the First Geneva Convention – was adopted by 16 States on 22 August 1864.[14] At the Conference, the Convention was signed by representatives of 12 States, and later, the total number of its States parties reached 57.[15] The ICRC summarised the significance of the Convention as follows:

> The main principles laid down in the Convention and maintained by the later Geneva Conventions are:
>
> – relief to the wounded without any distinction as to nationality;
> – neutrality (inviolability) of medical personnel and medical establishments and units;
> – the distinctive sign of the red cross on a white ground.[16]

The Convention was updated in 1906 and 1929.[17] Formally, it ceased to have effect in 1966 when its last State party (Republic of Korea) acceded to the 1949 Geneva Conventions.

[10] A Orakhelashvili, *Akehurst's Modern Introduction to International Law*, 9th edn (Abingdon, Routledge, 2022), 295.

[11] See Chapter 12, section I.D above.

[12] See Chapter 7, section II.B and Chapter 13, section II.B above.

[13] See Chapter 4, section I above.

[14] For the text of the 1864 Geneva Convention, see: ihl-databases.icrc.org/en/ihl-treaties/gc-1864.

[15] For the ratification status of the 1864 Geneva Convention, see: ihl-databases.icrc.org/en/ihl-treaties/gc-1864/state-parties.

[16] ICRC, 'Convention for the Amelioration of the Condition of the Wounded in Armies in the Field. Geneva, 22 August 1864: Historical treaty', see: ihl-databases.icrc.org/en/ihl-treaties/gc-1864.

[17] Likewise, in 1929, the first edition of the Convention relative to the Treatment of Prisoners of War was adopted. For the text, see: ihl-databases.icrc.org/en/ihl-treaties/gc-pow-1929.

B. The 1949 Geneva Conventions

From 21 April–12 August 1949, a Diplomatic Conference of 63 governments took place in Geneva and adopted four Conventions for the protection of victims of war.[18] The first three Conventions were revisions of pre-existing legal texts based on the experience of the Second World War. Convention (I) for the Amelioration of the Condition of the Wounded and Sick in Armed Forces in the Field was an update of the relevant texts adopted in 1864, 1906 and 1929.[19] It protected combatants who were wounded and sick, medical and religious personnel, and medical units and transports, and reaffirmed the distinctive emblems of the red cross, red crescent, and red lion and sun (see section I.D below).[20] Convention (II) for the Amelioration of the Condition of Wounded, Sick and Shipwrecked Members of Armed Forces at Sea codified the updated rules for the protection of victims of naval warfare.[21] Convention (III) relative to the Treatment of Prisoners of War updated and replaced the relevant Convention of 1929.[22] Convention (IV) relative to the Protection of Civilian Persons in Time of War was original.[23] All Conventions reaffirmed the relevant responsibilities of the ICRC and other humanitarian institutions.[24] Except for their Common Article 3, which applies in non-international armed conflicts,[25] the Conventions 'apply to all cases of declared war or of any other armed conflict which may arise between two or more of the High Contracting Parties, even if the state of war is not recognized by one of them' (Common Article 2, first paragraph). They also apply 'to all cases of partial or total occupation of the territory of a High Contracting Party, even if the said occupation meets with no armed resistance' (Common Article 2, second paragraph). At the time of writing, the 1949 Geneva Conventions have been ratified by 196 States,[26] and hence are universal. All Central Asian States ratified the 1949 Geneva Conventions in the early 1990s,[27] and are working on their implementation with ICRC advisory support.[28]

[18] Green (n 4), 41–42.

[19] ICRC, 'The Geneva Conventions of 1949 and their Additional Protocols', see: www.icrc.org/en/document/geneva-conventions-1949-additional-protocols.

[20] For the text of the First Convention, see: ihl-databases.icrc.org/en/ihl-treaties/gci-1949.

[21] For the text of the Second Convention, see: ihl-databases.icrc.org/en/ihl-treaties/gcii-1949.

[22] For the text of the Third Convention, see: ihl-databases.icrc.org/en/ihl-treaties/gciii-1949.

[23] For the text of the Fourth Convention, see: ihl-databases.icrc.org/en/ihl-treaties/gciv-1949. See also Y Salarain, 'Enforcing the Fourth Geneva Convention in Palestine: Between Legal Obligations and Political Deadlock', OpinioJuris, 31 July 2025, available at opiniojuris.org/2025/07/31/enforcing-the-fourth-geneva-convention-in-palestine-between-legal-obligations-and-political-deadlock/.

[24] S Sayapin, 'Rethinking the Responsibility of the International Committee of the Red Cross: A *Sui Generis* Regime' in A Berkes, R Collins and R Deplano (eds), *Reassessing the Articles on the Responsibility of International Organizations: From Theory to Practice* (Cheltenham, Edward Elgar Publishing, 2024), 248–50.

[25] Green (n 4), 42–43.

[26] For the ratification status of the 1949 Geneva Conventions, see: https://ihl-databases.icrc.org/en/ihl-treaties/gci-1949/state-parties.

[27] ibid.

[28] See section II below.

C. The 1977 Additional Protocols

Two Additional Protocols to the 1949 Geneva Conventions were adopted on 8 June 1977, in response to the wars of national liberation and non-international armed conflicts that took place in the decades following the Second World War. The First Additional Protocol fused selected aspects of the Law of Geneva with those of Hague Law, and was intended to reinforce the protection of victims of international armed conflicts.[29] In turn, the Second Additional Protocol developed and supplemented Common Article 3 of the 1949 Geneva Conventions, and was the first treaty devoted exclusively to the protection of victims of non-international armed conflicts.[30] The Additional Protocols of 1977 have not attained universality yet: at the time of writing, the First Additional Protocol has been ratified by 174 States,[31] and the Second Additional Protocol has 169 States Parties.[32] Nonetheless, both Additional Protocols of 1977 constitute customary international law to a significant extent.[33] The Additional Protocols of 1977 have been ratified by all Central Asian States, along with the 1949 Geneva Conventions.

D. The 2005 Additional Protocol

Protocol additional to the Geneva Conventions of 12 August 1949, and relating to the Adoption of an Additional Distinctive Emblem (Third Additional Protocol) was adopted on 8 December 2005.[34] Whereas the red cross emblem has been in use since 1864, and the red crescent emblem has been used since 1876, many more emblems were proposed in the twentieth century, which certainly may have decreased the protective value of the original distinctive emblems, and of the red lion and sun emblem, which was also recognised in the First Geneva Convention of 1949. In popular opinion, all three main emblems were considered to have religious connotations (although such was not intended by the International Red Cross and Red Crescent Movement). The 'Third Protocol emblem' – the so-called 'red crystal' – was therefore intended to be devoid of religious connotations, and to enable some National Societies to join the Movement. In accordance with Article 2(2) of the Third Protocol, the additional distinctive emblem is 'composed

[29] For the text of the First Additional Protocol, see: ihl-databases.icrc.org/en/ihl-treaties/api-1977. See also Hakimov (n 1), 140–44.

[30] For the text of the Second Additional Protocol, see: ihl-databases.icrc.org/en/ihl-treaties/apii-1977. See also E David, 'Internal (Non-International) Armed Conflict' in Clapham and Gaeta (n 6); Hakimov (n 1), 145–47.

[31] For the ratification status of the First Additional Protocol, see: ihl-databases.icrc.org/en/ihl-treaties/api-1977/state-parties?activeTab=default.

[32] For the ratification status of the Second Additional Protocol, see: ihl-databases.icrc.org/en/ihl-treaties/apii-1977/state-parties?activeTab=undefined.

[33] On customary rules of humanitarian law, see T Meron, 'Customary Humanitarian Law Today: From the Academy to the Courtroom' in Clapham and Gaeta (n 6).

[34] For the text of the Third Additional Protocol, see: ihl-databases.icrc.org/en/ihl-treaties/apiii-2005?activeTab=1949GCs-APs-and-commentaries.

of a red frame in the shape of a square on edge on a white ground'. Pursuant to Article 2(3), '[t]he conditions for use of and respect for the third Protocol emblem are identical to those for the distinctive emblems established by the Geneva Conventions and, where applicable, the 1977 Additional Protocols'. The 'Third Protocol emblem' has not yet achieved universal recognition: at the time of writing, the 2005 Protocol has been ratified by 79 States.[35] In Central Asia, it has been ratified by Kazakhstan (on 24 June 2009) and Kyrgyzstan (on 25 January 2019).[36]

E. Origins of Hague Law

The rules of Hague Law prohibit means of warfare (weapons and munitions), which cause superfluous injury or unnecessary suffering,[37] indiscriminate weapons,[38] and weapons harming the environment,[39] and regulate the use of permitted weapons. They also prohibit methods of warfare breaching any of the principles of IHL.[40] The most dangerous breaches are criminalised as war crimes.[41] The codification of these rules commenced soon after the adoption of the 1864 Geneva Convention – for example, in the 1868 St Petersburg Declaration[42] – and was consolidated at the First and Second Peace Conferences held at The Hague, respectively, from 18 May–29 July 1899,[43] and from 15 June–18 October 1907.[44] According to the Nuremberg Judgment, by 1939, the Hague Regulations acquired the status of customary law.[45]

F. Principles of IHL

The principles of IHL are key general rules which transcend all its more specific provisions.[46] They include:

(1) the principle of *distinction* between combatants and other persons taking a direct part in hostilities, on the one hand, and civilians and other persons

[35] For the ratification status of the Third Additional Protocol, see: ihl-databases.icrc.org/en/ihl-treaties/apiii-2005/state-parties?activeTab=1949GCs-APs-and-commentaries.
[36] ibid.
[37] Tsagourias and Morrison (n 1), 194.
[38] ibid, 194–96.
[39] ibid, 196.
[40] Hakimov (n 1), 114–29.
[41] See section II.F and Chapter 15, section IV.E below.
[42] Declaration Renouncing the Use, in Time of War, of Explosive Projectiles Under 400 Grammes Weight. Saint Petersburg, 29 November / 11 December 1868, see: ihl-databases.icrc.org/en/ihl-treaties/st-petersburg-decl-1868?activeTab=default.
[43] For the Final Act of the First Hague Peace Conference, see: ihl-databases.icrc.org/es/ihl-treaties/hague-finact-1899/final-act?activeTab=historical.
[44] For the Final Act of the Second Hague Peace Conference, see: ihl-databases.icrc.org/en/ihl-treaties/hague-finact-1907/final-act?activeTab=undefined.
[45] Green (n 4), 10–12. International Military Tribunal at Nuremberg, *Case of the Major War Criminals*, Judgment, 1 October 1946, Official Documents, Vol I, pp 253–54.
[46] Hakimov (n 1), 39–47.

taking no direct part in hostilities on the other hand.[47] The principle also requires that a distinction be made between civilian objects and military objectives;[48]

(2) the principle of *proportionality*, which prohibits attacks 'which may be expected to cause incidental loss of civilian life, injury to civilians, damage to civilian objects, or a combination thereof, which would be excessive in relation to the concrete and direct military advantage anticipated';[49]

(3) the principle of *military necessity*, which permits measures (ie, the means and methods of warfare) that are actually necessary to weaken the military capacity of the adversary, and are not otherwise prohibited by IHL; and[50]

(4) the overarching principle of *humanity*, which is probably best expressed both in the original Martens Clause,[51] and its modernised versions.[52]

The principles of IHL apply in all combat domains, including cyberspace.[53] They have exercised a fundamental influence on the development of Hague Law since the Second World War, and will retain their significance in the future.[54]

G. Biological Weapons Convention

A follow-up treaty to the Protocol for the Prohibition of the Use of Asphyxiating, Poisonous or Other Gases, and of Bacteriological Methods of Warfare (Biological Weapons Convention) of 17 June 1925,[55] namely the Convention on the Prohibition of the Development, Production and Stockpiling of Bacteriological (Biological) and Toxin Weapons and on their Destruction, opened for signature

[47] Tsagourias and Morrison (n 1), 102–22; N Melzer, 'The Principle of Distinction Between Civilians and Combatants' in Clapham and Gaeta (n 6).

[48] Y Dinstein, *The Conduct of Hostilities under the Law of International Armed Conflict*, 3rd edn (Cambridge, Cambridge University Press, 2016), 142.

[49] Additional Protocol I, Article 51(5)(b). See also Tsagourias and Morrison (n 1), 44–49; E Cannizzaro, 'Proportionality in the Law of Armed Conflict' in Clapham and Gaeta (n 6); T Kebebew, 'Evolutive Interpretation of Proportionality and Precautions to Strengthen Protections under International Humanitarian Law', OpinioJuris, 19 May 2025, available at opiniojuris.org/2025/05/19/evolutive-interpretation-of-proportionality-and-precautions-to-strengthen-protections-under-international-humanitarian-law/.

[50] ICRC, 'Military necessity', see: casebook.icrc.org/a_to_z/glossary/military-necessity.

[51] Preamble to the Hague Convention (IV) on War on Land (1899), para 8. On the significance of the Martens Clause, see Tsagourias and Morrison (n 1), 42–44.

[52] Additional Protocol I, Article 1(2) and Additional Protocol II, Preamble, para 4.

[53] K Mačák, 'Military Space Operations' in S Sayapin et al (eds), *International Conflict and Security Law: A Research Handbook* (The Hague, TMC Asser Press, 2022).

[54] cf Additional Protocol I, Article 36: 'In the study, development, acquisition or adoption of a new weapon, means or method of warfare, a High Contracting Party is under an obligation to determine whether its employment would, in some or all circumstances, be prohibited by this Protocol or by any other rule of international law applicable to the High Contracting Party'.

[55] For the text of the 1925 Geneva Protocol, see: ihl-databases.icrc.org/en/ihl-treaties/geneva-gas-prot-1925/protocol?activeTab=undefined.

on 10 April 1972 and entered into force on 26 March 1975.[56] At the time of writing, the Convention has been ratified by 189 States,[57] including all Central Asian nations. Under the Convention, States undertake never under any circumstances to develop, produce, stockpile, acquire or retain biological weapons (Article I); to destroy biological weapons or divert them to peaceful purposes (Article II); not to transfer, or in any way assist, encourage or induce anyone to manufacture or otherwise acquire biological weapons (Article III); to take any national measures necessary to prohibit and prevent the development, production, stockpiling, acquisition or retention of biological weapons within a State's territory, under its jurisdiction, or under its control (Article IV); and to take other relevant measures. Given that Renaissance Island (now a peninsula) in the Aral Sea was the Soviet Union's largest field test site for anthrax, plague, tularemia, and smallpox, and Stepnogorsk in Kazakhstan was home to the world's largest facility to produce anthrax,[58] post-Soviet Central Asia's resolute condemnation of biological weapons is crucial.

H. Chemical Weapons Convention

The Convention on the Prohibition of the Development, Production, Stockpiling and Use of Chemical Weapons and on their Destruction (Chemical Weapons Convention) of 13 January 1993 is another universal disarmament treaty,[59] which at the time of writing has been ratified by 193 States,[60] including all Central Asian States. Under Article III of the Convention, each State Party is required to submit a number of declarations to the Organisation for the Prohibition of Chemical Weapons (OPCW) within 30 days of the Convention's entry into force for that State Party. Article IV requires States Parties to destroy their chemical weapons. Article V requires that chemical weapons production facilities (CWPFs) be destroyed and / or converted. Article VI covers activities not prohibited under the Convention. National implementation measures are dealt with in Article VII. Article VIII regulates the structure and powers of the OPCW. Consultations, cooperation and fact-finding in cases of possible non-compliance are governed by Article IX. Importantly, Article X provides for assistance and protection if a State is attacked or threatened with attack by chemical weapons. The Central Asian nations' position against chemical weapons is determined.

[56] For the text of the Biological Weapons Convention, see: front.un-arm.org/wp-content/uploads/2020/12/BWC-text-English-1.pdf.

[57] For the ratification status of the Biological Weapons Convention, see: treaties.unoda.org/t/bwc.

[58] K Butler, 'Weapons of Mass Destruction in Central Asia', Nuclear Threat Initiative, 30 September 2002, see: www.nti.org/analysis/articles/weapons-mass-destruction-central-asia/.

[59] For an overview and text of the Chemical Weapons Convention, see: www.opcw.org/chemical-weapons-convention.

[60] For the ratification status of the Chemical Weapons Convention, see: https://treaties.unoda.org/t/cwc.

In compliance with the Convention, a chemical weapons production and testing facility was closed down in Nukus (western Uzbekistan).[61] On 17 July 2015, the Central Asia Regional Secretariat of the Chemical, Biological, Radiological and Nuclear (CBRN) Risk Mitigation Centres of Excellence Initiative was launched in Tashkent. The production, acquisition, stockpiling, transfer or use of chemical, biological and other weapons of mass destruction is a crime in all Central Asian States.[62]

I. The 1980 Convention on Certain Conventional Weapons (CCW)

The Convention on Prohibitions or Restrictions on the Use of Certain Conventional Weapons Which May be Deemed to be Excessively Injurious or to Have Indiscriminate Effects (CCW) of 10 October 1980 is an umbrella treaty with five Protocols annexed to it.[63] In accordance with Article 4(3) of the Convention, a State may be bound by the Convention if it expresses consent to be bound by any two or more of the annexed Protocols. The CCW currently has 128 States Parties, including all Central Asian nations, except Kyrgyzstan.[64] The Central Asian States have not ratified an amendment to Article 1 of the CCW of 21 December 2001, which extends the application of the CCW to non-international armed conflicts.[65] At the time of writing, the Protocol on Non-Detectable Fragments (Protocol I) has 121 States Parties, including all Central Asian States, except Kyrgyzstan.[66] Protocol (II) on Prohibitions or Restrictions on the Use of Mines, Booby-Traps and Other Devices of 10 October 1980 has been ratified by 96 States, including Tajikistan, Turkmenistan, and Uzbekistan.[67] Protocol II, as amended on 3 May 1996, has been ratified by 107 States, including Tajikistan and Turkmenistan.[68] The Protocol on Prohibitions or Restrictions on the Use of Incendiary Weapons (Protocol III) of 10 October 1980 has 117 States Parties, including Kazakhstan, Tajikistan, and Uzbekistan.[69] Protocol on Blinding Laser Weapons (Protocol IV) of 13 October 1995 has 111 States

[61] Butler (n 58).
[62] See below section II.F.
[63] For the text of the CCW, see: ihl-databases.icrc.org/en/ihl-treaties/ccw-1980.
[64] For the ratification status of the CCW, see: ihl-databases.icrc.org/en/ihl-treaties/ccw-1980/state-parties?activeTab=undefined.
[65] At the time of writing, the amendment to Article 1 has been ratified by 90 States: ihl-databases.icrc.org/en/ihl-treaties/ccw-amendment-art1-2001/state-parties?activeTab=default.
[66] For the ratification status of Protocol I, see: ihl-databases.icrc.org/en/ihl-treaties/ccw-protocol-i-1980/state-parties?activeTab=default.
[67] For the ratification status of Protocol II, see: ihl-databases.icrc.org/en/ihl-treaties/ccw-protocol-ii-1980/state-parties?activeTab=default.
[68] For the ratification status of Protocol II as amended, see: ihl-databases.icrc.org/en/ihl-treaties/ccw-amended-protocol-ii-1996/state-parties?activeTab=undefined.
[69] For the ratification status of Protocol III, see: ihl-databases.icrc.org/en/ihl-treaties/ccw-protocol-iii-1980/state-parties?activeTab=default.

Parties, including Kazakhstan, Tajikistan, and Uzbekistan.[70] The Protocol on Explosive Remnants of War (Protocol V) of 28 November 2003 has 99 States Parties, including Tajikistan and Turkmenistan.[71] It is hoped that Kyrgyzstan will consider acceding to the CCW and its relevant Protocols within the foreseeable future.

J. Nuclear Weapons

The Central Asian States are strongly opposed to nuclear weapons. During the Soviet period, Semey (Semipalatinsk) in Kazakhstan was home to a test site where 456 nuclear devices and radiological weapons were tested.[72] The test site was closed in August 1991. A total of 1410 nuclear warheads, which Kazakhstan had on its territory in December 1991, were transferred to Russia by the end of April 1995.[73] All Central Asian States have acceded to the Treaty on the Non-Proliferation of Nuclear Weapons of 1 July 1968.[74] The Treaty on the Prohibition of Nuclear Weapons of 7 July 2017 currently has 73 States Parties, including Kazakhstan (since 29 August 2019).[75] The other Central Asian nations have not expressed their consent to the latter treaty yet.

K. Other Issues of Hague Law

The other notable Hague Law instruments that already have relevance in Central Asia include the Convention on the Prohibition of the Use, Stockpiling, Production and Transfer of Anti-Personnel Mines and on their Destruction (Ottawa Convention) of 18 September 1997,[76] the Hague Convention for the Protection of Cultural Property in the Event of Armed Conflict of 14 May 1954,[77]

[70] For the ratification status of Protocol IV, see: ihl-databases.icrc.org/en/ihl-treaties/ccw-protocol-iv/state-parties.

[71] For the ratification status of Protocol V, see: ihl-databases.icrc.org/en/ihl-treaties/ccw-protocol-v/state-parties?activeTab=undefined.

[72] Butler (n 58).

[73] ibid.

[74] For the ratification status of the 1968 Treaty, see: treaties.unoda.org/t/npt.

[75] For the ratification status of the Treaty on the Prohibition of Nuclear Weapons, see: https://treaties.un.org/pages/ViewDetails.aspx?src=TREATY&mtdsg_no=XXVI-9&chapter=26.

[76] At the time of writing, the Ottawa Convention has 165 States Parties, including Tajikistan and Turkmenistan: ihl-databases.icrc.org/en/ihl-treaties/apmbc/state-parties?activeTab=default.

[77] At the time of writing, the 1954 Hague Convention has 137 States Parties, including all Central Asian States: ihl-databases.icrc.org/en/ihl-treaties/hague-conv-1954/state-parties?activeTab=default. See also VI Akulenko and VV Maksimov, 'Stanovleniye mezhdunarodnogo prava ohrany kulturnyh tsennostey kak novoy otrasli obshchego mezhdunarodnogo prava' ['The Evolution of International Law for the Protection of Cultural Property as a New Branch of General International Law'] in A Melnyk, S Melnyk and T Korotkyi (eds), *Mezhdunarodnoye pravo kak osnova sovremennogo miroporyadka* [*International Law as the Foundation of Modern World Order*] (Odessa, Phoenix Press, 2012).

its Protocol of 14 May 1954[78] and Second Protocol of 26 March 1999,[79] the ENMOD Convention of 10 December 1976,[80] the International Convention against the Recruitment, Use, Financing and Training of Mercenaries of 4 December 1989,[81] and the Arms Trade Treaty of 2 April 2013.[82] The Convention on Cluster Munitions of 30 May 2008 has not been ratified by any of the Central Asian States.[83] It is likely that the far-reaching effects of Russia's continued use of force against Ukraine and other security concerns will continue affecting the Central Asian nations' attitudes towards these treaties in the future.

II. IMPLEMENTATION OF INTERNATIONAL HUMANITARIAN LAW IN CENTRAL ASIA

IHL treaties require that States adopt legislative, administrative, and other measures at the national level to ensure the effective application of their provisions. The following subsections examine key aspects of national implementation and offer corresponding recommendations.

A. Dissemination

The 1949 Geneva Conventions and their Additional Protocols require their States Parties to disseminate knowledge of IHL among relevant professionals

[78] At the time of writing, the Protocol for the Protection of Cultural Property in the Event of Armed Conflict signed at The Hague on 14 May 1954 has 39 States Parties, including Kazakhstan, Tajikistan, and Turkmenistan: ihl-databases.icrc.org/en/ihl-treaties/hague-prot-1954/state-parties?activeTab=default.

[79] At the time of writing, the Second Protocol to the Hague Convention of 1954 for the Protection of Cultural Property in the Event of Armed Conflict, of 26 March 1999, has 91 States Parties, including Tajikistan and Turkmenistan: ihl-databases.icrc.org/en/ihl-treaties/hague-prot-1999/state-parties?activeTab=default.

[80] At the time of writing, the Convention on the Prohibition of Military or Any Hostile Use of Environmental Modification Techniques of 10 December 1976 has 78 States Parties, including all Central Asian States, except Turkmenistan: ihl-databases.icrc.org/en/ihl-treaties/enmod-1976/state-parties?activeTab=default.

[81] At the time of writing, the 1989 Convention against Mercenaries has 38 States Parties, including Turkmenistan and Uzbekistan: ihl-databases.icrc.org/en/ihl-treaties/conv-mercenaries-1989/state-parties?activeTab=default.

[82] At the time of writing, the Arms Trade Treaty has 116 States Parties, including Kazakhstan: ihl-databases.icrc.org/en/ihl-treaties/att-2013/state-parties?activeTab=default. See also W Worster, 'Assessing Assurances that Exported Arms Will Not Be Misused', OpinioJuris, 6 April 2024, available at opiniojuris.org/2024/04/06/assessing-assurances-that-exported-arms-will-not-be-misused/; and J Trittenbach, J Dorsey and O Spijkers, 'Dutch Appeals Court Blocks Deliveries of F-35 Parts to Israel: Overview, Analysis and Initial Reflections', OpinioJuris, 15 February 2024, available at opiniojuris.org/2024/02/15/dutch-appeals-court-blocks-deliveries-of-f-35-parts-to-israel-overview-analysis-and-initial-reflections/.

[83] For the ratification status of the Convention on Cluster Munitions, see: ihl-databases.icrc.org/en/ihl-treaties/ccm-2008/state-parties?activeTab=default.

and the general public.[84] The ICRC and Red Cross or Red Crescent National Societies play auxiliary roles in these processes. Thus, since the establishment of the ICRC Regional Delegation in Central Asia in 1992, manuals on the basics of IHL and humanitarian action intended for senior school children have been published in Kyrgyzstan, Tajikistan, and Uzbekistan, IHL courses have been introduced at leading law schools in all countries of the region, and military officers at various levels have been trained on the LoAC. Although the Geneva Conventions and Protocols require that such work be carried out 'in time of peace as in time of war',[85] in practice, the dissemination of IHL becomes more relevant against the background of armed conflicts and other situations of violence, and at other times States are more reluctant to spend resources on such work. For example, in Central Asia, dialogue between the ICRC and the Ministries of Education has been relatively easier in Tajikistan (where a civil war took place in 1992–97[86]) and Kyrgyzstan (which experienced a situation of violence in 2010). Likewise, dialogue with the higher education institutions in Kazakhstan and Kyrgyzstan has been relatively less complicated, due to their higher degree of academic autonomy. In the other Central Asian States, more administrative formalities were involved. On the other hand, such formalities have meant greater sustainability for the ICRC dissemination efforts. Thus, in Uzbekistan, the principles of IHL are integrated into the State educational standards for academic lyceums and professional colleges (in the 'Individual and Society' course), and the fundamentals of LoAC have become part of the Pre-recruitment Military Training course. Likewise, in 2022, a student team from Turkmenistan won the first place at the 22nd Martens Competition on IHL held by the ICRC.[87] It is recommended that the ICRC maintain an appropriate level of dialogue with the authorities and Red Crescent Societies in Central Asia, to ensure the sustainability and quality of IHL expertise offered to all national partners.

B. Military Statutes

The requirement to the effect that members of the armed forces must know and comply with IHL has been implemented in the relevant military statutes of the Central Asian States. Thus, paragraph 19 of the Interior Service Statutes

[84] ICRC, 'The Obligation to Disseminate International Humanitarian Law', available at https://www.icrc.org/sites/default/files/document/file_list/obligation-dissemination-ihl.pdf.

[85] ibid.

[86] See Chapter 10, section IX.A above.

[87] See TURKMENPORTAL, 'Turkmenskiye studenty zanyali pervoye mesto v Mezhdunarodnom konkurse imeni F.F. Martensa' ['Turkmen Students Won the First Place at the F.F. Martens International Competition'], 7 October 2022, available at: https://turkmenportal.com/blog/52620/turkmenskie-studenty-zanyali-pervoe-mesto-v-mezhdunarodnom-konkurse-im-ff-martensa.

of the Armed Forces, other troops and military formations of the Republic of Kazakhstan stipulates that

> [a] serviceman is obliged to know and strictly observe the provisions of international humanitarian law, including international rules on the conduct of hostilities, treatment of the wounded, sick, shipwrecked persons from among the adversary's armed forces, and the civilian population in the area of hostilities as well as prisoners of war.[88]

Analogous provisions are included in the Interior Service Statutes of the Armed Forces of Kyrgyzstan[89] and Uzbekistan.[90] At the time of writing, the relevant Statutes of the Armed Forces of Tajikistan and Turkmenistan appear not to be available online. On the other hand, the Interior Service Statutes contain somewhat contradictory provisions to the effect that '[a] military serviceman during hostilities, even when separated from his military unit … and fully surrounded, must show *resolute resistance* to the enemy, avoiding capture' (emphasis added).[91] It is not clear from the context what the 'resolute resistance' requirement means in practical terms – for example, whether it also includes methods prohibited by IHL such as perfidy. It is recommended that the content of this requirement be clarified, expressly in the Statutes or at least in official or academic commentaries.

C. Appointment of Legal Advisers to the Armed Forces

Article 82 of Additional Protocol I to the 1949 Geneva Conventions provides that

> [t]he High Contracting Parties at all times, and the Parties to the conflict in time of armed conflict shall ensure that legal advisers are available, when necessary, to advise military commanders at the appropriate level on the application of the Conventions and this Protocol and on the appropriate instruction to be given to the armed forces on this subject.

Although Protocol I formally applies to international armed conflicts, it follows from Article 82 that legal advisers to the armed forces should be available to perform their functions 'at all times' – that is, in peacetime and in non-international armed conflicts as well. Notably, the legal departments of the Central Asian States' Ministries of Defence are in charge of a variety of legal issues ranging from compliance with laws on military security and military

[88] Annex 1 to Decree No 364 issued by the President of the Republic of Kazakhstan on 5 July 2007, as amended by Decree No 187 of 2 February 2016.
[89] Law No 117 of the Kyrgyz Republic 'On the Interior Service Statutes of the Armed Forces of the Kyrgyz Republic' of 7 August 1998, as amended by the Law No 172 of 30 July 2013.
[90] Decree No UP-1571 issued by the President of the Republic of Uzbekistan on 9 October 1996.
[91] Para 20 in the Interior Service Statutes of the Armed Forces of the Republic of Kazakhstan and analogous provisions in the other Central Asian States' Interior Service Statutes.

service to those on property, labour, and housing.[92] However, it is essential to ensure the availability of legal advisers with specific competence on LoAC at the strategic, operational, and tactical levels. For this, regular in-service training involving theoretical instruction and practical exercises on LoAC ought to be offered nationally, regionally, and internationally. The International Institute of Humanitarian Law (IIHL) in San Remo offers numerous online and offline courses which may be of interest.[93]

D. Laws on the Use and Protection of Humanitarian Emblems

The Central Asian States have enacted laws on the use and protection of the emblems of the red cross, red crescent, and, as the case may be, red crystal.[94] The laws lay down the conditions for use of the emblems by the medical services of the Armed Forces as well as national and international humanitarian organisations, and set out grounds for the civil, administrative and criminal responsibility for violations.[95] More specifically, the laws provide that the emblems may be used exclusively for humanitarian and non-commercial purposes, and that misuses of the emblems must be prevented and penalised. The laws are generally complied with – for example, the instances of the use of the emblems by pharmacies or other commercial entities are at present very rare. It is recommended that the Central Asian States consider extending their legal protection to the red crystal emblem, in accordance with the emerging trend.[96]

E. Laws on the Legal Status of National Red Crescent Societies

There is an observable trend throughout Central Asia towards elevating the legal status of the National Red Crescent Societies, with due regard to their humanitarian mission. Although the National Societies technically are non-governmental organisations, the legal regulation of their activities goes beyond

[92] Ministry of Defence of the Republic of Kazakhstan, 'Yuridicheskaya rabota v Vooruzhennyh silah: normy – odnoznachnye, protsedury – prozrachnye' ['Legal Work in the Armed Forces: Rules are Clear, Procedures are Transparent'], 11 March 2021, available at: https://www.gov.kz/memleket/entities/mod/press/article/details/43172?lang=ru.

[93] See IIHL, Military Department: https://iihl.org/military-department-4/.

[94] See the Law of the Republic of Kazakhstan No 268-II 'On the Emblem and the Distinctive Sign of the Medical Service of the Armed Forces of the Republic of Kazakhstan' of 14 December 2001; the Law of the Kyrgyz Republic No 82 'On the Use and Protection of the Red Cross and Red Crescent Emblems' of 8 September 2000; the Law of the Republic of Uzbekistan No 65-II 'On the Use and Protection of the Red Cross and Red Crescent Emblems' of 29 April 2004; the Law of the Republic of Tajikistan No 26 'On the Use and Protection of the Red Cross and Red Crescent Emblems and Designations in the Republic of Tajikistan' of 12 May 2001; the Law of Turkmenistan No 268-V 'On the Use and Protection of the Red Cross and Red Crescent Symbolism' of 18 August 2015.

[95] cf section II.F below.

[96] cf section I.D above.

the applicable provisions of the Civil Codes and laws on NGOs. In Uzbekistan, the Red Crescent Society operates on the basis of a Decree issued by the President,[97] as now does the Red Crescent Society of Kazakhstan.[98] Yet, in Kazakhstan, a draft Law 'On the National Red Crescent Society of the Republic of Kazakhstan' is being considered,[99] which follows the example of similar laws already enacted in Kyrgyzstan,[100] Tajikistan,[101] and Turkmenistan.[102] The laws reaffirm the status of National Societies as institutions auxiliary to States in the performance of humanitarian functions in peacetime and during armed conflicts, outline their functions in relations with the State organs and partners in the International Red Cross and Red Crescent Movement, and stipulate privileges accorded to the National Societies. It is hoped that such laws will be enacted throughout Central Asia within the foreseeable future, and thus credit will be given to the Red Crescent Societies' important humanitarian work. Furthermore, the special status will endow the National Societies with special responsibilities, and will consolidate their role as national representatives of a worldwide humanitarian Movement.

F. Repression of War Crimes

War crimes are the most serious violations of IHL.[103] The concept covers crimes committed in connection with both international and non-international armed conflicts, in violation of the Law of Geneva or Hague Law.[104] War crimes feature in the Criminal Codes of all Central Asian States but the degree and quality of criminalisation are not uniform.

The 2014 edition of the Criminal Code of Kazakhstan contains four distinct provisions on war crimes (Articles 163–165, 167), whereas the first edition contained only one. The issuance by a superior or official of a manifestly unlawful order to commit a war crime is also criminalised (Article 166).[105]

[97] Decree of the President of the Republic of Uzbekistan No UP-411 'On the Red Crescent Society of Uzbekistan' of 28 May 1992. See also Hakimov (n 1), 74–77.

[98] Decree of the President of the Republic of Kazakhstan No 720 'On the Activity of the Kazakh Red Crescent and Red Cross Society' of 17 April 1992.

[99] For the text, see: https://legalacts.egov.kz/npa/view?id=7186635.

[100] Law of the Kyrgyz Republic No 19 'On the National Red Crescent Society of the Kyrgyz Republic' of 3 February 2018.

[101] Law of the Republic of Tajikistan No ZRT-923 'On the Red Crescent Society of Tajikistan' of 28 December 2012.

[102] Law of Turkmenistan 'On the National Red Crescent Society of Turkmenistan' of 22 December 2012.

[103] Dinstein (n 48), 298–331; P Gaeta, 'War Crimes and Other International "Core" Crimes' in Clapham and Gaeta (n 6).

[104] See section I above.

[105] For the text of Kazakhstan's Criminal Code (in Russian), see: online.zakon.kz/Document/?doc_id=31575252.

The 2021 edition of the Criminal Code of Kyrgyzstan contains Chapter 51 on War Crimes and Other Violations of the Laws and Customs of War. Although the title of the latter chapter appears somewhat confusing, it follows from its content that 'violations of the laws and customs of war' (Article 410) are essentially violations of the Law of Geneva, whereas 'criminal violations of the norms of international humanitarian law' (Article 413) are essentially those of Hague Law.[106] There is also criminal responsibility for violence against residents in the area of hostilities (Article 411), looting (Article 412), failure to act (to prevent crimes) or the issuance of a criminal order during hostilities (Article 414), misuse of emblems protected by treaties (Article 415), and mercenarism (Article 416).

Most notably, the drafters of Tajikistan's Criminal Code are to be commended for introducing, for the first time in Central Asia, a comprehensive criminalisation regime for war crimes.[107] Articles 403–405 are quite detailed and encompass war crimes committed in violation of the Law of Geneva and of Hague Law, both in international and non-international armed conflicts. Still, they are not as comprehensive as the provisions of Article 8 of the Statute of the International Criminal Court (ICC Statute), and it would have been more practicable to incorporate war crimes, for example, by reference to Article 8 of the ICC Statute, or by replicating its content in the Criminal Code. It should be recalled that Tajikistan is the only State Party to the ICC Statute in Central Asia, and further work should be accomplished to bring the country's penal legislation into conformity with the ICC Statute.

The Criminal Code of Turkmenistan contains four provisions on war crimes (Articles 167.4, 167.5, 167.6 and 167.8) from whose wording it follows that they apply to international armed conflicts as well as a provision on the responsibility of superiors or other officials (Article 167.7). The war crimes provisions include selected criminal violations of both the Law of Geneva and Hague Law, generally in accordance with Turkmenistan's obligations under IHL.[108]

Last but not least, as this author noted elsewhere:

> Article 152 of the current edition of Uzbekistan's Criminal Code is inconvenient in that it contains only an incomplete list of violations of the laws and customs of war, and in that it employs the plural forms of nouns to describe the victims of the respective crimes (e.g. the wounded, sick, prisoners of war, civilians and other protected persons), or the crimes as such (e.g. the employment of prohibited methods and means of warfare, attacking the civilian population or civilian objects, etc.). A literal interpretation suggests that acts committed against singular victims, or isolated acts, would not constitute war crimes (whereas, under international law, they should). Also, it is unclear from the provisions how many victims or acts are required to

[106] For the text of Kyrgyzstan's Criminal Code (in Russian), see: https://online.zakon.kz/Document/?doc_id=36675065.

[107] For the text of Tajikistan's Criminal Code (in Russian), see: https://online.zakon.kz/Document/?doc_id=30397325.

[108] For the text of Turkmenistan's Criminal Code, see: https://online.zakon.kz/Document/?doc_id=31295286.

> constitute a crime: a grammatical interpretation suggests that two victims or acts would be enough to meet the threshold of criminal responsibility but this would lead one to an absurd conclusion that a single act affecting a single victim should not be penalised at all but a second act affecting a second victim should also entail criminal responsibility for a previous act, which affected the first victim.[109]

It is recommended that the Central Asian States continue working on the penalisation of war crimes, with due regard to their obligations under IHL, and with a view to penalising war crimes as comprehensively as possible. Even though Tajikistan is the only State Party to the ICC Statute in the region, Article 8 of the Statute could serve as a helpful reference for the other Central Asian nations as well, as it codifies customary international law.

[109] S Sayapin, 'Crimes against the Peace and Security of Mankind in the Revised Edition of the Criminal Code of the Republic of Uzbekistan' (2020) 45 *Review of Central and East European Law* 36, 45. For the text of Uzbekistan's Criminal Code, see: https://online.zakon.kz/Document/?doc_id=30421110. See also Hakimov (n 1), 148–86.

15

*International and Transnational Criminal Law**

INTERNATIONAL AND TRANSNATIONAL criminal law regulate cooperation between States and international criminal justice institutions in the prevention, prosecution and punishment of individuals for transnational and international crimes.[1] To attain these goals, States put in place normative and institutional mechanisms at the international level and implement related substantive and procedural regulations in their domestic laws.[2] This chapter begins with an overview of the customary principles of penal jurisdiction, then examines the main principles of international criminal procedure, the modalities of international cooperation in penal matters, the 'core crimes' under international law and other international crimes, and concludes with a discussion of the direct and indirect enforcement of international criminal law.

I. APPLICABLE TERMINOLOGY

The concept of international criminal law (ICL) has a few meanings. In 1950, Georg Schwarzenberger offered six distinct meanings of ICL.[3] For our purpose, it will be useful to draw a distinction between transnational criminal law, international criminal procedure, and international criminal law *stricto sensu*.[4]

* This chapter uses the author's material published in S Sayapin, 'Transnational and International Criminal Law' in S Sayapin et al (eds), *International Conflict and Security Law: A Research Handbook* (The Hague, TMC Asser Press, 2022). Permission to use the published content is gratefully acknowledged.

[1] K Ambos, *Treatise on International Criminal Law*, vol III: International Criminal Procedure (Oxford, Oxford University Press, 2016), 44–56.

[2] HT Adilkariyev, *Mezhdunarodnoye pravo* [*International law*] (Tashkent, Tashkent State Law Institute, 2003), 383–432; II Lukashuk and AH Saidov, *Hozirgi zamon xalqaro huquqi nazariyasi asoslari* [*The theoretical fundamentals of modern international law*] (Tashkent, Adolat, 2006), 287–97.

[3] R Cryer, H Friman, D Robinson and E Wilmshurst, *An Introduction to International Criminal Law and Procedure*, 3rd edn (Cambridge, Cambridge University Press, 2014), 4; K Ambos, *Treatise on International Criminal Law, vol I: Foundations and General Part* (Oxford, Oxford University Press, 2013), 54.

[4] MC Bassiouni, 'The Discipline of International Criminal Law' in MC Bassiouni (ed), *International Criminal Law, Volume I: Sources, Subjects and Contents*, 3rd edn (Leiden, Brill, 2008), 3–40; C Safferling, *Internationales Strafrecht: Strafanwendungsrecht – Völkerstrafrecht – Europäisches Strafrecht* (Berlin, Springer, 2011), 3–6.

Transnational criminal law may be defined as the substantive rules of domestic criminal law (*droit pénal international*) having a bearing on crimes with a transnational element. Such an element may consist, for example, in the foreign nationality of a perpetrator of a crime or its victim, the commission of a crime abroad (with or without domestic effects of the crime), the commission of a crime affecting the interests of a foreign State, or the commission of a crime affecting the community of States as a whole. The focus of transnational criminal law is on the assertion of a State's penal jurisdiction with respect to a transnational crime.

In turn, international criminal procedure regulates bilateral or multilateral cooperation between States in criminal matters. As a rule, international criminal procedure is based on bilateral or multilateral treaties regulating extradition, mutual legal assistance, execution of foreign penal judgments, etc, although other ad hoc formats of inter-State cooperation in penal matters are also possible. Rules of international criminal procedure are usually implemented in domestic criminal procedure laws.[5]

Finally, international criminal law *stricto sensu* (*droit international pénal*) are rules of public international law establishing the criminality of a few 'core crimes' directly under international law, and regulating the prosecution of individuals for the commission of such crimes by international or 'hybrid' criminal tribunals, or within domestic legal systems.[6] International criminal law also serves as a normative foundation for States to penalise other international crimes, delicts and infractions.

II. TRANSNATIONAL CRIMINAL LAW

Whenever a transnational crime is committed, at least two States will have jurisdiction with respect to the crime. One of the States is the so-called territorial State – that is, the State within whose territory the crime takes places – and the other one may be a State of the perpetrator's nationality (if he or she is a foreigner), of the crime's victim (if he or she is a foreigner), a foreign State whose interests are injured by the crime, or another State, depending on the circumstances.[7] Domestic criminal laws contain principles on whose basis States assert their penal jurisdiction with respect to transnational crimes and crimes under international law, and make practical decisions about who will prosecute the perpetrators of such crimes.

[5] See section III below.

[6] Cryer et al (n 3), 6; G Werle and F Jessberger, *Principles of International Criminal Law*, 4th edn (Oxford, Oxford University Press, 2020), 34–37.

[7] Ambos (n 1), 233–42; É David, *Éléments de droit pénal international et europeén* (Brussels Bruylant, 2009), 273–83.

A. Territorial Jurisdiction

The main rule is the principle of territorial jurisdiction, and in most cases, the territorial State will have priority in prosecuting for a transnational crime committed in its territory.[8] On the one hand, the principle of territorial jurisdiction is a reflection of a State's sovereignty.[9] On the other hand, the principle is also very pragmatic, because it is practically easier to prosecute someone where the crime in question was committed, due to the evidence, witnesses, etc, being within reach. The principle means that every State may prescribe rules of penal law which extend to all of its territory,[10] and everyone, including foreigners, must obey these rules. The principle of territorial jurisdiction may have two variations, depending on where a crime originates and is completed. If a crime originates within a State but its effects occur abroad, the State has objective territorial jurisdiction. If a crime originates abroad but its effects occur locally, the State has subjective territorial jurisdiction.[11] A scenario like this can ensue, for instance, if a transboundary river is polluted by a natural person or legal entity located in an upstream State but the effects of the pollution are experienced in a downstream State. The Central Asian States apply both variations of the territorial jurisdiction principle.[12]

B. Active Personality Principle

When an individual travels abroad, he or she normally remains bound by the penal laws of a State of his or her nationality.[13] By extension, this principle may also apply to foreigners or stateless persons who are permanent residents of a State.[14] In practical terms, the principle means that if an individual commits a crime abroad and returns home before the territorial State is able to exercise its territorial penal jurisdiction, he or she may be held criminally liable by the State of his or her nationality or permanent residence (subject to the principle of double criminality).[15] The active personality principle is included in the Criminal Codes of all Central Asian States.[16] Conflicts of penal jurisdictions may occur

[8] Ambos (n 1), 242.
[9] Safferling (n 4), 14; Ambos (n 1), 206.
[10] David (n 7), 14–56.
[11] Cryer et al (n 3), 52–53.
[12] Kazakhstan's Criminal Code, Art 7(1)–(3); Kyrgyzstan's Criminal Code, Art 13(1)–(2); Tajikistan's Criminal Code, Art 14(1)–(3); Turkmenistan's Criminal Code, Art 7(1)–(4); Uzbekistan's Criminal Code, Art 11, first–third paras.
[13] II Lukashuk, *Mezhdunarodnoye pravo: Obshchaya chast* [*International Law: General Part*] (Moscow, Wolters Kluwer, 2008), 331.
[14] Ambos (n 1), 219–20.
[15] Cryer et al (n 3), 55; Safferling (n 4), 21–24; Ambos (n 1), 217–20; David (n 7), 188–203.
[16] Kazakhstan's Criminal Code, Art 8(1), first para; Kyrgyzstan's Criminal Code, Art 14; Tajikistan's Criminal Code, Art 15(1, 4); Turkmenistan's Criminal Code, Art 8(1); Uzbekistan's Criminal Code, Art 12, first para.

where a perpetrator of a transnational crime holds two or more nationalities. In such cases, the genuine link between the individual and a State may help determine which State should be given priority in prosecuting the perpetrator, on the basis of the active personality principle.

C. Passive Personality Principle

In turn, the passive personality principle offers protection to a State's nationals, if they become victims of a crime abroad.[17] This protection is in addition to the principles of territorial jurisdiction and active personality, and may apply if the territorial State or a State of the perpetrator's nationality is unable or unwilling to prosecute. The passive personality principle is explicitly provided for in the Criminal Codes of Kazakhstan, Tajikistan, and Turkmenistan.[18] Since both the perpetrators and victims of transnational crimes may change nationalities in the course of their lifetime, the relevant moment for determining nationality for the purpose of the active or passive personality principles is the time of the offence.[19]

D. Protective Principle

Although most crimes affect individual interests, some have a direct impact on the security of States. Such offences as espionage, currency counterfeiting, certain transborder cybercrimes,[20] and aggression are directed against the political, economic and other dimensions of States' national security – indeed, sometimes against their very existence. The protective principle of penal jurisdiction enables States to prosecute individuals for such crimes, irrespective of where the crimes were committed, and of the nationality of perpetrators.[21] The protective principle features in the Criminal Codes of all Central Asian States.[22] Notably, the passive personality principle is sometimes regarded as a spin-off of the protective principle: since a permanent population is an essential attribute of statehood,[23] an attack against a State's

[17] Cryer et al (n 3), 55–56; Ambos (n 1), 222–23; David (n 7), 203–17.

[18] Kazakhstan's Criminal Code, Art 8(1), second para; Tajikistan's Criminal Code, Art 15(2)(b); Turkmenistan's Criminal Code, Art 8(2).

[19] Cryer et al (n 3), 56.

[20] David (n 7), 1432–35.

[21] Cryer et al (n 3), 56; Safferling (n 4), 26–28; Ambos (n 1), 220–22; David (n 7), 237–41.

[22] Kazakhstan's Criminal Code, Art 8(4), second para; Kyrgyzstan's Criminal Code, Art 17(2); Tajikistan's Criminal Code, Art 15(2)(b); Turkmenistan's Criminal Code, Art 8(2). In Uzbekistan's Criminal Code, the protective principle is implicit in certain provisions of the Special Part – for example, offences such as assault on the constitutional order (Art 159) or espionage (Art 160).

[23] cf Art 1 of the Montevideo Convention on the Rights and Duties of States and Chapter 2, section III above.

nationals may be regarded as an attack against the State as such.[24] This adds weight to the passive personality principle, which may otherwise appear controversial.[25]

E. Exclusive Jurisdiction

As a rule, States retain exclusive jurisdiction over their diplomats and military personnel stationed abroad. Article 31(1) of the 1961 Vienna Convention on Diplomatic Relations provides explicitly that diplomatic agents enjoy immunity from the criminal jurisdiction of the receiving State. Article 32 of the Convention stipulates that the immunity from jurisdiction of diplomatic agents may be waived by the sending State but the waiver must always be express. Likewise, the Status of Forces Agreements (SOFAs) include standard clauses to the effect that the host State authorises the sending State to exercise criminal jurisdiction over its own personnel while in the territory of the host State.[26] The exclusive jurisdiction principle features in the Criminal Codes of all Central Asian States.[27] Such exclusive jurisdictional regime is a manifestation of State sovereignty inherent in the exercise of diplomatic and military functions.[28]

F. Vicarious (Representational) Jurisdiction

There may be scenarios where a State lawfully refuses to extradite an individual to another State (for instance, on the basis of the principle of *non-refoulement*) but nonetheless assumes penal jurisdiction 'on behalf' of the requesting State.[29] In other words, vicarious jurisdiction reduces instances of impunity in that it does not permit individuals who committed crimes to escape justice, and helps maintain the due process standards. The principle features in the Criminal Codes of all Central Asian nations, except Kyrgyzstan.[30]

[24] Safferling (n 4), 24–26; Ambos (n 1), 222–23.

[25] Cryer et al (n 3), 55.

[26] J Voetelink, 'The Status of Forces Agreements' in S Sayapin et al (eds), *International Conflict and Security Law: A Research Handbook* (The Hague, TMC Asser Press, 2022).

[27] Kazakhstan's Criminal Code, Arts 7(4) and 8(3); Kyrgyzstan's Criminal Code, Art 13(3); Tajikistan's Criminal Code, Art 14(4); Turkmenistan's Criminal Code, Art 7(5); Uzbekistan's Criminal Code, Art 11, fourth para.

[28] David (n 7), 56–136.

[29] Safferling (n 4), 32–33; Ambos (n 1), 230–33.

[30] Kazakhstan's Criminal Code, Art 8(1), third sentence, and Tajikistan's Criminal Code, Art 15(2)(a). The application of Art 8(2) of Turkmenistan's Criminal Code and Art 12, third para of Uzbekistan's Criminal Code is limited to crimes provided for by treaties or international agreements.

G. Universal Jurisdiction

Some crimes are so grave that they affect the international legal order as such. Habitually termed 'crimes against the peace and security of mankind', such crimes include the so-called 'core crimes' under international law – genocide, crimes against humanity, war crimes, and the crime of aggression – and a few other crimes that affect international peace and security, fundamental human rights, the integrity of the international system, and other values protected by international law. Although not without some controversy,[31] it is accepted that such crimes are subject to universal jurisdiction – that is, States may assert their jurisdiction with respect to such crimes irrespective of the place of their commission, the nationality of perpetrators and victims, and other customary jurisdictional links.[32]

There are two main approaches to universal jurisdiction. The 'pure' universal jurisdiction enables a State to prosecute anyone for genocide, crimes against humanity, or war crimes (and, as the case may be, other crimes against the peace and security of mankind) committed anywhere in the world,[33] with no regard to immunities attendant on a perpetrator's official position, and even *in absentia*.[34] A classic example is Belgium's law on universal jurisdiction (1993) whose scope of application was restricted in 2003.[35] The Criminal Codes of the Central Asian States (except Kyrgyzstan) have also implemented this model of universal jurisdiction.[36] In turn, the 'conditional' universal jurisdiction regime requires the presence of a suspect in the territory of the State asserting jurisdiction.[37] This approach is helpful, especially in scenarios where multiple States assert universal jurisdiction with respect to the same crime.

III. INTERNATIONAL CRIMINAL PROCEDURE

International criminal procedure serves the purposes of investigating, prosecuting and punishing transnational crimes and crimes under international law. The very nature of such crimes requires States to put in place bilateral or multilateral rules to enable transfers of criminal proceedings, evidence, and persons participating in such proceedings across international borders. As a rule, such cooperation is based on treaties, although States can also provide legal assistance

[31] Cryer et al (n 3), 56.
[32] ibid, 57; Safferling (n 4), 28–32; Ambos (n 1), 224–30; David (n 7), 242–71.
[33] Cryer et al (n 3), 57–58.
[34] ibid, 57.
[35] ibid, 61–62.
[36] Kazakhstan's Criminal Code, Art 8(1), second para; Tajikistan's Criminal Code, Art 15(2)(a); Turkmenistan's Criminal Code, Art 7(5); Uzbekistan's Criminal Code, Art 11, fourth para.
[37] Cryer et al (n 3), 57–58.

in penal matters unilaterally.[38] In the Central Asian context, the 1993 Minsk Convention[39] and the 2002 Chisinau Convention[40] as well as bilateral treaties on mutual legal assistance in penal matters are of particular relevance. This section highlights the essential principles of international criminal procedure, and offers a brief overview of the main forms of international cooperation in penal matters.[41]

A. Principles of International Criminal Procedure

Principles of international criminal procedure strike a pragmatic balance between State sovereignty and human rights. They enable States to cooperate in the prosecution of relevant crimes, while making sure that the rights of victims and perpetrators are upheld. Although States certainly have a common interest in combatting crime, they retain broad discretionary powers in arranging the specific modalities of cooperation through the medium of treaties and domestic laws, and the provision of assistance may be refused if an essential principle is breached.

B. Double Criminality

The principle of double (or dual) criminality is a standard rule in treaties on mutual legal assistance in penal matters. It means that States render each other assistance in the prosecution of alleged acts that already constitute crimes in both the requesting and the requested State at the time of their commission, and not (only) at the time of filing a request for legal assistance.[42] The principle of double criminality is closely related to the *nullum crimen sine lege* maxim, and to the principle of reciprocity.[43] The specific modalities of applying this principle may differ. Some treaties require identical crimes, whereas others specify that legal assistance will be rendered if a crime meets a minimum threshold of gravity in both jurisdictions.[44]

[38] DA Sadoff, *Bringing International Fugitives to Justice: Extradition and Its Alternatives* (Cambridge, Cambridge University Press, 2016), 327–29.
[39] For the text of the Minsk Convention of 22 January 1993 (in Russian), see: adilet.zan.kz/rus/docs/B930005100_.
[40] For the text of the Chisinau Convention of 7 October 2002 (in Russian), see: online.zakon.kz/Document/?doc_id=1034672.
[41] cf Kazakhstan's Code of Criminal Procedure, chapters 58–62; Kyrgyzstan's Code of Criminal Procedure, chapter 59–61; Tajikistan's Code of Criminal Procedure, chapters 48–52; Turkmenistan's Code of Criminal Procedure, chapter 52; Uzbekistan's Code of Criminal Procedure, chapters 64–65.
[42] Cryer et al (n 3), 94–95.
[43] ibid, 94.
[44] ibid.

C. Specialty

The rule of specialty derives from international comity,[45] and means that the pursuing State may hold a person accountable only for crimes for which he or she was extradited by the requested State, unless the requested State subsequently agrees otherwise, or the same underlying facts provide a basis for a lesser included offence.[46] The principle also applies to mutual legal assistance, for example, as far as the imposition of conditions on the use of information or evidence is concerned.[47]

D. Prohibition of Double Jeopardy *(Ne Bis in Idem)*

The prohibition of double jeopardy (*ne bis in idem*) is another standard rule in extradition treaties.[48] It means that an individual may not be prosecuted or punished again for the same criminal offence when he or she has already been finally convicted for, or acquitted of, the offence. Some extradition treaties prevent double punishment, whereas others aim at preventing double prosecutions as such.[49] The rule effectively applies within one jurisdiction and thus it may not always prevent multiple prosecutions in different legal systems,[50] especially where an offence is criminal in one jurisdiction and administrative in another.

E. Statutory Limitations

Statutory limitations may bar cooperation (and, in particular, extradition) where the passage of time makes a prosecution unjust or impractical. It should be noted, though, that statutory limitations do not apply to the 'core crimes' under international law,[51] and domestic penal laws may extend this regime to other crimes against the peace and security of mankind as well as terrorism.[52]

[45] A Abass, *International Law: Text, Cases, and Materials*, 2nd edn (Oxford, Oxford University Press, 2014), 263.
[46] Cryer et al (n 3), 95.
[47] ibid.
[48] ibid, 95–96; Ambos (n 3), 396–406. cf Art 14(7) of the International Covenant on Civil and Political Rights.
[49] Cryer et al (n 3), 96.
[50] cf Art 10 of the Criminal Code of the People's Republic of China or Art 5 of the Penal Code of Japan.
[51] See Convention on the Non-Applicability of Statutory Limitations to War Crimes and Crimes Against Humanity of 26 November 1968.
[52] Kazakhstan's Criminal Code, Art 71(6); Kyrgyzstan's Criminal Code, Art 58(6); Tajikistan's Criminal Code, Art 75(6); Turkmenistan's Criminal Code, Art 73(5); Uzbekistan's Criminal Code, Art 64, seventh para.

F. Non-refoulement

The principle of *non-refoulement* prohibits the extradition of an individual to a State where he or she would not have a fair trial, or where there are serious grounds to believe that the individual would be subjected to torture or other inhuman or degrading treatment or punishment in the requesting State.[53] If extradition is refused based on the principle of *non-refoulement*, the requested State may exercise vicarious jurisdiction to hold the individual accountable for the crime for which his or her extradition was requested.

G. International Cooperation in Penal Matters

M Cherif Bassiouni singled out eight main modalities of international cooperation in penal matters:[54]

- extradition;
- legal assistance;
- execution of foreign penal sentences;
- recognition of foreign penal judgments;
- transfer of criminal proceedings;
- freezing and seizing of assets deriving from criminal conduct;
- intelligence and law enforcement information-sharing;
- regional and sub-regional 'judicial spaces'.

H. Extradition

Extradition is the earliest form of international cooperation in penal matters. It dates back to a treaty concluded between Ramses II and Hattusili III around 1268 BC,[55] which means that historically, international criminal procedure is one of the oldest areas of public international law. Extradition means the physical relocation of a person from the requested State to the requesting State for that person's prosecution or punishment for an alleged crime, with respect to which the requesting State has penal jurisdiction.[56] As a rule, extradition is effectuated on the basis of a bilateral or multilateral treaty between the

[53] cf Art 3 of the Convention against Torture and Other Cruel, Inhuman or Degrading Treatment or Punishment of 10 December 1984.

[54] MC Bassiouni, *Introduction to International Criminal Law* (Ardsley NY, Transnational Publishers, Inc, 2003), 347–78.

[55] ibid, 348; S Sayapin, *The Crime of Aggression in International Criminal Law: Historical Development, Comparative Analysis and Present State* (The Hague, TMC Asser Press, 2014), 9.

[56] David (n 7), 436–558.

requesting and requested States. In the absence of such a treaty, alternative – more or less formal – procedural routes may be used to obtain custody of a suspect.[57]

I. Legal Assistance

In turn, Bassiouni explains legal assistance (or mutual legal assistance) as follows:

> This is when the courts of one state address a request to those of another state for judicial assistance in the form of taking the testimony of a witness or securing tangible evidence. The courts then transmit the oral or tangible evidence to the requesting court, certifying that the evidence has been secured in accordance with the legal requirements of the requested state …[58]
>
> The forms of legal assistance vary widely. They include: taking of witness testimony, securing tangible evidence such as business and bank records, and conducting investigations. These forms of legal assistance can be conducted by the judicial, prosecutorial or law enforcement personnel of the requested state. Sometimes, the requested state allows a judge or prosecutor from a requesting state to conduct the investigation on its territory, but under the supervision of the requested state's judicial authorities.[59]

It may be assumed that the best practices learned from a wider use of telecommunication technologies in the administration of justice during the COVID-19 pandemic will be used in the post-pandemic world as well, given that they reasonably expedite proceedings, and reduce associated costs.[60]

J. Execution of Foreign Penal Sentences

This modality of international cooperation means that the execution of penal sentences is transferred to convicted foreigners' countries of origin.[61] The procedure is not equivalent to the recognition of foreign penal judgments. According to Bassiouni, 'executing a foreign sentence does not imply the recognition of the penal judgment that gives rise to it'.[62] Instead, it 'separates the execution of the sentence from the recognition of the penal judgment which gave rise to the sentence',[63] and simply means bringing 'sentenced persons physically closer to family in their countries of origin'.[64] Hence, the purposes of the mechanism

[57] Sadoff (n 38), 389–550.
[58] Bassiouni (n 54), 352.
[59] ibid, 354. See also David (n 7), 409–31.
[60] Bassiouni (n 54), 354.
[61] David (n 7), 573–82.
[62] Bassiouni (n 54), 355–56.
[63] ibid, 356.
[64] ibid, 355.

are chiefly 'humanitarian and rehabilitative'.[65] Indeed, if a person was judged abroad but serves the sentence in his or her country of origin, he or she is likely to be in a closer contact with family than would have been the case if the penal sentence had been executed abroad. Likewise, the rehabilitation of offenders in a foreign country is likely to be complicated by practical matters – such as a possible language barrier.

K. Recognition of Foreign Penal Judgments

As noted above, the execution of foreign penal sentences is different from the recognition of foreign penal judgments. As a rule, States refrain from recognising foreign penal judgments, because these are regarded as a manifestation of national sovereignty.[66] Instead, international cooperation in penal matters is based on recognising the *consequences* of a foreign penal judgment (not the judgment as such), and extradition and other forms of international cooperation in penal matters are seen as the *effects* of the judgment.

L. Transfer of Criminal Proceedings

A State may choose to transfer criminal proceedings to another State, which, in Bassiouni's words,

> has more significant contacts with the parties, and is therefore a *forum conveniens*. This is in contrast to the transferring state being a *forum non conveniens*, or where some public policy interest exists that justifies the transfer of the proceedings to achieve the best interests of justice.[67]

Thus, this modality is different from the assumption of extraterritorial jurisdiction on the basis of any recognised principle.[68] It simply means that a State has a closer link to a case or its parties, and another State transfers proceedings to the former for pragmatic reasons, or in the interests of justice.

M. Freezing and Seizing Assets Deriving from Criminal Conduct

On the one hand, the freezing and seizing of assets deriving from criminal conduct is a specific form of enforcing foreign penal judgments. On the other

[65] ibid, 357. See also RadioFreeEurope / RadioLiberty, 'China Sends Four Convicted Kazakhs To Kazakhstan', 4 March 2016, available at https://www.rferl.org/a/china-kazakhstan-convicts-returned-home/27589355.html.
[66] Bassiouni (n 54), 357; David (n 7), 571–72.
[67] Bassiouni (n 54), 358; David (n 7), 559–65.
[68] Bassiouni (n 54), 359. See also section II above.

hand, it is specific enough to constitute a distinct modality of international cooperation in penal matters.[69] Such confiscation 'is predicated on a foreign penal judgment entered in the requesting state for a criminal activity that occurred in the requesting state or over which it had jurisdiction',[70] and cooperation can be based on a regional or universal treaty addressing such criminal phenomena as drug trafficking,[71] organised crime,[72] international terrorism,[73] or corruption.[74]

N. Intelligence and Law-enforcement Information-sharing

The fundamental difference between this and other modalities of international cooperation consists in that, unlike the latter, intelligence and law-enforcement information-sharing is not based on treaties.[75] Given the sensitive nature of information transmitted in the framework of this modality,

> [i]ntelligence and law enforcement agencies have historically shared information outside legal and judicial supervision. This de facto modality of international cooperation has historically been secretive, and the laws of almost all countries seldom deal with the regulation of this type of activity, except when national legislation limits or regulates the scope and context of these agencies' domestic work.[76]

In the current environment of mutual distrust between some of the world's major powers, 'potential for inefficiency, error, and infringement of the general right of privacy as well as for the specific rights of individuals'[77] is likely to grow.

O. Regional and Sub-regional 'Judicial Spaces'

Regional and sub-regional integration between States may lead to the emergence of 'judicial spaces'. This modality means an even closer integration than cooperation on the basis of multilateral treaties on mutual legal assistance as described above, to the extent that

> within the area determined as part of the 'judicial space' judicial orders shall be enforced automatically by the respective states without the need for the intermediation of a judicial order issued by the enforcing state. This would also mean that law enforcement officials from one member-state can pursue their investigations or

[69] Bassiouni (n 54), 359.
[70] ibid, 359–60.
[71] See the United Nations Convention against Illicit Traffic in Narcotic Drugs and Psychotropic Substances (1988).
[72] See the United Nations Convention against Transnational Organized Crime (2000).
[73] See the International Convention for the Suppression of the Financing of Terrorism (1999).
[74] See the United Nations Convention against Corruption (2003).
[75] Bassiouni (n 54), 368.
[76] ibid, 369.
[77] ibid, 371.

pursue fugitives outside their national boundaries (obviously, with some coordination with local law enforcement).[78]

It appears that efficient 'judicial spaces' emerge within otherwise successful integration formats with common approaches to penal policies, the rule of law, and respect for human rights. In the EU, for example, the European Arrest Warrant scheme is 'generally perceived as successful, at least from a law enforcement perspective'.[79] Theoretically, a common 'judicial space' could emerge, in the future, in the Eurasian Economic Union (EEAU),[80] of which Kazakhstan and Kyrgyzstan are Members. In turn, relations between Member States of a 'judicial space' and non-members are regulated by traditional mechanisms – that is, treaties on mutual legal assistance in penal matters.

IV. SUBSTANTIVE INTERNATIONAL CRIMINAL LAW

Substantive international criminal law comprises rules of public international law directly establishing the criminal responsibility of individuals for acts (or, more rarely, omissions), which affect the peace and security of mankind. In the twentieth century, the first attempts to criminalise such acts were made after the First World War[81] but the first trials on relevant charges did not take place until after the Second World War. The Charters and jurisprudence of the Nuremberg and Tokyo Tribunals laid the foundations for the General and Special Parts of the contemporary ICL,[82] and the rules were refined during the ensuing decades. Now, ICL is enforced in two main ways – directly (by the International Criminal Court and other international and 'hybrid' tribunals), and indirectly (by States, through their domestic systems of criminal justice). Given the limited capacities of international institutions, the indirect enforcement of ICL will continue gaining significance.

A. General Part of International Criminal Law

According to Werle and Jessberger, '[u]ntil the entry into force of the ICC Statute, general principles were of secondary importance in efforts to codify international criminal law'.[83] Indeed, during the Nuremberg and Tokyo trials, for example, the victorious Allied Powers held accountable the leaders of States

[78] ibid, 378.
[79] Cryer et al (n 3), 100; Safferling (n 4), 341–441.
[80] See Chapter 12, section II above.
[81] Werle and Jessberger (n 6), 2–5.
[82] ibid, 6–11.
[83] ibid, 205.

they had defeated but not their own nationals,[84] the prohibition of retroactivity of criminal law was obviously disregarded,[85] and some rules on evidence were below the normal legal standard.[86] When the International Criminal Tribunals for the Former Yugoslavia and Rwanda were established by the Security Council of the United Nations, respectively, in 1993 and 1994, some commentators questioned the authority of the Security Council, a political organ, to establish judicial organs.[87] The drafters of the ICC Statute had to take account of such criticisms, and to consolidate the general principles of ICL for the purpose of setting a high standard of justice at the ICC.

The general principles of criminal law are codified in Part 3 of the ICC Statute (Articles 22–33) and draw mostly on the common and civil law traditions.[88] The Islamic legal tradition is, unfortunately, largely disregarded in the ICC Statute. The Statute includes the following general principles of criminal law:

- *Nullum crimen sine lege* (Article 22);[89]
- *Nulla poena sine lege* (Article 23);[90]
- Non-retroactivity *ratione personae* (Article 24);[91]
- Individual criminal responsibility (Article 25);[92]
- Exclusion of jurisdiction over persons under 18 (Article 26);[93]
- Irrelevance of official capacity (Article 27);[94]
- Responsibility of commanders and other superiors (Article 28);[95]
- Non-applicability of statutes of limitation (Article 29);[96]
- Mental element (Article 30);[97]
- Grounds for excluding criminal responsibility (Article 31);[98]

[84] ibid, 9.

[85] ibid.

[86] cf Art 19 of the Nuremberg Charter (1945) and Art 13(a) of the Tokyo Charter (1946).

[87] TW Waters, 'The ad hoc tribunals: image, origins, pathways, legacies' in P Kastner (ed), *International Criminal Law in Context* (Abingdon, Routledge, 2018).

[88] Werle and Jessberger (n 6), 207; S Sayapin, 'The General Principles of International Criminal Law in the Criminal Code of the Republic of Kazakhstan' (2019) 9 *Asian Journal of International Law* 1.

[89] Werle and Jessberger (n 6), 48–50, 212–15.

[90] ibid, 48–50; K Ambos, *Treatise on International Criminal Law, vol II: The Crimes and Sentencing* (Oxford, Oxford University Press, 2014), 271–77.

[91] Cryer et al (n 3), 84–85.

[92] Werle and Jessberger (n 6), 233–64; Ambos (n 3), 102–79.

[93] Ambos (n 3), 430–32.

[94] Werle and Jessberger (n 6), 311–25; Safferling (n 4), 121–23; Ambos (n 3), 406–19.

[95] Werle and Jessberger (n 6), 264–76; Ambos (n 3), 197–232.

[96] cf Art 7 of the Nuremberg Charter (1945), Art 6 of the Tokyo Charter (1946). See also Ambos (n 3), 427–30.

[97] Werle and Jessberger (n 6), 215–33; Safferling (n 4), 119–20; Ambos (n 3), 266–300.

[98] Werle and Jessberger (n 6), 277–302; Ambos (n 3), 301–437.

- Mistake of fact or mistake of law (Article 32);[99]
- Superior orders and prescription of law (Article 33).[100]

At the international level, the general principles serve as common normative guidelines for the ICC Judges and Prosecutor, who represent various legal traditions of the world. Since their professional perceptions of international and criminal law are inevitably informed by their national academic and law enforcement practices, common normative guidelines are useful. At the domestic level, general principles of criminal law help maintain the appropriate standards of justice, both in the States Parties to the Rome Statute and States which have not ratified the Statute.

B. 'Core Crimes' under International Law

The 'core crimes' under international law are within the scope of 'crimes against the peace and security of mankind'.[101] They are 'the most serious crimes of concern to the international community as a whole',[102] and therefore are within the jurisdiction of the International Criminal Court. Genocide and war crimes are also widely criminalised at the domestic level. A common feature of all 'core crimes' under international law consists in the so-called 'context of organised violence' in which they are committed.[103]

C. Genocide

The term 'genocide' was suggested by Polish-American lawyer Raphael Lemkin (1900–59) to designate criminal acts committed with intent to destroy, in whole or in part, a national, ethnical, racial, or religious group, as such.[104] When designing the term, Lemkin bore in mind, in particular, acts perpetrated against

[99] Werle and Jessberger (n 6), 287–90; Ambos (n 3), 366–76.

[100] Werle and Jessberger (n 6), 290–95; Safferling (n 4), 121; Ambos (n 3), 376–86.

[101] David (n 7), 1190–95. See chapter 4 in the Special Part of Kazakhstan's Criminal Code; chapters 50–51 in Kyrgyzstan's Criminal Code; chapter 34 in Tajikistan's Criminal Code; chapter XXI in Turkmenistan's Criminal Code; chapter VIII in the Special Part of Uzbekistan's Criminal Code. See also S Sayapin, 'The Implementation of Crimes against the Peace and Security of Mankind in the Penal Legislation of the Republic of Kazakhstan' (2020) 10 *Asian Journal of International Law* 1.

[102] See Art 5 of the ICC Statute.

[103] Werle and Jessberger (n 6), 210.

[104] R Lemkin, *Axis Rule in Occupied Europe: Laws of Occupation, Analysis of Government, Proposals for Redress*, 2nd edn (Clark, The Lawbook Exchange, Ltd., 2008); Cryer et al (n 3), 205–28, Safferling (n 4), 155–78; S Sayapin, 'Raphael Lemkin: a Tribute' (2009) 20 *European Journal of International Law* 1157; Werle and Jessberger (n 6), 334–72. See Kazakhstan's Criminal Code, Art 168; Kyrgyzstan's Criminal Code, Art 405; Tajikistan's Criminal Code, Art 398; Turkmenistan's Criminal Code, Art 174; Uzbekistan's Criminal Code, Art 153.

Armenians during the First World War,[105] and against 'Jews, Poles, Slovenes and Russians' before and during the Second World War.[106] In 1948, the Convention for the Prevention and Punishment of the Crime of Genocide was adopted. As of this writing, the Convention has 153 States Parties, including all Central Asian States.[107] At times, genocide is confused with crimes against humanity, because both affect large numbers of victims as a matter of practice. The differences between the two crimes essentially consist in (1) the range of protected groups and interests, and (2) the *mens rea*. The crime of genocide is limited to four protected groups,[108] and does not include other identifiable groups (such as political groups or groups based on the sexual orientation of their members).[109] In turn, the 'genocidal intent' is aimed at the destruction of a protected group, in whole or in part, as such,[110] whereas the *mens rea* of crimes against humanity requires that 'the perpetrator must be aware that a (widespread or systematic) attack on a civilian population is taking place and that his or her action is part of this attack'.[111]

D. Crimes against Humanity

In practical terms, crimes against humanity are mass crimes against identifiable civilian groups.[112] The term was suggested by Hersch Lauterpacht (1897–1960) for the purpose of the Nuremberg Charter, where the concept appeared in Article 6(c).[113] It later appeared, with some modifications, in the Tokyo Charter (Article 5(c)), the Control Council Law No 10 (Article II(1)(c)), the Statutes of the International Criminal Tribunals for the Former Yugoslavia (Article 5) and Rwanda (Article 3), and in Article 7 of the Rome Statute of the International Criminal Court. There is an ongoing discussion regarding a possible adoption

[105] P Sands, *East West Street: On the Origins of Genocide and Crimes against Humanity* (London, Weidenfeld & Nicolson, 2016), 143.

[106] ibid, 178.

[107] See United Nations Treaty Collection (2025) Chapter IV: Human Rights, Convention on the Prevention and Punishment of the Crime of Genocide, available at treaties.un.org/pages/ViewDetails.aspx?src=TREATY&mtdsg_no=IV-1&chapter=4.

[108] Art II of the Genocide Convention.

[109] For a critical view on the definition of genocide, see MC Bassiouni, 'Challenges to International Criminal Justice and International Criminal Law' in WA Schabas (ed), *The Cambridge Companion to International Criminal Law* (Cambridge, Cambridge University Press, 2016), 383–84.

[110] Ambos (n 90), 18–45. See also NY Barigye, M Hendrickse and V Todeschini, 'Genocidal Intent in Armed Conflict: Unpacking the ICJ's "Only Reasonable Inference" Standard', OpinioJuris, 26 May 2025, available at opiniojuris.org/2025/05/26/genocidal-intent-in-armed-conflict-unpacking-the-icjs-only-reasonable-inference-standard/.

[111] Werle and Jessberger (n 6), 393; R Atadjanov, *Humanness as a Protected Legal Interest of Crimes Against Humanity: Conceptual and Normative Aspects* (The Hague, TMC Asser Press, 2019), 280–85.

[112] David (n 7), 1239–342; Cryer et al (n 3), 229–63; Safferling (n 4), 179–211; Werle and Jessberger (n 6), 373–440.

[113] Sands (n 105), 108–14; Atadjanov (n 111), 92.

of a Convention on Crimes against Humanity, which, if adopted, would not only consolidate the concept but also serve as a multilateral legal basis for mutual legal assistance in the prosecution of, and punishment for, crimes against humanity.[114] Modern discussions regarding crimes against humanity emphasise, on the one hand, positivist approaches explaining the crimes as widespread or systematic violations of the fundamental human rights of members of identifiable civilian groups,[115] and, on the other hand, approaches based on the natural law theory and focusing on multifaceted meanings of 'humanity' as a protected *Rechtsgut*.[116] In Central Asia, crimes against humanity are penalised only in Kyrgyzstan.[117]

E. War Crimes

War crimes are criminal violations of international humanitarian law (IHL).[118] Their legal basis is found in various treaties of IHL as well as in customary international law.[119] Like crimes against humanity, war crimes were codified in the Nuremberg (Article 6(b)) and Tokyo (Article 5(b)) Charters, the Control Council Law No 10 (Article II(1)(b)), the Statutes of the International Criminal Tribunals for the Former Yugoslavia (Articles 2 and 3) and Rwanda (Article 4), and in Article 8 of the Rome Statute of the International Criminal Court.[120] All war crimes share a few common attributes in that they are committed: (1) in connection with an armed conflict;[121] (2) by a person or persons belonging to one side in the armed conflict;[122] (3) against persons or objects belonging to another side in the armed conflict;[123] (4) in violation of one or more treaty-based or customary rules of IHL.[124] The Criminal Codes of the Central Asian States do not clearly distinguish between war crimes committed in international

[114] S Sayapin, 'Why a Crimes against Humanity Convention from a Perspective of Post-Soviet States?' (2020) 6 *African Journal of International Criminal Justice* 125, 135; A Chandran, 'A Future Crimes Against Humanity Convention and Asia: A New Tool for Accountability', OpinioJuris, 29 July 2025, available at opiniojuris.org/2025/07/29/a-future-crimes-against-humanity-convention-and-asia-a-new-tool-for-accountability/.

[115] S Sayapin, 'Crimes against the Peace and Security of Mankind in the Revised Edition of the Criminal Code of the Republic of Uzbekistan' (2020) 45 *Review of Central and East European Law* 36, 48–51; R Greta, 'Key Insights and Lessons from The First World Congress on Enforced Disappearances', OpinioJuris, 1 August 2025, available at opiniojuris.org/2025/08/01/key-insights-and-lessons-from-the-first-world-congress-on-enforced-disappearances/.

[116] L May, *Crimes Against Humanity: A Normative Account* (Cambridge, Cambridge University Press, 2005), 80–95.

[117] See Kyrgyzstan's Criminal Code, Art 403.

[118] Cryer et al (n 3), 264–306; Safferling (n 4), 212–46; Werle and Jessberger (n 6), 441–583.

[119] Y Sandoz, 'Penal Aspects of International Humanitarian Law', in Bassiouni (n 4).

[120] David (n 7), 1006–43.

[121] Ambos (n 90), 140–44.

[122] ibid, 145–46.

[123] ibid, 146–52.

[124] ibid, 160–83.

and non-international armed conflicts.[125] As IHL is developing, the law of war crimes is evolving accordingly. Emerging war crimes are related, for example, to the hostile use of information technologies.

F. Crime of Aggression

The crime of aggression is probably the most controversial of all 'core crimes' under international law.[126] As the Nuremberg Charter was being drafted, expert views on crimes against peace were divided,[127] and just a few pages were devoted to such crimes in the Nuremberg Judgment.[128] By contrast, already in the Tokyo Judgment, crimes against peace were much more prominent.[129] The Nuremberg follow-up trials reaffirmed that a war of aggression was an emerging crime under international law.[130] Unlike the other 'core crimes', aggression is usually regarded as a 'leadership crime',[131] and is now codified as such in Article 8 *bis* of the Rome Statute of the International Criminal Court.[132] Some 40 States – including all Central Asian nations[133] – introduced criminal responsibility for aggression and other crimes against peace.[134] In 2014, the concept of patriacide was introduced into academic discourse to denote the deliberate destruction of a State's constitutional, political, economic, or technical organisation. Patriacide is an extreme form of aggression consisting not only in the overt use of military force against a State in violation of

[125] Kazakhstan's Criminal Code, Arts 163–166; Kyrgyzstan's Criminal Code, Arts 410–416; Tajikistan's Criminal Code, Arts 401, 403–405; Turkmenistan's Criminal Code, Arts 169–172; Uzbekistan's Criminal Code, Art 152, 154.

[126] Cryer et al (n 3), 307–28; David (n 7), 1083–97; Safferling (n 4), 247–67; Werle and Jessberger (n 6), 584–614.

[127] Sayapin (n 55), 40.

[128] ibid, 149–61. International Military Tribunal at Nuremberg, *Case of the Major War Criminals*, Judgment, 1 October 1946, Official Documents, Vol I.

[129] ibid, 161–80. International Military Tribunal for the Far East, Tokyo, Judgment, November 1948.

[130] ibid, 180–90.

[131] Notably, Ukraine prosecuted for aggression not only its former President Yanukovych but also two Russian military servicemen, which constituted a departure from the customary understanding of aggression as a 'leadership crime'. See S Sayapin, 'The *Yanukovych* Trial in Ukraine: A Revival of the Crime of Aggression?' (2020) 50 *Israel Yearbook on Human Rights* 63; and S Sayapin, 'A Curious Aggression Trial in Ukraine: Some Reflections on the *Alexandrov and Yerofeyev* Case' (2018) 16 *Journal of International Criminal Justice* 1093.

[132] S Sayapin, 'A Great Unknown: the Definition of Aggression Revisited' (2008) 17 *Michigan State Journal of International Law* 375; Ambos (n 90), 186–220. From a human rights perspective on the crime of aggression, see T Dannenbaum, *The Crime of Aggression, Humanity, and the Soldier* (Cambridge, Cambridge University Press, 2018).

[133] Kazakhstan's Criminal Code, Arts 160–161; Kyrgyzstan's Criminal Code, Arts 402, 407; Tajikistan's Criminal Code, Arts 395–396; Turkmenistan's Criminal Code, Arts 165–167; Uzbekistan's Criminal Code, Arts 150–151.

[134] Sayapin (n 55), 202–22; S Sayapin, 'The Compatibility of the Rome Statute's Draft Definition of the Crime of Aggression with National Criminal Justice Systems' (2010) 81 *Revue internationale de droit penal* 165, 169–85.

international law but also encompassing 'hybrid' measures against the military, political, economic, legal and ideological organisation of the victim State, calculated to bring about its territorial and social disintegration, and ideally – the obliteration of its statehood as such.[135] Unlike aggression, which may not necessarily aim at the destruction of statehood, patriacide is defined precisely by its intent to dismantle the fundamental structures of a State and to obliterate its existence as a sovereign entity.

In recent years, several notable regional developments have emerged concerning the prosecution of the crime of aggression. In Africa, once the 2014 Malabo Protocol enters into force, regional prosecutions will become feasible.[136] In Central Asia, following the armed clashes between Kyrgyzstan and Tajikistan in 2021 and 2022,[137] both States initiated criminal prosecutions for aggression;[138] however, these proceedings have not resulted in any convictions. In June 2025, the Council of Europe took a significant step toward accountability by establishing a Special Tribunal for the Crime of Aggression against Ukraine, marking an unprecedented effort to address the unlawful use of force by the Russian Federation.[139]

G. International Violations

M Cherif Bassiouni identified 28 distinct categories of 'international violations'[140] on the basis of 281 conventions.[141] Depending on their gravity and the protected values they affect, he classified such violations under the headings of (1) international crimes, (2) international delicts, and (3) international infractions. Most of them are not within the jurisdiction of the ICC, either because they are not unequivocally defined in international law, or because relevant treaties explicitly assign penal jurisdiction with respect to such crimes to individual States.

[135] S Sayapin, 'Patriacide' in S Lee et al (eds), *Encyclopedia of Public International Law in Asia, Vol III: Central & South Asia* (Leiden, Brill, 2021).

[136] The Protocol on Amendments to the Protocol on the Statute of the African Court of Justice and Human Rights (Malabo Protocol) was adopted on 27 June 2014. In accordance with its Article 15, the Protocol shall enter into force 30 days after the deposit of instruments of instruments of ratification by 15 Member States. At the time of writing, the Protocol has 15 signatures and no ratifications. See S Sayapin, 'The Crime of Aggression in the African Court of Justice and Human and Peoples' Rights' in C Jalloh, MK Clarke and V Nmehielle (eds), *The African Court of Justice and Human and Peoples' Rights in Context: Development and Challenges* (Cambridge, Cambridge University Press, 2019).

[137] See Chapter 10, section IX.D above.

[138] J Emtseva, 'Small conflicts with big impact: The Tajik-Kyrgyz war no one talks about', EJIL:Talk!, 11 October 2022, available at www.ejiltalk.org/small-conflicts-with-big-impact-the-tajik-kyrgyz-war-no-one-talks-about/.

[139] Council of Europe, 'Ukraine and the Council of Europe sign Agreement on establishing a Special Tribunal for the Crime of Aggression against Ukraine', 25 June 2025, available at www.coe.int/en/web/portal/-/ukraine-and-the-council-of-europe-sign-agreement-on-establishing-a-special-tribunal-for-the-crime-of-aggression-against-ukraine.

[140] Bassiouni (n 54), 121.

[141] ibid, 116.

H. International Crimes

The first category mostly includes crimes that are part of *jus cogens*, and is 'typically characterized by the fact that their commission cannot occur without state action or a state-favoring policy'.[142] In addition to the four 'core crimes' under international law, according to Bassiouni, international crimes include:[143]

- unlawful possession or use of emplacement of weapons;[144]
- theft of nuclear materials;[145]
- mercenarism;[146]
- apartheid;[147]
- slavery or slave-related practices;[148]
- torture and other forms of cruel, inhuman or degrading treatment or punishment;[149]
- unlawful human experimentation.[150]

Bassiouni notes that, in addition to individual criminal responsibility, international crimes constitute internationally wrongful conduct, and entail the responsibility of States under international law.[151]

I. International Delicts

According to Bassiouni, the gravity of some 'international delicts' may amount to that of international crimes but as a rule, they are 'committed by individuals or small groups', and cause relatively lesser harm.[152] International delicts include:[153]

- piracy;[154]
- aircraft hijacking and unlawful acts against international air safety;[155]

[142] ibid, 121.
[143] ibid.
[144] ibid, 142–44.
[145] ibid, 144; David (n 7), 1378–81.
[146] Bassiouni (n 54), 144–45; David (n 7), 1154–69.
[147] Bassiouni (n 54), 145; David (n 7), 1342–49.
[148] Bassiouni (n 54), 145–46; David (n 7), 1211–27.
[149] Bassiouni (n 54), 146–47; David (n 7), 1353–78; Ambos (n 90), 241–45.
[150] Bassiouni (n 54), 147–48.
[151] Bassiouni (n 54), 121; David (n 7), 1392–94.
[152] Bassiouni (n 54), 122.
[153] ibid, 122–23.
[154] Bassiouni (n 54), 159; David (n 7), 1405–14; Ambos (n 90), 238–41; J Hartmann, 'Piracy and Undersea Cables: An Overlooked Interpretation of UNCLOS?', EJIL:Talk!, 6 March 2025, available at www.ejiltalk.org/piracy-and-undersea-cables-an-overlooked-interpretation-of-unclos/.
[155] Bassiouni (n 54), 149–50; David (n 7), 1424–27.

- unlawful acts against the safety of maritime navigation and the safety of platforms on the high seas;[156]
- threat and use of force against internationally protected persons;[157]
- crimes against United Nations and associated personnel;[158]
- taking of civilian hostages;[159]
- unlawful use of the mail;[160]
- use of explosives;[161]
- financing of terrorism;[162]
- unlawful traffic in drugs and related drug offences;[163]
- organised crime;[164]
- destruction and / or theft of national treasures;[165]
- unlawful acts against certain internationally protected elements of the environment.[166]

J. International Infractions

In Bassiouni's classification, international infractions are normative violations of ICL not included in the categories of international crimes or international delicts:[167]

- international traffic in obscene materials;[168]
- falsification and counterfeiting;[169]
- unlawful interference with international submarine cables;[170]
- bribery of foreign public officials.[171]

[156] Bassiouni (n 54), 150; David (n 7), 1414–16, 1427–31.
[157] Bassiouni (n 54), 150–51; David (n 7), 1169–77.
[158] Bassiouni (n 54), 151.
[159] ibid, 151; David (n 7), 1349–53.
[160] Bassiouni (n 54), 151–53.
[161] ibid, 153.
[162] ibid; David (n 7), 1098–1154; Ambos (n 90), 228–34; Fergana News, 'Grazhdanin Tadzhikistana osuzhden v Niderlandah za verbovku boevikov IGIL' ['Tajik Citizen Convicted in the Netherlands for Recruiting ISIS Militants'], 25 July 2025, available at fergana.agency/news/139125/.
[163] Bassiouni (n 54), 153–54; David (n 7), 1230–39; Ambos (n 90), 234–38.
[164] Bassiouni (n 54), 154; David (n 7), 1394–401.
[165] Bassiouni (n 54), 154–55; David (n 7), 1523–26.
[166] Bassiouni (n 54), 155–56; David (n 7), 1437–77.
[167] Bassiouni (n 54), 123.
[168] ibid, 156; David (n 7), 1228–30. See also Fergana News, 'Vlasti Kyrgyzstana monopolizirovali internet i zapretili dustup k pornografii' ['Kyrgyz Authorities Monopolise the Internet and Ban Access to Pornography'], 29 July 2025, available at fergana.agency/news/139163/.
[169] Bassiouni (n 54), 156–57; David (n 7), 1097–98.
[170] Bassiouni (n 54), 157–58; David (n 7), 1417–19.
[171] Bassiouni (n 54), 158.

Similarly, other transnational manifestations of corruption, as defined in the United Nations Convention against Corruption,[172] should be included within this category.

K. Direct Enforcement of International Criminal Law

Historically, ICL originated as a branch of public international law enforceable directly through the medium of international criminal tribunals. The Nuremberg (1945–46) and Tokyo (1946–48) trials[173] were followed half a century later by the International Criminal Tribunal for the Former Yugoslavia (ICTY)[174] and the International Criminal Tribunal for Rwanda (ICTR),[175] both established by the Security Council of the United Nations (respectively, in 1993 and 1994).[176] The jurisdiction of these international criminal tribunals extended to specific territories and armed conflicts, and was superior to the domestic penal jurisdictions of the States concerned.[177] Likewise, the personal, temporal, and territorial jurisdiction of internationalised or 'hybrid' tribunals was defined in limited terms.[178] The founders of the International Criminal Court, in turn, chose to establish the Court on the principle of complementarity,[179] thereby granting it a potentially universal reach without formally invoking the principle of universal jurisdiction.

L. International Criminal Court

The Rome Statute of the International Criminal Court (ICC) was adopted on 17 July 1998,[180] and entered into force, in accordance with its Article 126(1), on 1 April 2002. The eleventh preambular paragraph of the ICC Statute states that the Court was established 'to guarantee lasting respect for and the enforcement of international justice'. Indeed, a major difference between the ICC and all previous international criminal tribunals was precisely that the ICC was designed to be a permanent judicial institution having authority to prosecute individuals for the most serious crimes of concern to the international community as a whole (cf the fourth preambular paragraph of the Statute).[181] The ICC Statute is a potentially universal treaty but this potential universality

[172] David (n 7), 1177–90.
[173] Ambos (n 3), 4–6.
[174] ibid, 19–22.
[175] ibid, 22–23.
[176] D Scheffer, 'The United Nations Security Council and International Criminal Justice' in Schabas (n 109).
[177] Werle and Jessberger (n 6), 15.
[178] ibid, 158–61; David (n 7), 910–27.
[179] Ambos (n 1), 266–333.
[180] In 2010, this date was proclaimed as the World Day for International Justice.
[181] L Sadat, 'The International Criminal Court' in Schabas (n 109); David (n 7), 929–1002.

is made possible by virtue of the principle of territorial jurisdiction and the active personality principle whose customary character is beyond dispute. As the time of writing, the Rome Statute has 125 States Parties, mostly representing the common and civil legal traditions.[182] In Central Asia, only Tajikistan has ratified the Rome Statute.[183]

According to Article 5 of the Rome Statute, the ICC has jurisdiction with respect to the 'core crimes' under international law. The Statute originally contained the definitions of genocide (Article 6), crimes against humanity (Article 7), and war crimes (Article 8) for the purpose of the ICC, but the definition of the crime of aggression was left to a later date.[184] The latter crime was defined for the purpose of the ICC and included in Article 8 *bis* of the Statute at a Review Conference in Kampala, in 2010.[185] The same Review Conference adopted provisions regulating the exercise of jurisdiction with respect to the crime of aggression by the ICC (Articles 15 *bis* and 15 *ter*). The ICC jurisdiction with respect to the crime of aggression was activated on 17 July 2018 but remains limited in practical terms.[186]

Since 2002, the ICC – and more generally, international criminal justice as such – attracted notable criticism, including from some of its prominent founders.[187] The most significant grounds for criticism included the unwarranted length of the ICC proceedings, and their high cost.[188] Some members of the African Union were especially vocal in voicing their disapproving viewpoints about an alleged lack of impartiality in preliminary examinations, investigations and prosecutions.[189] The functionality of the Court is considerably weakened by reluctance on the part of some Islamic States,[190] and resistance on the part of such powers as China,[191] the Russian Federation,[192] and the United States.[193]

[182] Ambos (n 1), 1–4.

[183] For the States Parties to the Rome Statute, see: https://asp.icc-cpi.int/states-parties.

[184] Werle and Jessberger (n 6), 602.

[185] Safferling (n 4), 252–65.

[186] Werle and Jessberger (n 6), 603.

[187] See *passim* Bassiouni (n 109).

[188] ibid, 374–75.

[189] WK Shilaho, 'The International Criminal Court and the African Union: Is the ICC a bulwark against impunity or an imperial Trojan horse?', ACCORD, 21 July 2018, available at www.accord.org.za/ajcr-issues/the-international-criminal-court-and-the-african-union/.

[190] S Sayapin, 'A "Hybrid" Tribunal for Daesh?', EJIL:Talk!, 4 May 2016, available at www.ejiltalk.org/a-hybrid-tribunal-fordaesh/; KW Gray, 'Unrecognized Governments and the ICC Redux: Could Afghanistan Withdraw from the Rome Statute?', EJIL:Talk!, 1 August 2025, available at https://www.ejiltalk.org/unrecognized-governments-and-the-icc-redux-could-afghanistan-withdraw-from-the-rome-statute/.

[191] D Zhu, 'China, the International Criminal Court, and Global Governance' (2019) 73 *Australian Journal of International Affairs* 585.

[192] S Sayapin, 'Russia's Withdrawal of Signature from the Rome Statute Would not Shield its Nationals from Potential Prosecution at the ICC', EJIL:Talk!, 21 November 2016, available at www.ejiltalk.org/russias-withdrawal-of-signature-from-the-rome-statute-would-not-shield-its-nationals-from-potential-prosecution-at-the-icc/.

[193] W Schabas, 'United States Hostility to the International Criminal Court: It's All About the Security Council' (2004) 15 *European Journal of International Law* 701.

M. Indirect Enforcement of International Criminal Law

The indirect enforcement of ICL is essential for at least two reasons. First, States are sovereign, and the enforcement of their domestic penal laws is one of the most important manifestations of their sovereignty. Second, whereas the earlier international criminal tribunals (eg the Nuremberg and Tokyo Tribunals, the ICTY, or the ICTR) had primary jurisdiction, the ICC's jurisdiction already is complementary to the domestic systems of criminal justice, in recognition of States' primary role in prosecuting individuals for the commission of the 'core crimes' under international law and other crimes against the peace and security of mankind. A few notable domestic trials for crimes under international law have taken place since 1945,[194] as States took measures to implement ICL in their domestic laws and practices.[195] In Central Asia, States should continue working on the implementation of the General Part of ICL and the elements of relevant crimes in their Criminal Codes, in accordance with the principle of legality. Importantly, law enforcement officials and judges should be trained on the proper application of ICL.[196] Last but not least, bilateral and multilateral cooperation in penal matters among Central Asian States should continue to strengthen, with a view to preventing crimes under international law and transnational crimes, and to ensuring the effective prosecution and punishment of individuals responsible for such crimes.

[194] Werle and Jessberger (n 6), 162–79. See also K Sellars (ed), *Trials for International Crimes in Asia* (Cambridge, Cambridge University Press, 2016).
[195] Werle and Jessberger (n 6), 179–204.
[196] Sayapin (n 115), 46.

Index

www.ingramcontent.com/pod-product-compliance
Ingram Content Group UK Ltd.
Pitfield, Milton Keynes, MK11 3LW, UK
UKHW020228290926
15470UKWH00001B/417

9 781509 93549